D0900241

The Man Who Built the National Football League

Joe F. Carr

Chris Willis

THE SCARECROW PRESS, INC.
Lanham • Toronto • Plymouth, UK
2010

Published by Scarecrow Press, Inc.
A wholly owned subsidiary of The Rowman & Littlefield Publishing Group, Inc.
4501 Forbes Boulevard, Suite 200, Lanham, Maryland 20706
http://www.scarecrowpress.com

Estover Road, Plymouth PL6 7PY, United Kingdom

British Library Cataloguing in Publication Information Available

Library of Congress Cataloging-in-Publication Data
Carr, Joe F., d. 1939.
The man who built the National Football League / Joe F. Carr, Chris Willis.
p. cm.
Includes bibliographical references and index.
ISBN 978-0-8108-7669-9 (hardback : alk. paper) — ISBN 978-0-8108-7670-5 (ebook)
1. Carr, Joe F., d. 1939. 2. National Football League—History—20th century 3. Football managers—United States—History—20th century 4. Football. I. Willis, Chris, 1970- II. Title.
GV954.C368 2010
796.332640973—dc22 2010005351

∞™ The paper used in this publication meets the minimum requirements of American National Standard for Information Sciences—Permanence of Paper for Printed Library Materials, ANSI/NISO Z39.48-1992.

Printed in the United States of America

Contents

Foreword

It is a pleasure to introduce a book that I have watched grow from its inception to publication. It was at our Aunt Mary's "knee" that my four brothers—John, Michael, Dennis, and Gregory—and I were told about the life and outstanding accomplishments of our grandfather, Joe F. Carr. Now, thanks to his tireless efforts, author Chris Willis shares the life and career of Joe Carr for all to enjoy.

Like so many of our ancestors in the United States, Joe Carr's family fled the terrible conditions of mid-nineteenth-century Ireland. They came to settle in the town of Columbus, Ohio. Joe Carr was a railroader; a machinist; a sportswriter; a manager of the semipro football squad, the Columbus Panhandles; and the chief organizer of Major League Baseball's minor league system. He was also the devoted husband of his wife, Josephine Sullivan; the father of two adoring children, Mary and Joe Jr.; and a deeply religious man.

All of these factors came to fruition when, in 1921, Joe Carr was elected president of the APFA—the American Professional Football Association—which Carr immediately renamed the National Football League (in 1922). From 1921 until his death in 1939, he sowed the seeds of a sports organization that, arguably, has become one of the most popular in the world.

Chris Willis's extensive biography artfully expands upon this brief summary of the life of Joe Carr. I am fortunate to know Chris Willis, and I have been enormously impressed with his tenacity and tireless efforts in spending untold hours to create this biography of my grandfather. He is an author who leaves "no stone unturned" in his efforts to assemble all of the pertinent facts. For example, when researching his previous work on the Columbus Panhandles, Chris discovered that the team records had been destroyed. Undaunted, Chris researched *all* of the relevant local newspapers of the day covering a period of nineteen years to reconstruct the evidence of the Columbus Panhandles' past.

As in his prior books and articles, Chris Willis tells this story in a direct, readable, and entertaining style. The members of my family are very grateful to Chris for telling this story of our famous relative.

His work demonstrates that Joe Carr had a vision of a pro football league, and without that vision and a higher purpose beyond short-term profits and "relaxing the rules," the league would have perished. This vision and the singularity of purpose, shared with such pioneer owners as George Preston Marshall of Washington D.C., Art Rooney of Pittsburgh, Tim Mara of New York, Charlie Bidwill of Chicago, Bert Bell of Philadelphia, and George Halas of Chicago, made the dream of the National Football League the reality it is today.

I am confident that all who read this book, historian and the fan alike, will find it a very enjoyable and informative read.

Many thanks to Chris Willis for bringing the life of Joe Carr to light.

—James A. Carr
Grandson of Joe F. Carr

Preface

In 2002 while working for NFL Films, I pitched a project on the Nesser brothers—the group of six brothers who played for the Columbus (Ohio) Panhandles professional football team in the early 1900s. After my boss—Steve Sabol—approved the project, we found out that the Nesser family was holding their annual family reunion that fall at the Pro Football Hall of Fame in Canton, Ohio. It was perfect timing. While at the reunion I was planning to interview family members who had intimate stories on the famous Nesser brothers that would appear in one of our shows.

As I was preparing to shoot the reunion, I got an idea to invite a descendant from the Joe F. Carr family. Joe F. Carr had been the Panhandles long-time manager (1907–1922), and he had known the Nesser family for decades. Surely someone from the Carr family could talk about the Nessers. So I tracked down the family, who lived in my hometown of Columbus, Ohio, to see if they could send a representative to talk about Carr. The family's spokesperson was James Carr, grandson of the late Joe F. Carr, who agreed to attend.

On September 14, 2002, well before the reunion started, I sat down with James Carr to talk about his grandfather. For nearly an hour James discussed his grandfather's life and career with me, and I was totally fascinated. Being the head of the research library at NFL Films and part of the National Football League, I had heard the name Joe Carr and some of his accomplishments in starting the NFL. But after interviewing James I knew I wanted to know more about Joe's life. I knew right then that I wanted to write about the career of Joe F. Carr and preserve the legacy of one of pro football's most important pioneers. Also, the fact that Carr was born and had the NFL office in my hometown of Columbus made it a no-brainer for me to write the first-ever biography of him.

The following spring while back in Columbus to visit my family I made an appointment to talk with James to see about writing a biography of his grandfather. He was more than willing to allow me to write the book, and he also agreed to help me with any interviews with the family or any research the family might have. I couldn't have asked for a better situation. The Carr family opened its doors and hearts to me. Over the past eight years, I've researched the life of Joe F. Carr and the early history of the NFL. It has been a great journey.

Most people and football fans probably haven't heard the name Joe F. Carr. But he was the Henry Ford of the NFL. He laid the groundwork and foundation on which the NFL now stands. I hope this book can capture the legacy of Joe F. Carr and give football fans and readers a glimpse into what Carr meant to professional football and the NFL.

Acknowledgments

After spending nearly ten years researching the life of Joe F. Carr, I feel I don't have enough words to thank all of the people who helped me in completing this book. First and foremost I want to thank the entire Carr family for their support and generosity. Without their help this book could never have been written. I especially want to thank the grandsons of Joe F. Carr who spent so much time answering my questions in person, by phone, or through numerous e-mails.

I am extremely indebted to James Carr and his wife, Velda, for all their time and energy in helping me obtain the family material I needed to learn about James's famous grandfather. James helped in lining up family interviews; allowing me to use his home for the interviews; making copies of material; feeding a hungry researcher on occasion; and answering every question I had. In the end he made me feel like one of the family, and I am very grateful for all his help. Today I consider James a friend. Thanks also to his two children—Jennifer and Andy Carr.

Through James I met Joe Carr's other three grandsons. Thanks to the late Dennis Carr, who was always entertaining; Michael Carr, for giving me such passionate and honest answers during our interview; and Gregory Carr, for telling me all of his thoughtful stories about his grandfather. I also want to thank Gregory (and his wife, Karen) for allowing me to use the Joe F. Carr Scrapbook (which was on microfilm). You all went beyond the call of duty in helping me with my research, and I thank you.

Extra thanks goes to Margaret Mooney, great-niece of Joe F. Carr, and her husband, Pat. Margaret's knowledge and research of the Carr family tree (which included several trips to Ireland) gave me much needed insight into the early history of the Carr family. I will always treasure our visits and time together. I also want to thank Martha Sullivan, niece of Joe F. Carr, whose interviews about the Sullivan family were helpful in learning more about Carr's wife, Josephine. You gave me insight into events I didn't know about; thanks.

Special thanks goes to Joy Dolan and Kathy Frederick (brother Edward Carr's family); as well as Jim and Audey Heavey (brother John Karr's family), who made my weekend trip to Pine Island, Florida, an enjoyable one.

I want to thank Stephen Ryan, senior editor at Scarecrow Press, for believing in preserving the history of professional football. This is our third book together, and I can think of no other editor I would rather work with. Thanks to Jessica McCleary, production editor, for all her great help in getting this book done. I also want to thank Scarecrow Press and their professional staff for putting this book together. They are a joy to work with.

I want to applaud all the families of the former Columbus Panhandles players who gave me their time. Thanks to Irene and Al Cassady; Ted Schneider; Kate Benson; Terri Murdick; Thersea Graham; Sally Nesser; Connie Shomo; Joseph Nesser; Babe Sherman; Judi Doran; Tess Nesser; Bill and Linda Mulbarger; Sharon Ruh-Manhart; Joseph and Katherine Colburn; Andrea Lynch; Joann Franke; Marilyn Sue Hopkins; Joanne Distelweig; and Jerry Entingh. I especially want to thank James Brigham (and his wife, Mary) for talking about his father and making my trip to Detroit very productive.

I owe special thanks to all the NFL families, owners, and PR directors who helped me with my research. First, I want to thank Virginia McCaskey (daughter of George Halas) for agreeing to do two interviews—the first at her lovely home and the second in Canton, Ohio, on Hall of Fame weekend. Virginia's insight on her father, as well as her stories of Joe Carr's visits, are priceless. Meeting you, Virginia, was an experience I will never forget. Thanks to Scott Hagel, George McCaskey, and Patrick McCaskey of the Chicago Bears for all your help. Many thanks to the late Wellington Mara (son of Tim Mara); John Mara (son of Wellington Mara); Pat Hanlon; Doug Murphy; and Peter John-Baptise—all of the New York Giants. My gratitude to Dan Rooney (son of Art Rooney) of the Pittsburgh Steelers and Matt Barnhart and Deanna Caldwell of the Detroit Lions for their help.

Sometimes when researching a book you meet someone unexpectedly, a diamond in the rough, so to speak. In this case for me it would be locating the family of former NFL vice president Carl L. Storck. I am extremely grateful to Sandy Allen and her husband, Richard. Talking to Sandy led me to her mother Dolores (Storck) Seitz, who gave me an entire afternoon talking about her father, Carl. It was a very memorable day for me learning about one of the pioneers of the NFL. The Storcks are a special family. More thanks to Charles Seitz Sr. and son Charles Jr.

I also want to thank Jordan Wright (granddaughter of George Preston Marshall) for her interview and the wonderful time spent talking about her grandfather. My weekend in Alexandria, Virginia, was a great experience, and I learned so much. Many thanks to Bert Bell Jr. (son of Bert Bell) for giving me insight into his father. Additional thanks must go to Rozene Supple, and her husband, Ric, for her interview on her father, George A. Richards, original owner of the Detroit Lions.

Thanks go to Bob Lingo (son of Walter Lingo) for talking about his father and the famous Oorang Indians; Dr. James King (grandson of Ralph Hay) for his stories about the man who held the NFL's first organizational meeting in his automobile showroom; and Peg Holmes (daughter of Dutch Sternaman). I also want to thank the Tehan family—Kevin Johnson and Jeanne Johnson, Joe Deters and Nancy Deters, and Patrick Tehan—for their help in learning about their father, Dan Tehan.

Another unexpected find was locating the family of Kathleen Rubadue, the former secretary of Joe Carr. Special thanks to Robert Knapp (son of Kathleen [Rubadue] Knapp) for all his info on the NFL's first secretary.

I want to thank current NFL commissioner Roger Goodell and his staff—Joe Browne and Pete Abitante—as well as former commissioner Paul Tagliabue for all their support in trying to preserve the legacy of Joe F. Carr. I also want to thank Rita Benson LeBlanc of the New Orleans Saints for all her advice and support. You always have my best interests in mind, so thanks!

As with my previous projects, my favorite place to visit and do research is the Pro Football Hall of Fame in Canton, Ohio. I want to thank the staff in the research library—Pete Fierle, Saleem Choudhry, Jason Aikens, and Jon Kendle—for all their help. You guys are the best at what you do—thanks! I also want to thank Joe Horrigan, vice president of communications-exhibits, for all his support; I really appreciate it.

I also want to thank my friends with the Professional Football Researchers Association (PFRA). First, I want to thank the late Bob Carroll, who passed away in August of 2009, for all his help and guidance over the past fifteen years I've known him. Bob published my first ever article in the *Coffin Corner*—the PFRA publication—back in 1994, and I will always be grateful for his generosity. You'll be missed. Thanks to PFRA members Michael Moran (thanks for finding the Carr photo); Tod Maher; Sean Lahman; Roy Sye; Andy Piascik; and Ken Crippen, the new executive director of the PFRA. Lastly, thanks to coach T. J. Troup for all his support. I truly enjoy all our phone calls; can't wait for the next one.

I also want to thank fellow authors Sal Paolantonio (ESPN), Dan Daly (*Washington Times*), Allen Barra (*Wall Street Journal*), Jim Dent, and Ray Didinger for all their advice—keep up the good work. I would also like to thank my colleagues at NFL Films: Dave Plaut, Diane Kimball, Ray

Dominick, Lawrence Remsen, Kevin McLoughlin, Sue Nicholson, and, especially, Neil Zender, who gave his time to help read the manuscript. Special thanks to Steve Sabol, president of NFL Films, for allowing me every day to feed my passion for football.

I also want to thank Geoffrey Cutler, Matt Ball, and Tom Vogelphol for taping all my interviews. Special thanks go to former Columbus city councilwomen Maryellen O'Shaughessy for getting me (as well as James and Gregory Carr) into the vacant building of Joe Carr's office at 16 East Broad Street. The walk up to the eleventh floor where the NFL had their first office was an experience of a lifetime—I know James and Greg enjoyed it very much, too. I also want to thank Lelia Cady, Randy Black, Michael Broidy, Don Camerino, and Ted Poland (thanks for bringing the flashlight) for our access to the building.

Kudos go to all the libraries and organizations who helped me during my journey. Thanks to the staff at St. Patrick Church (Susan Livingston and father Andre LaCasse, O.P.) and St. Joseph's Cathedral (secretary Kathleen Finneran Slattery); Doug Motz (The Library Store); Jeff Lafever (Columbus Historical Society); Mike Foley (WCBE Radio); Bob Hunter (*Columbus Dispatch*); Mindy Drayer (NBC-TV); and Judy Williams.

Thanks to the Ohio Historical Society; Brown County (Wisconsin) Public Library; Greenwich (Connecticut) Library; the Ohio State University Library; Columbus (Ohio) Public Library; Egan-Ryan Funeral Home; Canton (Ohio) Public Library; Wayne County (Indiana) Historical Museum; Morrisson-Reeves (Indiana) Public Library; State Library of Ohio; Burlington County (New Jersey) Public Library; and Carneige Library of Pittsburgh. Also want to thank Ancestry.com and Newspaperarchives.com for their very helpful websites.

Lastly, I want to thank my family and friends. I want to thank my brothers, Rhu and Adrian, for all their support. Thanks to my best friend, Jennifer Heinz, for all her continued support and friendship. Although you couldn't care less about football, you are always there for me, and I couldn't have asked for a better friend. Thanks also to Jennifer's husband, Craig, and baby, Sean, a future quarterback. Thanks to my mother, Tina, for all her love and inspiration this past year in helping me finish this book. I know I couldn't have done it without you. Finally, I want to thank my father, Roy Willis (1941–2008). Thank you for giving me my passion for reading and writing while being a book dealer for nearly three decades. I miss you so much, and I hope you're proud of this book.

Introduction: One Man's Vision

On a cold and snowy day in Columbus, Ohio, a rather small, unassuming gray-haired man in his fifties, standing no taller than five feet nine, walked around the busy intersection at the corner of Broad and High streets on his way to work. He entered the building at 16 East Broad Street, a big skyscraper located in the middle of downtown Columbus that was right across the street from the Ohio Statehouse building, which the governor of Ohio called home. The unassuming man headed up to his small two-room office on the eleventh floor, unlocking the door—the door that read "Joe F. Carr, President of the National Football League."

After saying good morning to his secretary, he took off his hat and coat and made himself comfortable by lighting up one of his favorite cigars. Sitting down at his desk, he began to read the local newspaper dated January 27, 1933. His piercing blue eyes peered through his tiny rimmed glasses as he turned to the Sports section. A few moments later a friend walked through his door. Actually the friend was just a local sportswriter who wanted to interview him for his daily newspaper column. But to the man at the desk everyone was a friend, and he greeted his guest with his trademark handshake and cheery hello. "Come in young man. How have you been and what can I do for you?"[1]

"OK, Joe," the reporter asked. "You just finished another season of play in the National Football League. How do you think the league is progressing?" The man named Joe—the president of the National Football League, Joe F. Carr—responded by saying,

> This avid interest in football in all its phases is responsible largely for the amazing success of professional clubs. Because of the healthy increase in attendance at pro grid games each year since the National Football League was organized in 1920, I believe that I am making no mistake in predicting that in a few years it will outdraw baseball or any other sport, game for game.
>
> And in making this prediction, I am confident that baseball's best days are in the future. That there is an increase of interest in baseball but an increase that it not comparable to that in football. Professional football has progressed steadily . . . in a decade the helter skelter assortment of teams, several of which could not afford to play at home has been reduced from 22 to an organization which has financial backing in all of its cities and which now will be big league from start to finish.
>
> Professional football is for those who understand the game. College football was built with a background of tradition and pageantry. The professional game hasn't much tradition or pageantry yet, but it provides the hardest and most interesting competition for those who love the sport purely for its own merits.[2]

While looking outside the window of his office Carr noticed the snow slowly falling and gave the sportswriter another quote: "If only they knew how near our football league is to moving indoors and what a smashing success we are going to make of the pro game under cover, they would not hesitate for a moment to spend the additional money needed to size the building up to the requirements of the game."[3]

The sportswriter got what he came for. The always accommodating Carr thanked the writer; anything to help the progress of the National Football League (NFL) was well worth the time spent. The writer left and Carr finished his cigar. He thought about the idea he just revealed. The NFL played under a roof—a domed stadium; that would be spectacular for the sport of professional football. Pro football bigger than baseball? A domed stadium? In 1933 it was just a vision. It was Joe Carr's vision for the NFL.

For eighteen years, from 1921 until his death in office in 1939, Joe F. Carr was the president of the NFL. It was his guidance, leadership, and unbelievable vision that led the pro game from small-town obscurity to being a successful sporting venture located in major cities across the United States. The foundation on which the NFL sits today was established under the presidency of Joe F. Carr. His influence and integrity rubbed off on all the early NFL owners, and together Carr and the owners built a sport that is still seen every fall weekend; the NFL has become the most popular spectator sport in the country. But who was Joe F. Carr, and how did he build this foundation?

Starting with his humble beginnings in Columbus—before the start of the twentieth century—until the time of his death, Carr devoted his life to the promotion and organization of sports. Carr started his sports career as a sportswriter and assistant sports editor of the *Ohio State Journal.* He moved on to become the manager of the Columbus Panhandles, a very successful professional football team made up of employees from the Panhandle Division of the Pennsylvania Railroad. He was also the president of the Columbus Senators baseball team, was appointed the head of the minor leagues in 1933, and was an early leader in promoting professional basketball as president of the American Basketball League (1925–1927).

But this story is about his legacy in professional football. Starting with his election as NFL president in 1921, it was Carr's vision to have an NFL franchise in every major city. He thought this was the only way for professional football to survive as a successful business venture—to pattern itself after Major League Baseball and have franchises in the cities where the most people lived. So during his presidency Carr slowly moved the pro game from the small towns, which were the lifeblood of the early pro game, to the biggest cities east of the Mississippi.

In Carr's early years as president, NFL franchises came and went as quickly as the sun rises and sets. From 1920 through 1934 more than forty NFL franchises went through the league and twenty-four of those teams lasted just one or two years. After his first several years as president, Carr realized that the NFL's long-term success rested on better franchise stability just like Major League Baseball. In those same years (1920 to 1934) Major League Baseball had the same sixteen teams in just eleven cities.

In 1920—the first year of the American Professional Football Association (APFA), the forerunner of the NFL—the average city population for an APFA franchise was 753,176 (fourteen football franchises in thirteen cities), while the average city population for a Major League Baseball franchise was 1,326,124—almost more than double the population of the NFL cities. During the 1920s the NFL placed franchises in small towns and cities, such as Akron, Ohio; Decatur, Illinois; Duluth, Minnesota; Evansville, Indiana; Kenosha, Wisconsin; LaRue, Ohio; Pottsville, Pennsylvania; Rock Island, Illinois; Hammond, Indiana; Dayton, Ohio; Racine, Wisconsin; Toledo, Ohio; and Tonawanda, New York. This was not the big-time; this was a sport just trying to survive.[4]

But Carr was trying to buy some time to keep the sport alive so he could eventually find financially capable owners in larger cities to help build the NFL into a profitable business. These owners who he recruited would lose money in the beginning, but if they kept the league alive, they would see the sport become bigger than baseball and maybe make a little money in the process. Carr had that much faith in the NFL and was willing to sell it.

By using baseball as an example, Carr started to move his league to the big city. As the early 1930s roared by, the population of cities that housed NFL franchises started to go up. Carr's vision was starting to come true as professional football was beginning to resemble Major League Baseball. He reduced the NFL from twenty-one fledgling franchises in 1921 (his first year as president) to a more successful ten franchises in 1937. By then the National Football League and Major League Baseball (MLB) were almost identical, with nine out of ten NFL franchises existing in MLB cities:

1. Brooklyn
2. Chicago
3. Chicago (second team)
4. Cleveland
5. Detroit
6. New York
7. Philadelphia
8. Pittsburgh
9. Washington
10. Green Bay (the only NFL city not to have an MLB team)

By 1940 the average city population of NFL franchises had caught up with the average city population of MLB franchises. The NFL was now a big-city sport and was making strides into becoming a successful business for team owners—although big paydays for owners were still years away. By having teams in big cities, the NFL gained the stability it needed to succeed, and the foundation for the future was being built.[5]

In addition, Carr's recruitment of financially stable owners paid off in a big way. Carr and his close friend George Halas—who owned the Chicago Bears and was one of the original founders of the NFL in 1920—would only recruit men who had the same passion for the sport as they did. The owners Carr brought into the league during his presidency would turn out to be a who's who of NFL history. In 1925 he found a wealthy bookie by the name of Tim Mara to buy a franchise in the biggest city of them all—New York. After eighty years, the New York Giants are one of the longest-running NFL franchises and are still owned by the Mara family. Both Mara and his son Wellington are enshrined in the Pro Football Hall of Fame.

In 1933 Carr recruited Bert Bell and Lud Wray to purchase a franchise in Philadelphia, and the Philadelphia Eagles were born. Bell went on to be an NFL owner for over a decade and then became the commissioner of the NFL in 1946, serving in that role until his death in 1959. Bell put in over twenty-five years of service with professional football and earned a spot in the Hall of Fame.

Also in 1933 Carr wanted a franchise in Pittsburgh and selected Art Rooney, a local sports promoter and former boxer from the Steel City, to buy the team. The Pittsburgh Pirates began play that year and changed their name to the Steelers in 1940. The Rooney family still owns the franchise; Dan Rooney now runs his father's team. Both Art and Dan have been inducted into the Hall of Fame. The year before the Eagles and Steelers joined the NFL, in 1932, Carr persuaded George Preston Marshall to buy a franchise for the city of Boston. Marshall, who owned several successful Laundromats in Washington, DC, moved the Boston Redskins franchise to Washington before the start of the 1937 season. The Washington Redskins have played in the nation's capitol city for over seventy years, and Mr. Marshall is also enshrined in the Hall of Fame.

The cities of Detroit and Cleveland joined the NFL in 1934 and 1937, respectively, and the Lions and Rams franchises helped the NFL become a solid ten-team big-city organization. The foundation of the NFL was now established. The current NFL would look very different without the following franchises: the Chicago Bears (1920), Chicago-St. Louis-Arizona Cardinals (1920), Green Bay Packers (1921), New York Giants (1925), Boston-Washington Redskins (1932), Pittsburgh Steelers (1933), Philadelphia Eagles (1933), Detroit Lions (1934), and the Cleveland-Los Angeles-St. Louis Rams (1937).

Except for 1943—when there were only eight league teams because of World War II—the NFL would stay as a ten-team league for the next twelve years, until 1950 when the league grew to thirteen teams. When Joe Carr passed away in office on May 20, 1939—at the age of fifty-nine—the NFL he helped build was showing signs of becoming a successful sport that would eventually become more popular than baseball. On December 11, 1938, at the last game he ever saw, Carr and a then-record championship game crowd of 48,120 saw the New York Giants defeat the Green Bay Packers 23–17 at the Polo Grounds in New York City in an exciting, close game that decided the NFL title. Carr's vision of a big-time sport was complete; it was now time for the NFL owners, who he selected, to continue to build the great sport he loved so much and put so much energy and time into.

The men who were the pioneers of the NFL have names that are synonymous with the game of professional football. Names such as George Halas, Curly Lambeau, Jim Thorpe, Tim Mara, Art Rooney, George Preston Marshall, Charlie Bidwill, and Bert Bell have dominated the history of the sport, and rightly so. But for some reason the name of Joe F. Carr has been lost in time. Although Carr was the unquestioned leader of this group of pioneering men and guided the young league when nobody else wanted to, his accomplishments have been largely ignored.

The leadership, incredible vision, and solid foundation that Carr built while working from his rather small two-room office in Columbus can be seen today every fall weekend in what we now know as the NFL. His life and legacy are stories that shouldn't be forgotten and need to be told.

Part I

HUMBLE BEGINNINGS (1879–1919)

1

The Irish Way (1841–1878)

Sitting in his small two-room office on the eleventh floor in Columbus, Ohio, Joe Carr probably pondered more than a few times, how did I get here? How did the son of an Irish immigrant with a grammar school education get to become the president of the sport he loved? The sport he would go on to help build as the model of all sports leagues.

Joe Carr's values, work ethic, and personality, which guided the ways he would lead his life, were reflected and learned from his father. A man who looked to America to have a better life, he taught Joe how to live and how not to live. Michael Karr was born in Northern Ireland in County Armagh in 1841. The family's surname in Ireland was spelled K-a-r-r and would be changed later while living in America.[1] County Armagh was surrounded, to the west, by County Monaghan; to the east, by County Down; to the south, by County Louth; and to the north, by Lough Neagh, the largest lake in the British Isles.

According to the 1840 Irish Census, County Armagh had a population of 232,391 and the majority of the county residents made their living in the linen industry as weavers and spinners. A few years later, however, the Karr family and the rest of Ireland were affected by the famous Potato Famine. As a result of the famine, over 1 million Irish citizens died and another million were left to avoid starvation. Young Michael Karr survived, but most of his family it seems didn't. "Researching our family tree we never found out about his immediate family. We assume they didn't survive the famine, so considering that and his economic situation, it clearly shows he wanted to have a better life. America was the land of opportunity. So he went," says James Carr, the grandson of Joe Carr.[2]

From May 1851 to December 1860 nearly 30,000 residents of Armagh alone left the Emerald Isle. In 1864, at the age of twenty-three and by himself, Michael raised enough money and left Ireland for the United States. After traveling across the Atlantic Ocean he reached the "promised land" and arrived at the port of Baltimore. After landing in Baltimore he jumped on the Baltimore & Ohio Railroad line and headed west. Maybe thinking Ohio was the last stop on the ride, Michael stopped and settled in Columbus, Ohio. More than likely he heard Columbus had a big Irish contingent and that jobs were available to them around central Ohio.[3]

By the end of the year—with the finish of the Civil War just a few months away—Karr would make Columbus his permanent home. The city of Columbus was first laid out in 1812 and incorporated in 1816 to be the state capital of Ohio. Columbus was mainly chosen as the site for the new capital because of its central location within the state. The city was split down the middle by the famous intersection of Broad (running east–west) and High (running north–south) streets. At the time Michael arrived, the city of Columbus had a population of just 18,554, as well as having just six banks, seven schools, and twenty-nine churches. But the city was thriving with the railroads. In 1850 the city's first railroad, the Columbus–Xenia line, was established and shortly after that the more popular Cleveland–Columbus–Cincinnati railroad came transporting Ohioans to every part of the state.[4]

The two railroads (which would eventually be purchased by the Pennsylvania Railroad in May 1868) built a joint Union Station on the east side of High Street just north of North Public Lane, which ran along the established Irish neighborhood in Columbus. The new railroads created plenty of jobs in the railroad shops for the newly arrived immigrants in central Ohio. Although Michael did not seek this type of employment, Joe Carr would later use this railroad connection to start his career in sports and expose him to the game he would eventually love.

After settling in Columbus, Michael Karr lived at residences on East Gay and then McCoy streets in the Irish neighborhood that was north of the capital city's downtown. This wasn't the best end of town, as Columbus historian Ed Lentz would write, "with its patch of malarial swamp, the ever-growing town cemetery and the smelly, dirty and noisy railroads of Columbus, it was precisely these factors that attracted the new immigrants. The soil was poor but the land was cheap."[5] The neighborhood contained a fairly large contingent of Irish immigrants, and their language, dress, and lifestyle set them apart—including new citizen Michael Karr.

The place the Irish closed in on was North Public Lane—soon to be renamed Naghten Street (which it is still called today) in honor of William "Billy" Naghten, who became the first Irish-Catholic president of the Columbus City Council. Irish workers would empty out onto Naghten Street on Friday nights, as merchants, laborers, and railroader workers would make their way to the many shops, groceries, or saloons to enjoy the city's nightlife. Michael would jump right into the community feet first.

He quickly found work in one of the Irish shops as a shoemaker, which was becoming a booming business in the city. "Shoes were a big operation in central Ohio at that time. As a matter of fact, the well-known Wolfe family owned a shoe-making or a boot-making operation which I suspect may've spun-off other business types similar to the one that my great-grandfather would [have been] involved in," says Gregory Carr, grandson of Joe Carr.[6]

By 1870 the city of Columbus had close to sixty shoe-making/boot-making shops, and Michael was one of these hard-working employees dedicating ten hours a day to making shoes. Michael found the work to be rewarding, and he tackled it head on as only an Irish immigrant would. It was the "Irish way." Like most Irish immigrants he felt a hard day's work in America was better than dying of hunger back in Ireland. Spending ten hours making shoes was heaven and nothing to complain about. Michael earned a reputation of being a man of action, not words. He lived life like the old Irish saying, "The person of the greatest talk is the person of the least work."[7]

While living in the Irish neighborhood, Karr worked, socialized, drank, and engaged in what would have been the center of the Irish culture—attending church. The young Irish immigrant loved going to church, and because he was new to Columbus he attracted attention from the other churchgoers. "Michael wasn't a big man—he stood about five feet ten and around 200 pounds, he had that typical Irish look to him," says Michael Carr, grandson of Joe Carr, who was named after his great-grandfather.[8] Michael did have the tough Irish look. He had blue eyes, a strong jaw, and a small beard on his chin that was about an inch and a half in length, and like most immigrants he was a serious man.

Shortly after arriving in Columbus and getting settled, Karr met a fellow Irish immigrant, Margaret Hurley. Hurley was born in 1840 and her family was well traveled, having spent time in New York (where she was likely born), Connecticut, and Montreal. Just like Michael she eventually made her way to Columbus.[9]

"She had light eyes and dark hair and from the pictures of our great-grandmother, Margaret Hurley-Karr, you can tell that she was somewhat slim, not a big women, of slighter stature. Later on she looked more frail. She always looked older than she was. But that was typical of Irish immigrants, life was tough," says James Carr, grandson of Joe Carr. Michael fell in love very quickly with Margaret, and the two made a perfect Irish couple. Both were very simple and had typical Irish personalities. They also would go on to build together another famous Irish tradition—having a large family. After a short engagement Michael, age twenty-five, and Margaret, age twenty-six, married at the Columbus church where the Irish gathered.[10]

After just a decade St. Patrick Church was a staple in the Irish neighborhood. Purchased for $1,000, the first cornerstone was laid out in September 1852 at the northeast corner of Seventh Street (now Grant Street) and Naghten Street in the Irish neighborhood. The church's original layout—152 feet long and 52 feet wide—was done in Norman style architecture and patterned after the ancient castles of Ireland. One year later on Sunday, September 25, 1853, the church opened its doors to the Irish community.[11]

The following year a two-story brick school building was erected beside the church on Mt. Vernon Avenue. In August 1855 Father James Meagher of St. Patrick engaged the service of the Sisters of Notre Dame, from Cincinnati, who took immediate charge of the girls' school. Lay teachers were employed to teach the boys. Eventually the school would double its capacity, providing four rooms for the boys and four rooms for the girls. The Karr family would build a relationship with St. Patrick that lasted for over seventy years.[12]

Starting in 1867, Michael the shoemaker and his stay-at-home wife would have four children over the next seven years—two boys and two girls. These four children would travel very different paths and one would disappear altogether. Bridget Karr (1867), John Aloysius Karr (June 1869), James Karr (December 18, 1872), and Mary Therese Karr (September 22, 1874) were all born healthy and baptized at St. Patrick Church. After the arrival of child number five, Michael would change the direction of his family.

In 1877 the Karrs had their fifth child, another son, Michael Lawrence Karr (April 11, 1877).[13] At this time papa Michael decided to take charge of his own life and make his family more stable and comfortable. He was now on the verge of becoming a successful Irish story. After the birth of young Michael, the father decided to go into business for himself. Fourteen years after arriving from Ireland, he now owned and operated his own shoe-making business. He found a home where the family could work and live that was in the old Irish neighborhood located at 419 Mt. Vernon Avenue.

Over the next few years the business would also turn into a grocery store and a saloon for his customers. The tight-knit group of seven had now become a well-known established family in the city of Columbus as the Irish neighborhood and its citizens were becoming a positive influence in the city. Irish immigrants were running businesses, working on the railroad, running for political office, and making an impact in the capital city. The Karrs' new home on Mt. Vernon Avenue was right in the middle of what was now being called "the Irish Broadway."

But this home on Mt. Vernon Avenue was about to become the birthplace of a boy who would make his own success story and do it the Irish way.

2

Growing Up in Columbus, Ohio (1879–1893)

By 1879 the Karr family had been living in Columbus for nearly fifteen years and had seen the city start to grow up. The city now had a strong population of 51,647 that included forty-four churches, thirty schools, fourteen banks, over 140 grocery stores, and eighty-eight shoemaking shops—including the one owned by Michael Karr on Mt. Vernon Avenue. The Karr shop, which now included a grocery store and a saloon, became a place to meet and socialize for the local Irish citizens. The upbeat group of immigrants, mostly male, loved to hang out for a few drinks after a hard day's work, and Michael was no different. His store became a very popular spot.[1]

"As you look down Mt. Vernon Avenue at this time, there were quite a few saloons, but they were meeting places, places where people who couldn't entertain in their homes would go for the night and have a bite to eat and a bottle of beer," says Margaret Mooney, great-niece of Joe Carr, and great-granddaughter of Michael Karr. "My great-grandfather had a liking for the drink and that might've changed the opinion of the Karr boys about drinking as they got older."[2]

As summer turned to fall in Columbus everything seemed to be going very well for the Karrs, and Margaret was expecting again with child number six. But this child would be different; he would be special. On Thursday, October 23, 1879, Joseph Francis Karr was born at home on Mt. Vernon Avenue. A week and a half later on November 2, the family took baby Joe to be baptized by the Reverend Michael M. Meara at St. Joseph's Cathedral on East Broad Street. The bigger church was needed so the Karrs' new baby could be presented to God in front of his whole family and his two sponsors, James and Mary Edleman. James was a local bricklayer who, with his wife and seven children, lived in the neighborhood on Oak Street and knew the Karr family very well.[3]

Joe Karr spent the first six years of his life growing up with his family on Mt. Vernon Avenue. Four years after Joe was born, Michael and Margaret had their seventh and last child. On December 9, 1883, the clan welcomed Edward Karr to the family, giving them five boys and two girls. A year and a half later little Joe would attend his first year of Catholic school at St. Patrick following in the footsteps of his older siblings.

At this time Michael started to reevaluate his life and what his family needed. First, he saw that the home at Mt. Vernon Avenue was too small for his family, and they needed more room. Second, he also wanted to find something else to challenge him other than running the store. So in 1886 the well-established Karr family moved to a bigger home at 274 Hamilton Avenue. The new house was still located in the Irish neighborhood, and this would be home to Joe Karr for the next twenty years.

Michael, age forty-five, was now ready to change careers. After working for most of the past twenty years as a shoemaker, Michael became a sewer contractor. With his connections in the city and in particular the Irish neighborhood, it was an easy transition for him. The only drawback was that he was still drinking.

As his father changed occupations, the eldest son, John Karr, finished his schooling and at the age of seventeen went to work as a cigar maker in Columbus. But the big mystery in the Karr family at this time is what happened to the Karrs' first child, Bridget. According to the family, Bridget was accounted for in 1880 (at the age of thirteen) and appeared in the 1880 Ohio Census with the rest of the family. But suddenly she seemed to have disappeared, and the family couldn't find any records of her from 1880 on. Some think she might have married and moved away, but the consensus is that she became sick and died. But it has been a family mystery as to what happened to her.[4]

In the meantime Joe became a solid student, learning math, English, social studies, and Bible study. After three years at St. Patrick School he finished his education at St. Dominic's School. Michael made sure Joe and his siblings received a basic Catholic education, something he didn't have. To get to the new school Joe would leave the house early in the morning and gallop down Thorn Ally, which ran along the side of the house off Hamilton Avenue, and go the ten blocks to school. He always enjoyed the feel of running those ten blocks, and it made him ready for anything the teachers threw at him.

In 1890 the blue-eyed, light-brownish-haired (with a little red in it), eleven-year-old son of an Irish immigrant was not filling out physically as he would have liked. Fairly short and skinny, Joe was now interested in the sports being played in the neighborhood, but his lack of size and strength was obvious. Despite his small dimensions, he would usually be right in the middle of all the action; sometimes he would be the one organizing the games. He would take charge and pick the teams and set up the rules for the games—not typical of your average eleven-year-old. Joe looked like a born leader. He might not have known it then, but his love for sports was growing on the sandlots of Columbus. Like most sons of European immigrants who came to America, Joe and his friends gravitated to sports to assimilate with the population and prove they belonged. For the Columbus boys, the sport of choice was baseball.

While in the neighborhood Joe became familiar with an older boy who would have a big influence on his life and career. Robert "Bobby" Quinn was a Columbus native who was nine years older than Joe and had started to make a name for himself. Quinn, who grew up selling newspapers in the neighborhood to make money for the family, eventually left the city and played minor league baseball as a catcher in the 1890s for several teams. Then he became the general manager of the Columbus Senators of the American Association from 1902–1917. After leaving the Senators, Quinn spent the next twenty-nine years as a general manager, president, and owner for four Major League teams, including the St. Louis Browns (1917–1922), Boston Red Sox (1923–1933), Brooklyn Dodgers (1934–1935), and Boston Braves (1936–1945). It was Quinn who showed Joe that you could be successful in sports, and not as an athlete, but as an executive.[5]

Playing sandlot baseball in the neighborhood Joe would pretend to be Cap Anson, the best player in Major League Baseball, or John "Long John" Reilly, the first baseman for the Cincinnati Reds. While playing these games, Joe made another friend who gave him another future connection to Quinn and the sports world. Robert Drury was in the same grade as Joe, and the two became instant friends, with their love of baseball being the common connection. In the only photo from Joe's Catholic school years, a serious-looking Joe is standing (with his hands folded) right in front of his best friend, both dressed in their church robes. Drury's father was a prominent physician in Columbus and was the staff doctor of the Pennsylvania Railroad Company for many years. Drury was a talented ballplayer, himself good enough to play and manage for a few minor league teams in Ohio and the Eastern League. At the same time he was playing ball, he attended and graduated from medical school. After his playing career ended, Drury became a very successful surgeon in Columbus and became Joe's physician for many years.[6]

Drury also knew Quinn through the old neighborhood and would eventually strike up a close friendship with him. When Quinn needed investors to help him buy the Boston Red Sox, he asked Drury to be part of the ownership team and Drury agreed. For ten years (1923–1933) the two

Columbus natives helped run the ballclub, with Quinn as team president and Drury as a silent owner. The trio of Carr, Quinn, and Drury would make their mark as sports executives, and their connection through the Irish neighborhood would last a lifetime. The capital city of Ohio became a hotbed for sports leaders.

As Joe was going to Catholic school and playing sandlot ball, his father was now established as a successful sewer contractor. He made an easy transition from being a shoemaker, and it was done with the hard work he showed when starting his own business over twenty years ago. The Irish saying "a handful of skill is better than a bagful of gold" fit Michael perfectly. Over time this work ethic rubbed off on his children, and maybe a little too much for his two eldest sons, who wanted to make their own mark away from home.

In 1892 the eldest son, John, at the age of twenty-three, left Columbus and moved to Chicago, Illinois. After spending five years as a cigar maker in his hometown, he traveled to the Windy City and opened his own cigar shop located at 837 North Clark Street. John would keep the spelling of the family's last name of Karr and would go on to marry a German immigrant, Ada Abraham. The couple would have three children—Edward, Walter, and Virginia. "My grandfather was a very particular person. Very particular in the way he dressed and looked. Since he was twenty-one years old he never shaved himself; he always went to the barber shop to get a shave. He liked being very neat and he liked nice things," says Jim Heavey, grandson of John Karr.[7]

John was a sophisticated, well-read, very dapper man who always seemed to have perfect hair and a perfect mustache. The Karr cigar shop became a very popular place in the city, and John made many famous contacts there. But some of the clientele were very shady, and John contributed to this environment. In October of 1911 John Karr was arrested for running a gambling ring in back of his cigar shop. In a citywide crack down on gambling, Karr's store was raided; the *Chicago Daily Tribune* reported that "five detectives raided the handbook of Karr & Kennedy, just as bettors were getting into the action of the races. John Karr, who gave the name of Hammond at the police station, was arrested and betting sheets were confiscated."[8]

"Yes he was a bookie but he did quite well. He made a lot of money," says Heavey. Two years after John left his hometown, younger brother James, when he turned twenty-two years old, followed his brother to Chicago. Joe, who was a teenager, was happy for his brothers, that they were making it on their own, although in the future the gambling operation would always put a slight strain on their relationship. The rest of the family, however, didn't handle the departure of John and James too well, and it seemed that the Karr family was breaking up and drifting apart.

John Karr, who would reside in Chicago for the rest of his life, stayed in contact with his younger brother Joe by writing and visiting with him occasionally.[9]

In the fall of 1894 Joe was entering what would be the last two years of school, and he thought for an instant about furthering his education—maybe college. Besides school and church Joe would also hang out at the local amusement center, once saying, "I got more fun out of a penny arcade where we dropped a penny in the slot and saw the mother of present movie."[10] It was one of the few times Joe Karr would reveal something about his childhood to a reporter. But it was still sports that would top his list of things he loved. His experience of playing sandlot baseball in the neighborhood—and the connections he would make—became the start of a love affair that would eventually help Joe pave a road toward a career in sports. As the young teenager was getting this special feeling inside his gut for the sporting world, his family was drifting apart and it would get worse before it got better.

3

The Love of a Family Is Replaced by a Love of Sports (1894–1906)

With John and James in Chicago (and a missing Bridget), the Karr family had started to separate and Michael Karr was participating in that old Irish tradition—drinking. He was still working and providing for his remaining family, including helping Joe Karr get through his grammar school studies. But he was drinking more and more. As for Joe, he always enjoyed going to school, and later on he would preach getting an education as the number one priority for any young person—male or female. This is something he stressed with his children as well.

While at St. Dominic's he continued to be a good student. Once he won a school medal for excellence in Bible history, his favorite subject. The little gold medal (that was about two and half inches big) was presented to him by Father Mulhearn and was engraved with "Joseph F. Karr" on the back.[1] Around the age of sixteen, Joe finished his education. Although he thought about college (for about a minute), it wasn't in the cards. Most immigrant kids his age were already working and helping their families by making an income. Michael was a success but he wasn't a rich man, and Joe could be more helpful to the family by getting a job. There was no extra money to send a child to college.

After finishing school, Joe, like his older siblings John, James, Mary, and Michael, went to work at an early age. In between his sixteenth and seventeenth birthday, Joe gained employment as an apprentice machinist. He worked in the city as a machinist for Case Manufacturing Co. and Rarig Manufacturing Co. For a teenager, a machinist's job wasn't difficult to learn, and it was rewarding work and well respected within the community. "Well, I suspect given his age that he probably did not have the most important machinist, quote-unquote, job and I suspect that he generally worked twelve-hour workdays. So it might've been a 6 to 6 type of routine," says Gregory Carr, grandson of Joe Carr. As Joe started to work he never lost his passion for learning. After working all those hours, he would find time to read. "When he left school he would continue to read. He always said you can get an education by reading the newspaper," says Michael Carr, grandson of Joe Carr.[2]

Joe worked hard at these shops, and this led him to be hired by a company that would change his life. By using his connections in the Irish neighborhood and gaining a reputation as a very dependable and hard-working machinist, Joe was hired to work for the Pennsylvania Railroad. He would work in the Pennsy's Panhandle shops off of 20th and 22nd streets near the Irish neighborhood. He fit in well with the other shop workers, who were blacksmiths, boilermakers, carpenters, inspectors, laborers, clerks, welders, painters, drill operators, engine cleaners, and foremen. His daily job wasn't glamorous.

"The Panhandle yard here in Columbus was, for a long time, a repair yard. So they brought in a lot of machines or engines and so forth for maintenance and repair. Instead of maybe sending out for a part and that sort of thing, they would either repair or remanufacture a part along those lines, in order to repair and keep the engines running. His participation as a machinist would have been related to repair and maintenance of engines at the railroad Panhandle yard," says James Carr, grandson of Joe Carr.[3]

While Joe was making a living as a machinist, his sister Mary, age twenty-two, who the family nicknamed "Mayme," was working as a stenographer in the city, at one time being employed by New York Life and the Ohio Penitentiary. His brother Michael, age nineteen, found work as a clerk in a grocery-candy store, and Eddie, age thirteen, was still attending school. In the midst of their busy lives, the Karr siblings faced their biggest challenge. On July 20, 1898, Margaret Karr died at her home on Hamilton Avenue at the age of fifty-eight. The *Ohio State Journal* wrote this obituary (which never revealed cause of death) under the headline of "Another Pioneer Gone":

> In the death of Mrs. Michael Carr at her home at 274 Hamilton Avenue Thursday afternoon Columbus lost another pioneer. Mrs. Carr had lived in Columbus for 32 years and witnessed many remarkable changes in the city's growth. When she first came here the East End was not what it is at present. The land occupied now by beautiful residences and handsome streets was then a country field and under cultivation by those who owned it. She lived to see the city prosper and spread out until it is now one of the best and prettiest cities in Ohio.[4]

The Karr family was devastated by Margaret's death, especially Michael, who after thirty-two years of marriage, was now left alone. Three days after Margaret's death the family gathered to say good-bye. At 9:00 a.m. the family held a funeral for Margaret at St. Joseph's Cathedral (the same place where Joe was baptized). They would eventually bury her at Mt. Calvary Cemetery, the well-known Catholic cemetery in Columbus. Although she was only fifty-eight years old, Margaret Karr lived an immigrant life and probably felt more like she was eighty years old.

Joe was just eighteen years old when his mother died. In future years he never talked much about his mother, so we don't know how close he was to her or how he reacted to her death. He continued to work and helped his siblings look after their father. With a new century approaching the family got a new name. After a few years of trying it out (as you can see in Margaret Carr's obituary), the family officially changed the spelling of their last name to a more American version, C-a-r-r. Only the family rebel John Karr in Chicago kept the original spelling, mainly to keep his cigar shop's current name. For the rest of his life, Joe would be known as Joe F. Carr.[5]

Also that same year his brother, Michael L. Carr, married a local Irish girl named Margaret Megahan. Michael was built just like his younger brother Joe. "He had the same blue eyes like Joe with sandy blonde hair and the same body build. He had a deep voice and loved to smoke. He was a chain smoker just like Joe; maybe that's where Joe picked it up. He also was crazy about his wife and she was crazy about him," says Margaret Mooney, the granddaughter of Michael L. Carr. "Like his brother my grandfather loved sports. He played golf and he bowled. He played poker a lot too. I doubt Uncle Joe played poker though," says Mooney.[6]

Michael moved out of his father's home soon after getting married and continued to work as a clerk at the grocery store. The couple went on to have three children—Robert, John, and Margaret (although Robert would die before the age of ten). Joe's relationship with Michael and Eddie was the best among all his siblings, and it grew during this time. Joe liked working in the shops, but he wanted to do more and get involved in the one thing he truly loved—sports.

The new century had seen a new name, a new sister-in-law, and now a new career. Around this time Joe got his first job in the sporting world, as he was hired as an assistant sports editor at the *Ohio State Journal*, one of the big newspapers in the city, along with the *Columbus Dispatch*, the *Columbus Press-Post*, and the *Columbus Citizen*.

In 1811 the *Ohio State Journal* was founded in Worthington, Ohio, a small town just north of Columbus and was titled the *Western Intelligence*. After Columbus was named the capital, the paper moved to the downtown area. In 1840 the paper was renamed the *Ohio State Journal* and later became the Republican Party's main voice in central Ohio. This first sports job would come in handy down the road as Carr would continue to have a relationship with the *Ohio State Journal* for the next four decades.

Joe's title at the paper sounded bigger than the job, as the sports department wasn't very big and the pay was less. But it was a chance for Joe to be involved in the sports world, and that's all he wanted. He was able to attend local sporting events, and while doing this he got to know owners, promoters, athletes, team managers, coaches, and, just as important, other sportswriters. While covering the sports scene, he became well-known for his knowledge and writing on all sports, but it was his boxing stories that grabbed extra attention around Columbus. His boxing yarns were very popular, as well as his famous trademark line that would accompany every article: "the fighters went at it hammer and tongs."[7]

Joe was barely in his early twenties when he was gaining this much-needed experience in seeing from all angles how the sports world was being operated and run. His sports-writing days would always come in handy as he furthered his career, and the NFL would be the ultimate benefactor. Carr always saw the press as a dear friend and he treated it with respect. Once talking about the press he said, "Their support is the most important factor in the success of any sports venture. Be fair with the press and it will be fair with you." He lived by this motto for the rest of his career.[8]

Although Joe was covering sports for the *Ohio State Journal*, that wasn't enough. He wanted to more involved. He wanted to run his own sports team just like back on the sandlots in the neighborhood. He was smart and knew sports as well as anybody. He knew he could do it. So back at the Panhandle shops he formed a baseball team made up of employees of the railroad. The Panhandle Athletic Board approved the team. Because Joe was a fan of Chicago White Sox owner Charlie Comiskey, who was nicknamed "the Old Roman" and was one of the founders of the new American League, Joe named his team the Panhandle White Sox.

The Panhandle baseball team would go on to play in the Capital City League and the Saturday Afternoon League in Columbus for several years. About the same time Bob Quinn returned to Columbus to be secretary-business manager for the Columbus minor league baseball team in the new American Association. Joe would strike up a friendship with him and continue to see that one could make a career out of being a sports executive. Everything was falling in place for Joe to learn his true trade, as the machinist job was starting to take a back seat.

In the fall of 1901 a fairly new sport was starting to take off in central Ohio and in the Panhandle shops that would grab the attention of Joe

Carr. Professional football had gotten its roots in western Pennsylvania in the 1890s and now started to make its way west into Ohio. Columbus had several teams playing, including the Columbus Nationals, Columbus Northerns, and the Columbus Barracks (made up of soldiers who were stationed in Columbus). Colleges like Ohio Medical University and Ohio State University, which started football in 1890, would contribute to the excitement of the sport in Columbus by playing each other.

In the Panhandle shops there were whispers of a football team being formed. William Butler, a former fullback at Ohio Medical University and a blacksmith in the shops, decided to start the team and coach. The team would be called the Columbus Panhandles. Butler recruited players for the team through the employees of the railroad and contacted other local teams for games. In 1901 the Panhandles played three games; they faced the Columbus Barracks soldier team twice and traveled west to play the Logansport team once. They finished 1–2. Fans started to notice the new "physical" sport in Columbus, as crowds from 400 to 1,200 attended the games, but the leadership of the team was very poor.[9]

In the Panhandles first four seasons, the team had five different team managers and played only seventeen games. Nobody had the time (especially with no salary being ofered) or, more importantly, the passion to help run a football team. It took dedication to field a team, to schedule games, sell tickets, book travel, talk to the press about publicity for the team, and much more. In 1904 alone, the Panhandles had two separate team managers, with one quitting due to his railroad shop duties, and the team played just three games that season. The team went 2–1 with their only loss to the more skilled team from the Ohio State University. Carr, only twenty-five years old, witnessed all this confusion firsthand, and at the same time, this is where he started to fall in love with the sport. Football was just getting started in the Midwest and he thought this was a way of making his mark in the sporting world. Baseball was already established, but football needed some guidance.

Joe's experience the past couple of years with the newspaper and the company baseball team showed him that this type of mismangement could only hurt a team. He was proven right when the Panhandles would not field a football team in 1905 and 1906. Joe knew that a manager had to be hard working, fair, and honest with his players as well as the press, which at this time had a big influence on whether a team could be successful.

As Joe worked harder his father started to work less due to some reoccurring health issues. He was not working as a sewer contractor when another tragic death hit the family. While back in Columbus from Chicago, James Carr was stricken by the flu and never recovered. On December 9, 1904, at the young age of thirty-one, James died, just nine days short of his birthday; the family actually listed him at thirty-two years old on his tombstone. James was buried next to his mother at Mt. Calvary Cemetery. The family stood together in front of the two tombstones aching. Little did they know that in less than two months they would return to this very spot—grieving again.

Michael Carr was again hit hard by a death in his family. He wasn't working, his drinking was evident, and his health was in bad shape. The head of the Carr family had lived a typical Irish immigrant story in America. He left the troubled land of Ireland for a better life, and he succeeded. He was a hardworking, well-respected citizen, who provided for his large family and gave them a better life. It was now time to go home to meet his maker.

At 10:30 a.m. on the morning of February 6, 1905, and just two months after his son died, Michael Carr suffered a second stroke within a week and passed away at his home at 274 Hamilton Avenue. He was sixty-three years old. His death was reported by all of the Columbus newspapers, including the *Columbus Dispatch*'s evening edition of that day. After nearly forty years living in the capital city, Michael and Margaret Carr had both passed away. All five Carr children gathered to pay their respects to the father that gave them a better life.

The funeral was held on February 9 at St. Patrick Church. Family and friends said good-bye to an Irish life at the church that Michael loved so much. To describe Michael, the obituaries used the words "pioneer," as they had with his wife, and "one of the best known residents of the East Side." Joe and his siblings were proud of their father, and this going-away ceremony at the church was just what their father would want. After the funeral, the five Carr siblings marched over to Mt. Calvary Cemetery to bury their father. The patriarch of the Carr family was now laid to rest next to his wife and a few feet in front of his son James. The three tombstones were identical, made from white stone concrete, and stood about two and a half feet tall, with a solid stone base. The names were carved in the stone, the spelling of the family name being C-a-r-r, with the words *father*, *mother*, and *son* carved at the top. They were simple but elegant.[10]

Just as with the death of his mother, Joe Carr, in future years, didn't say anything about his relationship with his father; no quotes in any articles, interviews, or oral history passed down with his family. Joe's work ethic and dedication to God were definitely passed down from his parents, but what else? Nobody knows. He definitely didn't live in the past. One thing Joe learned from his father—probably the most important thing—was his dislike for drinking. For his entire life, Joe never took a drink of alcohol. "He was a teetotaler, no question about it," says Gregory Carr, grandson of Joe Carr.[11] This loss of family didn't stop Joe from working hard and trying to make his future better. He would work harder; it was the Irish way.

Shortly before and after her father's death, Joe's older sister Mary became romantically involved with a prison trustee, Frank Pratt, while working as a stenographer at the Ohio Pen. The slender, very attractive Mary didn't know how her father felt about Frank, but she had fallen in love with him and the two married. The couple started a family and eventually moved north to Toledo. The marriage didn't last though. The two divorced, which created some tension with her younger brother Joe, who like any good Catholic didn't believe in divorce. Mary found work as a secretary for St. John's College in Toledo and rarely saw her brother. Over the years the only way they would communicate was by writing letters, and most of Mary's letters were written by her children.

Pretty much from this point on, the Carr family in Columbus consisted of the three youngest boys—Michael, Joe, and Eddie. They would all remain in Columbus and have successful careers and lives in the capital city for the rest of their lives. While the three boys dealt with the loss of their father, the first thing they did was sell the Carr family home at 274 Hamilton Avenue. Michael was living with his wife and children, leaving Joe and Eddie to try and take care of a large house, so they agreed to sell it. After twenty years of living on Hamilton Avenue, Joe had to find a new home.

He and Eddie moved out and became boarders at the residence of a family friend, Charlotte Vanderau, who was a recent widower and had rooms for rent at her house at 295 North 21st Street. Her husband, Casper, had run a saloon on Mt. Vernon Avenue in the Irish neighborhood and had known Joe's father, who would stop by for drinks after work. It was an easy transition for the two brothers, considering the circumstance of losing their father and family home.[12]

Eddie Carr, age twenty-one, physically looked like his brothers, sharp blue eyes, slender build, deep voice, and a hard worker. Always good with numbers, after finishing school he became a clerk for several companies, including several buggy companies in the city. He would continue to do this type of work for the rest of his life. As roommates, Joe and Eddie got along well, although they lived separate lives. Joe was still working full-time as a machinist and socializing with his small group of friends. He was a member of the Monday Night club at the Buckeye Hall in Columbus, where a group of young men would meet to speak, sing, eat, and have a few cigars to pass the night. Joe was now a full-blown smoker, which would last the rest of his life. While mourning his father's death and finding a new place to live, Joe failed to notice that the Panhandles didn't field a football team in 1905 and 1906. But the sport was never too far from his mind.

During the two-year hiatus of the Panhandles, Carr heard about the gridiron exploits of two of his coworkers who had played for his baseball team. John and Ted Nesser were part of a large railroad family (they had eight family members working for the Pennsylvania Railroad at different times) who had played football the last two years with the Massillon (Ohio) Tigers. The Tigers were the best pro football team in the state of Ohio for those two seasons, compiling a record of 20–1–0 and attracting fairly big crowds for pro football games at that time. Their rivalry with the Canton Bulldogs (who were specifically set up to battle the Tigers) attracted crowds of 6,000 to 8,000 in 1905–1906 and gave the sport some national exposure, since the pro game at this time was still only played at the local level where small-town rivalries were the lifeblood of the sport.

Carr heard these stories from the two Nesser brothers and took note that the sport might have a future. College football had been around for nearly forty years, with the Ivy League schools being the standard bearers for the sport, and Ohio State University was slowly building a following in Columbus. But at the end of 1906, a scandal rocked the sport and Joe took notice.

There was no official football league in the early days of pro football; most teams played local and nearby teams, with team managers setting up games on the fly. At the start of the twentieth century, pro football was considered a criminal activity by the public and press and was frowned upon by the college game. Most teams would spend money to get the best players possible to try and beat their nearby rival for bragging rights and to collect a few bucks along the way. Stark County had the two best teams in the state do just that. In 1905 Massillon defeated the Canton team twice to claim the mythical title of "best pro team" in Ohio. So at the end of 1906 the Massillon Tigers set up two games with their archrival—the Canton Bulldogs. This was going to be the two best teams playing each other for bragging rights (since there was no actual league title to win), and it was to be the big paydays for each team, too.

Both teams spent money to bring in top talent (including players like John and Ted Nesser) to play in the two games. Canton won the first game 10–5, and Massillon won the second game 13–6. But shortly after the second game, there were rumors that the game was fixed so that there would be a third game to be played. Stories of betting by the managers and players on each team surfaced, and fans almost brawled in a hotel lobby hearing these rumors. It ruined a great season for professional football. Carr, a young executive and sportswriter, saw how this damaged the sport. The answer was simple to him: you needed to be honest and fair, and you needed rules to follow. Although gambling would be part of all sports (including pro football), Carr knew that in no way should a team manager or player gamble or try to fix a game for his own personal gain.

If the fans wanted to lay a bet on the game (something he couldn't control), that was fine, but a manager, coach, or player was unacceptable. In order for pro football or any sport to be accepted by the public it needed to be played clean and fair as possible. The Canton-Massillon scandal showed this to Carr. He took note.[13]

Carr was now hooked on football, and the past several years of working in the sports world gave him confidence to move forward in making this a career. "He definitely used this period to feel out if this was something he wanted to do. It grew on him. . . . He didn't play these sports; with his stature, he couldn't play them. So he went into other areas like organization," says Michael Carr, grandson of Joe Carr.[14] His family was now less a part of his life than the sporting world. It was time to make his family proud of him. He remembered his father's Irish work ethic, "a handful of skill is better than a bagful of gold." His parents were now gone. But what would Joe say to them if they were here? "Love you mom, love you dad, but now it's time to go to work."

Pro Football's Rag Days

Rutgers and Princeton played a college rugby-soccer-football game, the first ever, on November 6, 1869. The game used modified London Football Association rules, and during the next seven years rugby gained favor with the major eastern schools over soccer, and modern American football began to develop. The first organized attempt to establish a uniform set of football rules occurred on November 23, 1876, at the Massasoit House in Springfield, Massachusetts. Representatives from Harvard, Columbia, Princeton, and Yale were in attendance. The result was the first Intercollegiate Football Rules Book. From then on the professional game adopted the rules established by college football.

By the time the NFL was founded in 1920, football rules had already undergone significant change. Some pre-NFL rules that helped shape the American game include the following:

1879: scrimmage line replaced the rugby "scrum"
1880: eleven players on a side
1881: field dimensions reduced to 110 yards in length by 53 yards in width
1882: three downs to gain five yards
1893: kickoff must go ten yards unless touched by the defense to be in play
1895: seven men required to be on the line of scrimmage at the snap

1906: forward pass (with restrictions) made legal
1906: game made sixty minutes long
1910: game to be played in four 15-minute quarters
1912: fourth down added to series to make a first down
1912: the field was made 100 yards long with two 10-yard end zones

Professional football was a direct offspring of independent football, so titled by the press because of their independence from any college or university. The game was played mostly by local athletes in small blue-collar towns or cities in eastern Pennsylvania and Ohio. At the end of the nineteenth century, teams developed in other towns as far east as New York, as far west as Davenport, Iowa; as far south as Louisville, Kentucky; and as far north as Duluth, Minnesota.

Usually played on Sunday afternoons, the pro game didn't venture to the far south because the Baptists' and Methodists' influence didn't allow the game to be played on the Sabbath. Blue laws in Massachusetts, New York City, and parts of Pennsylvania (Pittsburgh-Philadelphia) hindered the progress of the pro game on the East Coast. But the small towns in eastern Pennsylvania and throughout Ohio were filled with blue-collar workers who slaved for six days a week and didn't mind shelling out the fifty cents to a dollar admission to see a professional football game on their one day off. The Sunday game had arrived.

Initially independent football was played by local athletes with maybe one or two "imports" brought in to play in crucial games. Most players played for the love of the game and would only make money based on the gate receipts. Over time teams would hire and pay imported players to help win the big game; this turned the independent player-team into "semi-professional." Most imported players were paid "ten and cakes" for their play on the field. Sometimes the team would pay for their travel. Eventually the whole team would be paid, and the transition to professional football was complete.

In eastern Pennsylvania the professional game would really take off. Strong local rivalries were the lifeblood of the early pro game as competing towns would build their teams up in order to defeat their chief rival. In 1892 an intense rivalry was growing between the Allegheny Athletic Association (AAA) and the Pittsburgh Athletic Club (PAC), and it led to the first documented professional football player. Former Yale All-American William "Pudge" Heffelfinger was paid $500 by the AAA to play against the PAC ($500 was an incredible amount at that time and not matched for decades) and thus became the first "pro." On November 12 the AAA won the game 4–0 when Heffelfinger picked up a PAC fumble and ran thirty-five yards for a touchdown.

The early pro game didn't quite look like the wide-open style we see today. The game didn't have any hash marks, and the ball was placed at the sideline if it was run out of bounds, making the next play very predictable with a run toward the middle. The ball used was a rugby type, very round and used more for kicking or drop-kicking than for passing, since passing wouldn't be legalized until 1906. The power running game or ball carrying dominated the sport and play was brutal at times. In 1888 the low tackle was legalized and the result of this rule tended to make the game more physical and dull. Until then teams used plenty of "open play," stressing laterals and backward passes to the halfbacks who were set out like a modern wingback. However, once it became legal to cut a man down at the knees, teams moved their halfbacks in behind the line and concentrated on power over trickery.

Starting in 1869, football's scoring system went through major changes, too:

1869: all goals count one point each
1883: safety worth one point; touchdown, two; goal after touchdown, four; goal from field, five
1884: safety worth two points; touchdown, four; goal after touchdown, two
1898: touchdown worth five points; goal after touchdown, one
1904: goal from field worth four points
1909: goal from field worth three points
1912: touchdown worth six points

Professional football at the beginning of the twentieth century was still played in small towns and was very much "unofficial." No football league was formed, as most teams would just compete to win their city or state championship, although there was no true way of declaring any type of champion. An informal number of sportswriters, team managers, and fan opinions would usually determine a "champion."

In the early days of professional football, with no league, no standings, no stadiums, no set rosters, and schedules done week-by-week, the team managers were vital to the success of a pro team. Team managers had to do everything; they had to find the players, arrange the schedule and travel plans, hire officials and security, advertise the game, sell the tickets, and disperse the gate receipts. A very competent team manager was the key to survival for early pro football teams, and this survival would be year to year for most pro teams.

At this time pro football would gravitate from eastern Pennsylvania to the state of Ohio and cities such as Akron, Canton, Cleveland, Columbus, and Massillon would field the strongest teams, eventually gaining the nickname "the Cradle of Pro Football." The rivalry between Canton and Massillon would grab national headlines and launch the sport to a new level. The popularity was just starting to take off but a couple of problems would affect the game for years to come. If those problems weren't bad enough, the play on the field was getting more violent.

4

The Columbus Panhandles and the Great Nesser Brothers (1907–1909)

In 1905 the sport of football was at a crossroad. For the past forty years the game was played mainly at the collegiate level, and it was played with brute strength. But now colleges and universities were being criticized by the public, school presidents, and press for its rough play and the proper role it had in the educational structure. In that year alone the sport saw eighteen fatalities and another 150 serious injuries. Even President Theodore Roosevelt, an avid sportsman who enjoyed football, put his two cents in and asked for reform.[1]

Since college football had a governing body that established rules and regulations, professional football managers followed their lead. The college officials started to think about what would make the game a little more wide open and not so brutal. In 1882 the college game set a rule of three downs to gain a first down and keep the ball. Thirteen years later (1895), they changed the rule where seven men had to be on the line of scrimmage, and that helped calm down the rough play a little. Then in 1906 they shortened the game to sixty minutes (in 1910 they set the game to be played in four 15-minute quarters) and came up with the most important rule change: they made the forward pass legal, although with some restrictions—for example, the forward pass had to be thrown five yards behind the line of scrimmage and an incomplete pass in the end zone would turn the ball over to the defense.

The forward pass opened up the game just enough to help curtail some of the criticism to abolish the sport, but it didn't change the basic fundamental play on the field. The game became more refined and less brutal, but it still was a sport built on strength and the power running game.

The strategy of the game would develop over the next decade, and the sport started to become more of a science for coaches. Men such as Walter Camp, Amos Alonzo Stagg, Glenn "Pop" Warner, Fielding Yost, and John Heisman would become legendary coaches at their schools and dominate the sport on and off the field. Nothing about the sport would be adopted without their knowledge or blessing.

The professional game was a different story. The pro game was played by the college rules because there was no governing body or no official football league that established any rules and regulations that each team had to follow. Because there was no league, there were no season-long standings to follow, like Major League Baseball, and no world championship game to decide who was the best team (like the World Series, which started in 1903). Much of the public and media looked down on the early pro game, thinking it was just a sport played by vagabonds or, worse yet, by young collegians who played under fake names for a quick dollar. With no rules, three big issues would affect the early years of the sport:

1. *Playing under assumed names while still in college.* Young athletes would play for their college on Saturday and then play professionally on Sunday. This upset coaches and school officials at many colleges and universities around the country, and most of the time, college football showed no support of or cooperation with professional football.
2. *Rising salaries.* Because pro football at this time was built on local rivalries, team managers would recruit the best players they could and pay rather large salaries. Usually the managers would spend ten dollars up to $100 a game for top players to field their team and try to win. Then the big game might only attract a thousand fans and the team would go broke by the end of the season.
3. *Hopping from one team to another.* Because team managers would entice players to play in the big games for good money, some players would hop from one team to another to go with the highest bidder.

These three issues would plague professional football in some way for the next fifteen years. For early pro football managers, these were big problems to overcome. Adding to the dilemma was the fact that the majority of team managers (who were mostly ex-players) during this era were guilty of all three issues, sometimes bragging about it. If you were going to win on the field you had to get the best players and usually that meant stealing a player from another team or recruiting a college player to play. So the sport continued this pattern, and it would take some time before they really solved the situation.

The Canton–Massillon football scandal of 1906 didn't help the pro game either. Joe Carr was not surprised by the fall-out of the gambling scandal, but there was one good thing for him and his dreams of being involved in football: the state of Ohio was now the place to be for the pro game. The best players and best teams still resided in the Buckeye state. Most of the teams in the state called themselves the "Ohio League," although the teams never met to establish rules or create an official way of declaring a champion. Cities such as Akron, Columbus, Cleveland, Dayton, Canton, Massillon, Shelby, Elyria, Toledo, and Youngstown would all build and operate successful professional football teams that would carry the sport to new heights over the next two decades.

This was the pro game in 1907, and Carr thought he was ready to tackle the sport head on. Was he ready to handle it? Although he wasn't a rookie in running a sports team, spending the last several years running the Panhandles baseball team, Carr was about to enter a sport that didn't have the direction and stability of baseball. After Carr talked to Ted Nesser about his playing experience with the Massillon Tigers, the two got to chatting more about starting a football team with the railroad. Once at the shops, Joe asked Ted who he thought would play on the team. "Well, there's six of us Nessers. We ought to be able to pick up a half dozen others in the shops. You go and see if you can get us a practice game and I'll see who might be interested."[2]

Sometime in the early fall of 1907, the twenty-seven-year-old Joe Carr approached the Panhandle Athletic Board to ask if he could reorganize the Columbus Panhandles football team. He said some of the employees wanted to play, and he thought he could make it work this time. He would put in the time and energy needed to make it successful, and he would do it for free. The team would just make money on how many fans came out for the game. The gate receipts would be the only way the team would make any money. The athletic board gave him the go-ahead. It was now official—Joe Carr had his very own pro football team.

He didn't have a salary (although he had left the newspaper he was still working as a machinist), and he didn't have any money to spend on acquiring players. He had to pick his squad from the employees of the Pennsylvania Railroad and the Panhandle shops. What a trade-off; you can field a team, but you have to get your players, not from the colleges and universities, but from the work shop at the railroad. Good luck. Of course, the athletic board didn't know that Carr had the nucleus of his team right there, a group of brothers that would make him famous. In 1907 there were five Nesser brothers working in the Panhandle shops as boilermakers, which was the toughest job physically in the shops. They all were very accomplished athletes, and Carr put his faith in their abilities. Carr would say that the Nesser brothers are "a family I will match for athletic ability against any in the land."[3]

The Nessers, like the Carr family, were very well-known in Columbus and had a long history with the capital city. Their father, Theodore Nesser, was born on January 20, 1850, in a small town in Germany called Kirsch, near Trier, Alsace-Lorraine, which used to be the border region between Germany and France. In 1870 at the age of twenty, he fought with the German army in the Franco-Prussian War and didn't care for all the fighting. Papa Nesser eventually got a job with the German railroad as an apprentice boilermaker, and the German government—which operated and controlled all the railroads—sent him to Metz, where he worked for twelve years as a boilermaker.[4]

Sometime around 1873 he met Katherine Steinbach and the following year the two were married and wasted no time in creating one large family. Theo and Katherine had five children in a six-year span while in Germany: John (April 25, 1875), Anna (April 17, 1876), Peter (October 22, 1877), Erminna (May 5, 1879), and Philip (December 10, 1880). By 1881 Theo had grown weary of the wars in Europe and looked to give his family a fresh start in America. That year he signed a contract to work with the Pennsylvania Railroad in the United States in exchange for boat fare. He left his family behind—until he could raise enough money to send for them—and agreed to work for three years to help the Pennsy develop improvements to their locomotive's fire box.

Theo came to America and the railroad sent him to the small town of Dennison, Ohio, to start working. In 1882 he finally had enough money to send for Katherine and the five children. While in Dennison, the Nesser family grew again as two more kids were born. Theodore Nesser Jr. (April 5, 1883) and Catherine (May 27, 1885). (Later on tragedy would strike the Nesser family, as Catherine would pass away in 1900, at the age of fifteen.) In 1889 Theo left the railroad, moved his family to Columbus, and opened up his own plumbing and pipe-fitting business.

While in Columbus the Nesser family continued to grow, and five more children were born: Fred (September 10, 1887), Frank (June 3, 1889), Mary Rose (May 7, 1891), Alfred (June 6, 1893), and Raymond (March 22, 1898). The grand total for the Nesser's reached eleven. Eventually seven of the eight Nesser boys would follow their father to work as boilermakers at the Pennsylvania Railroad. In 1905 the large family moved into a modest home at 1608 Harvard Avenue on the east side of the city within earshot of the Panhandle shop whistle.

Out of the eight boys, six of them would go on to play for Joe Carr and the Columbus Panhandles. The Nessers and Joe Carr made a great team. "The Nessers and my grandfather had a unique type of relationship. There was a great deal of mutual respect here and that carried onto the football field. They both respected what each other did," says James Carr, grandson of Joe Carr. "They called him Gentleman Joe. All of the Nesser brothers respected Joe Carr. They had great respect for him. They considered him more, I believe, as a friend than a manager. There was a close-knit relationship between the two," says Irene Cassady, niece of the Nesser brothers. "He and the Nessers were all good friends. When I talked to the Nesser family they all told me what great friends Joe Carr and the Nesser brothers were," says James Carr.[5]

Growing up the Nesser boys knew who was the boss of the house—Momma Nesser. She allowed the unruly boys to play rough in the backyard, until one of them drew blood, and then she would take a broomstick and break up the fisticuffs. The brothers were very physical in everything they did, whether it was playing sports or working as boilermakers in the railroad shops. The Nessers' raw strength and power was the key to the Panhandles success for years to come, and the whole family would enjoy everything about the sport.

There's a famous story that when the football team was going strong, Theodore served as water boy and Katherine washed and ironed the team's uniforms. The first part is probably an exaggeration, although Theodore may have gone onto the field a couple of times during timeouts to give his boys hell if they were losing. The second part of the story has to be true to some extent. Even if Mrs. Nesser (who worked sometimes as a seamstress) cleaned and repaired only her own boys' uniforms, she was practically laundress for the team since there were six of them playing. "Grandpa Nesser was about five feet seven and Grandma was just over five feet tall. Who would of thought that these two German immigrants would raise six big, tall, talented, tough football players," said Irene Cassady, niece of the Nesser brothers.[6]

The six Nesser brothers were all different in their personalities and playing abilities (described here in order of age):

John Nesser (five feet eleven, 195 pounds) was the midget of the family. He usually played quarterback, a position that called primarily for blocking and tackling ability in those days. He might have been the best all-around athlete of the brothers, once winning a medal as the all-around athlete of the Pennsylvania Railway System. Nicknamed "the Wolf," John would play eighteen years for the Panhandles, until the age of forty-one.

Phil Nesser (six feet, 225 pounds) was primarily a tackle, although he did carry the ball sometimes on end-arounds. Phil was probably the most unsung of the Nesser clan. His solid line play didn't make headlines—in eighteen seasons of playing with the Panhandles, he scored only four career touchdowns. "My father was a gentle giant. I never heard an excited word come out of his mouth. He was just very stoic," says Kate Benson, daughter of Phil Nesser.[7]

Ted Nesser (five feet ten, 230 pounds) was called "the greatest of the Nessers," playing seventeen seasons with the Panhandles. He would go on to play every position on the field and play each one well. When he played halfback, his best position, he had an uncanny ability to take a hit and stay on his feet. In an article published in the *Ohio State Journal* on December 7, 1917, Jim Thorpe was quoted as saying that Ted was "one of the great players of the pro game." But Ted did have a knack of putting his face right into the action a little too much. "My dad had his nose broken at least eight times. Dr. Turner [family doctor in Columbus] said, 'There's no use to set it. I'm not going to set it anymore; you'll just break it again.' After that he would say he had Knute Rockne's nose," says Babe Sherman, daughter of Ted Nesser.[8]

Ted was also the coach of the Panhandles for thirteen years. He would direct the practices and call most of the plays. He was the vocal leader of the group, and the team (as well as his brothers) always responded to him. He also was the closest of the brothers to Joe Carr. "My dad and Joe Carr were real close; he adored Joe Carr. I guess that's how Joe got into football; my dad coaxed him in to take care of the money end of it and scheduling the games. Carr did a good job of it," says Babe Sherman.[9]

Fred Nesser (six feet five, 250 pounds) was the tallest, but he was no string bean. He played fourteen seasons mainly as a tackle and end, but sometimes he would line up in the backfield at fullback, providing much-needed blocking with his big frame. Fred was also an accomplished boxer and was considered a prime contender for Jess Willard's heavyweight crown before a wrist injury halted his pursuit. But Fred's first love was playing football with his brothers. In one Columbus newspaper, Fred revealed that the highest salary he ever earned for a single season from gate receipts was $950. But the money didn't matter; he was doing something he loved.[10]

Frank Nesser (six feet one, 245 pounds) played fifteen seasons with the railroaders and at times his play was unbelievable. Playing mostly fullback, he carried his weight with the grace of a ballet dancer. He was also one of the greatest punters who ever lived, and seventy-yard boots were common. "Uncle Frank could kick a football from one field goal to another. He put on kicking exhibitions with Jim Thorpe and Thorpe never kicked the ball as far as Uncle Frank," says Irene Cassady, niece of Frank Nesser.[11]

Joann Frankie, daughter of Frank Nesser, says,

> He was a big guy but jolly. He had a good disposition. I believe he would've done anything for anybody he could. He was a big fella but he never threw

his weight around; he was a very nice person. He also respected Joe Carr for keeping the team together and making sure they had places to play and teams to play. There was a lot of work to it, come to think of it, because back in those days they didn't have all the telephones, cell phones, and e-mail back then. They had to get out and go. Just go. So he respected him. He would always say Mr. Joe Carr was one of the finest men I ever knew.[12]

Al Nesser (six feet, 195 pounds) was the youngest of the brothers and played eight seasons as a guard for the Panhandles. Al joined his brothers on the team in 1910, becoming one of the best guards in the early days of professional football and continuing to play pro ball until 1931. Because of his age, Al had more success playing in the NFL than did his older siblings. He played ten seasons in the NFL, with four different teams, winning two NFL championships on the way—with the Akron Pros (1920) and the New York Giants (1927). During his playing career Al Nesser usually played without a helmet and shoulder pads, and his durability earned him the title of "the Iron Man of Football." On November 20, 1922, the *Buffalo Evening-News* said this about Al Nesser: "There may be better ends than Nesser, but none have ever appeared here, there may be better tackles than Nesser, but again none have displayed their wares in Buffalo; the same holds for guards. Nesser was a team in himself. Big, powerful and fast he spoiled Buffalo on-slaughts time and again."[13]

Joe Carr used the Nesser brothers as the backbone of the Columbus Panhandles for the next fifteen years, and the group of boilermakers was perfectly built to play in the rough and tough early days of professional football. "Yes, they were rough. Absolutely. Ted was the captain and he called all the plays and what not. They played where they were needed, nobody had a specific assignment at that time. They had their little huddle on the sideline and they were told what to do and if they didn't do it, look out because they had five other brothers to answer to," says Irene Cassady, niece of the Nesser brothers.[14] Although none of the Nessers played in college they were about to become household names in the sport that desperately needed some positive press. After the 1906 Massillon-Canton scandal professional football needed some stability and the Panhandles were about to reorganize, singing a different tune. The new Columbus Panhandles—led by Joe Carr—wouldn't steal players from another team for more money; they wouldn't offer a college player a spot on the team for a quick buck, or allow a player to play under an assumed name.

With the five Nesser brothers on board (Al wouldn't join the team until 1910), Carr filled out the rest of his 1907 team with several players who would give him many years of service. Andy Kertzinger, a fellow machinist in the shops who played for the 1902–1904 Panhandles, rejoined the squad as a center and played until 1915 (missing only 1914). Chief Henry (three years) and Henry Spiers (three years) added depth to the

1907 squad. Carr now had a team and players. He then went to work on scheduling games. Using his sports connections, he went on to schedule six games in 1907, with four of them played on the road.

One of the perks for all railroad workers was having free passes to travel anywhere on the train. Carr used this to his advantage, although it would be several years until they became a full-fledged traveling team. Carr booked games with some of the best pro teams, such as the Pittsburgh Lyceum, the Shelby Athletic Club, the Massillon Tigers, and a local team called the Columbias. As Carr was scheduling games, the team began to practice under the guidance of Ted Nesser. The only problem was when and where to practice. Most of the players had families and responsibilities after work, so Ted and the squad decided to practice during their lunch hour.

"They would get an old melon-shaped football out and they would just practice there on the railroad yards. The men would eat their lunch in fifteen minutes, leaving forty-five minutes to practice. They wore no helmets or equipment, just work clothes. That's how they got started playing on the sandlots of the railroad yards," says Irene Cassady, niece of the Nesser brothers. "They would just throw the ball around and have light scrimmages, that sort of things, as well as doing the fundamentals because these folks were truly blessed. They were unusual. So they would spend most of the time working on basic fundamentals, throwing, catching, kicking, and punting," says James Carr, grandson of Joe Carr.[15]

Although in future years they would upgrade to several local parks for evening practices, the Panhandles mainly used the railroad yards as their primary practice site. Throughout September and early October the team practiced, as Carr set up their first game at Driving Park, against a local 160-pound squad called the Columbias. Carr knew his team outweighed the Columbias but he also knew that his team needed to ease into their schedule. As Panhandles manager, he would follow this philosophy of scheduling so-called warm-up games for his entire career. At 3:00 p.m. on October 13 at Driving Park, 400 fans saw the Panhandles play their first game under new team manager Joe Carr. The *Columbus Dispatch* recapped the action: "Manager [Joe] Carr's Panhandle football team opened its season yesterday at the Driving Park, defeating the Columbias 38 to 0. The Nesser boys were in evidence during the game, Frank getting three of the seven touchdowns. Lack of accurate knowledge of the signals on the part of the railroaders made their play less smooth than it would otherwise have been."[16]

The *Dispatch* article would be the first time that Joe Carr's name appeared in the paper as the Panhandles manager. It was Carr's team now, and the press knew it; Carr's name would regularly appear in Columbus papers detailing the team's successes and failures. The article also mentioned the less-than-smooth football skills of the Panhandles, who were still in the learning process. But it was a victory for Carr and his boys and they wanted more. Six days later the team traveled east to play the very talented Pittsburgh Lyceum. Because of Pennsylvania's blue laws (which prevented Sunday football), the game was played on a Saturday. Just another roadblock that faced pro football managers in the early days of professional football.

In front of a nice crowd of 3,000 fans the Panhandles lost a tough one, 11–6. The Pittsburgh papers had nice things to say about the railroaders.

> The Pittsburgh papers were loud in their praise of the Columbus team and, although the game was characterized as the most grueling contest seen in years, the Panhandles were highly complimented for the clean game they played.
>
> Commenting on the game, the Pittsburgh Post of Sunday said: "Although much heavier than Panhandle, the Lyceum met the most formidable bunch seen in Pittsburgh in years, and in the last half was perfectly helpless to the onslaught of the Columbus boys. Time alone kept the Panhandles from scoring another touchdown, as they were on the Lyceum 10-yard line and gaining continually."
>
> In discussing Panhandle's touchdown the Pittsburgh Press said: "A more spectacular football scene would be hard to imagine than when Frank Nesser went across Lyceum's line for the Panhandle's first touchdown. With five yards and the line to gain the two teams of giants lined up for the final struggle, the ball was passed and steadily Panhandle forced it over the line amid the plaudits of the 3000 spectators, who were loud in their praise of gameness of the boys from the Buckeye state. Lyceum wants a return engagement with the Panhandle and Manager Carr remained in Pittsburgh over Sunday to hold a conference for a return date."[17]

As impressed as the Pittsburgh papers were, Carr was unable to get a return match with the Lyceum. The following week Carr's team was to travel and play the Massillon Tigers, Ted and John Nesser's old team, but another "problem" facing early pro football managers came up that would be out of Carr's hands—mother nature. As both teams took the field, a torrential downpour soaked the field and forced the two managers to postpone the game. They agreed to play the make-up game on Thanksgiving Day in Massillon.

After the rainout Carr booked a road game against the well-known Shelby Athletic Club. Shelby had fielded very good teams for the past several years and had Charles Follis on its roster, the first documented black professional football player, who played on the squad from 1902–1906. Both teams played a rough game that ended in a 6–6 tie. The Panhandles were quick learners and looked like they could compete with the best teams in Ohio. Soon they would get a chance to prove it.

As the team prepared to face the Toledo Athletic Club and Massillon Tigers at home, Carr was trying to get his team a little publicity in Columbus. The next two games would be played in the capital city, and he wanted to get fans to come out. A day before the Toledo game (November 10), Carr had set up a photo opportunity for the team. In the Sunday edition of the *Columbus Dispatch*, the first ever team photo of the Columbus Panhandles, with new team manager Joe Carr, appeared. The team looked like your typical rough-and-tough early pro football players, while Carr looked like a million bucks. He was dressed in a nice overcoat, suit, and bow tie, topped off with his black derby, looking very stylish for a team manager. His experience as a sportswriter definitely influenced his decision to try and get more publicity for his squad, and it paid off.[18]

Nearly 2,000 people showed up to see the Panhandles destroy the Toledo Athletic Club 57–0. But Carr was not happy. The *Columbus Press-Post* revealed why: "Manager Carr of the Panhandles was quite disgusted at the showing made by the visitors. He had turned down other attractions to bring this team to Columbus, believing it would be capable of putting up some kind of game against the Panhandles. He added that it would be a long time before a Toledo team would again be given a game against the Panhandles."[19]

Carr kept his word. The Panhandles did not play Toledo again until 1911, when the respected Toledo Maroons played the railroaders. Carr knew that a quality opponent was more important than a blowout victory if he wanted fans to keep paying for professional football in Columbus. To finish the season off, the Panhandles played a home and away series with Ohio's best professional football team—the Massillon Tigers. The first game was played in Columbus at Neil Park, and on November 13 the *Ohio State Journal* reported on the pregame hype:

> No athletic event that Columbus has produced in a long time is the subject of so much comment as the big Panhandle–Massillon game at Neil Park next Sunday afternoon. Parties are already being formed and a number of tallyhos have already been bid for.
>
> Word comes from Massillon that followers of the Orange and Black will accompany the Tigers to the number of about 300 and are expecting a bunch from Canton and Salem. The Panhandles will give their rivals a strong play for the state trophy goes without saying and from the way bets are being laid around town by followers of both sides it looks from here that chances are about even.
>
> Panhandle Athletic field is the daily scene of much life in football, and judging from the crowd of interested spectators that daily journey out to witness practice, interest in the local champions is beginning to gain some proportions.[20]

On Sunday, November 17, the Panhandles and Tigers played before 4,000 spectators at Neil Park as the mighty Tigers came away with a tough 6–4 victory. Carr was ecstatic over the large crowd despite the unique setup for football games at local football fields in Columbus. "There was never any stands. People would just stand around like a little league game. But they would get crowds of 700 up to 2,000 for some of the bigger games, which was amazing at that time. But that spoke well early on of the reputation of the Nesser Brothers," says Ted Schneider, nephew of the Nesser Brothers.[21] Nonetheless, getting a win would have made it a little more sweet. The railroaders played with only four Nesser brothers, with Fred being absent, and Frank Nesser was the star of the game. The *Ohio State Journal* praised the big fullback:

> Many a college coach, after taking one look at Fullback Frank Nesser of the Panhandles, would welcome joyously that young man to his squad. Four of the brothers played yesterday, but Frank was the "king bee" not only of his family, but of all participants in the struggle. Staying on his feet was his principal strong point. By keeping from being thrown, he made it possible for his mates to push and pull him ahead for repeated gains. Then, when the P.H. attack went wrong because of fumbles, this big fellow kicked the ball over from placement and gave his side four points, all that could be secured, although a big bid was made for a touchdown in the second half.[22]

Eleven days later on Thanksgiving Day (November 28) the Panhandles traveled to Massillon for the rematch and the make-up game from earlier in the season. Once again the railroaders lost as the Tigers pretty much controlled the whole game and came away with a 13–4 victory. The two losses to Massillon were nothing to be ashamed of, as the Tigers finished the season as the Ohio League Independent Champion with a 7–0–1 record. Watching the Tigers, Carr knew he was watching the best pro team in the Midwest but he also knew that the Tigers had a lot more money to spend to get players. He came away knowing that his team could compete with the best.

The Panhandles finished the season with a 2–3–1 record, but the losing record wasn't the most important thing for the railroaders and professional football. Joe Carr had his own team, and he was gaining experience that first season that would launch a thirty-two-year career in professional football and make him a pioneer in the sport he wanted to be involved in. Writing a manuscript titled "Post-Graduate Football" in 1938, Carr made a short comment on his first year as team manager of the Panhandles: "My entry into the professional football game came in 1907. I fell in love with the sport then and the years that have passed have only added to my ardor."[23]

The love of pro football ran through his blood and he couldn't wait to build his team. He spent all his extra time, in between his baseball job and being a machinist, learning everything about the sport. He not only wanted to be a good team manager off the field, but he wanted his team to be good on the field as well. He was driven to prove to everyone that he could be great at something like he was proving himself on the sandlots in the old Irish neighborhood.

As the 1908 season approached, Joe Carr had pretty much the same team he had the previous year, with the five Nesser brothers leading the team. The Panhandles would play nine games against teams such as the Pittsburgh Lyceum (two games), Akron Giants, Canal Dover, Cincinnati Spauldings, and two games with the Dayton Oakwoods, starting a long-time rivalry with the best team from the Gem City in southwestern Ohio. Carr also would add a season-ending game against the other best team in Columbus for the Columbus city championship. Seven out of the nine games would be played in Columbus, giving the hometown fans plenty of opportunities to see Carr's Panhandles.

On September 28 the Panhandles played their warm-up game and defeated the Columbus Southerns very easily, 43–0. A week later they stepped up in competition playing the unknown Akron Giants at Recreation Park. The tough Giants played the Panhandles to a scoreless tie as things got a little chippy on the field. The *Columbus Press-Post* reported the action: "In the first three minutes of play Frank Nesser, the big fullback of the Panhandles, was put out of the game for slugging, thus reducing the strength of the local team very materially. Akron had been booked for a return date and will be seen at Recreation park later in the season."[24]

Carr knew his team would not back down from a fistfight (especially with the Nesser brothers), but he wanted to present his team of railroaders as a first class organization and not just a bunch of sluggers on the field—especially if he wanted to keep scheduling games. So to take away the spotlight from the fisticuffs against Akron, Carr announced before the next game that the Panhandles would look different. Carr's buddies at the *Ohio State Journal* made the announcement under the headline"May Appear in New Uniforms": "If completed in time, the Panhandles will be out in natty new uniforms of maroon and gold and the swell gold keystone will be a pretty sight. Gates for Sunday's game will open at 1 o'clock and play will start promptly at 2:30. The general admission is 25 cents."[25]

In an age where most pro teams didn't have matching uniforms, this was a brilliant idea for Carr to dress his team in identical jerseys—anything to help the Panhandles' tough-guy image. The only problem was that the new uniforms didn't come in time for the first game against the

Dayton Oakwoods. In front of a nice crowd of 2,000 fans at Recreation Park the Panhandles defeated the Oakwoods 25–0. Frank Nesser made up for his dismissal the previous week by scoring three touchdowns. Over the next month the Panhandles played consistent football, losing at Pittsburgh (16–0), beating the Canal Dover Giants (who were the Akron team located in a new city), and wearing their new jerseys, and crushing a very dismal Cincinnati Spauldings team, 66–0.

Then on November 8 the railroaders played at home in a rematch with the Pittsburgh Lyceum. For the third time under Carr, the Panhandles lost again (10–0) to the Steel City team. But Carr was pleased with the crowd of 2,500 who came out to Recreation Park. He would be even more pleased the next week when 3,500 fans in Dayton came out to witness the Panhandles 18–0 victory over the Oakwoods. Some of the hard work on the railroad yards was starting to pay off.

The Panhandles were now 4–3–1 and Carr began to set up the game that would decide the city championship of Columbus. Their opponent would be the Columbus Nationals, and both teams talked endlessly about the matchup, which was building up to be the game of the year in central Ohio. Even Ted Nesser gave the newspaper a quote the day before the game saying, "I am confident as to the outcome."[26]

The build up was tremendous and over 3,000 fans showed up at 3:00 p.m. at Recreation Park to watch the city's professional football championship game. The game was set up to witness the coming-out party for the Columbus Panhandles to show they were the best team in the capital city. But that wouldn't happen.

> "Nationals Win: Kern Still in His Old Form Wins Game"
> Bob Kern and his good right toe, which has broken up several games in years agone, again proved a winner, Sunday afternoon, at Recreation Park, when he dropped a goal from scoring the only points of the game which gave the Nationals the victory by the score of 4 to 0. The Nationals were aggressive all through the game, but the Panhandles held strong as their goal was neared. Kern made many efforts to kick the ball between the posts but failed to get the range again.[27]

The loss was devastating to Carr and the Panhandles—finishing the season with a 4–4–1 record—as they thought they had a game plan to win. But it didn't happen. The loss was very bitter to Joe Carr as for the past two years he had built a team he thought was the best in Columbus. Despite the loss Carr was gracious in defeat, giving a postgame quote to his former employee, the *Ohio State Journal*: "Much of the sting of the defeat is taken away because the winning team is made up of, as square and fair a lot of players as we have ever met. Those Nationals were working for each other all the time. The Panhandle team was in condition, we have no excuses whatever to offer."[28]

The loss to the Nationals would be a landmark game for the Panhandles and Joe Carr. After the loss Carr made two vows: (1) that the Panhandles would always make an effort to play the best Columbus teams each year, and (2) that the Panhandles would never lose to another Columbus team.

Carr kept his word, as the Panhandles would go on to play twenty-four more games against Columbus teams from 1909 to 1922, and they would go 24–0 in those games. The railroaders would outscore their opponents 608 to 13 in those twenty-four games, giving up only two touchdowns on defense and racking up 21 shutouts. The Panhandles would go on to dominate the pro football scene in Columbus.

Carr's first two seasons were a success as a team manager. He fielded a competitive team around the Nesser brothers, which in turn made it easy to schedule games with quality opponents (fifteen games in 1907–1908). He was a little concerned about the team's rough edges on the field, especially the physical play of his star attractions, the Nesser brothers. He didn't want anymore ejections or severe injuries that would keep them out of possible games. But it was almost impossible to tell the Nessers to take it easy on their bodies. In later years Carr commented on the brothers never wearing any padding by saying, "There aren't three good ribs amongst the lot of them."[29] The sandlot toughness of the Nessers would become a staple for the Panhandles for many years to come.

During the summer Carr got another opportunity to show off his leadership skills in the sports world. In August of 1909 Carr's good friend Bob Quinn, who was the president of the Ohio State (Baseball) League (OSL), had to fire the manager of the OSL's Newark minor league team and offered Carr the job. Carr accepted and finished the year as bench manager. The following year Quinn hired him as secretary of the OSL. Carr would serve five years (1910–1914) as secretary and then a couple years as president of the OSL, keeping the league going until World War I.

As Joe got this new job, his older brother Michael started his own business. After several years of being a clerk/grocer, he established a new company called the Franklin Coffee Company in Columbus. One of his first moves was to hire his brother Eddie to be secretary of the company and use his bookkeeping experience. The two brothers would work together for the rest of their lives. It was a busy summer, but Joe was looking forward to the fall and back to football.

As the season approached, he made a bold decision. Carr approached Ben Chamberlain about being the head coach for the Panhandles, allowing Ted Nesser to just concentrate on playing. Chamberlain had played local college football and then officiated several Panhandles games back in 1902, which led to him being hired by the Panhandles to be head coach in 1903 (he led the team to a 5–3 record) and 1904 (the team went 2–1 before folding).

So Carr knew Chamberlain well from those early years and knew his experience and expertise would be perfect for the Panhandles to try and make that jump to being a more polished product on the field. At worst they would be a little more disciplined. Chamberlain agreed, and in early September the team came together; all five Nesser brothers, Andy Kertzinger, and Henry Spiers were back. Through the railroad shops Carr added a big tackle, Oscar Kuehner, who would play for twelve years; Bob Kern (the man that beat the Panhandles in the city championship in 1908); and John "Pop" Schneider, a blacksmith in the shops, who would take being part of the "Nesser family" to a whole new level.

During one of the Panhandles games in Columbus, Schneider met Rose Nesser, one of the sisters of the famous Nesser brothers. "Rose Nesser very often would drive her brothers to the game in the family's horse-drawn cart. Because the field [Recreation Park] was about five or six miles away, she would stay and watch the game, then drive them back home," says Irene Cassady, daughter of Rose and John Schneider. "Well one time she drove the boys to the game and she met my father, John Schneider, who was playing on the team. My father said that once she stepped down off that wagon, he lost his heart, and the same with her."[30]

John and Rose fell in love, but it was tough for Schneider to convince the Nesser brothers that his intentions were pure. "My grandfather took a shine to my dad, he really liked my dad," said Cassady about her father. "My dad was a very likable guy and he knew he'd have no problem at all asking my grandparents, Theodore and Catherine, if he could marry their daughter. But he said the thing that just made him shake in his boots was having to ask the brothers, that scared him." On June 19, 1912, John Schneider and Rose Nesser were married, and "Pop" officially became a member of the Nesser family. Schneider would make his own mark as a player for the Panhandles starting at center or guard for eight years.[31]

Carr scheduled nine games (same as 1908), and after a 16–0 win over the Columbus Muldoons on September 26, the Panhandles began the start of one glorious season. With the combination of Chamberlain's coaching and the outstanding play of Bob Kern and the Nesser Brothers, the Panhandles made Joe Carr look like a genius.

On October 3 the Panhandles took care of the Columbus Barracks by scoring eight touchdowns (winning 44–5) and followed that up with a 17–0 victory over the Dayton Oakwoods. The Panhandles, now 3–0, were not only going to be tested by their next two opponents, but by Carr himself. Because of the blue laws in Pittsburgh forbidding Sunday football, Carr scheduled back-to-back games for the railroaders. On Saturday (October 16) they traveled to play the Pittsburgh Lyceum and then came home and played the Cleveland All-Stars on Sunday (October 17). This was pretty normal for the pro game with teams playing twice in a week or playing back-to-back games, especially when playing teams from eastern states such as New York and Pennsylvania, which still had blue laws in effect.

The Lyceum game was another low-scoring, rough football game, and for the fourth time the Panhandles came out on the losing end, a 3–0 heartbreaker. But the tough railroaders rebounded nicely the next day by crushing the Cleveland All-Stars at Indianola Park 57–5, led by three touchdowns by Frank Nesser. Carr's connections in the football world started to pay off as he made arrangements to play a new opponent in a familiar football city. The Canton Athletic Club would field a football team in 1909, and Carr's Panhandles would make their first visit to the city that was home to the famous Canton Bulldogs.

The scandal had set the city back the last couple of seasons, but Canton was pumped to see the Panhandles. A football ad in the *Canton Daily News* advertised the upcoming game:[32]

Football Sunday, Oct. 31—Booster Day—Be A Sport
Panhandles of Columbus, starring the 5 Nesser Brothers,
weighing over 1000 pounds
Vs Canton
Admission, 50 cents

The game was lopsided and the Panhandles proved they were an elite team, beating the Canton Athletic Club 34–0. The crowd even cheered the Nesser brothers throughout the game, especially John Nesser, who scored two touchdowns. The *Canton Repository* reported that "the game was devoid of rough tactics and there was no squabbling. It was the cleanest exhibition of the year."[33] Chamberlain's influence was very obvious as the Panhandles were getting the grasp of how to play the game of football, and Carr was pleased that his team was playing hard every week. The 5–1 record was no joke.

Up next would be the rematch with the Pittsburgh Lyceum, this time in Columbus at Indianola Park. Carr had only two more home dates left, this game and the city championship, so he wanted to get as many fans out to the games as possible. This time he came up with an idea that he would eventually take to the NFL. During the week Carr announced special admission for the game and once again he went to the *Ohio State Journal* to help him: "A splendid opportunity will be given the ladies to see this big game, as the manager [Carr] has decided to admit them free. Excellent arrangements are being made to care for an immense crowd and all will have an excellent chance to see the game. Plenty of seats, both grand stand and sideline bleachers, are assured. Added to this will be excellent street car service to handle the crowd to and from the grounds."[34]

Carr continued to find new avenues to help promote his team, and this was a perfect example. He wanted to encourage female fans to come to the game, which in turn would bring more men out. What man would turn down the opportunity to go to a sporting event with his lady friend? Carr always wanted to provide a positive experience for fans who paid to watch the Panhandles play, a philosophy that he would carry for all his years as Panhandles manager, and as president of the NFL.

Four hundred railroad workers and a near "capacity crowd" showed up at Indianola Park on November 7 and saw a closely fought game as the teams played to a 0–0 tie. But it was a game that ended in controversy. The *Ohio State Journal* ran a headline that said, "Panhandles Make Lyceums Give Up: Pittsburgers Get Off the Field When Final Danger Mark Is Reached." The article continued the story:

> Frequently driving the Lyceum eleven toward a corner and positively forcing the big Pittsburgers to show their fear of ultimate defeat—the Panhandle eleven fell just a trifle short of the good fortune to make even three points in the game played Sunday afternoon at Indianola gridiron, around which was banked a capacity crowd.
>
> Two minutes before time for the game to end, the Panhandle team was sweeping toward the Lyceum goal. Ted Nesser and [Bob] Kern worked a legitimate forward pass play for substantial gain. Instantly the Lyceum leaders rushed upon Referee Barker [who hailed from Latrobe, Pennsylvania] with a demand that it be declared illegal. Barker yielded and the ensuing argument continued for a time. Play was never resumed.
>
> Evidently the Lyceum players, who have never been beaten in these days of modern football, were more willing to convince Columbus people that they are not game to the core than to stand up in a sportsman like way and take their medicine. Their playing record will have a scoreless game added to it and their reputation for being top-notch sportsmen given a black blot.[35]

The *Ohio State Journal* might have been hard on the Lyceum team, but Carr was even tougher. It would be the last game the Panhandles played against the Pittsburgh team, ending a good rivalry. Following the controversy, the Panhandles were in need of some good publicity, and with the help of Carr, the *Columbus Citizen* on November 13 ran an article on the Nesser brothers titled "Five Famous Football Brothers." The article would be the first ever featured article written on all the Nesser brothers in a Columbus newspaper. Many more would follow. The *Citizen* had this to say about football's most famous family:

> The five brothers Nesser, whose aggregate weight is 1006 pounds, make the Panhandle football team a professional organization one of the best in the United States.
>
> The Panhandles have been constructed around the Nesser quintet, in whom football playing is almost an instinct. They are brawny, these Nessers, as the result of hard work in a railroad boiler shop, the same exercise which gave Jim Jeffries [heavyweight boxing champ] the constitution now standing him in good shape.
>
> Ted Nesser is the star of the family. He has years of experience on the whitewashed field, having starred with the famous Massillon Tigers when that eleven won the professional championship of the United States. Ted has until this year coached as well as played with the Panhandles. Every year he receives numerous offers to play with other professional organizations, but turns them down to play with his own team.
>
> The Panhandle Nessers, as someone called them, are: John, 34, who plays left half; Phil, 28, left tackle; Fred, 22, right half; Frank, 20, fullback; Ted, 26, left end.[36]

The article was accompanied by a photo showing all five Nessers with their weight written across their chest. Even though the article never mentioned Joe Carr, it was definitely his idea to get the photo and the publicity in the local paper. Just like allowing ladies to attend games for free, Carr would use photos to help promote and publicize the team for years to come.

The Nesser article gave the team some much-needed relief going into their annual trip to Dayton to play the Oakwoods (November 14). In front of a good crowd of 2,600, the Panhandles would beat the Oakwoods for the second time by a score of 16–0. Three different Nessers scored touchdowns—Frank, Fred, and Phil. The Dayton crowd was fascinated by the Nesser clan all day, even before the game started, the *Dayton Journal* would note:

> To these 2600 onlookers the five Nessers were the centers of attention. When the P.H. team left its hotel for the field it was found that hundreds of Daytonians were lined up in the streets just as eager to see the Nessers as the average citizen is to look over a circus parade.
>
> When it comes to playing, the brotherhood made good. It was strictly football with them and their teammates at all times. Never was there a wrangle at any stage of the game and the crowd was so well pleased with the show that it gave the Panhandle team a parting cheer.[37]

The Nesser clan was now becoming "rock stars" as professional football players—a must-see act. The rest of the Panhandle team also had reason to cheer: the season had just one game to go, and they had a 6-1-1 record. But all of that didn't matter to the railroaders; they only had one thing on their minds going into the last game. Revenge. All of the other games were just a tune-up for the finale, a rematch with the Columbus Nationals, the team that beat them for the 1908 city championship. The Panhandles had to win this game or it was a bad season.

The city of Columbus became excited about the upcoming game, and the press was doing its part in the hoopla. The *Ohio State Journal* ran daily articles previewing the game, but it was an article on November 17, four days before the matchup, that captured the city's interest in the gridiron battle. The article's title was "Chatter over a Championship: Football Fans Are Discussing Pro and Con Merits of Big Eleven":

> "On to Indianola" is the slogan of the National and Panhandle rooters. Everyone interested in the two teams is counting the minutes until the time will be called for the two big teams to take the field for the annual championship clash. Never before has an independent championship game caused as much talk among football fans of Columbus.
>
> "Do you think that the Nationals will repeat?" was asked by a prominent football coach yesterday of a Panhandle man and this was the reply: "Never in a thousand years." If it had been a National rooter the answer would have been, "We have won five times in a row and will not let the sixth attempt go by."
>
> News from the two camps is very scarce and hardly a line can be gotten on either team because everything is being kept quiet. The only thing said openly is that the teams will give the battle of their career. If this is the case, the good game of last year will be forgotten after Sunday's game.
>
> Both managers are working day and night to perfect every detail and will not leave the smallest stone unturned to have everything in the smoothest order.[38]

On the morning of November 21, both the city and the two teams were ready to battle. A crowd of 2,500 fans came out to Indianola Park and saw just how ready the Panhandles were, as the railroaders got their revenge in a big way, led by fullback Frank Nesser, who gave the greatest performance ever on a Columbus gridiron. The big 230-pound bulldozer had the game of his life, scoring six touchdowns as the Panhandles routed the Nationals 33–0. The Panhandles won the city championship title, and Carr was vindicated that his team was the best in central Ohio.

The big win over the Nationals capped what was the greatest season in Panhandles team history. The 7–1–1 record was a great achievement not only for the team but also for the management under Joe Carr and the coaching under Ben Chamberlain. The Panhandles had scored thirty-nine touchdowns in 1909, and twenty-six of them were scored by guys named Nesser. Frank Nesser scored seventeen by himself. The defense was even better, surrendering only thirteen points all season, with six shutouts in nine games. What would Carr do for an encore?

5

Starting a Family (1910–1913)

The success of the 1909 Panhandles put a lot of pressure on Joe Carr to see if he could duplicate the recipe. Before the season Carr's roster added a star and subtracted one. Bob Kern, who scored forty points, would leave the team. His running and kicking would be solely missed in 1910, but his presence would be replaced by the sixth member of the Nesser clan. Seventeen-year-old Al Nesser joined his brothers to give Carr six Nessers to help advertise his team. Al would play the next eight years with the Panhandles, mostly as a guard, and would quickly become one of the best at that position in the early days of professional football.

Just like the rest of his brothers, Al loved playing and practicing on the same team together with his siblings. "The brothers were like steel. When they came out to their lunch breaks they would practice on the cinders and not complain. My father would work at that hard [boilermaker] job and then for lunch he and the rest of the brothers would practice, then go back in and work their next eight hours. I think they worked twelve hours back then. For the weekend to relax they would play football games. They roughed it," says Sally Nesser, daughter of Al Nesser. "My father really liked Joe Carr, he said he was a very low-key guy, quite a scholarly person, smart. Joe Carr was a household name in our house for a long time," says Connie Shomo, daughter of Al Nesser.[1]

Joining Al as a rookie on the team was Roscoe Kuehner, who joined his brother Oscar, giving the Panhandles two sets of siblings. It looked like Carr's team would have another banner year, but in reality it would be a season full of turmoil and disappointment. Ben Chamberlain returned to coach, with help from Ted Nesser, and the season opened with mostly the new recruits playing (as Al Nesser would make his pro debut) in a 10–0 victory over the Columbus Northerns. The Panhandles first big test would be a road trip to play the competitive Queen City squad, the Cincinnati Celts, and the railroaders didn't look good settling for a scoreless tie. For the Panhandles it felt like a loss. After the Celts game the team held a special practice to learn some new plays. On October 20 the *Ohio State Journal* reported on the practice with a headline stating, "Secret Practice by Panhandles," which shows it wasn't really much of a secret since it appeared in the newspaper: "Panhandle eleven will practice today at the athletic field back of the shop, and every day this week, preparatory to the trip to Akron next Sunday. Coaches Chamberlain and (Ted) Nesser realize that a tough proposition is on hand at Akron and are very desirous that all be present for practice daily. A special lot of new plays are going to be rehearsed."[2]

The "secret" practice and the new plays didn't help the Panhandles as they (with four Nesser brothers in the lineup) were beaten badly by the Akron Indians 40–0 as a crowd of 5,000 fans in Akron saw the future of professional football. In the game recap from the *Ohio State Journal* the Akron squad was praised: "The Indians played modern football all the way through, swinging the ends and operating forward passes with great precision." The Indians would dominate professional football in 1910, going 7–2, with their only two losses to the Shelby Blues, who would finish the season undefeated. Years later Carr recalled this game, "Our boys had never seen the forward pass worked that well before. They saw plenty that day. I think we had possession of the ball just six times. The rest of the time those fellows were playing catch with each other and making touchdowns every play or two." The loss left Carr very dumbfounded about the abilities of his team.[3]

After the game the railroaders and Joe Carr faced their first big crisis since the team disbanded after the 1904 season. On October 27 the *Ohio State Journal* reported that three of the Nesser brothers had quit football. The article read,

> The Panhandle eleven will have its first practice since Sunday last at noon today. The team will undergo a little overhauling, as three of the Nesser brothers have decided to quit the game. They have found that they will be unable to practice at this time of the year. This will probably make the Panhandle back field a little lighter, but the line will remain the same.
>
> Several new men have already announced their intention of playing on the eleven. Some radical changes will be made with the intention of increasing the speed and agility of the team. The passing of John, Ted and Fred mark the passing of a great trio from the football ranks.[4]

Nobody knew why the three Nesser brothers suddenly quit; maybe the work at the railroad shops was too much to handle and playing a football game was impossible. Maybe Ted Nesser and Ben Chamberlain didn't see eye-to-eye on how to run the team.

On October 28 the *Ohio State Journal* reported more on the changes of the Panhandles as they prepared for their next game against the Cleveland Lyceum on October 30.

> Panhandles first practice with the reorganized team proved a hummer and 16 men were on hand. Three new men with long football experience were on hand, and will probably be placed in the regular positions. They are Wyant, Grimm and Stowall. All have played for two or three years on college elevens and will make valuable additions to the team. The line is just the same as before, and the new men will take places in the back field. The only shift made in the line was Kertzinger going back to the center and Schneider, who has been playing the position, will play a guard position. Busby made his first appearance and the little fellow took hold like an old-timer. The drilling will continue daily, and all candidates are to be on the field promptly at noon."[5]

On the day of the game the *Ohio State Journal* ran an article saying that "admission will be 25 cents, with this price it looks as if a capacity crowd will be on hand." The crowd saw the new-look Panhandles lose to an inferior Cleveland Lyceum team, 12–6, as Phil Nesser (the only Nesser brother to play) scored the only touchdown. The railroaders were now 1–2–1 and with more questions than answers. After a week of chaos, Joe Carr was able to find one answer: the trio of brothers would return. After the Cleveland game, Carr brought Ted Nesser back to coach the team. There was no more mention of Ben Chamberlain as coach; Carr gave all the power to Ted. With Ted back as coach, he brought back all his brothers—John, Fred, and Frank.[6]

Carr weathered his first big storm, but the team's stability was not where Carr wanted it to be, so he scheduled the city championship of Columbus early, against the Columbus Barracks. The Panhandles and five of the Nesser brothers beat the Barracks easily, 24–0. They followed that up with a 28–0 victory over the weaker Akron Tigers. The Panhandles had now won consecutive games for the first time in 1910 and had just one game left—a Thanksgiving Day contest against the Dayton Oakwoods. With ten days to prepare for the Oakwoods, the railroaders practiced hard and gave the fans of Dayton a historic event. This would be the first time in Panhandles team history that all six Nesser brothers would play together in the same game. It was a historic game indeed.

On November 24 the Panhandles and all six Nesser brothers took the field on a rainy Thanksgiving afternoon in Dayton, Ohio. On a sloppy gridiron the teams played to a 5–5 tie as the only score for the railroaders came on an eighty-yard fumble recovery by guard John "Pop" Schneider.

It was the only touchdown that Schneider scored in his career. It was a flawed and physical game for the Panhandles as the *Columbus Dispatch* reported: "[Dayton] Quarterback Weber suffered a broken nose and was carried from the field unconscious. . . . Six of the Nesser brothers were in the game."[7]

If anything, the game against the Oakwoods will be remembered for the participation of all six Nesser brothers, but the rest of the season might be forgotten. After having such great success in 1909, Carr's Panhandles should have been fighting for something more than a winning record in 1910. But with the constant shake-up of the starting lineup and the change in coaching, the Panhandles did all they could just to finish with a 3–2–2 record. But maybe there was a reason Carr was distracted.

About this time Joe Carr started to notice a beautiful young lady in his Irish neighborhood and became totally smitten. The Ted Nesser–Ben Chamberlain power struggle probably took a back seat to getting to know the woman he would eventually marry. Josephine Marie Sullivan was a slim, good-looking, blue-eyed brunette who came from a very well-known railroad family.

The Sullivan family also originated from Ireland, as Josephine's grandfather, James A. Sullivan, and his wife, Catherine, both came from County Kerry to America. They eventually found a home in Richmond, Indiana. James found work as a laborer on the railroad and would be described as having a "kindly disposition, [a man] who loved his church." He loved church so much that he became an original founder of St. Mary's Church (which is still operating) in Richmond. The couple had eleven children, but tragedy struck the Sullivan children often. By the time Catherine, age sixty-nine, died in 1907 and James, age eighty, died in 1908, only three of the Sullivan siblings remained: Josephine (Sullivan) Reece, James Sullivan Jr., and John S. Sullivan—the father of Josephine.[8]

John S. Sullivan was a powerfully built, no-nonsense man, who had a presence about him. He followed his father into the railroad trade, starting out as a blacksmith and working his way up to foreman, eventually becoming a superintendent with the Pennsylvania Railroad.

While in Richmond John met Mary Farrell and on September 19, 1877, the two married. "He was a very big man, a very attractive man who became a man of stature in the community in Richmond. He was a success as a person independent of his professional achievements," says Martha Sullivan, granddaughter of John S. Sullivan. "My grandmother, Mary Sullivan, was a very outgoing person; she enjoyed life. Sometimes she could be a little flighty but that made her fun to be around." Over the next twenty years the couple would live eight blocks from the railroad shops at 308 North 16th Street Street and have four children—Rose Sullivan (1878),

Josephine Marie Sullivan (November 20, 1879), William E. Sullivan (1880), and Francis John Sullivan (May 20, 1890).[9]

Josephine looked just like her mother. "She was a brunette and she had these very large blue eyes. She was just a very good looking woman, extremely attractive," says Martha Sullivan, niece of Josephine Sullivan. "Oh yes, she had a glorious sense of humor too. She just enjoyed life and she was a happy person. It just kind of radiated to all the people she came in contact with." The family called her "Josie," and when she turned twenty-one her father was transferred to Mill Township near Dennison, Ohio, to be a foreman there. After four years he was transferred one last time by the Pennsylvania Railroad to Columbus, Ohio. They made their home in the Irish neighborhood, near the shops, first on Monroe Avenue and then at 39 North 22nd Street. Older sister Rose married John Callahan and moved to Pittsburgh with their four children, while younger brother Frank Sullivan became a doctor and married a Columbus girl, Marie Ann Driscoll, and had three children. Josie's other brother William passed away in his early twenties before they arrived in Columbus.

Josie fit in well in the old Irish neighborhood. She worked occasionally as a seamstress, helped the family around the house, and attended church at St. Patrick's. With these connections to the railroad and church she was introduced to Joe Carr. Before Josie came along Joe didn't seem interested in too many women, but the beautiful brunette caught his eye. He would eventually take a road trip to prove his love. "He was just introduced to her and he found her very attractive. The story goes my grandmother was up at Lake Erie at Cedar Point and he came up to see her on a surprise visit. He sat next to her and said, 'Josie, I didn't come up here to see the lake.' She was enamored by that," says Michael Carr, grandson of Joe Carr. "She was a very slim and very attractive woman. That's what he liked about her. He also thought she was a very warm and tender woman. It was a perfect match."[10]

The couple quickly fell in love and it was obvious that Joe would propose. The wedding invitation was simple.

Mr. & Mrs. J. S. Sullivan
Request the honor of your presence
At the marriage of their daughter

Josephine
to
Mr. Joseph F. Carr
On the morning of Tuesday, the twenty-seventh of June,
One thousand nine hundred and eleven,
Seven o'clock,
St. Dominic's Church.[11]

They set a date for the summer of 1911 on the one day all railroad workers could get off. On a lovely Tuesday morning on June 27 at St. Dominic's Church (where Joe attended school), the couple gave their vows in front of their families and Rev. Thomas J. O'Reilly. The wedding was perfect and Joe couldn't have been happier. The Panhandles dismal 1910 season was the furthest thing from his mind. Joe was now married, and Josie moved in with him and Eddie at the boarding house at 295 North 21st Street until they could afford a home of their own.

Joe didn't stop keeping busy, as he continued to work as a machinist at the railroad, secretary of the Ohio State League, and his favorite job—manager of the Columbus Panhandles. The summer was very hectic for the young newlyweds. Joe's life with Josie had started, and he was now part of a family again. The Sullivan family adopted him warmly. "They were a very close-knit family; they got along very well. They seemed to thoroughly enjoy one another's company and spent a lot of time together," says Martha Sullivan.[12]

The 1911 Panhandles squad included all six Nesser brothers, Andy Kertzinger, John Schneider, and both Kuehner brothers. Two new recruits from the shops joined the team for the following three seasons. Parker Jarvis, a local high school star, and Earl "Cumpy" Colburn, a bookkeeper, would contribute to Carr's team. "My father was proud that he knew Joe Carr and the Nesser brothers. He told everyone. He was proud of the fact that he had been on the team with all of the Nessers," said Joe Colburn, son of Earl Colburn. "Carr paid him ten dollars a game in all the time he played for the Panhandles. That's it. But he thought it was great. He loved the fact that he played the whole sixty minutes. The only time they didn't play is when they were carried off the field."[13]

Ted Nesser returned to coach the railroaders and try to incorporate some of the new features of the pro game, especially throwing the ball a little more with big Frank Nesser, who had the best arm on the team. After scoring seventeen touchdowns in 1909 and five in 1910, Frank would score none in 1911, concentrating on passing from his fullback position. Carr again set up a very competitive schedule with ten total games, but only four would be on the road, as he wanted to spend a little more time home with Josie.

After a sluggish 3–0 opening-game victory over the Columbus Northerns, the railroaders followed up with a tough 10–5 win over the Cleveland Genesee Athletic Club (with only two Nessers playing). The Panhandles were now 2–0, but the always busy Carr got sidetracked from his football duties to be a guest at baseball's premier event, the World Series. The Philadelphia A's of the American League were facing off against the New York Giants of the National League. Carr's good friend Bobby Quinn set up a group of Columbus baseball executives and fans to be his guests at the first two games of the series. The first game would be played in New York and the second game in Philly.

As part of his trip Carr agreed to write a few daily stories for his former paper the *Ohio State Journal*. On October 13 Carr left his new wife and headed east to New York. Most of the Columbus delegation predicted that Connie Mack's A's would sweep the Giants. Joe's readers back in Columbus got a first hand report on the games.

October 14, 1911
Only the Result Displeases Them

By Joe Carr

The Columbus people in attendance at the World Series are just a little disappointed tonight over the defeat of the Athletics. About all are ardent rooters for the Mackmen and rooted lustily for them to bring home the bunting and keep it up until the last man was out in the ninth inning. The only member of the party who is pulling for the Giants is Mr. Louis Hoster and he had a lively time after the game in kidding the losers. Bobby Quinn had all arrangements complete and there was nothing for the tourists to do but enjoy themselves. Hotel accommodations had been arranged for and much sought-for tickets for the game were plentiful when the hustling Columbus promoter got to work, immediately after the arrival of the party this morning. The weather was simply made to order, being a bright sunny day with just enough cold to make an overcoat comfortable. A number of the party have arranged to remain during the entire series, while about half of them will remain to see the Monday game at Philadelphia, returning to Columbus on Tuesday.

October 15, 1911
Spend Their Off-Day Visiting in New York; Columbus Delegation Refuses to Weaken on the Chances of Mack's Team

By Joe Carr

Loss of the first game by the Athletics has not shaken the faith of the loyal rooters from Columbus and they are of the opinion that the Giants cannot repeat, all contending that the Giants have displayed all they have and that the Athletics were at their worst from the fact that (Eddie) Collins was responsible for the run-getting of the New York club in the early part of the game and that he will not make as many mistakes in all games yet to be played. The entire credit of the victory of Saturday is given to Christy Mathewson by all of the big fellows in baseball. It was surely a masterful performance by this grandest of pitchers.

October 16, 1911
Athletics' Stock Soars with Team; Plank's Clean Work Placates Columbus Men Who Expected to See Coombs

By Joe Carr

The Columbus contingent at the World's [*sic*] Series was in high glee tonight over the triumph of the Athletics in the second game. While many were disappointed that they were denied the privilege of seeing Jack Coombs pitch, they were all pleased with the masterful work of Plank and are more confident than ever that the Athletics will bring home the bunting. The setting for today's game could not have been more perfect, all things considered. The rain of Sunday put the playing field in the best of conditions and the day was perfect. Perhaps never in the history of the game have the spectators been treated to such a demonstration as that which followed the drive of Frank Baker. At first it appeared that the ball had struck high in the bleachers, but when it was seen that it had just cleared the fence the multitude was on its feet and the deafening applause continued long after Baker had reached the bench. It was a terrific drive and went straight on a line.[14]

After watching Game 2 of the series Carr headed back home. It was a joy for Carr to witness a World Series up close and seeing the likes of Christy Mathewson pitch and Frank "Home Run" Baker hit. Four games later Carr and the Columbus group would be happy again as the A's clinched the title by beating the Giants, four games to two. Carr's articles were well received and showed off his flair for writing and promotion. The grammar school kid was grown up now and could spin a yarn far beyond his years in the educational system.

While Carr was off at the World Series, Ted Nesser took the team north to play the Akron Indians, the same team that thumped the Panhandles 40–0 the previous year. This time the railroaders played their best game in a few seasons and brought out the best in the Indians, as the *Akron Beacon-Journal* stated:

(Akron) Fullback Hess was the hero of the Akron Indian-Columbus Panhandle contest Sunday afternoon at Nollan Park. It was he who carried the ball over the Panhandle line for a touchdown just four minutes before the end of the game.

For a time it looked as if the Indians would be defeated but this great bunch of gridiron stars who never give up went after their opponent and finally won the day. It was a great contest and one which will linger in the memory of those who saw the game. Hess not only made it possible for his team to win but he was so severely injured in the attempt that he had to be carried off the field and a doctor summoned. In falling on the ball over the line with the Panhandle men on top of him he hurt his chest and for a time it was impossible for him to breathe.

The forward pass was not worked very successfully by either team, only once or twice was either side able to pull it off with any degree of success. Both teams preferred to punt the ball out of danger and take a chance on getting it back. In the early stages of the game rough tactics were used by the visitors but after being warned several times by the officials they stopped. The star of the visitors was without a doubt Frank Nesser. He was able to punt the ball so high in the air that the rest of the team had sufficient time to get down the field and be at the point where it fell almost as soon as it came down.

The game was without doubt the best which the Indian team had ever played.[15]

It was a tough loss for the team and when Carr returned the squad continued to lose close games. After suffering a tie (5–5) against the Cleveland All-Stars, Carr's Panhandles lost back-to-back home games against the Cincinnati Celts (5–2), by scoring only a safety, and the Toledo Maroons (9–0). The railroaders were now just 2-3-1 and didn't look like the dominant team they were just two years ago. The annual trip to Dayton to play the Oakwoods (on November 12) was next for the Panhandles, and it was perfect timing for the railroaders. Playing on an icy field, the Panhandles survived a tough game and defeated the Oakwoods by a single point, 6–5. After a touchdown by Phil Nesser, brother Frank provided the difference by kicking the extra point. Despite the tight score, the *Ohio State Journal* gave the Panhandles the edge throughout the game:

The Panhandles of Columbus defeated the Oakwoods of Dayton this afternoon by the score of 6 to 5, before a comparatively large crowd, considering the extreme cold and ice covered field. The low score does not tell the story of the game, as the Columbus eleven were by far the best team and only the condition of the field, which made fast play impossible, kept the score down. It was not until the last period of the game that the real strength of the Panhandle eleven took the field. When they entered the locals were comparatively at their mercy, being compelled to kick on the first down.[16]

The big win in Dayton seemed to take something out of the Panhandles as the following week the railroaders came back down to earth. Without the services of Fred Nesser—out with a bad knee—the team was buried by the Shelby Blues 40–0 at Shelby. Despite the margin of victory, this was not that bad of a loss; the Blues, led by Peggy Parratt and Homer Davidson, would go on to have an undefeated season (beating the tough Akron Indians three times) and made a claim to the mythical Ohio League championship. Most of the best clubs in Ohio—including pro teams from Akron, Canton, Cleveland, Columbus, Dayton, Elyria, Massillon, Toledo, and Youngstown—were now playing each other consistently and the team standing at the end of the year usually claimed the so-called title. But no official standings or rules were followed and nobody was in charge of policing the clubs. That would be years away, but it was obvious that the state of Ohio was the place to be to see the best of professional football.

After the Shelby loss Joe Carr looked to wrap up the season with another city championship. The *Ohio State Journal* would report the matchup on November 21:

> Arrangements were completed last night between the managers of the Panhandles and the Mendel Muldoons for the much-talked-of game between these two teams for the championship of the city. The Panhandles are the present holders, having taken the title from the Nationals two years ago, and have since defended it. The Muldoons have played and defeated all other teams in the city with the exception of the Panhandles, which gives them the right to contest with the Railroaders for the title.
>
> The game will be played next Sunday at Indianola Park. Perhaps never in history of professional football in the city has the interest been so great as in the coming contest.[17]

The game would be a big one for the Panhandles; not only did they have a mediocre season, with a 3–4–1 record, but they didn't want to lose the city championship to top it off. Ted Nesser's team was ready to play on November 26 against the Muldoons, as all six Nesser brothers, Oscar Kuehner, Andy Kertzinger, and John Schneider were in the lineup. The game kicked off at 2:30 p.m. at Indianola Park, and the railroaders took control early behind a Ted Nesser touchdown run. Frank Nesser added the extra point and a 6–0 lead. The Panhandles' defense did the rest as they shut out the Muldoons the rest of the way and the railroaders had another city title.

The 'Handles defense was dominating as the Muldoons couldn't move the ball all game. The *Columbus Citizen* praised the performance of the champions:

> By a score of 6 to 0 the Panhandles yesterday defeated the Muldoons at Indianola Park thereby retaining their title of professional champions of the city.
>
> The score fails to show how much the railroaders put it over their opponents, as no less than 11 times, when on the verge of crossing the Muldoon goal, they received penalties which made the scoring out of the question. The single touchdown came early in the game. The Panhandles intercepted a forward pass on the Muldoons' 25-yard line. Two forward passes and two line plunges sent Ted Nesser over the goal line. Frank Nesser kicked goal.

> For the Panhandles, Ted and Frank Nesser were the stars. The former was a "bear" at line plunging, while the punting and onside kicking of the latter aided the railroaders materially.[18]

The Panhandles had defended their city title and Joe Carr rewarded his team—not with a cash bonus or celebration dinner, but with another game. On November 29 the *Ohio State Journal* reported on the game: "Panhandles will go to Wellston on Thanksgiving Day, where they play the team of that city. The Wellston eleven are thought very well of in the southern section of the state, having won every game this year. They boast of a heavy and fast team and think they will give the Panhandles plenty to do to come back with the long end of the score." [19]

The team left Columbus on Thanksgiving morning at 7:30 a.m. for the sixty-seven-mile trip down south to Wellston, and the early wake-up call definitely affected the Panhandles in the first half. Wellston scored two touchdowns early and took a 10–6 lead into halftime. But the second half was a different story as the railroaders woke up and dominated the game. By using the passing game, the railroaders scored two second-half touchdowns to defeat Wellston 17–13.

The seventeen points scored was a season high for the Panhandles, and they needed every point to defeat the scrappy team from Wellston. The *Wellston Telegram* reported on the Nesser style of play:

> A great many fans thought the visitors played "dirty" ball, and cited the injury to Gallagher and Grinnell as evidence. In the case of Gallagher it must be remembered that Joe weighs 122 pound, while Ted Nesser, who made the tackle weighs 232, a difference of 110 pounds, and when Nesser fell on Joe there was small chance of Joe coming out uninjured. Grinnell says the play in which he was knocked out was strictly legal; Nesser wanted to get at the man with the ball—he tried to keep him away—the bump on the head resulted from the collision.[20]

Manager Carr noticed that the offense was coming around late in the season and looked to schedule one last game, a rematch in Dayton against the Oakwoods. The game was scheduled to be played on December 3, but a snowstorm would affect the game as the *Dayton Journal* would report:

> Amid the swirl of snowflakes and blustery winds of December the Dayton football season came to a discouraging close on Sunday afternoon, when the Columbus Panhandles were scheduled to play the Oakwoods for the southern Ohio championship. The season was not closed on the gridiron but came close through communication with the management of the Pan Handle team over telegraph wire.
>
> When Manager Harry Huckins of the Oakwoods arose from his bed Sunday morning he went to the window and threw up the blind. He fell back

with a gasp, for it was then apparent that the game would have to be called off. Snow was coming down out of the sky and wind was blowing around the corner of the house at a fifty mile gait. Harry shivered, pulled down the blind and then debated with himself as to whether or not he should 'hit the hay' or go down and telegraph the Panhandles not to come.[21]

Carr could relate to manager Huckins's situation, being a manager of an early pro football team was tough business. The 5–4–1 record of the Panhandles wasn't what Carr was looking for in 1911; he knew something was missing and he wanted to get the team back to the success it had in 1909. It was a long season professionally for Carr but a glorious one personally. Getting married, writing about his experience at the World Series, and continuing to learn about the football business made for a very challenging year.

Over the past five years, Carr saw the Panhandles and professional football go through some changes as the sport had overcome the gambling scandal of 1906. But the sport did lack the leadership and guidance of honest team managers like Carr. "Our grandfather was known for his integrity. At this time the league, which really wasn't a league at all, but a group of pro clubs, if you will, that got together and played on a Sunday afternoon and would be promised x-amount of dollars," says Gregory Carr, grandson of Joe Carr. "The manager or the person who owned the stadium collected the money from the fans and blew the pop stand. My grandfather never did that. He was known for his integrity, his honesty in terms of dealing with people. That's why he was so successful in knowing that the Columbus Panhandles are coming to Dayton or Massillon, that the players from the opposite team knew that they were going to be compensated and treated fairly."[22]

In the region where the scandal reigned they were about to get a shot in the arm as the city of Canton would again dominate the sport. Jack Cusack was a young office employee at the East Ohio Gas Company in Canton who became the secretary-treasurer of the Canton professional team in 1912. He eventually worked his way up to being the team's manager and would rename his team the Canton Bulldogs. Cusack had a philosophy and passion for the game similar to Joe Carr. He thought the sport would become a huge success if operated properly. Although he had more resources (and wasn't shy on spending money) from the city to help field his team (like Carr he also worked for free), he would always promote the positives of the game. At this time Cusack was already an avid football fan and in his short autobiography, titled *Pioneer in Pro Football,* he wrote about his experience as an early pro football manager:

I have called 1912 the Renaissance period for pro football because it was in that year that so many teams were organized in that part of the country—the

> Cleveland Erin Braus, Toledo Maroons, Columbus Panhandles, Cincinnati Celts, Shelby Blues, Elyria Pros, and Pittsburgh Lyceums. Soon other cities were getting into the revival act—Salem, Youngstown, Dayton and Detroit—all on an individual basis. The spirit of pro football was on the march again, even without formation of an official league.
>
> I was brightly aware that if professional football was to be a success we had to live down the scandal of 1906 and gain the public's confidence in the honesty of the game, and I felt that this could be done only with proper understanding among the managers and backers of the various teams. It was my theory that if we could stop players from jumping from one team to another, it would be a first step in the right direction.[23]

By 1912 most of the teams Cusack mentions were already established (not formed) but he was right that the pro teams in Ohio had established themselves as the best teams, with the best players. The sport now had some passionate supporters, but it also had many problems—mainly, no official league to run the sport and the continuation of players still hopping from team to team. An article that appeared in the *Hamilton (Ohio) Evening Journal* on November 15, 1912, with the headline "Championship Decision in Ohio Comes on Saturday" was a perfect example of the sport's many problems: "The professional football championship of Ohio will be decided at Dayton Sunday, when the Dayton Oakwoods play the Shelby Blues, who at present hold the state championship. Both teams include in their lineup some of the best known eastern college stars whose work in the last few years has made football history, but most of these men play under assumed names, on account of their college connections."[24]

In one article you had the claim of a "championship game," although there was no official league or standings to support that proof, so each week there was a title game advertised in every town or state. Then you had college athletes playing professional football under an assumed name to protect their eligibility, which was just as big a problem as players hopping from one team to another during the season for more money. Carr, as well as managers like Cusack, believed that the sport could gain some stability if player hopping was controlled, because the public could be reasonably sure of seeing the same players all year. It would take a while for this philosophy to take over the sport.

Even the Nessers faced the sport's evil doings. In later years the six Nesser brothers would claim to have played against Knute Rockne, the great Notre Dame coach (who was one of the better ends in the early days of professional football), six times with six different teams in one year. This was probably an exaggeration but it shows that players, especially ones as good as Rockne, were so willing to play for multiple teams during a single football season. The year 1912 might have felt like a renaissance to

Jack Cusack when he became involved in pro football, but Carr was still going through growing pains with his squad.

He was about to enter his sixth season as manager of the Panhandles and his team was still falling behind while trying to play the more modern game, as speed with a little passing mixed in seemed to dominate the sport. The only things going for them were (1) they were still a very physical team that could keep the score close and (2) the very talented Nesser brothers were still a great attraction for opposing teams to schedule.

Maybe Carr's marital responsibilities distracted him, but 1912 would be worse than 1911. Carr retained the same roster, although he adjusted it some throughout the season as he had players on his own team hopping to other teams for more money. Frank and Al Nesser, for example, played a few games with the Akron Indians to make a few bucks. Carr also continued to schedule the best pro teams in the Midwest as well as the city championship game. After winning their opener over the Columbus Parthians 26–0, the Panhandles suffered a brutal home loss to the Dayton Oakwoods, 7–2, scoring only a safety. This was the first time the Panhandles had lost to a team from Dayton.

Once again Carr took a break from football and attended the World Series, this time the National League's New York Giants faced off against the American League's Boston Red Sox, and Carr gave his opinion on who he thought would win: "Outside of [Smoky] Joe Wood, the Red Sox have shown little or nothing. There seems to be no organization in the club, and the base running is bad, and coaching is infinitely worse. But as for Wood. In my opinion he is the best player on either club. He is a wonder."[25]

In the series known for Fred Snodgrass's "folly," the Red Sox upset the Giants to capture the world's championship of baseball. Carr repeated his duties as a correspondent for the *Ohio State Journal* in relating all the activities of the Columbus baseball executives. He also missed the Panhandles tough 12–6 road loss against the Akron Indians on October 13. The following week he returned to take his team back up north to play the Canton professional team managed by the young Jack Cusack, who welcomed the very popular Panhandles in a big way. The local press was building up the game under the headline of "Columbus Panhandles, with 7 Nesser Brothers, Will Play Here Sunday."

> "If there were two Nessers playing football in 1906, five in 1911 and seven in 1912, how long will it be until the Columbus Panhandles are composed entirely of Nesser?"
>
> That query might suggest itself to the minds of many of the Canton football bugs right now, for the famous Panhandles, with their tribe of seven Nesser brothers, will be here Sunday to give the Canton eleven its first real

> fight of the season. The answer to the problem could easily be ascertained by finding out how many more of the same kind Nesser, Sr. has at home. Only four positions remain to be filled by Nessers.
>
> The entire backfield is made up of brothers. Frank, with over 200 pounds of beef and the huskiest of the seven, plays fullback and is rated one of the best in the state. He is a powerful punter, his boots averaging over 60 yards last season. Ted, the old Massillon Tigers star, plays one of the half positions, and Fred, the tallest of the bunch and dubbed "Greyhound," plays the other half. John directs the attack of the team from quarterback. On the line there are three more of the family. Phillip, much the same build as Frank and also over 200 pounds, plays right tackle, and Alfred, the kid of the septet, takes care of one end. The other end also has been assigned to a Nesser, but his name has (sapped).[26]

The publicity was there for a big game, and over 1,500 fans came out to League Park in Canton to watch the event. All six Nessers played as Canton gave the home crowd plenty to cheer about in a 25–6 victory. The Panhandles and manager Carr were extremely impressed with the Canton squad, and before they left town, they let the Canton newspapers know it. In the *Canton Daily News* Ted Nesser and Carr were quoted about the Canton squad.

> "I don't know why we couldn't get started. Maybe it was because the other fellows were getting into the plays quicker. We expected to win, and hadn't any idea that Canton would run up 25 points. That means that Akron will have to play hard to beat Canton. I think the teams will be evenly matched when the series starts."—Ted Nesser

> "Football is something like horse racing. There's form in every sport. One week ago, the Panhandles played methodically and in unity against Akron. Theirs was a 50 percent better game in every department. Today they seemed like strangers in a strange land. I doubt if Canton can defeat Akron, but Canton played better ball against us than did Akron."—Joe Carr[27]

The praise bestowed on the Canton team was a rarity as most opposing teams didn't give quotes in the paper too often. It was another way of Joe Carr getting his team some publicity—even if the predictions weren't correct. The Akron team proved its worth by defeating the Canton team twice in 1912, despite losing their team manager in the middle of the season. The *Newark (Ohio) Advocate* detailed the shocking news.

> Death was the victor in one of the most valiant fights for life ever made by a patient at the Akron City Hospital, when John E. "Key" Wilson, manager of the Indian football team, leading contenders for the professional football championship of Ohio, succumbed to an operation for appendicitis.

> Staging his favorite songs and whistling to keep up his courage almost until the last spark of life remained, Wilson fought death with that same spirit which characterized the work of his gridiron heroes. Mr. Wilson continued to repeat to the nurses and friends that he must live until his team had won the state football championship. "I cannot and must not die—I shall be out of here in time to see the boys win the state title," he said. And then he would proceed to sing or whistle one of his favorite songs.[28]

Carr could relate, as most early pro football team managers would do anything to win a game; it meant that much to them. Years later Carr would face his own battle with an ailing appendix. The Panhandles had suffered another loss and the rematch with the Dayton Oakwoods wouldn't be any better. On October 27 in Dayton the railroaders took an early 6–0 lead on a John Nesser touchdown catch from his brother Ted—but Ted would miss the point after. The lead held up until late in the fourth quarter when the Oakwoods blocked a punt, which led to a touchdown. The Dayton team converted the extra point and gave the Panhandles a heartbreaking 7–6 loss. The railroaders had now lost four consecutive games (three by six points or less) for the first time in team history. Could the season get any worse? Yes.

After an uninspiring 6–0 home win over the Cincinnati Celts, the Panhandles followed that up it with probably the most embarrassing loss in Joe Carr's career. The following week the Panhandles played another team from Cincinnati, this time the Cincinnati Christ Church. The team name didn't instill fear or toughness as the Panhandles name did, but the railroaders weren't ready to play. The Christ Church football team pounded the Panhandles 25–3 as a fifty-yard drop kick for a field goal was the only highlight for the Panhandles. The disappointing loss to such an inferior opponent left the railroaders with a disappointing 2–5 record.

The season did end on a high note with a tie against the Toledo Overlands and a nice 19–0 win in the city championship game against the Columbus Muldoons, behind two touchdowns by John Nesser. After the season Carr turned his attention to his family, and his team's first losing season since his first year as manager in 1907 slipped from his mind. Not too far after the holidays and the beginning of the new year, Joe and Josephine announced they were expecting their first child. With this big news the couple went looking for a new home.

After living the past year and half at the boarding house, the parents-to-be looked just outside the old Irish neighborhood and found a small house located at 1285 East Long Street as their first "baile." The new baby in the fall would call this home. Carr continued his work as secretary of the Ohio State League, but the machinist job at the railroad shops was starting to weigh him down. He saw his future as a sports executive, not as a railroad worker, and saw this as a perfect time for a change. His great relationship with the Panhandle shops guaranteed his continuation as team manager, but he was ready to leave the daily grind. Late in the summer before the season started, Carr was offered a job he wasn't even looking for.

> Carr Is Secretary of County License Board: Well Known Pennsy. Railroad Employee Gets Place With-out Applicant.
>
> Joseph F. Carr, of the motor department of the Pennsylvania railroad, has been chosen for the secretaryship of the Franklin County liquor licensing board. He was not an applicant and did not know he was being considered for the position. He has been secretary and treasurer of the Ohio State Baseball League for five years, and the efficient manner in which he handled the finances of that organization made such a favorable impression upon the board that it was decided to tender him to place.[29]

Carr now had another job. It wasn't that he wanted a career in the liquor industry but it was an opportunity to help control alcohol in the city he loved. It was also a well-respected position that probably had a very nice salary, and with a baby on the way this was something he couldn't pass up.

Even with the new house and job and a baby on the way, Carr didn't forget about his beloved Panhandles. The summer of 1913 might have been his best year of recruiting new players for the team since he took over as manager, though it didn't start off well. Frank Nesser left his brothers to play full time for the mighty Akron Indians; the lure of making good money was too strong for him.

The running, passing, and kicking of the bruising fullback was the heart and soul of the Columbus attack, and the team struggled to find a replacement for Frank. But Carr found a trio of players that changed the fortunes of his team for the next four years. Lee Snoots and Emmett Ruh were high school stars in the city of Columbus that Carr wanted badly. They were two of the fastest players to ever play in the capital city, and Carr knew they would adapt to the new pro game that was emphasizing speed. At the start of the season, Ted Nesser decided to put Fred Nesser at fullback and play Ruh at end, not really knowing how much speed he had. Snoots played in the backfield, and over time Ruh and Snoots would team up and provide the speed needed to match up with the physical play of the Panhandles.

The third player Carr wanted happened to play right under his nose. While watching a game being played by the Fahrney's Tailors, a local professional team sponsored by a tailor shop, Carr noticed Hi Brigham, who was making a name for himself as a pretty good center in the Columbus professional football scene. Carr offered Brigham twenty dollars a game, with two dollars for expenses on road trips and a job at the railroad for a salary of seventy-five dollars a month. Brigham took the offer and worked first as a clerk and then as a repairman in the railroad shops.

Ted Nesser started practice with just five Nesser brothers, Earl Colburn, Andy Kertzinger (who Brigham would replace at center), John Schneider, Ruh, Snoots, and both Kuehner brothers. Carr scheduled nine games with six of them on the road as he was getting closer to making the railroaders a full-fledged traveling team and taking advantage of those free passes. Instead of a "cupcake" to start the season, Carr scheduled a heavyweight—the Akron Indians with Frank Nesser. But Carr had his reason for choosing the Indians, as well as the late date for an opening game. On October 12 the railroaders (without Snoots and Brigham) traveled north and played before 2,000 rain-soaked fans, who saw the Indians defeat the Panhandles 19–0.

The Indians, led by Peggy Parratt, would once again field a strong team and finish as the best team in Ohio with a 9–1–2 record. But the game was secondary to Joe Carr—who probably didn't make the trip to Akron—as the following day Carr's life changed forever. On Monday, October 13, 1913, Mary Agnes Carr was born as Joe and Josephine welcomed home the baby girl to the house on East Long Street. The little princess of the well-known sports executive instantly became daddy's girl.

Two weeks after the birth (and the day after the Panhandles lost 6–0 to Canton), Mary Carr was baptized at St. Patrick Church, with Joe's younger brother, Eddie, and his new fiancé, Kathryn Traynor, as her godparents. The new baby brought quick joy to the young Irish couple, and she would not disappoint them. For the rest of her life she would dedicate herself to her loving parents, especially her father, who she just worshipped. "She idolized her father," says Martha Sullivan. "He was the end all, be all for her."[30]

From an early age Mary would show the flair of a movie star. In the earliest photos of her, the curly brunette is seen smiling while posing for the camera wearing her best white dress. In another one she poses with her favorite children's book, *Little People's A-B-C: A Picture Alphabet Book for Little People*, as she sits on a small wooden chair. She was a natural for the camera and her biggest fan was her father. But daddy's girl wouldn't have been happy with her dad's start to the 1913 season. The Canton loss was a tough one to swallow and the team's fighting didn't help. The *Canton Daily News* described the brawl. "A sidelight to the engagement was found in the belligerency of right guard [Al] Nesser of Columbus and guard Schlott of Canton. The pair was ejected from the contest for slugging in the third quarter, but both returned by agreement. Canton being without the services of an eligible player under the rule of substitution."[31]

The "new game" of professional football (with passing and speed) was slowly being used by the railroaders as the new recruits needed time to get used to playing the pro game; but when would it click? After back-to-back scoreless ties against the Dayton Oakwoods and the McKeesport (Pennsylvania) pro team, the Panhandles lost a tough one to the Cincinnati Celts, 7–0. After five straight road games and a winless record (0–3–2), Carr stayed close to home and scheduled mostly games against Columbus teams to end the season. The next four games would change the team's fortunes forever and change the way they played on the field.

Before the game with the Columbus Muldoons, coach Ted Nesser decided to make some position changes in the starting lineup. For the upcoming game Ted moved his brother Fred from fullback to end and moved speedy Emmett Ruh to halfback. Ted moved himself from halfback to fullback. This switch helped the team go on to win three of their last four games. With a backfield of Ted Nesser, Emmett Ruh, Lee Snoots, and John Nesser, the Panhandles finally put some points on the scoreboard, defeating the Muldoons 23–0 at Indianola Park. Ted tallied two touchdowns and Emmett Ruh accounted for eleven points (one touchdown, two extra points, and one field goal).

After a tough Thanksgiving Day loss against the Wabash (Indiana) Athletic Association (played before 2,500 fans), the Panhandles won their second game of the year by defeating the Barracks 23–0 in front of 1,500 spectators. Emmett Ruh, Ted Nesser, and Lee Snoots all scored touchdowns. After beating the Barracks, Carr arranged one last game to decide the Columbus city championship. This time the railroaders played their old rivals—the Columbus Nationals. On December 2 the *Ohio State Journal* officially announced the game. "The Panhandles will meet the Fahrney Nationals next Sunday. After the defeat of the Muldoons and the Barracks by the champions, the Nationals contend that, inasmuch as that their goal line was not crossed by either the Muldoons or the Barracks, they were entitled to consideration before the final announcement making the Panhandles the undisputed champions of the city."[32]

But on the day of the game, the weather didn't cooperate, as the *Columbus Dispatch* explained:

> Held off by the blizzard, which struck Columbus early Sunday morning the Panhandles and Fahrney Nationals were forced to postpone their battle for the city professional championship, which was to have been staged at Indianola Park, Sunday afternoon.
>
> Although the weather prevented the teams from meeting it did not stop hundreds of football fans from journeying to the park in hope of seeing the

> game played, despite the storm. "If arrangements can be made the game may still be played later in the year, although it is not likely," said Mr. Fahrney of the Nationals Monday morning.[33]

The game was cancelled because of the storm, but Carr and the team got together anyway. The *Ohio State Journal* reported on the team's nighttime activity with the headline "Panhandle Entertained at Ruh Home": "Mr. and Mrs. Ruh, parents of Emmett Ruh, who has been one of the stars of the champion Panhandles this year, entertained his teammates at dinner at their home on Sunday evening. The party was in the nature of a surprise for the popular Panhandle player. After an elegant dinner, the boys were entertained by some of their number and the Misses Ruh and Caldwell."[34]

The surprise dinner party seemed to reenergize the team and Carr worked to reschedule the game against the Nationals. Four days after the cancelled game the two teams agreed to play again. On December 14 the two teams finally took the field at Indianola Park and the Panhandles played their best football in years. The final game capped off a difficult year on a positive note and gave the team some momentum for the 1914 season.

The railroaders simply pounded the Nationals by scoring ten touchdowns and claimed the city title with a convincing 68–0 victory. Emmett Ruh and Lee Snoots scored four touchdowns each, and the *Ohio State Journal* praised the railroaders on their big win.

> Panhandles 68; Fahrney's National All-Stars 0, briefly tells the story of the last independent football game of the season to determine finally the Columbus championship. The Panhandles have demonstrated beyond the shadow of any doubt that they are far and above any other team in the city at the game called football.
>
> Eliminating each team that claimed any right to the title by first defeating the Muldoons and then defeating the Barracks, the Panhandle heard the Nationals contending that they were to be considered before the champions could wear the laurels. As a closing number for the season, the Panhandles got to work early in the game yesterday and in less than five minutes of play, Emmett Ruh went over the goal line for the first touchdown. This was the stiffest resistance the Nationals offered. After the first scores by the champions, they romped up and down the field almost at will."[35]

A season of frustration was released against the Nationals as the team scored 117 points and won three of their final four games. Carr was disappointed that the team finished under .500 for the season but was very happy that his roster was now set to challenge for the mythical Ohio League pro football championship. He now had the perfect blend of speed (Snoots and Ruh) and power (Brigham and the Nesser brothers) and for the next three seasons the Columbus Panhandles would play their best stretch of football.

The year 1913 was pivotal for Joe Carr, as he found a new home and a new job, had his first child, and established a new roster that would soon make his talented bunch of railroaders a household name. He had found that magic touch again, as in 1909, and now he was ready to take his team on the road and show them off to the rest of the pro football world.

6

Pro Football's Most Famous Traveling Team (1914–1916)

After a disappointing season, Joe Carr would start out 1914 on a positive note, as Eddie Carr would tie the knot with his fiancé Kathryn Traynor. On February 18 the godparents of little Mary Carr exchanged their wedding vows in a very small ceremony at St. Patrick Church. Kathryn was a very tiny (five feet three), independent, private woman, whose father worked at the Pennsy railroad and attended church at St. Patrick's with the Carr family. "Katie always liked the Carr brothers and thought they were really wonderful. She was totally in love with Eddie. Although they never had any children, they were totally devoted to each other," says Joy Dolan, great-niece of Kathryn Traynor-Carr.[1]

"Eddie Carr was a very gentle man and I would say that he was the most serious of the Carr brothers," says Margaret Mooney, granddaughter of Michael Carr. Eddie and Kathryn would remain married for thirty-eight years, and he would continue to work as secretary-treasurer for his brother Michael at the Franklin Coffee Company in Columbus. "Katie always knew that Joe Carr wasn't wasting his time with the football team and later with the NFL. She knew he would make it work because that was the type of guy he was. When he set his mind up to accomplish something he usually did," says Joy Dolan.[2]

Joe continued his work at the Liquor Licensing Board and as secretary of the Ohio State League under Robert W. Read, who had replaced Carr's good friend Bobby Quinn in 1910 as president. But during the summer his thoughts quickly turned to his football team. During some of those days at the ballpark, or staying up late with Mary, he would think about how he could give his team the best opportunity to display its skills. This was going to be his best team to date, and he wanted to showcase them to the football world in the best way possible—especially in the state of Ohio. For the past couple of seasons Carr was able to take advantage of the railroad's perk of free passes for all railroad employees, which included himself (although he know longer worked there). His good relationship with the Pennsylvania Railroad insured his free pass. Over his first seven seasons as manager, he had slowly increased the team's road games:

1907—four road games
1908—two road games
1909—three road games
1910—two road games
1911—four road games
1912—five road games
1913—six road games

The six road games in 1913 proved to him that he could take his team on the road and promote his squad as a traveling team. By taking them on the road, Carr would keep the team's expenses down for the entire year because he didn't have to pay for a home field, officials, promotion, and so forth, and in turn they would be able to make a little money. With his roster set with the perfect blend of speed and power—as well as the attraction of the six Nesser brothers to bring out the fans—this was the right time to hit the road. Using his experience as a sports promoter and writer, Carr built pro football's greatest traveling team. "The Nesser brothers had developed a reputation of being hardnosed football players, certainly. One of them broke their leg one time and came back into the game to play. That shows you how tough these guys were. So with this reputation they were able to barnstorm around Ohio and the Midwest," says James Carr, grandson of Joe Carr. "At this time the Nesser brothers were getting a reputation as being some of the most well-known pro football players in the country. I've talked to people who watched them and they all said they were awesome. So everybody wanted to play them, and it made it easier for my grandfather to schedule road games for the Panhandles to play," says Michael Carr, grandson of Joe Carr.[3]

In 1914 Frank Nesser returned to play with his famous siblings, and the Panhandles fielded a talented team comprised of the six Nesser brothers (who played every position possible), Lee Snoots, and Emmett Ruh in the backfield; Hi Brigham, Charlie Dunn, and Roscoe Kuehner (Oscar Kuehner sat out the year) on the line. Throughout the season the railroaders would explode on offense, scoring 210 points, and flex their muscle on defense, allowing only 60 points in nine games. After playing the opener at home (a 57–0 warm-up game against an overmatched

Columbus Wyandottes team), the team would play six straight road games, from October 4 to November 15, before finishing the year with two home games.

Coach Ted Nesser prepared his team for the upcoming season, and Carr rewarded his squad with a gift even before the first game. On September 24 the *Ohio State Journal* explained under the headline "Togs Are Gorgeous Ones."

> Panhandle football uniforms and blankets, which have been on exhibition at Spalding's, will be distributed Friday evening to the regulars and subs who have made the team and weather permitting will be in use for the first time next Sunday when the railroaders meet the Wyandottes at Indianola Park.
>
> The color scheme is maroon and gold, emblematic of the club. The body of the jerseys is of maroon with one and one-eighth inch alternating stripes of the club's colors the full length of the sleeves. The stockings also have alternating bands of the same colors and the material is of double thickness. The blankets are of extra high-grade wool and were made from a special design by William Gracey, the club's trainer. They are maroon in color and in the middle of each blanket is a large sunburst of gold, encircling a keystone, which in turn encloses the club's monogram composed of the letters P and H.
>
> Few football clubs will be better or more completely equipped than the Panhandle squad when it makes its initial appearance on the playing field."[4]

The team now had new uniforms and new sideline blankets. Carr made sure his team looked first class, as most early pro teams barely made money to have matching uniforms. Carr used his resources to make his team look good to the paying public. Carr knew professional football had a future, so he wanted to make the Panhandles look like a first-class organization, especially since he was about to take his team on the road for good. The first trip was to Akron to play Peggy Parratt's Indians, who were pro football's best team in 1913 and who beat the Panhandles 19–0.

The railroaders played a perfect football game against the Indians and came home with a convincing 26–0 win. The *Akron Beacon-Journal* praised the Panhandles performance, and the *Canton Repository* reported on their fashion style.

> Just a few words about the Panhandles. The Columbus aggregation looked trained to the minute. The Nesser boys never played the brand of football they are putting up this fall. Ruh, Snoots and Brigham proved valuable assistance. The Panhandles not only used the old style game to advantage, but made the forward pass count for many long gains. They played solid, consistent football and deserved to win.

> The Panhandles gave the Indians their first drubbing. That is not all. They will go along winning from the other professional teams in Ohio. Canton looks to be the only team which had a chance to make the Panhandles extend themselves. Manager Parratt admitted Sunday that he must secure new material to brace his team. Parratt never sleeps on the job. He says he will give Akron a winner, and Peggy can be depended upon to plug up the holes which showed in the Panhandle game.
>
> Columbus Men Finely Garbed
>
> In past seasons the Panhandles have never drawn any prize for the cut or pattern of their uniforms. They were never considered the Beau Brummels of the professional grid. This fall, however, hats must be lifted to the Columbus troupe. The Panhandles have been newly outfitted from head to heel with uniforms that have attracted considerable comment wherever they have played. Peggy Parratt, whose [Akron] Indians the Panhandles defeated 26 to 0, dubbed them the most fashionable team in the state.[5]

Who would have thought that the rough-and-tough Panhandles would be the most stylish-looking team in professional football? As Parratt went in search for better players (as most early pro football managers did after a bad loss), the Akron victory propelled the Panhandles into a position of competing not only for the city title but for the mythical Ohio League championship. The city of Columbus was getting excited and the *Ohio State Journal* was also on board with the railroaders:

> With the chances brighter than ever for the state independent football championship to fall to the lot of the Columbus eleven, fans feel that the Panhandles are closer to the goal through their defeat of the Akron Indians last Sunday. Manager Carr is arranging a schedule that will include every first class team in Ohio, Pennsylvania and Indiana. The team is determined for once, if possible, to have the state championship rest in Columbus. On next Sunday the Panhandles will tackle the strong eleven at New Philadelphia. Coach Nesser has his men at work daily.[6]

The next game took the railroaders north to face the pro team from New Philadelphia (Ohio). Behind the play of the six Nesser brothers, the Panhandles won their third straight game with an easy 37–0 victory. During the three-game win streak, the Panhandles had outscored their opponents 120 to 0. It seemed nothing could stop the Panhandles momentum. The following week that momentum came to a screeching halt when a game with the Dayton Oakwoods was cancelled: "Just as the Panhandle team was ready to start for Dayton yesterday, a message was received from the management of the Dayton Oakwoods that play would be impossible. A heavy rain was falling and the field was muddy from the week's downpour. The two teams will meet later in the season."[7]

Mother Nature was the only thing that could have stopped the Panhandles. Joe Carr was never able to reschedule the game with Dayton, and the week off hurt the team's momentum as the next game would show. On October 25 the Panhandles traveled to Stark County to face the talented Canton Bulldogs managed by Jack Cusack, who threw the first shot at Carr and his famous Panhandles by giving the *Canton Repository* a pregame quote: "We must hand Columbus a beating. Victory will give us the title, for a time at least. Canton has never been able to boast of a state championship, not even for a week or two, but I think a precedent will be established Sunday."[8]

Cusack respected Carr but he knew if his team was going to be taken seriously he needed to beat the Panhandles, and if a boastful quote put a few more people in the stands, all the better. Canton's management was confident in a victory and the Bulldogs played like champions, defeating the lifeless railroaders 40–10 before a crowd of 4,000 screaming Bulldog fans. The *Canton Repository* gave the home team all the praise.

> It is doubtful whether a Canton team ever played better football than did the squad Sunday. Not once did Capt. Hamilton make a mistake in generalship, only a few times did a play go wrong and only once did Canton fumble. This one foozie did no damage as the ball was recovered without a loss of a yard. Brilliant individual plays and smooth team work marked the progress of the Canton machine, bringing six touchdowns over the noted Panhandles combination which three weeks ago triumphed over the Akron Indians 26 to 0. The Columbus stars played their best and never showed signs of quitting but they were up against a foe of greater skill and ability.[9]

The Bulldogs went on to finish the season with a 9–1 record, but it was still a bad loss for the Panhandles and the hangover from the Bulldogs whipping carried over to the following week. The railroaders made their second trip to Akron for the rematch with Parratt's Indians, who had added a few more players to the roster. The outcome this time was much different, as the railroaders lost any chance at the state championship by losing to the Indians 14–0. With a record of 3–2 the season was starting to slip away from Carr's boys. How would the team finish? The answer would be found in the team's last four games.

First up was a trip to Indiana to play the tough Wabash Athletic Association—the champions of the Indiana Valley. On November 8 the railroaders got touchdowns from John Nesser and Emmett Ruh to help shut out Wabash 13–0 on a muddy gridiron. It was a great rebound win and the team needed it.

The following week the railroaders played their sixth straight game on the road by facing the Toledo Maroons for the first time ever. The Maroons would become one of the Panhandles biggest rivals and would later play in the NFL in 1922–1923 (compiling a two-year record of 8–5–4). On November 15, however, the Maroons first game against the Panhandles was a tough one as the railroaders came away with a 7–4 win.

Playing on another muddy field, fullback Frank Nesser scored the game's only touchdown. The *Ohio State Journal* reported on the game and the field conditions with the headline "Columbus Players Better Mud Horses Than Maroons in a Very Close Game":

> The Toledo Maroons lost their reputation as "mud beavers" this afternoon when the beefy Columbus Panhandle eleven "outmired" them in a "marine" encounter at Armory Park. After an hour's maneuvering about the rain-swept field, the Pennsy crew, wearing an inch thick coat of clay, emerged with a 7 to 4 victory.
>
> The Panhandles' lone touchdown came in the initial period, and was the result of a blocked kick which Frank Nesser rescued on the locals' 12-yard line, and crossed the final marker. Ruh added another point by kicking goal. The Maroons sacrificed an opportunity to register a touchdown on two occasions in the second quarter, but were forced to be content with a safety."[10]

The team now had a solid 5–2 record and would finish the season with two home games against opponents from Columbus who wanted to challenge for the Panhandles' city title. Coach Ted Nesser wasn't about to have his squad let up now; his boys would be ready to face any challengers. After six straight road games, Carr was pleased with his team's effort on the field, as well as the financial side of the enterprise, as the team made a small profit. Heading into the last two games in Columbus, Carr met with *Columbus Citizen* sportswriter Clyde Tuttle to help him promote his team and try to get fans to come out to the games, as they spent the last two months on the road. Tuttle wrote a colorful article on the great Nesser siblings.

> It is doubtful if any other family in the country can equal the Nesser family of Columbus. So far as is known the Panhandles have the only football team in the country on which six brothers are playing a wonderful game and making Columbus talked about.
>
> All of them are employed at the Panhandle shops and for years all of them have been prominent in athletics. While football has been the forte of all of them, several of them are crack bowlers and basketball players and one of them, Frank, plays baseball professionally.
>
> In height they range from Fred, the tallest, who is six feet five inches tall, to Ted, the shortest, who standing five feet 10 inches, is taller than the average man. The six brothers average about 190 pounds. Frank, the heaviest, tips the beam at 235 pounds, while John, the lightest, weighs about 160 pounds. There is a difference of 20 years of age. John, the oldest, is 41 years of age,

while Alfred, the youngest, is just 21. In age they rank this way: John, Phillip, Ted, Fred, Frank and Alfred. All of them are perfect specimens of manhood. All of them are married and have families.

Their parents are both living and both of them take an active interest in the athletic activities of their sons. It's as much of a certainty as anything in this world can be that both of them though more than 70 years of age will be at Indianola Park Sunday afternoon rooting for their sons when they line up with the Panhandles against the Bates Pirates, for the professional football title of the city, for announcement has been made that all of the six brothers will take part in this game.[11]

The publicity seemed to work. A day after the Nesser article ran, 3,000 fans at Indianola Park saw the brothers and the rest of the railroaders go out and score thirty-five second-half points to defeat the Columbus Bates Pirates 41–0. Ted Nesser scored three touchdowns to lead the attack. The score was lopsided and the play on the field looked odd as the railroaders played against one of their own when John "Pop" Schneider switched sides and played halfback for the Pirates. "Sometimes when the team would go out and play different teams, if the opposing teams they were playing didn't have enough players, they would take a player from the Panhandle team and put them on the opposing team. Most of the time it would be my father who would play against the Panhandles," said Irene Cassady, daughter of John Schneider. "My father was only five feet ten and weighed about 190 pounds, but he was strong, strong as an ox. But he would say the Nessers annihilated me. They would beat the tar out of him."[12]

During the game Schneider had a punt blocked by Hi Brigham, which led to one of the Panhandles touchdowns. Another name on the Bates team looked familiar, too, as Homer Ruh lined up against his brother Emmett. After defeating the Pirates, Joe Carr scheduled one last game, against the Columbus Mendel's All-Stars, a team consisting of former college stars around Ohio. Behind two touchdowns by Ted Nesser and one by Lee Snoots, the railroaders came away with a convincing 19–2 victory. The All-Stars did manage to accomplish one thing as they became the first Columbus team in thirteen games to score a point against the Panhandles. Not since the October 3, 1909, game against the Columbus Barracks did the railroaders give up a score.

The railroaders finished the season strong, winning their last four games and retaining the Columbus city championship. After all the roster changes and frustrating losses over the previous four seasons, Joe Carr saw his Panhandles finally put everything together. The backfield consisting of John Nesser (quarterback), Lee Snoots (left halfback), Emmett Ruh (right halfback), and Ted Nesser and Frank Nesser (fullbacks) combined strength with speed and helped the Panhandles finish with one of their best seasons ever. The 7–2 record was a tremendous achievement, and the winning ways would continue in 1915, which became a landmark year in professional football.

Shortly after the season Joe Carr received some more good news; he and his wife were pregnant with their second child. As Carr heard this news he once again decided to put his future in the area of sports management. On March 16 he was named president of the Ohio State League, replacing William Read. Later in the year before the football season started he would resign his post as secretary of the County Liquor Board and concentrate all his time on being a sports executive.[13]

After a tremendous season in 1914, the Panhandles responded with another great campaign. The win-loss record, a very respectable 8–3–1, didn't quite show it, but the 1915 Panhandles might have been their best team ever. Joe Carr's addition of quarterback Lou Pickerel, former Ohio State University star, added a great deal of versatility to an already powerful attack. He was a fine passer and adding his arm to Frank Nesser's gave the team an excellent air attack. It also was the first time Carr actively recruited a college star to play for the Panhandles by offering him a job with the railroad.

The railroaders would go on to score 192 points (averaging 16 points per game), but once again the team's strength would be its hard-nosed defense. The Panhandles only allowed thirty-seven points in twelve games, including eight shutouts. The combination of offense and defense made the team worthy of the Ohio League championship. Joe Carr brought back most of the great 1914 team—all six Nessers, Hi Brigham, Roscoe Kuehner, Lee Snoots, and Emmett Ruh. The big additions were Pickerel and the return of Oscar Kuehner. These fourteen men played almost every game for the Panhandles in 1915. The two new additions would be needed as Carr set up the most challenging schedule any pro team in Ohio would play. The team played only four games in Columbus—two at the beginning of the season and two at the end. These games bookended eight straight road games with new trips to Detroit (Michigan), Fort Wayne (Indiana), Marion, and Youngstown, as well as old stops in Canton, Dayton, Massillon, and Toledo. This would be the first time in Panhandles history that they would play twelve games in a single season.

After a 40–0 victory in the Panhandles' opener at home against the Columbus Smokers, Joe Carr would step back from football and join his wife Josephine in welcoming their new baby boy. On Friday, October 1, 1915, Joseph Francis Carr Jr. was born at home, and the whole city celebrated his arrival. In the morning edition of the *Ohio State Journal* his pals at the paper congratulated him: "President Joe Carr of the Ohio State League was shelling out cigars last night. A son arrived yesterday afternoon at his home, 1285 East Long Street."[14]

Joe and Josephine soon decided to have only two children, devoting their time and energy to giving the two Carr siblings everything possible. As Carr was at home with his family, the Panhandles defeated the Columbus All-Stars 45–0 at Indianola Park, showing Carr that they were ready to hit the road. The team prepared to play eight consecutive weeks away from Columbus and the first stop on the long road trip was a game north of Columbus in Marion to play the Marion Questions. The small town was excited about seeing the Panhandles and the famous Nesser brothers. On October 6 the *Marion Daily Star* ran a feature article on the Nesser clan.

> In booking the Panhandles, of Columbus, for a game at Marion, next Sunday, the management of the Questions football team has shown, football lovers say, that nothing will be spared to give the football fans of the city the very best that is to be seen in this section of the country. The Panhandles have long been looked upon as one of the leading teams in the professional game in the country and in their ranks they have a feature that is possessed by no other team in the history of the game. Six brothers, the famous Nessers, are all members of the team and will play in the line-up against the Questions.
>
> The six Nessers brothers average close to 200 pounds each and each is a finished athlete. Two of them formerly played on the famous Massillon Tigers champion team and have played with the Panhandles since.
>
> **Holder of a Medal**
>
> John, who plays quarterback, is the holder of the Pennsylvania lines diamond medal for being the most finished athlete among the many thousand employees of the railroad system.
>
> Ted, who plays fullback and also coaches the team, has been pronounced one of the greatest football players of all time by college coaches and officials and has been offered a college course in many of the big institutions of learning in order that his service might be had on the college elevens. He was a half back on the Massillon team and today is one of the ranking players of the country in the professional game.
>
> Frank, the largest of the brothers and the one who does the punting, is a wonder at kicking the ball. Standing over six feet and weighing 220 pounds, his kicking alone is a feature of any game of football. College coaches readily admit that his equal as a punter and drop kicker is not to be found among the colleges of the Middle West.
>
> **Star with Forward Pass**
>
> Fred, who plays one of the end positions, is also a star in a particular way. He is also the man who does all of the forward-passing for the famous eleven and he can handle a football with the dexterity of a baseball player handling

> a baseball. Before the game he will give an exhibition of long distance throwing of the football that will in itself be an attraction.
>
> The remaining members of the team all balance up this great aggregation and with the exception of the Nesser brothers have all had college experience on the gridiron. The Kuehner brothers, one playing a tackle position and the other one of the end positions, were the stars of the Wellston High football team in 1912. The two half backs, Emmett Ruh and Sid (Lee) Snoots, have had experience on college elevens and their services have been sought by about every high-class eleven in the Middle West. Altogether the Panhandles present a line-up of stars that are seldom seen in one team and their coming to Marion marks a real event in the professional game.[15]

On game day the small town of Marion was just that, a small town, as only 400 fans came out to see the game. Just four Nesser brothers played—no Al or John—as the railroaders won 21–0 behind two touchdowns by Emmett Ruh and one by rookie Lou Pickerel. After three convincing wins by a combined score of 106–0, the railroaders were ready for some better competition and they got it. Next up was the great Canton Bulldogs. The Bulldogs were in midst of a season that would change the face of professional football. Late in the season (November), Bulldogs Manager Jack Cusack signed pro football's first national superstar—Jim Thorpe—to play two games against the Bulldogs' chief rival, the Massillon Tigers.

But in October Thorpe would miss out on playing the Panhandles. Bulldogs manager Cusack made sure the railroaders were in the news as the *Canton Daily News* promoted the game. "With a reputation of having struggled undauntedly for season after season for the Ohio professional football title, the Panhandle A.C. of Columbus comes to Canton Sunday armed with up to date plays and wonderful striking ability and fully prepared for the meeting with Mgr. Cusack's Canton pro gridders."[16]

The *Canton Repository* had more to say about the Panhandles and they chose to write about the new star of the team.

> The Columbus Panhandles, perennial aspirants to the professional honors of Ohio who battle the Canton "pros" at League Park Sunday, have made just one notable change in their array for this season from that which they used last fall. They have inserted at quarterback a chap named Pickerel who is far from being a dud at the gridiron game.
>
> In fact, this Pickerel was last season one of the leading men of Ohio college elevens. He wore the scarlet and gray of Ohio State and was named for the All-Ohio by the conference coaches, the critics who are in the best position to form an opinion. Pickerel is a flash on the field, full of speed and hard to stop. He has but one noticeable fault—he is not strong enough physically to stand the gaff of a hard conflict. Although the Panhandle–Canton struggle will be no place for any but a husky, Pickerel will be on the job at quarter for the Columbus bunch.[17]

The scene was set for a big Panhandles victory and they gave it their best shot. In front of "two thousand rabid fans," the two teams slugged it out in a back-and-forth defensive battle. In the fourth quarter during a scoreless game, Emmett Ruh fumbled a punt that led to the only touchdown of the game and a 7–0 win for the Bulldogs. The *Canton Daily News* reported on the rough tactics by the railroaders.

> Rich was the harvest reaped by Canton's professional football outfit at League Park Sunday. The big Red and White eleven, in the first important battle for the state title, conquered the vicious Panhandle A.C. of Columbus, founded by the Nesser family, 7 to 0. The Panhandles produced probably the most glaring exhibition of what in football is called "dirty playing" ever seen on a Canton gridiron. Three Canton players were injured, one very seriously.
>
> The Columbus umpire refused to call penalties for holding and there was constant slugging and unnecessary roughness of the viciously-playing Panhandles. Profanity from the field was heard in the stands. For over 40 minutes the battle scarred rivals struggled scorelessly. Canton's sole touchdown came like a bolt from Jove. A punt by Axtell, a tackle of halfback Ruh of Columbus by Gardner, the contact causing the invader to fumble, a cat-like and successful leap for the uncovered ball by Edwards who [brought the ball back] to the P.A.C.'s 5-yard line—there you have the wedge. Two plays later, both line plunges by fullback Peters, the locals were six points to the good. The touchdown came three minutes and 15 seconds after the beginning of the fourth period.
>
> Time and again the contest was stopped to quell actions frowned upon by rule makers. In the last half, the feeling ran high due to the rough mark always inaugurated by the visitors. Two injuries, both coming to Cantonians, cast shadows. Dagenhart, local product, retired on the first kickoff after fiercely tackling Fred Nesser. He was aided from the field. Truesby, Cleveland lad playing halfback, went to the sidelines with a broken collarbone, giving Van Allman the opportunity of which he made the most. Gardner went out near the close with an injured leg.[18]

Despite the big hits laid on the Bulldogs, it was a tough loss for the Panhandles, and just like in 1914, the Panhandles would have another hangover after their first loss of the season. The Panhandles next game was against the Toledo Maroons, and Joe Carr tried to motivate his team as well as get fans to come out and see the game. On October 21 the *Toledo Daily Blade* reported on Carr's big statement with the headline "Pan Handles to Win by 3 Touchdowns—Carr":

> Columbus Panhandles will beat the Maroons by three touchdowns was the statement made by Joe Carr, manager of the railroaders to Art Gratop Tuesday evening at Columbus. Carr figures that despite his 7 to 0 defeat at the hands of the Canton outfit, the Pan Handles have one of the strongest ag-

> gregations in the state and are capable of giving any team, with the possible exception of the Canton giants, a good trimming.
>
> On the other hand the Maroons are as confident as ever and figure that by their open style of football they will be able to eliminate the Pan Handles from State Championship consideration. From all indications it will be one of the best contests of the year.[19]

Carr always believed his team would win, and if his statement put a few more fans in the stands then the publicity worked. The game turned out to be a hit with the fans, as over 3,500 spectators came out to Armory Park and watched the hometown Maroons beat the railroaders 20–0. Carr's prediction wasn't even close as his team didn't play very well and once again slugged its way through the game. The *Toledo News-Bee* sent writer Mart Manley to describe the game and he would focus on the fight.

> Took Punch at Sala
>
> Errett Sala, Maroon end, whose hard tackles jarred the Pan Handle backfield men, was put out of the game for his clash with Fred Nesser, the giant end of the visitors. Sala, a 140-pounder, and Nesser, a 210-pounder, swapped punches. Both were put out by Referee Wright. Nesser started the trouble.
>
> The Maroon line seemed to be cement to all of the Pan Handle plungers except Snoots. He was the only one of the visitors who could gain consistently. Jule Wise broke through the visitors' line time after time and nailed his man before the Pan Handle could get started.[20]

It seems every newspaper wanted to point out the rough "tactics" by the railroaders. The Panhandles and the Nesser brothers physical play—learned on the railroad yards in Columbus—was now the team's trademark and would follow them forever. After a tremendous start the Panhandles were now 3–2, and the rest of the season was in jeopardy. After the consecutive losses the railroaders headed back to Stark County to play the Massillon Tigers. It would be the first meeting between the two teams since 1907. On October 30 the *Massillon Independent* prepared fans for a great game.

> Massillon Sunday will be the scene of the biggest game of football played here since the old Tiger days of 10 years ago.
>
> The Tigers, Massillon's professional team, seeking the state title, will receive its first severe test of the season tomorrow when the orange and black stars trot upon the field at the Driving Park grounds to battle the Columbus Panhandles, a team controlled by Nesser Bros. & Co.
>
> Players whose names have been connected with All-American teams, others who have achieved fame with college teams, and still others who have never played college football but have learned the game on sand lots, will

be in the aggregation of gridiron talent that assembles here Sunday for the big game.

The Panhandles are demons on the football field. Big as mountains and strong as lions the railroaders from the capital are among the most feared teams in the state. Led in their efforts by the six Nesser brothers, football players of renown, the Columbus aggregation balks at nothing.

They fight from the start to finish. Possessing a clever backfield and a heavy line the Panhandles present a battle front hard to pierce. Directed by Pickerel, former Ohio State quarterback and all Ohio choice last year, the Panhandles display an effective brand of football.[21]

Two weeks after losing a tough one to the Canton Bulldogs the "big as mountains and strong as lions" Panhandles—with all six Nessers—played perhaps their best game of the season, defeating the Tigers 16–0. In front of 3,000 fans, the railroaders' passing game came alive as John Nesser and Roscoe Kuehner caught touchdown passes from Lou Pickerel. The *Columbus Dispatch* described the passing attack of the Panhandles.

By clever use of the forward pass the Pan Handle team of Columbus threw a blanket over the state championship hopes of the Massillon Tigers here Sunday afternoon by defeating the home football players 16 to 0.

Two of the Pan Handles' touchdowns were down to the expert throwing of the ball by Pickerel at quarter for the Railroaders. The other points were taken when Pickerel shot a drop kick over the bars in the final period. In the second quarter Fred Nesser went over the line when Pickerel gave him a short forward pass and the second Columbus touchdown was made in the fourth period when Kuehner nabbed a Pickerel thrown ball and scampered across the final bar for the six points.[22]

The aerial attack helped snap the team's two-game losing streak, and it showed that the railroaders could win a big game. It also was the only time the Panhandles would defeat the famous Massillon Tigers, going 1–4 all time against the Tigers. But the team did suffer one loss; John Nesser's injured leg would keep him out of the next five games. After a month on the road, the traveling didn't affect the team's effort, and most of the players were just happy to get away from work.

"My dad didn't really mind the traveling at all because it was part of the package. They were working six days a week and then on Saturday you're done at 4 and then you're on a train going to play on Sunday. Then they would return late Sunday night and be right back at work in the railroad shops early Monday morning," says James Brigham, son of Hi Brigham, former Panhandles center. "My dad admired Joe Carr. He thought he was really a great guy. I also think he was somewhat in awe of him despite the both of them being good friends. On the road he roomed with Carr from time to time when they stayed in rooming houses on the road. I never heard the word hotel mentioned. I'd hear rooming houses. But he certainly admired Joe Carr and he was quite proud to have known him."[23]

Carr would save money by having the team stay in rooming houses, but every once in a while if they arrived very late into town they would hit the nearest barn. In a 1948 Columbus newspaper interview, former Panhandles halfback Lee Snoots explained traveling with the Panhandles.

> Our trips were wonderful. We preferred the yearly trek to Toledo. We would leave on Saturday night and stay over at a small town called Carrothers. Here I learned how to eat Nesser style. P. Regula owned a saloon and boarding house in Carrothers and in the rear of the house was a barn with the upstairs furnished somewhat. The Nesser boys preferred this barn to the house and after a card session, off to bed they would go. The snoring from that barn was a fright from midnight on. There wasn't a tenor among them. All bassos.[24]

It's hard to believe that Joe Carr would hang out and sleep in a barn; he would always stay in the rooming houses while traveling on the road. But anything to save a dollar was definitely something Carr would try at any time during the season.

The momentum from the Massillon win carried over into the following week when the team traveled to Dayton to play the Gym-Cadets. The Cadets had replaced the Oakwoods as the best pro team in Dayton, and they were no match for the Panhandles. In front of another nice crowd of 3,500, the railroaders gave up an early touchdown before getting the offense rolling. Once again the passing of Lou Pickerel led the attack, as the Panhandles scored twenty-four straight points, and the *Ohio State Journal* praised the performance: "The Panhandles gave such an exhibition of classy play as has seldom been seen in this city. The team changed its style of offense so often that it completely bewildered the Cadets. First by plunging the line, then a long forward pass, to be followed by a triple pass, the Columbus boys carried the Dayton aspirants for the state championship off their feet."[25]

After the back-to-back victories, the railroaders were feeling really good about their chances of having a great season. Manager Carr then scheduled a unique road trip as the team traveled north to play the Detroit Maroons. The pro game was growing outside of the state of Ohio, and this was the first time the Columbus boys played a squad from Michigan. The Panhandles would go on to make five more trips to play teams from the city of Detroit. On November 14 the Panhandles came away with a close 7–0 victory against the tough Motor City crew. Oscar Kuehner scooped up a bad snap on a punt attempt for the only touchdown of the game. The *Ohio State Journal* reported that "both teams played sensational football,"[26] which meant that it was sensational on the defensive side.

The railroaders were now 6–2, and for the second straight week they traveled to play a team they had never faced before. Joe Carr took his team back up north to play the Youngstown Patricians, a pretty good independent team sponsored by the St. Patrick's Church in the city, who started playing football in 1911. Carr had the team arrive in Youngstown the day before the game and the first thing he did was head over to the local newspaper office and hand them a write-up and a team photo of his squad to help promote the game. On the day of the game (November 21), the *Youngstown Vindicator* wrote about the Panhandles' arrival:

> The Pan Handles under the direction of Manager Joe Carr, Columbus newspaper man, arrived in this city last night and according to their pilot, are in the finest fettle possible for a strenuous contest. The squad numbered 18 last night, and four others are due to arrive early in the morning, bringing the total up to 22 men eligible for duty.
>
> The Pan Handles were met at the Pennsylvania station at midnight by Manager Omier of the Patricians, and escorted to the Ohio hotel where they will quarter while in Youngstown. Manager Carr called the Vindicator office soon after his arrival, and while he was strong in his praise of his own outfit, declared the Patricians had won an enviable reputation throughout the state.
>
> Carr naturally was confident of victory. He declared Youngstown fans might be prepared to see a classy contest and one that would be clean and snappy throughout. The Pan Handles have been in existence for 14 years and during that time have met and defeated some of the best grid teams in the country. He declared he would have no apologies to offer if defeated, and added that if the Patricians won they surely could honestly claim the state title.
>
> The six Nesser brothers were in the squad which arrived last night (really there was only five). They form the nucleus of the Pan Handle team which is strongly augmented by a half dozen college stars headed by Pickerel, former Ohio State star.[27]

After all of the publicity, the two teams were ready to play and over 5,000 fans paying fifty cents a ticket came out to Wright Field to witness the battle. For sixty minutes the two teams slugged it out, but mistakes on both sides cost either team any chance of scoring and the game ended in a 0–0 tie. The railroaders were much heavier than the Pats, but they never took advantage of their size and Carr's team went home disappointed in the final score. But he was extremely pleased with the turnout; his extra work in advertising the game definitely helped. Carr was now hitting his stride as a team manager and being able to see the entire picture. He always went the extra yard to promote the games and his Irish work ethic never took a break. Just like Carr the Panhandles couldn't rest for too long, as Carr arranged two games for the upcoming week. First up was a Thanksgiving Day game against the Fort Wayne (Indiana) Friars, and three days later the railroaders would play the Columbus Barracks in a rare home game.

On November 25 the Panhandles took the rail to Fort Wayne and lost a close game to the Friars, 3–0. After the game the Nesser brothers, Joe Carr, and the rest of the squad were rewarded with a special holiday treat from the victorious Friars. The *Fort Wayne Journal-Gazette* described the postgame celebration.

> The football players who toiled so faithfully throughout the season just closed for the Friars were banqueted last night at the Anthony by the local club. This is an annual event in local football circles and last night's spread was easily the best ever, probably because of that pleasant surprise in the nature of a victory over the Columbus crowd. The Panhandle players were also on hand as guests of the Friar management and the crowd numbered about seventy. After the eats the Nesser brothers quartet sang several songs and (John) Schneider, the clever Columbus guard, told a number of stories which were great.[28]

Despite the loss the Panhandles knew how to have a good time, and they were grateful for the Friars' hospitality. Joe Carr made sure the two teams would see each other again, saying, "The Panhandles will be back next season. So many times in independent football the home players and fans will take advantage of the visiting players and hand out some miserable treatment. You seldom get anything like a square deal from the officials and the fans are always looking for a chance to hand you a bum deal. Just the opposite is the case here. Your officials certainly treated us fairly and I like the spirit shown by the crowd which had cheers for the visiting as well as the home players."[29]

The loss to the Friars wasn't all that bad as the team from Indiana would finish the season with a 7–1–1 record. When the railroaders returned home—after an amazing eight straight Sunday games on the road—pro football's most famous traveling team was ready to defend its title as city champions. After two tough games over the previous seven days, the railroaders took care of business against the overmatched Columbus Barracks team. Four different players scored a touchdown—Lee Snoots, Charlie Dunn, Frank Nesser, and Ted Nesser—as the Panhandles won easily 26–0.

Carr's boys were again city champs but his team suffered a big blow in the Barracks game. Center Hi Brigham was badly injured. Two days after the game, on November 30, the *Columbus Dispatch* reported the bad news under the headline "Pan Handle Player Near Death: Center Brigham Hurt When He Falls on Bucket."

Crack Lineman Who Was Formerly an Ohio State Student Has Scarcely Even Chance for Recovery at Mt. Carmel Hospital—Accident Sustained in Barracks Game Not Noticed Much at First

From an injury received in the Pan Handle-Barracks game played Sunday afternoon on the United States post gridiron, Haven Brigham, center on the Panhandle team, is lying in the Mt. Carmel hospital today, suffering from injuries that may prove fatal.

Brigham was hurt in the second period of the game when he missed a tackle and fell astride a water bucket that was near the playing field. While he suffered some pain from the injury and was forced to take time out, he continued to play at his position until the contest was completed.

After the game he did not suffer any serious trouble and the injury passed without further notice until he had retired for the evening at his rooming house at 332 North Garfield Avenue. Then it was that the effects of the fall first caused trouble.

He was attacked with severe pains in the abdomen and Dr. Charles E. Turner of Mt. Vernon and Monroe avenues was called. A perfunctory examination showed that the trouble was serious and the injured athlete was taken to Mt. Carmel hospital Monday morning. A more thorough examination there showed that Brigham was suffering from severe internal hurts. Tuesday morning an X-ray photograph was made so as to make a complete diagnosis of the case. While the injury is serious, the attending physicians were unable to state Tuesday morning whether they would necessarily prove fatal, but it was said that Brigham's condition is very grave. Brigham is a former student at Ohio State, but never played on the varsity team, being ineligible through professional activity. His home is in Bowling Green, Ohio. His mother, who was called to Columbus, Monday, is at his bedside.[30]

The team rallied around Brigham in the hospital, and Carr went about his business as he scheduled a final game for 1915 against an all-star team from Columbus comprised mostly of ex-college stars from Ohio. Carr wanted the football fans of Columbus to see a high-class event to end the football season and he told the *Ohio State Journal* what he expected of his team.

We have been meeting an array of stars every Sunday during the season and we will be in shape to take care of the aggregation being gathered in this city for the game next Sunday, regardless of how strong it is. We have the team and are ready and willing to meet all comers. Coach Nesser has passed the word that each and every man on the squad must appear for practice every day at noon and every evening this week. Nothing is to be left undone in the Panhandle camp and there will be no excuses to offer if the long end of the score is carried off by the all-college men.[31]

Shortly before the big game the Panhandles received some good news about their fallen teammate. On December 2 the *Columbus Dispatch* reported on Brigham's condition: "Haven Brigham, center of the Pan Handle eleven, who was injured in Sunday's game with the Barracks, is still in serious condition at Mt. Carmel hospital. His condition is some what improved, however, and the attending physicians feel confident that the injury will not prove as dangerous as at first thought."[32]

The good news was just what the Panhandles wanted to hear, and Brigham soon made a complete recovery. He missed the game against the Columbus All-Stars but returned to play in 1916 and continued playing center for the railroaders until 1920.

On December 5 at the Barracks Grounds in front of 3,000 fans, the two teams took the field. With all six Nesser brothers (John returned to the lineup) playing, the railroaders scored quickly, as Lee Snoots went over for a touchdown and Emmett Ruh's extra point made it 7–0 with just two minutes gone. One minute later Frank Nesser scored on a fifty-five-yard touchdown run, and a missed extra point made it 13–0. The rest of the game the railroaders kept the ball away from the All-Stars and came away with a 13–0 win.

Playing one of the toughest schedules in professional football, the Panhandles finished with an 8–3–1 record with wins against the Massillon Tigers, Dayton Gym-Cadets, and Detroit Maroons. The eight wins would be a franchise high for victories. With a balance of offense (192 points scored) and defense (37 points allowed), the railroaders were hitting their peak. They also were one of the biggest shows in professional football, as over the course of the season more than 20,000 spectators (figures from newspaper accounts) came out to watch the Panhandles and football's greatest attraction—the Nesser brothers.

But the big news coming out of professional football in 1915 came from Canton, Ohio, as Canton Bulldogs manager Jack Cusack basically ushered in the "modern" era of professional football and changed the landscape of the sport. In 1915 the Massillon Tigers fielded a new team to compete with the Canton Bulldogs, and in order for his Bulldogs to beat the Tigers, Cusack went out of his way to hire a big name to help his team win. He also happened to hire the greatest football player in the country.

Cusack set out to recruit Jim Thorpe to play for Canton. In his memoir, *Pioneer in Pro Football*, Cusack explained how he was able to sign the great Thorpe to a pro contract.

> I sent Bill Gardner, his old Carlisle teammate, over to Indiana University, where he was coaching the backfield, to see him, and shortly thereafter I had Thorpe under contract to play for the Canton Bulldogs for $250 a game. Some of my business "advisers" frankly predicted that I was leading the Bulldogs into bankruptcy by paying Jim the enormous sum of $250 per game, but the deal paid off even beyond my greatest expectations. Jim was an attraction

> as well as a player, and whereas our paid attendance averaged around 1,200 before we took him on, we filled the Massillon and Canton parks for the next two games—6,000 for the first and 8,000 for the second. All the fans wanted to see the big Indian in action.[33]

At this time Thorpe was America's finest all-around athlete. He was twice an All-American while playing football at Carlisle; winner of two gold medals at the 1912 Olympics; and a professional baseball player with the New York Giants. In the 1912 Olympics held in Stockholm, Sweden, he won the pentathlon and decathlon while compiling 8,412 of a possible 10,000 points. King Gustaf presented the two gold medals to Thorpe, proclaiming, "You are the greatest athlete in the world." Thorpe modestly responded, "Thanks King."

But it was football that Thorpe really excelled in, and it was why Cusack was willing to pay him the unheard amount of $250 a game. There was nothing that Thorpe couldn't do on a football field. He was the best passer, best runner, best defender, and the best kicker, and when he signed to play professional football in 1915, he put the sport on the front pages across America. In the first game against the Massillon Tigers, 6,000 fans watched as Thorpe was a nonfactor, in a 16–0 win by the Tigers. But the second game saw a larger crowd, 8,000, and Thorpe at his best. In a hard-fought, low-scoring game, Thorpe kicked two field goals in a 6–0 victory over the Tigers.

Cusack had succeeded in hiring Thorpe, as his Bulldogs made a profit in the two games against the Tigers, and this turn of events once again showed Joe Carr the potential of professional football. In the long run the most important thing about the 1915 season wasn't who won or lost but who played and how much money it had cost. After years of carefree "independent" football dominated by sandlot players, the game began to move toward bigger name, college-trained players who now would lead the way. Although some sandlot players would linger around in pro football for another decade, most pro teams would now consist of full squads of former college players. Even Carr, who had a sandlot team, signed Ohio State star Lou Pickerel that season. The Thorpe signing just speeded up the process for early pro football managers, and the influx of better-prepared players now meant better quality of play on the field.[34]

However, the Thorpe signing also brought a great increase in the cost of doing business, as players' salaries jumped, with Thorpe's salary setting the bar. Those teams willing to pay top salaries usually prospered on the field, if not in their ledger books; those that refused to spend the money and attempted to continue with lower-paid talent usually dropped to second class status. Carr had to decide where his team fit in.

In 1916 Cusack couldn't take a step backward and built a strong Canton Bulldogs squad with Thorpe as the key player. That fall he signed former college stars Cub Buck (Wisconsin), Clarence "Doc" Spears (Dartmouth), Unk Russell (Penn), Bull Lowe (Lafayette), and Milt Ghee (Dartmouth). The Bulldogs dominated professional football in 1916, and in October the Panhandles got their shot at seeing how good Thorpe's Bulldogs really were.

Carr now had two children and a wife at home, but most of his time was spent thinking about his Panhandles and how they would compete in the new era of professional football. The game was becoming more popular, and there were even some rumblings about a new pro football league being formed to give order to the loose affiliation of teams. On September 21 the *Portsmouth (Ohio) Daily Times* reported about a league being formed out of Columbus, Ohio:

> May Form Football League
>
> Reports are being circulated here [Columbus] that plans for a professional football league comprised of Columbus, Toledo, Canton, Youngstown, Massillon and Cleveland are being formed, the season to start at the expiration of the baseball season. According to reports, "Peggy" Parratt, who has managed professional teams in Canton [Akron] for several years, is signing star players and making plans for the Cleveland team if the proposed league, which plans to play its games in the American league baseball park.[35]

The report appeared in several more newspapers, and it showed that some of the early pro football managers might be serious about organizing their sport. The report didn't mention any names but did say that it circulated from Columbus, Ohio. Was Joe Carr behind this movement to organize? Nobody really knows, but certainly he would have wanted to be involved if there was such a movement. The 1916 season would start with no other mention of the proposed league.

After compiling an overall record of 15–5–1 over the past two seasons, the Panhandles remained one of the toughest aggregations in professional football, despite a rather up-and-down year in 1916. They opened with four straight victories and then dropped five of their next six games before ending the year with two straight wins. Three of the team's losses were to Toledo, Canton, and Massillon, with the latter two battling for the Ohio state championship, although the Bulldogs claimed the title with a 9–0–1 record. The Panhandles' other two losses were to Fort Wayne and the Cleveland Indians. There was not one defeat to be ashamed of.

Joe Carr's team returned its core players with all six Nessers, Hi Brigham, both Kuehner brothers, Emmett Ruh, and Lee Snoots. Gone were some talented players, including longtime linemen Charlie Dunn, Andy Kertzinger, and John "Pop" Schneider, who all retired. Lou Pickerel, star of the 1915 team, decided not to come back after just one season. To fill out the 1916 roster Carr added Sam Compton, a guard, and recruited end Homer Ruh, brother of Emmett Ruh, to join the Panhandles. The Panhandles now had three sets of brothers—the Nessers, Kuehners, and Ruhs.

Carr's Panhandles were getting ready to not only play some games but also do some serious traveling. The team would play eleven straight games on the road before closing the season with one home game. The Panhandles were now a full-fledged traveling team, and in 1916 the fans at opposing cities came out in great numbers to see pro football's most famous and toughest team. On September 27 the railroaders played their typical warm-up game, defeating the Lancaster (Ohio) Independents 69–0, scoring a whopping ten touchdowns. The following week it was another lopsided game beating the Marion Questions, 54–0.

After two games the Panhandles had scored eighteen touchdowns and won by a combined score of 123–0. The next game would be a different story as the Panhandles moved up in competition, playing the Detroit Heralds. On October 14 the *Ohio State Journal* wrote, "Detroit critics contend that the Panhandles are better than the Heralds and a lot of Columbus people who are in Detroit are anxious to see the two elevens clash. Football has gained a big foothold in Detroit and Sunday's game is booked as one of the big attractions of the season. The entire Panhandle squad will make the trip. All members are in great condition. While in Detroit, the team will be quartered at the Cadillac Hotel.[36]

The trip paid off handsomely for Joe Carr and the Panhandles. Not only did they win a tough game, 13–7, but the railroaders played before a huge crowd of 7,000 fans. The payout to Joe Carr was very nice and made the return trip home twice as sweet. The *Detroit Free Press* praised the Panhandles and the famous Nesser brothers.

> Many came out to see the six Nesser brothers and were not a bit disappointed. The six of them were all in the game for the first two periods. J. Nesser, quarterback, was then removed. He is only 41 years old and his younger brother, Ted, who is coach and captain, probably figured that the old gentleman had done quite enough in piloting his team to a 13-point lead. But then Ted is only 33 years old and as soon as he gains a little more experience he will acquire the discretion which comes with years.
>
> As for the other brothers, all they can do—is kick, run, forward pass, block and tackle. Over and above the possession of these few talents they are on the team only for advertising purposes.
>
> The Panhandles are the smartest football boys that have ever played in Detroit. They are heavy and fast and when one of those Nessers hits an opponent flush there usually is work for the water boy and field physician. The

> Panhandles are the smartest pro football team Detroit has ever seen. They have any amount of trick plays and strategy. It is a nice team to look at: tricky but always clean.[37]

The Nessers were on a roll after their third straight win, and the press and pro football fans were getting to know the traveling Panhandles. Their next game was against the Cleveland Indians, a team organized by Peggy Parratt. It would be the first time the Panhandles would play a game in the city of Cleveland and again the railroaders didn't disappoint.

Before a crowd of 6,000 fans at League Park the Panhandles defeated the Indians 9–6 behind a Ted Nesser touchdown and a clutch field goal by Emmett Ruh. The *Cleveland Plain Dealer* was very impressed by the Panhandles.

> Ted and John and Fred and Frank and other members of the famous Nesser family may be getting ancient in years, and may be battle-scarred veterans and old timers and all that sort of thing. But about 6,000 Clevelanders will bear testimony to the fact that Ted and John, etc., haven't lost the art of playing football with advancing years.
>
> Working with the enthusiasm of youngsters and with the power that comes with two hundred or more pounds of bones and flesh per man, the Nesser brothers and teammates, composing the Panhandle team of Columbus smashed and kicked their way to a 9 to 6 victory over the Cleveland Indians at League Park yesterday.
>
> Ted, who earned the admiration of Clevelanders here eleven years ago when he was a prime factor in the victory of the Massillon Tigers over the Carlisle Indians, yesterday showed consistent flashes of Ted of old and literally scored the victor's sole touchdown unaided in the second period. Just as the period ended the Indians tied the score on a beautiful forward pass from Hanley to Williams over the goal line. Both teams failed in the attempts for goal after touchdown.
>
> **Goal from Field in Fourth Period Turns Tide of Fray**
>
> The visitors registered the deciding points when in their fourth period they were held on downs after marching almost under Cleveland's goal posts and then Emmett Ruh drop kicked the ball between the goal posts.[38]

Accompanying the article was a great action photo of Fred Nesser carrying the ball behind a wall of blocking. Fred got a little glory from the photo, but that's where it ended, as he left the game with a broken hand. The injury would force Fred to miss the next three games. Fred's misfortunate did not dampen the team's enthusiasm as they had just won their fourth consecutive game (six in a row counting the last two in 1915), and next up was the best team in pro football—the Canton Bulldogs.

Led by Jim Thorpe, the Bulldogs would give the Panhandles their toughest test of the year. On October 26 the *Columbus Dispatch* wrote on the upcoming game.

> To meet one of the greatest aggregations of stars grouped under the colors of one team, Ted Nesser and Joe Carr will escort the Panhandles eleven to Canton Saturday evening, where on the following afternoon, the Canton professional squad coached and managed by James Thorpe, famous as an All-American fullback and declared to be one of the greatest performers of the gridiron game ever developed in America, will be played.
>
> Thorpe has gathered about him a coterie of supporting stars whose names are a part of every school boy's education in the great college sport. This is the kind of eleven the Panhandles meet Sunday after Sunday. Since the football season was inaugurated the Panhandle eleven has had but one or two easy tasks. Since those first games were played the Nesser boys and their five helpers have been hot footing it about the country meeting the best that each town has had to offer and in each instance they have brought glory both on themselves and the town from whence they hail.[39]

Even Bulldogs manager Jack Cusack was nervous about playing the Panhandles. "Canton knows it will need every bit of beef and speed to offset the Panhandles and check their winning streak which is growing to unusual proportions," Cusack would say to the Canton press.[40] The undefeated Panhandles were a challenge to the Bulldogs championship aspirations and the game was starting to become the game of the year in professional football—not just in Ohio. On October 28 the *Canton Repository* ran an ad for the game.

> Sunday, October 29th, 1916
> Columbus Panhandles vs. Canton
> General Admission $1.00—Ladies 25¢—Reserved Seats 25¢
> GAME CALLED AT 2:30 P.M.
>
> Advance sale at Altman's and Simpson's cigar stores, Riehl's and the Great Northern Billiard Rooms and Arcade Saloon.[41]

The hype continued on game day as the *Repository* ran a full page article previewing the game—with a great photo of the six Nesser Brothers.

> Long and short, lean and stocky, the six Nesser "boys" and eight or ten other panthers in human form come to Canton today. That statement alone is sufficient to tell the whole tale. It means that the Canton professionals are in for a scrap, a battle royal against the most fearless football crew in existence—the Columbus Panhandles. There's always something doing when the Panhandles come to town.

These Nessers are no strangers by any means. Canton first became acquainted with the name about 11 years ago, when Ted held down a backfield position with the great Massillon Tiger team that ripped Canton's aspirations toward a world's championship into little shreds. He's been playing football, brilliant football, ever since and has gradually introduced other Nessers into the game. He has five of 'em helping him this year, all from the same sturdy stock.

The invasion by the Panhandles means a tough, rough game for Canton, but Big Jim Thorpe has his red and white machine in readiness to repel the attack. He and Manager Jack Cusack have assembled what looks like the most powerful gridiron crew that has ever represented Canton, not even barring the Bulldogs of a decade ago. The present Bulldogs, every one of them a star, present an array of which a Percy Haughton or a Hurry-up Yost might well be proud.

What betting has been done favors the Bulldogs to win. Some of the more optimistic have gone so far as to wager that Canton will pile up 30 points or more. Others have placed the limit at 25 and still others, entertaining wholesome respect for the prowess of the Columbus huskies, will go no higher than three touchdowns. A few have such regard for the Canton defense that they will bet on no touchdowns for the Panhandles. It's a bold risk.

There's one safe bet though. This is that Canton will have to fight, and fight hard, for every inch and every point. That's the beauty of any scrap between the Panhandles and a strong opponent. There's never a dull moment or a relaxation in the efforts of the principals. Just one continual battle, with the breaks of the game playing a leading role.[42]

The Panhandles were prepared to play the Bulldogs tough and facing the great Jim Thorpe for the first time didn't intimidate them. On October 29 over 4,500 fans filled League Park in Canton to watch the big game. Playing without an injured Fred Nesser, the railroaders fell behind by two touchdowns in the first half and never recovered. The second half became a hard-hitting affair, and the Bulldogs came away with a 12–0 win. The railroaders played a good game but couldn't control Thorpe. The *Canton Daily News* recapped the action.

Canton's Bulldogs did not bite off more than they could chew Sunday at League Park in meeting the Panhandles of Columbus. The local professional footballers, scenting the U.S. title, managed to digest a 12 to 0 victory over the five Nessers—Fred Nesser accompanied the team but did not don a uniform having broken a small bone in his right hand in the game with Cleveland the previous week—and their associates in the presence of a crowd which went above the 4500 mark.

True to form played the Panhandles. The spectator was unschooled who didn't know the invaders delighted in roughing matters. Rough it they did likewise Canton. Both lines were miniature productions of English "tanks"

> and if the British government ever runs short of such vehicles a mistake would not be made to write Ohioward.
>
> Players tackled with abandon; they threw themselves against the advance like lost souls, caring not for consequences. Every yard meant something to the 22 strugglers, zealous in protecting their territory, and hungry for some of the enemy's. Despite titanic maneuvers, only one player was injured to the extent of being carried from the field—halfback Conley of Canton being dazed by a collision with Capt. Ted Nesser of Columbus. Conley was severely stunned, but he did not lose consciousness.
>
> Individually, no player ranked higher than fullback Julian of Canton, ex-Michigan Aggie star. He made the biggest impressions on the rushline of the foe, and was omnipresent in backing up the Bulldogs' first stretch of defense. It is safe to say that Julian played his most spectacular game since joining Canton in 1915.
>
> But arm in arm with the lanky fullback was "Indian Jim" Thorpe, whose educated toe, gained yard after yard in a punting duel with Frank Nesser, and who came through on several occasions when Canton needed ground for first downs. The untiring defense of Canton's line also brought comment, as well as the sensational play of ends Soucy and Stewart. Thorpe as a windup to his work lifted two punts, each over 75 yards, the first one rolling an additional 15 yards to the back of Columbus' goal line. For Columbus the bulk of the offense fell to Ted and Frank Nesser who bored through Canton's forwards several times for 10 yards or more, much to the excitement of the crowd which was orderly, despite the tension, and which was admirably handled by the Canton management.[43]

Joe Carr was so impressed by the Canton team he gave the *Canton Daily News* a quote as he left town with the headline "Panhandle Manager Rates Canton Team To Sky; His Reasons."

> "The greatest football team I've ever seen," declared Joe Carr of Columbus, manager of the Panhandle team who has been in charge of the railroaders' business affairs for the last nine years.
>
> Carr's statement pertained to Canton's professional aggregation. He was enthusiastic over Columbus' showing up to Sunday but did not hesitate to throw a bouquet to the Red and White.
>
> "I know this much about forming football elevens: Nothing but a big expenditure of money and the devotion of a lot of time can bring such a team together, and it will take miraculous work from Massillon, Cleveland and Youngstown to lay the Canton team in defeat.[44]

Carr also gave his thoughts to the *Columbus Citizen* about seeing Thorpe for the first time: "Thorpe is the only man I ever saw that it took two or three of our men to stop. In every department he played a most wonderful game, and I never saw anyone who can kick as he did. At one time he stood back of his own goal posts and punted back of ours."[45]

Thorpe was the best player in professional football and he helped lead the Bulldogs to a record of 9–0–1 and the Ohio League professional championship. He also brought out the biggest crowds of the season. At the end of the year in the two games (November 26 and December 3) against the Massillon Tigers, Thorpe brought out over 20,000 fans total for both games, once again proving that he was the biggest draw in pro football. The railroaders might have lost to the Bulldogs—snapping their six-game winning streak—but the team continued to grab headlines. On November 2 the *Toledo Daily Blade* ran an article previewing the Panhandles upcoming game against the Toledo Maroons.

> The Columbus Pan Handles are staging the greatest "come-back" in Ohio professional football. Up to two years ago they were one of the strongest elevens in the country, but then something went wrong and they began losing games—by small margins, to be sure—but losing, nevertheless.
>
> Everybody figured that the Nesser brothers had shot their bolt; that age was beginning to tell and that the grand old Pan Handle machine was about to throw a tire. The Panhandles, however, came right back, upset the dope, and are playing a better game than ever—and as good an article of football as any team in the country.
>
> They are doing it with the same six Nesser brothers, the Kuehner brothers, the Ruh brothers and Brigham, and Snoots. Up to date they have defeated Lancaster, Marion, Detroit Heralds, Peggy Parratt's Cleveland Indians and last Sunday held Thorpe's wonderful all-college star Canton team, 12 to 0.
>
> The Pan Handle team as it stands is as good as the Massillon team that played here. The team is at the top of its game and the Maroons will have to travel faster than ever if they hope to defeat them.[46]

At this time the press was very positive for the Panhandles and it was paying off in a big way. The railroaders played before 17,500 fans in their last three road games—at Detroit, Cleveland, and Canton. Carr's hard work and ability to promote his team was now convincing him that there was a big future in the sport of professional football. This was where his heart was. The big crowds continued as the Toledo game was also getting some major headlines and one big advertisement in the *Toledo Daily Blade*.

FOOTBALL—SUNDAY, NOV. 5
2:30 P.M.—Armory Park
Maroons
And Johnny Barrett
Vs.
Columbus Panhandles
(with Six Nesser Brothers)

One of the Best Games of the Season
???REMEMBER LAST YEAR'S GAME???
Admission—Gentlemen 75¢, Ladies 50¢, Children 8 to 12, 25¢
Reserved Seats on Sale at Covert's and Mecca Sporting Goods
COVERT BROS.[47]

Only seventy-five cents admission would get the fans of Toledo a chance to see the great Nesser brothers—what a bargain. On the eve of the game though the Panhandles and the Nesser brothers suffered a family tragedy. Geneva Nesser, the infant daughter of Frank Nesser, suddenly died and big Frank would not make the trip to Toledo. The rest of the team traveled to Toledo with a heavy heart, including four of Frank's brothers, Phil, Al, John, and Ted, who all played the next day. Fred was still out because of the broken hand. With their minds elsewhere, the railroaders lost 23–7 to the Maroons. Under the circumstances the result was just about right. The *Toledo News-Bee* recapped the game with the headline "Maroons Down Nesser Family."

> Johnny Barrett's wonderful 43-yard dodging, side-stepping, twisting and straight-arming run was the spectacular splurge in the Maroons' 23 to 7 triumph over the slashing, battering and rough-housing Panhandles at Armory Park on Sunday afternoon.
>
> It was one of the most intensely interesting gridiron contests ever played here during the regime of professional football. It was a rough battle a give-and-take fracas, where knees and elbows and roughly-shod feet played a conspicuous part.
>
> As is customary, the massive Columbus gladiators left their drawing room manners somewhere along High St. They played the kitchen or woodshed variety of the sward pastime, but it was very successful for two-thirds of the game.[48]

The *Toledo Daily Blade* reported that Phil Nesser was the "chief offender" of the rough play and "time and time again dropped upon tackled men with his knees, slugged, or stopped runners by means of a forearm thrown against their necks. He seldom tackled according to the code."[49] Who could blame the Nessers for trying to take out their grief against the Maroons. The Panhandles headed home with a loss, and the team had now suffered numerous injuries heading into their next game against the Massillon Tigers. In a letter sent to the *Massillon Independent*, Carr explained to the Massillon fans what happened against Toledo.

> Fred Nesser was out on account of an injured arm and the doctor insisted that he stay out of the game until next Sunday. Emmett Ruh was hardly able to move and about two hours before the team left Columbus the infant child of Frank Nesser died. The child became ill Saturday morning. One can re-

ally see that news of this kind would affect a team that had been together for years. With Frank and Fred Nesser out of the game we were without a kicker or a passer and were practically at the mercy of our foes. However, we are coming to Massillon with our strongest lineup and we expect to take the Tigers into camp.[50]

Carr wanted to assure the folks in Massillon that his team was still competitive and would put up a great effort. Then, for the second straight week, the railroaders had a death in the family as halfback Lee Snoots lost his father. But just like the week earlier the team showed up and played a football game. The Panhandles would play their hearts out, as five Nesser brothers were in the lineup, including a still grieving Frank. On November 12 over 4,000 fans came out to Driving Park in Massillon to watch the Tigers win 10–0 over the tough Panhandles. Playing with a depleted roster, the railroaders played a great game against a team that would finish the season with a record of 7–1–2 with their only loss to the unbeaten Canton Bulldogs.

It was the third straight loss for the Panhandles, and nobody would have blamed the team if they didn't win another game under the current circumstances, but that wasn't the Panhandle way. It was time to prove how good they could be, and on November 14 the *Columbus Citizen* reported on Carr's next move: "Arrangements were consummated Tuesday morning where-by the Panhandles will play an All-Star eleven at Neil Park on Sunday, Dec. 10. The makeup of the All-Star aggregation is as yet indefinite, but there is more than a possibility that Jim Thorpe will be on the team which will oppose the railroaders. His presence here will depend on whether the Canton eleven has finished its season by that time or not."[51]

Carr was preparing his squad for a strong finish to the season and next up for the team was a return trip to Detroit to face the Heralds—a team they defeated 13–7 earlier in the season. Fred Nesser and Lee Snoots returned to the lineup and helped the railroaders get back in the win column with a 15–0 victory. Both Homer Ruh and Al Nesser scored touchdowns. The team celebrated the big win on the trip back to Columbus; after a month of losing football games and family members, the team deserved to let off some steam. The win made the work week a little easier and practice was fun again as the team prepared to play three games in seven days.

First up was a rematch with Peggy Parratt's Cleveland Indians, who wanted revenge against the railroaders. "If we defeat the Nessers we will have broken even at least with every team played this season. We were caught napping early in the season, but I think I have the team now to stop the Panhandles," said Parratt to the *Cleveland Plain Dealer* the day before the game.[52] Parratt loaded up his team with some top talent but that didn't matter to the Panhandles, who never brought in any "ringers" to help the cause; they always played with the same players. With all six Nesser brothers in the lineup the Panhandles matched the Indians hit-for-hit but a touchdown early in the third quarter was the difference as the Indians won a close one 7–0.

Four days after the tough loss to Cleveland the railroaders followed it up with an equally tough loss at Fort Wayne on Thanksgiving Day. A second quarter field goal by the Friars' Al Feeney gave the home team a 3–0 win. It was the same score the Friars defeated the railroaders by in 1915. The Panhandles were now 5–5 with two games remaining. The team was getting healthier and had the confidence to finish the season with a winning record.

Two days after the Thanksgiving contest, Carr took his team north to Youngstown for their next game against the Patricians. Playing on a soggy gridiron—and in front of only 1,500 fans—the healthy Panhandles defeated the Patricians 13–0 behind touchdowns by Lee Snoots and Ted Nesser. As in previous seasons, the Panhandles were finishing the year on a high note; all that was left was a rare home game against the Columbus All-Stars. It would be the only home game of the season for the Panhandles after eleven straight road games.

Instead of a city championship game, the season finale was against a collection of professional players from different teams. Some of the players who would play on the All-Stars team would be Howard "Cap" Edwards (Canton Bulldogs), Dave Reese (Cincinnati Celts), Red Fleming (Massillon Tigers), and Bart Macomber (Pine Village). But one player would not come to Columbus, as the *Ohio State Journal* reported the bad news.

> Following the plan of giving no false impressions, the men who are producing the Panhandle-All Star game Sunday afternoon at Neil Park deny the rumor that Jim Thorpe, famous as a Carlisle star, will play with the team that is to oppose the Keystones.
>
> Thorpe will not come to Columbus. By Sunday afternoon he will be on his way to Oklahoma, where he has planned a two week hunting trip. A sincere effort was made to land the Redskin for Sunday's game, but he flatly refused a substantial offer to play just one-half of the game. He declared the offer to be the most handsome he had ever received.[53]

For the Columbus football fans it was a disappointment not to be able to watch the great Thorpe play, but for the locals it would be an opportunity to see the famous Nesser brothers show their stuff on a local gridiron. After all the publicity the two teams took the field in front of 2,500 spectators at Neil Park. The two teams were evenly matched and played a close game. A forty-yard punt return for a touchdown by Lee Snoots was the only score of the game, giving the Panhandles a tough 6–0 victory. They had played a talented All-Star squad on their home turf and once again came out victorious. After the game it was time to celebrate as the *Columbus Dispatch* reported under the headline "Railroaders Celebrate Successful Football Season at 'Feed' Prepared by Mrs. H. Ruh": "Pan Handle football players who closed their season Sunday by defeating the College All-Stars, were tendered a dinner Sunday evening after the game by Mrs. H. Ruh, mother of Emmett and Homer Ruh, players on the eleven. Twelve games were played during the season, of which seven were victories. All the scores were close. The financial season was one of the best in the history of the team."[54]

The railroaders were definitely a family, and after a season of family losses the squad deserved to celebrate together. For Carr it was a season of financial success as the Panhandles played before a total of over 25,900 fans in five games (the other seven games didn't have a newspaper account of the actual attendance). The Panhandles completed the season with a 7–5 record. Considering that the team overcame injuries, played eleven straight road games, and experienced personal losses, the 1916 season was a complete success.

It was the third consecutive season of great play, as the team went 22–10–1 over that time period. But this would be the last great year for Carr's squad, as the sport of professional football was making strides toward being a serious business. And with any business, money was the key. Because of rising salaries, most of the pro teams in the Midwest went into the red. Despite the record crowds for the two Canton–Massillon games (over 20,000 fans total), Massillon lost money and Canton made a small profit.

Every player knew that Jim Thorpe was making $250 a game, and most agreed that he was worth it. But players of considerably less skill would hold out for $100 or $125. Team managers had to produce stars to draw crowds, but the crowds could never be big enough to pay for the stars. Teams desperately needed some type of organization or rule against teams "raiding" other teams to help keep the salaries down, or have a "gentleman's agreement" to not recruit players from other teams. Only something like that would keep the salaries down. A league was needed.

7

Making a Name for Himself (1917–1919)

In December of 1916 a published report out of Toledo, Ohio, mentioned that the manager of the Toledo Maroons, Art Gratop, favored a plan to start an official pro football league that would resemble Major League Baseball. A month later more reports came out trying to get the owners of Major League Baseball teams to help finance a football league by renting the baseball parks—which weren't in use after the baseball season ended in October—to help get the league organized. Even the Chicago White Sox owner, Charles A. Comiskey, thought it was a good idea. "If professional football can be made to pay it will be the answer to the problem confronting baseball owners since the game was started. Now, we use our parks only six months in the year. If I find that there is money in the professional end of the college game, I will go to the limit."[1]

Teams mentioned for the proposed league were from the cities of Chicago, New York, Detroit, Pittsburgh, Indianapolis, Cleveland, and Columbus. Joe Carr was one of the staunchest supporters of this new proposed league, and with his baseball connection, he probably encouraged the baseball owners to really consider it. But the backing of the baseball owners would have to take a back seat as the owners of Major League Baseball teams had more important things to worry about in the spring of 1917.

It is quite likely that the pro football team managers would have formed a new football league during the summer of 1917 had the United States not entered World War I on April 6 of that year. The game was ready to take on some structure at least by some of the major teams in the Midwest, but more troubling were the salaries continuing to rise, as more college stars followed Thorpe into the pro ranks. The sport needed a league binding all the major teams together in a way that controlled spending by establishing a salary limit that all teams would abide by and that would, in turn, eliminate players "hopping" from one team to another. But the war would push this idea of a pro football league onto the back burner.

The war affected Joe Carr immediately as the Ohio State Baseball League (which only played sixty-six games in 1916) ceased operations for good. So to make up for the lost income, Carr took a job with a local auto dealership. The thirty-seven-year-old sports executive had a wife and two young children to think about. Working for dealership owner Thomas E. Curtin, Carr used his experience as a sports promoter and team manager to help sell cars. He was a successful salesman and also got a lot of attention wherever he went. Once the *Portsmouth (Ohio) Daily Times* reported that Carr was in town under the headline "Joe Carr in City": "Joseph Carr, former president of the Ohio State League, was a business visitor to Portsmouth Wednesday. He represents the Curtin-Williams Automobile Co., of Columbus, and is working on a big order here."[2]

Carr continued selling cars for several years and was well-known for his honesty in trying to sell his product. It didn't matter whether it was sports or cars, the little Irish worker from Columbus did it the right way. His father would have been proud of him. As the summer continued Carr's thoughts turned to his football team and how they would stack up against the ever-improving pro football squads in the Midwest. He was also concerned about how the other pro football teams would fill their rosters given that some players joined the war effort. Writing to the *Massillon Independent*, he hoped the Tigers would be ready for the fall: "I sincerely hope Massillon has a football team this fall. For Massillon without football is like Ohio without a governor."[3]

But the war hadn't slowed down the pro football teams; the season would go on. Massillon, Canton, Akron, Detroit, Fort Wayne, Toledo, and the other top squads would play, and the press reported the good news to Ohio football fans: "Pro-Football Grips Ohio. Profesisonal football is again rampant in Eastern Ohio, the war or nothing else being apparently able to stem the popularity of this sport in many of New Castle's neighboring cities. Canton, Akron, Massillon and the Pan Handle club of Columbus already have teams in action, while Youngstown has several teams, including the strong Patrician eleven. Mansfield will likely have her aggregation out soon."[4]

Carr was pleased that his team would play games in the fall, but what type of team would he have? After playing their best football over the previous three seasons, the 1917 campaign was a huge letdown for the Panhandles, the beginning of the downfall for pro football's most famous traveling team. The season started out with promise with two early victories, but it was all downhill after that. The team only won one of its last seven games. The railroaders finished with a 3–6–0 record, and all six losses were shutouts. All nine games played were on the road, and for the first time the Panhandles did not play a game in Columbus.

The losses were bad, but the saddest part was not that the railroaders lost, since they had lost before; the sad thing was the way they lost. They were not just beaten—they were bludgeoned; outscored 157 to 65 all season.

The 1917 season also saw a change in the philosophy of the Nesser family, as Al Nesser, who played just one game with the Panhandles, and Frank Nesser, who played just two games, decided to take the money and play elsewhere for better-paying teams. Al played for the Akron Pros most of the season, and Frank split his season playing for Akron and the Detroit Heralds.

Without the two most talented Nessers, the Panhandles' roster was affected all year. Also gone from the 1916 squad was the speedy backfield of Lee Snoots and Emmett Ruh, who would serve in World War I. Both players were lost for the entire season; the railroaders had now lost four key players before the year even started.

Joe Carr did add two local players. Hal Gaulke, a former star quarterback at Columbus South High School, who was a prep teammate of the Ruh brothers. Gaulke was a solid player and would play five years for the railroaders but did not have the speed of Snoots or Emmett Ruh, and that would be very apparent during the 1917 season. Another addition was Joe Mulbarger, a five feet nine, 221-pound guard-tackle who was a former star at Columbus East High School. Mulbarger was a high school teammate of Chic Harley, the former All-American great at Ohio State University. He would go on to play six years with the Panhandles. The team would also welcome back guard Charlie Dunn to join old pros Homer Ruh, the Kuehner brothers, Hi Brigham, and the other four Nessers.

Under the guidance of Ted Nesser, the team's first practice took place on September 17. Carr had arranged early games with lightweight teams in Newark and Lancaster to ease the team into their tough part of the schedule. The railroaders traveled the forty miles to Newark with Al Nesser (playing in his only game with his brothers) to take on the Newark Stars. The Panhandles came away with a 14–6 victory behind touchdowns by Ted Nesser and Joe Mulbarger, who played halfback. The final score was closer than the Panhandles expected, but it was a win.

The following week the railroaders made another short trip, this time to play the Lancaster Independents, who they had defeated 69–0 the year before. This year they took it easy on the Independents and won by a 38–0 score. The Panhandles scored six touchdowns as Frank Nesser and Hal

Gaulke led the way with two touchdowns apiece. The Panhandles won their second straight game, and Carr thought his team was looking a lot like the Panhandles of the last couple of seasons, but that was about to change. Next up was the trip to Akron, and the Rubber City was ready to see the famous Nessers. On October 11 the *Akron Beacon-Journal* welcomed the football playing brothers.

Nesser Brothers On Opposite Sides In Sunday Grid Battle

> Ted Nesser, the first of the famous family of footballers, and father of a flock of younger Nessers who will keep up the family trait in the next generation, is playing in his last season at the game and will make his final Akron appearance Sunday when the Columbus Panhandles take issue with the Welch-McGuiness outfit of All Stars at Grossvater Park.
>
> Ted Nesser started chasing the pigskin 20 years ago and has probably played in more contests than any other athlete in the state. Every warrior that was ever tackled by the husky boilermaker remembers well the occasion and every linesman that ever made an effort to down him when in his prime, remembers well when the light went out.
>
> Jim Thorpe, the Indian athlete, once said that if he ever felt a tackle in his life, Ted Nesser was the man who made him feel it.
>
> Besides Ted, Frank, Fred and the rest of the Nessers will accompany the Panhandles here. Al Nesser resigned and will play against his brothers with the Akron club.
>
> "I have a nice little surprise package for the Panhandles," said [Suey] Welch, "and it will also be a big surprise for local fans. We will have a team on the field Sunday that will do credit to Akron."[5]

The Panhandles took the field at Grossvater Park, with five Nesser brothers in the lineup, as they battled Akron with little brother Al at left tackle for the Pros. The two teams battled to a scoreless tie well into the third quarter, when an Akron field goal gave the home team a 3–0 lead. The kick was the only score of the game as the Akron Pros handed the railroaders a tough loss. It was an especially sour note for Frank Nesser, as he missed three field goals in the last game he would play with the Panhandles and his brothers in 1917. Big Frank would go on to play the rest of the season mainly with the Detroit Heralds and a few games with the Akron Pros and Massillon Tigers.

Carr didn't like that he was losing his best player, but what could he do? He couldn't pay him as much as the other pro teams so he let Frank go, but he burned up inside. He knew that if there was a league he could hang on to Al and Frank Nesser and keep them from jumping, but for now he couldn't do anything about it. And he had bigger problems looming. The tough loss to Akron was followed up by a game with the 1916 pro champs—the Canton Bulldogs. Carr was determined to beat his friend

Jack Cusack and sent him a wire to let him know, stating that his "team is coming to Canton on Sunday to resort to every method to dislodge the world's champions. It has been our ambition for years of the Columbus aggregation to win from Canton."[6]

All the pregame hype was just that—hype—as the Panhandles suffered the worst defeat of their storied history, and to top it off they played before a crowd of just 2,000 fans. The Canton squad, led by Jim Thorpe, scored eight touchdowns and routed the railroaders 54–0. The *Canton Repository* had nothing but good things to say about the Bulldogs' defense.

> To back up this powerful attack the Bulldogs presented a defense that was really the proverbial stone wall. It would not yield an inch to the determined assaults of the Panhandles, led by the veteran Captain Ted Nesser. Not once did the Panhandles succeed in making a first down. In fact only three Panhandle plays gained any ground at all. Ruh made eight at center in the second period. Mulbarger made five at Fisher's end and Ted [made] five at center in the third quarter. Thirteen Panhandle plays were stopped without an inch of gain. All of which shows the caliber of the Canton defense.[7]

The Panhandles were completely dominated by the Bulldogs on both sides of the football. The Thorpe-led Bulldogs would finish the 1917 season at 9–1 and for the second straight year would claim the title of pro champs. The back-to-back losses were bad enough, but the way they lost to the Bulldogs is what sent the team reeling. Joe Carr and Ted Nesser tried to rally the team, but they weren't prepared for what was about to happen in the next two weeks. After hearing about the 54–0 result of the Canton–Columbus game, Youngstown Patrician manager Joe Mullane sent a Western Union telegram questioning the talent on the Panhandles team. Joe Carr wasn't happy about this, and the *Youngstown Vindicator* reported on the verbal sparring of the two managers.

> The Western Union Telegraph company ought to pay handsome dividends after the immense controversy staged on their lines since Sunday night between Manager Joe Mullane of the Patricians and Joe Carr, manager of the Columbus Panhandles.
>
> Mullane, after Sunday's game here, got a report of Canton's 54 to 0 victory over the Columbus aggregation, and immediately sent a wire to Carr, telling him that the Pan Handles would have to strengthen or lose their date here next Sunday. The attitude of the local manager was, of course, as a thunderbolt to Carr, but the latter could readily see that the Patricians were not going to be hoodwinked by an inferior club.
>
> Carr replied at great length—and great expense—that at least three of Canton's touchdowns were of the fluke variety, but that he had already started to pull strings to strengthen for the game here next Sunday. Mullane would take no chances on booking another outfit in here after that horrible

> nightmare of last Sunday, so he laid the case before Carr without even a bit of regard for telegraph tolls.
>
> Carr came right back and declared the Pan Handles would beat the Patricians because the score at Canton did not indicate what they had done in the way of offense. The final chapter of the costly controversy was written last night when Mullane declared in a wire to Carr that the Pan Handles were coming here at their own risk unless they displayed some good football. Carr is willing to take the chance.
>
> This year there are but four of the seven Nesser brothers playing with the Columbus team. Two of them are with the Akron eleven, and one is in the army. Carr has added some high class college talent to take the place of the Nessers and he promises to give the locals a merry argument here. "Don't worry about us; build up your own team if you want to avoid a beating," came back the Columbus boss. The Panhandle aggregation has always been a favorite here.[8]

Carr always believed in his team, and his words were reiterated a day before the game in the *Vindicator*.

> Last Sunday the Pan Handles were defeated by Canton 54 to 0 in what the fans thought was an uninteresting one-sided game, and Manager Carr laid the defeat to the fact that his team was due to arrive in Canton about midnight but did not land until morning due to a wreck on the railroad. He says they will take no such chances today.
>
> Carr also advises that the Patricians are going to get a drubbing, despite the fact that Canton walloped them. He says the locals do not need to think they will have easy picking because Canton defeated them because his men had not the proper rest to enable them to play the football of which they are capable.[9]

Regardless of what happened in Canton the Panhandles had traveled on trains for years so getting into a visiting town at a late time had happened before. The logical answer to the bad loss is that they lost to a great team, but Carr wasn't about to have his team questioned. He knew if other teams questioned the talent level of his team that scheduling games against quality opponents might become tougher. This was the first time the Panhandles' talent was being called out; how would they respond?

But just like the previous week all the pregame hype was nothing but hot air for the Panhandles and Joe Carr. In front of a "large crowd of fans," the Panhandles lost 30–0 to the much faster Patricians. The railroaders' backfield was missing the speed of Lee Snoots and Emmett Ruh, and despite the presence of the four Nesser brothers it was obvious the team lacked their normal offensive production. After three straight losses, the season was slipping away and things only got tougher with the Massillon Tigers next on the schedule.

After returning to Columbus, Joe Carr told the *Canton Daily News* who he thought would win between Canton and Youngstown since his team had just played both.

> Canton is going to win over the Patricians of Youngstown in the Steeltown Saturday in the first hard fight the Bulldogs have been called to make in the defense of the U.S. professional football title.
>
> This is the word sent here by Joseph Carr, manager of the Panhandles of Columbus who have met the big rivals and who play the Tigers of Massillon at Massillon Sunday.
>
> Carr's statement comes from Youngstown, Canton downed the "Pans" by a count of 54 to 0: Youngstown held the down staters pointless and succeeded in tolling off 30 points.
>
> "Columbus believes Canton will defeat Youngstown," said the Columbus mogul after the defeat at Youngstown last Sunday. "The score will be close, but I think the Bulldog eleven is better rounded."[10]

This time Carr was right on his predication, as the Canton Bulldogs would go on to defeat the Patricians twice in 1917 (3–0 on November 4 and 13–0 on November 18). Carr was now ready to fix the Panhandles' problems, but he just couldn't get it done. Another small crowd came out (as the war had affected attendance everywhere) the following week as the Panhandles played at Massillon. Columbus played poorly again as the Tigers scored at will and won easily 28–0. The railroaders had now hit rock bottom by losing four straight games without scoring a point. After three successful seasons, Carr's Panhandles were in jeopardy of taking a major step backward.

Next up was a trip to Toledo to play the Maroons. The press was still kind to the Panhandles despite their 2–4 record. Years of good playing allowed the railroaders a free pass in 1917. On November 8 the *Toledo News-Bee* previewed the game.

> You always see a football game when the Maroons and the Panhandles of Columbus clash on the gridiron. Every season for several years they have furnished splendid sport, and each battle has been a fight for victory. This fall both teams have been losing games with unaccustomed regularity, but they are still strong and should furnish an interesting combat in Sunday afternoon at Swayne Field.
>
> Joe Carr, manager of the Panhandles, declares that his team is as good as ever, but that the elevens it has faced this fall are much stronger than in other seasons. Carr says that the army camps are full of football players who are able to get Sunday furloughs and to play with the professional teams[11]

Pro football continued to have problems with so-called ringers in the game, but the Panhandles still lined up against these teams and played.

In talking with sportswriter Dick Meade of the *Toledo News-Bee*, Carr declared that he still had a great team but "these athletes performing under assumed names are making things hard for the elevens that are going along with their same old squads."[12] It would be a problem that professional football would have to deal with soon.

The railroaders turned their attention to the Maroons and got a much needed win, defeating the Toledo squad 13–0. But the winning ways didn't last long. The Panhandles gave up two early touchdowns and lost 13–0 to the Fort Wayne Friars the following week. Despite the nice crowd of 3,500, it was the third consecutive year the Panhandles had lost to the Friars. The railroaders' bad luck continued the following week against the Detroit Heralds, who featured Frank Nesser. On November 25 in Detroit the railroaders were soundly beaten 23–0 on a snow-covered field, behind a touchdown and a field goal by big Frank. The Panhandles' season was officially a disaster with a disappointing 3–6 record.

The team was missing something, maybe it was the loss of Frank and Al Nesser, maybe it was the backfield losses of Lee Snoots and Emmett Ruh. Four days after the loss to Detroit, the Panhandles boarded a train to Lafayette, Indiana, to play the talented Pine Village squad on Thanksgiving Day. When the team arrived in Lafayette, the railroaders got a big surprise. The Pine Village football team wasn't there. The *Ohio State Journal* told why, under the headline "Panhandles Get Only a Ride": "In keeping with terms of a contract, Columbus Panhandles players arrived here this morning to meet the Pine Village team. However, the Pine Villagers did not show up, but went to Wabash, Ind. It is probable that legal steps will be taken to force the Pine Village management to settle in accordance with terms of the original agreement."[13]

The Panhandles and Joe Carr weren't very happy with the situation, but what could they do? After stewing around for awhile, the team boarded the next train and headed back to Columbus. It was a missed game, and Carr thought to himself that the season couldn't get any worse. He was wrong. The Sunday after Thanksgiving Carr gave his team the day off and worked to schedule the game of the year for the Panhandles. Instead of setting up a game with a Columbus team to decide the city championship, Carr decided to talk to Jack Cusack. Carr wanted to arrange a game between the two teams to be played in Columbus to give the capital city fans a chance to see the hometown Panhandles and the great Canton Bulldogs—led by Jim Thorpe. On December 2 the two teams agreed to a game to be played the following week (December 9) at Neil Park in Columbus. The following day in the *Canton Daily News*, Joe Carr was quoted on the big game. "Columbus will see a good game. Canton shouldn't have been defeated by Massillon. There was a nut loose somewhere. Columbus will be a good town for the sport, but the fans have never seen a championship combine, and that is why I've persuaded Cusack to sign for a game. I expect to secure one or two college men to strengthen the Panhandles, but it cannot be construed as loading in any sense of the word. I want to have enough talent to make the game interesting."[14]

Carr was excited about the matchup (he even thought about bringing in some ringers) as he was able to bring the great Canton team to Columbus to play in front of the Panhandles fans. After a somewhat disappointing campaign, he thought bringing in a big-time drawing card would be the event to turn the season around and make a little money. The impending game was going to be the biggest pro football game ever held in Columbus. But like most of the 1917 season, the game would be a big disappointment as the Bulldogs never made it to Columbus. The *Canton Daily News* reported the bad news.

Columbus Trip Called Off, Bulldogs Cancel Last Game in Capital City

> King Winter scored his first touchdown Saturday. His armies stopped the last drive of Canton's professional team. Captain Thorpe and his celebrated troupe will not go to Columbus this evening to meet the Columbus Panhandles.
>
> The deal was brought to an end Saturday morning when Mgr. Jack Cusack wired Mgr. Carr of the Columbus team that on account of the snowfall every Canton Bulldog had been notified not to report for the contest which would have been labeled "finis" by the squad, the majority of whose member have been here for two seasons only being defeated once, said feat being due to the accuracy of Stanley Cofall's booting in the last game of the Massillon series.
>
> Cusack denied the report that Thorpe hadn't planned to make the trip to Columbus with Canton, and that he had accepted an offer to play with the Heralds of Detroit against the Hammond, Ind., team at Hammond Sunday, the Hammond star being Paddy Driscoll, former Northwestern U. captain.
>
> "Thorpe hasn't departed from Canton, and he doesn't intend to go for several days at least," said Cusack. "The Detroit story was buncombe. Jim will go to his home at Yale, Oklahoma, to spend the winter with Mrs. Thorpe and their two children."[15]

The season from hell ended with the Panhandles losing out on a big payday with the Canton Bulldogs. The team finished the year with a losing record (3–6–0) for the first time since 1913. Despite some of the roster losses, the 1917 season proved to Carr that his team was getting old and might be in decline. In the Panhandles' six losses, they were outscored 151–0. The increasing age of some of its players, the war in Europe, and the improvement of professional football teams everywhere made the future very bleak.

Joe Carr was starting to lose his team as the core of the squad was getting old, and he wasn't in position to go out and pay a star player, like Jim Thorpe, $250 a game. The Pennsylvania Railroad wasn't in the business of developing potential pro football players. In 1918 the team would be affected by things out of its control and would barely play a game, but as for the 1917 season, it was one to be forgotten.

Talk of a real football league kept circulating but remained only talk as none of the team managers really wanted to bind themselves to an organized league. They still wanted the freedom to pay for any player they wanted. As a result, most teams in 1917 lost money, and salaries were still very high. For example Massillon lost over $5,000 for the season.

But thoughts of a league took a break in 1918 as World War I dominated the country and most of the pro football teams took the year off. Some of the best teams such as Canton, Massillon, Akron, Youngstown, and Cleveland didn't bother to field a team. After the disastrous season Carr thought about what to do with his team. In the meantime he went back to the future, as he accepted a job as assistant sports editor at his old stomping grounds—the *Ohio State Journal*. It was another way to keep close to the sports world as well as making a few extra dollars.

As fall approached it looked like Carr would have a team playing; Ted Nesser started preseason practice at the railroad yards on September 24. The *Journal* reported on the progress.

> Panhandles football players will start practice today. Coach Nesser will get the men out for the first workout of the season and it is likely that most of last year's team and some crack material, that is out at the shop, will be found in the lineup this year.
>
> Owing to the fact that all practice by the big eleven is done at the noon hour and the games played on Sunday, no interference whatever will be made with the working plans of the team members, who are all employed in the railroad shops, which need so much help now.
>
> Early reports indicate that most of the big teams, with which the Panhandles have competed with each year, will be back on the field and, in some instances, stronger than ever before, owing to the presence in Akron, Canton, and Massillon of many football stars with concerns engaged in work essential to the war.
>
> While many old-timers will be out for the Panhandles, the team is open to all and the coach will welcome any players desiring to make it. Any recruits should present themselves to Coach Nesser on the athletic field in the rear of the shops any noon from now on.[16]

The *Journal* article wasn't completely accurate as Carr's Panhandles and other pro teams didn't field a team to begin the season. Most of the railroad employees were putting in time for the war effort, and playing a football game at this time wasn't plausible. However, later in the year, the work load at the Panhandle shops lightened up and the thought of playing a football game became a reality. Joe Carr's boys wanted to play, and he made arrangements for a game in the middle of November with the Dayton Triangles. The Triangles (who were basically the same team as the Gym-Cadets) were managed by Carl L. H. Storck, a stocky, fun-loving sports junkie, who would become one of Carr's closest confidants and friends.

Carl Louis Horrell Storck was born on November 14, 1893, in Dayton, Ohio, as the only child of German Americans Charles and Margaret Storck. The Storcks operated a very popular family-owned restaurant that was known in Dayton for its ice cream and milkshakes. Just like Carr in Columbus, Carl Storck in Dayton became a pretty good student who fell in love with sports. "He liked sports. At Stivers High School he was a star basketball player, captain of the high school football team, and ran track. He just fell in love with all sports but football was [his] favorite," says Dolores Seitz, daughter of Carl Storck.[17]

After high school Storck graduated from the George Williams YMCA College in Chicago, devoted his life to athletics and gained a very unusual nickname. "He had a horrible nickname. They called him Scummy but no one knew where he got it from. My mother never knew. The only thing they can figure out was that he was so immaculate and always so well groomed that they did it by teasing him. It's the worst name I've ever heard," says Seitz.[18]

Despite the bad nickname Storck was a very outgoing and likeable man who got along with everyone. Rarely did he walk down the streets of Dayton without someone yelling hello, and his athletic interests were very well-known around the city. Being a rotund man (six feet and over 220 pounds), he was definitely hard to miss. After graduating from college in the spring of 1917, he returned to Dayton and was hired by Mike Redelle to be an assistant manager of the Triangle Park recreation program, which included the company's football team—the Dayton Triangles.

The Dayton Triangles were the brainchild of two business giants, Edward Deeds and Charles Kettering. The team was sponsored by the duo's three factories—Dayton Engineering Laboratories Company, Dayton Metal Products Company, and Domestic Engineering Company—that formed an industrial triangle of plants in downtown Dayton. Triangle Park was the site for the company's athletic events and where Storck would get his pro football start. In 1917 Storck was the comanager of the team and also played fullback. The following year he replaced Redelle as the full-time manager.

That same year on April 10, 1918, Carl married Edythe Martz in Dayton and the couple would have one child, a daughter, Dolores. "My mother was very refined. I think she wanted to add a little of finesse and polish to her sporting husband. But football was his first love. My mother always said football came before she did because that was his first love and she accepted that. It was true," says Dolores Seitz, daughter of Carl Storck.[19]

In his first year as a full-time manager, Storck was very aggressive in scheduling games for the Triangles. The war didn't slow him down. When the Panhandles traveled to Dayton to play, Carr met Storck for the first time; they would strike up a professional relationship and a unique friendship that would last for the next twenty-one years. "They both were very interested in sports and this brought them together. Their thinking was so similar that this was a perfect relationship for both of them," says Seitz.[20]

With four Nessers (Phil, John, Fred, and Frank) Hi Brigham, Joe Mulbarger, and Oscar Kuehner all in the lineup, the Panhandles traveled to Dayton to play the Triangles (on November 17). On a muddy field at Triangle Park, the railroaders acquitted themselves honorably as they lost to the Triangles 12–0. The Triangles had played five games to that point and looked a lot better on the field than the rusty Panhandles, who were playing their first game. The Panhandles held the Triangles scoreless for three quarters before Dayton halfback Lou Partlow scored two fourth-quarter touchdowns to give the Triangles the win.

The Panhandles played hard, but the Dayton game would be the only one the railroaders played in 1918. With the lack of teams, Joe Carr decided not to find another game. The war was over, and the managers of the major pro football teams would get back to business in 1919. But for Joe Carr, the future of the Columbus Panhandles was coming to a crossroad.

By 1919 the country was prepared to get back to normal, including the sports world. In early July, Carr was given his first assignment for the *Ohio State Journal*, covering the big heavyweight boxing championship fight between Jess Willard, the champion, and Jack Dempsey, the challenger. On a hot Independence Day in Toledo, Ohio, Carr would attend the title bout and describe the action for his readers back in central Ohio. While sitting in 100 degree temperatures in section G with the other sportswriters, Carr typed the following article:

Barrier of Age Is Plainly Seen; Willard Not Fast Enough to Ward Off Attack of Young Challenger, Now Champ

By Joe Carr

This time honored saying, "youth will be served," was surely dragged out here today, when the youthful Jack Dempsey won so decisively over his

> older opponent Jess Willard, for it was only for a second at the very beginning of the first round, when Willard landed the first blow of the battle, a light left jab to the face, that the now ex-champion had a ghost of a show. The confident Dempsey sailed right into his older and much larger opponent and with his good left hand had Willard on the floor and on the way to championship retirement before the first round had progressed a full minute.
>
> The blow that really did the work for the challenger was delivered just before Willard went down the first time. It was a short left hook to the jaw, delivered in Willard's corner. The champions staggered to the opposite side of the ring, where he received a right to the body, when he went to the floor for the first time. However, this blow was more of a push than a hard jolt, as the left received previously had taken the steam out of the champion.
>
> Willard took a terrific lacing in this first round and was brave enough to come back for more, but the aggressive Dempsey could not be denied. The much-touted left hand of the new champion surely helped him into his new title, as time after time he landed with terrific force on Willard's jaw and head. He had the entire side of Willard's face a sight to behold. The right eye was closed and his jaw was swollen as if a bone was broken.
>
> After the battle was all over and Willard was in his dressing room, he made a statement in which he said that he realized that he was trying to put up a game, losing battle, and that, rather than take a knockout punch, he ordered his seconds to toss the towel in the ring.[21]

Carr enjoyed being one of the media "scribes" again, and covering a marquee sporting event was very rewarding, considering what the country had gone through the past year. When Carr returned to Columbus to be with his family, talk of a new professional football league started up again. On July 14 owners of three teams in northeast Ohio met at the Courtland Hotel in Canton to discuss guidelines to be used for the upcoming season. The small get-together was called by a new name on the pro football scene, someone who just happened to be taking over the best team in professional football.

Ralph E. Hay, a successful Canton automobile dealer, bought the Canton Bulldogs from former manager Jack Cusack, who had entered the oil business during the war and had moved to Oklahoma to seek his fortune. "My grandfather got involved in the automobile business at a very early age, about the age of twenty-three, and he went on to run his own dealership called Ralph E. Hay Motors," says James King, grandson of Ralph Hay. "He was one of the most prominent auto dealers in Ohio and he was considered to be a live wire. Very active. He was a great dresser, he always had nice suits and nice dress shoes to match. But he was known to be a very energetic, ambitious and a very astute businessman.[22]

"Ralph was interested in all sports but especially football. He was a close friend to Jim Thorpe while he played with the Bulldogs so that's why he bought the team," says King.[23] Although he was now out of the pro football business, Jack Cusack's contributions to the early days of the pro game can't be ignored. His signing of the great Jim Thorpe in 1915 had started the modern growth and popularity of the game, while showing the public, press, and other team managers the potential of the sport.

Years later when the sport was more established, Joe Carr sent Cusack a book on football and signed it, "To my pal Jack Cusack. He helped to make pro football what it is, Joe F. Carr." In his memoirs Cusack would comment on Carr's kind words by saying, "I would like to say that this tribute, from one who knew, is ample reward for my contributions to this great game." Cusack's team was now in the hands of Ralph Hay, who had a reputation of being a "great hustler," he would use his salesmanship personality in getting his team as much publicity as possible. The bigger the headline the better.[24]

The Canton meeting in July included teams from Canton (represented by Hay), Akron (Vernon "Mac" Maginnis), and Massillon (Jack Donahue and Jack Whalen). The trio of teams would agree to refrain from stealing other teams' players, but Donahue of Massillon refused on setting a salary limit. "If a manager wants to pay $10,000 for a player, that's his business," Donahue said at the meeting. This type of thinking wasn't going to help professional football and is probably why Massillon lost money in 1917. It also didn't help them in 1919 as the Tigers would play their last year of pro football.[25]

But this meeting didn't solve anything, as the three teams couldn't even agree on two major issues, let alone trying to convince other pro teams to join the cause. Reporting on the meeting, the *Akron Beacon-Journal* wrote that another meeting will take place and "a league will be formally organized at the next meeting and officers elected." The only flaw in this plan was that no other meeting occurred as the pro teams went their separate ways, just happy to be playing football again.[26]

As the season approached, pro football teams signed many new players who had finished their college careers within the past couple of seasons, giving the sport some much needed star power. Hay's Bulldogs signed two future Hall of Famers, Joe Guyon (Georgia Tech) and Guy Chamberlin (Nebraska). Akron signed former Brown All-American Fritz Pollard, one of the first early black stars in professional football. In his first game with Akron against the Massillon Tigers, 10,000 fans came out to Liberty Park in Akron and saw Pollard score a touchdown despite the Tigers winning 13–6.

In Wisconsin Earl "Curly" Lambeau, a Notre Dame dropout, helped start a pro team in Green Bay that was sponsored by a local meatpacking company. That team would eventually be called the Green Bay Packers. Another team gaining big headlines was the Hammond (Indiana) All-Stars, who signed former college stars Paddy Driscall (Northwestern), Milt

Ghee (Dartmouth), Paul Des Jardien (University of Chicago), and George Halas (Illinois)—a man who would make his own mark in helping organize professional football and would become a close friend of Joe Carr.

The Hammond All-Stars played their home games at Cubs Park (which would be renamed Wrigley Field) and intended to pay their all-star roster close to $20,000. Throughout the season the Hammond All-Stars played to huge crowds; in their six home games they averaged over 7,000 per game, which they needed in order to pay all those big salaries. Other pro teams that also made headlines were the Minneapolis Marines (managed by Joe Dunn), the Rock Island (Illinois) Independents (managed by Walter H. Flanigan), and of course the teams that comprised the mythical Ohio League.

The pro football scene was now full of a few passionate owners and more talented stars than every before, and Carr got excited about the prospects of the gridiron game in 1919. While addressing a group of local sportsmen in Akron, Carr spoke about the birth of pro football: "It started in 1901 when West Point Cadets were stationed in the Columbus barracks and they tossed a challenge into Columbus for a football match. The boys came to me and asked me to manage a team, so I did, and went over and played them. That was in September and every Sunday from then to Christmas, we played back and forth. As the season grew older we started hiring players and next year organized a professional team. That's how professional football started in this country."[27]

Maybe Carr was thinking how pro football started in Columbus for his Panhandles' team (which played the Columbus Barracks in their first game in 1901 under William Butler), but it was not how pro football started in this country. But anything for a headline, as the *Akron Beacon-Journal* ran the quote in its sports section to promote the sport. Despite the lack of an organized league, Carr was now excited about the prospects of professional football; the only thing worrying him was how his sandlot squad would compete in this new environment of college star-filled teams.

After playing just one game the previous season, Carr brought back most of the old stars to play in 1919. Back were the five Nesser brothers (everyone except Al), Hi Brigham, Hal Gaulke, Joe Mulbarger, Homer Ruh, and Oscar Kuehner. Walt Rogers, Oscar Wolford, and Will Waite added some new blood to the Panhandles' lineup. Emmett Ruh and Lee Snoots returned to the team after serving in the army. But the Nessers were getting old, four of them were over the age of thirty—John was forty-three, Phil was thirty-six, Ted was thirty-five, and Fred was thirty-one—and Frank turned thirty that summer. Plus, Emmett Ruh and Lee Snoots had lost two years due to the war, and Carr was at the mercy of hiring his players from the Panhandle shops, which wasn't going to help him compete with the other fully loaded pro squads.

The schedule was tough as always, with most professional teams in Ohio and around the Midwest still wanting to schedule the famous Panhandles. The Nessers still had the ability to attract fans. All ten games would be played away from Columbus as Carr took his team on the road again. Columbus was becoming more and more "gaga" over the Ohio State Buckeyes football exploits, and Carr could see his hometown building a special relationship with the campus, which later would contribute to the demise of pro football in Columbus.

The season started on a positive note with a 53–0 victory over the Newark (Ohio) Stars, but the Panhandles offense would stall and score only twenty-four points in the next nine games. After the Newark game Carr received another marquee writing assignment from the *Ohio State Journal*, as he was asked to cover the 1919 World Series between the Cincinnati Reds of the National League and the Chicago White Sox of the American League. Carr had no idea he was about to cover one of the darkest moments in sports history; the 1919 World Series would be known as the "Black Sox" Series, as eight members of the White Sox were eventually accused of throwing the series.

Joe Carr invited his brother Michael to attend Game 1 in Cincinnati, as well as his older brother John Karr, who wanted to watch his adopted hometown team, the White Sox. Carr covered almost every game, and his writing didn't reveal suspicion of any wrongdoings by the White Sox players. He wrote about the atmosphere and action with just a few sprinkles of questionable play.

Game 1 (October 1, 1919—at Cincinnati)

> Crowds jammed every available place within a block to witness the game. Seats are built to witness the game. Seats are built extending over the park wall over two streets that are closed. People covered the tops of large factories close by. While on a hilltop, that looks to be at least a half a mile from the park, a big crowd stood all afternoon watching the game. A demonstration worth going miles to see was pulled shortly before the teams took the field for play when John Philip Sousa entered the grounds. The band immediately struck up "The Star Spangled Banner." Every one of the many thousands immediately stood up and the spectacle was one long to be remembered.
>
> With the pitching "ace" of the American League [Ed Cicotte] chucked temporarily into the discard, stock of the Reds has taken a rapid advance. Before the game the most ardent followers of the Moran tribe were anything but confident of the outcome. But, after seeing the Reds outplay the hirelings of Comiskey at every turn of the game, both friend and foe are agreed that

the White Sox will have to use everything at their command and then some to come through on the long end of the series.

Game 2 (October 2, 1919—at Cincinnati)

The day was like one in July, and the sun shone brightly. The crowd, while not quite as large as yesterday, filled all of the stands, but fewer were standing along the outfield fences. Many women were among the spectators, even in the bleachers, and when the immense throng would stand from time to time to stretch, it looked as though a great white wave was rising, as all had coats off on account of the extreme heat.

The thought that many had that the Reds would falter when they faced a left hander [Lefty Williams] was dispelled after today's game, for in addition to taking advantage of Williams' wildness, they seemed able to solve his delivery when hits meant runs. However, it is a matter of record during the championship season that the Reds lost few games in which the flinging was done by a portsider.

Game 3 (October 3, 1919—at Chicago)

It was left for the smallest battery in the American League to halt, at least temporarily, the fast-going Reds in their rush for the world's premier honors in baseball. Dick Kerr, the miniature lefthander of the Sox, and his little battery mate, Ray Schalk, today turned the trick. The Reds did not have the slightest chance to score in the entire game. They, as losers, did not look as bad as the White Sox did when they were on the short end of the score.

Game 5 (October 6, 1919—at Chicago)

Even the most ardent White Sox fans are willing to quit after the performance today. With the coming of the blues to the followers of the Chicago club the enthusiasm of the Red followers increased, as they made an awful din in the stands, and the Red players on the bench were making plenty of noise kidding the White Sox players. In that eventful sixth inning you would have thought that the game was being played in Cincinnati rather than on the grounds of the enemy, so great was the cheering and noise that followed each play that added to the [Reds] scoring.

The general cry on all sides tonight is "On to Redland and finish it up tomorrow." Even the Sox players want to get it over as the gate receipts, in which they share, have stopped. They consider themselves out of the running.

Game 6 (October 7, 1919—at Cincinnati)

The crowd today was the largest of the series in Cincinnati. Every available space was packed and the housetops all around the park were packed to the guard rails. Three women, far outside the left field on a building were waving small American flags during most of the play.

In the first extra-inning of the present series and in the most weird game of the entire six played to date, the White Sox came from behind and won over the Reds, 5 to 4. It was a game full of errors of both commission and omission, with the latter style of misplay far in the majority. For were it possible to record the errors of the brain that were made by players of both teams and especially, the Reds, it would take a longer column than has ever been seen recording a baseball game.[28]

The Reds would end up winning the series in eight games (as the World Series was the best of nine in 1919) and upsetting the heavily favored White Sox. The following year eight members of the White Sox would be accused of fixing the series, but on August 2, 1921, the defendants were acquitted of all charges. Despite this verdict, baseball commissioner Kenesaw Mountain Landis banned all eight players for life, showing once again gambling among players had no business in professional sports, something Carr took note of, again.

When Carr returned to his football team, he saw his squad lose a tough one to the Akron Indians, 13–0, before heading into their annual battle with the Canton Bulldogs. The Panhandles brought only one Nesser (thirty-five-year-old Ted) to face Ralph Hay's powerful Bulldog aggregation, which didn't make the car dealer too happy. A disappointing crowd of 2,000 fans saw the Bulldogs win 22–3 over the railroaders. It would be one of the smallest crowds to see the Bulldogs play all season—compared to the games against Akron (9,000), Massillon (10,000 for first game; 7,000 for second), and the two Hammond games in Chicago attracting 20,000 fans combined—and Hay was fuming at the Panhandles' crowd.

In order to pay his talented and very pricy squad, Hay needed more than 2,000 fans per game, and he took out his frustration on Joe Carr. Their relationship would become very "icy" over the next few years when the sport was going to organize itself. One thing was for sure—Hay didn't think highly of the Panhandles, as the Bulldogs never played Carr's team ever again, ending a great rivalry that had played every season since 1912 (excluding the war year of 1918).

A couple of weeks after the Bulldogs–Panhandles game, Hay once again brought up the potential of a pro football league. Speaking at a luncheon in Cleveland, he was quoted as saying the Bulldogs "will be on the ground floor when a meeting for the formation of a league is called."[29] Hay's "hustler" personality and flamboyant way of doing business didn't sit well with the more thoughtful and humble Carr, whose nearly twenty years of experience backed him up. Hay had only been an owner for one season so the idea of this "novice" talking about a new pro football league disturbed Carr.

Carr now had a lot of things to think about, but the most important thing occupying his mind was how to salvage his team's season. After back-to-back wins against the Dayton Triangles and Detroit Heralds, everything went south for the Panhandles. As the aging Nessers and the rest of the railroaders played late into the 1919 season, they lost their last three games to finish the season with a 3–6–1 record. The only highlight was the trip west to play in Illinois against the Rock Island Independents in front of a big crowd of 6,000 fans. The Nessers were still an attraction to pro football fans, but their play on the field was a different story, as the Panhandles were steamrolled 40–0.

Some of the fire was still there, but the skills had diminished for most of the players on Carr's roster. Also, the team was getting less publicity, as most of the teams in Ohio and in the Midwest were either equal to or better than the once mighty Panhandles. So Carr had a lot to think about going into next season. But the one thing he didn't have to think about was the future of the sport he loved. On the whole pro football was improving as a viable sporting venture, as teams in Canton, Akron, Chicago, Dayton, Buffalo, Rock Island, Hammond, and Detroit were running teams that were very successful.

On November 15 the *Columbus Citizen* wrote an article on the potential of professional football.

Pro Football Can Be Made Success

There is something besides the "nine rahs" missing in professional football. The pros lack condition, team work, speed and spirit. Outside of that it closely resembles the good old gridiron game indulged in by husky collegians for many decades.

But professional football is growing in popularity and if the men backing the teams will insist on rigid training and plenty of practice sessions the game may be made worth while.

There is a demand for such a good healthy sport as football. The sport fans have baseball in the summer and up until the first autumn crispness is in the air. The baseball is adjourned until the next spring. There remains two months of generally good weather. Football fills it nicely. The fans are willing to pay for it.

Should Pep Up

But the footballers should make it snappier. There is plenty of talent. Men out of college only two or three season should be capable of playing good football if they'd only practice with their teammates and perfect offensive work. They're fairly good on the defense as is evidenced by the fact that in Ohio, where pro football is strongest, most games have been won by field goal kicking. That shows the defense work of the teams is much better than their offensives for failing to gain distance in line plunging, end runs and forward passes, they win their games with field goals.[30]

But despite these encouraging signs, the sport of professional football had several major problems that needed to be addressed by the passionate team managers. "Moguls," as newspapers called them, had to face the escalating prices of players. In 1915 Jack Cusack had lured Jim Thorpe to Canton for the unheard of sum of $250 dollars per game. He was worth the price, but it inflated prices for the rest of the players, and teams now had to shell out over $2,000 for an entire team, which would be tough to cover when most ticket prices didn't go for more than one dollar each. Moreover, most of the parks in these small towns of Ohio didn't seat more than a few thousand and were usually only filled for the bigger games. More cities such as Detroit or Chicago were needed to see the game grow.[31]

Because of the escalating salaries, players could play one team manager against another better than they actually played their positions. Players still played for multiple teams during a season, and this bothered fans and the press. Fan loyalty was hard to maintain when this week's star halfback who ran ragged last week for one team would sometimes be scoring touchdowns against you the next. Most team managers readily admitted they were their own worst enemies in these bidding wars and insisted they were forced to do it in order to be competitive. They would say, "If we didn't do it, someone else would," and fans wouldn't support a loser. Most of this was true for team managers, but the sport couldn't grow without settling these issues.[32]

Probably the worst offense was using college coaches and players under assumed names. Over the past several years pro teams lined up with more "Smiths" than could be read in the phone book. One advantage of using college players was that they came cheaper than a more established star. This practice gave pro football a bad reputation within the sports world and earned it the unyielding opposition of the more popular college game. College football was the "king" on the gridiron block, and it commanded big headlines on the sports pages, filled large stadiums, and pressured graduates to avoid the pro game. For example, in December of 1919 the Western Conference (forerunner of the Big Ten Conference) passed a rule that banned any former player, coach, or official who participated in professional football from ever working in the conference.

Several columnists suggested that the only solution to these problems would be the organization of an official league just like Major League Baseball had done some fifty years earlier. Joe Carr couldn't have agreed more. He knew pro football was going to be big, maybe even bigger than baseball, and he wanted to make his mark in the sport he had helped grow over the past thirteen years as team manager of the Columbus Panhandles.

After a year where he made a name for himself by covering two of the biggest sports events in 1919 (Willard–Dempsey fight and the World Series) and continuing to run the popular Panhandles, Carr was about to start the job he was destined for. Although he didn't know what the future held for his "aging" team, what he did know was that he wanted to be at the forefront of developing a new professional football league. The year 1920 would see a landmark meeting in sports history, changing the course of the sport, and the life of Joe Carr forever.

Part II

THE PRESIDENCY (1920–1939)

8

The American Professional Football Association (1920)

After spending the holidays with his family, Carr quickly turned his thoughts toward organizing a new professional football league. He knew it was time. In early January, Carr traveled south by train to the small city of Martins Ferry, Ohio, to visit an old friend. J. Francis Mullaney, a foreman at the local tin plant, was also a sports promoter from the city who was known for booking exhibitions with Major League Baseball teams for his hometown. Carr spent a full day speaking about putting together a professional football league and came away with a good feeling that it could be done. Several newspapers in Ohio wrote about this meeting, but it was the *Massillon (Ohio) Evening Independent* on January 8 that gave Carr the headline he was looking for.

> Joe Carr Plans Pro Grid League; Tigers on List
>
> Massillon will draw a berth in a new professional football league which Joe Carr, for years manager of the Columbus Panhandles, is now trying to swing, according to reports emulating from Martins Ferry where Carr is now in conference with J. F. Mullaney, football promoter in the southern Ohio city, in an effort to draw up plans for the proposed league.
>
> According to the report cities to be included in the league would be Columbus, Cleveland, Canton, Akron, Dayton, Toledo, Massillon, Cincinnati and Fort Wayne, Ind. It is proposed to put the Panhandles and Pitcarin (PA) Quakers on the circuit as road teams.[1]

Carr looked to use the core franchises of the Ohio League to help build his football league, and he envisioned his Panhandles as a traveling team in this new setup. But after hearing the news of a potential pro football league, the National Collegiate Athletic Association, at its annual winter meeting, made its own headlines by telling its former players to stay away from the pro game. The Western Conference adopted a rule that stated any football letter winner who participates in professional football would have his letter rescinded. Speaking at the conference, famous college coach Glenn "Pop" Warner, who coached Jim Thorpe at Carlisle and was currently the head coach at Stanford University, put down the pro game even more: "Football should not be encouraged as a professional sport, because it is not adapted to it. Football requires strict supervision to keep down abuses, needs skilled, well-trained players and pure spirit. Professional football would have a harder time embodying all those essentials than a college team. Soccer is an ideal sport for professional players and I would not be surprised to see it more generally approved when it is introduced to the strong holds of the professional Rugby game."[2]

Warner's thinking reflected that of most of the college coaches in America—they just wanted the pro game to go away, so much so that Warner suggested that soccer, which had no real following or popularity throughout the country, would make a better professional sport than football. This was a big slap in the face to Carr and the passionate team managers who were trying to organize the sport into a stable enterprise. Even more than before, the college game didn't give the pro game any support and would make life difficult for the pro grid "moguls."

Carr's momentum in organizing a pro league took a break during the spring as he continued to work as a salesman and sportswriter to help support his family. At this time in Chicago, another pro football pioneer would get his big break in the grid game. George Halas was a former star athlete at the University of Illinois who played football for the great Bob Zuppke. After he played his last game, Halas attended the football team's annual banquet and later remembered a statement that his coach made about his players. "Zuppke said, 'why is it that just when you players are beginning to know something about football I lose you and you stop playing. It makes no sense. Football is the only sport that ends a man's career just when it should be beginning.' I always remembered that," Halas would comment years later.[3]

George Stanley Halas was born in Chicago on February 2, 1895, as the eighth child of Bohemian immigrants Barbara and Frank J. Halas. Frank was a tailor, while his wife Barbara would make buttonholes for him in the family shop. Halas's early childhood, just like Carr's, revolved around school, church, and sports. After a successful athletic career at Crane Tech playing baseball and football, the six-foot, 140-pound Halas enrolled at the University of Illinois and went out for the football team. Playing for Bob Zuppke made a lasting impression on Halas. "He was a careful teacher," Halas would say about his former coach. "He knew how to get the best out of young men."[4]

Over time Halas would use many of Zuppke's teachings, especially the use of the T-formation, while running his own football team.

After graduating college with a degree in civil engineering, Halas played Major League Baseball for the New York Yankees, where a hip injury ended his career, and then professional football with the Hammond (Indiana) All-Stars in 1919. While playing with Hammond, Halas took a job working for fifty-five dollars a week as an engineer, designing bridges at the Chicago, Burlington & Quincy Railroad. Halas would go on to marry Wilhelmina Bushing, a young girl who everyone called "Min," who lived three blocks from him while they were in high school. They had two children, a daughter, Virginia, and then a son, George Halas Jr. "My father just assumed that his first born child would be a son because they planned to name him George Halas Jr. They had no girl's name picked out. Took him awhile to decide upon the name Virginia Maryann. It was entered on my birth certificate weeks after the certificate was filed," says Virginia McCaskey, daughter of George Halas.[5]

In March of 1920, Halas received a phone call from a Mr. George Chamberlain who offered Halas a unique job that would give professional football its "Papa Bear." Chamberlain was a superintendent at the A. E. Staley Manufacturing Company, a starch business located in Decatur, Illinois, about 172 miles southwest of Chicago, in corn country. Augustus Eugene Staley was the founder of the Staley company and always believed sports were a positive force for developing human character and stimulating a wholesome attitude of spirited competition for his employees—as well as for the community. He fielded successful sports teams, especially baseball squads, managed by former Major League star Joe "Iron Man" McGinnity. In 1920 Staley wanted his football team to be just as successful as his baseball squad, so he sent Chamberlain to Chicago to talk to this very passionate football star who played brilliantly for the University of Illinois.

"Chamberlain made a date with me and we met at the LaSalle Hotel. He asked if I would like to move to Decatur to work for the Staley Company," Halas wrote in his autobiography. "I would play on the baseball team and manage and coach the football team as well as play on it. I don't know how much money he offered. It may have been a little less than the $55 the railroad paid me. The magnet for me was the opportunity to build a winning football team." So Halas demanded three conditions from Chamberlain: (1) he wanted to recruit players from major colleges, at Great Lakes (service team), or on semi-pro teams; (2) he wanted to offer the players full-time jobs with the company; and (3) he wanted the team to practice daily on company time for at least two hours. Chamberlain agreed to all three. "I was elated. I saw the offer as an exciting opportunity but did not suspect the tremendous future Mr. Staley was opening for me," recalled Halas.[6]

The twenty-five-year-old Halas was now in charge of his own professional football team and went about signing players for his squad. With the resources provided by Mr. Staley, Halas signed a team full of former All-Americans, including Hugh Blacklock (Michigan State), Jimmy Conzelman (Washington of St. Louis), Burt Ingwersen (Illinois), George Trafton (Notre Dame), and Guy Chamberlin—who played for the Canton Bulldogs in 1919. Now he was ready to schedule games for the fall.

As the summer rolled on, Carr and the other pro football managers started to talk again of forming a pro football league, but this time Carr wasn't at the forefront of the discussion. The Ohio League owners had the most to say in shaping the new arrangements of a proposed league, as the four northeastern teams—Cleveland Tigers, Canton Bulldogs, Massillon Tigers, and Akron Indians—who were the sport's marquee teams (although that didn't help Massillon and Akron from losing money) were now starting some dialogue. A few of the other clubs from around the state that were considered second tier—the Toledo Maroons, Dayton Triangles, Cincinnati Celts, and Joe Carr's Columbus Panhandles—could help the big four form a legit league.

Strong teams emerging from Illinois, Indiana, Michigan, and western New York, which were threatening Ohio's pro football leadership and bidding on the best players on Ohio teams, would fill the league out even more. From a fan's standpoint, a pro football league was a great idea that sounded big-time and could produce a legitimate champion. But from an owner's standpoint, especially those from Ohio, a league was a chance for survival. The three major issues affecting pro football—escalating salaries, players hopping from one team to another, and the use of college players—were still there and still needed to be addressed. Then in August one man took charge to organize a football league that would change the structure of the sport.[7]

Ralph Hay, manager of the Canton Bulldogs, sent out word for a meeting with Ohio's best teams but excluded Carr. Maybe their icy relationship, brought out by the bad turnout for the Panhandles–Bulldogs game in 1919, was the reason. Nobody knows for sure, but when four pro football teams met to seriously discuss a pro football league on August 20 at the office of Ralph Hay in Canton, Ohio, Carr wasn't there.

Representing the Bulldogs were Hay and his star player, Jim Thorpe—who was available because he was playing minor league baseball in Akron. From Akron came cigar store proprietor Frank Neid and his partner Art Ranney, who were promising to put a new team in Akron to replace the defunct Akron Indians. (Neid and Ranney basically signed a lot of the former Indian players, including Fritz Pollard and Al Nesser.) Cleveland Tigers manager Jimmy O'Donnell, an experienced, albeit small-time, sports promoter and his coach and star player, Stanley Cofall, came from that city. Lastly, the fourth team that showed up was the Dayton Triangles and their stocky manager Carl Storck.

Although sports pages lauded these gentleman as "magnates," they were in reality five middle-class businessmen and two football players who had come together to try and make a few bucks from the sport they loved. The group gave itself a name—the American Professional Football Conference—and elected Hay as temporary secretary. This was an effort to form a league and marked the most ambitious effort to date. The minutes from the meeting are a little sketchy, but the newspapers described what the owners agreed on:

> The purpose of the A.P.F.C. [American Professional Football Conference] will be to raise the standard of professional football in every way possible, to eliminate bidding for players between rival clubs and to secure cooperation in the formation of schedules, at least for the bigger teams.
>
> Members of the organization reached an agreement to refrain from offering inducements to players to jump from one team to another, which has been one of the glaring drawbacks to the game in past seasons. Contracts must be respected by players as much as possible, as by club managers.—*Canton Repository*

> The league voted unanimously not to seek the services of any undergraduate college player. . . . Last season there were quite a number of intercollegiate stars who padded their bankrolls by slipping away on a Sunday, and performing with a pro team, using every name under the sun but their own to hide their identity. Some startling disclosures came later that brought the wrath of the intercollegiate heads down on the pro game.—*Dayton Journal*

> A maximum on financial terms for players.—*Cleveland Plain Dealer*[8]

Although the three major problems had been addressed, the solution only bound the four teams attending the meeting. Perhaps that is why the group called itself a "conference" instead of a "league." Regardless of what the conference did, if the other teams didn't honor those provisions, the Ohio foursome would find itself victimized by the very practice it was swearing to forgo. After the meeting Secretary Hay was instructed to contact the other nation's leading pro football teams and invite them to another bigger meeting to discuss the "conference."[9]

Carr was not bothered by the snub and started to put his team together and schedule games for his Panhandles, booking a contest with the new Akron team for October 10. Before the 1920 season started, the Panhandles lost a few big names, as Fred Nesser and John Nesser decided to hang it up. They would return in 1921, but their loss would be felt all season. Emmett Ruh would also miss the season. Al Nesser chose to play for more money with rival Akron and Phil Nesser would only play one game. The rest of the roster did consist of some of the usual suspects, with Frank Nesser, Ted Nesser, Hi Brigham, Lee Snoots, Homer Ruh, Oscar Kuehner, Joe Mulbarger, Will Waite, and Oscar Wolford playing the majority of the games. The team even brought back John "Pop" Schneider—at the age of thirty-one—to fill in for a few games at halfback.

Carr was still trying to find more talent for his team, but he couldn't locate any in the railroad yards. Once again he was limited in what he could add to his roster. The team would play a tough schedule, adding the Dayton Triangles for the opening game on October 3, but it was time to organize professional football on a grand scale. Once again Carr would not be given an invitation. After the first meeting, Hay received letters from several other pro football managers who wanted to join the newly organized conference, so Hay set a date for the next meeting.

On a hot and muggy Friday night in Canton, Ohio, on September 17, ten professional football teams convened at the automobile showroom of Ralph Hay. It would be a historic meeting. The football managers arrived by train, but nobody really stopped the presses to announce their arrival. Hay really didn't know how many owners would actually show; since his small office wasn't big enough to have the meeting, they moved out in the spacious showroom with the cars on display. It was quite a scene as these milestone men meet in the showroom of an automobile dealer. One of the ten owners would always remember the trip to Canton. George Halas, in *Halas: An Autobiography*, described the experience: "Morgan O'Brien, a Staley engineer and a football fan who was being very helpful in administrative matters, and I went to Canton on the train. The showroom, big enough for four cars—Hupmobiles and Jordans—occupied the ground floor of the three-story brick Odd Fellows building. Chairs were few. I sat on a running board."[10]

At the meeting were the four teams who were at the August get-together with the same representatives; Hay and Thorpe for Canton; Nied and Ranney for Akron; O'Donnell and Cofall for Cleveland; and Storck for Dayton. Also present were Walter H. Flanigan, the veteran manager of the Rock Island (Illinois) Independents; Earl Ball of the Ball Mason Jar Company and the backer of the Muncie (Indiana) Flyers; Halas and O'Brien, representing A. E. Staley's Decatur team; Chicago contractor Chris O'Brien, who operated the Chicago Cardinals; Leo Lyons, representing his Rochester (New York) Jeffersons; and Dr. Alva A. Young, owner of the Hammond (Indiana) Pros.

Not everybody showed up. Missing were the Minneapolis (Minnesota) Marines, Ft. Wayne Friars, Detroit Heralds, Toledo Maroons, and of course Carr and his Panhandles. Some earlier histories on pro football would put Carr at this meeting, but there is no historical proof to back this up. There was no mention of Carr in the league minutes or any newspaper articles reporting on the meeting. It's possible he arrived earlier in the day and gave his input, but that doesn't sound correct. If he made the effort to make the two-hour trip to Canton, Carr would have stayed for the meeting. Maybe it was Carr's icy relationship with Hay that doomed his participation in this meeting, or maybe he didn't think the "hustler" from Canton would pull off this meeting to help organize the sport he loved. Whatever the reason was, Carr didn't attend this meeting.

After some informal discussion beforehand the meeting was started at 8:15 p.m. by Hay. Frank Nied of the Akron squad took the minutes and had them typed up on the letterhead of the Akron Professional Football Team. A copy of the league minutes from the NFL's first meeting is now on display at the Pro Football Hall of Fame.

In the minutes the ten teams were listed, then Old Business was taken care of; the only topic discussed was that "Massillon had withdrawn from professional football for the 1920 season." Then it was on to New Business and the league minutes covered the rest of the meeting.

> It was moved and seconded that a permanent organization be formed to be known as American Professional Football Association. Motion carried.
>
> Moved and seconded that officers be now elected, consisting of President, Vice-President, Secretary and Tresurer. Carried.
>
> Mr. Jim Thorpe was unanimously elected President, Mr. Stan Cofall, Vice-President, and Mr. A. F. Ranney, Secretary and Treasurer.
>
> Moved and seconded that a fee of $100.00 be charged for membership in the Association. Carried.
>
> Moved and seconded that the President appoint a committee to work in conjunction with a lawyer to draft a constitution, by laws and rules for the Association. Carried. Mr. Thorpe appointed A. A. Young of Hammond, Chairman, and Messrs. Cofall, Flanigan and Storck associates.
>
> Moved and seconded that all clubs mail to the Secretary by January 1, 1921, a list of all players used by them this season, the Secretary to furnish all clubs with duplicate copy of same, so that each club would have first choice of services for 1921 of his team of this season. Carried.
>
> Moved and seconded that all members have printed upon their stationery, "Member of American Professional Football Association." Carried.
>
> Mr. Marshall of the Brunswick-Dalke Collender Company, Tire Division, presented a silver loving cup to be given the team awarded the championship by the Association. Any team winning the cup three times should be adjudged the owner.
>
> It was moved and seconded that a vote of thanks be extended by the secretary to Mr. Marshall.

The meeting was adjourned. Next meeting to be called by the President sometime in January.

[signed] A.F. Ranney.[11]

Although the meeting officially started at 8:15 p.m., some of the main issues might have been decided before Hay suggested they go on the record. What they did decide was to change the name of the organization to the American Professional Football Association (APFA). The managers might have felt that the use of the word "association" was much more loose and general than using a word such as "league," denoting maybe less of a commitment. Several managers urged Hay to take the association's presidency, but he realized that the organization needed a bigger name to earn respect from the public and the nation's sports pages. "Thorpe should be our man. He's by far the biggest name we have. No one knows me," Hay said. So they chose the biggest name in pro football to be president—Jim Thorpe.[12]

Old Jim was elected and sure enough, Hay was right, as headlines in sports pages across the country led with the naming of Thorpe as the league's president. Most of the managers in the room knew that Thorpe's executive abilities didn't match his athletic prowess, but they expected Hay to work behind the scenes to help guide the league. Stanley Cofall was named vice president, and Art Ranney was elected secretary-treasurer, giving the three main Ohio clubs all the executive positions.

The group decided to charge a fee for membership but this was just for show. "We announced that membership in the league would cost $100 per team. I can testify no money changed hands. I doubt if there was a hundred bucks in the whole room. We just wanted to give our new organization a façade of financial stability," Halas later admitted. Other business discussed was the appointment of a committee to draw up rules and regulations and the decision to furnish a list of all players used during the season to all clubs by the first day of the new year.[13]

At the end of the meeting, a Mr. Marshall presented a silver loving cup to be given to the team "awarded the championship by the association."[14] This phrase is very significant because it declared that the champion would be decided by a vote of the association teams instead of a mathematical won-loss formula or standings. No time was spent discussing rules; everyone assumed the pro game would follow college rules, like they always did.

According to the league minutes, the three major problems in professional football had not been directly addressed. But the association must have talked about them because the media coverage of the meeting would stress the action of the managers not mentioned in the minutes. Most of the newspapers announced that the association would not use undergraduates and that all contracts would be honored. News of the new pro football league spread across the country, but it was not the main headline in every sports page. Even in the *Canton Repository* the day's big news was the Canton Bulldogs' signing of Pete "Fats" Henry, the former Washington and Jefferson All-American tackle. Only on the following page did the paper mention the birth of a new pro football league.

In Carr's hometown the *Ohio State Journal* reported on the meeting but on a much smaller scale.

> Jim Thorpe, leader of the Canton Bulldogs, was chosen to head the American Professional Football Association, the only professional football organization in existence. Representatives of 11 cities [including Massillon] assembled and unanimously voted Thorpe to the presidency, with Stanley Cofall of Cleveland as vice-president, and Art Ranney of Akron, for secretary and treasurer.
>
> A decision was reached to refrain from luring players out of college for the professional game.[15]

It was now official, the sport of professional football had a league. The ten teams represented at the September 17 meeting are considered charter members of the APFA, and by extension, the NFL. Over the next couple of weeks four more teams joined the APFA—the Buffalo All-Americans, the Chicago Tigers, the Detroit Heralds, and Carr's Columbus Panhandles. No evidence or actual date exists as to when the Panhandles joined the association; the only proof is that the railroaders played five games against members of the association in 1920. The APFA would have fourteen teams play in its initial season, but for historians it has always been difficult figuring out who actually played in the 1920 season.

The truth is that the organization was almost never mentioned in the sports pages of any of the cities involved in the APFA until the association met again in 1921. There were no final standings from which to get a list of members—the association just didn't keep standings. They also didn't keep any team or player statistics or establish a league office anywhere. I guess Thorpe was too busy to set up these minor details. The APFA was organized, and now it was time to play the games.

On October 3, 1920, the newly formed APFA—the forerunner of the NFL—played their first full weekend of games. Although some APFA teams got into action as early as September of that year, the first meeting between teams listed as APFA members occurred on October 3. On that date, the Dayton Triangles hosted Joe Carr's Columbus Panhandles, winning 14–0, and the Rock Island Independents hosted the Muncie Flyers, winning 45–0.

Here's where it gets interesting; which one of these games was the first in NFL history? A glance at the map of the Midwest will show that Dayton is in the Eastern time zone and Rock Island is in the Central. So

Dayton being an hour earlier has been given credit for playing the first-ever game in NFL history. Kickoff times were far from being standardized in 1920, and no proof of the actual kickoff times has surfaced, so the time zone theory is all we have to go on.

As for the Panhandle–Triangle game itself, a small crowd gathered at Triangle Park to watch a hard-fought game between two old rivals. After a scoreless first half, the Triangles took control of the game. Early in the third quarter Triangles fullback Lou Partlow scored on a seven-yard touchdown run—scoring the first touchdown in NFL history. George "Hobby" Kinderdine kicked the extra point—another first in NFL history—giving the Triangles a 7–0 lead. Later in the fourth quarter Panhandles fullback Frank Nesser got off a booming punt that Triangles halfback Francis Bacon fielded at his own forty yard line. Bacon weaved his way through the railroaders tacklers on his way to a sixty-yard punt return for a touchdown. Kinderdine added another extra point and the Triangles won 14–0.

At the time Joe Carr and his Panhandles didn't realize this would be the first game in NFL history; to them it was just another loss by an aging team. Next up the Panhandles headed north to play the Akron Pros, led by Al Nesser. During the week the *Akron Beacon-Journal* wrote a nice article on the Nesser family and the current state of the Panhandles. It would be one of the last lengthy articles written on the Nessers.

Nesser Clan at Least 50 Per Cent Better, Says Their Manager

Coach Tobin of the Akron Pro gridders is running his men through long workouts this week so that when the eleven faces the Columbus Panhandles at League Park next Sunday they will be as fit as the proverbial fiddle. Tobin denies that he is frightened by the stories being sent out from the Nesser camp. But he does say that it is well to be prepared and "you never can tell." Joe Carr, veteran manager of the capitol [*sic*] city announces that his squad is stronger by fifty per cent than it ever was in all previous history, which is saying a mouthful.

Ted Nesser, oldest of the clan, will hold down either fullback or tackle positions. John Nesser is scheduled to appear on the line. One brother of the famous family, and probably the best in football, is Al, now with the Akronites. Last Sunday Brother Al played a sensational game for the local team, scoring three successive touchdowns on fumbles.

Some fans may have been disappointed in the showing made by the much advertised Fritz Pollard last week-end. But Coach Tobin says that the dark skinned one was ill all last week, and in weak condition when he arrived here Saturday night. He insisted on playing and even then made a creditable appearance. However next week he is expected to be in something nearer his old time form. And if he is, watch your step you Panhandles.

> The Panhandles crew was defeated last Sunday by the fast Dayton eleven, but they think they are still in a class with Akron and Canton, so it is up to Tobin & Co. to waken them up next Sunday.[16]

On October 10 in Akron the Panhandles were never in the game as the Pros, led by the blocking of Al Nesser and the running of Fritz Pollard, won easily 37–0. The Panhandles would be a nonfactor in the race for the first APFA championship, not that Carr thought he had a title contender on the field, but he would be disappointed in his team's 2–7–2 overall record—including a winless 0–5 record in APFA games.

Another disappointing team was the Cleveland Tigers, who in the middle of the season cleaned house and signed several new players before they played the Panhandles in late October. One of the players leaving was Stan Cofall, the APFA's current vice president. Playing the Tigers didn't help the psyche of the Panhandles, as the railroaders lost a close one 7–0 in front of a nice crowd of 5,000 fans. The Panhandles were once again shut out—seven straight games without scoring—and their losing streak stretched to eight games going back to 1919.

On the same day of the Cleveland–Columbus game, the APFA's biggest game was played at Lakeside Park in Canton between the Akron Pros (4–0 overall, 2–0 APFA) and the Canton Bulldogs (3–0–1 overall, 1–0–1 APFA). Before a huge crowd of 10,000 fans, the Pros handed the Bulldogs a surprising 10–0 loss on a fifty-five-yard interception return of a tipped pass by Akron tackle Pike Johnson.

As November began four APFA teams were still undefeated, Buffalo All-Americans, Decatur Staleys, Dayton Triangles, and Akron Pros; the first three were no surprises, but Akron was. No one outside the Rubber City saw this coming, despite the presence of the game's best breakaway runner in former Brown All-American Fritz Pollard, one of the APFA's first black stars, and who enjoyed his time playing in Akron. "I didn't have any problems playing with Akron. They adopted me very well. On the football field, they blocked for me and everything else. The town would cheer for me. Akron was a very southern-like town. Some southerners came up to work here when the war started, but when I played, they would cheer, 'We want Pollard! We want Pollard!' Throughout that year (1920), the team treated me right and I had a good year," Pollard would say in a 1976 interview.[17]

In 1920 the APFA didn't have any rule against black players playing in their organization, as professional football had black players as early as 1904 with Charles Follis playing for Shelby Athletic Club. Carr's teams had played against black players before. But it would be an issue that he would eventually face head-on as president of the NFL.

Akron continued to win, beating Dayton (spoiling their chances) and the Canton Bulldogs on Thanksgiving Day for the second time. Three days later saw George Halas's Decatur Staleys upset by the Chicago Cardinals, 7–6, behind the play of future Hall of Famer Paddy Driscoll. Both touchdowns in the game were scored by the defense, with Driscoll's point after touchdown in the third quarter making the difference. Five thousand fans came out to Normal Park to watch the first ever game between the future crosstown rivals. This left the door wide open for the upstart and undefeated Akron Pros to finish the season with the best record.

The season now came down to just a few games in December, but first was a unique game scheduled for a city that didn't even have an APFA franchise. Frank McNeil, the manager of the Buffalo All-Americans, came up with an idea to help his team make some extra money by scheduling his game against the Canton Bulldogs—and star attraction Jim Thorpe—for Saturday, December 4 in New York City at the Polo Grounds. Then his team would play the Akron Pros in Buffalo the following day. The day before the game, the Bulldogs worked out at the stadium and the Big Apple was ready to see professional football at its highest level. The move by McNeil paid off.

Over 10,000 paid customers (some newspaper reports had the crowd at about 20,000) saw the All-Americans defeat Thorpe's Bulldogs 7–3. Most eastern writers looked down on the pro game, as college football was the king of the gridiron, but most game recaps were impressed by the quality of the game and gave the sport some positive reviews. "The little Ohio league of football clubs, which started a few years ago with an even chance of failure has proved itself a tremendous success. Every city of any size in the west today has its pro aggregation. Professional football may or may not be a good thing, but it is with us, and it is here to stay. The thing now is to make the best of it and attempt by building it clean from the start to ward off the stigma which has fallen upon organized baseball."[18]

"Tiny" Maxwell, former college star at the University of Chicago and Swarthmore, who refereed the game, was impressed too, calling it an "errorless game of football."[19] The following day Decatur won a rematch against the Cardinals in front of 11,000 fans at Cubs Park, and Akron tied Buffalo, 0–0, in front of just 3,000 in Buffalo (keeping Akron unbeaten), and it looked like the APFA was getting a "small" foot hold in the bigger cities. The next week the season came down to one final game as the Akron Pros traveled to Chicago to play Halas's Decatur Staleys.

At the beginning of the season the Staleys played their home games at Staley Field in Decatur, but Halas didn't think the field or small town of Decatur was going to make his team profitable. Staley Field sat next to the starchworks factory and had a grandstand that would only accommodate

1,500 people. "We charged only a dollar for admission to Staley Field, which maybe wasn't enough. Employees got in for half price. When the season ended, the 18 players on our squad received $1,800 each for three months of action. This was a lot of money considering they were making only $50 a week as plant and office workers," Halas remembered.[20]

So late in 1920 Halas scheduled a few games to be played at Cubs Park in Chicago, including the season finale against the Akron Pros. Halas know he needed to win this game if he wanted any shot of winning the APFA title and decided to break one of the "league rules" to do it. A few days before the game, Halas hired Paddy Driscoll of the Chicago Cardinals (who just the week before played against the Staleys). The move—similar to McNeil's idea of playing a game in New York—would also pay off. Before 12,000 fans at Cubs Park, the two teams played to a scoreless tie, and the 1920 APFA season ended with a whimper. For Akron the tie was just as good as a win. They were the only unbeaten team in the APFA with a league record of 6–0–3.

The first year of the APFA was less than triumphant, despite the brave promises of August and September; the season saw players still "hopping" (like Halas's signing of Paddy Driscoll late in the season, and furthermore he wasn't punished), the use of college graduates; and higher salaries. At best these practices had been slowed. After the season, the *Buffalo Courier* even reported about the failures of the new pro league. "A sort of association was formed last September, but it did not go to the lengths demanded in a regular organized league. There was no way of enforcing contracts or preventing contract jumping and no rules for disciplining players on the field."[21]

Most of the APFA teams lost money. The Chicago Tigers and Detroit Heralds folded after the season, and the Muncie Flyers folded after that one bad game against the Rock Island Independents way back in week one. The teams from the Ohio League had pushed for the APFA, and they could be proud of the fact that the Akron Pros were the best team, but the biggest crowds were in Chicago, New York, and even Philadelphia, where the Union Athletic Association (a non-APFA team) was attracting over 11,000 fans at home—including playing before 17,000 on December 11 against the Canton Bulldogs.

But everything wasn't doom and gloom for the pro game, and support came from an unlikely source. Speaking to a reporter, Walter Camp, dean of football, who developed more rules for the college game than anyone and was a former Yale star, put his stamp of approval on the game of professional football.

> I am practically satisfied that professional football will be a success. We must prepare for it. We must define its position and place in the athletic curriculum

> of the nation. Once a perspective is gained by the professional player and I believe it will be gained then we may look for the professional game to grow and expand.
>
> I have studied the professional game situation and I am convinced it is with us to stay. There is no reason why it should fail, unless it be that college stars desire to quit the game immediately after the close of their college careers. This seems unlikely in view of the fact that most men graduate from school when they are anywhere from 22 to 25 years old. The football ability of a man does not cease to exist at that age. The man, himself, in most cases, is unwilling that his career be terminated at such an age in life when really he is at his best in so far as athletics are concerned. For these reasons and a number of others, the men still want to play the game. The more of these men who continue in the game as professionals, the finer becomes the brand of football offered by the professional teams. The finer the brand of football offered the public, the larger the crowd that will attend the games.
>
> If men at 25 or 26 desire to play football, and the keener the better teams are those of professional standing, what is wrong with the player offering himself as a candidate for these teams? I believe that the money involved really is of secondary importance to the young men who love the game.[22]

Camp was very astute in explaining why the pro game could be successful, knowing that football players at the age of twenty-five or twenty-six were hitting their prime years of athletic abilities, and if they wanted to, they would find a way to keep playing. Imagine football addict Peyton Manning not wanting to play football after graduating from the University of Tennessee and retiring at the age of twenty-two. Camp was also right about another thing—the pro game was here to stay. "The 1920 season confirmed my belief that professional football had a great future. It confirmed the correctness of Coach Zuppke's statement that college football players are only reaching their peak when they are graduated," George Halas wrote in his autobiography.[23]

In the end, the APFA of 1920 was not a true league as most sports leagues were supposed to be. It did not set schedules, keep records (or standings), make official announcements or decisions, or even publish rules or regulations. League members played nonleague teams, and there was no provision for determining the season's champion. The APFA needed a leader, someone with a vision that would guide the sport to new heights.

9

President Elect (1921)

The Panhandles' poor season didn't sit well with Joe Carr, and he knew deep down the team was probably on its last legs. But Carr had faith in the sport of pro football and knew all the years with the Panhandles were going to pay off in a big way. If anything, the founding of the American Professional Football Association (APFA) proved to Carr that he wanted to be part of the growth of pro football.

Now that the 1920 APFA season had ended, the owners planned a league meeting to try and answer the problems that faced the young organization. The first question that needed to be answered was, who would provide the leadership to move the sport forward? The current president, Jim Thorpe, was not the right man for the job; he was a great athlete, not an administrator, and most of the league's owners knew this. The league needed a stronger leader, someone with a vision who could see what the sport could become. Going into the meeting, Carr had some ideas he wanted to share, and this time he wasn't going to be left out of the party.

So on April 30 at the Portage Hotel in Akron, Ohio, the league met to decide the fate of the year-old APFA. Besides Carr (representing Columbus), other team owners who attended this meeting were league secretary-treasurer Art Ranney (Akron); Carl Storck (Dayton); Frank Nied (Akron); Chris O'Brien (Chicago Cardinals); Doc Young (Hammond); Leo Lyons (Rochester); Ralph Hay and his brother-in-law, treasurer Lester Higgins (Canton); Frank McNeil (Buffalo); and Morgan O'Brien (Decatur Staleys), who was sitting in for George Halas who couldn't make the meeting. Also there was Leo Conway, who was applying for a league franchise for his team from Philadelphia, and Dr. Charles Lambert, a well-known game official, who Carr brought with him as an advisor.

At 7:20 p.m. Secretary Ranney started the meeting and Dayton owner Carl Storck took the minutes. The first order of business was to officially award the previous year's championship to the Akron Pros. Jimmy Bryant of the Brunswick Balke Collender Company was present to award the cup to the Akron officials. The owners set a bad precedent the year before by awarding the title after the season by a league vote, but that was what they set up. After the title presentation the owners got down to the business at hand.[1]

At this time each owner got up and made a short speech outlining the state of his franchise and outlook for 1921. Most of what they said was bad, and most were disappointed in the league for not providing any answers to the problems facing the sport. The owners revealed they had lost money during the season (due mainly to the high salaries) and were serious about disbanding the league. To top it off Jim Thorpe—who failed to show up at the meeting—wasn't getting anything done as the league's president. As the negative tone of the meeting reached its peak, Joe Carr finally spoke up.

Carr started out by saying that there was a bright future for professional football as a successful business. He had seen the potential of the sport as the manager of the Columbus Panhandles, and with the right leadership the sport would succeed. Carr's words grabbed the attention of the owners, and they were all starting to get excited about the prospects of the APFA. After he completed his enthusiastic speech, the owners knew they had the type of man who could lead them.

The owners quickly motioned to vote for a new executive staff for the APFA. For the post of president, the owners nominated Carr. After giving his passionate speech, Carr couldn't turn down the job, so he accepted the post and he was elected unanimously. In his 1953 book *The Story of Pro Football*, Howard Roberts writes that Carr accepted a salary of $1,000 for the year, although there was no mention of his salary in the league minutes. No salary was set. In later years the humble, unassuming Carr would give his own version of being elected president by saying, "I was elected much against my will and while I was out of the room." Made for a good quote, but to be honest, Carr absolutely wanted the job.[2]

"Jim Thorpe, although he was the greatest athlete of the century, he was not an administrator. So they looked at my grandfather. Through his experience with the Panhandles and baseball he had become a first rate administrator and that was his forte. They needed somebody with a good business sense to develop the league because the other folks who were involved, that was not their area of expertise, but it was my grandfather's," says James Carr, grandson of Joe Carr. "At this time, for him, there was something very special about football and that was his passion, his love. He loved football and he wanted to make his mark."[3]

After Carr accepted the post, the owners went on to elect Morgan O'Brien as vice president (mainly because Halas would have been the choice if he were there) and Carr's good friend Carl Storck as secretary-treasurer. At this point Ranney turned the meeting over to Carr, and for the next eighteen years, he would be called Joe F. Carr, Mr. President. Carr would now use his middle initial of "F" to sign his name, he would tell a reporter once to "never omit that 'F' because no issue would be complete without it." Carr's first act as the leader of professional football was to name a committee to help draw up a league constitution and bylaws, which Thorpe had never done. The league needed rules to make progress, and these rules had to be in print so everybody could follow them.[4]

Carr selected Storck, Dr. Charles Lambert, and Art Ranney (chairman) as the men to do it. He then announced that the next meeting would be held on June 18 in Cleveland, and at that date the constitution would be ready—showing how serious he was about the league's rules. To make his point even more clear, the league carried the following rules stated in the league minutes:

- that all players of last year's teams are not to be approached by any other managers of any other teams until managers notify the President of the Association that a player is a free agent.
- to prohibit players playing on two different clubs in the same week.
- deadline of all players of last year's club to President by May 15th.
- all clubs present send check $25.00 to Treasurer, take care miscellaneous expenses of Association.[5]

Carr also reiterated that no player with college eligibility was allowed to play in his league or that club would be barred from the association. This topic would provide Carr with some serious headaches in his first years as president, and he would take it more seriously than any other rule that he established. On the financial front, the price of an association membership dropped from $100 to just $50, but each team would have to pay this fee, unlike 1920. Carr also set up territorial rights for league franchises, giving teams exclusive rights to play their home games without another APFA team coming into their area and playing the same day. This gave APFA team owners and their franchises a little more value. Carr then finished his first meeting as president.

The forty-one-year-old Carr hadn't gone into the Akron meeting looking to become president, but his passion and unquenchable belief in the sport was revealed in a big way to his fellow owners. Now the other owners were starting to see in him what Carr felt all along, that he was the right man for the job. Even though he wasn't at the meeting that initially elected Carr, George Halas could always see it in Carr, too. "Before Joe came along, teams were run by coaches and ex-players," Halas recalled. "Joe was the first non-sportsman to become involved in this area of sports management. He had what the rest of us lacked and that was real business-sense. All we were interested in was winning games. He was a born organizer. It was Joe who said our real concern should be the future of the sport."[6]

Carr would be the first to think about the league first, and that philosophy is still used today by the NFL. When Carr arrived back home he got right to work. He first announced that the league's headquarters would be located in his hometown of Columbus, and he would work at his desk on the third floor of the *Ohio State Journal*. Newspapers around the country revealed Carr's new job, including his hometown paper.

Joe Carr, Head of Pro. Football Men

> Ten professional football clubs of the United States were represented at the annual meeting of the American Professional Football Association here [Akron] today. Fourteen other cities sent word that they would become members of the association before the next football season.
>
> Joe F. Carr was elected president of the association, Morgan P. O'Brien vice president, and Carl Storck, secretary-treasurer.
>
> A committee of three was appointed to amend the constitution and bylaws to be submitted at the next meeting in Cleveland, June 18. Iron-clad rules were adopted prohibiting the jumping of players from one team to another. Any club which harbors or plays a man who has not completed his college course will be barred from the association. Other teams will refuse to play with any team using college players. A regular set of officials will be chosen to officiate at all games played by teams in the association.[7]

The press's reaction to Carr being elected president was very positive; the *Canton Daily News* stated Carr "should make a strong head for the organization" and the sport got a big shot in the arm by making the decision. The June 18 meeting at the Hollenden Hotel in Cleveland was another step for the young league. At this meeting the owners would first approve franchises in Rock Island (Independents), Illinois; Detroit (Tigers), Michigan, who replaced the Heralds franchise; and Toledo (Maroons), Ohio, although the Maroons didn't field a team in the APFA in 1921. Then after a short dinner break they came back to officially accept the league's new constitution and bylaws. After two months of work, Carr was extremely thrilled with the new constitution. The league now had a list of rules and regulations that helped established a solid foundation for the owners and franchises to follow.[8]

With these rules Carr now had the power to see that professional football would be operated as a respectable sport—especially in the eyes of the media and public who deserved to know. As part of the new constitution, Carr introduced one of the major rules that would finally give the sport some much needed stability. On June 19 the *Canton Daily News* would comment on this new rule under the headline "Professional Football Men Adopt Reserve Clause Similar to That in Baseball": "Adoption of a reserve rule similar to that now existing in professional baseball was the outstanding feature of the meeting of the professional football league here [Cleveland] tonight. Official records will be kept and those under contract to play with a professional football team will not be permitted to 'jump' to some contender offering a higher salary, it was declared."[9]

The APFA now had some stability as Carr reached back to his baseball background to use the unique reserve clause to keep player movement limited. The reserve clause would give teams the first right to sign their players each season, unless they wanted to release them, essentially allowing that player to become a free agent. This would eliminate the days of players hopping from one team to another.

Carr also addressed the issue of using college players, as the bylaws would include a rule—under Article IX, Section 1—that would say "that no college player shall participate in any games of the Association while he is in college."[10]

This rule was highly publicized by the press and garnered the APFA even more praise, but it would be tested by pro teams and players. The rule and its "specific wording" would cause Carr much stress over the next couple of seasons. It was a busy three months for Carr after he was elected president of the APFA, establishing a home base for the league in his hometown; creating a new constitution; and expanding the sport with several new franchises. It was now time to go home and take a break.

After returning to Columbus, Carr would spend most of his summer with his family and celebrated his tenth wedding anniversary with Josephine on June 27. The ten years had passed in a blink of an eye, and for the couple they were very happy. The two kids were healthy and preparing for the new school year, and Joe was about to embark on the first season of his presidency that would change the course of his career. At this time the family would begin to keep a scrapbook chronicling the achievements of the head of the household.

As the season approached, Carr and the owners held one last meeting to finalize everything. On August 27 at the LaSalle Hotel in Chicago, the owners would put the finishing touches on the upcoming season. Five new franchises—from Minneapolis (Marines), Minnesota; Evansville (Crimson Giants), Indiana; Tonawanda (Kardex), New York; Green Bay (Packers), Wisconsin; and Buffalo (All-Americans), New York—joined

Carr's association. The Buffalo franchise was the same as in 1920, as this transaction was just a formality, but it was the small-town Green Bay Packers that would be the surprise entry in Carr's new pro loop.[11]

Pro football played in Green Bay, Wisconsin, can be traced back to as early as 1895, but it would be the Green Bay Packers, formed on the city's far east side, that would become the NFL's most unlikely success story. The story starts with a University of Notre Dame dropout. Earl Louis Lambeau was born in Green Bay on April 9, 1898, to parents Marcel and Mary Lambeau. Marcel ran a successful construction business in town and would eventually build the stadium in which the Packers and his son played. Earl Lambeau was born with a thick shock of black hair that was so "curly" that he would be known by that nickname the rest of his life.[12]

Curly grew up to be a five feet ten, 186-pound triple threat football star at Green Bay's East High School, making him an instant legend in his hometown. Just like Carr and Halas, he also fell in love with the game and would dream of playing for his city's team. But first his father wanted Curly to go to college, and in the fall of 1918 Lambeau enrolled at the University of Notre Dame to play for the school's new head coach—Knute Rockne. Lambeau was there for just one reason, to play football; despite his father's dream, Curly had no illusions that he was there for the academics.

Rockne's intense, sure-minded personality, as well as his football formations and emphasis on the passing game as an offensive strategy, rubbed off on young Curly. Because of the war freshman were eligible to play, so Lambeau got plenty of playing time. After the season Curly returned home and was suddenly stricken with a severe case of infected tonsils that kept him home for six weeks. By the time he recovered he thought it was too late to return to Notre Dame, plus there was no football to go back to. So he decided to stay in Green Bay and was offered a fantastic job that led him to his ultimate destiny.

Frank Peck, an executive with the Indian Packing Company (a local meatpacking business), had followed Lambeau's high school exploits just two years earlier, and offered Lambeau a job as traffic manager with his company. "The Indian Packing Company offered me a job at $250 a month and I thought that was all the money in the world," Lambeau recalled years later. Since he was engaged to his high school sweetheart, Marguerite Van Kessel, he was ready to settle down in the small town. Then he had a chance encounter with another local citizen that changed the course of professional football.[13]

George Whitney Calhoun was the cantankerous, cigar-smoking sports editor of the *Green Bay Press-Gazette* who everyone called "Cal." Like Peck, Cal knew of Lambeau's football exploits while writing for the paper and ran into Curly one day while in town. "I met Calhoun on the street one day in August (1919) and after talking it over, we decided to organize a football team and ask the company to sponsor it," Lambeau recalled. Some historians say they agreed to form the team over a beer but wherever it was, Curly Lambeau was about to establish the team he would lead for the next thirty-one years.[14]

After the meeting Curly went to his boss, Frank Peck, and asked if the company would sponsor a team and help buy football uniforms, equipment, and balls. Peck responded by giving Lambeau $500 and the use of the vacant field the company owned next to the plant so his team could practice. He only asked that the team use the name Indian Packing Company to help advertise the company. Curly said no problem. Lambeau would be the captain of the squad on the field and run the business matters, and Calhoun would write about the team in the *Gazette*—giving the team free publicity.

Calhoun and other sportswriters started calling the team the Big Bay Blues (the jerseys were blue and gold), as well as the Packers. Lambeau wasn't thrilled with either name but would soon be fond of the name Packers. "It's a great name, but we didn't realize it then," Lambeau later recalled. The team practiced three days a week with most of the roster loaded with local Wisconsin boys, and in 1919 they played their home games at small Hagemeister Park. They didn't charge any admission that first year and only made money by passing the hat; usually it was Cal's fedora accepting the coin. "We just wanted to play for the love of football. We agreed to split any money we got and each man was to pay his own doctor bills," Lambeau remembered.[15]

Like George Halas in Decatur Curly Lambeau knew football. He understood and evaluated players as well as anybody, and his weekly practices helped his team dominate opponents in the state of Wisconsin. The pro game's coaching and practice habits were starting to take shape (although not every team had daily practice sessions), and with the likes of Halas and Lambeau running these powerful squads, they were going to prove to the likes of Pop Warner—and his comments back in 1920—that the pros could field a true "team" that played as one. The Packers proved that in 1919–1920 by beating almost every opponent they faced, including an 87–0 whipping against Sheboygan.

Lambeau was the star, especially his passing, and Calhoun would praise his partner. "Lambeau was shooting 'em all the way from 20 to 40 yards with the other back fielders and ends making sensational catches" was a typical Calhoun description of the flamboyant passing ace. After two great years, the Packers were now ready to join the big boys. Calhoun found out about the newly reorganized APFA and that sometime in August they were going to meet again in Chicago to talk about new franchises. Once again Lambeau went to his boss; this time it was John

Clair (whose ACME Packing Company bought the Indian Packing Company) who gave him the go-ahead. John sent his brother Emmett Clair to the meeting to pay the fifty dollar franchise fee. The small town of 31,643 now had a team in the APFA.[16]

For the twenty-three-year-old Curly Lambeau, it was now time to prove he belonged with the best teams in the country. He bolstered his squad by signing Howard "Cub" Buck, former star at the University of Wisconsin, who had played four years with the Canton Bulldogs, to a contract of $75 a game. They would also charge fifty cents admission at all home games. This was the big time, so it was now time to start acting like they belonged.

To wrap up the Chicago meeting, applications from Gary, Indiana, and Davenport, Iowa, were to be delayed and investigated at a later date. The APFA now had nineteen teams—five more than in 1920. Carr thought that to build his league, the more franchises the better (plus the fifty dollars for each team padded the league's bank account), but this was a philosophy that would hurt the APFA, and over the next couple of seasons Carr would map out a plan to move the league to the big cities. This philosophy of accepting any franchise was done to keep the sport alive, but most early pro teams would be broke at the end of the season or the manager of the team didn't have the financial resources to lose money and continue to operate a team on a yearly basis. It would take nearly a decade for Carr to establish a plan to solidify franchise stability.

At the end of the August meeting the owners passed one final issue that Carr suggested. The move was to allow the president to ensure "that season passes be sent from the President's office to newspaper [men] & prominent officials."[17]

This would turn out to be a good public relations move for the young league. Carr's newspaper and promotional experience saw the advantage of getting the press and other prominent individuals out to the games and this would only help the image of the league. Over his entire time as president, Carr made sure the press would be taken care of even if it meant that he would personally accompany these passes. Carr would not only give free passes to games but he would make sure they were the best seats in the house. *Columbus Citizen-Journal* writer Lew Byrer once asked Carr why he would give up a good seat for free, and Carr replied, "The usual thing is to give a pass-holder a seat right in back of a post. That doesn't make sense to me. If I give a man a pass it's because I want his good will. Why, then risk losing the good will you're trying to get by giving the man poor seats?"[18]

Some time between the August meeting and the beginning of the season Carr accepted eastern franchises in Washington (Senators), D.C., and New York City (Brickley's Giants). The New York franchise was backed by Billy Gibson, a well-known boxing manager and promoter, who signed two-time Harvard All-American Charles Brickley to coach and play. There is no league record to say when both teams joined the association, but they were the last two teams to be allowed in the league. The Senators played three league games and the Giants played only two, so neither team would be a factor during the season. Although neither city embraced the pro game in 1921, Carr did not give up on the sport in those well-populated eastern cities. Carr's league now had twenty-one teams, and the first season under his presidency was about to kick off. Speaking to the United Press, he predicated a big year:

"Professional football last year drew crowds as large as many big league baseball games did. With the popular interest already shown and with the successful fight we are making on contract-breaking and other wildcat practices, we are confident of a big league standing before long."[19]

League standings were to be kept by Carr, and only games between league teams would count in the final standings. Despite the rather large league, the race for the championship came down to three teams—the Buffalo All-Americans, the Decatur Staleys, and the 1920 APFA champion Akron Pros. Carr's own Columbus Panhandles would go through another bad season, finishing with a 1–8 league record (3–8 overall).

During the summer of 1921, George Halas went about making his team even stronger than the previous year. He set his sights on Ohio State University star Chic Harley, but Harley would only listen to his brother Bill on what he should do. Acting as Chic's agent, Bill Harley told Halas he could have Chic, as well as fellow Buckeye stars halfback Pete Stinchcomb and guard Tarzan Taylor, if Bill could get 15 percent of what was collected at the gate. Halas reluctantly agreed but he had the guy he wanted. The thrill of trying to get that special player would be a trait that Halas would constantly seek, and he usually got his man.

With a roster that featured Harley, Stinchcomb, Taylor, Hugh Blacklock, Guy Chamberlin, Ralph Scott, and Dutch Sternaman, the 1921 Decatur Staleys were a talented and very expensive team. After beating Waukegan American Legion to warm up for the APFA season, the Staleys prepared to play the Rock Island Independents at Staley Field. Then Halas was summoned to the boss's office to discuss the football team. In his autobiography Halas remembers the conversation.

> Mr. Staley asked me to come to his office. I had no idea what he wanted. We talked only on the field but there was no question in my mind that the sports program would continue. Mr. Staley greeted me warmly and said, "George, I know you are more interested in football than starch. As you know, there is a slight recession in the country. Time lost practicing and playing costs a huge amount of money. I feel we can no longer underwrite the team's losses.

"George, why don't you take the team to Chicago? I think football will go over big there. Professional teams need a big city base. I'll give you $5,000 seed money to pay costs until the gate receipts start coming in. I ask only that you continue to call the team the Staleys for one season." I said I will do it. Thank you, thank you, thank you very much. We shook hands.[20]

A written agreement was signed on October 6 by both Halas and Staley that stated the following:

- A sum of $3,000 was given in return for two pages of advertising in team programs, plus pictures and 100-word biographies of the chief Staley company officers.
- The other $2,000 would be paid at the rate of $25 a week per player up to a total of nineteen players.
- The team would operate in Chicago as the Staley Football Club.
- The new arrangement would terminate at the end of the 1921 season.[21]

After signing the written agreement, Halas immediately telephoned William Veeck, president of the Chicago Cubs, and asked if he could see him. Veeck said come on in. Halas took the train into Chicago and laid out the situation to Veeck. "I'm bringing the Staley team to Chicago and I would like to use Cubs Park as our home, for practices as well as our home games," Halas told him. Veeck welcomed the idea as his ballpark would be empty after the baseball season. Halas asked the terms, and Veeck said 15 percent of the gate and concessions sales. "I considered that very fair and rejoiced silently. All right, providing I can keep the program rights, which sold for ten cents in those days. He said done and I left the park a happy man," Halas said later. After playing the Rock Island Independents at Staley Field in front of just 3,600 fans, Halas's team played their first game of the season in Cubs Park in Chicago against the Rochester Jeffersons on October 16. Nearly 8,000 paid customers saw the permanently new Chicago team come back and win a thrilling 16–13 game over the Jeffs.[22]

Once in Chicago, Halas set up headquarters at the Blackwood Apartment Hotel where he rented ten rooms (two dollars a week for the players) and was in walking distance of the field. He also picked out the Staley's uniform colors as orange and blue—the same colors as his alma mater the University of Illinois. But Halas recognized the many problems of running a team and decided to take on a partner. "I wanted Paddy Driscoll but he wasn't available (Driscoll was under contract with the Chicago Cardinals) so I looked around the team and I settled with Dutch Sternaman. I offered him a 50–50 partnership," Halas later said.[23]

The move to Chicago would pay off in a big way for Halas, as big crowds (averaging well over 5,000 fans for nine home games) showed up in the big city, despite some bad weather. Although his partnership with Sternaman would cause him some future headaches, the move was a success. By early November the race for the APFA title started to get really tight. The defending champs, the Akron Pros, got off to a great start winning their first seven games of the season. After a 0–0 tie against the tough Buffalo All-Americans on November 13, the Pros met an unsuspecting foe the following week. The Pros traveled south to face Carl Storck's Dayton Triangles (who had a league record of 3–3–1) at Triangle Park. In a close game the Triangles' Russ Hathaway kicked a field goal in the third quarter for the only points and gave Dayton a 3–0 upset victory. It was a devastating loss for the defending champs, and they went on to lose back-to-back games and finished the season with a 8–3–1 record, good for third place in the APFA standings.

So it was down to the Chicago Staleys (6–0 record) and the Buffalo All-Americans. On Thanksgiving Day (November 24), the Buffalo All-Americans upset the undefeated Staleys at Cubs Park 7–6. The All-Americans were now 7–0–2 and continued to play great football by beating Dayton and Akron at home to set up a rematch with the Staleys, in what was being billed as the APFA "championship game." The All-Americans had played Akron the day before, and it affected their play early as Guy Chamberlin returned an interception seventy yards for a touchdown and a 7–0 lead. But the Buffalo squad came back and scored a touchdown early in the third quarter to tie it at 7–7. A few minutes later Dutch Sternaman kicked a twenty-yard field goal, and the Staleys defense made the 10–7 score hold up. It looked like the Staleys were champs, or were they?

After defeating the Buffalo All-Americans, Halas scheduled a game with the Canton Bulldogs, and the teams became confused as to what would happen to the title if the Staleys lost. The deadline for the season was an issue that teams debated with Carr, and he issued a statement: "The game in Chicago Sunday between the Canton Bulldogs and [Chicago] Staleys will have no bearing on the championship of the national professional league. Our season closed last Sunday. The championship will probably be awarded at a meeting of directors of the league here next week."[24]

With this ruling Carr essentially awarded George Halas his first pro football championship (although it wouldn't be official until the league meeting in early 1922). It was a very hard and busy 1921 season for Joe F. Carr, but seeing his Panhandles complete another difficult year (compiling a 1–8 record in league games) was probably the toughest thing he endured. It would also be the last season for four of the Nesser brothers as Fred, John, Phil, and Ted would play their last professional football games in 1921. But the season wasn't all bad for the Nessers.

That fall saw Ted Nesser play the whole season with his nineteen-year-old son Charlie Nesser. The two would make history by becoming the only father-son combination to play together in APFA-NFL history. The historic twosome made the family proud and set a record that might never be equalled. Carr knew his squad was too old to compete in the newly organized APFA, but he decided to give the Panhandles another year to see if they could turn it around.

The election of Carr as the APFA president would be an inspired choice. Personally a kindly, unassuming, religious man, Carr (who was now prematurely gray, balding, and bespectacled) looked like someone's grandfather. But when push came to shove, he would be tough as a seven-ten split. He would slowly bring his vision to the sport of professional football and follow a simple philosophy—strive for the highest standards and always consider the fans first, keeping in mind the league was the most important thing.[25]

10

The National Football League (1922)

It had now been fifteen years since Joe F. Carr reorganized the Columbus Panhandles in 1907 and threw his hat into the world of professional football. But it had all been worth it for the son of an Irish immigrant who was now the leader of the sport he loved. He did it the "Irish way" by working hard and gaining the respect of his fellow football executives. They were now looking at him to solve the problems facing the sport.

After his first year as president, Carr looked to rectify some of the financial difficulties plaguing some of the American Professional Football Association's (APFA's) franchises, but it wasn't an easy task. Ralph Hay revealed that his Canton Bulldogs lost between $8,000 and $10,000. "Running a pro football team at that time did have its problems. It cost us $3,300 to put a team on the field for a game," said Lester Higgins, former Canton Bulldogs treasurer, in a 1976 NFL Films interview. "Sometimes attendance would be a problem. Here in Canton, our field would only hold about 7,000 or 8,000 capacity. When we played Akron we would have an overflow of people. But we didn't have any reserve seating; it was first come, first served. We'd get about 12,000 people in there. They'd break the fence down and didn't pay. Then there were games when we didn't get any more than a couple of hundred people."[1]

Most of the money Hay put into the team came from his automobile business. He would continue to invest his own cash in the Bulldogs for the 1921 season, and the rest of the league would see greatness from them the next two years.

After relaxing with his family for the holidays, the new year started with a scandal for Joe F. Carr. Carr had announced that the owners would have a meeting on January 28 in Canton to discuss league matters. But right before the meeting, a report came out stating that several college football players from several prominent universities played for money with professional teams. Speaking at a banquet in New York, Fielding Yost, head coach at the University of Michigan, claimed that the pros "robs the game of many of the greatest character building qualities, and destroys the ideals of generous service, loyalty, sacrifice and whole-hearted devotion to a cause, which mark the college player."[2]

Carr had only been on the job for a year and now had his first black eye to show for it. Colleges and universities everywhere took their shots at the pro game, and they had the proof to do it. There would be two instances of college players playing for pro teams that put the issue right in front of Carr. First was the small-town Green Bay Packers' use of three Notre Dame players late in the 1921 season. For their game against Racine, Curly Lambeau signed Hunk Anderson, Hec Garvey, and Ojay Larson to play. Some reports had the trio playing against the Chicago Staleys too, but regardless, the Packers were found guilty of breaking the association's rule against playing a college player.

Although the Packers weren't the only APFA team using college players, there was proof against them; the Pack would soon be dealt with. The other instance of illegal players occurred with two nonmembers of the APFA who would get caught up in an even bigger scandal.

In the fall of 1920, the town of Carlinville, Illinois, defeated its semipro rival Taylorville, 10–7. The rooters of Taylorville (who lost a lot of money) vowed to beat their rivals the next year, this time playing in Taylorville. Carlinville didn't stand pat; they decided to ask several Notre Dame boys to play for them in 1921, paying up to $200 a body. The Notre Dame boys said yes. Everybody in Carlinville heard about the "ringers" and were so confident that they wagered most of the town's money. It looked like a full-proof plan—except the town talked, and word got back to Taylorville.

Taylorville didn't want to look like fools, so they went to the University of Illinois (which had its share of good players too) and offered their boys some cash to help them win the big game. They said, why not? Game day came, and both towns claimed that each one bet as much as $50,000 on each side. The Taylorville team actually led 7–0 at the half, playing with mostly their regulars against the Notre Dame squad of Carlinville. But in the second half they inserted the Illinois kids and little Joey Sternaman (younger brother of Dutch Sternaman) dominated the rest of the game. Joey kicked three field goals and Taylorville won 16–0 and their $50,000.[3]

If anyone expected to keep a $100,000 football game a secret they must have been living on the moon. Before some of the boys reached their dorm rooms, news came out about the big game and soon an investigation started. "A while later, back at school one day, I got a call from George Huff [Ilinois Athletic Director]. He wanted to see me. He said 'I understand you played down in that Taylorville game.' He knew it, and that was that," said Joey Sternaman to author Richard Whittingham in a 1983 interview.[4]

Dick Simpson, manager of the Taylorville team, readily admitted to using the Illinois players but refused to say whether he paid them. The Illinois players say he didn't. On the evening of January 27 the University of Illinois disqualified nine of its athletes from further sports competition for having played in the game as professionals—including Laurie Walquist and Joey Sternaman (both went on to play for George Halas's team). Carlinville coach Rivers Anderson revealed later that he personally "hired and paid Notre Dame men." Notre Dame followed suit, suspending eight players.

"There's always been the story going around that I wore paint on my face and adhesive bandages to disguise who I was, but that wasn't really so. Everybody at the game knew who we were," said Sternaman. The Taylorville–Carlinville mess instantly grabbed Carr's attention and he quickly responded: "Our league, of which such teams as Taylorville and Carlinville, which figured in the Illinois-Notre Dame scandal are not members, has no desire and in fact is unalterably opposed to the use of college men who are still eligible for intercollegiate competition. We will wipe out this evil sooner or later, but we could do it immediately if assured cooperation on the part of college coaches."[5]

Carr's relationship with the colleges and universities across the country had now escalated into a war of words and neither was happy with the situation. But for the time being, college officials looked at Carr and the owners to see how they would respond to this current crisis. Carr knew something needed to be done to show the public (especially the fans) that the sport was stamping out this "evil."

The day after the Illinois verdict was reported, the APFA opened its meeting in Canton at the Courtland Hotel. They woke up to the *Canton Repository*'s story on the Illinois suspensions, which was directly below its story of the league meeting under the headline of "Pro Football Moguls Here Today to Thrash Out Many Problems for Next Season." With all the bullets flying, Carr and other league owners gathered together to discuss the important issues facing their sport. First up was the matter of the Staley franchise in Chicago.

Although George Halas's Chicago-based team was a first-rate outfit in 1921—best in pro football—he did not actually own the franchise. The Chicago Staleys were still the property of starch-maker A. E. Staley of Decatur, Illinois. Halas and his partner, Ed "Dutch" Sternaman, were managers of the team (as well as coaches and star players), but old A. E. still had the official ownership according to the APFA. Based on the agreement between Halas and Staley, the two owners needed to secure the franchise after the 1921 season. At the meeting, Bill Harley (brother of Chic Harley) wanted a team for Chicago too and applied. So did Halas and Sternaman. Having been on the scene since 1920 gave the Staleys the inside track.[6]

Carr and the other managers telephoned A. E. Staley in Decatur to get his version of the 1921 arrangement with Halas. Halas and Sternaman were able to sit in on the conversation. "A. E. said he had transferred the team to me the previous fall. The company, he said, was quitting all paid athletes," Halas would write in his autobiography. "The members debated all day and into the evening. In the end, they decided to vote on whether the franchise should be given to Sternaman and me or to Bill Harley. Eight votes for us, two for Harley."[7]

A couple of years later Harley took his argument to court; he lost that too. Halas was elated and relieved that he still had his team, but he needed a new name. "I considered naming the team the Chicago Cubs, out of respect for Mr. William Veeck, who had been such a great help. But I noted football players are bigger than baseball players, so if baseball players are cubs, then certainly football players must be bears. The Chicago Bears were born!" said Halas.[8]

Next the owners voted the Chicago Staleys the 1921 APFA champion. Halas was now two for two. Though the procedure of voting the league's champions at the first league meeting after the season was clearly a horrible way of deciding a champion, the owners didn't have any reason to change it. It would stay that way. Halas might have been happy in that Canton meeting, but Carr was just starting to sweat, as it was time to handle the issue of college players participating in pro ball. Carr knew someone would have to pay a price. A motion was made to listen to the case of the Green Bay Packers, probably brought up by John Clair who was there representing the Pack, as Curly Lambeau didn't make the trip. But the motion lost, Carr needed more time to think, and the owners broke for dinner at Bender's restaurant.

At dinner there was much discussion between Clair and the other owners about the evidence against the Packers, which was supplied by the *Chicago Tribune*. Some historians think that George Halas supplied the information, turning in the Packers to get a chance to sign Hunk Anderson, but it sounds too far-fetched that Halas would cause all the trouble of punishing the small-town franchise just to sign a guard—albeit a good one. Clair was then given the floor, and he asked the association to consider withdrawal of the Green Bay franchise, and he personally apologized to the association. The motion carried.[9]

After one year the Packers were out of the APFA. "My grandfather said he knew that some of the teams have been fudging on this particular rule of using college players. But this is the first time [he had] caught somebody in this infraction. So he pulled the league franchise from the Packers and Curly Lambeau and that franchise certificate that was originally sent to Lambeau was returned to my grandfather as a sanction for him breaking the rule. That original certificate still belongs in our family," says James Carr, grandson of Joe F. Carr.[10]

After the Packers had withdrawn from the APFA the election of officers took place. Once again Carr was reelected as president; he would work on a one-year contract for most of his eighteen-year tenure. John Dunn, owner of the Minneapolis Marines, replaced Morgan O'Brien as vice president, and Carl Storck (who was absent) was reelected secretary-treasurer. Carr then set up a few new rules. First was that each team must post a $1,000 guarantee against hiring any college grid players, showing that he was serious in stamping out the "evil" of this terrible practice.[11]

Next up he established a player limit of eighteen players per team, which pleased Ralph Hay very much because it might keep his team's cost down (although the teams couldn't agree on a pay scale). Carr was also voted to assign the referee for each league game, eliminating the practice of home teams hiring the referee. Once the meeting ended, most of the owners headed back to Bender's for a drink. Carr headed home. There was more work to do.

Three days after the meeting, Joe F. Carr released a statement declaring the APFA's stance on the recent scandal of pro teams using college athletes, and how his office would stamp out the practice:

> There's no one in the world who regrets the unfortunate Taylorville football game between stars of Notre Dame and Illinois more than myself and my associates in the American Professional Football Association.
>
> Our association was formed, mainly, for the purpose of stamping out the practice of professional football teams signing college players before they have completed their college career. Our rules are very definite on this matter. The only member of the association to break this rule this fall was the Green Bay, Wis., Packers. This team was dropped from the association by unanimous vote of directors of the association at the recent meeting of the league's directors in Canton.
>
> At this meeting we put teeth in the rule. We made it necessary for every one of the 20 teams in the association to post a forfeit of $1000 with the association to guarantee observance of the rule against tampering with college stars. If we could have secured the co-operation of college coaches the rule would also include a clause in which a former college star would be compelled to present a signed release from his coach stating that he was no longer eligible for college athletics of any kind, before being signed.

What League Includes

The association includes 20 teams in each of the 20 large cities east of the Rocky Mountains in the United States. On these teams as managers and players are some of the highest class college athletes of recent years. They love football, college football as well as professional, and would be the last men in the world to do anything to jeopardize the grand old sport.

Purpose of Association

In organizing the association the founders realized that professional football was growing to a point where it needed some governing body to protect it and college football against such abuses as the recent one in Illinois. We attached the name of professional association to our organization so that everyone would know just who we are and what we are trying to do.

Our rules absolutely prohibit the use of any player under an assumed name, under penalty of expulsion from the association and also absolutely forbid gambling in any form on football games. As a further precaution against being deceived by college players playing under assumed names we employed collegiate officials to officiate our games until the colleges prohibited it.

When I heard that a team in our association had been guilty of using college players I immediately wrote to Knute K. Rockne, Notre Dame coach as the first step in the investigation which led to the ousting of that team from our league.

I didn't wait for the college to ask for such action.

If any college official can tell me any way in which the association can be fairer I can assure him that his suggestion will be carried out.[12]

Most of the colleges and universities around the country still continued to criticize the pro game, and there was no direct dialogue between the two organizations. Carr's statement appeared in many newspapers, and his strong stance continued to emphasize that his association just wanted peace, honesty, fair play, and anything else the colleges wanted. His door was open to dealing with this issue, but he got no response from college football.

The off-season was just getting started, and Carr made one decision that needed no help. He decided that his own Columbus Panhandles would play in 1922. That season the team would no longer belong to the Nesser family, as only one Nesser was on the roster, and a new coach would be calling the shots. Frank Nesser would be the only member of his family to wear the maroon and gold, as Fred, John, Phil, and Ted all retired from professional football before the season started. With their retirement, the Panhandles as a professional football team ended; even though the railroaders would play in 1922, the aura of the Panhandles was now totally gone.

Carr hired a new coach as Ted Nesser also decided not to lead the team. Carr looked toward a friend to help guide the team, as he hired Herb Dell, a Columbus man who had refereed Panhandle games since 1911, to take over the team. It would be the first time since 1910 that Ted Nesser would not coach the team. It was definitely the end of an era. Carr then announced that the next league meeting would be June 24–25 in Cleveland.

Eighteen teams arrived at the Hollenden Hotel in Cleveland to discuss the association's business. First up was the short but ground-breaking discussion to change the name of the organization. On a suggestion by George Halas the owners decided to change the name of their "little group" to the National Football League (NFL). "I lacked enthusiasm for our name, the American Professional Football Association. In baseball, 'association' was applied to second-class teams. We were first class. The Chicago Cubs baseball club belonged to the National League, not the American League. 'Professional' was superfluous. I proposed we change our name to the National Football League. My fellow members agreed," Halas recalled in his autobiography.[13]

The "Football" part of the name was true enough, and so was the "League," but "National" it wasn't. With New York and Washington out, the farthest eastern team was Rochester and the farthest southern team was Louisville. Rock Island was the farthest west. Despite the technicality of not truly being "national," the name was a thousand times better than the awkward and lengthy American Professional Football Association.[14]

After officially changing the league's name, Carr awarded franchises to four new teams and eliminated Cleveland when no backer came forward. Youngstown, Ohio, which never actually fielded a team in 1922, Racine (Wisconsin), LaRue (Ohio), and Green Bay (Wisconsin) were admitted to the NFL. Was Green Bay back in the NFL? The heat had lessened a little in the summer for Carr and his league, and most people had forgotten about Taylorville. Plus, nobody knew the determination of Curly Lambeau.

Not long after getting the boot by Carr, Lambeau was thinking about how he could get his team back in the league. He communicated with Carr and other league members about obtaining a franchise that would be in his name. On June 9 he even received a blank franchise application form and letter from league secretary Carl Storck, which also mentioned that the next meeting would be later that month in Cleveland.

When Lambeau heard about the June meeting, he made up his mind that he wanted his team back and went about getting it. The only problem was that he didn't have any money. He would have to pay the $1,000 guarantee plus the $500 franchise fee. Once again Curly had a friend help him out to achieve his goal. Don Murphy knew Lambeau was looking to get Green Bay back in the league and lent him the money. Some historians have written that Murphy sold his car to get Lambeau the money, but that was only coincidental. With the money in his pocket, Lambeau arrived in Cleveland to get his team back. Carr and the other owners voted yes. The NFL franchise was named the Green Bay Football Club with E. L. Lambeau of Green Bay, Wisconsin, as its owner.

While Carr accepted the Packers' application, he would keep an extra eye on Lambeau and his small-town team—so much so that he scheduled a game in Green Bay for his Panhandles to play. Besides Green Bay (population 31,634), the NFL approved another small-town franchise that made the Wisconsin city look like New York City. The town of LaRue, Ohio, had a population of about 800 citizens in the early 1920s, and its entry into professional football was the idea of a man who organized and formed the most colorful team in NFL history.

Walter Lingo was born on October 12, 1890, in tiny LaRue and grew up working in his father's general store, which sold mainly dry goods and groceries. The store would shift locations a couple of times but eventually became a landmark at the corner of High and Vine Streets in LaRue. In the early twenties the town consisted of several grocery stores, four automotive garages, three automobile dealers, a post office, a high school, and eventually, one famous dog business.[15]

"He started the dog business when he was about twelve or thirteen years old. He started on a very small scale with the hounds. Then he had a desire to raise a particular breed of dog, so he came up with the Airedale, the Oorang Airedale, which is different than the Airedale terrier because of his breeding," says Bob Lingo, son of Walter Lingo. "It has a stronger jaw, broader head. It was a more muscular dog. It was designed for hunting, especially big game hunting like bear, mountain lion, and so forth. It was a dog that required a lot of stamina in the field, not so much showmanship. At that time, nobody else was breeding that type of dog. It was a unique breed. He was very careful in the breeding of those dogs. He would only sell the most select dogs. He worked very hard to keep the breed pure."[16]

Lingo's passion for dogs led to him to start his own full-time dog-selling business that he called the Oorang Dog Kennels. Located in Lingo's hometown of LaRue, the kennel was named after his famous new breed of hunting dog and the kennels were anything but a neighborhood dog pound. They were the "Airedale" of pet stores, a mail-order puppy factory that spread over acres of Lingo's land and neighboring towns. He employed over forty workers who made his business and his Oorang dogs a national sensation. A price for his dogs ranged from $25 for a pup to $500 for a full-trained Red Cross, scout, or army dog.[17]

"During the heyday of the kennel, when so many dogs were being shipped, my dad didn't breed the dogs at the kennel. He had a contract with several farmers to help. He didn't believe in raising the dogs in pens like they do today," says Bob Lingo. "He would take them and put them out on a farm. There they would have the pups, and he would select the pups he wanted and bring them back to the kennel for training. Depending on what their mission was going to be, the dogs would be trained for hunting, for show, or whatever."[18]

According to *Oorang Comments*, the company's catalog published by Lingo to sell and advertise his dogs, Lingo sold roughly 15,000 dogs and puppies a year during the company's peak years and sometimes as many as 300 a day. Although Lingo would exaggerate his numbers, one thing was certain: his business was a success. He was also a fairly wealthy man too, especially in the small town of LaRue, where he became somewhat of a local celebrity. The dogs were so popular around the country that "stars" like Ty Cobb, Tris Speaker, Gary Cooper, and Jack Dempsey would come to LaRue to visit Lingo and pick up their Airedale.[19]

Lingo was always promoting his dogs, spending as much as $2,000 a month for advertising in nearly a dozen or more leading magazines, but what he needed was to lure thousands of people at one time into watching his Airedales perform. Enter Jim Thorpe. As Bob Lingo explains,

> My father was not an athlete; he was an outdoorsman. He loved to be outdoors. He loved working with the dogs. I think that was one of the things that joined him with the Indians, the fact that they both loved the outdoor life. They liked working with the animals. He was also a fan of the Wild West shows. That was the start of his idea for halftime shows during the professional football games. He felt people needed something to do at halftime, so he came up with the idea to have halftime shows to help promote the dogs.[20]

Next to Airedales, Lingo loved Indians second best. He had grown up hearing Indian tales—LaRue was the site of an old Wyandotte village—and was convinced that the Indians could teach the dogs things that the best white hunters couldn't. Through his dog kennel, Lingo met Jim Thorpe when he was playing for the Canton Bulldogs years before, and the two became close friends with their mutual love for hunting and animals bringing them together. After the 1921 football season, Thorpe visited Lingo and heard about his new promotional idea.

Lingo suggested that he purchase a franchise in the new professional football league and that Thorpe would run the team—which would be comprised entirely of Indians. They would play as a traveling team and put on shows during pregame and halftimes to help advertise the dogs. Lingo also offered Thorpe (and the Indians) a job training the dogs at $500 dollars a week. Thorpe, who played and coached the 1921 Cleveland Indians to a 3–5 record, was a free agent and agreed to join Lingo's company.

"It was a unique marriage. Lingo wanted to promote his dogs and Dad, in addition to being a great athlete, was a great lover of dogs," said Grace Thorpe, daughter of Jim Thorpe, in a 1995 newspaper interview.[21]

Thorpe put together his team with former players from Carlisle and Haskell Indian schools, including signing future Hall of Fame running back Joe Guyon and fullback-end Pete Calac. The team was now ready to join the NFL, and Lingo would name his team the Oorang Indians. "My father named the team after the dog business, the Oorang Indians. Most people thought he named the team after an Indian tribe but Oorang was the name of his famous dog breed," says Bob Lingo.[22]

Carr probably didn't know what to think of this unusual new franchise, but he could relate. His Panhandles were pretty much a sandlot traveling team comprised of railroad workers who crisscrossed the Midwest to play and put people in the stands. That was what he hoped the Oorang Indians would actually do, especially with the great Jim Thorpe and his name providing the star power to attract fans.

Now that Green Bay and LaRue were admitted, the two-day June meeting in Cleveland continued with Carr and the other owners approving a rule that each NFL team play at least seven league games but no more than thirteen in the final standings; that the president assign the referee for each league game; and that the season start on October 1 and end December 10. Carr also brought up a motion that a new Code of Ethics be put into the bylaws (Article X, Section 1), which carried with no objection. This Code of Ethics was put into the bylaws and was printed in NFL programs.

> Members of this League are expected to conduct themselves as gentlemen and sportsmen. Any flagrant violation of this principle may subject the offending member to suspension or expulsion.
>
> No member shall knowingly make false representations through advertising as to the personnel of his or a competitive team in an effort to deceive the public for his own financial betterment. The confidence of the public is to be desired above all else.
>
> No member shall have a player on his team under an assumed name.
>
> Tampering with players on College teams shall not be tolerated by this League. The same creates much unfavorable public sentiment against professional football and is deplored and discouraged by this League. An adequate supply of football players who have completed their academic status exist and by confining ourselves to these men much favorable public sentiment shall be ours.[23]

Carr was probably looking right at Curly Lambeau and George Halas as he made this statement. He ended the meeting warning Mr. Halas to lay off Paddy Driscoll, who was the property of the Chicago Cardinals, until he received his release. Halas's attempt to sign Driscoll was common knowledge, and Carr wanted to make a point to the league's most influential owner. So much so that this scolding actually made the league minutes and was carried unanimously.[24]

Even though this was only his fifth league meeting, President Joe F. Carr was making it very clear that the shenanigans with professional football owners were going to be a thing of the past, and the bottom line was that the public deserved to know that the NFL was being operated in a first-class manner. The young league was far from a polished product, but it was going to learn from its mistakes and move forward.

On August 20, in Carl Storck's hometown of Dayton, the NFL had their final league meeting—accepting the Toledo (Ohio) Maroons as the newest franchise, managed by Bill Harley, who finally got his own team. The owners passed a resolution that an official's salary shouldn't exceed $35 per game and a team's salary shouldn't exceed $1,200 per game, which would be stretched to the limit by some teams. Harley's Toledo squad fired the first big bullets by signing Chic Harley, Pete Stinchcomb, and Tarzen Taylor away from the Chicago Bears (although none would actually play any games for the Toledo squad). When George Halas was awarded his "new" franchise, his players technically became free agents. Most of them would eventually re-sign with the Bears, so losing the Ohio State trio didn't cause Halas any sleepless nights—but the signing of Guy Chamberlin by the Canton Bulldogs did.[25]

Ralph Hay's team had slumped into the middle of the standings the past two years, and he needed a spark. Everyone knew that Guy was the best player and maybe the best coach in the league, so Hay had his man. "I was paid $7,000 the two years I was at Canton. That was quite remunerative," said Guy Chamberlin in a 1965 Canton radio interview when he was enshrined in the Pro Football Hall of Fame. In the same interview, he gave his opinion on Joe F. Carr. "He had a lot of ability in the executive capacity. He was absolutely honest. You couldn't argue him out of anything but his ideas were always right. Every year he did something to build this league up. Never let anybody tear it down, so the league was very fortunate in having him because everyone was taught to be honest, straightforward and not tamper with the rules. Joe F. Carr should be given quite a little credit in establishing the sounds of our NFL."[26]

Chamberlin began his two-year run in Canton by building a very talented team. He started with tackle Pete "Fats" Henry, who was already on the roster, and he paired him up with another future Hall of Fame tackle, Roy "Link" Lyman. The tandem of Lyman and Henry—along with Duke Osborn, Dutch Speck, and ends Chamberlin and Bird Carroll—gave the Bulldogs the best line in the league. The Canton backfield looked weak at the start of the season but would take advantage of the great line play and become very dominant throughout the 1922 season. Wooky Roberts, Tex Grigg, Lou "the Hammer" Smyth, Harry Robb, and Doc Elliott rotated to give the offense a balance and versatility that would give their opponents big headaches.

After the craziness that happened off the field, Carr's league was now ready to play, and after those two lackluster seasons the Bulldogs would rise to the top of the standings. After five games in October the Bulldogs were 4–0–1 including a big 7–6 win over the Bears in front of 10,000 fans at Cubs Park, which actually made George Halas very happy. "The sight of 10,000 fans in the stands softened the loss," Halas remembered. The Bulldogs defense gave up only 6 points all month. The following week the Bulldogs played a scoreless tie with the Toledo Maroons, leaving the Canton team with a 4–0–2 record, but that would be the last time they were challenged.[27]

On the same day the Bulldogs tied the Maroons, Joe F. Carr traveled with his Panhandles to play the Green Bay Packers and see Curly Lambeau's small-town team in person. The Panhandles brought just one Nesser brother (Frank) and were in the middle of another horrible year with an 0–4 record, but they played a very competitive game on this Sunday. Playing during a steady downpour, the Packers pulled out a 3–0 victory on a thirty-four-yard field goal by Cub Buck. After the game while at the Beaumont Hotel Joe F. Carr had plenty to say to the sportswriters about his first visit to Green Bay.

> Seeing is believing and I take my hat off to Green Bay. I've heard a lot about Green Bay as a football community and to my estimation it has more than lived up to all the nice things which have been said about it. I think it is the greatest football town in the country for its size.
>
> This is sure a great football town. The spirit which at times is sadly missing in post-graduate football is on tap here. It seems to me as if everybody from the urchin on the streets to the gray haired retired business man thinks, eats and sleeps football. I've been in the game twenty years but never in my football career saw a better display of football spirit and community pride than was on tap Sunday afternoon at the ball park. Think of all those people who flocked to the park in the driving rain to see the game. To me it was wonderful.
>
> Your Green Bay town, in my opinion, right now is equal to any club in our organization, it is a credit to your city and is making the 'Bay what you call nationally famous in the football world. Your management has worked harder than some other teams, due to a limited field to draw from but they are going ahead splendidly against much bigger odds than one can imagine and all I can say is to back them to the limit and even farther if necessary because post graduate football in Green Bay is too big a proposition to be passed up.
>
> And I am going to tell all that Green Bay is the best little football city in the country.[28]

It looked like Carr had a school boy "crush" on the city of Green Bay, as he could see the potential the town had with its passionate fan base, despite the limited population. As for the Panhandles the rest of the season would not get any better as they finished the season winless in the NFL with an 0–8 record. As for the Canton Bulldogs, the rest of the season would be a breeze. They won their next five games by outscoring their opponents 84–9 to set up a rematch with the Toledo Maroons. On December 10, Canton (9–0–2 record) and the Maroons (5–1–2) played before 5,000 fans in Toledo. This time the Bulldogs got their revenge for the tie earlier in the season by pounding the Maroons 19–0. The fairly large crowd (between two of the league's best teams) paled in comparison to the Chicago Cardinals–Chicago Bears game played on the same day in the Windy City, as 15,000 fans came out to see Paddy Driscoll kick three field goals to give the Cards a 9–0 win.

Carr was torn seeing these attendance figures—he was happy to see 5,000 fans come out to see the league's best play in a small town like Toledo, but hearing 15,000 spectators in Chicago to see two teams battle for second place put an even bigger smile on his face. But he knew that could only be done in the big cities. Which way to go? Restrict teams to big cities or let small towns play? Carr was definitely pleased with the "clean" ending to the season, and there was no debate as to who was champion. The Bulldogs were now 10–0–2 and kings of the NFL.

As Carr was preparing for the future, he was about to end one chapter of his life. His Columbus Panhandles were wrapping up the season, when he decided that this was to be the last season for his squad. On Thanksgiving Day Carr gave the city of Columbus one last treat as he scheduled a rare home game at Neil Park for the Panhandles to play the Oorang Indians with their star Jim Thorpe. It would be the first time Thorpe would play in the capital city, and Carr made sure everyone, especially the young boys of Columbus, would have a chance to see the legendary athlete. The *Columbus Citizen*'s headline read "Youngsters Get Chance to See Big Game."

> It's not hard to imagine where most of the Columbus youngsters will be after they have done ample justice to the Thanksgiving turkey. They'll be at Neil Park in a body and they'll be there because Joe Carr, who is staging the professional football game between the Panhandles and the Oorang Indians, announced Monday morning that all boys under 12 years of age will be admitted to Thursday's game on the payment of the nominal fee of 25 cents. A section of the bleachers will be reserved for them.
>
> This is the only game of the Professional Football League scheduled for Columbus this season.[29]

Over 3,000 fans came out and witnessed the Indians defeat the Panhandles 18–6. Thorpe's Indians would end the season with a 3–6 league record, but they did attract a few big crowds and provide some good promotion for Lingo's dog kennel. So the experiment seemed to work. After the Indians–Panhandles game, Carr scheduled two more local games for the Panhandles, with the railroaders beating the Columbus Wagner Pirates 13–0 and the West End Athletic Club 9–6.

The Columbus Panhandles had played professional football nearly every year since 1901 (only missing 1905–1906) and had taken part in over 160 games during the sports' rag-tag days. But Carr's Panhandles had just suffered their sixth straight losing year and couldn't compete with the big-time pro teams who had the resources to pay top-flight college stars. So Carr knew it was time to let his team go. It was a great run, but now it was time to turn his full attention to building the NFL.

With the league's strongest lineup and the championship won, Canton couldn't keep its payroll below the $1,200 per game limit. Whether Ralph Hay planned to sacrifice his own money for the honor of his city or really expected to pay the bills out of the gate receipts, the simple fact was the Bulldogs were winners on the field but losers off. Despite the big crowd in Chicago and a nice crowd in Milwaukee, the Bulldogs just couldn't get the crowds to pay the bills. Although Lakeside Park in Canton had plenty of enthusiastic fans, they just didn't have enough of them. Only 3,000 came out for the games against Dayton and Louisville, and 2,500 for the Chicago Cardinals contest. Once again, Hay's Bulldogs lost money. Would the Bulldogs be back in the league in 1923?

Right before spending Christmas at home with his wife and family, Carr wrote a press release recapping the 1922 season that appeared in newspapers around the country, including his hometown *Ohio State Journal.*

> Canton Bulldogs Undisputed Champs of Professional Loop: League Has Wonderful Season, According to President Joe Carr—400,000 See Games

> The Canton Bull Dogs, managed by Ralph Hay and coached by Guy Chamberlin, former Nebraska star, won the undisputed championship of the National Professional Football League, whose 75 games this fall were watched by more than 400,000 spectators, Joe Carr, president of the league, announced yesterday.
>
> The two Chicago teams, the Bears and Cardinals, finished in second and third places, each of them dropping three games, while the Bull Dogs were going through the season with-out a loss of a single battle, although they were twice tied, once by Toledo and once by Dayton.
>
> Until the middle of November Toledo, which finished in fourth place, was an undefeated eleven. Then the Maroons were trimmed by both Canton and the Chicago Bears.

Dayton Surprised

While for the most part scores were small, and all of the teams showed defensive ability, there were occasional upsets. Probably the most notable one of the entire season was the 42 to 0 defeat handed the strong Dayton eleven by Rock Island. That defeat prevented Dayton from finishing in a tie with Toledo for fourth place.

It was the third season for the professional league. President Carr said play was notably clean. Only seven men were disciplined in the 75 games, he said.

According to Carr, there were no infractions of the rule adopted prior to the start of the season, which prevented each club from making any offers or playing any men who were still eligible for college play.

The innovation this year of the appointment of all officials by the league president proved to be a marked success, Carr declared. Competent officials were obtained for all of the games and the usual bickerings between rival clubs as to the officials was lacking, Carr points out. The annual meeting of the league will be held in Chicago in January.[30]

According to newspaper accounts, attendance was more around 180,000, but that was for thirty-six of the sixty-six APFA games since most papers didn't always list actual attendance. In the end, the league had a new name—the National Football League—that would endure and gain in stature in 1922, but the league itself was far from a success. Despite the presence of the league's first great team, the money situation made pro football still a very shaky affair. But with no team to operate, Carr now had all the time in the world to think about the future of his eighteen-team loop, and he would pull out his boxing gloves because it was time to fight.

11

Defending Professional Football (1923)

During the 1922 season, the Green Bay Packers saw themselves suffering major financial losses, and the rest of the season looked to be in jeopardy of not being played. They were only averaging about 2,000 fans at home and bad weather was contributing to the small crowds. Curly Lambeau wasn't a great businessman and saw the team slipping away from him. The team was in debt for $5,400, and when playing the remaining teams on the 1922 schedule, they needed $1,500 for the guarantee and franchise fee and another $1,200 to place a Green Bay team on the field; other expenses included traveling, printing tickets, security, and paying the officials. In total, they needed to take in approximately $3,600 to make ends meet.[1]

George Calhoun and Lambeau even sought out the advice of Joe F. Carr when he visited Green Bay for the Packers–Panhandles game. He wrote a letter telling them,

> You have only one way out. Increase the admission prices. Your field here is limited. At the outset, you probably can't get over 3,500 in your park. Other cities in the league, remember Green Bay is the smallest, are drawing from 8,000 to 15,000 crowds every Sunday and what's more, with but three exceptions, their admission prices are higher than at Green Bay. It is an unfortunate situation here because I consider Green Bay the best 'little' football city in the country. However, I feel confident that if the matter is put before the public in a true light, the fans will rally at the club's support just as loyal as they did on Sunday when some 1,500 braved a driving rain storm to see their team meet my club. It isn't fair that a handful should be called on to carry the financial load for all. Play fair with your fans and they will meet you square.[2]

The Packers were charging $1.65 and $1.10 for tickets with mostly the $1.10 ticket being sold, so if the Packers attracted only 2,000 fans, they would always come up short in paying expenses. Joe F. Carr recognized this bad business sense and so did Andy Turnbull, the business manager of the *Green Bay Press-Gazette*. Neither Lambeau or Calhoun were businessmen, and Turnbull wanted to help them, because he knew the Packers team was good for the city. He also knew that Lambeau and Calhoun were the heart and soul of the team. He asked a few friends for advice on how to save the Packers.[3]

So Turnbull meet with three of his closest friends—Leland H. Joannes, a very successful wholesale grocer; W. Weber Kelly, a doctor; and Gerald F. Clifford, a local attorney. They all agreed that professional football in Green Bay was a good thing, and it should be preserved. Turnbull asked Calhoun to write an article about a town meeting on saving the Packers. Approximately 150 businessman and boosters showed up on December 7, 1922, at the Elks Club in the city; plans were made to sell stock; and the Green Bay Football Corporation was set up.

Pledges were taken for five dollars a share and eventually a fifteen-man board of directors was established with a five-man executive committee heading the team. The "Hungry Five," as they were named by Milwaukee sportswriter Oliver Kuechle, was composed of Lambeau, Turnbull, Joannes, Kelly, and Clifford. Nobody (not even Kuechle) revealed how the term *Hungry Five* came about, nor what it meant exactly. There is no doubt, however, that the group was "hungry" to make the Packers a success, and these five men saw that Green Bay kept their team in the NFL through the leanest years. The Packers would now have the solid financial backing to survive, although the road would always be bumpy for the small-town franchise.[4]

As the 1922 calendar flipped over to 1923, most NFL teams were still losing money. One of the owners not in debt was George Halas, who in his autobiography revealed that the 1922 Chicago Bears actually made a profit of $1,476.92. He also said that he was "offered $35,000 for our franchise. We turned it down."[5] But Halas was the exception. Nonetheless, Joe F. Carr had a personal crisis to handle before he could turn his attention to the financial state of the NFL.

John S. Sullivan, Josephine's father, began to have health issues that limited his time working at the railroad, and his wife, Mary, had a tough time taking care of him by herself. So Joe and Josephine and the two Carr children moved out of their home on East Long Street and into the Sullivan house at 39 North 22nd Street. Carr made sure that Josie could help her mother take care of her father. "They were a very close-knit family and Josie had a pretty good relationship with her mother," says Martha Sullivan, niece of Joe F. Carr. "They had their ups and downs, just like any other family, but they were very close like your typical Irish family."[6]

The Sullivan's two-story brick house was located just at the edge of the Irish neighborhood and became a place for the Carrs to enjoy the company of the entire Sullivan family. "My father Frank would take us over there often to see grandma Sullivan and it was a wonderful place to visit. In the summer we'd always be on the porch. The porch had a swing and when the adults were on the porch we'd be on the front yard playing," says Sullivan. Despite the circumstances, Carr felt this was the right move for his family and it made Josie very happy.[7]

Carr announced that on January 20, the NFL would have its annual winter meeting in Chicago. Sixteen teams—with Carr representing the Canton Bulldogs and not his Panhandles—met in the afternoon on that day at the Sherman House. The first order of business was to award the 1922 NFL championship to the unbeaten Canton Bulldogs. The league also awarded the Bulldog players eighteen gold footballs and a championship pennant. George Halas made a motion to incorporate in the bylaws that the gold footballs be awarded each season to the champion, and it was carried. Then Carl Storck brought up a motion that NFL teams should allow that children under twelve be charged twenty-five cents to games. The motion failed, but they compromised by charging children under sixteen an admission of fifty cents.[8]

The owners then discussed and approved that the president form a committee on how the colors of uniforms and socks be improved. There was much confusion among the teams that would wear the same color jerseys, so Carr named Dutch Sternaman (Chicago Bears), John Dunn (Minneapolis Marines), and chairman Babe Reutz (Racine) to come up with a way to identify teams better, something that probably was long overdue.

The meeting ended with the owners approving the updated "Constitution and Bylaws," and adding that each club must play at least seven league games against seven different clubs. This figured to help the weaker teams, ones that seldom played more than a few games against league opponents, by forcing major teams like the Bears to schedule a few more games against the small fries and helping the weaker teams with one or more quality gates. Carr ended the meeting at 10:00 p.m.[9]

When Carr returned from Chicago he announced to the press that he would surrender management of the Columbus Panhandles and devote his time to administering the affairs of the league. He also said he would probably be drawing a regular salary to be the chief of the organization, although he never mentioned what that salary might be. The Panhandles were now gone, but Carr kept the city of Columbus in the NFL by setting up another franchise to be owned by a group of local businessman led by team president Mike O'Rourke and managed by his good friend Jerry Corcoran. The Columbus Tigers would join the NFL in the fall of 1923.

After sixteen years as Panhandles manager, Carr was now ready to leave his team behind and move forward to guide the NFL. But Carr wasn't the only manager leaving professional football. As the summer began, Ralph Hay, who had owned the Canton Bulldogs since 1919, wanted out of the pro football business. He was losing too much money, and his asking price for the NFL's best team was $1,500, which after a great deal of wrangling among several Canton businessmen, was about $500 more than they wanted to pay. Things were still up in the air when Hay and Guy Chamberlin left Canton for Chicago to attend the NFL's summer meeting.[10]

Carr knew there was a possibility that Canton might not play in 1923, so he investigated the other applications for new franchises. It looked like they were going to accept franchises in Duluth (Minnesota) and St. Louis, but it was the city of Cleveland he wanted the most. While visiting the city, Carr spoke to the local media of the potential of a new Cleveland team in the NFL.

> I feel pretty sure that the pro grid game will be revived in Cleveland this coming fall, though we have no idea who will get the franchise. This is too good a sport city to go without pro football and besides it's right in the heart of the region where pro football has its strongest hold on popular favor.
>
> But you can rest assured of one thing, that the national pro football league will not grant the Cleveland franchise until it is given plenty of assurance that those who get that franchise will put the game on a sound footing here. There will be no experimenting next time and Cleveland will be given a real team that will be right up among the contenders. We all want Cleveland in the league and that makes it pretty certain Cleveland will be in.
>
> Several parties have taken up with me the situation here and we'll be ready to talk turkey after we thrash the matter out in our coming national annual meeting.[11]

The summer meeting was held over two days, July 28–29, at the Hotel Sherman in Chicago, and the main topic was money—getting it and saving it. In addition to the guarantee fee, new franchises that applied for a spot in the league had to pay a $500 application fee, just extra money for the league's bank account. St. Louis, Duluth, and the new Cleveland franchise were admitted. Also, teams had to pay $140 to cover the salaries of the NFL president and secretary, to be paid in quarterly installments. This fee was part of a motion by George Halas that would set the president's salary at $1,000 per year and the salary of the secretary at $750. Cardinals' owner Chris O'Brien amended the motion that the salary for each be $1,000 per year. The motion carried.[12]

Then the owners declared nominations for the league's executive positions. Carr was once again elected president unanimously, with Dunn (vice president) and Storck (secretary-treasurer) also reelected. This was the first time in the NFL's league minutes that Carr was given a set salary, and showing he had no ego about his salary, he was willing to accept the same yearly contract as the secretary. It was league first for President Carr.

To end the meeting the owners set the start of the upcoming season for September 30 (but forgot to establish an ending date) and held a lengthy discussion on splitting the gate. Visiting teams were given 40 percent of the gross receipts, minus 15 percent for park rental. The max guarantee to be paid to the visitors for games not played or poorly attended was set at $1,200 plus $100 for traveling and hotel expenses, so long as a team's salaries came to $1,200. This would be the league's attempt to keep each team's salaries down and hopefully to save some money.[13]

Before leaving town Carr met with the press to go over the just-ended proceedings, and his regular statement about use of college players took on a different form—not a single complaint about the practice occurred in 1922.

> We have no desire to interfere with college players who cannot play on our teams then go back to their organizations. As it is more than 90 per cent of the college football stars who graduated in 1923 are signed by professional clubs for the coming year. In addition to the forfeit money posted against the securing of amateur players, I have the word of each of the twenty presidents of clubs in the league, who attended today's meeting, that they will not try to steal college players from their college allegiance. It is true that in the past much of this sort of thing has happened, but it has been such a blow to amateur football that we have no desire to continue.[14]

Carr couldn't have made a more forceful stance on the use of college players in his league, but this didn't ease the tension between the NFL and college football officials. The issue would soon be thrown back into Carr's lap, and he was ready to defend his league. While Carr returned to Columbus pleased with the summer meeting, Ralph Hay went back to Canton with the Bulldogs still in the NFL and ready to talk price. He eventually unloaded his franchise to a group of local investors who formed the Canton Athletic Company (CAC). The CAC listed eighteen stockholders, including H. H. Timken (owner of Timken Bearing), Guy C. Hiner (Canton Bridge Company), and Ed E. Bender (owner of Bender's restaurant). Guy Chamberlin's coaching ensured the team's success on the field but not off it.

In four years as owner, Hay brought two national titles (1919, 1922) to Canton, helped organize the NFL, gained a lot of publicity for his Hupmobile business, and lost a ton of money. Four years doesn't sound like a long time, but Ralph Hay, just like his predecessor Jack Cusack, made a vital contribution to the growth of professional football and in turn the NFL. Before he left the scene, Hay got in a few last words of thanks to the city of Canton.[15]

> The height of my ambition in the five years (1919–1923) that I handled the Canton Bulldogs Pro. Football Team was accomplished by winning the 1922 World's Championship.
>
> The assistance of my organization, the loyal support of the Canton fans and the wonderful harmony that Coach Chamberlin brought in to the heart of every player who was with this team in 1922 was the fundamental reason for our success.
>
> I, therefore, wish every member of the new organization worlds of success and trust that in 1923 they will retain the World's Championship Pennant of the National Football League. I am,
> Ralph E. Hay[16]

The 1923 season (with twenty NFL teams) would be a very eventful one, except for the championship race, as the Bulldogs would cement their spot as the NFL's first great team. As the season approached, on Thursday, September 27, Joe F. Carr took a short train trip north of Columbus to LaRue to visit Walter Lingo and check in on the Oorang Indians. Talking with Lingo he told the dog kennel king "that the club looked 100 percent better than it did last year." Carr witnessed the Indians practice on what was just an open field, since the small town didn't have a full-length football field.[17]

At times the Indians held their practice on the small field at the same time as the high school team, an experience that former LaRue High School player William Guthery remembered. "We didn't really know how to handle the ball or how to catch it. They showed us what to do. The Indians showed us how to tackle, how to straight arm, how to pass and kick. I think the Indians kind of enjoyed helping us out."[18] Carr enjoyed his visit but was probably still a little unsure that the Indians would go beyond one more year of play. His prediction that the squad looked 100 percent better was way off base, as Jim Thorpe's Indians lost their first ten games (scoring only thirty-one points), before winning the season finale against the equally terrible Louisville Brecks. The Brecks played only three league games and were outscored 83–0.

Three days after visiting Lingo's Indians, Carr accompanied the Columbus Tigers on their road trip to Dayton to face Carl Storck's Triangles. As the first full weekend of play began (with eight games), Carr was part of a crowd of 5,000 spectators who saw the hometown team pull out a hard-fought 7–6 victory. Upon returning to Columbus Carr wrote in his

Gridiron Gossip column that he "was congratulated repeatedly by well known sportsmen over the intensity that players of both teams put into their efforts. It's a fact that there's spirit spread all over the big organization."[19]

Carr was very pleased with the start of the new season and worked hard getting the news of the league out in his weekly column that appeared every Friday in the *Ohio State Journal*, as well as in other newspapers. Carr's colorful and expert reporting would give the reader an insight into the league that only a true "insider" could give. He would list the standings and the schedule of games for that Sunday and then usually write three columns about the players in his league that were doing well or poorly, the players who had injuries, the upcoming matchups, and almost anything to do with the NFL.

> *October 19*—Eyes of the Pro. Football world will center on Cubs' park, Chicago, Sunday, where the Bears and Canton Bulldogs will have it out. Odds favor the Bulldogs as the Bears are not up to snuff behind the line.
>
> Duke Slater, big colored star, who gained fame at Iowa, is in tip-top shape and he is playing his usual aggressive game when on the defense.
>
> *October 26*—[Curly] Lambeau, the Green Bay captain, is continuing his brilliant performances as a forward pass hurler. The air attack is the Packers' best stock in trade due to Lambeau's ability to shoot the pigskin like a bullet.
>
> *November 2*—[Link] Lyman, the husky Canton tackle, made himself solid with the Bulldog followers when he grabbed a pass in the closing minutes of the Akron game, scoring the touchdown that pulled the argument out of the fire.[20]

As the NFL season moved into November, the Canton Bulldogs continued their dominance over the rest of the league. Guy Chamberlin's boys put on a weekly clinic, going unbeaten at 6–0–1 after their first seven games and outscoring their opponents 107–9, not allowing a single touchdown. This was a special team. But just when Carr thought he could relax and enjoy the end of the season, an old foe resurfaced and threw a punch right into the face of the NFL's president.

Amos Alonzo Stagg, the sixty-one-year-old head coach and athletic director at the University of Chicago, was in the midst of a season where his Maroons would finish with a 7–1 record while playing in the Western Conference. Stagg, who never cared for professional football and was one of the most vocal college football officials expressing his distaste for the postgraduate game, once again tried to bury the sport. In a letter sent to college coaches and athletic directors, Stagg wrote about how "professional football is a menace and I urge you to refrain from in any manner encouraging the professional sport." The Associated Press released the letter on November 1, and almost every newspaper in the country ran an excerpt from it, usually accompanied with a bold headline of "Pro Football is a Menace."

> It seems like a matter of little consequence for one to attend the Sunday professional football games—nothing more than attending any Sunday event—but it has a deeper meaning than you realize, possibly a vital meaning to college football. Intercollegiate football will live only so long as it contributes to the well being of the students, that is, while the influences of the game are predominantly on the side of amateur principles, right ideals, proper standards and wholesome conditions.
>
> For years the colleges have been waging a bitter warfare against the insidious forces of the gambling public and alumni and against overzealous and short-sighted friends, inside and out, and also not infrequently against crooked coaches and managers who have been anxious to win at any cost, and victory has not been completely won. And now along comes another serious menace, possibly greater than all others, viz, Sunday professional football.
>
> Under the guise of fair play but countenancing rank dishonesty in playing men under assumed names, scores of professional teams have sprung up within the last two or three years, most of them on a salary basis of some kind. These teams are bidding hard for college players in order to capitalize not only on their ability, but also, and mostly, upon the name of the college they come from and in many cases the noised abroad, mystery of their presence. The well-known Carlinville and Taylorville incident of 1921 is likely to be repeated in essence on different occasions. There is nothing that a bunch of gamblers will not do for their purpose and quite often they carry along with them the support of a thoughtless group of business men and well-meaning citizens.
>
> The schools and colleges are struggling to combat the various evils connected with football which when played with the amateur spirit possesses more elements for the development of character and manhood than any other sport I know of.
>
> To co-operate with Sunday professional football games is to co-operate with forces which are destructive of the finest elements of interscholastic and intercollegiate football and to add to the heavy burden of the schools and colleges in preserving it in its ennobling worth. If you believe in preserving interscholastic and intercollegiate football for the upbuilding of the present and future generations of clean, healthy, right-minded and patriotic citizens, you will not lend your assistance to any of the forces which are helping to destroy it.[21]

Stagg's letter brought up on old issue that Carr thought was well under control, especially after the Carlinville-Taylorville incident. Calling the pro game a "menace" and portraying the players of the NFL as unclean, unhealthy, and unpatriotic was so grossly overstated that Carr took immediate action and responded with a punch of his own. Writing with the passion he had in his heart for the sport and the league he was in charge of, he wrote a nine-paragraph press release that rebutted Stagg's comments.

> Speaking for the National Football League, I think that a glance at the personnel of the ownership of the various teams will convince any person that leading men in the various communities, which support the teams, would not lend themselves to any of the things outlined in this overview. In most cases they are prominent business and professional men of their cities and all are either [established] football players or alumni of [pledges] that support teams.
>
> Increasing attendance of thousands each Sunday also indicates the—ace that the professional game is—king. It is a matter of common knowledge that the National Football League has done more in its few years of existence to purify football generally and make young men walk the straight and narrow path in regard to amateur status than any other agency that has ever tried it.
>
> Fear that attendance at professional football will be a menace to the development of college football is entirely without foundation, as with the increased numbers attending professional football each week, new followers for the game are developed, with the result that today, with the professional game at its best, colleges are unable to have enclosures that will take care of the crowds. This increase is more notable in the Middle West where the professional game flourishes.
>
> Another fact that points to the mistaken idea that professional football is a menace is the fact that many of the highest class and most successful college coaches in the country at some time or another have been associated with the professional game.
>
> Regarding players using assumed names and the participation of a certain Western Conference official under an alias, detection will mean banishment from the National Football League, as our organization will not countenance a thing that savors of deceit in any way.
>
> Inspection of the constitution and bylaws of the National Football League will convince any open-minded person that there is really no menace to the future of the college elevens, but rather a great help in the provision that any player who violates his college status is forever barred from playing with any club in this organization.
>
> If space permitted, statements by innumerable former college stars, who are playing to pay off debts contracted while going to college, and others who are using this means to help members of their families in securing educations, would discredit much of the unnecessary criticism that is aimed at the professional game.

> It is hardly fair to cast suspicion on the many creditable men who are backing teams as well as the attempt to discredit the many former college stars of the gridiron, as the pick and flower of the players of the past few years are to be found in the lineups of the various teams now playing post-graduate football.
>
> It is gratifying to know that the view is not shared by all college men, for there are many who feel that the post-graduate or professional game, when properly conducted is an asset rather than a menace to the college branch of the sport.[22]

Carr's statement was precise and effective. He knew he had to respond quickly because the public, the press, and the college football community would be wanting to hear the NFL's response to Stagg's words. Carr was up to the challenge; he did not back down from what he and the NFL were trying to accomplish the past couple of years with their rules and regulations—especially stamping out the practice of using college players. His press release also reinforced to George Halas and the other team owners that Carr was the right man for the job and that he would fight for the honor and integrity of the league.

Because of Stagg's comments, the sport of football at all levels became more aware of the practice of using college players in professional games. Even a young sophomore from the University of Illinois, who was making a name for himself, was answering questions about playing professional football. Harold "Red" Grange was having a great fall season that would lead him to being named on Walter Camp's All-American team. He responded to the question about allegedly playing for the Green Bay Packers: "I don't even know where Green Bay is. I never played football anywhere but at Wheaton, Ill. High School and Illinois."[23]

Carr's sports-writing experience also shined through in a big way by calming the storm that followed Stagg's comments. He also followed his philosophy that the public and all football fans deserved to know that the NFL and professional football were operating honestly and fairly. In early December as the NFL season was winding down, Carr's Gridiron Gossip revealed that he was definitely looking toward the future as well as seeing the great Canton Bulldogs go for back-to-back NFL titles.

> *December 7*—Columbus [Tigers] will attempt to put a crimp in the Canton Bulldogs' string of wins in Sunday's game. The Columbus club is playing at top form these days and Chamberlin's aggregation is a mighty tough nut to crack.
>
> With the close of the season at hand the Pro League magnates are beginning to look forward to another year. Some of the clubs had bad breaks financially but none of the teams are thinking of giving up the ghost.[24]

Off the field, Carr's honesty, leadership, and optimism were revealed to the public and the owners of the NFL, while on the field nobody could touch the Canton Bulldogs. The great team from Stark County finished the season at 11–0–1 by winning their last five games. The Bulldogs' defense allowed only nineteen points all season and just *one* touchdown—against the Cleveland Indians on November 25. The Bulldogs and the city of Canton could now celebrate back-to-back NFL championships.

Aesthetically the Bulldogs were purebreds, but financially they were once again mutts. The Bulldogs' home attendance was just comparable to smaller cities with less talent. Canton showed in 1920 and 1921 that they wouldn't support an ordinary team. In 1923 they showed they wouldn't support a great one. The Bulldogs were a fine draw on the road—attracting nice crowds in Chicago (6,000 versus the Cardinals), Buffalo (10,000), and a whopping 17,000 fans at League Park in Cleveland—and were always welcomed at rival parks. But few of the important NFL teams (Bears, Cardinals, Packers) would want to travel to Canton for a game where the best they could hope for was the minimum guaranteed percentage of gate sales. Canton was looking at another difficult off-season.[25]

The other Ohio League teams weren't doing much better than Canton. Massillon had been gone since 1919, and after the 1923 season so were Toledo, Cincinnati, and the colorful but poorly coached Oorang Indians; hanging on were Akron, Canton, and Columbus. The only two franchises that looked somewhat strong were Dayton (because of Carl Storck's involvement as NFL secretary-treasurer) and the Cleveland Indians operated by Sam Deutsch. The Indians had showed they could draw fans, but they were boring and not very strong. That would change for the 1924 season.[26]

Now that the season was over the *Green Bay Press-Gazette* published an All-Pro team, encouraged by George Calhoun, selected by a poll of sportswriters from fifteen NFL cities around the league. The poll would become an annual event that eventually led to the NFL making an "official" All-League team. The first team included the following:

End—Inky Williams, Hammond
Tackle—Ed Healey, Chicago Bears
Guard—Bub Weller, St. Louis
Center—Harry Mehre, Minneapolis
Guard—Swede Youngstrom, Buffalo
Tackle—Pete "Fats" Henry, Canton
End—Gus Tebell, Columbus
Quarterback—Paddy Driscoll, Chicago Cardinals
Halfback—Jim Thorpe, Oorang
Halfback—Al Michaels, Akron
Fullback—Doc Elliott, Canton[27]

Of course, Canton dominated the first team with two choices, but the big surprise was that Guy Chamberlin didn't make the first team (placing on the second), though winning the NFL title probably softened his disappointment. Also making the first team was Jay "Inky" Williams, one of the early black players, who was one of at least six black players in the NFL in 1923. Joe F. Carr was happy to see that the NFL was still standing and operating at the end of the season despite all the negative publicity heaved on his delicate league. But one thing was sure, Carr was a fighter, and he wasn't afraid to mix it up with the big boys.

12

Baby Steps for President Carr (1924)

Carr began his fourth year as president with another trip to Chicago for the annual winter meeting. On January 26–27 the league's magnates gathered at the Hotel Sherman to further establish the NFL. Eighteen of the twenty teams showed up, with representatives from Duluth and St. Louis not able to attend. After Carr began the first day of the meeting, at precisely 4:00 p.m., a very interesting proposal was brought up. The owners voted the president to appoint a committee of five members to draw up a plan to divide the league into two geographical divisions and adopting a schedule based on the divisions.[1]

This was the first time the idea of splitting the league into divisions—similar to major league baseball's National and American leagues—had come up. The motion carried unanimously, and Carr nominated Lester Higgins (Canton Bulldogs), Andy Turnbull (Green Bay), Chris O'Brien (Chicago Cardinals), Mike O'Rourke (Columbus), and chairman Babe Ruetz (Racine). The committee would talk the rest of the night to see what they could come up with.

Then the owners awarded the 1923 NFL championship to the Canton Bulldogs and once again the title-winning team was awarded gold footballs and a championship pennant. The first day's proceedings ended with the election of the NFL's officials and to no one's surprise Joe Carr (president), John Dunn (vice president), and Carl Storck (secetary-treasurer) were all reelected.[2]

The following day Carr accepted the application for a new franchise from Kansas City (Missouri) and passed a resolution that the referee would be paid thirty-five dollars a game and traveling expenses. Also carried was that the umpire and head linesman are to be agreed upon by the two teams (assigned at least four days in advance), that the visiting club chooses the head linesman, and that each is to be paid no more than twenty-five dollars per game.[3]

Lastly the topic of scheduling with the two-division setup came back up, and after much discussion, complaining, and rewording, nothing was approved. Each club was to submit to Carr a seven-game schedule by June 1 that would be ratified at the July meeting. A nine-game schedule was to be drafted with at least the first five games to be divisional games. In the end, when all of the owners returned home, the idea of having two divisions died. Its time would come a decade later.

Six months later Carr and the owners returned to the Hotel Sherman in Chicago to put the finishing touches on the upcoming season, which meant approving new franchises and completing the schedule. Meeting on July 25–26, Carr and the owners first established the NFL season by agreeing to start the year on September 28 and finish on November 30. Ignored was the fact that teams usually contended and scheduled games into December. Then Carr accepted the applications of the Kansas City (Missouri) Cowboys and a new Philadelphia team. With the removal of the Toledo, LaRue, St. Louis, and Louisville franchises, the NFL in 1924 would have eighteen teams.[4]

At the end of the meeting the owners finalized the schedules that each team did on their own and voted on increasing the player limit from sixteen to eighteen, allowing teams some flexibility in case injuries happened during the season. After wrapping up the two-day meeting, President Carr was exhausted but noticed that the league was continuing to take baby steps to gain the stability it needed to succeed. His eighteen-team loop had gone through some changes, and two franchises (one new and one old) would make things very interesting for the upcoming season.[5]

The newest member of the NFL was the Frankford Yellow Jackets. Frankford was a suburb northeast of Philadelphia and had built a worthy reputation as the strongest team in the city—succeeding Leo Conway's Philadelphia Quakers. The Yellow Jackets were founded in 1899 by the Frankford Athletic Association (FAA), a nonprofit organization composed of sports lovers of the community who paid annual dues to belong. The president of the FAA was H. S. "Shep" Royle, a former tackle for the Yellow Jackets, who was also the president of a large textile mill and a state representative and would do anything to build a successful squad. Being in a fairly big market got Carr very excited despite the fact the Yellow Jackets couldn't play on Sundays.

Pennsylvania Blue Laws forbade football on Sundays, necessitating Saturday games for the Yellow Jackets. Very quickly they fell into a pattern of playing home on Saturday, then jumping a train to play somewhere else on Sunday. As a consequence, in some years, they would play twice as many games as some of the other NFL teams. Lesser teams would have crumbled, but from the start the Yellow Jackets were one of the league's best teams. Better yet, for Carr, Frankford drew big crowds as the FAA had just built a new stadium that cost roughly $100,000 and would seat about 15,000 fans. The Yellow Jackets would be that big-city team Joe F. Carr was now leaning toward. Having the Yellow Jackets in the league also gave the western teams someplace to go east where they could make some money.[6]

The other franchise that would make a big move was the NFL's two-time champions the Canton Bulldogs. Once again the Bulldogs were a financial disaster. High salaries, traveling expenses, and low attendance combined to put the team in red ink. On August 24 the *Canton Repository* reported the news that due to staggering losses of approximately $13,000, the team would be sold to Sam Deutsch.[7]

Deutsch was a sports promoter from Cleveland who was involved in both minor league baseball and boxing in the city, but he really wanted to have a big-time pro football team. He took over the Cleveland franchise vacated the previous year by Jimmy O'Donnell and named his team the Cleveland Indians, matching the baseball squad. His team went 3–1–3, and its only loss was a 46–10 blowout to the Bulldogs, giving Deutsch a front-row seat to watch Guy Chamberlin's powerful team. So seeing the Canton team in financial distress, he made an offer of $2,500 to buy the team that was essentially the old Canton Bulldogs team with a few exceptions. So after nearly two decades of sitting on top of the pro football world, the city of Canton and the Canton Bulldogs would not field a professional team in 1924. The game was definitely changing, and Carr could see the day that the small towns (that started and nurtured the game) would eventually fade. But when that would finally happen he didn't know.

As the Cleveland Bulldogs situation resolved itself, the 1924 season started on the weekend of September 28. Carr continued to write his Gridiron Gossip column, and his positive and truthful writing was never sharper.

> *October 4*—"One of the big games, Sunday, will be the tilt between the Chicago Bears and Cleveland. The Windy City combination will have to step on the gas. Guy Chamberlin's lineup looks mighty powerful.
>
> Green Bay is booked to invade Chicago for a fracas with the Cardinals. Quite a kicking duel should be on tap when these clubs clash as Paddy Driscoll and Cub Buck are past masters at booting the pigskin.[8]

The gossip gave the league some constant publicity and was a great example of Carr using the press/media to help get his league some exposure that would put people in the stands. They were the first "unofficial" press releases sent out by the NFL office, an example of blogging or putting up short stories on the Web for the 1920s. In the second week of October, Joe F. Carr planned a trip with the officials of the Columbus Tigers to check out two eastern teams. Traveling with team president Mike O'Rourke and team manager and friend Jerry Corcoran, Carr planned to watch the Tigers play the Frankford Yellow Jackets on Saturday, October 18, and then accompany the team to see the Tigers play the following day against the Providence Steam Roller, a nonleague team. He heard good things about the Steam Roller and wanted to see if it could be a potential NFL team. The Steam Roller was another one of those teams that played in a bigger market and would expand the NFL's population circle.[9]

In Frankford Carr saw the Tigers lose 23–7 to the talented Yellow Jackets in front of a large crowd of 10,000 spectators, a number that impressed Carr very much. The following day Carr saw 7,000 fans show up for the Columbus–Providence game, and Carr was once again impressed by the fairly large crowd. He definitely thought Providence had the potential to be a good NFL town, and its proximity to Boston (forty miles) would help attract some new fans.[10]

As the NFL was settling into the teeth of its season, the biggest news coming out of the football world was about the exploits of Harold "Red" Grange, the junior halfback for the University of Illinois. In a game against the University of Michigan on October 18, Grange made sports history. In a matchup of the two best teams in the country, Grange returned the opening kickoff ninety-five yards for a touchdown. Then he ran sixty-seven, fifty-six, and forty-four yards for three more touchdowns—all in the first twelve minutes of the game. Tired, Grange sat out the second quarter. He came back to run eleven yards for a fifth touchdown and passed twenty yards for a sixth, as Illinois won 39–14 to end Michigan's twenty-game unbeaten streak. He totaled an amazing 402 total yards and became a national hero. The national press would follow his every move, and the owners of the NFL started to line up for his talent.

Joe F. Carr would also take notice of the best football player in the country. He knew Grange could help his league as fans wanted to watch the redhead perform. But Grange was only a junior, so Carr and the rest of the NFL would have to wait. On November 9 the Columbus Tigers traveled west to play the Chicago Bears. During the Bears' 12–6 win, the 10,000 fans at Cubs Park saw a strange play that caught the whole crowd by surprise. While on offense, the Tigers fumbled and Bears fullback Oscar Knop picked up the loose ball, got mixed up, and started running toward his own goal line. After rumbling thirty-five yards, Knop was brought down at his own five yard line by his teammate Joey Sternaman. The big crowd got a laugh, but George Halas didn't. His Bears were right in the middle of trying to win another NFL championship.[11]

The Bears might have been running the wrong way, but Carr was hoping his sport was heading in the right direction and taking the necessary baby steps forward. One team that was running the right way was the Cleveland Bulldogs. To start the season the Bulldogs defeated the Chicago Bears in a close contest (16–14) and suffered a tie against the Frankford Yellow Jackets. But after that, the Bulldogs won four straight games and found themselves at the top of the standings heading into the final weeks of the season.

After getting off to a slow start (losing to Dayton, tying Cleveland, and losing to the Bears by the lopsided margin of 33–3), the Frankford Yellow Jackets then turned it on by winning their last eight games. The most shocking victory was on November 16 when they handed the Cleveland Bulldogs their first defeat of the season, 12–7. This game gave Guy Chamberlin his first loss as a head coach. He was unbeaten at 26–0–4 in his first thirty games as head coach of the Canton-Cleveland Bulldogs. Nobody has ever matched Chamberlin's start, and it's probable that nobody will.

Although the Yellow Jackets would not win the championship, finishing with an 11–2–1 record, they were winners at the box office. In their ten home matchups (nine games were played on Saturday and one Thanksgiving Thursday), the Yellow Jackets averaged close to 7,500 fans per game.

September 29—Rochester (7,000)
October 4—Kenosha (7,000)
October 11—Cleveland (not available)
October 18—Columbus (10,000)
November 1—Akron (6,000)
November 8—Kansas City (10,000)
November 15—Minneapolis (8,000)
November 22—Milwaukee (5,000)
November 27—Dayton (15,000)
November 29—Buffalo (7,000)
ten home games (averaging 7,500)[12]

The Bulldogs rebounded with two straight wins to finish with a 7–1–1 record on November 30—the supposed ending date of the season. At the same time, the Bears were 6–1–4. The NFL didn't count ties, so the Bulldogs had a better winning percentage than the Bears at .875 to .857. Had everyone stopped playing on November 30, the Bulldogs' championship would have been cut-and-dry. Moreover, the general public was still not at all clear on how the NFL champion was to be chosen. In the days before the league existed, settling the championship by the "last win" method always took precedence in any dispute between two teams with fairly similar records. The Bears were close and invited the Bulldogs to Chicago to settle the matter.

George Halas set up the game for December 7 at Cubs Park, and the Chicago newspapers billed the game as being "for the championship." Chamberlin and his Bulldogs treated the game as an exhibition, thinking that November 30 was the end of the season. Close to 18,000 fans saw a very close game through three quarters, after which the Bulldogs trailed 7–0. Then they let everything slide as the Bears scored several times in the fourth quarter and won easily 23–0.[13]

The Chicago press, as well as other newspapers across the country, immediately awarded the Bears the championship. Mass confusion ensued, and Carr took his time on clearing the air. Well aware that the end of the season was established early in the year as November 30, Carr knew that the Bulldogs were the champs, and according to the bylaws, the decision to award the title wouldn't happen until the following winter meeting in January. Writing in his Gossip column, Carr didn't even bother to mention the dueling title winners and wrote about the league's just finished season.

> *December 14*—The Chicago Bears administered a stinging 23-to-0 defeat to the Cleveland Bulldogs. Chamberlin's crew simply could not get going and they went down grade fast in the fourth quarter, when the Bruins ran wild.
>
> Walter Camp, dean of collegiate football, was an interested spectator at the Bear-Bulldog game. Sir Walter admitted it was a great exhibition of pigskin chasing, adding that the brilliant offense rather surprised him.
>
> This is the time of the year that the moguls begin figuring up their profits and losses. If it hadn't been for several months' bad breaks in the weather, the majority of the clubs would have, at least, come through about even.
>
> Reports from Notre Dame have it that the "Four Horsemen" will not play pro football together. From this it would seem that several of the players may be seen on the post-graduate grid. Any one of them would be an attraction.
>
> Chris O'Brien is looking around for new blood in his Cardinal eleven and it is understood that there will be a thorough house-cleaning before it is time to start another season of professional football.[14]

But the confusion and the Bears' contention (led by George Halas) that they had a shot at the title just added to the hysteria. At the root of the controversy was a very basic question, one that had been hovering for five years ever since the idea of a league had first surfaced in Ralph Hay's Hupmobile office in 1920: was this a league of equals, all following the same rules, or was it a business in which economic might made right? At the league meeting in January of 1925, Carr came down on the side of his bylaws and awarded the championship to the Cleveland Bulldogs. The championship went to the team with the best winning percentage on November 30, just as the owners decided the summer before.

Furthermore the league didn't have a "championship" game and individual clubs—like the Bears—had no right to invent one. In other words, only the league could establish a title game. So Guy Chamberlin had his third straight NFL championship, and Sam Deutsch his first. On December 21 Carr wrote an in-depth season-ending article for the *Ohio State Journal* titled "Pro Football Takes Better Hold on Fans."

> Professional football came into its own during the season of 1924. The press and some of the great football authorities have been willing to admit that the post-graduate gridiron game has made rapid strides into public favor. It wasn't so long ago that the "money-tainted" footballers were looked upon with disfavor and the critics of the pro game were losing little time heaping gobs of abuse on those who attempted to foster Sunday football with the dollar sign as the goal.
>
> However times have changed and this season planted professional football solidly in the ranks of fall sports. There is no question but that the post-graduate has improved rapidly. The class of play is much better and the club owners are making progress towards handling their teams in collegiate style.
>
> **Hold Daily Practice**
>
> Back in the olden days, the players used to arrive just a few hours before the game and run through signals in a hotel corridor or back alley. But today, the majority of the teams keep their players on the scene of action all week and the squad has its daily practice. Under this new working order, the class of play measures up pretty close to a 100 percent to the collegiate brand. Possibly the individual condition of the pro players is a bit below the college grade but each year this weakness is being wiped out as the club owners are fining heavily those players who stray off the straight and narrow path.
>
> The National Football League knows its place in the gridiron world and the circuit is watching its steps with greatest care. There is no tinkering with players in college as each spoke in the wheel has on deposit a forfeit of $1,000 guarding against this or other violations.
>
> **Stage Blanket Finish**
>
> The class of play this fall was brilliant. Eighteen teams stepped off at the opening gun and they were going strong at the finish. The race for the cham-

pionship narrowed down to a blanket finish with a half dozen clubs in the running right up until the final lap. Good football packed them in at the gate and, despite inclement weather conditions, several of the clubs were money-makers while a number of others got an even break on the financial ledger.

Too much defense. That was one of the main complaints about the professional game in other years. Small scores were the rule and the touchdown thrills were not quite frequent enough to whet the appetite of the fans. But it was different this year. Scores were numerous and in many of the games, good sized total counts were marked up by both elevens. Followers of the post-graduate sport said that the increased scoring was traced directly to the improved offense. Practice makes perfect and the pro gridders drilled more often this past fall than ever before.

Show Civic Pride

Civic pride is beginning to cut a figure in professional football. In Wisconsin and Ohio, the followers of the gridiron migrate with the team. This gives the game something of a college spirit which has been lacing in other seasons. When the Bears and Cleveland Bulldogs played in Chicago, Walter Camp, dean of collegiate football, was an interested spectator. Camp has always been on the edge about pro football, but after seeing the former college stars perform, he admitted that the post graduate football appeared to gaining in popularity. The paid gate amounted to over $13,000.

Making Many Fans

The post graduate game is making many football fans. Thousands of the sport followers are unable to get into college games for love nor money and these same fans are flocking to the pro contests. If they can't see the stars while in college, they do get a chance to glimpse them while performing on the pro gridiron.[15]

The season-ending article also included the annual All-Pro team. Carr had now put an end to the 1924 NFL season and was ready to take a break, but he hoped not a step back. What he was really hoping for was a peaceful Christmas with Josie and the kids; apparently the year before hadn't been so peaceful, as he told a fellow writer at the *Ohio State Journal*:

In my opinion this Xmas business is very much overrated, says Joe Carr the other day. You see this tie I got on Joe says, pointing to a string around his neck. Well, he says, that is the most expensive tie I ever bought. It cost me $235.43, he says. It don't look it I says. No he says that it don't, but $235.43, or a little more than a down payment on a Buick is what it cost.

Last year he says, I loosened up the heart string and the purse strings and went out and did Xmas shopping early and late and I bought a present for all my friends and the whole total was $11.44. Then he says, I gave the wife cart blanch to get what she and the kids wanted. You gave her what I says? That's French for the whole works, Joe says.

Well, he says, they did plenty shopping, running here and there and buying presents for first this one and then that and the total came to the amount mentioned in the beginning. Well, I thought that at least I would have a fine Xmas, Joe says, and all my friends would remember me as handsomely as I remembered them and when I stole down the steps on Xmas day to see what Peter Rabbitt had left for me I find 42 Xmas cards and this necktie. The most expensive tie in the world, and I'll wear it as long as it stays with me."[16]

It was one of the few times Carr showed his sense of humor to the press, and after a year of taking some baby steps forward he needed to relax with his family and close friends. He would need it because the next year and a half would be the most difficult of his career. He would be challenged more than ever mentally, professionally, and physically.

13

The NFL Comes to New York City (1925)

The Carr family did not have a good start to 1925. John S. Sullivan, the father of Josephine Carr, suffered a heart attack at home on the morning of January 4 and died at the age of seventy. The former superintendent at the Pennsylvania Railroad who brought his family to Columbus twenty years ago had been ill for the past couple of years, but his death still stunned the family. Joe F. Carr was there to comfort his wife, and the couple was glad that they moved into the Sullivan home back in 1923 to be there for just this situation.[1]

Josie spent the following days with her mother, while Joe handled the two children, keeping their minds off what had just happened to their grandfather. After the funeral Joe started thinking about scheduling the annual winter meeting of the NFL and set the dates for January 24–25. This time instead of Chicago, the meeting was to be at the Statler Hotel in Cleveland, a location much closer to home. Carr didn't want to make it more difficult on his family, so he chose the two-hour train ride instead of the longer trip to the Windy City. Eighteen teams showed up and heard Carr's opening remarks on the state of the NFL. He reported on the success of several professional teams, telling the owners about the positive stories by the press on the league, including the statements by Walter Camp, and that indicated the league had made progress. After hearing the report the owners again reelected Carr, Dunn, and Storck as the NFL's executive committee.[2]

The owners also passed a motion that all three game officials (referee, umpire, and head linesman) were to be appointed by the president. Just another task for President Carr; no problem. After the dinner break the league voted on starting the season on September 20 and closing on December 20—much later than the previous season. The ending date would become a hot issue at the conclusion of the 1925 season.[3]

The following morning Carr started the session at 10:45 a.m., and the owners awarded the 1924 pennant to the Cleveland Bulldogs, finally settling the argument of last season. Carr also said in the league minutes that playing any "postseason" games made in agreement between two teams to play for a championship is "positively forbidden and to insure conformity to this resolution the season is extended to December 20 for 1925." Carr wanted to make sure the league, as well as the public and press, knew that his organization had a concrete ending date and they would keep to it.[4]

Before ending the meeting, applications for new franchises were received from Providence (Rhode Island), Pottsville (Pennsylvania), Cincinnati, and a new Detroit team that Carr especially wanted for the Motor City. Carr announced that the applications would be acted on by the executive committee in Columbus next month. Before Carr headed home, he was given an assignment by the owners, and this one would change the future of the league. While in Cleveland, Carr had a few small meetings with several of the owners about expanding the league to at least twenty teams, and he wanted to start by placing an NFL franchise in New York City. Seeing the big crowds in Chicago, Frankford (Philly), and Cleveland, Carr saw the future of the sport located in the bigger cities and knew that if the sport was to survive and prosper, he needed to move the game from the struggling small towns to the more populated hubs. The NFL needed to resemble Major League Baseball in this way, and Carr's discussions with owners like George Halas paved the way for him to seek a permanent franchise in the biggest city of them all.

Halas was on board with this movement from small towns to big cities. "The increased popularity of the sport was producing pro teams in many towns and cities. Membership stabilized between sixteen and eighteen teams, but there was one major lack—a team in New York City. We oldtimers thought this to be a severe hindrance to the development of professional football as a popular sport and as an economic proposition, so in the summer of 1925, we assigned President Carr the task of trying to plug the hole," Halas later wrote in his autobiography.[5]

In between the January meeting and the executive discussion in Columbus the following month, Carr got some much-needed information on how to find the right person in New York to invest in an NFL franchise. He wanted an investor who knew sports, knew how to promote a team in a big city, had connections within the city to get things done, and, finally, wouldn't be afraid to lose money—a large amount of money—especially in the first year or two. Carr's first choice was Billy

Gibson, the very successful boxing promoter who was the manager for Gene Tunney (who would win the heavyweight title in 1926) and who invested in the first attempt of a New York franchise back in 1921. He knew Gibson fit all of his criteria for an investor and Carr planned to approach him initially to see what he thought. But first he called Dr. Harry March, an old friend who had a background in the pro game going back to the original Canton–Massillon rivalry.

Dr. Harry March was born outside of Canton in 1876 and went on to graduate from Mt. Union (Ohio) College and the medical school at George Washington University. He served in the Spanish-American War as a correspondent and as a lieutenant (medical corps) in World War I. He returned to Stark County and became the county coroner as well as the city's biggest football enthusiast. He became the official team doctor for the Canton Bulldogs and Massillon Tigers during the teams' bitter rivalry in 1905–1906, before the gambling scandal took place. Besides continuing his practice, March dabbled in the entertainment field too, putting on plays at Meyers Lake Park Theatre in Canton. With this love for the theater and desire to be closer to Broadway, March moved his wife and one son to New York.[6]

March was always interested in putting a professional football team in New York, especially for the football fans who couldn't afford to see a college game in the city. With the likes of Fordham, Columbia, and New York University charging up to five dollars a ticket, and some fans working on Saturday and thus unable to attend college games, March always thought the pro game would go over well in the Big Apple. March also, and maybe more importantly, knew talent. He was very much up on the college game and the talent the universities were turning out.

Carr knew March from the Canton Bulldogs days back in the Ohio League and could use him if he was going to establish a presence in New York. After setting up a meeting with March and Gibson about his plans for an NFL franchise in New York, Carr then made arrangements for a trip to the biggest city of them all—to find the man he needed to start his vision of making the NFL a big-city league.

In the middle of May, Carr left Columbus for a three-day conference for the sole purpose of getting an investor for an NFL franchise in New York City. He would keep to his criteria and give the potential buyer one more big incentive to join the league: the owner would have exclusive rights to a franchise in New York, protected by the league's territorial rights rule. After arriving in New York, Carr made plans to meet with Dr. Harry March and then head over with March to the office of Billy Gibson to try to convince the promoter to invest. Carr reiterated to March that he needed a New York franchise to pair with the two Chicago franchises to anchor his league. He knew professional football would be a big-time sport, but if they didn't have a presence in New York, the NFL was never going to be as big as baseball.

But after arriving at Gibson's office, Carr found that his first choice of an owner wasn't too keen in putting up the money for a professional football team. Despite the fact that New York had just repealed the city's Blue Laws to allow Sunday football, Gibson remembered the failure of 1921 and was very reluctant to invest in a team by himself. He didn't know if the sport would sell in New York, but Gibson thought he had the right man for Carr. While the three men continued to talk, in walked a tall, affable Irishman, with a wide smile, who Carr knew to be a man of integrity and honesty. Tim Mara was visiting Billy Gibson to see if he could get a piece of Gene Tunney, but what he joined was a conversation about a sport he knew very little about, a sport that would change his life forever.

Timothy James Mara was born on July 29, 1887, in New York City and grew up working as a newspaper boy to help support his widowed mother. He also worked as a theater usher and sold programs at Madison Square Garden, all the while attending grammar school at Public School 14. As a newspaper boy his route ran along Broadway from the old Wannamaker store up to Union Square.[7]

This route happened to be filled with a large number of bookmaking establishments, which grabbed the attention of young Mara. Once he laid a bet on a horse that was being jockeyed by a former newspaper boy; he lost the bet, but was hooked. With this connection Mara started running bets for the bookmakers, and he learned very quickly how to play both sides of the betting action. On his route, some of his customers were bookmakers; others were guests in the east side hotels. The bookmakers often asked him to pick up wagers that had been lost by their customers, and they paid him a 5 percent commission for the service. They also used him to make payoffs, and the pleased winners usually gave him a tip. Either way young Tim Mara would come out with some type of payoff.

Mara loved the bookmaking lifestyle, which at this time was a legal profession in New York, and dropped out of school at the age of thirteen. His reason for choosing bookmaking was very simple—he would always say, "They lived the best and worked the least." After leaving school, Mara began to take small bets on his own and by the age of sixteen, he had his own clientele. Over time he became one of the most successful bookmakers in the city. But Mara wasn't a gambler; although he would lay a bet down occasionally, he was a bookmaker and he would become a wealthy man doing it.[8]

Horse racing would become his staple, with offices at Saratoga Springs, Jamaica, Belmont, and several others racetracks throughout the New York metro region. With his success, Mara appeared regularly in the society columns in the New York papers and rubbed elbows with the likes of the Astor, Vanderbilt, and Belmont families. All of this gave Mara the opportunity to be right in the epicenter of the New York sporting scene, and he became a man everyone knew. He made connections in boxing, horse racing, golf, and baseball, and he always looked for new challenges. "I never passed up the chance to promote anything. Not just because of the profit but for the challenge of promoting something. But you have to remember that New York City was virgin area for a smart promoter. There was money around, and people would buy anything, or at least come to see or hear it," Tim Mara would once say.[9]

At this time in 1925, the thirty-seven-year-old Mara was married to Lizette Barclay; had two sons—John V., who everyone called "Jack," and Wellington, who both loved football; had a successful bookmaking business; and had a place on Park Avenue. He didn't quite know what was about to happen the moment he walked into the office of Billy Gibson on that May afternoon. Gibson would make the introductions.

"Tim, I'd like you to meet Joe Carr. He's president of the National Football League. That's the new professional league, you know." Mara shook hands with the smallish unassuming leader of this organization called the NFL. "And this is Dr. Harry March," continued Gibson, indicating the tall pipe smoker. "The doctor is a New Yorker and is also interested in pro football." The four men sat down.[10]

Carr then revealed his plan. "I've just been trying to interest Billy in investing in a New York franchise for our league. Until we can establish ourselves in a New York franchise for our league, we'll stay small-time. I don't want to sound like a visionary, but I can see the day when pro football will be as big league as big league baseball. What do you say, Billy?"

"No, I don't really want to buy a football team. But maybe Tim Mara would," said Gibson from behind his desk.

"What would it cost?" Mara asked.

"A franchise in our league costs $2,500." Carr explained that the cost included the application fee; the guarantee fee, which guaranteed teams would not sign any players playing college football; and other expenses. Mara paused and then said, "A New York franchise in anything should be worth $2,500, including one for shining shoes. I'll take it."

Mara put out his hand, and Carr shook hands with the new owner of a New York franchise in the NFL. Previous historians and writers describe how Tim Mara just randomly showed up at Billy Gibson's office and bought an NFL franchise, like they were just giving them out for free. Also, in later years, Tim Mara would play up this scene, stating that he accidently bought the franchise. It was his way of showing how professional football was in the early days, and sometimes he would say that he paid $500 for the franchise. This was simply not true. This wasn't a fly-by-the-seat-of-your-pants meeting. This was a meeting that had a purpose and was planned in advance.

After they shook hands, Mara wrote Carr a check to cover the cost for applying for a franchise, and to make the transaction even stronger, Billy Gibson gave in, agreeing to help as a partner-in-debt. But the team belonged to Mara, who would eventually buy out Gibson a few years later. Tim Mara was now the owner of an NFL franchise in the league's biggest city. There was just one problem: Mara had never seen a pro football game. "I was betting on the city of New York. Sports have always been important in New York, and the franchise was worth that money even if it would have been in a shoe-shining league," Mara said.[11]

Mara would name his team the New York Football Giants, a name necessary to differentiate between the new, risky venture and the safely established baseball team of the same name. "I don't think I had seen more than two football games in my life, but here I was with a team, and I had to do something," Mara recalled about buying the team. At that point Mara hired Dr. Harry March as team secretary. March became more than secretary, however; he was a player scout, business manager, accountant, ticker seller, general manager, and bill collector. Mara now had the support he needed to run a pro football franchise, despite not knowing what he was getting into. Mara would always give the same quote on how the Giants were founded: "The Giants were founded on a combination of brute strength and ignorance. The players supplied the strength. I supplied the ignorance."[12]

Carr left the meeting and the city of New York with a good feeling that he had the right man to run the New York franchise that the league so desperately needed. After a couple of months of work, Carr had accomplished the task given to him. The press across the country announced the new big-city team that would play in New York. On May 15 the *New York Times* gave the meeting some big headlines and more than just a mention.

Plan Pro Football Here Next Season
Billy Gibson Applies for a Franchise after Conference
with National League Head
May Use Polo Grounds
New York Promoter Also Says He Will Build Stadium
Here If Venture Is a Success

Another attempt will be made to put professional football on a paying basis in New York next season. After a three-day conference with Joseph F. Carr of Columbus, Ohio, President of the National Football League, Billy Gibson,

New York promoter, yesterday announced that he had filed application for a franchise for New York in the organization.

While all the details have not been definitely settled concerning the New York team and its operations, it is known that Gibson will be at the head of the club and that in all probability at the [Polo] Grounds, although negotiations for a field have not been completed. Gibson said yesterday that he and his associates were seeking a coach of national reputation to run the eleven and that he expected to be able to announce the name of the mentor in a few days. He also said that it is his plan to erect a stadium here if the games prove a success and the team gains a following.

Professional football has been attempted before in New York, but has never been very popular. However, in other cities, such as Buffalo, Rochester, Philadelphia, Cleveland, Chicago and Milwaukee, the game has been very successful and officials of the National Football League expressed their belief that with such a man as Gibson behind the new project the game also could be made popular in this city.

No doubt the new organization will make every attempt to obtain the services of prominent college football players after they graduate, and have New York represented by players of national reputation. At least it will be a chance for New York to see many of the gridiron stars in action.[13]

Most of the articles mentioned that Billy Gibson would head up the team. This was Carr's idea to keep the "bookie" out of the headlines initially and use Gibson's name to get the team out there to the pubic nationally. Several articles mentioned Dr. March as an associate, but it would be Tim Mara paying all the bills. First up was for the Giants to hire a head coach. March and Mara decided on Bob Folwell, the former head coach of Lafayette University of Pennsylvania and head coach at the U.S. Naval Academy for the past five years. Folwell was excited about joining the Giants and being part of the NFL:

As for entertaining the public, I am sure professional football can be made to flourish in New York as it has in the West. I know of no greater thrills in professional sport than the sight of twenty-two highly trained experts engaged in a game of football. It is my plan to organize a football machine in New York on the same basis that I would a college team, and when it is realized that instead of having only one or two stars for a nucleus, I will have a skilled man with four years of college training in each position it should mean that the public will see some spectacular football.[14]

Mara gave March the go-ahead to start signing players, and he spared no expense. "Get me the best pro football talent in the business. New York likes a winner and we've got to come up with one fast," Mara told March. Knowing that they would need a big name, the Giants signed Jim Thorpe to a very unique contract. They knew the thirty-seven-year-old probably couldn't play a whole game, so they paid Thorpe $200 per half. They were counting on his name to put a few people in the stands.[15]

March then went out and spent Mara's money. He signed center Century Milstead (Yale) for $250 a game and continued the spending spree by securing contracts with center Joe Alexander (Syracuse), fullback Jack McBride (Syracuse), offensive tackle Bob "Nasty" Nash (Rutgers), guard Joe Williams (Lafayette), halfback Heinie Benkert (Rutgers), and probably the biggest signing, halfback Hinkey Haines (Penn State). In all the Mara-Gibson partnership would be on the hook for $25,000 with the cost of player's salaries, equipment and uniforms, ball park rental, transportation, and front office operations, even before they played their first game. The Giants were now a very talented squad with a competent head coach. The big-city team was very much looking like it could be big time. Now it was time to officially join the league.

The NFL's summer meeting took place at the Hotel Sherman in Chicago on August 1–2. Carr called the meeting at 2:00 p.m. on the first day with twenty teams represented. Franchises that dropped out of the league were Racine, Kenosha (Wisconsin), and Minneapolis (Minnesota), and the Canton Bulldogs were reinstated, led by players Pete Henry and Link Lyman. Carr presented the four new applicants to the owners for membership, and all four were approved. Providence (Rhode Island) Steam Roller, Detroit (Michigan) Panthers led by star player Jimmy Conzelmen, Pottsville (Pennsylvania) Maroons, and the New York Giants. Billy Gibson and Dr. Harry March were in town to accept the franchise for Tim Mara.[16]

The small-town Maroons were a surprise entry, but owner Dr. John Striegel raised enough funds to get his coal region squad into the NFL. His team would cause Carr some unnecessary headaches at the end of the 1925 season. After awarding the new franchises, the owners heard from the Spalding Company about being the official football supplier. The owners would also hear a proposal from the Wilson Sporting Goods Company. In the end the NFL adopted the Spalding J-5 football that would cost $6.75 per ball and have an NFL stamp placed on it. As determined at the first meeting, the season would start on September 20 and end on December 20. Lastly, Dutch Sternaman made a motion that before six o'clock local time, the home club should send the NFL secretary the result of the game by wire or be fined twenty-five dollars. The motion was carried.[17]

The second day of the meeting saw the owners schedule games and approve an increase in the president's salary to $2,500 a year (effective on August 1). The NFL's owners could see that Carr was getting the job done, and securing a franchise in New York just cemented his commitment to the league. "We knew Mara would tap a rich market and bring the game of professional football to the attention of sportswriters for the New York papers and for the burgeoning news agencies which distributed reports to newspapers throughout the league. We all applauded Joe Carr's success," George Halas said in his autobiography.[18]

The raise in salary was unexpected for Carr, and he would earn every penny of it in 1925. Besides running the NFL, Carr was offered another sports executive job to test his abilities. George Preston Marshall, a wealthy entrepreneur who owned a Washington, D.C., business called the Palace Laundry, was also a big sports fan and collaborated with George Halas and Cleveland department store tycoon Max Rosenblum to organize the American Basketball League (ABL). It is regarded as the first national basketball circuit. Halas's team was named the Chicago Bruins and Marshall called his ABL team the Palace Big Five; the league fielded nine teams. The owners asked Carr to be the president and of course he said yes. He was now involved in pro football, minor league baseball, and professional basketball. Carr lasted three years as ABL president (1925–1927). Through his involvement in the ABL, Marshall cultivated a strong relationship with Halas and Carr. This wouldn't be the last time Marshall's name would be heard.

As the season approached, Tim Mara and Dr. Harry March went about selling the New York Giants to the city of New York. "We mean to give New York a good, clean, hard game of football of the highest type. We are picking up where Charlie Brickley left off four years ago and are confident that after this season professional football will be a permanent institution in this city," Dr. March declared. The team's first two games would be on the road (the baseball Giants were still using the Polo Grounds), and the initial home game in New York was scheduled for October 18 against the Frankford Yellow Jackets. Ticket prices ranged from fifty cents up to $2.75, and the fearsome duo of Mara and March would do anything to get people out to the games in that first year.[19]

They handed out free tickets in restaurants, theaters, and subways in hopes of building up crowds that would later pay their way into the Polo Grounds. "I can remember how he used to walk around the streets handing out free tickets and half-price tickets. And if [he] couldn't get half-price, those became free, too," Wellington Mara, son of Tim Mara, remembered. "All he wanted was to get some people in the stands. He had to do that before he could hope to get their money." Mara knew that establishing a fan base would take time and giving out free tickets was just part of the job. "Tickets were a problem. They must have been, because nobody wanted them," Tim Mara would always say.[20]

Along with the slow ticket sales, Mara's team on the field got off to a sluggish start, losing their first two games on the road—a 14–0 shutout against Providence and a 5–3 loss in front of 15,000 fans at Frankford on Saturday, October 17, a day before the home opener, which was also against Frankford. The rematch between the two teams took on a bigger meaning because this would be the first time Tim Mara would see his team play in New York City. After attending mass on the morning of the 18th, Wellington Mara heard his father casually say, "I'm gonna try to put pro football over in New York today." As if this was just another day.[21]

The Giants' first home game in the NFL saw a crowd of 27,000 fans, which was one of the largest crowds to ever witness a league game to that point. How many actually paid nobody knows, but Mara-March did what they wanted to accomplish, and that was to get people in the stands. Most of the New York newspapers led with the attendance figure, the *New York Times* printing the number twice in its headline of the game, written by well-known sportswriter Allison Danzig. As for the action on the field, the Giants were still a work in progress. The Yellow Jackets, led by player-coach Guy Chamberlin (who had left the Cleveland franchise), scored two touchdowns in the first half and won 14–0. The game left an impression on nine-year-old Wellington Mara. "I recall going to the game and I wanted to sit on the bench. I remember our coach, Bob Folwell, a former Navy coach, turning to one of the players on the bench, his name was Paul Jappe, and saying 'Jappe get in there and give them hell!' I thought, boy, this is really a rough game."[22]

The Giants' rough start wouldn't last very long, as the team started to jell. The first thing they did was release Jim Thorpe, as the aging veteran didn't have any skills left, and insert Hinkey Haines at halfback. The high-priced talent then rattled off four wins in a row (all at home) against Cleveland (18,000 fans), Buffalo (20,000), Columbus (4,000), and Rochester (10,000). The Giants were now 4–3, but the attendance figures slowly began to head south with each game. In the middle of November, they got ready to host a very important visitor.[23]

On November 15 Joe F. Carr traveled east to see the Giants play the Providence Steam Roller. The Giants' front office brass put out the red carpet for their special guest, and Carr was very impressed with what he saw. At the game Carr saw a beautiful fall day in New York and 20,000 fans in the stands at the Polo Grounds. It was a long way from those early days of the Columbus Panhandles with 2,000 fans lined up on the sidelines or sitting in three rows of a hand-built grandstand. As for the action on the field, Carr saw the Giants pull out an exciting 13–12 victory over the Steam Roller.[24]

Before leaving New York, Carr talked to the press about his new idea for the makeup of the NFL and its presence on the East Coast.

Football League Planned
Banding of Eastern Pro Elevens Contemplated, Says Official

Joseph F. Carr of Columbus, Ohio, President of the national Professional Football League, while attending the victory of the Giants over the Provi-

> dence Steam Rollers at the Polo Grounds yesterday intimated that plans were developing for the formation of the professional league of Eastern elevens.
>
> Investigations are being conducted relative to placing teams in Brooklyn, Washington, Newark, Atlantic City, Boston and Hartford, Conn. New York State is already represented by the Giants in this city, Buffalo and Rochester.[25]

Carr's big plans for the NFL consisted of the league's franchises being in major cities and having an eastern and western division with the winner of each division playing in a championship game—pro football's World Series. The owners had discussed splitting the league into divisions before, and seeing the type of crowds the big cities could generate, Carr used the New York media to reenergize the idea. Carr would have to face two major issues and a near-death illness before tackling his newest plan.

14

The Galloping Ghost and Pottsville Controversy (1925)

Harold "Red" Grange was a six-foot, 180-pound halfback, who burst onto the sports scene in 1924 with his historic performance against the University of Michigan. Not since Jim Thorpe had there been a football player who gained such national attention for his gridiron exploits. Entering his senior year in the fall of 1925, Grange's every move was closely followed as the press and public couldn't get enough of him.

On the field Grange would change the game of football. Before he arrived, most of the action on offense would be three yards and a cloud of dust, and if you managed to move the ball downfield you settled for a field goal. If you were extremely effective, you plowed over for a short touchdown. But Grange would bring the "home-run" threat to football. Although there had been plenty of long scoring plays before, nobody did it with the flair of Red Grange.

At a time when sports fans during the Roaring Twenties were cheering long home runs by Babe Ruth, crushing drives by Bobby Jones, or knockout punches by Jack Dempsey, football fans wanted to see Grange run eighty yards for a touchdown, and usually he delivered. So much so that he earned the nickname "the Galloping Ghost." The image of Grange as an evasive "streak of fire, a breath of flame, . . . a gray ghost thrown into the game," as famed sportswriter Grantland Rice lyrically described him, captured America's attention. As a senior he was ready to finish his career in style.[1]

After a slow start to the season, Grange was presented a perfect opportunity to prove how great he was. On October 31 Illinois traveled east to play the University of Pennsylvania. It was the ideal situation for the Ghost to show the eastern press that the Midwest could play the game that the Ivy League "invented." If he could dominate an eastern powerhouse, then just maybe he could be the greatest player to put on a football uniform. The game was highly anticipated, and the most well-known sportswriters in the country were in attendance to see what Grange would do. Grantland Rice, Laurence Stallings, Paul Gallico, Damon Runyon, and Ford Frick were all in the press box at Franklin Field to witness another remarkable performance by Grange.

On a sloppy field and in front of a sellout crowd of 65,000 fans, Grange amassed 363 yards rushing and three touchdowns in a stunning 24–2 victory over the Quakers. Grange proved he was the best player in the country. Everybody wanted to know everything about him and what he would do next. Rumors started to fly about the future of Red Grange. There were even a few linking him to professional football for roughly $40,000 a year with the Chicago Bears or the New York Giants. While George Halas was quiet in hearing these rumors, Tim Mara set the record straight with his Giants. "In the first place we are limited under the league rules in the amount of money we can pay a player, and for three games this limit would not reach $1,000, much less $40,000. In the second place we are under agreement not to tamper with football players while they are in college and I believe in the rule."[2]

There were other rumors that Grange would become an actor, run for political office, become a writer, or go into coaching. His every move was now being monitored, and it seemed everybody had their own opinion on what he should do:

> *George Huff, University of Illinois athletic director*—I have no fight with professional football, but I hope Grange never again puts on a suit after he finishes college. It is by no means a crime to play after leaving school but Grange has so many better opportunities before him. After I talked with him for an hour he thanked me for my advice and I believe I convinced him that it would be wise to proceed cautiously.
>
> *Bob Zuppke, University of Illinois head coach*—Keep away from professionalism and you'll be another Walter Camp. Football isn't a game to play for money.
>
> *Fielding Yost, University of Michigan head coach*—I'd be glad to see Grange do anything else except play professional football.
>
> *Westbrook Pegler,* Chicago Tribune *writer*—To be an imitation writer or a fake movie actor would surely be less virtuous than becoming a real football player.[3]

Of course most of the college coaches and officials wanted to see Grange do anything else but play professional football. After hearing all of this for weeks Grange went to see his father to hear his opinion.

> Every time I read the papers that Harold has accepted a contract from this or that team, it gives me a shock. I sincerely hope that he does not do this, although he has not confided in me what his plans are. I have a notion, however, that he will drop out of school for a while after the football season and accept one of the offers made him.
>
> I think he's entitled to "cash in" on the long runs his gridiron fame has brought him. It is expensive for me to send Harold and his brother Garland through the university. We are not rolling in wealth and I think the public would approve of anything Harold does.[4]

Grange had an idea of what he was going to do, but he was keeping it to himself. The only thing he would say was that he would announce his future plans after his final collegiate game against Ohio State. One thing was for sure—the whole country was watching and everybody wanted to see the Galloping Ghost—even Joe F. Carr. Using his connections, Carr contacted Lynn St. John, the athletic director at Ohio State, and asked his good friend for a favor. Carr wanted a ticket (the hottest ticket in town) to see Grange's collegiate finale against the Buckeyes on November 21. St. John agreed and sent Carr a ticket. Carr now had a front seat to see the famous redhead in action and maybe get a glimpse of the future of professional football.

After Carr returned from his trip to New York to watch the Steamroller–Giants matchup, he prepared to attend the most talked about game of the year. First he had to answer the rumors of Red Grange signing a contract with one of the teams in the NFL. On Wednesday, November 18, he made a statement to the press on the Grange issue.

> No college player may participate in any game of the National League while he is still eligible to play on his college team and that he cannot play in the same year in which he finishes his football career, in the event he remains in college.
>
> Of course if Grange retires from school after Saturday's game he is a free agent and cannot be restrained under the rules of the National League. It would be absurd for the National League or any other organization to try and restrain any athlete from capitalizing on his ability when he is no longer a member of any amateur organization and has retired from college.
>
> We have done everything possible to keep the college players clean and above board, but, inasmuch as all who would like to see the stars of the gridiron in action and are unable to gain admittance to the big college games, we feel that we are doing a public service when we promote professional football on the high plane we have it, thereby making it possible for the country at large to see the stars in action. This applies not only to Mr. Grange, but

to other stars too numerous to mention who elect to enter the professional ranks after they have done their full share for their Alma Mater.

After careful investigation I am fully convinced that Mr. Grange has not been approached by any club in the National Football League.[5]

With this statement, Carr, very uncharacteristically, was giving permission for any NFL club to sign Grange if they wanted to, as long as he dropped out of college. Carr knew this was a unique situation for his league, and he had to act quickly. The NFL might only have one shot at getting Grange to play professional football, and he wanted to give his teams the chance to do it. The specific wording of the rule to not sign players still in college was once again a matter of interpretation.

The bottom line for Carr was that if Grange dropped out of college, he was fair game and Carr couldn't deny the young man a chance to make a living. In turn Carr and the NFL would get a superstar who would give the organization some publicity, respectability, and media coverage that it had never had before. It was a chance Carr was willing to take. Now it was time to actually see what all the fuss was about. Unfortunately for Carr he never made it to the game. Instead, he almost died.

On Thursday, a day after writing the press release on Grange, Carr became very ill and showed symptoms of a high fever, nausea, drowsiness, and sudden loss of appetite. Feeling sick he decided to stay home and get some rest, hoping that a day of no stress would allow him to attend the big Illinois–Ohio State matchup on Saturday. Carr's illness became big news in Columbus and in subsequent days the reporting of his health would take on a dramatic play-by-play scenario. The *Columbus Citizen* reported the story, under the headline "Joe Carr Is Ill": "Joe F. Carr, president of the National Professional Football League, is confined to his home, 39 N. 22nd St., suffering from an attack of acute indigestion. Carr was stricken Thursday. His condition Friday was much improved."[6]

But instead of feeling better, Carr suffered a setback. While relaxing at home on Friday night he started having some extreme abdominal pains that would send him to the hospital. The forty-six-year-old Carr suffered a ruptured appendix and went straight to the operating room at Mt. Carmel Hospital. While there his close friend Dr. Bob Drury, as well as his brother-in-law Dr. Frank Sullivan, took care of him. The surgery was performed and the front page of the *Ohio State Journal* told the rest of Columbus the state of Carr's condition.

Joe Carr Operated on for Appendicitis

Joe F. Carr, president of the National Football League, is in serious condition as result of an operation yesterday for appendicitis. He is in Mt. Carmel Hospital.

> The sudden illness prevented Carr from carrying out a long cherished desire to see Red Grange in action in his final game.[7]

The *St. Patrick Church Bulletin* encouraged people to say a little prayer for one of their most dedicated church-goers: "Joe Carr is fighting for his life with the help of thousands of friends who are praying for him at Mt. Carmel Hospital. Joe is battling as he has battled for clean, wholesome athletics all his life. Yes, say a prayer that God in His mercy will spare Joe Carr to continue his activities for young men to help them in developing themselves into healthful practical Christian citizens."[8]

The whole community in Columbus held their breath that Carr would pull through, and saying a little prayer couldn't hurt. Over the next few days Carr's condition would go from critical, to stable, and back to critical. Monday morning Dr. Drury announced that his good friend was "progressing satisfactorily, but was not yet out of danger." The *Portsmouth (Ohio) Times* reported that Carr was "seriously ill and in critical condition." Then it looked very bleak for Joe F. Carr when, at the bottom of the front page of the November 25 edition, the *Ohio State Journal* reported on Carr's condition under the headline "Carr Sinking": "Hospital physicians last night said the condition of Joe F. Carr, president of the National Professional Football League, operated on for appendicitis last week, was critical. Doubt was expressed as to his recovery."[9]

Less than a week after arriving at Mt. Carmel Hospital, the family of Joe F. Carr had gone through the complete range of emotions. Surrounded by his immediate family, Carr slowly fought to stay alive and eventually showed improvement. He had too much to live for and so much more to accomplish with his family and career. His doctors saw his condition improve and let the *Ohio State Journal* know that he might pull through. Under the headline "Attaboy, Joe!" the *Journal* reported, "Joe F. Carr, is steadily improving in Mt. Carmel Hospital, and physicians said last night his condition is now more favorable than at any time since his recent operation for appendicitis."[10]

When the good news spread through Columbus that Carr was getting healthier, the little sports executive was swamped with tons of well-wishes. He received cards and flowers from several NFL people, including his friend Carl Storck, Jim Durfee (an NFL referee), the Frankford Athletic Association, and other Columbus citizens. His former coworker at the *Ohio State Journal* Clyde Tuttle wrote a special tribute to his friend.

> Test of Popularity
>
> A fellow never knows how many friends or how few friends he has until he is in trouble.

We feel that if Joe Carr, president of the National Football League, who is now recovering at Mt. Carmel Hospital from an operation for appendicitis, had been able to be around this office this week, he would know that his friends are legion.

When Mr. Carr's condition was the worst, when it looked for a time that he might not be able to pull through, calls came to this department by the hundreds, and telegrams and long distance telephone calls came from all over the country.

People may sometimes be fooled regarding a person, but they are not long fooled, nor are all of them always fooled. A fellow with the sterling characteristics that Joe Carr possesses will never want for friends. And he shouldn't.[11]

The tremendous show of support really touched Carr, and he became even more determined to make a full recovery. As he started to feel better, he responded to the support he received from his colleagues and friends. If he wasn't in a good mood already, a letter from his boyhood friend Bob Quinn probably sealed it for him.

Dear Joe—

The past two weeks have been long ones for me, for like many of your friends we were fearful [that] our Dear Lord would call you home not that we begrudged you the wonderful place we all felt sure God had preferred for you but we were sure that you could do so many things here for his honor and glory and for your family and friends. So you see we were really selfish, and we prayed hard that you be spared to us although we were sure that you yourself would have been happier with our Dear Lord. However we are thankful that you are to remain with us and we shall thank God and His Blessed Mother, also the Little Flower for their kindness. Do not get out too soon and begin to hustle about remember it takes at least six months to get the ether out of you so do not be impatient if you do not feel yourself for sometime. When you are able to write me as I have some things I want to write you about your football league, nothing that will not [keep] just a few ideas that have come to me recently.

Hoping God will let you soon get home,
most sincerely yours,
Bob Quinn[12]

Carr was now on his way to a full recovery. While Carr was stricken with his illness and recuperating in the hospital, the circus surrounding Red Grange arrived in Columbus. The game between the two Midwest rivals was secondary to the anticipation of what Grange would decide to do after his college finale—the game Carr would miss. Before the Galloping Ghost played his final game, the rumors of him turning pro intensified. The *Champaign News-Gazette* interviewed the redhead and accused him of signing to play professional football. Grange recalled, "I replied that I had not affixed my signature to any contract and defied them to produce evidence to the contrary. At this point I put on my hat and walked out."[13]

More than 100 newspapers and correspondents arrived at Ohio State's massive stadium, along with over 85,000 excited fans to witness Grange's final college game. The contest was unremarkable. Grange ran for 113 yards to lead his team to a 14–9 victory. After the final gun sounded, Grange was surrounded by reporters, and then he announced that he "would drop of college and play professional football for the Chicago Bears. I have nothing to say right now." Then the Galloping Ghost left in a hurry.[14]

After leaving the stadium, Grange hopped on a train and headed for Chicago where he met up with his "agent," Charles C. Pyle, better known as C. C. Pyle, a theater owner who met Grange at a Champaign movie house earlier in the year and laid out a plan for Grange to capitalize on his famous name, by playing professional football. The man who'd tabbed Grange "the Galloping Ghost," Warren Brown of the *Chicago Herald-Examiner*, cautioned Grange. "People who know C. C. Pyle claim the initials stand for Cash and Carry. Mr. Grange is hereby forewarned." Pyle revealed his plan for Grange to sign with an NFL team and go on a coast-to-coast tour to large crowds and big paydays.[15]

The previous summer Grange had agreed to let Pyle represent him and shook hands on it, but he didn't sign anything. For Grange a handshake was as good as a signed contract—plus it kept his collegiate eligibility still intact. Despite Pyle's rapacious reputation, Grange was impressed by him. "Pyle was about forty-five when I met him. He was a shade over six feet tall and weighed about 195 pounds. He had gray hair and a neatly trimmed mustache. An immaculate dresser, his clothes were made to order by the most exclusive tailors. He always carried a cane, wore spats, a derby and a diamond stickpin in his tie," Grange wrote in his autobiography. "Pyle came up with more ideas in one day than most men come up with in a lifetime."[16]

Grange took the train to the Windy City where Pyle had already worked out an agreement with Bears co-owners George Halas and Dutch Sternaman. Grange had never meet Halas or Sternaman before, and later that day he sat on the Chicago bench in street clothes and watched the Bears trounce the Green Bay Packers, 21–0. The next morning the contract was signed. Halas-Sternaman agreed with Pyle to split the earnings fifty-fifty, with the Bears paying the tour costs, and Pyle would provide Red. The two parties put it in writing. Grange later announced why he chose professional football over all the other offers: "I have received many alluring offers to enter fields of enterprise in which I have no training or experience. I believe the public will be better satisfied with my honesty and good motives if I turn my efforts to that field in which I have been most useful in order to reap a reward which will keep the home fires burning."[17]

About the same time as Grange signed his Bears contract, New York Giants owner Tim Mara arrived in Chicago thinking he would have a chance to sign the Galloping Ghost. He got the next best thing. "We got a telegram from my father saying: 'Partially successful. Will arrive on train and explain.' We didn't really know what that meant. We had already heard that he had been unable to sign Red Grange because Red had signed with the Bears. As far as we were concerned, he was totally unsuccessful. But what he meant was that he had booked a game in the Polo Grounds with the Bears and Red Grange," Wellington Mara remembered about his dad trying to sign Grange.[18]

After only three days of practice with the Bears, Grange would make his professional debut on Thanksgiving Day against their cross-town rivals, the Cardinals. Interest was so great that 20,000 tickets were printed up and sold in three hours on the Monday after Grange signed. Halas had more printed and a standing-room only crowd of 36,000 jammed Cubs Park—it was the largest crowd ever to see a pro football game anywhere. Too bad Joe F. Carr was laid up in a Columbus hospital struggling for his life.

The Cardinals held Grange to only thirty-five yards, and the Cards' star player Paddy Driscoll kept punting away from Grange, not giving him a chance for one of his famous long-distance touchdowns. Driscoll later explained, "It was a question of which one of us would look bad—Grange or Driscoll. I decided it wouldn't be Paddy." When the game ended in a scoreless tie, thousands of fans surrounded Grange as he left the field, but the police escorted him to safety. Halas reportedly cried when counting the gate receipts. "There had never been such evidence of public interest since our professional league began in 1920. I knew then and there that pro football was destined to be a big-time sport," Halas recalled.[19]

The following Sunday the Bears hosted the Columbus Tigers, and 28,000 fans braved the snow to see Grange play his second game, a 14–13 win. After the Columbus game, Halas signed Earl Britton—former fullback for the University of Illinois—to a pro contract, opening the flood gates for any collegian to sign with a pro team as long as they quit school. Once again, the NFL didn't endear itself to the coaches and athletic directors in college football.

The Bears then launched the first of two tours that Pyle and Halas-Sternaman set up. The Bears had NFL games on the road against Frankford

(December 5), New York (December 6), Providence (December 9), and Detroit (December 12), as well as a rematch with the Giants in Chicago on December 13. In between, Pyle set up nonleague games in St. Louis (December 2), Washington (December 8), and Pittsburgh (December 10). In just a twelve-day period, the Bears and their star Red Grange would play eight games. A murderous schedule clearly showed that C. C. Pyle didn't know anything about pro football, and it proved that this tour wasn't about winning games or trying to claim an NFL championship. It was about trying to make as much money as possible by exploiting the Grange phenomenon.

On Wednesday, the Grange-Bears squad played a pickup team in St. Louis before only 8,000 fans as snow fell during the game and the temperature dropped to twelve degrees. On Saturday, a rainstorm hit Philadelphia, but 35,000 came out to Franklin Field to watch Grange score both touchdowns in a 14–0 win over the Frankford Yellow Jackets. After taking a train overnight to New York, the Grange-Bears were prepared to play Tim Mara's Giants the following day.

At this time Mara was facing a financial deficit of about $40,000, and failing to sign Grange as an attraction made the tall Irishman rethink his investment. Even his good friend New York governor Al Smith questioned his decision, "Pro football will never amount to anything, why don't you give it up?" Mara responded, "The boys would run me right out of the house if I did." Mara thought the arrival of Grange would change everything, and he was right.[20]

Although attendance figures for that game have varied, based on the gate receipts of $142,000 it seems that about 70,000 spectators filled every seat in the Polo Grounds to watch Grange play. It was the largest ever gathering at a professional football game—topping the previous mark set just ten days earlier in Chicago when Grange made his professional debut. "When I saw that crowd and knew that half the cash in the house was mine, I said to myself, 'Timothy, how long has this gravy train been running,'" recalled Tim Mara. Over 125 newspapermen from across the country covered the game. Damon Runyon described the wonderful scene: "Seventy thousand men, women and children were in the stands, blocking the aisles and runways. Twenty thousand more were perched on Coogan's Bluff and the roofs of apartment houses, content with just an occasional glimpse of the whirling mass of players on the field below and wondering which was Red Grange."[21]

The Bears won 19–7 (although the outcome seemed secondary), with Grange scoring the final touchdown on an interception return. Grange made an estimated $30,000 for that game alone. The game likely saved Mara's New York franchise, wiping out Mara's $40,000 debt and giving him a tidy profit of $18,000 for the year. The Grange-Bears tour was making the NFL and professional football more popular than ever and giving the sport the expanded coverage it needed. Some historians credit Grange for saving professional football, but this was not true. Pioneers like Carr, Halas, and Lambeau had already accomplished this; the sport was going to survive with or without Grange. What Grange did was bring the sport, and in turn the NFL, to a mass audience like never before. Halas summed up Grange's debut, "I believe that as a result of our Grange tour, pro football for the first time took on a national stature."[22]

Although most NFL teams weren't seeing profits, the publicity generated by Grange in the large eastern cities proved to the league that the future of the young organization would be in the big cities. Carr knew this was going to be the direction his league would be moving in; Grange's arrival just sped up his grand plan. First Carr had to get healthier if he wanted to see his vision of the NFL come true.

The Grange-Bears tour continued in Washington, then traveled to Boston, where Grange only gained eighteen yards and was booed by the crowd of 25,000. Ford Frick, the newsman who later became baseball commissioner, who was accompanying the tour wrote, "The strain of this tour is starting to show on Grange. He is tremendously human, in his quiet, shy way, and just a little bit nervous and bored by the laudations which suddenly have come his way. And the pace has begun to tell." On Thursday, December 10, against a team of locals in Pittsburgh, Grange was kicked in the arm, tearing a muscle, and a blood clot began to form. The injury forced him out of the game, and the crowd booed again. Grange was diagnosed with a broken blood vessel and was told to rest for at least two weeks. He missed the Detroit and Giants games as the first part of the tour ended.[23]

In the first eight games of the eastern tour, Grange wore down and didn't play at the standard he set in college. The brutal schedule contributed mainly to Grange's physical problems. Guy Chamberlin commented that "Grange broke down mentally and physically, because more was asked of him than any human being could perform. The pro players on other teams were affected by the Grange splurge, and the public disillusioned."[24] As the public went gaga over Grange, the actual championship race for the 1925 NFL title was being decided. If Carr rejoiced at Grange's arrival from his hospital bed, he probably wanted to remain in the recovery room because of the controversy over the championship.

The race for the NFL title came down to two teams, the Chicago Cardinals and the surprising small-town Pottsville Maroons. After opening the season with a defeat by Hammond, the Cardinals reeled off eight consecutive wins before battling the Bears to a scoreless tie in Red Grange's professional debut on Thanksgiving Day. At 8–1–1 the Cardinals sat atop of the NFL standings, just a half game ahead of the Maroons, who took advantage of Pennsylvania's famous Blue Laws. Before joining the NFL, the Maroons were members of the "Anthracite League," playing games on Sundays against other mining communities, such as Coaldale, Shenandoah, Gilberton, and Mount Carmel. Lawmakers didn't want to tell the miners—who worked six days a week—that they couldn't play football on their only day off.

When Carr admitted the Maroons into the NFL, one of the big reasons was that teams traveling east could schedule two games to be played on back-to-back days; Saturdays against the Frankford Yellow Jackets, and Sundays against the Pottsville Maroons. The Maroons took full advantage of this situation by winning six of seven Sunday games when their opponent played the previous day in Frankford. The day after Thanksgiving the Maroons (8–2) were just a half game back of the Cardinals (8–1–1). On November 29 the Cardinals defeated Rock Island (7–0) and the Maroons destroyed the Yellow Jackets (49–0). Cardinals owner Chris O'Brien now wanted a game with the Maroons, but he also wanted another shot at playing against Red Grange for a bigger payday.

At this time Maroons owner Dr. John Striegel was looking to make some money as well. By joining the NFL, his team's payroll had ballooned in 1925, and the crowds at tiny Minersville Park weren't filling his pocket with dollars. As December approached Striegel had arranged for exhibition games in Atlantic City (December 6), and by virtue of their victory against the Yellow Jackets, a game against the Notre Dame All-Stars (a team made up of former Irish players). But Carr wanted the NFL season concluded before his teams starting playing meaningless games. So he contacted Striegel and recommended his team play the Chicago Cardinals to help decide the NFL championship. In a telegram sent to Striegel, Carr voiced his opinion. "Can't allow your game with Atlantic City until after the regular season. Several clubs [Chicago Cardinals] have kicked to me as they desire your services."[25]

On the front page of the December 2 *Pottsville Journal* sports section, the headline read, "President Carr Orders Maroons to Play at Chicago on Dec. 6th."[26] Carr knew the game and the much-needed media coverage (along with the ongoing Grange circus), was getting the NFL more publicity than ever before. Reluctantly the Maroons' owner—who seemed more interested in making money than winning a championship—agreed. The Atlantic City game was postponed so that the Maroons–Cardinals could pretty much decide the NFL championship on December 6 in Chicago.

On an eighteen-degree day at Comiskey Park the Maroons scored two second-quarter touchdowns to take a 14–7 halftime lead. In the second half, the Maroons ground game behind the play of Walter French, controlled the clock, and led the small-town Maroons to a 21–7 victory.

Although there were two weeks to go in the season (the season's ending date was December 20), the Maroons claimed to be "NFL champions." For all intents and purposes, it looked like the Maroons would win the title, but in the early days of the NFL nothing was that easy.

After defeating the Cardinals in Chicago, Dr. Striegel went about organizing his team's exhibition game against the Notre Dame All-Stars. This would be his big payday. This is where Striegel made his big mistake. Instead of trying to finish the season as NFL champion, he went for the money. Although most newspapers around the country declared Pottsville champions, they were a bit premature. The Maroons had merely taken over first place. Before those two critical weeks were over—with President Carr in a hospital bed—the NFL would face another season-ending controversy.

As Striegel kept his word to play the Notre Dame All-Stars, the Maroons were still scheduled to play the Providence Steam Roller the day after. The Notre Dame game figured to be a big moneymaker, and Striegel wanted to cash in more by playing the game at spacious Shibe Park in Philadelphia. But Striegel forgot one big thing—Shibe Park was inside the protected territory of the Frankford Yellow Jackets. The Yellow Jackets protested to the league office to have the game cancelled. Because of the league's territorial rights rule, the Yellow Jackets were well within their rights to do so.

A Pottsville trespass might not have seemed so awful had the Yellow Jackets already disbanded for the season, but they actually had a game scheduled against the Cleveland Bulldogs at Frankford Stadium on the same day. In other words, Dr. Striegel had signed a contract to go head-to-head against a fellow member of the league. When Carr got word of this, he immediately sent a warning to the Pottsville owner to cancel the game or face suspension from the league. Striegel claimed to the press that he had received permission from the league to play the game. He admitted—while Carr was in the hospital—that he received the go-ahead from the NFL secretary—Jerry Corcoran. The only problem was that the NFL secretary was Carl L. Storck; Corcoran was the manager of the Columbus Tigers and had no power to set league policy. He was probably just helping out Carr with league matters until the president was healthy enough to do it himself.

Three days before the Pottsville–Notre Dame exhibition game, Carr sent another telegram to warn Striegel about not playing the game. On December 10 the *Philadelphia Ledger* reported the news under the headline of "Pottsville Club Intends to Fullfill Its Contract": "The Pottsville Maroons, national pro football champions, intend to go through with their contract to play the Four Horsemen at Shibe Park, Philadelphia, on Saturday afternoon, despite threats of President Carr, of the National

League, that such a procedure is against his orders and rumors that the Frankford Yellow Jacket management will ask that the Pottsville league charter be revoked."[27]

After hearing the second warning, Striegel contacted Carr to ask him if the league would cover the loss if he backed out of his contract with the promoter of the exhibition game. Carr offered all reasonable protection, but the NFL wasn't going to pick up the tab. Striegel had never backed out of a contract and he wasn't going to do it now—conveniently forgetting about his obligation to the NFL. The game would be played.

In Chicago Chris O'Brien still believed he had a great chance of getting a rematch with the Bears and Red Grange. When the two teams played on Thanksgiving Day in Grange's debut, O'Brien made the mistake of taking the $1,200 dollar guarantee. So O'Brien thought if he could schedule two more league games to leapfrog the Maroons in the standings, he could get the big game against the Bears. Because Grange was the big star at this time, O'Brien wanted to get a second game with the Bears. Thinking Grange and the Bears would only play attractive teams, O'Brien thought he needed his team to keep winning to be an attractive team to schedule the Bears again. A big crowd for a Grange game would make more than the $1,200 guarantee—which he received for the last game against Grange.

O'Brien set up games with two weaker NFL teams who had basically disbanded for the season. On Thursday, December 10 (two days before the Pottsville–Notre Dame contest), the Cardinals pounded a makeshift Milwaukee Badgers team that was so patched together that O'Brien decided to throw open the gates and forego any admission charge. The Cardinals won easily 59–0. Little did O'Brien know that on the field were four high school kids recruited to play for the Badgers. Then on Sunday (December 12), the Cardinals defeated the Hammond Pros 13–0 to finish the regular season with an 11–2–1 record. Ironically, the purpose of all O'Brien's maneuvering went down the drain during that same week. Red Grange suffered his arm injury, and the Cardinals didn't get their rematch with the Bears. As far as O'Brien knew, the season was over.

At this time Maroons' fans had already decided their team was NFL champs. However, those who looked at the NFL schedule realized the season was not yet completed. The Maroons were scheduled to play at Providence on Sunday, December 13, a day after the exhibition game against the Notre Dame All-Stars. But most of Pottsville—as well as owner Dr. Striegel—was interested in the game against the Irish. A victory over the Irish would mean the "world" title—and a lot of money. In the end, Dr. Striegel would overplay his hand. On Saturday, December 12, four things happened:

1. The Pottsville Maroons defeated the Notre Dame All-Stars, 9–7, on the strength of a Charlie Berry field goal before a disappointing crowd of just 8,000 fans at Shibe Park.
2. The Cleveland Bulldogs defeated the Frankford Yellow Jackets, 3–0, in front of 8,000 fans at Frankford Stadium.
3. Dr. Striegel received a telegram from NFL president Joe F. Carr stating that the Pottsville Maroons would be suspended by the NFL for playing a game in the territorial rights of the Frankford Yellow Jackets after being warned.
4. The Providence Steam Roller received word that they were not permitted to play Pottsville (on December 13) the next day.

After repeated warnings, Carr had nothing else to do but suspend the Pottsville franchise—officially ending the Maroons chances of winning the 1925 NFL championship. At this point, the Maroons were not a member of the NFL and in turn not eligible to win the NFL title. But in the early years of the NFL everything was never that clear. As the NFL season came to a close, events began to unfold that would make the 1925 season the most controversial in history. First, the Cardinals found themselves in trouble when the truth about the December 10 game against the Milwaukee Badgers came out in Chicago. In order for the Badgers to have eleven men on the field, they put four high school boys in uniform. While still in bed at the hospital, Carr received word of the four high school boys, and immediately started an investigation.

> If the reports are well founded both the Chicago and Milwaukee teams will be fined heavily. Our rules prohibit any team playing a man eligible for college football. The fine is $50 to $1,000 with possible expulsion from the league. I will enforce the rules, if the charges are true.
>
> I can see no reason why either Chris O'Brien, president of the Cardinals or the Milwaukee management would need to call on high school boys. Both teams have plenty of players. This is the first case of flagrant rule violation called to my attention.[28]

After quickly gathering the information, President Carr passed down punishment that was swift and harsh. On December 30 the *Chicago Tribune* reported the penalties:

1. The Milwaukee team was not suspended; but the owner, Ambrose McGurk, was fined $500 and given ninety days to sell his club.
2. Art Folz, a Cardinals player who admitted procuring the four high school boys for McGurk, was banned from the NFL for life!

3. Although everyone agreed that he hadn't known about the arrangement, Cardinals owner Chris O'Brien was still fined $1,000 and placed on probation for one year by Carr.
4. Following up on the Pottsville resolution, the Maroons, for violating territorial rights in Philadelphia on December 12 after it had been forbidden to by the president, were fined $500 and the club was suspended as a member of the league, which meant forfeiture of its franchise.[29]

Carr's quick and rather harsh response to the end of the 1925 season was universally praised across the country. And Carr was still in the hospital recovering from appendicitis. Chris O'Brien readily admitted his mistake:

> No one is as sorry over what happened to those four Englewood high school boys as I am, and I want to give my story to the public and am willing to take my share of the blame, because I will admit selfishness on my part. I was selfish, perhaps, because I wanted another game with the Bears. I hadn't experienced a very good year, I saw the chance of getting even with such a game. I expected to get it by beating Pottsville in our game with them on Dec. 6. But were beaten.
>
> Just before time to start [game], I learned that there were high school amateurs on the Milwaukee team. Now I know the mistake I made was in not cancelling the game right then. But there were several hundred people out there to see the game. Things were moving fast. I didn't sit down and think it out carefully. Probably thought the best way was to go ahead and play the game, thinking that the high school boys never would be caught. Anyway, I didn't stop it.
>
> I have written our president, Mr. Carr, in Columbus about it. . . . I am willing to do anything to save those schoolboys and put professional football in the right light.[30]

The four high school boys were also punished for playing in the game. James Snyder, William Thompson, Jack Daniels, and Charles Richardson were declared ineligible to play any high school activities by participating in a professional sport—although they were not paid to play. As for the NFL, Carr's decisions were solely based on upholding the rules and regulations of his league. For over eighty-five years, the city of Pottsville has claimed to have had the 1925 NFL championship "stolen" from it, but that couldn't be further from the truth. Their owner—Dr. Striegel—broke a league rule and paid the ultimate price.

For President Carr it was a simple choice to suspend the Maroons and make them ineligible for the 1925 NFL title. It was all about moving the young league forward. In speaking to the press, Carr clarified his stance on all the controversy.

Rules of our league are going to be enforced as long as I am President. That's the only way professional football can continue to exist and hold popular favor. The violators knew what the rules were when they violated them. Now they'll have to pay the penalty.

We are trying to build up the National Professional Football League by trying to merit confidence of the public and press through observance of all rules, especially that pertaining to the use of players who still are eligible for college competition. My only regret is that in this instance league rules do not permit more drastic fines and I propose to ask that stringent regulations and much heavier fines be placed in the league rules when the league convenes in its annual meeting next month.[31]

15

The Grange League (1926)

After a tumultuous month and a half, Joe F. Carr was nearly at full strength and felt physically ready for anything. He announced that the NFL's winter meeting would be held on February 6–7 in Detroit, Michigan. In preparing for the meeting Carr put together an itinerary that was sure to be very eventful, since the owners had several major issues that needed to be resolved. The public and press would watch this meeting more closely than any previous league get-together—something Carr and the other owners were very aware of.

The most important topic was the NFL's fragile relationship with the colleges and universities around the country. Carr knew he had to regain (or according to some, gain for the first time) the trust of the coaches and athletic directors who ran college football, or life could be very difficult. For the past five years he had fought this issue, stating that his league would do the right thing to protect the eligibility of college players. It was now time to put up or shut up.

The weeks before the Detroit meeting, Carr had conversations with Tim Mara, Dr. Harry March, and James Dooley (a lawyer and one of the Providence owners) to get their input on writing a new bylaw for the NFL to finally put this issue to rest. It was time to get the "specific wording" correct and ironclad, so there wouldn't be any argument. After getting all the input he needed, Carr came up with the answer he was looking for. He would reveal the new bylaw at the meeting.

Carr would also address the Pottsville issue and explain for the final time his ruling on the subject. He hoped that issue would be put to rest too. While Carr was very busy in getting ready for the league meeting,

Red Grange was wrapping up the second half of his barnstorming tour on January 31. In the end Grange and the Bears played nineteen games in two months before over 469,000 fans. It is estimated that Grange and Pyle cleared about $250,000 on the second part of the tour (including endorsements). The newspapers and promoters of the two tours tended to overstate attendance, as well as Grange's share of the gate receipts; the actual amount he collected is unknown. The Bears organization netted about $100,000, which George Halas described as "the first financial cushion we'd managed to accumulate." The bottom line for all the parties involved is that they all made money giving professional football a major boost in respectability.[1]

During the long trip back, Pyle huddled with Halas and Dutch Sternaman to discuss his plans for the 1926 season and his star player Red Grange. The Bears' owners thought the 1925 deal heavily favored Pyle, but they were willing to accept the same arrangement to keep Grange in a Bears uniform. Pyle was amenable to the fifty-fifty split, but he also asked for one-third ownership of the franchise. Halas and Sternaman said no way, "No, no, no! In no way. No, first, last and always! The matter was not negotiable. A percentage of earnings, yes, that was negotiable, but a share of ownership, no!" Halas said in his autobiography. The Grange-Pyle team then parted company with the Bears. Pyle then looked to get his own NFL team. He would go to Detroit with his own agenda and was willing to ruffle some feathers to get what he wanted.[2]

The Motor City would be the stage for an unexpected battle among two moguls, who suddenly showed a nasty dislike for each other. At 2:00 p.m. on February 6 at the Hotel Statler, President Carr called the league meeting with twenty NFL teams in attendance. Carr opened the session by giving the "President's Report," and it set the tone for the rest of the meeting.

> In making my annual report of the affairs of the National Football League, I feel that the past season has been the most remarkable in many ways of any year in the history of the organization. Attendance at most cities increased many times and the feeling of the Press and public was better than ever before. True, the addition of New York and Providence added much to both the class and prestige of the League, but the outstanding development of the past season was the increased publicity that the organization received on all sides.
>
> Shortly after the opening of the past season, your President received a letter, after an exchange of much correspondence, from the General Manager of the Associated Press, in which he stated that he felt the National Football League had kept faith with the public in all matters, and that beginning with that date the Associated Press would carry the results of our games and the League standings on its trunk wire, giving us publicity throughout the United States, Canada and Mexico, and we had won a place that we had been striving for since the League was organized.

With increased attendance as recorded above, and with much publicity, both were augmented when Mr. Grange elected to become a professional and play on one of the teams in the National Football League. Much discussion followed the entry of this most talked of athlete of modern times into our League, but I am firmly convinced that the net result has been all in favor of our organization.

Thousands upon thousands of people were attracted to their first game of Professional football through a curiosity to see Grange in action, and many of these newcomers became profound advocates of the Professional game. I quote one of the New York's writers, who said, "I have always been an advocate of Professional Football. Last Sunday I went to the Polo Grounds to see Red Grange. I was invited to sit on the bench of the New York Club. Never in my long experience have I ever seen so much spirit, so much perfect play, so sure tackling, and I came away from the game an avowed advocate of the Professional game, and you may expect to see me on the bench at every game the Giants play next season." This is only one of the many, many who have spoken in the same vein.

Just when it seemed that our organization had gone fairly well toward its goal last season, two events happened that threatened to tear the very foundation from under our League. First Milwaukee and the Chicago Cardinals engaged in a game of football at Chicago, in which four high school boys were permitted to play with the Milwaukee club. Then over the positive orders of the President of the League, and against all of its rules and regulations, the Pottsville team invaded the territory of another club in the League and played a game with a team that was not a member of the League.

In the case of the Chicago Cardinals and the Milwaukee club, I made a very thoro [*sic*] investigation and at its conclusion I fined the Milwaukee Club the sum of $500.00, and gave the management ninety days in which to dispose of its assets at Milwaukee, after which he must retire from the League. The Cardinal management was fined the sum of $1,000.00 and placed on probation for one year.

I could not find where the management of the Cardinal team had guilty knowledge of the status of the boys who played until after the game had been played.

In the case of Pottsville, I had been appraised through reports from League members and the Press that the Pottsville team intended to play a game at Philadelphia on Saturday, December 12. I immediately notified the management of the Pottsville club that the game should not be played under all penalties that the League could inflict. The Pottsville management wired me that they had signed a contract and that they desired the League to insure them against a damage suit. I advised that the League would give them every protection possible and again forbade them to play in the protected territory of another club, and with a team which was not a member of our organization. Three different notices forbidding the Pottsville club to play were given and the management elected to play regardless. Hence I fined the club the sum of $500.00, and suspended them from all rights and privileges, and declared their franchise forfeited in the League.

All of the foregoing were acts and penalties assessed by me against men whom I have come to know and mingle with as friends and still have the kindliest feeling toward all of them. However, as your President pledged to both the members of this organization and the public to sustain both the rules of the League and play fair with the public, and do my plain duty as I saw it, the penalties were imposed in keeping with the rules and regulations of our League.

As I have stated before in this report, while the penalties that were imposed on those who violated our rules sound severe, nevertheless I felt that in many cases in our League, immense sums of money have been invested and still greater sums will be expended. The only protection this money has is the protection your officers give it through the enforcement of the rules, and if clubs feel that the rule may be broken with impunity and are permitted to do it, then the history of the National Football League is already written.

Dr. Striegel of the Pottsville club and his brother called at my home after notification of the penalties as recorded previously in this report. They contended that they had been punished without a hearing. I contended that having been forewarned, no hearing was necessary, but in a spirit of fairness I would be glad to have them come before the League and state their case. However, I advised them that under no consideration would I retract from the penalties that had been imposed, unless instructed to do so by the League, and if it is the pleasure of the organization before we adjourn, the Pottsville club will be given a hearing and also the facts re-stated by your President and it will then be up to the organization to either sustain the President or give the Pottsville team a mitigation of sentence.

In closing, I again state that I have tried to do my duty as I saw it, and I feel that every act of mine will stand the strictest scrutiny of the public, Press and the courts if necessary, and I will gladly invite discussion of this report and will be glad to give additional information that any member may desire.[3]

Carr's report and all his decisions were then approved by all of the owners. His powerful words finally put to rest the Pottsville issue and reiterated that no player, team, or owner was above the rules and regulations that he was trying to establish. Although the bylaws weren't perfect (the league was still only six years old), Carr knew that the rules had to be followed in order for the league to progress and move forward. The owners continued to see that Carr was going to be the man with the answers, and he was the right person for the job.

The owners then reelected Carr as their president, as well as John Dunn as vice president and Carl Storck as treasurer. After putting 1925 behind them, Carr then presented a new resolution that would put the eligibility of college players coming into the NFL in a more clear and concise manner. With help from James Dooley (lawyer) and Charlie Coppen of the Providence Steam Roller the resolution was presented to the other owners.

> That the National Football League, assembled in annual Meeting at Detroit, Michigan, this 6th day of February, 1926, hereby places itself on record as unalterably opposed to any encroachment upon college football, and hereby pledges its hearty support to college authorities in maintaining and advancing the interest in college football and in preserving the amateur standing of all college athletes.
>
> We believe there is a public demand for professional football as has been clearly demonstrated by the wide interest manifested notably thruout [*sic*] the past season, and, to the end that this League may not jeopardize the amateur standing of any college player, it is the unanimous opinion of this meeting that every member of the National Football League be positively prohibited from inducing or attempting to induce any college player to engage in professional football until his class at college shall have graduated, and any member violating this rule shall be fined not less that One Thousand Dollars, or loss of its franchise or both.
>
> The President of this League is hereby authorized and directed to appoint a committee of League members to confer with a Committee from the Inter-Collegiate Athletic Association, with a view to carrying out the purpose set forth in this Resolution.[4]

The resolution was passed and Carr nominated George Halas to be chairman of the committee to confer with the college officials to present the resolution. After six years, Carr and the owners finally got the specific wording correct, and it seemed that the new resolution would be ironclad. After the meeting, Carr spoke to the press about the resolution.

> What more could we do to prove our regard for college football than rule that a lad who matriculates in any institution of learning cannot play in our league *until his class has graduated*? This means that if a boy enters the University of Pennsylvania, say, this fall, joins the freshman squad, and quits college two weeks after he matriculates, *he cannot play football in the National League until 1930*. That may work a hardship on some boys. I could cite several cases where it has appeared to be a little harsh already. But it is the only way we can prove to the college men that we are not going to do anything to weaken amateur athletics as the recreational part of higher education.[5]

The rule became one of the NFL's proudest badges of altruism. The league always took pride in its "class-has-graduated" rule as an example of how it protected both college football and student athletes. Sixty years later, some student-athletes would challenge that rule in the courts as a violation of their right to earn a living.

Just when it looked like the NFL was feeling good about itself, another war was about to start. C. C. Pyle (with his star player Red Grange at his side) had arrived in Detroit to apply for an NFL franchise. But Pyle never did anything by the books. He took the floor and announced that he and Red had just secured a five-year lease on Yankee Stadium for all the

Sundays and holiday dates from October 15 to December 31. "I have the biggest star in football and I have the lease on the biggest stadium in the country and I am going into your league whether you like it or not," Pyle boldly announced. He proposed running his own franchise right in New York City. Pyle painted a convincing picture: with the biggest stadium in the country and the biggest star in football playing in it, all the league members stood to profit greatly. All but one.[6]

Pyle didn't discuss his idea with Tim Mara, who just a year ago purchased his Giants franchise with the thought he was buying an exclusive franchise in New York. Wasn't that the purpose of a franchise? In the name of profit, would the league set aside Mara's rights and allow a new franchise in Yankee Stadium across the Harlem River, less than a thousand yards from the Polo Grounds? A couple of owners didn't think twice before jumping on the Grange bandwagon. A. H. Bowlby of Rock Island bubbled over, Dutch Sternaman went for it, and Halas was noncommittal, knowing that Grange in the league would only help the NFL. But as much as the other owners wanted Grange in the NFL, he couldn't be in New York unless Mara said it was okay. The NFL's territorial rights rule gave him the power.

Mara didn't care for the way Pyle moved into his territory and assumed the league would just give him a franchise. He told Pyle no way. That evening a couple of the owners attempted a compromise. Perhaps Mara would be willing to countenance a team with Grange in Brooklyn. Perhaps Pyle would be willing to back off and go to Ebbets Field some ten miles from the Polo Grounds. Pyle dug in for a fight, saying to Grange, "No blasted Irishman is going to keep me out of New York!"[7]

After roughly five hours of discussions, a meeting was arranged between Mara and Pyle. It was doomed. Mara had developed a dislike for Pyle's arrogance, and now C. C. was treating him as a tiresome obstacle to more "riches." According to one witness, Mara came close to punching C. C. In the end it looked like Mara would get his wish with no NFL franchise for Pyle-Grange. Mara's decision to not allow Pyle a team in his territory was well within his rights, and Carr backed his owner 100 percent. He, like Mara, didn't care for the way Pyle did business, assuming he could have any franchise in any city he wanted. Everyone knew that Pyle was only capitalizing on Red's fame, something that every man in the room was anxious to do. The only difference was that, unlike the others, Pyle was determined Grange would receive the biggest share of the capitalization, which in turn would put more money in Pyle's pockets. Carr couldn't bankrupt his league so Pyle could become rich. Everybody in the league had to follow the same rules, right?

That Mara's refusal to be bulldozed was fueled by self-interest goes without saying. He saw no profit in allowing his Giants to become New

York's "second" team. But beyond that, he could think of long-term profits as opposed to quick riches. If the league caved in this time, what would happen when next year's "Grange" came along and wanted a slice of Chicago? And the year after that; would Philadelphia be given away to another college star? Mara, Carr, and the others owners had to ask, who was running this show anyway—the league or the stars? This was a battle worth fighting.

The first day of the winter meetings ended with C. C. Pyle being shut out of the NFL. Pyle and Grange knew the door was pretty much closed, so Pyle did the only thing he knew how to do and that was think big. Pyle slowly got the word out he was going to organize his own league with Grange's team playing in New York at Yankee Stadium. The entire dynamic of professional football was about to change, and Carr's NFL was about to face a war against what historians have called the "Grange League."

After a restless night for everyone, the second day started at 1:15 p.m. with Carr and the NFL owners increasing the roster limit from sixteen players to eighteen, helping teams who had suffered late-season injuries. The owners also approved raising the guarantee fee from $1,000 to $1,500, and the application fee was increased from $500 to $2,500. This was done to reduce the number of applications coming into the NFL. Then to wrap up the very eventful meeting, one more curveball was thrown. The league awarded the 1925 NFL championship to the Chicago Cardinals and their owner Chris O'Brien. But O'Brien declined the title, saying that "the Chicago club wanted only a title won on the playing field," although they were the NFL's champions for the 1925 season on the basis of having the best record.[8]

Just like Mara and his decision to block Pyle in New York, O'Brien was well within his right to decline. But the bottom line was the Cardinals were still the NFL's champions in 1925 based on Carr's ruling that made Pottsville ineligible. The owners voted the Cardinals champions regardless of O'Brien's choice, and Carr's proper ruling regarding Pottsville has remained correct for nearly eighty-five years. The way it should be. The evidence in the Pottsville case is simple. The owner of the Maroons was warned repeatedly by the president of the NFL about not playing the game. He broke a league rule and paid the price.[9]

The meeting ended, and while heading home Carr must have thought about what a hectic two days he had just spent in Detroit. To be honest, it was a crazy nine months since he left for New York to seek an owner for an NFL franchise—a franchise nobody wanted. Now he had two rich moguls, and the sport's biggest star, all fighting over which would survive in the Big Apple. Carr thought the publicity and attention the sport was getting was positive, but he also knew this was just the beginning of a financial battle. How would his league survive?

In the beginning of this conflict, Carr fully, and silently, supported one of his owners. But Tim Mara began the struggle with a war of words.

> I didn't make enough money last year to stuff a hat brim. I remember one game where our net profits were something like $105, which was absurd compared to what the players got. Of course, we expect to do better next year but it's a cinch the revenue won't increase to the point where there will be room for two clubs. Under those conditions, all of Jake Ruppert's [owner of the New York Yankees baseball team] money hardly could save Grange from going broke.
>
> I can see that brand new bankroll of his melting right away. If he attempts to go it alone here, he will have the same chance of an independent running against a solid organization, to wit: None.
>
> If he tries to organize a rival league, he will find the player market low, even if he could locate adequate grounds in paying cities which I doubt. The thing would mean the lining up of 150 players for eight clubs and I don't think there is anything like that many good ones available. Of course he might get the services of a few stars. So did the Federal League in baseball and most of the backers lost plenty. The playing strength would remain with us, knowing from experience that we can meet our obligation.
>
> Incidentally, I'm far from alone in my stand against an invasion of New York territory. President Carr has telephoned me with the assurance that the league is behind me to a man. As for the report that Grange and his manager, Pyle, might persuade the Chicago Bears to desert in a body, I am pleased to say that they have told me they are with the New York Giants one hundred per cent.
>
> If Grange carries out his threat to promote a team in New York and conflicts with our Sunday dates, neither one of us will make a nickel. But we are in a better position to survive as we are in an organized league and any other team that invades our territory without a franchise will have to play as an outlaw.[10]

Mara didn't hold back, but his right hand man—Dr. Harry March—was a little more diplomatic saying, "Competition is the backbone of all sports, and the New York Football Giants welcome the coming of a new league in this city."[11] President Carr was definitely in Mara's corner, and speaking to Don Maxwell of the *Chicago Tribune*, he explained the history of making money in professional football.

> O, it's a great game—this pro football. But it's never been a great money making game. Take that old team we called the Columbus Panhandles. I organized that bunch 20 years and more ago. We made some money, but I didn't get rich. Nobody has in this pro grid game. A lot of us have gone broke thinking we would. I managed those Nesser boys and the rest of the Panhandles because I got a kick out of it. Of course I wanted to make money. But money wasn't all of it—you get what I mean?

We kept on playing pro football and getting fun out of it and then in 1921 some of the other professional promoters got me to come down to Akron and they made me president of a new league. They called it the National Professional Football League. Chris O'Brien, the boss of your Cardinals, was one of them.

Five years—that's the life of the league. We started with a loose organization—no bylaws, no constitution, just a sort of gentleman's agreement to play the game square and let the colleges alone. I believe pro football has a big future. I believe that games in New York and Chicago will be drawing crowds rivaling baseball attandances—not next year, or the next, but in five years.

We're not worried over this new league. If it's successful it will help all of us. Competition's all right. But don't let any one kid you into thinking that any new league, or old league, either, is going to make a million dollars next year. Somebody might lose a half million. Running a football club is the most risky business I know. You stand a chance of injury to your stars and you run the chance of bad weather. Tim Mara went into New York prepared to lose thousands of dollars. It's a great game.[12]

Carr and the fellow owners would get in line to support Mara, and the "league first" mentality was taking shape. Cardinals owner Chris O'Brien was next to fall in line and throw his support: "We have most of the high class stars under contract and a war chest on which to draw—and we certainly intend to protect our investment to the best of our financial ability. If the newcomers think they can break in without a fight, they are welcome to try it."[13]

As the NFL owners were talking the talk, Pyle began to organize his new league. On February 17—all of eight days after his negotiations with the NFL broke down—Pyle announced that his league would have ten teams and start play that fall. The first four teams were the New York Yankees (Red Grange), Boston, Newark, and Milwaukee. Other possible cities included Chicago (to compete with the Bears and Cardinals), Brooklyn, and a West Coast team to be led by George "Wildcat" Wilson, former All-American halfback at Washington. Pyle also would talk the talk.

Our league will be limited in the number of clubs. It will follow a schedule that is arranged before the season opens and there will be no deviation from this schedule, no games tossed in, or out, as the race is under way. We intend to have one of the most influential figures in the football world as the head of our league. We will insist that each club given a franchise, put up a substantial sum, which will go into a sinking fund.

We are not preparing to start a football "war," as has been announced, but if there has to be a "war" our army will be strong enough to win it.[14]

There was no doubt professional football was about to see a "war." At this time Carr took a break from all the bickering and trash-talking to help promote the game. In a national article written by *Liberty Magazine* on Red Grange and the money involved in professional football, Carr selected his NFL All-Star team for 1925. He named the following players on his first team:

Ends: Lynn Bomar (New York Giants); Paul Goebel (Columbus Tigers)
Tackles: Ed Healey (Chicago Bears); Link Lyman (Cleveland Bulldogs)
Guards: Butch Spagna (Frankford Yellow Jackets); John Alexander (New York Giants)
Center: Herb Stein (Pottsville Maroons)
Quarterback: Joey Sternaman (Chicago Bears)
Halfbacks: Red Grange (Chicago Bears); Red Barron (Coral Gables All-Stars)
Fullback: Jack McBride (New York Giants)[15]

Carr included stars who played on the Red Grange tour; thus Grange and Barron were selected. In the midst of dealing with the issues facing the NFL, Carr was also asked to be president of the Columbus Senators, the capital city's minor league baseball team, and of course he said yes. But baseball took a back seat to Carr's football duties, and he quickly arranged a meeting with an unlikely source. Dr. John Streigel, the embattled owner of the Pottsville Maroons, made a trip to Columbus to visit with Carr.

Carr had heard that Streigel was in negotiation with C. C. Pyle to join his new league, which was now being called the American Football League (AFL). Carr might not have wanted to bring the Maroons back into the NFL, but he knew that blocking them from joining the AFL was probably more important. So Carr gave Streigel a second chance by reassuring him that the NFL would readmit his team to the league during their summer meeting. Then Carr struck another blow to Pyle's loop.

In order to make a big splash, Pyle announced the hiring of William "Big Bill" Edwards—the former Princeton All-American tackle who had held jobs as collector of internal revenues and street cleaning commissioner in New York—to be the president of the AFL. Pyle signed Edwards to a three-year contract at $25,000 per year. Edwards ascended to his office with a ringing speech about preserving "high-class football" and "red-blooded sport." The huge salary made big headlines but it also turned off potential investors.[16]

After hearing about the big salary that AFL owners would pay Edwards, the owners of the Milwaukee franchise started backing out of joining Pyle's league. Carr stepped in with a compromise—join the NFL. Carr was willing to sell the old Milwaukee franchise, which was disposed by Ambrose McGurk for playing the four high school kids, to Johnny Bryan (who had played halfback the last couple of seasons with the Chicago Bears) and his partners. They quickly said yes to Carr. "We were all set to support Pyle when he first started to organize. We attended his meetings and we got our franchise. Things moved along nicely until Pyle gave Edwards a contract of $25,000 a year. Even this might have been all right had Pyle let us in on the secret but he never told us a word about what he intended to do and we found out only through the papers."[17]

With the potential of ten clubs in his league, Pyle was asking his investors to contribute $2,500 a season up front, just to pay the salary of the league's president. That was a big chunk of change to put up even before an owner tried to sign any players. Pyle was limiting his field of possible owners if he was asking for that type of money, and eventually he had to invest his own money just to get the league off the ground. Plus his way of doing business wasn't what pro football owners were used to, by spending "lots" of money.

Carr felt good going two for two against Pyle, getting both Pottsville and Milwaukee to join his league. In April Carr sent a letter to all the NFL owners, keeping them updated on the current state of the league—including a bombshell.

To All Club Owners in the National Football League

Gentleman: Much publicity has appeared since our meeting at Detroit in connection with Professional football, and especially about the proposed new League. I deem it necessary therefore, to let you know that your President has been attempting to take good care of the interests of the National League; and I am giving you herewith, a brief resume of what has been done.

Have consummated the transfer of the Milwaukee franchise from Mr. McGurk to Messrs. Bryan and Mulkern. I consider the entrance of these gentlemen into the national League as a distinct asset, as both are highly representative citizens of Milwaukee, and I am sure they will put the team over in a real big way for the National League.

Was in the East two weeks since we have secured Ebbett's Field in Brooklyn, and just as soon as the personnel of the Officers [are] ready to be announced we will give the news out. We are trying to get a gentleman who will be a real asset to serve as President of the Brooklyn club, but are not ready just at this time to make the announcement.

Cleveland newspapers carried several stories about attempts being made to interest Cleveland citizens in the proposed new League, but according to last reports, two prominent men who had been approached had turned down the proposition.

While in the East, I had a conference with a group of business men of Newark, N.J. They are looking over the situation and if they feel Professional Football will be profitable in Newark, they will file an application for membership in the National League.

Very truly yours,
Joe F. Carr, Pres.[18]

In the end Newark would join Pyle's league, giving Carr his only loss to the new organization. But the intriguing news in the letter was that the NFL would have a franchise in Brooklyn. Tim Mara noticed the need for more teams to compete with Pyle's league so he agreed to allow a team to be placed in the borough across the city. Carr saw the extra franchises coming in as a way of keeping players off AFL teams and fans away from AFL games.

On June 9 Carr traveled east to Philadelphia to be a guest speaker at a rally for the Frankford Athletic Association. Speaking in front of a few thousands members at the Frankford High School gymnasium, Carr detailed the NFL's activities and the current outlook for the 1926 season. After his speech Carr watched three boxing matches (which were refereed by Guy Chamberlin), a wrestling exhibition, and a performance by the Yellow Jacket Band. The year 1926 would be a big one for the Yellow Jackets.[19]

Carr so enjoyed his visit to the City of Brotherly Love that when he returned to Columbus, he announced that the league's summer scheduling meeting would take place in Philadelphia. So on July 10–11 the NFL met at the Ben Franklin Hotel to discuss league matters. On the first day Carr began the meeting by naming a small committee, which included George Halas and Dr. Harry March, to meet with the Intercollegiate Athletic Union in New York the following week. The owners then approved the use of the *Official Collegiate Spalding Football Guide* for the upcoming season, as the NFL still followed the rules used by the college game.[20]

After a dinner break that saw the Frankford Athletic Association serve lobster, clam chowder, fried potatoes, coffee, pie, and Yellow Jacket cigars, the owners got back to business. The new Brooklyn franchise was accepted and the old Pottsville franchise readmitted. The new additions helped the NFL compete with the upstart AFL, but the war was just beginning. The Rock Island Independents defected to the AFL, and Pyle then tried to woo Chris O'Brien and his Cardinals to the new league. Even though the Cardinals were not a moneymaker, they were the 1925 NFL champions, and their loss would have really hurt the older league. But O'Brien was loyal to the NFL, forcing Pyle to make his arrangement with

Joey Sternaman, taking "Little Joey" away from the Chicago Bears, to run the other Chicago franchise. When the AFL Chicago Bulls gained the right to play home games in Comiskey Park and pushed the Cardinals to the smallish Normal Park, O'Brien was in trouble.[21]

Carr saw that O'Brien needed help so he quietly rescinded the $1,000 fine levied on him for participating in the "high school" game with Milwaukee. Finally, before the season started, O'Brien was forced to sell his star player, Paddy Driscoll, to the Bears for $3,500 in order to keep his team operating. "His financial outlook was dismal. He had to cut expenses. The most expensive player was Paddy Driscoll, and common sense told Chris that Paddy deserved a raise, not a cut," Halas recalled. Driscoll eventually signed a contract for the year at $10,000. With this golden contract, Driscoll became the first—and maybe only—player to profit from the war between the two leagues.[22]

The Cardinals stayed in and Louisville returned, but the Rochester Jeffersons, Cleveland Bulldogs, and Minneapolis Marines begged out for the 1926 season. On the second day of the league's meeting a new traveling team, the Los Angeles Buccaneers, headquartered in Chicago, was accepted and featured mostly West Coast players—the biggest name was two-time All-American end Harold "Brick" Muller. But the most important news from the two-day marathon meeting came from a tiny town in Minnesota.

For the past three years, the Duluth Kelleys had played winning football (9–7 overall record) in the NFL, but they never played enough games to challenge for any league championship. Plus nobody wanted to travel the great distance to Duluth to play in the league's worst weather conditions. The team seemed to be a financial loser. Four players operated the franchise in 1925, and on two occasions they had to chip in their own money to pay the guarantee for visiting teams. Ole Haugsrud, the club treasurer, was given the franchise in 1926, and to make things legal, he handed the players a dollar bill to complete the transaction.

Before the summer meeting began, Haugsrud had an idea to make his Duluth team more competitive and profitable. Haugsrud had been a high school teammate of Ernie Nevers in Superior, Wisconsin, and had maintained a friendship with the football star. Nevers had been an All-American running back at Stanford and was second only to Red Grange in star power and ability. Most of the NFL owners thought he would sign with Pyle's AFL, but Haugsrud knew if he could talk to Nevers, he could get him to play for Duluth.

So Ole hopped on a train and headed to St. Louis to meet with Nevers, who was playing major league baseball with the St. Louis Browns that summer. "Ernie was glad to see me, and I was glad to see him. Ernie showed me a letter he had from C. C. Pyle, and Ernie told me, 'Ole, if you can meet the terms Pyle is offering in this letter, it's okay with me. I'll play for Duluth.' And really, that's all there was to it," said Ole Haugsrud to author Myron Cope in an interview. "I would have to pay Ernie fifteen thousand dollars, plus a percentage of the larger gates. I had the money to do it. I believe I was only twenty-two or twenty-three years old, but I had various holdings—buildings and things like that. I had inherited a little money."[23]

The NFL had outfoxed Pyle once again. Haugsrud then contacted Tim Mara to give him the news.

> I had called Tim Mara and let him know about the contract with Ernie Nevers. He was like a father to me from the beginning, he said "I'll tell you kid. We got to do something here to make this a *league*. Now we'll go through with the regular meeting and when it gets halfways through and you got two, three ballgames, I will give you the high sign, then you go up to the league president with your option on Nevers." Well, I did as he told me to. I showed the option to Joe Carr and he said, "Gentleman! I got a surprise for you." He read the option paper and some of them out front got up and yelled like a bunch of kids.[24]

When the owners heard the NFL had a new attraction who nearly rivaled Grange in appeal, they cheered. Then the other owners scrambled to schedule the Duluth team that was now being called Ernie Nevers (Duluth) Eskimos. Only one game would be played in Duluth as the Eskimos would become a full-time traveling team. "Duluth was greatly handicapped in not having anything like a modern stadium. The games were played in Athletic Park in the west end. Seating arrangements were inadequate and at many of the games even the women patrons had to stand," said Haugsrud.[25]

Nevers signed for $15,000 and a share of the bigger gates, making him the highest paid player in the NFL. Carr's league was now feeling good, boosting its membership to twenty-two teams. The president's strategy was to fight the AFL with numbers—teams in the league, players under contract, and games available to fans. To wrap up the meeting, the owners set an opening date (September 19) and a closing date (December 19). The owners then applauded the Frankford Athletic Association for the banquet dinner and their fine hospitality.[26]

Two days after the meeting in Philadelphia, Dr. Harry March, on behalf of the NFL, met with General Palmer A. Pierce, president of the Intercollegiate Athletic Union, in New York to discuss professional football's relationship with the colleges and universities around the country. "Our strong stand in regard to approaching undergraduate athletes in the colleges and the writing into the league constitution forbidding the practice received the hearty approval of General Pierce," March announced after the meeting. Pierce concurred saying the NFL's stance is "in line with what we want."[27]

Carr must have felt relieved hearing this news and finally put the issue behind him. But that news was quickly followed by C. C. Pyle's big announcement on the future of his new league. On July 17 Pyle issued a statement saying that his new AFL would have nine teams and would start play on September 26. The league consisted of three teams clustered around New York: Pyle's New York Yankees, featuring Red Grange; the Brooklyn Horsemen, so named because the team signed two members of the famous Four Horsemen of Notre Dame (Elmer Layden and Harry Stuhldreher); and the Newark Bears.

Other franchises included the Boston Bulldogs (a team mainly of former Ivy Leaguers); the Philadelphia Quakers, owned by Leo Conway; the Cleveland Panthers; the Rock Island Independents (NFL reject); and the Los Angles Wildcats, a traveling team named after their star attraction, George "Wildcat" Wilson.

The last franchise was the Chicago Bulls, led by quarterback Joey Sternaman, who left the Bears (and his brother Dutch) to run his own team. Supposedly, Pyle was no more than the owner of the New York franchise, but that was just for public consumption. The Wilson Wildcat franchise was definitely his concoction and very likely the Chicago squad was also being funded by "Cash and Carry" Pyle. He probably owned nearly a third of the league; the public thought of the AFL as the Grange League, but in reality it was Pyle's.

As the summer came to an end, both leagues finally prepared to do battle on the field. AFL president Bill Edwards proclaimed the league's slogan as "football for all and all for football."[28] Carr ignored the competition when speaking to the press about the NFL's outlook in 1926.

> The National Football League, ready to start the 1926 season, faces the best and brightest prospects in its history. We have 22 teams in our league and every one is backed by good substantial business men. There will be no tampering with players, no contract jumping, no luring away of college stars, nothing but high class sport served in a high class way. Professional sport promotion is always difficult when one starts out to do anything and many evils and many undesirable figures get in before a solid foundation is built. I believe we have eliminated all this by the adoption of stringent rules and a policy of fair dealing with the public.
>
> College men decry the growth of pro football but I believe their attitude is prompted by selfishness. There is no good reason why pro football should not thrive if conducted along clean, sporting lines.
>
> Baseball has become successful because of the excellent way in which it is organized and I can honestly say that I believe the National Football League

Joe's father, Michael Carr (1841–1905), was born in the county of Armagh in Ireland. He came to America at the end of the Civil War and eventually resided in Columbus, Ohio. He married Margaret Hurley in 1866 and passed away in 1905 at the age of sixty-three. Photo from circa 1880–1885. *Courtesy of James Carr.*

Joe's mother, Margaret (Hurley) Carr (circa 1840–1898), married Michael Carr and the couple went on to have seven children—five boys and two girls. Margaret was a stay-at-home mother who passed away in 1898 at the age of fifty-eight. Photo from circa 1880–1885. *Courtesy of James Carr.*

This is the only known photo of Joe F. Carr's Catholic school days. Carr is in the back row, fourth from the right, with his hands folded together. Sitting directly in front of him is his close friend Robert Drury, who would go on to be a part owner of the Boston Red Sox and a successful surgeon in Columbus. The school photo is from circa 1889–1890 when Carr was about ten years old. *Courtesy of the Carr Family Scrapbook.*

As a teenager Joe F. Carr worked as a machinist at the Pennsylvania Railroad and in 1900 began his professional career in sports as the assistant sports editor of the *Ohio State Journal*. This photo of Carr is circa 1903–1905 when he was in his early to mid-twenties. *Courtesy of Margaret Mooney.*

In this photo a young Joe F. Carr is seen throwing a baseball at a family picnic. Carr always liked to wear nice clothes; he is wearing a white dress shirt, bow tie, and derby hat for the occasion. This photo is from circa 1910. *Courtesy of James Carr.*

Joe Carr (in the middle wearing the bow tie) was the team manager of the Columbus Panhandles for sixteen seasons (1907–1922), guiding the railroaders to great success as pro football's most famous traveling team. This photo was taken in 1907—Carr's first year as team manager of the Panhandles. On the right is Harry Greenwood, an assistant manager, and on the left is Ed Hughes. *Courtesy of James Carr.*

For nearly twenty years, the six Nesser brothers were the backbone of the Columbus Panhandles football team. In a photo from 1916, left to right, are Ted, Al, Fred, Frank, Phil, and John. None of the six brothers played college football; instead they all worked as boilermakers in the Panhandle Division of the Pennsylvania Railroad. *Courtesy of the Ohio Historical Society.*

On June 27, 1911, in Columbus, Ohio, Joe Carr (back row, second from right) married Josephine Marie Sullivan (back row, first from right). In this photo from circa 1910–1911, Carr and Josephine pose with the whole Sullivan family. *Courtesy of Martha Sullivan.*

Mary Carr was born on October 13, 1913, the first child of Joe and Josephine Carr. In these two photos, Mary, age two, poses for the camera in her favorite white dress, sitting on a wooden chair, reading her favorite book *Little People's A B C. Photos courtesy of the Carr family.*

Joseph Francis Carr Jr. was born on October 1, 1915, the second child of Joe and Josephine Carr. This photo is from circa 1933, the year he graduated from Holy Rosary High School. *Courtesy of James Carr.*

This photo was taken before Game 1 of the 1919 World Series in Cincinnati, Ohio. At this particular gathering, the Carr brothers were joined by John Philip Sousa, the famous American composer and conductor, who was nicknamed "the March King." Sousa composed 136 marches during his career and performed the "Star Spangled Banner" before the first pitch of Game 1. In the photo are—in the back row, from left to right—Michael Carr (Joe's brother), John Philip Sousa, and Joe F. Carr. In the front row, from left to right, are unknown, John A. Karr (Joe's brother who lived in Chicago), and James Wilson. *Courtesy of James Carr.*

This 1922 Columbus Panhandles team photo was taken at Neil Park. The 1922 Panhandles would be the last Panhandle team ever. The railroaders finished with an overall record of 3–8–0, including a horrible 0–8–0 record in NFL games. In the front row, from left to right, are John Conley, Lee Snoots, Bob Rapp, Frank Nesser (wearing helmet), Morris Glassman, Emmett Ruh, and Oscar Wolford. In the back row, from left to right, are assistant manager Jerry Corcoran, Walt Rogers, unknown, Joe Mulbarger, Homer Ruh, Hal Gaulke, Mark Stevenson, Ted Hopkins, coach Herb Dell, and team manager Joe Carr. *Courtesy of Ohio Historical Society.*

NFL president Joe F. Carr, on the right, shakes hands with baseball commissioner Kenesaw Mountain Landis at a football game in Chicago. Landis was the man responsible for cleaning up baseball after the 1919 Black Sox Scandal that rocked baseball. He was elected to the Baseball Hall of Fame in 1944. This photo is from a game circa 1922–1923. *Courtesy of Carr Family.*

In 1925 New York bookie Tim Mara met with NFL president Joe F. Carr and invested in a NFL franchise. Starting that fall the New York Giants began play. In 1963 Mara was inducted as a charter member of the Pro Football Hall of Fame. *Courtesy of the New York Giants.*

Because of Joe Carr's traveling schedule, the rest of the family found ways to entertain themselves. In this photo from circa 1925–1927, the family poses for a formal photo. From left to right are Joe Carr Jr., Josephine Carr, and Mary Carr. *Courtesy of Carr family.*

Carr, Pyle in Conference

In 1926 sports promoter C. C. Pyle, along with his star player Red Grange, formed their own league to compete with the NFL. Pyle's American Football League failed after just one season. In this photo Pyle poses with NFL president Joe F. Carr. *Courtesy of author's collection.*

During his time as NFL president, Joe F. Carr traveled to many NFL contests. In this photo taken on Saturday, November 6, 1926, Carr (in the middle tipping his hat) acknowledges the crowd in Frankford, Pennsylvania—just outside of Philadelphia—as he attends the game between the Chicago Cardinals and the hometown Frankford Yellow Jackets. The Yellow Jackets beat the Cardinals 33–7 in front of 8,000 fans. Frankford Athletic Association president Theodore Holden (far right) stands next to Carr, while the Frankford Girls Football Team hangs out in the back. *Courtesy of Michael Moran.*

Kathleen Rubadue was hired by Joe F. Carr to be his secretary starting in 1929. She was the first and only NFL secretary during Carr's tenure as NFL president. Rubadue worked in the NFL office located on the eleventh floor at 16 East Broad Street in Columbus, Ohio, from 1929 to 1939. This photo was taken in 1936 and shows her taking a call at her desk. *Courtesy of Robert Knapp.*

In this photo from 1931 NFL president Joe F. Carr, standing in the middle (shielding his eyes from the sun), presents the game ball to Spartans captain Father "Pop" Lumpkin at midfield while attending the Spartans–Giants game. *Courtesy of Spartans Historical Society.*

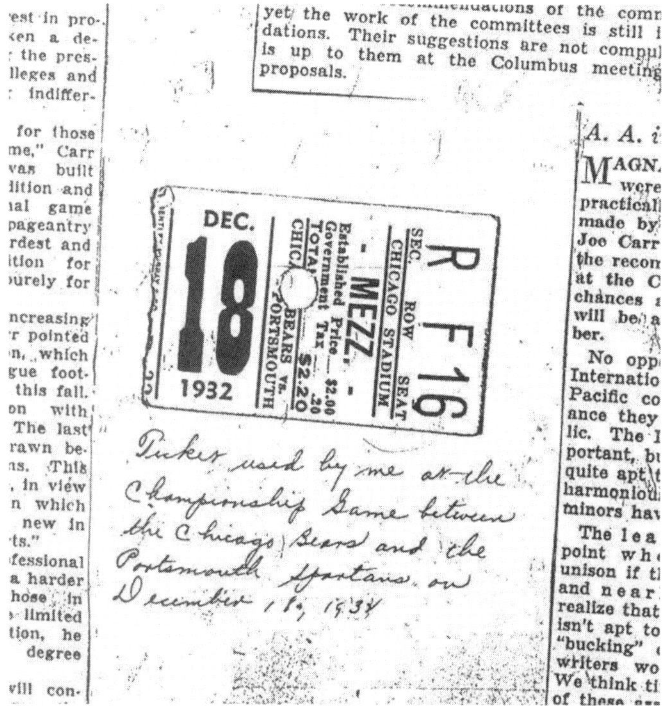

yet the work of the committees is still
dations. Their suggestions are not compul
is up to them at the Columbus meeting
proposals.

DEC.
18
1932

R F 16
SEC. ROW SEAT
CHICAGO STADIUM
- MEZZ. -
Established Price... $2.00
Government Tax... .20
TOTAL... $2.20
CHICAGO BEARS vs. PORTSMOUTH

Ticket used by me at the Championship Game between the Chicago Bears and the Portsmouth Spartans on December 18, 1932

On December 18, 1932, the Portsmouth Spartans played the Chicago Bears in the NFL's first ever postseason game. Because of a snowstorm the game was moved indoors to Chicago Stadium. The Bears went on to defeat the Spartans 9–0 to win the NFL championship. This ticket stub was used by NFL president Joe F. Carr. After the game he placed the historical stub in his personal scrapbook. This is the only known action photo from the indoor game. Number fifty-six, Bears end Bill Hewitt (no helmet), is lead blocking for Bronko Nagurski, who is getting tackled around the neck by Spartans halfback Glenn Presnell. *Courtesy of Carr Family Scrapbook.*

In 1933 the NFL saw three new owners come into the league: Bert Bell, on left (Philadelphia Eagles); Art Rooney, on right (Pittsburgh Pirates); and Charlie Bidwill, in middle (Chicago Cardinals). All three owners ended up in the Pro Football Hall of Fame. *Courtesy of author's collection.*

On December 7, 1933, in Columbus, Ohio, NFL president Joe F. Carr met with team owners Jack Mara of the New York Giants and George Halas of the Chicago Bears to discuss details for the upcoming NFL Championship Game to be played on December 17 in Chicago. After the meeting Carr took the football moguls for a visit to meet the governor of Ohio, George H. White. From left to right are Halas, Mara, Carr, and Governor White. *Courtesy of Carr family.*

This photo was taken on Monday, December 10, 1934, one day after the New York Giants defeated the Chicago Bears 30–13 for the 1934 NFL championship, in a game that has become known as "the Sneaker Game," where the Giants used basketball sneakers in the second half to battle the frozen field. In this photo all the NFL owners watch NFL president Joe F. Carr hand the 1934 NFL championship trophy to Giants owners Tim Mara and his son Jack Mara. In the front row, from left to right, are Dr. Harry March (Giants executive), Carl Storck (NFL vice president), George Halas (Bears), George Richards (Lions), Joe F. Carr (NFL president), Tim Mara (Giants), Jack Mara (Giants), Dan Topping (Dodgers), William Alfs (Lions executive), Charles Bidwill (Cardinals). In the back row, from left to right, are Bert Bell (Eagles), George Preston Marshall (Boston Redskins), Lud Wray (Eagles), Frank Halas (Bears), Dick Guy (Pirates executive), and Art Rooney (Pittsburgh Pirates). *Courtesy of New York Giants.*

George A. Richards, a Detroit radio mogul, was persuaded by NFL president Joe F. Carr to invest in an NFL franchise. In 1934 Richards purchased the struggling small-town Portsmouth Spartans and relocated the team to his hometown. Richards named his team the Detroit Lions. In 1935 the Lions—in just their second year—won the NFL championship. *Courtesy of the Detroit Lions.*

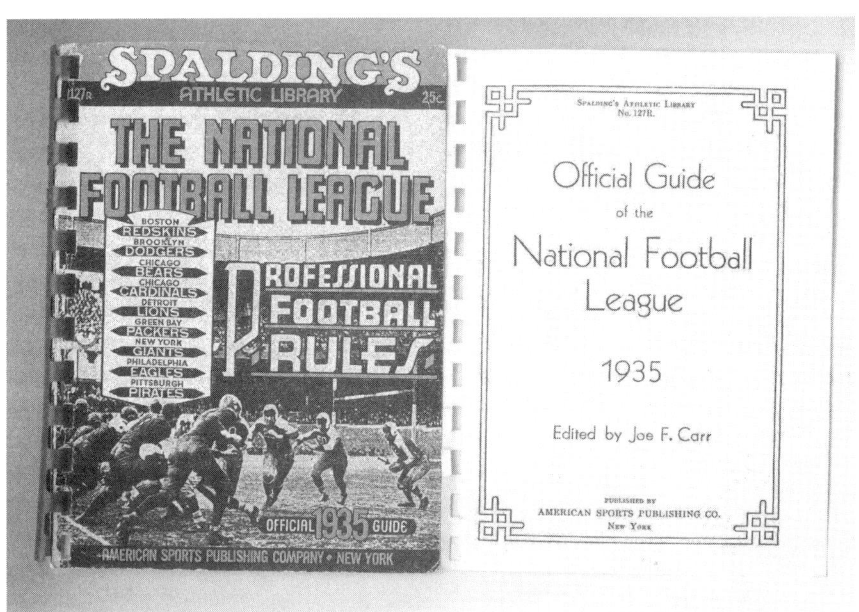

In 1935 NFL president Joe F. Carr edited the first-ever *Official Guide of the National Football League*. The fifty-eight-page guide was published by the Spalding's American Sports Publishing Company. The NFL's official guide is now titled the *Official NFL Record & Fact Book*, and in 2009 it celebrated its seventy-fifth edition. *Photos courtesy of the Spalding Sporting Goods Co.*

NATIONAL FOOTBALL LEAGUE

Season of 1936

OFFICIAL "WHO'S WHO" COUPON

For Ladies Only

This coupon may be exchanged at any box office of any club in the National Football League for a ticket entitling a lady to a grandstand seat at any one of the official games listed on the back of this coupon during the 1936 season . . . PROVIDED the holder of this coupon is accompanied by a gentleman escort who purchases a ticket to the same game.

Signed

Joe. F. Carr

President National Football League

NFL president Joe F. Carr was always trying to find new ways to get fans, sportswriters, and special guests to attend NFL games. These two passes were examples: the top pass from 1936 was given to media personnel and special guests; the bottom pass came in the 1936 copies of *Who's Who in Major League Football*, and it allowed women to attend selected NFL games for free. *Courtesy of author's collection.*

George Preston Marshall, on the left in a fur coat, bought the Boston Braves NFL franchise in 1932. After the Braves struggled for five years in Boston, Marshall moved his team south to Washington and renamed them the Washington Redskins. *Courtesy of Jordan Wright.*

In early September of 1937, Joe F. Carr suffered a mild heart attack that kept him at home in bed for several months. In this photo, Carr–who poses with his trademark cigar–is at his desk in his Columbus office at 16 East Broad Street. Smoking cigars contributed to his heart problems. *Courtesy of the Carr family.*

On December 11, 1938, Joe F. Carr presents the first ever NFL MVP award—a nice watch—to New York Giants center Mel Hein moments before the 1938 NFL Championship Game between the Giants and the Green Bay Packers at the New York Polo Grounds. This would be the last NFL game Carr ever attended before dying of a heart attack in 1939. Starting in 1939 the league's MVP award was named the Joe F. Carr Memorial MVP Trophy. *Courtesy of the author's collection.*

In February 1939, the NFL owners meeting was held in Chicago, Illinois, at the Congress Hotel. NFL president Joe F. Carr was reelected by the owners and given an unheard-of ten-year contract at $10,000 per year. This would be the last owners meeting Carr would attend; three months later he died of a heart attack. Front row, from left to right: Jack Mara (New York Giants), Carl Storck (NFL vice president), NFL president Joe Carr, Dan Topping (Brooklyn Dodgers), and Lee Joannes (Green Bay Packers). Back row, from left to right: George Halas (Chicago Bears), Bert Bell (Philadelphia Eagles), George Preston Marshall (Washington Redskins), Art Rooney (Pittsburgh Pirates), Thomas Lipscomb (Cleveland Rams), and Charlie Bidwill (Chicago Cardinals). *Courtesy of Sandy Allen-Storck family.*

On Wednesday, May 24, 1939, over 300 people attended the funeral of Joe F. Carr at Holy Rosary Church in Columbus, Ohio. Carr had over thirty honorary and eight active pallbearers, including NFL vice president Carl Storck (standing in front of the casket, partially hidden, second from left) and George Halas, owner of the Chicago Bears (in the middle wearing the dark suit). *Courtesy of Margaret Mooney.*

On May 25, 1939, five days after Joe Carr passed away, Carl L. H. Storck was named president of the NFL. In 1941 Storck resigned as president when the league wanted to hire Elmer Layden as the first NFL commissioner. Feeling betrayed by the owners with whom he had worked, Storck never got over the way he was replaced as president. His health declined, and he died in a Dayton nursing home in 1950 at the age of fifty-six. *Courtesy of Sandy Allen.*

In 1963 former NFL president Joe F. Carr was inducted as one of the seventeen charter members of the Pro Football Hall of Fame in Canton, Ohio. In this photo former NFL official Dan Tehan—who was hired by Carr to work NFL games—accepted on behalf of the Carr family. He stands next to the Hall of Fame bronze bust of Carr. *Courtesy of Tehan family.*

Starting in 1939 the NFL honored the memory of Joe F. Carr by naming its MVP award after him. The last Joe F. Carr NFL MVP award came in 1946 when the Associated Press discontinued naming an MVP. In this photo from 1963, Mary Carr (daughter of Joe F. Carr) holds a replica of the former MVP trophy, surrounded by the five grandsons of the former NFL president. In the front row, from left to right, are Gregory, Mary (holding trophy), and James. In the top row, from left to right, are John, Dennis, and Michael. *Courtesy of Carr family.*

On May 24, 1939, Joseph F. Carr (1879–1939) was buried at St. Joseph's Cemetery in Columbus, Ohio. The headstone is made of pinkish granite with the Celtic cross in the middle. *Courtesy of author.*

> is just as strongly entrenched as any league in baseball. The fly-by-night birds are now on the outside looking in, and we intend to keep them there.[29]

Was Carr thinking of Pyle when talking about the "fly-by-night birds"? Who knows, but despite the "war" approaching, Carr always kept a positive spin on the sport he loved. Building that foundation was proving difficult, and this was just another step in the process. The 1926 professional football season would have two leagues, thirty-one teams, and over 600 players; now, would the fans show up?

Early in the season, President Carr went to several games. On Saturday, October 16, he watched the Kansas City Cowboys visit the Columbus Tigers at Neil Park in Columbus. Carr and a crowd of 5,000 fans watched the Cowboys shut out the Tigers, 9–0. Carr was watching the last season of NFL play in his hometown, as the Tigers would not return to the NFL in 1927. The crowds were just too small, as most football fans in central Ohio were paying for tickets to see the Ohio State Buckeyes play, rather than the NFL. The following day Carr was in Stark County to take a look at the traveling Los Angeles (LA) Buccaneers play the aging Canton Bulldogs. Arriving before the game Carr met with both teams on the field and welcomed the LA team into the NFL: "Athletes of Los Angeles, you are meeting members of a football team that carries with it great tradition; you are in a city where players have been trail blazers, who always have fought honorably. Canton is a credit to the National League and we know Los Angeles will be."[30]

An average crowd of 5,000 spectators and Carr showed up at Lakeside Park and saw an exciting game as the Buccaneers came from behind to win 16–13 over the Bulldogs. Canton's glory days were definitely behind them, as they finished the season with a 1–9–3 record. Three weeks later Carr traveled to the East Coast to see games in New York and Philadelphia. In the Big Apple he watched the Bulldogs play a special Tuesday election-day contest against the Giants. Only 4,000 fans showed up at the Polo Grounds to watch a 7–7 tie; it was a sight that disappointed Carr.

In Philadelphia on Saturday, November 6, Carr was introduced to a crowd of 8,000 Yellow Jackets fans. After giving a short speech at midfield, Carr tipped his hat and received a standing ovation. As for the game, Carr saw one of the NFL's best teams put on a show as Guy Chamberlin's Yellow Jackets destroyed the Chicago Cardinals 33–7. At this point the NFL was barely getting by, as crowds were mostly small, and the rest of the season wouldn't get any better. Carr had witnessed some of the smallish crowds personally, but he took some solace in the fact that the AFL was doing even worse. Then Mother Nature threw the knockout punch to C. C. Pyle.[31]

"I'll never forget that it rained every Sunday all fall. I don't think we had one sunny Sunday," Red Grange would recall about the fall of 1926. The competition with the NFL and the bad weather that hit finally took its toll on the AFL. Halfway through its inaugural season, Pyle's league hit a financial crisis. Cleveland and Newark quit by the end of October, and the Boston franchise surrendered in the middle of November. Rock Island followed next, and in an unusual move, the AFL's Brooklyn Horsemen merged with the NFL's Brooklyn Lions, becoming the Horse-Lions. By the end of the season, the AFL had become a four-team loop consisting of the Philadelphia Quakers, New York Yankees, Chicago Bulls, and Los Angeles Wildcats.[32]

The Quakers defeated the Yankees twice in late November to finish the season with an 8–2 record and the AFL title. But by then nobody was watching. The final game of the AFL season was played on December 12 as Red Grange returned to Chicago with his Yankees to play the Bulls. The game was won by the Yankees 7–3, and it bankrupted Joey Sternaman. "We actually had a pretty good team but we didn't get the crowds. We sure tried. But everywhere in that league it was tough. We had plenty of big names and fellows who tried to make it work. But it went under at the end of the year. I came out broke after it; it was a bum gamble," Joey Sternaman recalled in a 1983 interview.[33]

The teams in the AFL were undercapitalized, and when the league didn't capture the fans' interest, the owners—meaning C. C. Pyle—couldn't cover the promised salaries. "He lost a bundle," Grange would later recall. A particularly rainy autumn compounded the problem. Plus most of the teams in the AFL weren't very good; they had been hastily assembled, lacked acceptable linemen, and were badly coached. The games, though often close, were always low scoring or dull. Despite some famous backs scoring was rare. In forty-one league games, the AFL teams scored only forty-two touchdowns.[34]

Most of the problems that afflicted the AFL were present in the NFL too. Talent was spread thin, and most of the twenty-two teams were weaklings. The traveling Louisville Colonels didn't score a point in their four league games, and Hammond only a field goal in their four contests. Neither of those two teams, nor Racine or Milwaukee, finished the season. Akron, Brooklyn, Canton, Columbus, Dayton, Detroit, and Hartford all limped to the end.

The Nevers Eskimos drew fans here and there but not enough to completely offset heavy losses for even the stronger teams. Tim Mara's Giants, going directly against Grange's Yankees, reportedly lost $40,000. In Chicago, where three teams squared off, both the Bears and Cardinals were badly hurt. "I wasn't happy. We were back to the small gates, the search for fans, the pinching of the penny. Mara learned the Red Grange euphoria had vanished. The Giants drew only 3,000 or 4,000. Mara would look through binoculars at Yankee Stadium and say, 'There's no one over there either,'" Halas said in his autobiography.[35]

Ironically, the NFL had a strong finish to the season. By the end of November, the Bears were undefeated (11–0–2) and the Frankford Yellow Jackets had one loss (12–1–1). On December 4 the Jackets and Bears faced each other at Philadelphia's Shibe Park. A nice crowd of 10,000 turned out for the game of the year. For fifty-five minutes the teams battled back and forth across the fifty yard line. The closest anyone came to scoring was Paddy Driscoll's third-quarter field goal attempt that was blocked by Chamberlin.

Suddenly, in the fourth quarter, Bears halfback Bill Senn broke away for a sixty-two-yard touchdown scamper. Driscoll tried the extra point, and once again Chamberlin blocked it. With time running out, Frankford took over the ball. After a long pass to move the pigskin to the Bears' twenty-seven yard line, the Jackets won the NFL championship on the next play. Fading back to pass, Houston Stockton hit Henry "Two-Bits" Homan, the smallest man on the field at five feet five and 144 pounds, who made the catch of the day just as he crossed the goal line. When fullback Tex Hamer split the uprights, the Jackets moved into first place with a 7–6 "miracle" win.

The Yellow Jackets finished the season with a win over the Providence Steam Roller and a tie against the Pottsville Maroons. Guy Chamberlin's squad was now 14–1–2 and it was his fourth NFL championship in the past five seasons. Philadelphia added the NFL crown to the AFL's won earlier by the Quakers. After the Quakers had their title in hand, Leo Conway tried to wangle a game with the Yellow Jackets but they refused. Joe F. Carr also issued a statement saying no NFL club would play the AFL's Quakers.

However, Tim Mara agreed to let his Giants play the Quakers at the Polo Grounds on December 12 in an odd sort of "Super Bowl" with the champions of one league playing against the seventh-place team of the other. There is no evidence that has been found to say whether Carr gave his blessing for the game or that Mara was punished. Maybe Carr felt this was Mara's way of sticking it to Pyle. "Everybody on the Giants wanted to win that one. The Quakers thought the Giants were pushovers, but we kicked the bleep out of them," recalled Babe Parnell, Giants tackle. Only 5,000 die-hard fans braved the snow and cold to see the Grange League's best team get embarrassed. The Giants crushed the Quakers 31–0. There could be no doubt; the AFL was dead.[36]

Although it looked like the NFL had won the war against the Grange League, it definitely lost its share of money. "The National League must have lost at least $250,000. I am sure that eleven of its twenty-two teams lost $150,000 among them. Our club finished the season at least $35,000 in the red," said Jack McDonough, manager of the NFL's Los Angeles Buccaneers, to a Universal Services sportswriter. "Tim Mara was a heavy loser. Only four clubs in our organization made money, the Philadelphia Yellow Jackets, the Chicago Bears, the Providence Steam Roller and the Green Bay, Wisconsin team."[37]

Just a year after rejoicing the big crowd of the Grange tour game, Mara's heavy losses in 1926 made him rethink his involvement in the unpredictable sport of professional football. "Many times my father had second thoughts about football, advancing money and writing off losses. His friends told him he was foolish to keep the Giants but he stayed firm, I am sure, because my brother Jack and I were so interested in the sport," remembered Wellington Mara.[38]

In the end Carr's more structured league was better prepared to lose money and still be able to survive than Pyle's AFL. The NFL had survived its first war against a rival league. The war also proved to Carr, Mara, and Halas that the franchise—not the star—would guide the league and be the most important property. And these franchises would be more successful if the NFL lost some of its dead weight. Now was the time to get rid of some of those extra pounds.

16

Traveling for a Cause (1927–1928)

The 1926 season was a costly war financially for NFL owners, and it showed President Carr what had to be done in order for the league to prosper. Carr's ultimate vision of the NFL becoming a big-time sport, played in big cities, needed to be put into motion. There was no time to wait. Raising the guarantee league fee to $2,500 in 1926 and increasing the application fee were the first big steps to eliminate some of the league's "fat."

In 1927 Carr and the NFL were now ready to get rid of the weaker franchises. For the league's initial seven seasons, franchises came and went as fast as the sun rises and sets, with most of the failed franchises drowning in their own red ink. A few of them had been removed forcibly for not paying league fees, but no owner had been kicked out or told to go away simply because his team couldn't hack it and was, as a result, costing other owners' money. Until now.

One year earlier it was essential for the NFL to field as many franchises as possible to battle the American Football League. Anything to keep players away from AFL rosters, fans away from AFL games, or the league itself out of the sports pages. But now the crisis had passed as "healthy" franchises in larger cities, such as the Chicago Bears, New York Giants, and Frankford Yellow Jackets, who had lost money in 1926, were looking at a better situation in 1927. They needed to avoid being pulled into the abyss by the NFL's weaklings, such as the Canton Bulldogs, Akron Indians, Hammond Pros, Columbus Tigers, Racine Tornadoes, and other such losers.

A sellout in Canton's tiny Lakeside Park would earn the Bears less as a visitor than the Halas men could reap from playing host before a modest crowd at Cubs Park. Also, fans in Chicago, New York, and Philadelphia didn't want to see the likes of Canton or Akron—certainly Canton or Akron wouldn't be involved in the championship race in 1927 (and hadn't for awhile)—because they were old news.

Teams in Green Bay, Providence, and Cleveland were caught in the middle; they could attract medium-size crowds for visiting teams—like the Bears and Giants—and they were good enough to get a home-and-home series with the larger cities; but in the end neither wanted too many Cantons cluttering up their schedule. So Carr started to get the word out that his league would be eliminating some of the weaker franchises starting at the NFL's annual winter meeting.

Carr announced the meeting was to be held in New York on February 5–6 at the Astor Hotel. Twenty-one teams showed up; word got to Canton that they weren't wanted, so they didn't even send a representative. The owners heard Carr's report about the state of the NFL the previous year and Halas's brief statement on the meeting last July with General Pierce of the Intercollegiate Athetic Union.[1]

After hearing the reports the owners got down to business. It was soon made clear to the representatives of teams like Akron, Louisville, Rochester, and such that the league had no more use for any weak teams who couldn't fill their 4,000-seat stadiums. Nor could it abide any more anemic road teams, whose only use was to show up in Chicago or New York on an odd weekend and provide a practice game for the local teams; such clubs as the Columbus Panhandles, Oorang Indians, or Los Angeles Buccaneers, once useful, were now considered leeches. Instead of by addition, in 1927, the NFL was about to grow by subtraction.

Shortly after the discussion started, Dr. Harry March, president of the New York Giants, proposed that President Carr appoint a committee of nine to consider the "reorganization of the league." Carr appointed a nice mix of representatives of the strong, middle, and weak.

Strong—Chicago Bears, New York Giants, and Frankford
Middle—Providence, Pottsville, and Green Bay
Weak—Kansas City, Akron, and Columbus[2]

After a short fifteen-minute break to discuss the matter of reorganization, most of the time was spent telling Akron, Kansas City, and Rochester they were about to be lopped off; a battle ensued, with the weaker teams fighting to stay in the league. Somehow Carr had to find a suitable way to get the unproductive teams to agree, however grudgingly, to their own demise.

Carr started day 2 at 10:00 a.m. but immediately deferred the meeting until 2:00 p.m. to continue the dialogue. A motion was then brought up by March that the league be divided into two divisions, to be known as class A (teams in) and class B (teams out), which was carried unanimously. A committee of five was established to help divide teams into two classes; Carr chose Charles Coppen (Providence) as chairman, Shep Royle (Frankford), Johnny Bryan (Milwaukee), Jimmy Conzelman (Detroit), and Jerry Corcoran (Columbus). But who would decide on who was A and who was a B. It came as no shock that when the committee of five returned from the break that the only member in charge of naming a B team was Corcoran, Carr's right hand man. It was clear Carr would decide who was in and who was out. Suggested A teams:

Brooklyn
Buffalo
Chicago Bears
Chicago Cardinals
Cleveland
Detroit
Duluth
Frankford
Green Bay
Kansas City
New York
Pottsville
Providence

B teams on the endangered list:
Akron
Canton
Columbus
Dayton
Hammond
Hartford
Louisville
Minneapolis
Racine
Rochester[3]

Note that the B list included the heart of the old Ohio League and most of the teams that originally founded the league (Hammond, Rochester) less than a decade before. A few minutes after the list was presented, everything began to fall apart. Corcoran, head of the B teams, reported that the only thing his owners would accept would be the sale of their franchise back to the league for the current application fee of $2,500 per. In some cases, that was $2,400 more than had been paid for the originals. The ten B teams were proposing to sting the league's treasury for nearly $25,000 (more than was there). The A teams quickly voted no.[4]

The owners then put the ball in the president's court. He was instructed by the owners to come up with an acceptable plan to reorganize the league by April 15. (It took him until April 23.) The heated meeting ended with Carr passing a rule that was brought on by Tim Mara's Giants playing the AFL's Philadelphia Quakers without his permission. The league adopted an amendment of the present rule that no club in the NFL be permitted to play an exhibition game "prior to, during, or after" the playing season without permission in writing from the president of the league.[5]

Shortly after the winter meeting Carr took a surprise road trip east to, of all places, Pottsville, Pennsylvania. On March 6 Carr was the guest of honor at the Supporters of the Pottsville Maroons rally at the Hippodrome Theatre in the small town. A year ago Carr visited the small town and was given a tiny coal football fob by the Maroons supporters that was inscribed "Pottsville—J.F.C.—1926." A nice souvenir for the president who just one year earlier had suspended the Maroons for breaking a league rule. The original fob is now in the possession of the Carr family.

After getting back to his hometown, Carr had a few months to reorganize his league and put his plan into writing. Before taking action, he decided to make things easier on his family. Just like his father Carr was now a well-established citizen in Columbus, and after spending the past four years at the Sullivan home, it was now time for his family to branch out on their own again. The situation following the death of Josie's father was now stable for her mother, so Joe looked outside of the Irish neighborhood to find a new home for his family.

To the southeast of the old Irish neighborhood, Carr found a brand new house in the Bryden Road district. "It was very much a middle class neighborhood, which it remains today," says Gregory Carr, grandson of Joe F. Carr. "The house they bought just off Main Street had everything, a grocery store, dry cleaners, restaurants, a dentist, and a barbershop. The neighborhood was like a suburb and a main corridor and thoroughfare that led right into downtown Columbus."[6]

The working-class neighborhood attracted Carr to the area, and it was the perfect place for Josie and the kids, Mary and Joe Jr., to make their new home. The two-story brick double broke into two homes, with the Carrs buying the home on the left side at 1863 Bryden Road. The beautiful home had a very small front yard with enough space for a few flower beds about ten feet from the street's sidewalk. There were four concrete steps leading to the front porch, which had room for a two-person bench or swing. One large window looked out from the front living room.[7]

Once you entered through the front door, the first floor had a fairly large living room accompanied by a gas fireplace; a dining room next to the stairways that led to the second floor and basement (which was used to keep coal for the furnace, a laundry area, and food storage); and a medium-size kitchen, which contained a gas stove, refrigerator, and oak breakfast table.

Up on the second floor, the Carr family had three bedrooms; Joe and his wife had the front bedroom (with a small fireplace like the living room); Mary took the middle room; and Joe Jr. had the back bedroom, which also had a screened-in porch, which was nice for enjoying the summer nights. Besides the bedrooms there was one bathroom on the second floor, as well as a finished attic that could have been used as a fourth bedroom.

The house's backyard was approximately fifty feet by eighty feet with a cement walk down the middle. Josie kept several flower gardens on either side of the yard all the way down the sidewalk. The home also had a two-car garage in back. "It was a very modest home. They didn't have a lot of fancy type of furniture or items like that. They lived a pretty modest life," says James Carr, grandson of Joe F. Carr. "The house they bought on Bryden Road was just recently built and they were the first people to occupy the house."[8]

Josie quickly made the new home comfortable for her family and made sure it was a place where people felt at ease. "We visited the Carrs often and it was always a pleasant house to go to," says Martha Sullivan, niece of Josephine and Joe F. Carr. "Aunt Josie was a very gracious, charming hostess. She always had something kind of special for you if you went. We went frequently as kids. We would trailer into the kitchen and she'd have some goodie waiting for us there."[9]

The Carr family also continued to attend services at St. Patrick Church in the Irish neighborhood. Being the head of the family, Joe contributed to St. Patrick by donating five dollars every month. According to the church's *Monthly Calendar* newsletters, Carr did this throughout the next decade. His name would usually appear as the first name on the donation list. In November of 1929, he donated ten dollars to the annual collection for Dominican Novitiate, showing his love and dedication to the church.[10]

Joe F. Carr did a lot of traveling to help reorganize the NFL, and that put a lot of pressure on Josie. "Well he was gone a lot. He was dedicated to the league. So when you're on a path, on a venture of that sort, you have to devote most of your time to that, to the league and to that goal. So he was gone a lot," says James Carr, grandson of Joe F. Carr. "He did have a good relationship with my father, Joe Carr Jr., and he adored his daughter, my Aunt Mary Carr. I think that the fact that his children idolized him gives a good indication that the time that they did spend together was quality time."[11]

"Well, he was the head of the household. There was absolutely no question about that and he adored the both of them [his children]," says Martha Sullivan. "He was very indulgent insofar as he saw that they had most anything they wanted. But he also was very, very strict with them. He had a fantastic sense of right and wrong and there was no in between, and he never mixed them up. He was a very special kind of man. He was strict, kind of stern but he was very warm and caring. You just had the feeling he liked you. He created that kind of atmosphere."[12]

The family accepted that their father would be traveling for a cause, and they enjoyed any circumstance they could to be together. In the spring of 1927, Josie (age forty-seven), Mary (thirteen), and Joe Jr. (eleven) showed that Carr spirit to see their dad off to work. James Carr says,

> He was on the road quite a bit and going from town to town and for the owners meetings and so on. Most of the major meetings were in Chicago and New York and so forth. But down the street there are some railroad tracks that go along Nelson Road here in Columbus on the west side of Bryden Road. At one point in time the railroad tracks were flush, now they're elevated, but back then they would walk the 150 yards down to the train tracks. My grandmother, my dad, and my aunt would go down to the end of Bryden Road and watch the train. My grandfather would come out on the caboose and wave to them as he went on his trips. They would wave back as he went on his journey to further the business of the NFL.[13]

The very close and tight Carr family seemed to understand what Joe F. Carr was trying to accomplish, especially Josie. "She just took it as part of the package. She rolled with the punches," says Martha Sullivan. The whole family supported him and Carr in turn appreciated their encouragement. It was the perfect setup, or was it? Carr didn't want to work away from home if he didn't have too, so besides the new home for his family, he also set out to find a new home for the NFL.[14]

Six years after establishing Columbus as the headquarters of the NFL, it was now time to find a permanent home for the league. The president looked toward the city's downtown area, specifically at the busy intersection of Broad and High, just a few blocks from his old stomping grounds at the *Ohio State Journal*. The very busy corner of Broad and High was the heartbeat and epicenter of the capital city. To the southeast of the corner was the state capital building where the governor of Ohio worked; across from the Statehouse was the Neil House, the city's most popular hotel with its famous restaurants and entertainment venues; just to the south of the hotel was the city's most successful bank, the Huntington Bank; as well as several other businesses, restaurants, and theaters sprinkling the intersection. In 1927 the corner became the official home of the NFL.

When Carr went looking for an office in the area, he only went to one destination and that was the New Hayden Building. The estate of former Columbus industrialist Peter Hayden hired well-known Chicago architects George Nimmons and William Fellows to design the New Hayden Building, which was built next to the original Hayden Building. Completed in 1901 the thirteen-story steel frame and brick office building was located at 16 East Broad Street in the heart of downtown Columbus.[15]

The building faced the north side of Capitol Square across the street from the Ohio Statehouse and was sandwiched between the four-story Hayden Building (built in 1869) at 8 East Broad and the sixteen-story Capital Trust Building (1906). The building's design by Nimmons-Fellows was an example of the commercial style of architecture that was popularized in Chicago's office and mercantile buildings of the 1890's. The interior of the skyscraper was designed around the historic building stairs and three elevator shafts on the first floor.

When the building was being built, the *Ohio State Journal* described Columbus's newest addition as "truly artistic in design and a monument of good architecture is more than usually important on account of its prominence, as the character of its design will play a large part in fixing the character of commercial architecture in Columbus. . . . It is of interest to note that the style of design for the building follows the latest designs of the modern office building style, a style that is distinctly American and entirely the outgrowth of the American steel construction."[16]

Carr knew the New Hayden Building was a perfect spot to establish a home base for the NFL. He rented two rooms on the eleventh floor and set up shop. After entering through the front door vestibule, Carr could have taken one of the elevators, or if he wanted a little more time to think about his upcoming day, he might have walked up the iron and marble stairs, all the way up to the eleventh floor. Down the hall from his two-room office were the offices of Stalter & Essex Coal Company; Frankfort Lumber Company; and the law firms of Allread-Armstrong and Summers-Poor.[17]

The two rooms in the new Hayden Building numbered 1115–1116, the first ever office of the NFL. In 1927 for the first time Carr had the NFL listed in the Columbus City Directories and printed up official NFL stationary with NFL letterhead. The NFL office had a wooden door with a clear glass nameplate that nearly took up half the door. The clear misty glass had the president's name printed on it in black:

Joe F. Carr
Pres.
National Football League[18]

After entering the door, the first room was very small with a desk and office cabinets/supplies for use. The second room was larger than the first but not by that much. It was no bigger than a thirty-by-twenty office space and was a very plain room with light-colored walls. Carr had an eight-foot wooden desk that he always kept very neat and organized, with note pads, daily newspapers, pens, and, of course, an ashtray for his favorite cigars. In the corner of his office were a few file cabinets that contained the league's bylaws, players' contracts, franchise information, and other paperwork. Next to the cabinets was a wooden coat rack for his overcoat and trademark hat. Carr's new office was just three miles away from his new home on Bryden Road. In one off-season Carr had found new homes for both his family and his league.[19]

The NFL's second meeting of 1927 occurred on April 23 at the Hotel Statler in Cleveland, and Carr had come up with a six-point plan to reorganize the league. At the meeting were sixteen teams, mostly A teams from the previous meeting. The only representatives from the B teams who bothered to show up at all had some type of league connection—John Dunn (NFL vice president) of Minneapolis; Carl Storck (NFL treasurer) of Dayton; and Aaron Hertzman (committee) of Louisville. Carr started the meeting at 2:00 p.m. and quickly outlined his plan to, according to the league's minutes, "re-organize the League, either to reduce the number of members or to divide it geographically in order to increase the efficiency of the organization." Carr went over the six points and the owners absorbed it.

> 1. Each Club which so elects may suspend operation for the season of 1927 without the payment of dues and any club which desires to retire definitely from the League shall upon the surrender of its franchise certificate to the League President be refunded its pro-rata share of any money in the League Treasury at the time said certificate is surrendered.

A pro rata share of the league treasury, about one-twentieth, would have been a few hundred dollars at best—a far cry from the $2,500 the B team owners had asked for in February. It was a clever bylaw to keep the weaker teams from draining the league's funds just to get back at the league for booting them out. The better part of the deal was the chance to remain a member of the league without paying dues. A team could sit out a year for free, hoping for a better situation in 1928.

> 2. In the event a club elects to suspend for the season of 1927 . . . the League will give such clubs the privilege and right of selling any player's contract up to and including September 15, 1927, providing they are going to disband their team. If a club elects to withdraw from the League as per the above plan, but elects to operate an independent Club, the League will respect the rights of their player during the entire season of 1927. The above protection and privilege to sell players shall be restricted to such players as are under contract at present or on the reserve list of said club as of April 23, 1927.

Although it would be a buyer's marker, the B teams could try to sell their players to the A teams before the next season to offset their 1926 losses. Or, if they wanted to continue operating outside the NFL, they'd have a season's grace before their rosters were raided.

> 3. In the event a number of clubs elect to accept the above proposal to form a league among themselves, the National Football League agrees to respect their player's contract and territorial rights, and to extend in every manner possible help in the organization and operation of their league, agreeing to play exhibitions games with them whenever possible and extending such other courtesies that may be within its power.
>
> 4. In the event a club elects to suspend as per the foregoing, the League will agree to permit such club to retain its franchise certificate in the National Football League and to dispose of it to any new member that may be voted upon favorably by the League. The League further agrees that no new franchises will be issued until all suspended franchises have been sold or cancelled, and that an applicant for a franchise in the League who may be acted upon favorably by the League President or the Executive Committee will be referred to the clubs holding the suspended franchises certificate to purchase them. However, any such owner of said suspended franchise certificate shall be limited to asking as its purchase price the amount that shall be the application fee for the time said sale or transfer is proposed.

Point 4 wasn't as good as it sounded. In theory a team could suspend and then sell its franchise for $2,500, and the league had to approve the new buyer. The only problem was the NFL wasn't looking for any new members. The only team that really benefitted by this clause in 1927 was Tim Mara's New York Giants.

> 5. All the foregoing agreements which the League makes with any club which elects to avail itself of this voluntary retirement privilege is contingent upon said club refraining from having any connection, association or friendly relation in any way, shape or form with any other Football League, or organization of any kind that does not have the approval or sanction of the National Football League.

Carr included this based on the demise of the American Football League but he wanted to be sure if the B teams messed around with the likes of C. C. Pyle then all signals were off.

> 6. All of the foregoing shall be operative for a period of one year from the date of the schedule meeting of 1927 or until the schedule of 1928, at which time the foregoing agreements may be revised or broadened as the membership of the League decide.[20]

Carr made it clear that the B owners needed to take this deal because within a year it would get more difficult to join the league. The next move by the owners was to adopt Carr's plan, and they did with a unanimous vote. Although the next move wasn't part of Carr's plan, it definitely added more incentive for the B teams to drop out of the league. George Halas proposed that the guarantee fee that each club was to deposit at the schedule meeting in July be raised a thousand dollars to $2,500. Storck suggested $5,000, but the league settled on Halas's proposed figure.[21]

The one-day meeting ended with the owners agreeing to follow the rule book adopted by the collegiate game. One of the new rules adopted by the collegiate officials in 1927 was to move the goal post to the back of the end zone. Leaving Cleveland, Carr thought his plan to trim the "fat" off the NFL was pretty solid and would eventually stabilize the league for a successful future.

The summer scheduling meeting was held on July 16–17 in the small town of Green Bay, Wisconsin. This was the first time the "little" city in the north hosted the group of NFL moguls, and the league was now ready to see who was "in" and who was "out." Sixteen teams showed up at the Hotel Northland, with a few other teams represented by Carr, and the first thing they did was take roll call. Each club was asked to come forward and deposit their $2,500 or withdraw from the league.

Teams that were out included Akron, Columbus (both of the old Ohio League), Detroit, Hammond, Kansas City, the Los Angeles traveling team, Minneapolis, Milwaukee (which operated as an independent team), and Rochester. The Brooklyn franchise was sold to Tim Mara. The teams that plucked down the guarantee fee were Buffalo, Chicago Bears, Chicago Cardinals, Cleveland, Dayton, Duluth, Frankford, Green Bay, New York Giants, Pottsville, and Providence. These eleven teams would make up the NFL in 1927.[22]

The only surprise was Carl Storck's Dayton Triangles, who were one of the weakest teams in pro football. The Triangles had gone a combined 4–23–3 the previous four seasons and strictly played on the road. But Storck put down his money; football was too close to his heart to give up his team. The second day of the meetings started bright and early at 9:00 a.m., with the owners agreeing to raise the visiting guarantee to $2,500 and then filling out the schedule for the 1927 season. Curly Lambeau raised a motion for the league to use the Spalding J-5 football in games, and it was passed. Finally the owners gave Lambeau and the Packers officials a standing ovation for hosting the meeting.[23]

Carr and the owners left the summer meeting thinking their league work was finished for the year, but there was one more item to discuss before the season started—what to do with C. C. Pyle's New York Yankees. After the summer meeting, Tim Mara figured out what to do with his Brooklyn franchise. He'd rent it to Pyle. Mara disliked Pyle intensely, but he was no fool. He knew Pyle still had Red Grange, a football team, and a lease on Yankee Stadium. By taking Pyle into the NFL, Mara could put a leash on him.

As an outsider Pyle could have scheduled independent teams all season for Yankee Stadium and cut into attendance for Mara's Giants. But once inside the NFL, Pyle was stuck with whatever Mara wanted him to do. In the middle of August, the two groups met at Saratoga Springs Racetrack to discuss the matter. Mara, Pyle, AFL president Bill Edwards, and by request of Joe F. Carr, William Veeck, president of the Chicago Cubs, attended the meeting. The four men hammered out an agreement for Pyle's team to join the NFL.[24]

Mara dominated the discussion, and Pyle and Edwards agreed to basically everything he wanted. The Yankees would be kept out of New York and on the road, playing only one game at the same time in New York as the Giants. The Giants and Yankees then would play a home-and-home series on December 4 and December 11. The New York Yankees became the NFL's twelfth team in 1927. Newspaper reports on the agreement called it a "merger" of the NFL and AFL; while technically correct, the only AFL team to join was Pyle's Yankees. Some of the players from the AFL's Chicago Bulls were divided among the Cardinals and Bears. Joey Sternaman returned to the Bears.

On September 4 in Cleveland, the owners met one last time as President Carr outlined the purpose of the get-together. He explained negotiations had been completed to transfer the Brooklyn franchise to Pyle. Teams then had a chance to schedule the Yankees and Red Grange for the season. Pyle then spoke briefly about his plan for the Yankees and stated that "all past controversies were to be forgotten and he was for the National League, its rules and its members one hundred percent."[25]

Other players who joined NFL teams that fall were George "Wildcat" Wilson with Providence; Century Milstead and Al Nesser with the Giants; Bull Behman with Frankford; Grange with the New York Yankees; Joey Sternaman and Paddy Driscoll with the Chicago Bears; Wilson and Jimmy Conzelman with Providence; newly signed quarterback Benny Friedman with the Cleveland Bulldogs; and Ernie Nevers still with Duluth. The NFL had assembled the most stars in its history. And with a tighter, twelve-team league to divide the loot, everyone was looking forward to 1927 being the best year ever. But early on one of the league's stars would be crippled.

"We were playing in a game against, of all teams, the Chicago Bears at Wrigley Field," Red Grange told author Richard Whittingham. "I had my cleats dug into the ground and it was a kind of wet day and somebody fell over my knee. It was nothing deliberate just one of those things. I was hit from the side by somebody [George Trafton] and boom, out went my knee. After the injury I was just another halfback." Grange would miss the 1928 season but come back to play for Halas's Bears in 1929 as one of the league's best defensive backs. But Grange would never again be that impossible-to-stop "Galloping Ghost," and Pyle's Yankees limped to a 4–8–1 record in 1927.[26]

While the Yankees struggled, the New York Giants rolled to their first NFL championship. The team Mara put on the Polo Grounds gridiron was a veteran group that included Jack McBride (the NFL's best player in 1927), Hinkey Haines, Century Milstead, Cal Hubbard, Al Nesser, and stout Steve Owen. After their first four games, the team stood at just 2–1–1 with a tie and loss to Benny Friedman's Cleveland squad. But after the October 16 setback to Cleveland, they wouldn't lose another game.

The Giants then rolled off nine consecutive wins, seven by way of shutouts, as Tim Mara's team finished with a league best 11–1–1 record. In just three seasons Mara had gone from novice NFL owner, to battling C. C. Pyle for New York City, to NFL champion. He also had a decent showing at the gate, as the Giants' eight home games averaged 18,500 fans per game, including a league high 38,000 fans for the November 8 game against Providence.[27]

But Carr's league did have its problems. In the middle of the season the Buffalo Bisons disbanded after suffering five straight defeats. Manager and coach George "Dim" Batterson gave the reason for quitting as "lack of cooperation from players and interference by club managers," while Bisons president Ray Weil said "small crowds and financial losses" were the real reason.[28] The bottom line was that the Bisons were not a very good team, and the city was not ready to support an NFL franchise. On October 12 the Bisons hosted Red Grange before his knee injury occurred and only attracted 3,000 fans. The club lost $7,000 in their two home games and left Carr's loop.

Carr's plan to reduce the number of teams in the NFL to a smaller, stronger organization seemed to pay off in 1927. Compared to 1926 and its super-sized twenty-two-team loop that attracted 490,800 fans in 116 NFL games, the twelve teams in 1927 generated 557,100 fans in just 72 league games—averaging about 7,737 per game—and the future of the league seemed to be on the right track to become that big-city sport that Carr envisioned.[29] After the season, Carr attended the second annual *Ohio State Journal* Sports Department Christmas party, conceived by Carr's former colleague and friend Clyde Tuttle, the paper's sports editor.

Santa showed up to give out gifts to all the special guests, Carr received a souvenir baseball, as other giveaways went to Chic Harley (a book), Dr. Bob Drury (a book on how to play baseball), Clyde Tuttle (a poem), and John McNulty (derby hat). Carr's holiday with his family was always short-lived as preparation for the upcoming season was quickly upon him and the other owners.[30]

Carr traveled north to attend the winter meeting in Cleveland on February 11–12 at the Hotel Statler. The first day Carr read the "President's Report," stating that the 1927 season's "fan attendance was the greatest in the history of the League and the general condition the best in its history," and treasurer Carl Storck said that the "league's finances are in very good condition." But you couldn't prove it in Cleveland, Buffalo, or Pottsville.[31]

Cleveland owner Herbert Brandt pulled the plug for 1928 and the city, which Carr thought was a perfect NFL location. The Buffalo franchise that disbanded during the middle of 1927 would also not field a team in '28, and neither would Duluth. After five seasons in the NFL (last two with Ernie Nevers), the city of Duluth was now out of pro football. Nevers's Duluth Eskimos would be the last true traveling team in NFL history. Carr needed his franchises to be in larger cities with some stability, and Duluth didn't fit the plan.

Pottsville was also in trouble, but Dr. John Streigel would let star player Pete Henry run the team for one more year. If half the NFL's active franchises were a little sick, at least half were in reasonably good health. Carr's plan to scale down the league had worked for now. At the end of the meeting, the league awarded the 1927 championship to Tim Mara's New York Giants to cheers from the other owners.

Before leaving Cleveland, Carr announced that the summer's scheduling meeting would be on the East Coast in Providence on July 7. Nine owners arrived in Rhode Island at the Biltmore Hotel to schedule games for the 1928 season. Carr read a letter from Mr. Brandt that confirmed that Cleveland wouldn't field a team, and then the owners got to arranging games. After a dinner break the league again approved the official game ball from Spalding, and with no other matters to discuss Carr cut the meeting to just one day. But the owners weren't quite done.[32]

Carr called for one more meeting on August 12 in Detroit to welcome the newest NFL franchise. After lying dormant for one season, the Motor City franchise was reactivated under new ownership by a consortium of Detroit businessmen. Just like the city of Cleveland, Carr had a soft spot for Detroit. He thought the city was the ideal location for professional football and was willing to bring them back into the league. As for players, the newest team signed several men from the defunct Cleveland franchise, including star quarterback Benny Freidman, the former Michigan All-American, and because of that the team was nicknamed the Wolverines.

All the teams put down their $2,500 guarantee fee; the NFL would only field ten teams in 1928 (two less than in 1927) and the season was prepared to start on September 23 and end on December 16.[33] For Carr this would be the NFL's seventh league meeting in the past nineteen months;

the league's president was becoming a traveling fool. He was confident his league would continue its run of improvement and progress. The 1928 season saw more baby steps in between another personal loss.

In 1928 the NFL's New England outpost was the Providence Steam Roller. Organized as a professional team in 1916, the Steam Roller played a schedule of games mostly against independent teams in the area before joining the NFL in 1925. In three seasons, the team had a 19–17–3 NFL record under the ownership of sportswriter-lawyer Charles Coppen, former judge James Dooley, and realtor-promoter Peter Laudati. Laudati was such a fixture at games that he held the first-down marker, a job the wealthy businessman enjoyed. Coppen was the sports editor at the *Providence Journal* and suggested the unique nickname of the team. "We did have quite a debate as to whether it should be singular or plural. Mr. Coppen, who as club president made most final decisions, insisted that the singular sounded better and made more sense," recalled Pearce Johnson, a young "stringer" at the paper who was made the team's manager. "So we became the Providence Steam Roller."[34]

The Steam Roller's home field was the Cycledrome, located near the Providence-Pawtucket city line, and was built mainly to host bicycle races. The stadium sat approximately 10,000 spectators in an oval of bleachers surrounding a wooden banked cycle track. This wooden track, steeply banked around the turns and flatter on the straightaways, enclosed just enough ground to fit a football field, with some slight problems.

The track equipped with seats and a bench for the players on one side, ran so close to the sidelines that players tackled near the boundary line frequently caromed into the front row of seats. The Cycledrome had an intimate ambiance, so that all the seats, priced at $2, $1.50, and $1, were actually good seats from which to view a football game. The dressing quarters for the players were less agreeable; the dressing room used by the Steam Roller players had been built with a couple of bicycle racers in mind, so that a football team of eighteen men found the room to be cramped, with only two showers at their disposal.

"There was probably more room in a phone booth," said Pearce Johnson in a 1988 interview. "With 18 giants changing all at the same time, somebody was always getting an elbow in the eye or a sock in the chops from an arm struggling with a jersey. Jim Conzelman used to say we got more injuries dressing than on the field." There was no visitor's quarters, so the visiting team had to dress at the hotel, come to the stadium, then return in uniform to the hotel to shower and change.[35]

The 1928 Steam Roller were coached by Conzelman, who was getting a salary of $292 per game. He not only coached the team, but he also played quarterback in the single-wing formation. Joining Conzelman was All-Pro lineman Clyde Smith, tackle Gus Sonnenberg, and halfback George

"Wildcat" Wilson. Despite Conzelman blowing out his knee in the fourth game, the Steam Roller became the NFL's best team. "We had no fights or feuds," Johnson recalled. "They were paid players but they wanted above all else to win the NFL championship. It probably sounds odd today but salaries were secondary considerations."[36]

After losing the second game of the year (10–6 loss) against the Frankford Yellow Jackets, the Steam Roller won four consecutive games. With a 5–1 record the Steam Roller were prepared to play the Yellow Jackets again on back-to-back days in the middle of November; first playing in Philly on Saturday, November 17, and then the following day in Providence (Sunday, November 18). The Jackets were 7–1–1 going into the biggest weekend of the 1928 season. Carr made sure he was there.

Conzelman and his squad traveled to Philly on Friday night and stayed at the Hotel Adelphia. Carr also arrived in the City of Brotherly Love and with a crowd of 8,000 spectators witnessed a very tight game between the NFL's two best teams. The hometown Jackets scored on a blocked punt for a touchdown in the third quarter to take a 6–0 lead, missing the extra point. But late in the fourth quarter the Steam Roller offense caught a break with a poor punt deep in Jackets' territory. After seven straight running plays Wildcat Wilson plowed over for a twelve-yard score, but like their counterparts, they too missed the extra point. The game ended in a 6–6 tie.

After relaxing for a few hours, both teams hopped on a train and headed to Providence for the rematch. The Yellow Jackets usually played back-to-back games, so this wasn't unusual, but the Steam Roller didn't and would be playing the most important game on just a few hours of rest. Rain threatened to drench the Cycledrome, but an overflow crowd of 12,000 fans came out to root for their local heroes. In the opening quarter, the Steam Roller had the ball on the Frankford forty-six yard line when Wilson threw a short pass to Curly Oden, who raced the remaining distance for a touchdown.

The extra point failed but that didn't matter; the home team had more than they needed. For the rest of the afternoon, the Steam Roller defense kept the 1926 NFL champions out of the scoring column. When the final gun sounded, the Cycledrome scoreboard read 6–0 and the Steam Roller had rolled into first place in the NFL standings. When Carr arrived back in Columbus, he should have been rejoicing the league's fantastic weekend of play on the field. Instead he got a heavy dose of reality.

On the same day that Carr arrived in Philadelphia, Dr. Frank Sullivan suffered a stroke due to pressure in his brain and was admitted into Mt. Carmel Hospital in Columbus. When Carr returned that Monday morning (November 19), Josie's younger brother passed away at the age of thirty-eight. The successful doctor left a widow and three young children, including his eldest child, Martha Sullivan.[37]

"When my father died we were very young and Joe Carr became a surrogate father. He always had time to visit with us. He always had time to listen to us," says Martha Sullivan. "He thought we needed the attention and of course we got too much attention as it was. We were all spoiled. He would talk to us and just made us feel important. He was very sensitive toward us. One thing I remembered is that one of his brothers was in the coffee and candy business, so Uncle Joe would always have a supply of candy and he was always very generous in sharing those candies with us. In retrospect you realize how sweet it really was."[38]

Josie and the rest of the Sullivan family were still in a state of shock as Joe took care of the children. The funeral service took place at St. Patrick Church with the whole family there, and Josie's brother was buried in St. Joseph's Cemetery in the south end of Columbus. It would take some time for everything to get back to normal, and for Carr the end of the NFL season seemed to take a back seat in his world.

The following week after the Steam Roller's big win over the Yellow Jackets, the Providence squad crushed the NFL's defending champs, the New York Giants, 16–0. Then the team escaped the Pottsville Maroons, 7–0, to set up a season finale matchup with the Green Bay Packers at the Cycledrome. All Providence had to do was not lose to the Pack, and it would capture the NFL championship. In front of 10,000 fans the hometown team struggled early on, trailing 7–0 into the third quarter. Then the Steam Roller put together an eleven-play, seventy-two-yard drive to tie the game. George Wilson's well-placed punts kept the Packers away from the goal line the rest of the game and secured a 7–7 tie. Although the Packers weren't fighting for the NFL title, they let the rest of the league know that their time was about to come.

Later that afternoon the Frankford Yellow Jackets lost 28–6 to the Chicago Bears, making the Steam Roller the undisputed champions. The following Tuesday the team, a delegation of city and state officials, and approximately 200 fans celebrated the success of the football team at a victory banquet held at the Hotel Biltmore. Each member of the squad received a gold watch and a loving cup was presented to coach Jimmy Conzelman as team Most Valuable Player. Conzelman praised his players, saying that "there had not been a cross word between any two of the players in three months, on or off the field."[39]

The Providence owners of Coppen, Dooley, and Laudati rejoiced in the team's profits, but it would be the only time the Steam Roller would finish higher than fifth place in the NFL. In Chicago, Chris O'Brien's Cardinals barely survived the season with an odd schedule. They opened with a 15–0 loss to the Bears before only 4,000 fans at Normal Park; skipped a week and then beat a dreadful Dayton team 7–0; then a week later they were pounded by the Packers 20–0. Then they took five weeks off, apparently because O'Brien couldn't arrange any games. With his team out of Comiskey Park and back at smallish Normal Park, the only visitors were the Bears and the Dayton Triangles, who would take any guarantee. O'Brien had a big decision to make about what to do with his team in 1929.

Near the end of the season, Carr spoke to Newspaper Enterprise Association sportswriter Henry Farrell, a former beat writer in Columbus, for a feature article on the NFL. He was asked by Farrell why pro football wasn't a success. "It is a success and if you don't know it you have turned sap. To make a success of any business or undertaking it is necessary to apply intelligent business sense. Pro football is a business. So is college football. College football is one of the biggest businesses in the country and smart men are running it. How do you get that way?"[40]

Carr and the NFL were still learning how to make the sport a successful business but the groundwork was there. Carr knew the league had to be in the big cities, and these big-city franchises needed to be operated by financially capable owners. He also knew that this would be a long process and wouldn't happen overnight. He would be in it for the long haul. On Christmas Eve, Carr attended the *Ohio State Journal*'s third annual Christmas party hosted by his friend Clyde Tuttle. This time Carr brought thirteen-year-old Joe Carr Jr. to the party, who was very happy when he received a model plane set as a gift. Nearly 300 employees and guests ate sandwiches and drank refreshments provided by The Clock, Columbus' most popular restaurant. Music played all night, and enough Chesterfield cigars were available to make everyone satisfied. After a tough year traveling and losing a family member, Carr cherished this time with his son. Soon it would be back to work.[41]

17

How Do We Get to the Big Cities and Stay? (1929–1930)

Going into the NFL's annual winter meeting, Carr's loop was now looking to put a few more teams on the field and those teams had to be in big cities. But events off the field that fall would have a far greater bearing on the health of pro football than any games played in 1929. At 2:00 p.m. on February 2, President Carr called the one-day meeting to order at the Hotel Sherman in Chicago. After Carr read his annual state-of-the-NFL report, treasurer Carl Storck read his financial statement, which was received with "considerable comment, all very complimentary." But some teams weren't rejoicing.[1]

The owners then awarded the 1928 NFL championship to the Providence Steam Roller, with Judge Dooley accepting. After the back-slapping ended, the moguls elected Joe F. Carr again as their president. A motion was then brought up by Mike Redelle of the Dayton Triangles and seconded by C. C. Pyle, who actually showed up to represent his Yankees, to raise the president's salary to $3,000 per year and to have the league pay for office rent, a secretary, and office maintenance. Carr was to get a check for $250 a month. Carl L. Storck was then elected as vice president—to replace John Dunn—and treasurer at a salary of $1,000 per year. Shep Royle (Frankford), James Dooley (Providence) and George Halas (Bears) were selected members of the NFL's executive committee.[2]

Pyle's appearance was somewhat of a surprise as he was one of the owners who was in deep financial trouble. His New York Yankees had been without their main attraction, Red Grange, in 1928, but Pyle's problems also included some bad investments that lost a bunch of money. At the end of the season, Pyle owed his players over $7,000. If he couldn't pay them, all of his players would become free agents. Pyle told the owners he had paid $1,200 to his players and asked to be given until April 15 to come up with the rest. Carr gave him until May 1.

Another issue that was presented to Carr was what to do with the Buffalo franchise and its $2,500 guarantee fund. The Buffalo team had quit in mid-1927 and not operated in 1928. The $2,500 they'd put into the fund was still sitting there, and former owner Ray Weil advised the league he wanted his money back. After the meeting Vice President Storck wrote Carr a letter saying, "I met Mr. Weil of the Buffalo Club in the hotel on Sunday and he advised me that they were going to start legal proceedings with reference to their guarantee fund. I imagine that we will have some problems on our hands with this before we get through."[3]

In view of the league's modern million-dollar lawsuits, it's rather quaint to see the NFL officers nervous over a mere $2,500. But for Carr everything was scaled down in those years, and anything dealing with money had to be treated with care. Carr adjourned the meeting, with both Detroit and Pottsville (who didn't even bother to attend the meeting) pretty much out of the league. Carr now had just seven healthy teams, one on life support (New York Yankees) and one about to sue (Buffalo). It was time to look toward some new blood.

Two days after returning from the owners meeting, Carr had a special visitor to his office at 16 East Broad Street in Columbus. C. C. Pyle was in town to promote his second annual "Bunion Derby"—a 3,455-mile cross-country foot race from New York to Los Angeles—that was scheduled to arrive in the capital city in April. Carr reiterated to Cash and Carry that he must pay his players or he would have to give up his team. This time Carr wasn't going to back down; he was pretty fed up with Pyle's lack of "fiscal responsibility," and the league needed smarter businessmen running their teams. It would be the last time Carr would talk to Pyle as an NFL owner.[4]

In the spring Carr dealt with his baseball issues (remember he was also a baseball executive) and went about hiring a secretary to help him with his NFL duties. Carr was swamped with all the paperwork and public relations he had to deal with as NFL president, plus with all the traveling he had to do with all his jobs, he finally realized that he needed help. At the winter meeting he was given permission by the owners to hire a secretary, and Carr looked to the Irish neighborhood to find his partner for life.

Kathleen Rubadue was born in the Irish neighborhood in Columbus on July 15, 1910, to Ernest and Mary Rubadue. Ernest was a pharmacist who owned a drug store on East Livingston Avenue, and Mary was a stay-at-home mother. The couple had four children—two daughters, Regina and Kathleen, and two sons, Clare and Ernest Jr. The family of six lived at 672 South 22nd Street, which was just a couple of blocks from the Sullivan home at 39 North 22nd Street where Carr and his family lived from 1923 to 1926.[5]

Young Kathleen grew up going to school and church, but unlike some of her female friends, she also began a love affair with sports. "She was very outgoing. Oh yeah, she could talk to anybody. She also had a good sense of humor, sort of a dry humor. She could take a joke and she liked any kind of sports," says Robert Knapp, son of Kathleen Rubadue. "She was an extremely sports-minded individual for a lady in those days.[6]

"She taught me how to bowl. Taught me how to play baseball. Taught me how to play football. She knew all the rules and the positions and all that kind of stuff. If I had a question, I'd go ask her," says Knapp. Kathleen grew up to be a very tall (five feet ten), attractive brunette, with beautiful green eyes, and after graduating high school from the all-girls St. Joseph's Academy in 1929, she was hired as the NFL's first secretary.[7]

Joe F. Carr knew the Rubadue family from the neighborhood, and he was aware of Kathleen's love for sports. He knew of her exploits as a basketball player, and her understanding of all of the different aspects of each game made it a no-brainer to hire her. "She thought he was a great guy to work for. It took both of them to run the league. Two people, Carr and my mother. They worked together. I think she probably was a little more than a secretary," says Robert Knapp. "Back in those days she would work nine to five but during the fall on Sundays she would go into the office."[8]

In the only interview Kathleen Rubadue would give about her time as NFL secretary, she told the *Columbus Dispatch* in January 1982 about working on Sundays.

> The one big thing that really stuck with me is that when I went to work for him, none of the wire services or news agencies would even carry the scores of the game. Mr. Carr finally got them to agree to carry the scores and standings. The referees would wire in the scores on Sunday afternoon and I'd figure out the standings and take them over to the Associated Press and the rest. That was the only way they had a chance of getting into the newspapers. I think he expected the league to grow, but I don't think there is any way he could have foreseen what it has become now. But he worked hard to make it better every year. Football was his whole life.[9]

Even fifty years after being hired, she still called him Mr. Carr. "They were very close. It was like a little family setting at the office. She was friends with my grandmother and so on," says James Carr, grandson of Joe F. Carr. "It was a very friendly, homey atmosphere. He would always greet her in the morning with some niceties, ask her how she is doing, and so forth." Asking Rubadue to work on Sundays was no problem for the nineteen-year-old sports lover. "Being single and liking what she did I wouldn't think that would've been a problem for her," says Robert Knapp. The NFL office on the eleventh floor at 16 East Broad Street now had two people working in it. Kathleen took over the front office in room 1115 and made herself feel at home. Her outgoing personality made everyone who visited the office feel special.[10]

"It was just about as ordinary an office as you can imagine. It wasn't luxury; it was not that deep, just terribly ordinary. The secretary had a separate area. I used to go with my mother and she would go to see Uncle Joe and he had a secretary and she entertained me while they had their meeting," says Martha Sullivan, niece of Joe F. Carr. "She was nice to me. She talked to me or gave me a picture book to look at."[11]

When Carr took off on one of his trips, Rubadue would be in charge of the NFL office by herself and she handled it with little problem. "She knew everything that he was doing when he wasn't there, she handled it. When he was out, she took over and you had to deal with her! Somebody told her one time that Joe Carr was basically the NFL and she was the other half of it. They had two employees, not hundreds like we got now," says Robert Knapp.[12]

Ms. Rubadue would be the NFL's first secretary, and she would go down in history as the only secretary Joe F. Carr ever had. The NFL was now operating as a two-headed machine, and it was moving along to the beat of Carr's vision. On the eve on the league's summer scheduling meeting Carr was once again looking at NFL franchises (and different owners) coming and going.

At this time in New York, Tim Mara made headlines when he purchased the entire Detroit Wolverines franchise and its players. The main reason Mara swung the deal was to get the great Benny Friedman. The star quarterback made the Giants a profitable enterprise in the next couple of years, after Mara had lost about $40,000 in 1928. Friedman's salary was said to be $10,000 and it was well-earned for the best passer in the NFL.[13]

In Chicago the headlines read that one of the NFL's pioneers was calling it quits. On July 18 Chris O'Brien announced that he had sold the Chicago Cardinals to wealthy Chicago physician Dr. David Jones for a reported $25,000. The Cardinals had been around in one form or another since the turn of the century and were one of the NFL's charter members. But they never really recovered from the war with the American Football League (AFL) in 1926.[14]

With help from George Halas, the Cardinals and O'Brien found a very capable successor. "It [the Cardinals franchise] was losing money and Chris O'Brien could not subsidize it. I was concerned the buyer might be undesirable. I induced a great Bears' fan, Dr. David Jones, to buy the club. He had served as city physician under four mayors," recalled George

Halas. Dr. Jones and Halas had been partners with the Chicago Bruins professional basketball franchise in the American Basketball League and were friends, so Carr was confident that the Cardinals were now in capable hands. Jones also brought some bravado with him. "I believe the South Side will support winning football and I'm going to give 'em that or bust."[15]

Jones was brimming with confidence and ideas. First he rented Comiskey Park instead of tiny Normal Park. Then he hired Ole Haugsrud and Dewey Scanlon from the old Duluth franchise to help run his team. Although Duluth would sell their franchise in 1929, the duo of Haugsrud-Scanlon had several of the players still under contract, including Ernie Nevers. Jones had his star, locking up the big blonde fullback to a contract and continuing his boasting: "The South Side club is going to be the best in the professional game. The acquisition of Nevers, along with Howard Maple (Oregon QB), reputed to be the greatest quarter in recent years, is only a starter. We will have a team and a schedule which will be representative of what pro football really should be."[16]

So even before the summer meeting started, Carr had answers to two of his problems, and most of the meeting was taken up with the rest of who was in and who was out. Carr headed east to attend the summer gathering on July 27–28 at the Seaside Hotel in beautiful Atlantic City. The first big news to be brought up was the no-show of C. C. Pyle. His absence pretty much sealed the fate of his New York Yankees. Speaking to the press, Carr revealed the status of the franchise and Pyle: "The franchise of the New York Yankees has been forfeited. Mr. Pyle does not see fit to attend this meeting, therefore, there was nothing left for officials of the league to do but declare the franchise forfeited . . . apparently [he] just did not wish to attend."[17]

At 2:00 p.m. on the first day, Carr called the meeting to order. Among those who showed up were Ray Weil and Albert Lowe of Buffalo, and the fight for $2,500 went to the gentlemen from Buffalo. In effect Carr caved in to the threat of a lawsuit and gave them another chance as long as they promised they'd really and truly play a whole season in 1929. To control the situation Carr had the duo post an extra $2,500 and ordered his right hand man Jerry Corcoran as team manager. Another problem solved.[18]

After the Cardinals were officially transferred from O'Brien to Jones, the owners announced that the dormant Duluth franchise was sold to the Orange Athletic Club (OAC) of New Jersey. The OAC had operated a strong independent pro team known as the Tornadoes, managed by Eddie Simandl. After a dinner break Dr. Harry March announced that the old Brooklyn franchise had been sold to the city of Staten Island, New York.

The Staten Island Stapletons were owned by Dan Blaine, a native of the working-class neighborhood known as Stapleton, who was a good halfback and formed the team with three other players in 1915. In 1919 he took over sole ownership of the team, and at the same time his businesses started to prosper. His ownership of several restaurants on Staten Island made him wealthy, although some people say the night spots were actually speakeasies where one could get a drink during Prohibition, but nothing was ever proved. He continued to play in the Stapes' lineup until retiring in 1924 at the age of thirty-three.[19]

By 1928 Blaine was in full pursuit of an NFL franchise. He bolstered his squad by signing several former New York University players and luring Doug Wycoff away from the New York Giants to be his player-coach. Wycoff had just helped Mara's Giants to the 1927 NFL championship. Despite the liquor rumors, Carr took a chance on the financially stable Blaine, who would schedule his home games at cozy Thompson's Stadium, the Stapes minor-league ballpark.

Built in the early 1920s by the wealthy owner of a local lumber company, Thompson's Stadium nestled against a hill in the working-class Stapleton neighborhood and doubled in the summer as a home for a semipro baseball team. Inside its stockade façade fence, the stadium could hold about 8,000 fans on its uncovered bleachers. Another 3,000 or 4,000 could line the sidelines and end zones, making for a very quaint setting. Although dwarfed by places like the Polo Grounds, Comiskey Park, and Wrigley Field, little Thompson Stadium would host four years of NFL action in an often electric atmosphere.

At the end of the first day and into the second day, the owners discussed what to do with the Pottsville franchise. In the end Dr. John Striegel found new financing in Massachusetts, as the Providence Steam Roller acted as guardian angel for the deal, guaranteeing the check that brought the Boston Bulldogs into the league. Several of the Pottsville players would go to Boston, while a few of the others found new teams, including one that would land in Green Bay and become a legend.

The last franchise to get approved was Minneapolis, returning to the league and reincarnated by John Dunn. The Minneapolis Redjackets and Dunn signed former Minnesota All-American fullback Herb Joesting to build his team around. By adding teams in larger cities like Boston, Buffalo, Minneapolis, the New York borough of Staten Island, and Orange, a suburb of Newark, New Jersey, Carr and his vision of a big-city league would be put to the test for the first time. The NFL would have twelve teams playing on gridirons in 1929. For more than a decade, the college game had been controlled by three officials, and in the final piece of business, the NFL finally added a fourth man, a field judge, to go along with the referee, umpire, and head linesman. Meeting adjourned.[20]

Before leaving Atlantic City, league vice president and treasurer Carl Storck handed Carr the league's financial report dated from January 1, 1929, to July 15, 1929. This report stated that the NFL had a bank balance of $27,514.36, a very nice cushion for the league considering what was about to happen to the stock market in October. Also in the report, Storck listed all the money spent by the president for the past year.[21]

Expense of Office of President
Office rent—$369.00
Postage—$10.00
Telegrams—$15.67
Telephone—$110.90
Printing—$14.25
Office supplies—$4.10

Traveling Expenses of Officers
John Dunn to Chicago—$65.82
Joe Carr to Chicago—$40.00
Joe Carr to Chicago—$45.00
Joe Carr expenses to East—$123.00
Carl Storck expenses to Chicago—$35.00

The report revealed that the rent of the NFL office was $369.00 ($30.75 per month) and that Carr spent $154.92 on everyday supplies. In 1929 he would add the salary of Kathleen Rubadue (which was unknown/no record) to the payroll. As Carr added personnel to his organization, NFL teams were doing the same. After graduating from New York University in the spring of 1929, Ken Strong, the best college football player the previous fall, signed his first pro contract to play baseball with the New York Yankees, as a power-hitting outfielder. He hit twenty-one home runs and had a batting average of .285 for New Haven (Connecticut) in the Eastern League. On one afternoon while leaving the ballpark, Dan Blaine and Doug Wycoff walked up to Strong to see if he would like to play professional football for the Staten Island Stapletons.

There was no college draft, so Strong was free to sign with anybody who made the best offer. The Stapes offered him a very high salary of $300 per game. Strong liked the offer but said he had a meeting set up with the New York Giants soon and wanted to hear what they would offer. Blaine gave Strong his phone number and asked him to call right away if things didn't work out with the Giants. The Giants coach Roy

Andrews met with Strong and only offered $200 per game, so Strong called Blaine and bent the truth, telling him that the Giants offered $350 a game. Blaine countered with an offer of $5,000 for the season plus a rent-free apartment. Strong accepted on the phone, and the story broke the next day.[22]

In Green Bay, Curly Lambeau was busy building a team that would dominate the NFL for the next three years. At this point Curly had a solid team that had their best finish in 1927 when they landed in second place behind the New York Giants. In 1928 Lambeau played very little and started to put more time in at finding players and coaching them. Lambeaus's last year as a player would be 1929. In the off-season he signed three newcomers who eventually ended up in the Pro Football Hall of Fame. Cal Hubbard was an All-Pro tackle the past two seasons with the Giants who wanted out of New York, and he set his sights on Green Bay. The six-feet-two, 250-pound "giant" gave the Packers' line some much-needed toughness. Lambeau followed up that acquisition by signing free agent guard Mike Michalske who was just recently released from his contract by Pyle's New York Yankees. Michalske was the best guard in pro football and provided unbelievable quickness to go with Hubbard's toughness. The front wall of Hubbard, Michalske, center Jug Earp, end Lavvie Dilweg, and tackle Claude Perry gave the Packers the best line in the NFL.

The third newcomer signed by Lambeau was the well-traveled and very colorful Johnny "Blood" McNally, who picked up his pseudonym from a movie marquee. On his way to playing a semipro game while in college, he passed a theater playing the Valentino film "Blood and Sand," and he chose "Blood" to protect his eligibility. After college he put in four years of play in the NFL with weaker teams in Milwaukee (1925), Duluth (1926–1927), and Pottsville (1928) before signing with the Packers.

McNally always had great talent as an end and halfback, and most teams saw that he could help you win football games. With a team coached by Lambeau, Blood could really showcase his skills. He could outsprint most players, was a slashing inside runner, caught passes better than any back or end in the league, and was a great defensive player. He also could get into trouble with his famous off-the-field lifestyle that included drinking, women, and tons of missed curfews. His abilities on the field were so great that Lambeau had to live with his antics, but Lambeau fined Blood more than any other player.

"Green Bay was definitely the place for me. My destiny, maybe," said Johnny McNally once about playing in Green Bay. "I loved the place and, I have to say, the place, the people, loved me. If you play for the Packers, the people in Green Bay know you better than they know their own brothers. And they care more about what you do. I imagine that's not so good if the team isn't going well, but I was lucky to be there during those great years."[23]

With the Packers preparing for a special season, City Stadium in Green Bay was getting an upgrade that would expand the seating capacity to seat more than 10,000 fans. Lambeau was now getting paid $2,500 per year by the Packers and was working two off-season jobs with Massachusetts Life (selling insurance) and Steifels Clothing Store (selling men's clothing). The race for the 1929 NFL title would pit small town versus big city.[24]

Both the New York Giants and Green Bay Packers raced through the first two months of the season without a loss. The Packers won their first five games, all at home, by allowing their opponents a total of four points—including a 23–0 dismantling of the Chicago Bears in front of an overflow crowd of 13,000 at City Stadium. The Giants, meanwhile, had opened their season with a scoreless tie against the Orange Tornadoes. After that slow start, Benny Friedman got the offense rolling and the Giants reeled off eight straight wins by scoring 204 points (averaging 25.5 per game). Then the unexpected happened.

On Thursday, October 24, the country was hit hard by the news that the stock market had crashed. After the weekend, the market took more hits on Black Monday and even blacker Tuesday, as the whole country would be tossed into the Great Depression; the NFL, like everyone else, would be heavily affected for years to come. As for the 1929 season, the Dayton Triangles, who played only six games, were the only team hurt by the crash, playing only one game after October. Carl Storck's team would be playing their last season in the NFL, and the squad's final game was a 19–0 loss to the Chicago Cardinals in front of a crowd reported as "300 spectators." Not the best way to say good-bye.

The same weekend as the crash, Carr attended the Staten Island–Frankford contest outside of Philadelphia, seeing a 6–6 tie along with 7,000 other spectators. Not a bad turnout considering what was happening. As the country's mood turned sour, Carr's league rolled along with the season's biggest game. On November 24, the Packers invaded New York to battle the Giants for first place and the inside track to the championship. The season's biggest showdown featured two unbeaten teams (Packers at 9–0 and the Giants 8–0–1) doing battle in front of a large crowd of 25,000 at the famous Polo Grounds. "This was the first time that I really got the feeling that I was in the big leagues. The New York papers devoted a lot of space to pre-game publicity, which we'd never seen before. And it was really something to get out here in front of all those people," said Johnny "Blood" McNally years later about the 1929 matchup.[25]

One of the largest NFL crowds of the past several years saw the coming-out party of a dynasty. In the first quarter the Packers scored early with a touchdown pass, and the small-town team led 7–0 at the half. A Benny Friedman touchdown in the third quarter cut the lead to 7–6, as they missed the extra point. Then the Packers dominated the final quarter by scoring two touchdowns, the last one on a short run by Johnny Blood. The Packers' 20–6 victory over the Giants put Lambeau's squad into first place and just three games away from the city's first NFL championship.

Neither the Giants nor the Packers lost any of their remaining games. The Giants finished the season at 13–1–1 but the Packers' big win at the Polo Grounds was the deciding factor. The Packers played a scoreless tie at Frankford on Thanksgiving Day, then routed Providence (25–0); to wrap up the season, they destroyed the Chicago Bears 25–0, defeating Halas's Bears for the third time in 1929. Until the 1929 season, George Halas had owned Curly Lambeau by holding a 7–3–3 overall record, but this season saw a new Packers team against the rival Bears.

"Halas and Lambeau were friends, like coaches would be friends. But when it comes to playing, hell, you're not friends. You're out to win and you win any damn way you can," recalled George Musso, former Bears guard. In the three games that the Packers defeated the Bears, they outscored the Monsters of the Midway 62–0. After six games the Bears had a record of 4–1–1, but their final nine games resulted in eight losses and a tie. It was the Bears' first losing season. The worst defeat occurred on Thanksgiving Day when Ernie Nevers scored six touchdowns and kicked four extra points as the Cardinals slaughtered the Bears 40–6. The forty points that Nevers scored is still an NFL record for most points scored in a single game.[26]

Part of the problem was that the Bears had too many past-their-prime regulars, but even more destructive was their trouble at the top. The team's co-owners, George Halas and Dutch Sternaman, were having a hard time agreeing on anything. The biggest issue was how to handle the offense, and consequently, the offense suffered. Over the next couple of years the relationship would get worse.

Although the Packers–Giants game was the most important of the season, there was another game that would have a lasting impact on the NFL. The Providence Steam Roller had scheduled a visit from the Chicago Cardinals on November 3, but heavy rain forced a postponement. The Steam Roller management certainly didn't want to miss out on the drawing power of Ernie Nevers, so they convinced the Cardinals to stay and play a make-up game on Wednesday. The catch was the Steam Roller rescheduled the contest for a night game—the first night game in NFL history.

Temporary floodlights were installed at little Kinsley Park (instead of the Cycledrome), and 6,000 fans filled the tiny park. Nevers played a phenomenal game by throwing for a score, running for another, and kicking a field goal as the Cards won 16–0. The night game experience was a novelty, but Carr took notice of the event and thought the idea of night games could work for his league. It would be a matter discussed by Carr and the owners shortly after the season.

When the Packers returned home after defeating the Bears in the last game of the season, they were greeted by 20,000 shivering fans at the train station. The fans and a police escort led Lambeau and his team to City Hall, where Lambeau was presented a key to the city. Speaking to the large crowd, Lambeau was looking to the future: "It is pretty hard to say anything. This welcome is something that we didn't expect and is a complete surprise. Speaking for the boys, I can say that they appreciate it and the only answer we can make is a championship again next year."[27]

The following evening the team and 400 guests held a special banquet at the Beaumont Hotel complete with a dinner, speeches, and dancing. Johnny Blood spoke for the players. "I'm in the greatest town in the world and I'm glad to be here in Green Bay, the home of the perpetual fatted calf." Lambeau spoke again about what the Packers' faithful could expect from his squad. "When a city responds as it has done to our efforts, I'll say it certainly deserves a championship. It is going to take a lot of hard work, energy and loyal support of all fans to give Green Bay another championship team next year."[28]

Several telegrams were read at the banquet, congratulating the team on their championship, including one from Carr; one from Tim Mara, saying "the best team won"; and one from Halas, who wrote "the West is proud of the Green Bay Packers but look out next year." After the losing season, Halas was still very positive that his team would turn it around, but they now had to go through Lambeau's Packers if he wanted another title.[29]

Carr's off-season was once again struck by tragedy. In November his close friend and former colleague Clyde Tuttle, the sports editor at the *Ohio State Journal*, died at his desk of a heart attack. The annual Christmas party at the *Journal* was a somber affair and was renamed in his honor. The 1929 season was a very exciting and successful one for the NFL, and Carr prepared his loop for the challenges of trying to run this organization under the cloud of the Great Depression.

At the winter meeting held on January 25, 1930, in Dayton, the owners met at the Van Cleve Hotel to prepare for life after the crash. NFL vice president and treasurer Carl Storck hosted the event as Carr began the proceedings at 2:00 p.m. with his annual report:

> The 1929 season of the National Football League considered from all angles was the most successful in the history of the organization. Report of our treasurer will show that we had the largest average attendance per game, notwithstanding that the average weather conditions were poor.

There were fewer complaints than in any previous season and the Executive Committee has less for its consideration than at any time in the history of the organization. The publicity was extended and in a general way the season was a great success. It is my belief that the general character of the players was improved over previous years. This is determined by the closeness of the scores in most instances and clubs which were far down in the race most of the season gave very creditable accounts when they were pitted against clubs that were much higher in the race. The four additions to the League, namely: Buffalo, Minneapolis, Orange and Stapleton did very well from an attendance standpoint and each of these cities presented clubs in the League that were well worthy of membership in the organization.

The year of 1929 was not only a remarkable one for professional football as exemplified in the National Football League but several individual teams of outstanding importance were developed in various sections of the country, as Portsmouth and Ironton, Ohio, Ashland, Ky., and Memphis, Tenn., all practically new to the professional world had clubs backed by reputable organizations that met with favorable comment throughout the country.

Though our league has made remarkable strides in its few years of existence I am quite sure you will agree there is much room for improvement. Personally I feel that the most stringent need at this time is capable coaches and to this end I would recommend that every club owner in the League give as serious thought to the person who is to have charge of the club as to the personnel of the club itself, for after all we must agree that team work at all times will outshine individual efforts.[30]

Carr's initial report of the new season hit the duo of Halas-Sternaman the hardest and they responded by hiring themselves a new coach. For years it was said that George Halas and Dutch Sternaman, the Bears' co-owners and co-coaches, always took opposite sides in every minor argument at league meetings but presented a united front on all major issues. But, by 1929, their bickering had spread from league politics to how their own team was being directed. The absence of a united front split the team, and the result was the first ever losing season in Bears' history with a 4–9–2 record. A change was necessary.

Neither Halas nor Sternaman was willing to let the other take charge, so they resolved their differences by agreeing neither would coach the team. In effect they fired themselves and vowed to just run the front office matters. The Bears' owners hired Ralph Jones to be their new coach; Jones was the head man at Lake Forest (Illinois) Academy and a former assistant coach under Bob Zuppke at the partners' old school of the University of Illinois. Jones had faith in the T-formation, the attack mode the Bears had used since they began as the Decatur Staleys. While other teams lined up in more modern formations, like the Notre Dame box used by Knute Rockne, Jones continued to use the basic T. But Jones added new refinements such as split ends and a man in motion in the backfield, opening up the Bears' offense for more passes and end runs. Along with Jones, the Bears signed the biggest college star in the country by inking Minnesota All-American fullback Bronko Nagurski. In 1930 the Bears rebounded with a 9–4–1 record and a third place finish.

The owners awarded the 1929 title to the Packers; discussed the potential of adding a new franchise, with Portsmouth, Ohio, being the leading candidate; looked into the process of scheduling night games; and reelected Carl Storck as vice president and treasurer and Joe F. Carr as president and secretary (adding a new role to his job). The owners also approved a motion "that beginning in 1931 the League should meet just once a year, instead of twice, during the second week of July. Yearly meetings shall be in alternate years in Atlantic City, NJ and Chicago, Illinois."[31]

After the meeting Storck talked to his hometown paper, the *Dayton Journal*, about one of the most important issues discussed by the moguls: "The 12 clubs, playing a total of 90 games [in 1929], had an average paid attendance of 6,000 to the contest. Every team made money, and were looking forward to bigger and better things this year. Things have not always been thus in pro football, and we were naturally curious to know what brought about such a decided change in the fortunes of the National grid league. NIGHT FOOTBALL."[32]

Storck's belief that night football would be an instant hit and change the fortunes of the league would have to wait until the night games were played later that year. But it was an experiment that the NFL was willing to try for the 1930 season. The country was in the midst of a depression, and if a few more fans could attend an NFL game at night because they were working on Sunday or trying to find employment, it was an idea worth trying.

When he returned to Columbus, Carr set up a meeting with the officials of the Portsmouth (Ohio) Spartans to see if they were prepared to join the NFL. Once again a few of the NFL franchises were in trouble—despite the declaration by Carl Storck that every NFL team made money, which wasn't the case—with three teams in jeopardy of folding. Carr had looked to replace the Boston Bulldogs, Buffalo Bisons, and the last of the original Ohio League teams, Storck's Dayton Triangles.

Harold Griffen, the coach and manager of the Spartans, traveled to Columbus and met for a couple of hours in Carr's office. Griffen filed a formal application for admittance, and Carr virtually assured him that the Spartans were going to be guaranteed a spot in the NFL. Before turning the application in to Carr, the NFL's executive committee of Dr. Harry March, Dr. W. W. Kelly, and George Halas had given their approval to Carr. Formal acceptance would be made at the annual scheduling meeting in July.

On February 21 the *Portsmouth Times* announced the news that President Carr and the NFL had virtually accepted the Spartans. Carr stated that he "was anxious to see Portsmouth become one of the league teams and that the Spartans had the strongest team outside the league."[33]

In 1929 the city of Portsmouth, Ohio, had a population of 42,000 citizens who were very proud of their independent professional football team. That year the Spartans—who were owned by local businessmen as a nonprofit corporation—had just finished a successful season with a 12–2–1 record. So after the season the directors of the Portsmouth Football Corporation announced their intention of gaining membership to the NFL.

The addition of Portsmouth was against Carr's prevailing trend of locating franchises in large, well-populated cities, and despite a good record in 1929 as an independent team, the Spartans might have seen their bid for an NFL franchise go unheeded except for its location. The league was badly split geographically. Minneapolis, Green Bay, and the two Chicago teams were in the upper Midwest, while New York City, Frankford, Brooklyn, Staten Island, Providence, and Newark were all on the East Coast. Portsmouth, situated on the Ohio River, made a convenient stopover payday on trips east or west. Chicago and three other teams could play night games on Wednesday in Portsmouth and then continue on to play a league game on Sunday.

Besides its location, the city of Portsmouth had another positive thing going for it in the eyes of Joe F. Carr. The community had just agreed to build a brand new stadium to meet the needs of a big-time professional football team. The Universal Stadium Corporation, named specifically for its mission, was the creation of Harry Snyder, a prominent and longtime building contractor in the city (who would also invest money in the team). In his bid of fifty dollars annually for the lease of LaBold Field (the old field in Portsmouth where the new stadium would be built), he proposed to construct a stadium far larger and costlier than the city council had originally required. Instead of accommodating 4,000, it would seat 8,000 to 10,000; instead of costing as little as $30,000, it would run as high as $100,000.[34]

The new Portsmouth franchise hired Harry Doerr as general manager and retained Harry Griffen as head coach. They sold season tickets at $12.00, having fans pay $1.00 down and the rest in installments. They set their game day prices at $1.50 for a general admission ticket and a souvenir program at ten cents. Stockholders transformed their nonprofit corporation, and they changed the name to the Portsmouth National Football League Corporation.[35]

Carr stuck his neck out for the small-town Spartans, and it was definitely a big gamble on his part to include them in his big-city vision. On

July 12–13 the owners and Carr returned to the Seaside Hotel in Atlantic City for the summer meeting to put the finishing touches on the NFL schedule and award new franchises. Starting at noon, Carr announced that Boston and Buffalo were out of the league. For the city of Buffalo, it would be the last time they would be in the NFL until the Buffalo Bills came along in the AFL merger. But Carr wouldn't give up on Boston as he would get them back into the league in 1932.[36]

The owners officially accepted the Portsmouth Spartans (and their $2,500 guarantee fund) and admitted Hal Griffen to the meeting. After a short dinner break, Carr announced that he and the NFL's executive committee had approved the transfer of the Dayton franchise to Brooklyn. Carl Storck, who missed the meeting to attend to work for General Motors in Detroit, was out as an NFL owner. For the next twelve years he would just serve the NFL in a front office capacity. The Triangles were sold to William "Bill" Dwyer, a Brooklyn businessman, and John Depler, former Illinois star, for $2,500 (the price of the guarantee fee). Depler coached the previous season with the Orange (New Jersey) Tornadoes and assumed those duties for the new club, which adopted the baseball team's historic nickname: the Dodgers. They would, of course, play their home games at Ebbets Field.[37]

Dwyer had business interest in several sports around the city, including football, hockey, and horse racing, and he owned several racetracks. The year before he purchased the Triangles, Dwyer acquired a controlling interest in the National Hockey League's (NHL) New York Americans, and he served on the NHL Board of Governors from 1929–1937. The addition of the Dodgers now gave the city of New York three teams, joining Tim Mara's Giants and Dan Blaine's Stapletons. The NFL now had eleven teams.

1930 NFL Franchises
Brooklyn Dodgers
Chicago Bears
Chicago Cardinals
Frankford Yellow Jackets
Green Bay Packers
Minneapolis Redjackets
Newark (Orange) Tornadoes
New York Giants
Portsmouth Spartans
Providence Steam Roller
Staten Island Stapletons

The eleven teams that made up the NFL definitely gave the league a big-city look, with just two franchises in small markets—Green Bay and

Portsmouth. But just like every year, Carr asked himself,, which teams would survive? Which teams could generate the money to pay players and then attract fans to the stadiums to help offset their expenses? And if they didn't accomplish this by making a profit, could the owner absorb the financial losses and not give up on the sport? Carr had found a few owners like Tim Mara, James Dooley–Charles Coppen, Dr. David Jones, Dan Blaine, and John Dunn to invest in the NFL without showing much profit over the past several years. Frankford, Green Bay, and Portsmouth were financed by either an association, a city, or a corporation. Then there was George Halas, who was in the business of professional football for life, so Carr knew he would be sticking around. To make matters worse for Carr and his plan to try and keep the NFL in large metropolitan cities was that the Depression would have a say in who would survive.

On the second day of the meeting, the league approved the schedule for the 1930 season (will start on September 14 and end on December 14) that included eleven Wednesday night games in four different cities—New York (Giants), Newark, Portsmouth, and Providence. With night games in tow, the owners approved a new rule stating "that all League games played at night where a white football is used, no part of the uniform of either team shall be predominately white. However, should the regulation football [brown] be used white may be used as part of the uniform."[38]

Carr had now wrapped up his twenty-sixth NFL meeting as league president, and his passion and commitment for the league was at an all-time high. It had also been twenty-six years since he became the manager of the Columbus Panhandles and began his career in professional football. He had seen the growth of the sport ranging from the players on the field to the crowds of 20,000 plus in cities like Chicago and New York. It was now up to him and the owners to continue the drive to keep the league on the right track to becoming that big-city sport. This year would be their biggest challenge.

Going into the 1930 season, Carr finalized the schedule and took care of a few minor details but he also made a unique hire. Over the years Carr selected his game officials very carefully, and usually he looked for men who had a lot of experience in officiating. Some of the officials he hired had played professional football or officiated at the college level. In 1930 he hired a young man who would eventually play a small part in Carr's legacy nearly twenty-five years after his death.

Dan Tehan was a son of an Irish immigrant who became a very well-known prep athlete in the city of Cincinnati. After a decorated athletic career at St. Xavier High School, he went on to be a two-sport (football and basketball) star at Xavier University in his hometown. Tehan's love of sports continued after his graduation in the spring of 1929, when he played semipro football and officiated high school and college football games. That fall he quickly gained a reputation of being a very knowledgeable and fair official on the gridiron. "He knew the rules. He was a big rule man and he knew them," says Patrick Tehan, son of Dan Tehan. "I can remember when I was a kid, he'd be laying in his bed at night. I'd go in and he'd be there reading. Every night he read his rulebook."[39]

Tehan would also get married in 1929 and find employment with the Cincinnati Athletic Goods Company. But the following year he was offered a great opportunity to work in the fledgling NFL. In a 1976 interview with *Referee Magazine*, Dan Tehan recalled how he was hired to be an NFL official.

> It was funny how I got started in the pro league. Joe Carr was President of the league at the time. He lived in Columbus, Ohio, and was running the whole show from there. He wanted Frank Lane [a top football and basketball official before he became a baseball executive] to work for him. But Lane, who was working in the Big Ten at the time, turned him down because he was getting $50 a game in that conference and the pay in the pro league was only $25. But Frank recommended me to Carr and I was hired in 1930.[40]

At this time NFL referees were getting thirty-five dollars a game and the other three officials were getting twenty-five a game, so there was no way Carr was going to match the fifty bucks to get a top-of-the-line official like Lane. Instead he hired the tall (six feet two), very athletic, very young Tehan to be a head linesman. In 1930 Tehan would start a thirty-five-year NFL career as one of the league's greatest whistle blowers, and he always took his job seriously with a touch of reality. "Since he is engaged in this duty alone, the official must put forth enough intelligent effort to justify his being on the field. He must be prepared mentally and physically for each game. It is hard work and a serious business—but it is fun, too, and all the money in the world could not beat the friends you make in sports."[41]

Carr's ability to judge talent and his personal affinity for good Irish lads gave his league another building block. As the 1930 season approached, Carr was invited to attend the NFL debut of the Portsmouth Spartans on September 14. While there Carr was to tour the new stadium and participate in the pregame ceremonies with the mayor of Portsmouth to dedicate the new stadium. After traveling the ninety-mile trip south from Columbus, Carr was given the royal treatment.

On a perfect day for football, Carr took a tour of the brand new Universal Stadium and came away very impressed by the facility. Before the game started between Newark and Portsmouth, Carr joined Mayor Robert C. Bryan and city manager C. A. Harrell for pregame ceremonies. After short speeches by the political bigwigs over the stadium's new PA system, Carr shook hands with the team captains, Father Lumpkin

(Spartans) and Stu Clancy (Tornadoes), before presenting the game ball to referee Bobbie Cahn. Carr then sat in a special box on the fifty yard line with the mayor and other city officials to watch the action. What he saw was an uneventful game, with the Spartans pulling out a 13–6 victory to give the small town its first NFL win. Carr then spoke to the press, giving his opinion of the city: "I was amazed at the size of your stadium and its completeness. It is a credit to a city much larger than Portsmouth. Your city is aflame with football enthusiasm and it looks to me like the Spartans are in for a great year. Of course the opposition will be tougher than the fans have been seeing and for this reason there will not be many touchdowns scored. All the teams are made up of college stars and are about evenly matched."[42]

Carr was impressed with the atmosphere of the game, but he wanted more from the small town. In giving his quote he was very disappointed in the turnout of just 4,000 fans, because he knew better teams would be visiting Portsmouth (Newark would finish with a horrible 1–10–1 record), and the team needed to attract bigger crowds in order to make a profit. In speaking to the *Portsmouth Times*, Spartans coach Hal Griffen said it would cost $60,000 to pay the players (up to twenty-two men) for the season, and after adding the cost of traveling by rail, food, accommodations, and equipment, the annual expenditure rose to nearly $85,000. The small-town Portsmouth National Football League Corporation had a big challenge ahead of it.[43] After the game Carr had dinner with his friend William Gableman, who he knew from his old days as president of the Ohio State League, then headed home.

The season was now under way as the Packers began their defense of their title by adding 2,000 additional seats to City Stadium, as well as adding a special flag pole (painted blue and gold) placed prominently at one end of the field inside the stadium. At the season opener against the Cardinals, the Packers raised the championship flag proclaiming the Packers "1929 Champions."

The Packers returned basically the same squad as the year before, and they didn't miss a beat, winning their first seven games. But the Packers strong start was overshadowed by another big event going on around the NFL—night games. Throughout the 1930 season the league saw eleven night games, all on Wednesday evenings—except one Thursday night contest hosted by the New York Giants on October 16.

September 17—New York Giants at Newark (10,000)
September 24—Frankford at Newark (2,000)
September 24—Brooklyn at Portsmouth (6,000)
October 1—Staten Island at Newark (8,000)
October 1—Frankford at Providence (3,500)

October 8—Frankford at Portsmouth (No Figures Found)
October 8—Chicago Cardinals at Newark (5,000)
October 16—Chicago Cardinals at New York Giants (15,000—Thursday night)
October 22—Chicago Bears at Portsmouth (7,500)
October 29—Newark at New York Giants (5,000)
November 5—New York Giants at Portsmouth (7,000)

The eleven games attracted a total of 68,500 fans—averaging about 6,227 per game—which wasn't a bad number, but it didn't change the course of professional football. The eleven night games would be a season high for twilight contests during the entire decade of the 1930s, but, of course, night games in the NFL wouldn't really become a staple until 1970 with *Monday Night Football*. On October 16 the Giants played their first ever night game at the Polo Grounds. Tim Mara had as his special guest former New York governor and friend Al Smith, among the 15,000 fans, which was the largest crowd of any of the eleven night games.[44]

The week after the Giants hosted Smith, Carr attended the Bears–Spartans night game with several friends as the guest of George Halas. A crowd of 7,500 saw the Spartans upset Halas's Bears 7–6, as the team near the Ohio River got off to a 4–1–1 record. But the Spartans won just one more game during the rest of the season to finish with a 5–6–3 record. After the game Carr gave another shot in the arm to the Spartans, saying to the press that "you can say Portsmouth is in the league to stay." Carr knew it was premature to start making promises like that, but he wanted the fans in Portsmouth to know he was behind them 100 percent. He definitely wanted the city to make it in his loop.[45]

The NFL's other rookie team had a little more success. The Brooklyn Dodgers were led by former Giants star running back Jake McBride, who guided Bill Dwyer's team to a fourth place finish at 7–4–1. But the wins and losses didn't impress Carr. It was the attendance figures that did. In the Dodgers' five home games, they totaled 64,000 fans and an average of 12,800 a game, including a season-high crowd of 20,000 at Ebbets Field for the December 7 matchup with the cross-town Giants.[46]

The contrast between the small town and the big city would be waged over the next couple of seasons, but 1930, both on and off the field, belonged to the big city. By November 10 the Packers stood at 8–0 and the Giants at 10–1, with their only loss to the Pack, but surprisingly both teams lost their next game. So the following week both teams faced off in the Big Apple to pretty much settle the NFL title, with the Packers looking to repeat as champs.

Before a stunning crowd of 37,000 fans at the Polo Grounds—the largest crowd for an NFL game since Red Grange's New York invasion in

1925—the Giants pulled off a huge upset victory, defeating the Packers 13–6. Behind a Benny Friedman–to–Red Badgro touchdown pass and an eighty-four-yard run by Hap Moran that led to Friedman's one-yard sneak, the Giants, at 11–2, moved into first place ahead of the 8–2 Packers. But four days later on Thanksgiving Day, the Giants came crashing down to earth by losing to Staten Island, 7–6. On the same day the Packers thumped the Frankford Yellow Jackets 25–7.

As the Carr family celebrated turkey day, the NFL president had an unexpected crisis come across his desk. In early November Notre Dame star fullback Joe Savoldi was forced to withdraw from school after an investigation disclosed he had been secretly married in 1929 and was filing for an annulment. Three weeks later, Savoldi signed a contract with the Chicago Bears to play the final three games of the season. Co-owners George Halas and Dutch Sternaman issued a press release announcing the signing: "Because of the extraordinary circumstances surrounding this case we do not feel that we are making any encroachment upon college football, nor does this set any precedent of jeopardizing the amateur standing of any college player, as Savoldi is no longer classed as a college player. We are happy and proud to announce that Joe Savoldi will appear in uniform as one of our regular players to participate in our big game next Thanksgiving morning against the Cardinals."[47]

Just as with the signing of Red Grange in 1925, Halas had to have the next big "star," but this time he had crossed the line. Halas contended that the new roster addition was legal since Savoldi was forced to leave school and was not a member of a graduating class. Carr understood Halas's claim and said this case was "without parallel" in the history of the league. Savoldi did play against the Cardinals on Thanksgiving in front of just 8,000 fans at Wrigley Field, and Halas gave him a chance to be the hero. In a scoreless game in the third quarter, Savoldi scored a one-yard touchdown to give the Bears a 6–0 victory.[48]

The day after the game, Carr fined the Bears $1,000 for breaking the league rule against signing college players before their class had graduated. "It's an unusual case but the violation is plain and I have no choice in the matter. The only recourse for the owners of the Bears is to appeal to the executive committee of the league. The ruling will in no way affect Savoldi's future in professional football after his class is graduated from Notre Dame next spring."[49] On November 28, 1930, Carr sat with his secretary Kathleen Rubadue and wrote Dutch Sternaman a letter explaining the ruling and how to pay the fine.

Dear Mr. Sternaman:

In keeping with the provisions of Section 1 Article 10 of the Constitution and By-Laws of the National Football League you are here-by notified that *the Chicago Bears have been fined the sum of $1,000 for permitting player [Joe] Savoldi to participate in a game with your club on Nov. 27.*

I have given full consideration to your claim that the circumstances surrounding Savoldi are not a violation of the League rules and consideration of this fact will permit an appeal to the membership of the Executive Committee. However, in the meantime I would suggest you forward your check covering the above fine to our Treasury who will hold same until the matter is finally disposed of.

In this same mail I am returning to Mr. Halas the agreement signed by your club with this player covering his services in games during the season of 1930 which cannot be promulgated in this office. However, his contract for 1931 will be retained until the matter is finally disposed of.

Trusting you will give the forgoing your usual attention and with kindest personal regards, I am,

Very truly yours,
Joe F. Carr
President[50]

Carr quickly resolved the issue without it getting out of control, and the press was very favorable to the way he handled it. Most of the headlines around the country led with the $1,000 fine in big bold letters, which caught the attention of the public. Halas-Sternaman paid the fine, and Savoldi played just two more games in 1930, and then retired to pursue a career in professional wrestling. The week after the Savoldi decision was made, the NFL's championship race ended. The Packers crushed the Stapletons 37–7, and the Giants were upset again, this time by the Dodgers 7–6. The Giants slump cost head coach Roy Andrews his job, and players Benny Friedman and Steve Owen took over coaching duties in the final two games—both wins. On the last day of the regular season (December 14), Joe F. Carr attended the Packers–Spartans game in Portsmouth. Once again he sat in the box at the fifty yard line, and after the game he talked to sportswriters George Calhoun (*Green Bay Press-Gazette*) and Ollie Kuechle (*Milwaukee Journal*), who were there covering the Pack. After watching a hard fought 6–6 tie he told the group of writers, "It was a great game and Portsmouth should be proud of its team. It is a real fighting football eleven. When the smallest city in the league can win the championship two years in a row it is something to be proud of. And I'm as proud of the Green Bay Packers as any of their fans up there in Wisconsin."[51]

Speaking to the *Portsmouth Times*, Curly Lambeau also said a few kind words about the city of Portsmouth: "With a little revamping the league will be ready to start its most successful season next fall. Portsmouth has certainly taken its football seriously and I wish to compliment your real city and the spirit of the fans. That fine crowd Sunday on the eve of the holidays was a real testimonial to the loyalty of your supporters."[52] Little did Lambeau know that one year later the two small towns would be engaged in a bitter controversy that would put Carr right in the middle of the argument. But for now the Packers had won back-to-back NFL championships, joining the 1922–1923 Canton Bulldogs as the only teams to accomplish that feat.

On the same day when Carr saw the Packers–Spartans game end the NFL season, three other league teams played two charity games that would have a great impact on the history of the league. In Chicago the city's two rivals—Bears and Cardinals—planned a charity contest to benefit the Illinois Unemployment Relief Fund in a very unique environment. The game was played indoors at Chicago Stadium—the home of the NHL's Chicago Blackhawks—to avoid the bad weather. A near capacity crowd of 10,000 showed up to watch the Bears score a safety in the third quarter to break a tie and give them a 9–7 victory. The crazy idea of an indoor football game would make a comeback two years later and forever change the history of the NFL.[53]

The other charity game occurred in New York. With the Great Depression growing worse, the New York Giants agreed to meet an all-star team of Notre Dame graduates in the Polo Grounds with all the proceeds going to the New York Unemployment Fund. Knute Rockne coached the Notre Dame squad, which included the Four Horsemen and other recent graduates of college football's most dominant program. Rockne and much of the public still held pro football in low regard and expected an easy Notre Dame victory. The debate of who played better football—the colleges or pros—was still hotly discussed.

However, Benny Freidman and the Giants found the game a great opportunity to convince Rockne and the public of the quality of pro ball. "The best professional team could spot the best college team two touchdowns and win the game," Friedman had said on WDR radio in New York earlier in 1930. "Although a college eleven may have as much offensive power as a professional team, the latter is much better defensively. Some pro lines average 230 pounds and you need a stick of dynamite to dent a wall like that," said Red Grange when asked about his opinion of the upcoming matchup.[54]

Before a crowd of 55,000 Freidman led the Giants to a pair of quick touchdowns while allowing the Notre Dame players not even a first down. Legend has it that Rockne went over to the Giants dressing room at halftime and begged the pros to take it easy on his boys. The Giants cruised to a 22–0 win. The New York Unemployment Fund collected

$115,153. Mara turned over every cent to the fund, and his Giants profited from the enormous publicity the press gave the contest. No longer could the public shrug off the pros as clumsy goons.[55]

Carr was very pleased with the contributions his teams were making in the fight against the Great Depression. He also saw that his league could only grow in the big cities and not just on the field but off the field as well. The publicity of the charity games and the media coverage of his league in cities such as Chicago and New York could only be available in the cities with the bright lights. The only problem was how to stay there.

18

Small-Town Green Bay Is Titletown (1931)

Joe F. Carr had just finished ten seasons as NFL president (1921–1930), and there were some incredible numbers to digest. From 1921 to 1930, the NFL had forty-eight different franchises in thirty-eight different cities. Then there were the attendance figures, which were taken by actual newspaper accounts from the local press. It is clear that as the decade moved on, more attention was given to reporting attendance figures. Although some writers embellished the numbers of fans in their articles, this is the only source we have to gauge these figures. The NFL didn't keep official attendance figures. Also, in the second list, the average attendance per NFL game showed a steady increase in fans attending NFL games—except for the big spike in 1925 with the arrival of Red Grange, and a small deduction in 1930, a year after the stock market crash. Comparing 1924 (3,655 fans per game) to 1930 (7,027 fans per game) the average attendance per game nearly doubled.[1]

Attendance by Year

1921 APFA (66 league games) = 172, 804 fans (36 out of 66 games reported in papers)
1922 NFL (74 league games) = 187,752 fans (42 out of 74 games)
1923 NFL (88 league games) = 252,596 fans (57 out of 88 games)
1924 NFL (80 league games) = 292,444 fans (61 out of 80 games)
1925 NFL (103 league games) = 680,361 fans (74 out of 103 games)
1926 NFL (116 league games) = 490,800 fans (82 out of 116 games)
1927 NFL (72 league games) = 557,100 fans (64 out of 72 games)
1928 NFL (56 league games) = 440,400 fans (50 out of 56 games)

1929 NFL (71 league games) = 554,600 fans (61 out of 71 games)
1930 NFL (73 league games) = 513,000 fans (63 out of 73 games)

Average Attendance per Game
1921 APFA = 2,618 fans per game
1922 NFL = 2,537 fans per game
1923 NFL = 2,870 fans per game
1924 NFL = 3,655 fans per game
1925 NFL = 6,605 fans per game
1926 NFL = 4,231 fans per game
1927 NFL = 7,737 fans per game
1928 NFL = 7,864 fans per game
1929 NFL = 7,811 fans per game
1930 NFL = 7,027 fans per game

The first ten years had been a challenge for President Joe F. Carr, and he responded by building a solid foundation for the league. He established the NFL's "Constitution and Bylaws"; made peace with the colleges/universities; recruited financially capable owners; set franchise fees, territorial rights, player contracts; had a working relationship with the press; set up the league's headquarters in his hometown; and hired competent officials to officiate games. The building blocks were being laid down by Carr and the other owners, but each group knew that more work needed to be done. The Roaring Twenties saw this growth, but the 1930s (right in the midst of the Great Depression) would see the league's foundation grow from being a small barn to a huge mansion.

For the first time the league didn't hold a winter meeting, agreeing to only meet in the summer. Carr was given more time to go over applications for new franchises. In 1930 the NFL had eleven teams but two franchises weren't returning—Minneapolis and Newark were out—leaving the NFL with just nine teams. The nine franchises gave Carr on paper what he was looking for—franchises in large, populated cities with suitable playing fields:

Brooklyn Dodgers (population 2,560,401)—Ebbets Field (32,000 capacity**)
Chicago Bears (population 3,982,123)—Wrigley Field (38,000 capacity)
Chicago Cardinals (population 3,982,123)—Comiskey Park (52,000 capacity)
Frankford Yellow Jackets (population 1,950,961)—Frankford Stadium (15,000 capacity)
Green Bay Packers (population 70,249)—City Stadium (15,000 capacity)

New York Giants (population 1,867,312)—Polo Grounds (56,000 capacity)
Portsmouth Spartans (population 81,221)—Universal Stadium (8,200 capacity)
Providence Steam Roller (population 540,016)—Cycledrome (10,000 capacity)
Staten Island Stapletons (population 158,346)—Thompson's Stadium (8,000 capacity)
** Capacity seating numbers are estimates because of additional and standing-room seating.

Just like the previous ten years, franchise stability was at the top of Carr's to-do list, and adding to his headache, playing facilities were becoming a bigger issue when looking at a potential team. In the spring of 1931 Carr focused on two familiar cities to get his loop to an even number of franchises—Milwaukee and Cleveland. In the middle of May, Carr traveled to Milwaukee to meet with potential investors led by local sports promoter Eddie Stumpf.

The city of Milwaukee had one previous team, the 1922–1926 Badgers, and made a strong case to field another. Speaking to the Milwaukee press Carr gave his opinion on the city's chances.

> I'm here today to interest a responsible promoter in a National League franchise. Unless I get the man I want, I would not care to have a National team in Milwaukee, for I know that irresponsible promoters have given the game a black eye here.
>
> Milwaukee is an ideal spot for a team. Why, the two games with the Green Bay Packers would draw huge gates and there would be a natural rivalry between the Bears and Cardinals in Chicago and the Milwaukee club. There you have six games a year for a Milwaukee team with little traveling expense involved.
>
> Milwaukee has had professional teams before but never before a team that has had the financial backing that this one will have. I expect that within two years, Milwaukee will be one of the best drawing teams in the league.[2]

Carr was impressed by Stumpf—he was a football guy—but his ability to raise money and field a competitive squad was still a question mark, despite the vote of confidence to the press. Carr, as always, would paint a positive picture of professional football, especially when it came to the financial stability of the NFL. Even potential investors needed to appear stable. Carr then turned to his favorite city without an NFL team, the only city in his beloved home state that he thought could handle an NFL franchise—Cleveland.

A month after visiting Milwaukee he traveled to the city by the lake, but not before he gave his family and daughter a "tiny" scare. Mary Carr was seventeen years old at this time and was about to finish high school and soon attend college at the St. Mary's College of the Springs in Columbus. In a two-page letter written by Mary Carr to her father, she explains her feelings toward her dear dad.

Dearest Daddy,

You'll never know how scared I was when the Union Station called to tell us that you forgot your tickets, you were in such a hurry and I'll bet you just left without your wallet—you carry that wherever you go.

Are you all right—please, please—take care of yourself—don't rush around much remember you're not quite as young as you used to be!

I have said 2 Rosaries for you—so I know you will be safe.

Come home as soon as you can—I miss you so much. You know I love you more that I can tell you.

Please be careful & take it easy—and I'll continue to pray for your success.

Until I hear from you, please write—Be sure & get your proper rest,

I remain your Lammy.
Love + 1000,000,0000,000 kisses.[3]

Mary's undying love for her father was obvious to the family, and Carr loved getting the attention of his little girl. Carr's tiny family crisis didn't slow him down as he made his way to Cleveland. For Carr the idea was to give the city another try mainly because of the presence of a new stadium, Municipal Stadium, which was to have a capacity of over 70,000. Cleveland had fielded teams in the NFL in 1920–1921 and again in 1923, a team won an NFL championship (in 1924) using former Canton players. But that team only lasted one more year. Another try in 1927 with star attraction Benny Friedman didn't last long either.

So, in the midst of the Depression when every team was being challenged to stay afloat, Carr looked to Cleveland to be the NFL's newest franchise. Deep down Carr always believed in the city but he just couldn't understand the lack of support. He thought this time it would be different.

I never before really felt Cleveland could be developed into a good town for our league but now things are different. After looking over your wonderful stadium I am genuinely enthusiastic. With that arena and our great players I don't see how the pro game could miss here now.

Cleveland fans never will recognize pro football as the same game they witnessed in the old days. We not only have classy individual players, but every team drills daily just like the best college elevens. These fellows devote their full time to the game and have the very best of team work. Few college

> teams could give them a battle. If we come in here we will be packing the stadium within a couple of years—and that's no idle boast, for we know how our game has picked up in New York and other towns where the wise folks told us we never could make it pay.[4]

Always the optimist, Carr gave the press an uplifting quote before leaving town. One thing was for sure: he was very impressed with the new football stadium, saying, "I have seen all the well known stadia in the country, but none of them comes up to this Cleveland one. It's in a class by itself."[5] Cleveland now had the inside track to be the tenth NFL team, but the decision would not come until the summer meeting, scheduled for July 11–12 in Chicago at the Edgewater Beach Hotel.

At 11:00 a.m. on the first day in the hotel's conference room, Carr and the executive committee—made up of Jim Dooley, Dr. Harry March, and Dr. Kelly—met early to outline the actions taken against the Bears (Joe Salvodi), Packers (Arnie Herber), and Spartans for using college players who hadn't graduated with their class. Each team was fined $1,000, and the committee agreed with the punishments.[6]

The regular meeting started at 8:00 p.m. with all nine teams present. The owners agreed to a new bylaw stating "that the maximum number of franchises to be permitted in league be twelve (12), which number shall not be increased unless approved by two-thirds vote of the active members present at any meeting."[7] With the country in the middle of a depression, the owners and Carr knew that the league wouldn't be expanded that much, so it was a good rule to adopt.

The league awarded the 1930 NFL championship to the Packers and then gave a standing ovation to Tim Mara and the Giants for the "commendable manner in which the exhibition game was played at the close of the 1930 season between the Giants & Notre Dame All-Stars, for the unemployment fund. The entire assembly arose with a cheer." After the standing ovation the owners reelected Joe F. Carr and Carl Storck to their respective positions for another year.[8]

On the second day the moguls put together the 1931 NFL schedule; agreed to use the Spalding J-5 football; raised the roster limit to twenty-two; and, probably most important, approved the city of Cleveland as the NFL's tenth franchise. The Cleveland Indians were a league-sponsored team that was to be managed by Jerry Corcoran. Carr's intention was to locate the franchise permanently in Cleveland after a suitable backer was found. The Indians would play mainly on the road and didn't take advantage of the big new stadium. Once again the city wasn't ready for professional football.

After returning to Columbus, Carr was hit with some sad news, as John Nesser died at the age of fifty-five of a liver aliment. Carr recalled his former player and one of the great Nesser brothers: "That fellow didn't know what fear was. He was a rugged, aggressive player, a great field general and a sterling defensive player who tackled hard and surely."[9] John was the first of the football-playing Nesser siblings to pass away.

As the season approached, Carr released the 1931 NFL schedule, which would appear in newspapers nationwide and cause a big controversy in Green Bay and Portsmouth. In the September 11 edition of the *Portsmouth Times*, the paper listed that on Sunday, December 13, Green Bay was to play at Portsmouth. In the *Stevens Point (Wisconsin) Daily Journal* and other Wisconsin papers, there was no game listed on December 13 that had the Packers playing on the road in Portsmouth. The potential matchup would cause Carr a couple of sleepless nights.[10]

Before the season started big news came out of Chicago. Ed "Dutch" Sternaman, feeling the crunch of the Depression, decided to sell his interest in the Chicago Bears to his partner George Halas. "In the summer of 1931, my partner, Dutch Sternaman, couldn't meet mortgage payments on his apartment house and his gas station. His only asset was his partnership in the Bears. He asked if I would buy him out for $38,000, enough to meet his financial needs," recalled Halas in his autobiography. "I did want control of the Bears. My faith was boundless." Eventually Halas borrowed $5,000 from Ralph Brizzolara, Jim McMillen, and close friend Charlie Bidwill. He also borrowed $20,000 from the mother of former player George Trafton and a small amount from his mother. "On July 3, 1931, I did buy out Dutch. I paid him $25,000 in cash and promised to pay $6,000 on January 25, 1932 and the final $7,000 on July 31, 1932," remembered Halas.[11]

When the NFL season got under way, Carr took the train south to attend the league's opening weekend at the Brooklyn–Portsmouth game. On a 100 degree day he would sit in his box on the fifty yard line watching a completely different Spartans team from the previous season. In 1931 the Spartans' front office brought in Potsy Clark as their new head coach at an annual salary of $5,000. Clark wasn't a big household name but had great credentials. After a solid playing career at Illinois under Bob Zuppke, he served as an assistant coach with Dr. Clarence Spears at Minnesota and also had head coaching stints at Michigan Sate, Kansas, and Butler.

Potsy brought to the Spartans new ideas and very tight discipline. He also brought in another Clark. He signed former Colorado College All-American Earl "Dutch" Clark, who was a truly remarkable player. He was a triple-threat quarterback-halfback, who became one of the best players in the league over the next decade. The Spartans also signed halfback Glenn Presnell (semipro Ironton Tanks), guard Ox Emerson (Texas), tackle George Christensen (Oregon), center Clare Randolph (Indiana), and end Bill McKalip (Oregon) to strengthen the squad. The Spartans were about to give the Packers a run for their money. In their opening game, the Spartans shut out the Dodgers 14–0 in front of a nice crowd of 7,000 fans.

As the season began, Carr was faced with a minor infraction that needed his attention. Several teams complained to his office that the Packers were using more than the twenty-two players allowed. The new league rule stated that teams had to have just twenty-two players (not only meaning players in uniform but under contract) after the third league game. Carr threatened to fine the Green Bay club $500 and throw out all games played by the Packers after the third contest if they didn't adhere to the new rule.[12]

Carr called Curly Lambeau to explain the situation and gave him the ultimatum. Lambeau quickly reduced his squad by cutting five players, including Arnie Herber, who wasn't getting much playing time. The released players didn't stop the Packers as they continued to be the best team in the NFL. In 1929–1930 the Pack's main competition came from the New York Giants, led by quarterback Benny Friedman, but in 1931 the Giants slumped to 7–6–1 under new head coach Steve Owen. Owen would coach Mara's team for the next twenty-three years (1931–1953).

Despite the disappointing season in New York, the Giants did find themselves a building block at center. Owen signed Mel Hein out of Washington State for $150 a game, and he would play the pivot for the next fifteen seasons and earn a place in the Pro Football Hall of Fame. The Chicago Bears, with the backfield of Red Grange and Bronko Nagurski, finished in third place with an 8–5 record. One of the high points in the Bears' season was the team's first ever "Ladies Day" at Wrigley Field on October 25. Halas put an advertisement in the local newspapers stating that female fans should "write to the ladies' ticket office at Wrigley Field, sending self-addressed, stamped envelopes to obtain two free ducuts for the game."[13] The promotion worked, as 26,000 fans came out to see the Bears–Frankford contest; the only thing Halas wasn't happy about was the 13–12 loss to the Yellow Jackets.

The new Cleveland franchise got off to a very bad start, losing three of their first four games on their way to a 2–8 record, and it looked like it would be one and done for the Indians. A more shocking demise was that of the Frankford Yellow Jackets. The Philadelphia-based club had been one of the strongest members during the 1920s, consistently fielding strong teams and drawing a nice crowd despite ample competition from local colleges when they played home games on Saturdays due to the city's Blue Laws.

But the Depression was killing them. After winning the 1926 championship, they badly slipped in 1927 and then rebounded the next two years. The Frankford Athletic Association (FAA), which owned the team, was suddenly not a good financial base. Whereas an individual owner like Tim Mara had his own money tied to the fate of the Giants, the FAA depended on the largesse of its members to help run the team. Once the Depression hit, too many members found it necessary to cut back on their contributions to the club.

The hired talent also dropped in quality for the Jackets and it didn't help that, as always, Pennsylvania Blue Laws forced the team to play its home games on Saturdays opposite the college teams. The 1931 Yellow Jackets managed a scoreless tie with Providence in their second game, but there wasn't another bright spot until late October when they upset the Bears on "Ladies Day" in Chicago. Two games later, several thousand dollars in debt, the Yellow Jackets threw in the towel. One of Carr's big-city teams was out of the NFL.

After starting the season with five straight home games and five straight victories, the Portsmouth Spartans headed east to play four games on the East Coast. Potsy's team came up big, defeating Brooklyn, Staten Island, and Frankford and outscoring their opponents 53–7. Sporting an undefeated record (8–0), the Spartans rolled into their next game against the New York Giants at the Polo Grounds. In front of a crowd of 32,500—that included New York mayor Jimmy Walker—the Spartans suffered their first loss. The 14–0 setback left the Packers as the league's only unbeaten team.[14]

The Pack won (9–0 record) the next week as the Spartans lost their second straight game, this time to the Bears. On November 11 the Spartans hosted a Wednesday night game against the Stapes with Carr in the crowd. The Spartans rebounded with a nice 14–12 win, and then on Sunday the race got a little tighter. The undefeated Packers suffered their first defeat, a 21–13 setback to the pesky Chicago Cardinals, as the Spartans won their second game of the week beating the weak Cleveland Indians.

With four weeks to go, the Packers' lead was down to half a game with a potential season-ending matchup in Portsmouth on the last day of the season (December 13). That is what the Spartans and their fans thought:

Packers 9–1 (four games left)
Spartans 10–2 (two games left)

On November 22 the Packers traveled to the Big Apple and played the Giants in front of an NFL season high of 35,000 fans. The Polo Grounds saw a very entertaining game as the Pack showed how great they were. Red Dunn connected with Johnny Blood on a fifty-three-yard touchdown pass to give the Pack an early 7–0 lead. But the Giants came roaring back in the second quarter behind the play of halfback Hap Moran, who scored a touchdown and kicked a field goal to give the Giants a 10–7 halftime lead.

After a scoreless third period, Dunn threw his second touchdown pass of the game to give the Packers a thrilling 14–10 win. On the same day the Spartans suffered a tough 20–19 loss to the Cardinals. It now looked like Lambeau's team was clear for title number three in a row, barring a miracle. A miracle then happened.

On December 6 (with the Spartans on a bye week) at Wrigley Field (18,000 fans), the Bears shocked the Packers 7–6, as Red Dunn's missed extra point in the second quarter was the difference. The Packers' loss gave them just a one-game lead going into what the Spartans and their fans thought was the final week of the season and their game against the Pack on December 13.

Packers 12–2
Spartans 11–3

All their Spartans had to do was beat Lambeau's club and they'd tie for the NFL championship in only their second year in the league. Then, the plan went, the Spartans would beat the Packers in a playoff game to win the title. They had it all figured out. So did Curly Lambeau. Before the Bears game, he announced that, should his team lose, it would not play in Portsmouth. Or anywhere else. Should they beat the Bears as expected, of course, they'd probably play the game, but the Pack would not put its championship at risk.

Immediately Spartans president Harry Snyder began lobbying President Carr to get the game played. Here was the problem: at the summer scheduling meeting the two teams said let's make the December 13 contest a "tentative game" because of the prospect of bad weather in December. The Spartans' management put the game on its schedule and had it printed in the *Portsmouth Times* (remember back in September), but Lambeau and the Packers thought differently; they didn't put it on the original schedule that they released; who suspected the Spartans to be this good?

At first Lambeau declared he wouldn't play the game no matter what Joe F. Carr decided. Later, his sanity restored by the prospect of fines and suspensions, he changed his tune. On the day of the Bears–Packers "miracle" game in Chicago, the parties involved met to discuss the situation. At the meeting was Spartans president Harry Snyder, Packers executives Lee H. Joannes and Dr. W. W. Kelly, and Joe F. Carr. The Packers held firm that the game was just "tentatively" scheduled, and the Spartans contended that the game was agreed upon.

Carr agreed with the Packers, saying that the "Green Bay–Portsmouth arrangement was made after the regular schedule had been drawn up." He also said that "he had no power to force Green Bay to play the game, or that he could not forfeit the game to Portsmouth, if Green Bay did not play."[15] Under league rules a game "tentatively scheduled" may be cancelled by either of the clubs involved. Carr was following his own bylaws. After the three-hour meeting it looked like the Packers would *not* be playing the game in Portsmouth. Snyder sent a telegram back to the *Portsmouth Times* revealing the bad news: "Just concluded about three hours conference with Green Bay officials and Joe Carr, president of the league. Green Bay refuses to jeopardize its league standing by playing Portsmouth. They would give us no answer until after the Bears game. Continued pressure is being brought by influential parties, however, and they change their decision."[16]

Later that day after the meeting, the Packers lost their game to the Bears and with no need to put their title on the line with the Spartans, the Pack told the Spartans they would not be playing in Portsmouth. The Packers were now three-time champs. The press criticized the Packers for not playing the game. Robert Hooey of the *Ohio State Journal* called them the "cheese champions."[17] A *Portsmouth Times* editorial took a shot not only at the Packers but at Carr too.

> The National Professional Football League will suffer as the result of Green Bay's decision not to come here. What respect can a team, no matter how many championships it claims, expect to gain when it deliberately backs out of an agreement—tentative though it was—and refuses to meet an eleven that has been proved just as good and perhaps better?
>
> In refusing to come to Portsmouth the Green Bay Packers have revealed that they are more anxious about the safety of a paper championship title than they are about the future of the National League. It is as if the Packers said, "What do we care if the future of professional football in Portsmouth is at stake? Why should we worry if Portsmouth loses its professional team?"
>
> Harry Snyder, president of the Spartans, has admitted that the scheduling was tentative, depending on the weather conditions. If that is true, than there is absolutely no reason for Green Bay to back out of the agreement.
>
> It is quite apparent now that Spartan officials should have notified Joe F. Carr of the league about these arrangements. But, tentative or not, the game was on the official schedule sent out by Carr, and it should be played.
>
> The present Portsmouth–Green Bay mixup appears to be an indication of the loose way in which the National League is operated. It has been revealed that any number of Spartan games this season were played without more than a verbal agreement. If that is true then President Carr and other National League officials would do well to put their organization on a business-like basis if they expect it to continue to prosper. And President Carr would do well to take a firmer grasp on his official duties and make the office more than a titled position. There's plenty of work for a National League president.[18]

The Portsmouth editorial made its point (sticking up for its hometown team), but it took a cheap shot at Carr and the other pioneers of the NFL

(Halas, Storck, Mara, Lambeau). The writer failed to see that these men were keeping a sport alive, losing a lot of money, and learning on the job. Who knew a small town like Portsmouth would be in the running for an NFL title? Yes, the confusion at the end of the season over whether the game between the Packers and Spartans was officially scheduled was poorly handled, but it didn't mean that Carr and the other NFL officials weren't trying to make the organization a "business-like" success. The league was just twelve years old, and its leaders would learn from their mistakes; just as with the constitution and bylaws, franchise stability, or the Red Grange rule, it was definitely a work in progress.

On December 12 Carr announced that there would be no game between the Packers and Spartans, giving the Green Bay Packers their third straight NFL championship. Carr explained that while the additional game was arranged tentatively, league rules proved that games not on the official schedule may be cancelled at the option of the teams involved. Spartans head coach Potsy Clark didn't care for the ruling by President Carr.

> I don't see how a team can claim the pennant when they haven't played all the teams in the league. That is what happened to the Packers. I feel sure and so do the fans in this city and all around the circuit that if the Spartans had played the Packers here and tied them they would have beaten them on neutral soil.
>
> I think Mr. Carr has overstepped his authority in awarding something to a team over which he has no control. The Packers didn't finish the season and if a pennant is to be awarded it should go to the Spartans. I think my boys are entitled to gold footballs and not the Wisconsin eleven.[19]

Potsy and the city of Portsmouth weren't big fans of the Packers or Carr at this time, but when you lose a championship some people handle the disappointment differently. But Carr was well within his rights to award the Pack the title by following the bylaws, so Potsy couldn't have been more wrong. Carr's word was final. One thing was certain: the relationship between the two franchises, once cordial, now turned sour. The Spartans would look for revenge against their small-town rival.

While the controversy calmed down, the Packers' front office awarded its players a $100 bonus and celebrated the "three-peat." Lambeau described the town of Green Bay "as a community project and a regional religion." Future Hall of Fame tackle Cal Hubbard recalled his time in Green Bay saying, "I think Green Bay is a wonderful town and no doubt about it being the best town in the league to play in."[20]

Carr put the finishing touches on the 1931 season by talking to the press and saying, "The season as a whole was the best in the history of the organization. The attendance at several places was the best the league has experienced." The NFL saw 606,500 fans attend fifty-nine league games in 1931—an average of 9,727 per game (newspapers reported figures on fifty-three of fifty-nine games). Carr saw an increase of 2,000 fans per game, as well as marked improvement on the field as "the player limit proved its importance in the caliber of play. The play was hard but no player was injured seriously."[21] Besides the scheduling issue, the only big negatives were the poor showings of Cleveland, Frankford, and Providence.

While the league continued to look stable and the Packers claimed their new moniker of "Titletown," Joe F. Carr settled down with his family to enjoy the holidays. "That Christmas it wasn't a big group; it was just us visiting. My mother with her three kids and the four of them. So we had eight there for dinner. It was relatively small," says Martha Sullivan, niece of Joe F. Carr. "Well, you know how Christmas dinners are. Wonderful food, all kinds of pie, cakes, just a very bountiful amount of food. We had a nice, long leisurely dinner that would take a couple of hours to eat. Uncle Joe was so relaxed. When I close my eyes I can see him very plainly and he had a wonderful deep laugh. There was no question that it was a sincere thing. Just that real strong sincere laugh. He was a great guy.[22]

"Mary was about nine years older than I was but whenever we'd visit she would take us upstairs and show us her collection, her vast collection of hats. We really enjoyed seeing that. Joe Carr Jr. was just a typical boy and had a great personality. We called him 'Buddy' to distinguish him from his father. He was just fun to be with," says Sullivan.

> Well, Buddy at that stage just started to drive. He just got his driver's license. We had been there at the Carrs' for Christmas dinner and he was going to take us home. This was a big deal because he was a brand new driver. The Carrs lived a few blocks from us so we started home. It was a wretched night. It was still snowing, very slippery and as we went down the block from the home on Bryden Road the car swerved and jammed into the curb. Buddy couldn't get the car started, so he trudged back. We all trudged back to the house. Oh, his father was so annoyed with him and Buddy was just, oh, he was just in terrible shape. He was so upset because I'm sure he had envisioned not being able to drive again, at least for a while. We ended up taking a cab home. All's well that ends well.[23]

Carr didn't stay angry for long at his only son, who was able to get back into the family car. President Carr saw his son learn from his own mistakes, and he took that philosophy when thinking about his league. He had to learn from his mistakes and in 1931—with the scheduling fiasco—he had a big one to correct. The progress of the young league was increasing, but over the next two years the NFL would change forever.

19

Indoor Circus (1932)

The Portsmouth Spartans were one game away from tying for the NFL title in 1931, but the outlook for 1932 was bleak. Despite the team's success on the field, Spartans management announced that they were severely in the red, and that it would take about $30,000 to cover the debt. President Joe F. Carr made it a priority to "save the Spartans." Although he knew the future of the league was to establish solid franchises in big cities, he also thought the Spartans were doing all the right things—they had solid ownership, a great coach, and a young, talented team that looked to be on the verge of winning a championship. They just needed more money.[1]

After the season, the Spartans' organization agreed to take on a few more investors—local prominent businessmen—to help with the growing cost to operate the team. One of those investors was Homer C. Selby, a well-known shoe manufacturer, who was chairman of the board of the Selby Shoe Company. Selby quickly became involved in the affairs of the team, so much so that he made a trip to Columbus to visit Carr to reveal the team's plan to sell stock. The two talked in depth about the state of the team and Carr said he "was anxious for Portsmouth to retain its franchise as the team was now in shape to be more than self sustaining after two years of real experience."[2] Carr gave Selby his word that he would attend a pep rally to kick off the stock selling campaign.

The backers of the Spartans brought back Potsy Clark to coach and then made plans to sell stock in the team to raise the money to keep the Spartans in the NFL. The goal was to sell 3,000 shares of stock, which would raise roughly $40,000. Local businessmen purchased 1,200 shares of stock to get the campaign started, with the public sell scheduled to launch on January 12. The day before the sell was to begin the team held a giant "Save the Spartans" pep rally. A parade led by the Portsmouth High School band ended at the Selby gym with a large crowd waiting to hear about the upcoming sell. Speakers included Potsy Clark and Homer C. Selby. Carr kept his word by attending the rally.[3]

While Carr was in Portsmouth, rumors circulated that other cities were seeking franchises in the NFL and that the small town could be on its way out. Carr said yes, that four other cities had made inquiries, but he reassured the town by saying, "I feel sure that the Spartan drive is going over and have made no other plans relative to shaping up the size of the league next season."[4] Always positive, Carr used the press again to make everything in his league appear well and good. But Carr was investigating other potential cities just in case Portsmouth couldn't continue as a franchise. He had his sights on Charleston (West Virginia), Boston, St. Louis, and Cincinnati.

After returning from Portsmouth, Carr received some surprising news from New York. His good friend Dr. Harry March (the man who helped him establish a franchise in New York), had resigned as Giants president. Known as the "father of professional football" in New York, March was replaced by Jack Mara, the twenty-four-year-old son of Giants owner Tim Mara. Just two years before Tim Mara split ownership of the team to his two sons. Jack was now ready to run his father's team, but Wellington (age fourteen) was a few years away from being fully active in the team's front office. March said he was determined to devote his time to the practice of medicine, but he would continue his work on the NFL's executive committee.[5]

Another good-bye would come from Ernie Nevers, who retired to take a coaching position with Pop Warner at his alma mater, Stanford. On March 1 President Carr returned to Portsmouth to continue his support in helping the city "Save the Spartans." This time his friend Jerry Corcoran accompanied him and he gave a very uplifting speech as the guest of honor:

> This is my second visit to your city in two months and I'm not going to bore you with a long, tedious speech. You fans know, as well as I, what National League football has done for your city. It has given it your greatest advertisement. Thousands of people know all about Portsmouth and the Spartans by reason of your great team last year. It would be a pity to lose this team and judging from your enthusiasm here tonight I don't believe you have any ideas of doing this. I want to impress upon you that if Portsmouth gives up its present franchise, no other small city will be admitted into the league.
>
> We have too many big cities knocking on our door and will have some interesting arrangements to make later. Portsmouth is mentioned with New

> York, Chicago, Brooklyn, Green Bay and other cities in the loop and gives your city real boosting and I believe you could not get it any other way. You have the local foundation for a permanent berth in the league. Green Bay wouldn't take half a million for its franchise.
>
> The pioneering has been done in Portsmouth. The fans have pledged $25,000 for the continuance of football in Portsmouth and I think that is wonderful spirit. I doubt if you can duplicate this spirit in any city anywhere near the size of Portsmouth. I really look for Portsmouth to almost double its crowds next year, I know you drew well last year, I'm banking on the Spartans being retained here and that is why I have refused to give another city a franchise which has raised the money and is crying for it. I stuck to Portsmouth in the Ohio State [baseball] league days and it stuck to me and now I'm going to stick to it again, but this time it is football.[6]

Carr was given a standing ovation for his support of the Spartans, but his strong words also gave the fans and the team's management a warning that they better get their financial situation straightened out. It also told the rest of the sporting world that this would be the last small-town experience the NFL would try. As much as the league was struggling to get through the Great Depression, with franchises in Cleveland, Frankford, and Providence out of the league for the 1932 season, Carr's vision of a big-city league was the only way the NFL was going to not only survive, but be able to prosper as a profitable business.

The NFL was now entering its thirteenth season and had come a long way from its humble beginnings. But it still had a long way to go. Pro football was still a distant second to the college game in popularity, and football in any form couldn't match baseball's hold on the nation's sports fans. Carr and the other owners had now built a solid foundation, and until the NFL established itself exclusively in major league cities, it was unlikely the league would be considered "major league." The NFL now had just seven franchises:

1. Brooklyn Dodgers
2. Chicago Bears
3. Chicago Cardinals
4. Green Bay Packers
5. New York Giants
6. Portsmouth Spartans
7. Staten Island

Among the potential cities Carr looked at, in order to get the league to an even eight teams, only one stood out—Boston. Just like New York, finding an investor was probably just as important in finding the right city. In looking for the right owner, he contacted an old friend to help. The man had the right financial profile to operate an NFL team and would bring a "genius mind" for promotion that had never been seen before in the NFL. But his rather rough and brash personality would always cause conflict among his fellow owners.

George Preston Marshall was born on October 11, 1896, in the small town of Grafton, West Virginia, as the only child of Thomas Hill Marshall and his wife, Blanche Marshall. While in Grafton, Marshall's father published a local newspaper called the *Grafton Leader*, until he moved his family to Washington, D.C., to operate a laundry business, located on the corner of 9th and H streets. In the nation's capital, George was exposed to the Friends Select School and then Randolph-Macon University. He also liked acting and became an extra in the stock company shows at the Poli's Theater in Washington.

"Well, he was about six feet two, had blue eyes, black hair, and a very strong face. People thought he was a very good looking guy," says Jordan Wright, granddaughter of George Preston Marshall. "He was a fun-loving guy. He was very sophisticated and urbane and they all thought that he was really something else. By the time he was twenty-one he was going to have made his first million because he never wanted to drive a car. He wanted to be driven around. He always had a car and a driver his entire life. He never had a driver's license. I think that was the motivating factor that drove his ambition to want to be successful. He was very ambitious."[7]

Marshall always said, "I wasn't much of an actor." But he liked the limelight and the ability to meet famous and powerful people, a lifestyle he would lead for the rest of his life. But in 1918, when Marshall was twenty-two, his world was interrupted when his father suddenly died and left the laundry business to him and his mother. Marshall took over his father's business, and like the showman in him he built the most successful laundry kingdom on the East Coast. Located in the Washington area would be over fifty Palace Laundry stores, and these places would show off his flair for promotion. "It was the first time people started living in apartments and that sort of thing. It was the first time that there was a real huge need for this [type of business]," says Wright.[8]

He dressed his employees in blue-and-gold uniforms and disguised his stores with such simple décor that they barely resembled laundries. A showcase for instance, would have nothing except a blue vase containing white flowers. "My grandfather felt very strongly that the business should be a very attractive place. So the only thing that you would see is a beautiful window. He would display a big spray of flowers; he then would change them based on the season. The customer would go into this elegant store and drop off their bag of laundry. It was elegant and it was attractive and people liked it," says Wright.[9]

Marshall also had a certain way of advertising. He would take out a full-page ad and the only thing on the white page would be a line of type at the bottom saying, "This space was cleaned by the Palace Laundry and Dry Cleaning Company." The laundry business made him wealthy and very popular around the nation's capital. Marshall eventually married Elizabeth Mortensen, and they had two children—George Preston Marshall Jr. and Catherine Marshall. In time Marshall's thirst for the nightlife got the best of him, and he eventually divorced Elizabeth. He then moved on to dating starlets and movie actresses, including Louise Brooks, the former Ziegfeld Follies girl who was famous for her "bobbed haircut" and appeared in silent hit films such as *Pandora's Box* and *Diary of a Lost Girl*.

Brooks nicknamed Marshall "the Wet Wash King." Because of his wealth and success, Marshall became a man about town. "He was quite the man to be seen with and go around with," says Wright. "He liked to go out all the time. He liked to have fun all the time. He was a party guy and yes he did have a huge booming voice. He was brash in that respect but I think he got away with it because he had a certain charm. And he was successful."[10]

As Marshall's success blossomed he branched out into other interests, and one of his projects led him to meet two sports pioneers who offered him an opportunity to join their club. In 1925 Joe F. Carr had been asked by a few owners to be president of the American Basketball League (ABL), a new professional league that would start play in the fall. Carr encouraged George Halas to invest in a team and then heard about a potential investor in Washington. Carr and Halas convinced George Preston Marshall to put up some money for a team, and the three started a professional relationship that would come full circle in the spring of 1932, when Carr approached Marshall about investing in an NFL franchise.

Carr told Marshall that his league was going places and that in a few years the sport would be bigger than baseball. Now was the time to get in. "Carr and I worried about the shrinking League. We needed new clubs. We proposed that George Preston Marshall start a club in Boston, a good baseball town. George Preston Marshall knew little about football but he was a promoter. He had good connections and a source of money. His father had died and left [his] son the Palace Laundry, a small but growing enterprise in Washington. He made it grow and grow," said George Halas in his autobiography. Marshall said yes to Carr and Halas.[11]

Carr sold the franchise rights of the defunct Newark Tornadoes to Marshall for the fee of $2,500. Carr then mandated that Marshall locate his team in Boston, as he thought that Washington was a little too south for his league. Marshall then recruited a syndicate of three investors to help finance the team—Jay O'Brien, a New York investment banker; Vincent Bendix, an automobile and aircraft components inventor and manufacturer from South Bend, Indiana; and Larry Doyle, a New York stockbroker.

Marshall then signed a lease to use Braves Field—the ballpark used by the Major League Baseball team—and named his squad after the ball club, the Boston Braves. Carr then suggested to Marshall that he hire Roy Andrews, who led the Giants to back-to-back second place finishes in 1929–1930, as his new head coach. Marshall and his partner Jay O'Brien wanted Lou Little, the famous head coach at Columbia University, who wasn't interested. But Little suggested someone else.

Little played college football at the University of Pennsylvania and was a teammate of Lud Wray, who was replaced as head coach at their alma mater in 1931 after just one season in which he finished 5–4. Little (who also played two years in the NFL with the 1920–1921 Buffalo All-Americans) wanted Wray to get the job with the Boston Braves and set up a meeting with the Braves' officials to discuss the situation. In a letter typed on April 4, 1932, Little tells another Penn teammate, Bert Bell, how the meeting went.

Dear Bert:

Yesterday I was due to have lunch with George Marshall and Jay O'Brien in order to help them select a coach for the coming fall. They have been after me for quite some time so finally on Saturday when they called me I suggested Lud Wray only to find out that you had done the same thing. When I arrived Sunday for lunch I was dumbfounded when Marshall told me that Wray was in New York. They informed me that they were going to decide on [Roy] Andrews, former coach of the New York Giants. It seems Joe Carr recommended him. I immediately went to work and talked Marshall out of that idea and also Jay O'Brien when he arrived with Lud. I told Lud to wait outside and after talking with both of them, they decided to take Lud. Lud was uncertain whether he should take it as he wanted this Amherst job. I told him that $5,000 jobs with the possibility of a bonus were not hanging around just now and also that it was always easy to break back into the college ranks and that he should accept the Boston job. Finally he decided to accept but the funny part of it all is that after making Marshall and O'Brien change their mind and take Wray, he does not know whether he wanted to take the job or not. The same old Lud. Keep this confidential as they want to break the story from Boston and having it found out here [in New York] would ruin their publicity.

I hope that everything is going along nicely and with best wishes, I am,

Sincerely yours,
Louis Little[12]

Wray got the job, and Little stayed at Columbia as head coach until 1956. As for their fellow Penn teammate Bert Bell, he would get to know Carr and the other NFL owners soon enough.

On July 9–10 at the Ritz-Carlton Hotel in Atlantic City the league met for their only meeting in 1932. Carr began the session at 4:00 p.m. on the first day with eight teams represented—including Providence, which didn't field a team in 1932. The first piece of business was to admit the Boston franchise as George Preston Marshall attended his first league meeting.[13]

Marshall then quickly made his presence felt. After the league accepted the current rules made by the Intercollegiate Rules Committee, he seconded a motion brought by Dr. Harry March that the NFL go on record as favoring placing the goal post on the goal line. The collegiate rule at this time had the goal post at the back of the end zone. Marshall and March thought the move would increase scoring by encouraging field goals. After considerable discussion the motion went to a vote, with the owners voting no. Although he lost this motion, Marshall would eventually get his fellow owners to see his way of thinking—the game had to be more entertaining for paying fans. By the end of the 1932 season they would agree.[14]

After the rules discussion the owners awarded the 1931 title to the Green Bay Packers and then decided that players would be allowed two dollars maximum per day for traveling expenses. The rest of the meeting saw the teams put their deposits in the league's bank account; the election of officers (Carr and Storck reelected); the player roster limit set at twenty players; approval to use the Spalding J-5 football in games; and the official schedule drafted.[15]

But the biggest news coming out of the summer get-together was the approval of a motion brought up by George Halas that the president be instructed to appoint a league publicity director with headquarters in New York City. The motion was carried, unanimously, as well as a fifty-dollar expense for the publicity department. Carr would eventually hire Ned Irish to be publicity director for the NFL.

But the off-season fireworks weren't over yet for George Halas, as he faced a big deadline on July 31. According to the agreement he signed the previous year to buy out Dutch Sternaman, Halas had one last payment of $7,000 that was due. On that day, Halas was short $5,000. Under the agreement if Halas didn't make the payment, Dutch would assume control of his stock and the team. Dutch's lawyer sent Papa Bear a letter stating that Dutch's stock would go up for public auction on August 9. Desperation set in for Halas as he had till noon on the ninth to gain full control of the Bears.

"I tried everywhere to raise the $5,000. I called everyone I knew. No one could help me. Many banks were closed and those open would make no loan. I was desperate. At noon I would lose my Bears," Halas remembered in his autobiography.

> About 11 o'clock Mr. C. K. Anderson, the president of the First National Bank in Antioch, phoned. He said he understood I needed $5,000 urgently. "How true! I must have the money by noon or I will lose my Bears!" He said he would lend me the money. I raced from my office at 111 W. Washington to his Chicago office at Randolph and LaSalle Streets and collected his check. With grateful but quick thanks, and then ran to the lawyer's office and handed in a check. It was 10 minutes to noon . . . I had firm control of the Bears. Again, adversity had bestowed its benefits upon me.[16]

Halas had avoided disaster and was now the sole owner of the Chicago Bears. It was hard for Carr to think about what would have happened if the Bears went up for public auction.

What Carr was thinking about was what the publicity department in New York would be doing. The money spent for the department would change the landscape of the NFL. In 1932 the NFL would keep "official statistics" for the first time ever. With the help of Ned Irish and the newly developed publicity department in New York, the stats and league scores/standings would reach newspapers nationally each Monday.

A month before the season was to start, the Portsmouth Spartans held another rally with over four hundred fans showing up to hear Harry Snyder talk about the state of the team, the upcoming schedule, and ticket prices. The Spartans set tickets at seventy-five cents for a general admission, $1.50 for bleachers seats and $2.00 for stadium seats. They also announced they would have a special $1.00 coupon for a stadium seat (in sections A–B, F–G) that would be in the *Portsmouth Times* for the October 2 game against the Chicago Cardinals.[17]

Several teams felt the crunch of the Great Depression. The Packers reduced their ticket prices going into the season by cutting season tickets (six games) from fifteen dollars to twelve dollars and box seats from twenty-five dollars to twenty dollars. They hoped the lowering of ticket prices would bring out fans to NFL games to watch the action, even though the 1932 season would go down as one of the truly remarkable seasons, despite the sometimes "boring" play on the field (which made absolutely no sense since Carr's loop featured a bevy of current and new stars). Returning All-Pros and future Hall of Famers included Bronko Nagurski (Bears), Red Grange (Bears), Mel Hein (Giants), Red Badgro (Giants), Dutch Clark (Spartans), Ken Strong (Stapletons), Benny Friedman (who had just joined Brooklyn), Cal Hubbard (Packers), and Johnny Blood (Packers).[18]

The new crop of rookies was equally impressive. With no NFL draft, graduating college players were free to sign with the highest bidder. In 1932 four future Hall of Famers inked NFL contracts. Fullback Clarke Hinkle (Bucknell) signed with Lambeau's Packers; end Bill Hewitt (Michigan) with the Bears; halfback Cliff Battles (West Virginia Wesleyan); and tackle Turk Edwards (Washington State) with Marshall's new Boston Braves.

Although the NFL had more stars than they could possibly dream of and the league played under virtually the same rules as college football, the perception of the two games by the fans was very different: college football, awash in ancient rivalries and hoopla, was exciting; pro football, with its low scores and ties, was not. The only major change in the rules for 1932, a substitution change allowing a replaced player to return in a subsequent quarter, had no effect on the lack of scoring. In 1932, NFL games averaged only 16.4 points per game for both teams, the lowest per-game average since 1926. At the end of the season, the NFL owners would see a light at the end of the tunnel.

But Carr did have to put out one fire concerning a new player. The Boston Braves filed a complaint against the New York Giants over the signing of former University of Southern California star halfback Ernie Pinckert. It seems that Pinckert signed contracts with both teams, so on his way east from California, he stopped in Columbus to visit with Carr. The president declared him the property of the Braves since he signed with them first. As the off-season fireworks ended, the eight NFL teams were now ready to hit the field.

On September 18 the Packers kicked off the NFL's thirteenth season by raising the championship banner for the third consecutive year. Then in front of a disappointing crowd of just 3,500 fans, the Pack defeated the Chicago Cardinals 15–7. The following week, Carr allowed his precious daughter to take a trip to Portsmouth to visit a friend. He was so well-known in that area that the news made the local paper there: "Miss Mary Vallee Harold of Ninth and Gay streets will have as guest this week, Miss Mary Carr of Columbus, who was a classmate of Miss Harold at St. Mary's of the Springs College, is the daughter of Joe Carr, president of the National Football League. Mr. Carr will come to Portsmouth Sunday [September 25] to attend the Spartans–New York Giants football game and his daughter will return home with him."[19]

Carr did attend the Giants–Spartans game. After chatting with Tim Mara and Dr. Harry March before the game on the Giants sideline, he sat in his customary fifty-yard-line box seat and watched the Spartans pull out a 7–0 victory behind a Dutch Clark touchdown. Following the game, he told the press it was "one of the greatest games he has ever seen" and he "praised both teams."[20] I guess only Carr could appreciate a game that featured just one touchdown and call it one of the greatest games. Something needed to be done to increase the thrills on the field.

The following week Carr traveled east, leaving Mary at home this time, to Boston to see the first ever NFL game for the newly minted Boston Braves. Leading up to the game ads were taken out in Boston papers, proclaiming the Braves to be part of "Big League Football," and listing ticket prices at $1.50 for box seats, $1.00 for grandstand, and fifty cents for a bleacher seat. At 2:30 p.m. on October 2 Carr, Marshall, and over 6,000 fans (*New York Times* reported 8,000 fans) from Beantown gathered at Braves Field to watch the Braves tackle the Brooklyn Dodgers—led by new quarterback Benny Friedman. What they saw was a clinic by the best passer in the league. Freidman fired two touchdown passes to Jack Grossman to help the Dodgers to a 14–0 victory.[21]

Despite the shutout, the reviews were positive, but not spectacular for Carr's newest team. The crowd in the big city was somewhat disappointing too. Small-town Portsmouth was capable of getting 6,000 fans—so for a city that had a population base of over 780,000, it wasn't quite what Carr was expecting. In writing to the directors of the Portsmouth Spartans (who were to play the Braves on November 20), Carr said the Braves' debut "was a big success. Two bands furnished the music and the crowd exceeded the 10,000 mark and Boston looks like a real city for the National league."[22] This time Carr's positive outlook got the best of him. The crowd was nowhere near 10,000, and Boston would struggle in its first year in the NFL.

Carr's comments on the Braves were written by Will P. Minego and appeared in the October 7 edition of the *Portsmouth Times*. In that same column Minego also wrote about the eligibility of Joe Lillard, a black halfback just signed by the Chicago Cardinals. Lillard was the only black player in the NFL in 1932 and had played just one year of college ball at Oregon before it was revealed that he had played professional baseball. Declared ineligible, Lillard claimed that he only got paid for driving the bus and only played when an emergency arose. The *Times* wrote, "The Spartan owners have asked Joe Carr to look into the eligibility of Joe Lillard, Negro flash with the Chicago Cardinals. Carr says he has already started the investigation. He says the eligibility rules were amended at the annual meeting in Atlantic City last July and Lillard may be eligible."[23]

Lillard shouldn't have been allowed to play since his class had not yet graduated, so it's very odd that Carr and the other owners would allow Lillard to play. Maybe Carr thought in the midst of a depression—where the number of unemployed Americans had climbed from 2 million in 1929 to 8 million in 1932—that it would have been difficult to see a young man who was forced to give up his college eligibility under distressful circumstances not be given a chance to make a living. Nobody really knows why Lillard was able to play, but he made the best of his opportunity.[24]

Lillard became the Cardinals' biggest attraction on a team that finished with just two wins, as he helped attract big crowds in Boston (15,000) and Brooklyn (17,000). Lillard also saw the potential of the pro game, as was clear when he spoke to the press about comparing the pro game to the college game:

> The crowd goes to a football game for the thrills, and the pros are giving the customers as many sensational plays as the college gridders. In a college game, you see stars in two or three positions on the team, while in a professional contest every man needs to be a star to retain his place on the team.
>
> This is why pro football is a more finished product than the amateur sport.[25]

But Carr's charity toward black players would take a different turn after the 1933 season.

Two weeks after seeing the Braves play their first game, Carr went west to watch the Packers–Bears game at Wrigley Field. On an overcast day Carr was extremely thrilled to see the stands filled with over 17,000 fans. After mingling with Packers officials, team president Lee Joannes, board members Gerald Clifford and Dr. W. W. Kelly, and coach Curly Lambeau, Carr then watched a game that would have bored the most enthusiastic pro football fan.

A blocked punt by Tom Nash late in the second quarter went out of the end zone for a safety and gave the Packers a 2–0 lead. It would be the only score of the game, as the Pack won 2–0. Carr must have been thinking that with all the stars on the field for both teams, it seems inconceivable that a Packers–Bears game could end with a 2–0 final score. How would Carr put a positive spin on that display of NFL football? In speaking with the press he praised the Packers and their fearless leader, but not the performance: "Another great Green Bay team. To me, it is remarkable how Curly Lambeau continues, year in and year out to consistently produce a winner. Around the league, the other managers are rating him as a 'gridiron magician.'"[26]

The 1932 NFL season was turning into a year of no scoring and meaningless tie games, which, per the NFL bylaws, didn't count in the standings. After several seasons of gaining in popularity and momentum, Carr was seeing it slip away. The sport had too many dull, low-scoring games to this point. After the first two months of action—twenty-four league games—the NFL saw thirteen shutouts (which was 54 percent of the games) and seven ties (with four of those games ending in a 0–0 tie). Ironically, at a time when the NFL saw the least offense in years, the league had decided to keep official statistics. This is probably not what Carr envisioned. In speaking with

Ralph Teatsorth of United Press International, Carr defended his league against the popularity of the collegiate game.

> Professional football is for those who understand the game. College football was built with a background of tradition and pageantry. The professional game hasn't much tradition or pageantry yet, but it provides the hardest and most interesting competition for those who love the sport purely for its own merits.
>
> We started in Boston with crowds of less than 5,000. The last two games there have drawn between 15,000 and 20,000 fans. This was somewhat a surprise in view of the conservative way in which Boston receives anything new in the line of professional sports.[27]

Carr's unyielding confidence in his league always shined through when talking to the press, and during this small crisis he once again showed his true leadership by emphasizing the positives. Boston had attracted some large crowds against the Bears (18,000) and Packers (16,500), but they didn't produce a winning team, finishing with a 4–4–2 record. By midseason the Packers looked like a sure bet to win their fourth straight NFL championship. On the eve of their annual trip east, they were 7–0–1. Lambeau's squad had pretty much stayed the same (Hubbard, Michalske, Dilweg, Blood), but they added Hinkle and started to play Arnie Herber in the backfield.

The road trip started with a 21–0 victory over the Boston Braves (November 13), and then one week later the Pack faced the Giants in New York. The Giants were a different team than in 1929–1930 as Benny Friedman was playing across the river for Brooklyn. Without Benny the Giants were scuffling with a 3–5–1 record, but Mara's men pulled off a big upset, shutting out the Pack, 6–0. That same day, both the Spartans and Bears won. On Monday, November 21, the standings looked like this:

1—Green Bay Packers 8–1–1** (.888)
2—Portsmouth Spartans 5–1–3 (.833)
3—Chicago Bears 3–1–5 (.750)
4—New York Giants 4–4–1 (.500)
5—Brooklyn Dodgers 3–6–0 (.333)
5—Boston Braves 2–4–2 (.333)
5—Chicago Cardinals 2–4–2 (.333)
8—Staten Island Stapletons 2–6–2 (.250)
** In 1932 the NFL did not count ties in the standings.

After Thanksgiving Day games (November 24) and regularly scheduled games on Sunday (November 27) in which the Packers went 2–0, the Bears went 1–0–1 with a tie against the Spartans, who were playing their only game of the week. The Packers took a slim lead (Packers at .909, Spartans at .833, Bears at .800) into the league's final two weekends, but they would have to face the Spartans and the Bears on the road to wrap up the season. If they wanted to win their fourth title in a row they would have to do it the hard way.

On their way south to Portsmouth, the Packers stopped off in Columbus for a couple of days to visit with President Carr and get in some practice before the big game. On December 4 the Spartans hosted the Pack and in a couple of hours the Green Bay dynasty was over. In a game that the Spartans team and fans had been waiting nearly a year for they took it out on the great Packer team. Playing only eleven men, Potsy Clark got his revenge as the Spartans simply destroyed the Pack 19–0. Behind the play of Dutch Clark (two touchdowns), Father Lumpkin, and Glenn Presnell (one touchdown), the "cheese champs" didn't have a chance.

Despite one last game on the schedule the Packers were out of the championship race. As the Spartans were moving into first place the Bears defeated the Giants 6–0 and were still alive in the hunt for the NFL championship.

NFL standings as of Monday, December 5
1—Portsmouth Spartans 6–1–4 (.857); regular season completed
2—Green Bay Packers 10–2–1 (.833); next game—December 11 at Chicago Bears
2—Chicago Bears 5–1–6 (.833); next game—December 11 versus Green Bay Packers

The two-team race was down to one last game, with the Bears having a chance to tie the Spartans for the title. Both teams couldn't have had more different emotions going in—one playing for a title and a proud champion not. How would each team play? Green Bay faced the Bears at Wrigley Field in a heavy snowstorm. The Packers' offense continued to flatline, and after three quarters the score stood at 0–0. A tie wouldn't help the Bears. Then in the final quarter the Bears scored twice to give them a hard-fought 9–0 victory, a 6–1–6 record, and a tie for first place with the Spartans (6–1–4). Despite all the disputed championships in the league's first dozen years, this was the first race to actually end in a tie.

Had the league compiled its standings as it does now—counting a tie game as a half-win, half-loss—the championship would have gone to Green Bay. However, the rules established in 1921 were in effect. Winning percentage, based strictly on wins and losses, determined the order of finish; ties were simply ignored.

Right after the Bears defeated the Packers in the snow on December 11, George Halas conferred with Spartans owner Harry Snyder about a playoff game to decide the NFL title. They agreed that it would be the best thing for the NFL, and Halas called Carr to ask if this game could take place. Carr was on board with the idea and gave the two teams permission to play the game at Wrigley Field the following Sunday (December 18).

Carr's decision to play the game would make football history as the NFL was about to play its *first ever* postseason game. Although the game would be an extension of the regular season rather than a championship game, the playoff would count in the standings, which meant the loser would slip to third place behind the Green Bay Packers.

For George Halas it had been one of the most unusual seasons in Bears history, as they started the year with three scoreless ties. Then their fourth game was the 2–0 loss to the Packers on a safety, which turned out to be the Bears' only defeat. "The start of the season was totally frustrating. We had devoted two years to developing the modern T-formation with man-in-motion to open up the game and bring in new skills for scoring. We had so many good players. . . . Yet, we went through our first four League games without scoring. Not one touchdown. Not one field goal. Not even a safety. Finally we took off and went through the rest of the season unbeaten," recalled Halas.[28]

One of the Bears' biggest fans that season was the future Virginia McCaskey, the nine-year-old daughter of Papa Bear, who was now devoted to the game her father loved. "I was very much involved then. Loved the game, mostly because it was so important to my dad and everything that was so important to him was important to me too," says Virginia McCaskey.[29]

The NFL president could relate to the love of a daughter for her father, and his friendship with the Halas family would always bring back happy memories. "My memory of Joe Carr is his coming to dinner in our apartment on Campbell Ave. during my grammar school and high school days," says McCaskey.

> He was always well reserved and well dressed with his business suit, and his white shirt, and his tie and his glasses. He would always ask Mugs [her brother] and me about our school work and our activities. He paid special compliments to my mother because she fixed a chicken dinner, which was his favorite. She also had a chocolate icebox cake recipe that we all enjoyed. She didn't make it very often, so we were always happy when we heard that Mr. Carr was coming for dinner, because then we knew we'd get the chocolate icebox cake.
>
> Then after dinner he and dad would go into the living room to have their business discussions. Mugs and I would help mom clean up the dishes or something just to keep us out of the way. Now I look back and think, wouldn't it have been wonderful to sit in on some of those discussions. At that time I had no idea.[30]

The first obstacle to this first postseason game was the weather. The Bears had played the Packers in a driving snowstorm in front of just 5,000 brave fans and the week of the playoff game it didn't get any better. For a week, bitter cold and heavy snow continued to pound the Windy City, and the possibility of playing the game at Wrigley Field—with any type of fan support—looked to be a bad idea. Halas remembered his team and the Cardinals playing a charity game indoors at Chicago Stadium in 1930, and he suggested to the Spartans that they move the game to the indoor stadium if the snow continued to fall.

Although the weather looked to be the biggest problem for the Spartans, they had another dilemma. On Tuesday before the game it was announced that star halfback Dutch Clark would miss the game. Clark was scheduled to go back to his alma mater Colorado College to start his duties as head basketball coach. Since the playoff game wasn't on the original schedule, the Spartans didn't see this coming. Management contacted the school's athletic director and asked for permission to allow Clark, just this once, to show up late so he could play. In a Western Union telegram Portsmouth received the bad news.

Dec. 14—1:17 PM

To: HOMER C. SELBY, PRESIDENT PORTSMOUTH NATIONAL LEAGUE FOOTBALL CORP.

REGRET IMPOSSIBILITY OF PERMITTING MR CLARK TO LEAVE HIS IMPORTANT DUTIES AS BASKETBALL COACH.

CHARLES C. MIEROW. [Athletic Director][31]

The Spartans were dealt a big blow even before the game started. Despite the loss Potsy Clark—whose team arrived in Chicago on Thursday—was still confident in his squad to pull out the victory. "I'll have the boys clicking again and we know the offense of the Bears and will plan to break it up. If the boys play any kind of ball at all, we should win."[32] The two teams played twice during the regular season and tied both games, 13–13 (November 13) and 7–7 (November 27). Halas suggested to the press that if the teams were tied after four quarters they would play a ten-minute overtime to break the tie. There is no proof if this was agreed upon by the league before the game or not.

Carr arrived in Chicago late in the week, and on the Friday before the game he announced that the contest would be played indoors at Chicago Stadium because of the snowstorm. Chicago Stadium was the perfect size for the events usually held there—hockey games and circuses. It was absurdly small for football—only forty-five yards wide (regular width is 53⅓ yards) and eighty yards long, including the end zones. At least they wouldn't play on hockey ice. Fortunately for the players, a circus sponsored by the Salvation Army had just performed in the arena the week before, leaving a six-inch bed of tanbark on the cement floor.

More than a few players and fans noted the peculiar aromatic quality of the playing surface. "It was stinking and dirty," recalled Charles "Ookie" Miller, who played center for the Bears that game. "One of our players got sick in the stomach and threw up. Oh it was bad. I could tell you something else. We had a couple of nips the night before. That smell wasn't too good either. I could hardly get my head in that huddle."[33]

"I remember being there, because I was nine years old. I remember the odor," says Virginia McCaskey. "The field was not your ideal field. It certainly was a lot more comfortable than being at Wrigley Field that particular week." "It didn't smell very good," remembered Glenn Presnell, former Spartans halfback who replaced Dutch Clark in the starting lineup.[34]

Because of the confined playing environment, several rules were put into place to make the game easier. Little did they know these rules and the game itself would open the eyes of everybody involved in the NFL. To accommodate football indoors the two teams agreed to the following rules:

1. The field would be only eighty yards long, including the end zones, with a single goal post placed at one goal line. Kickoffs would originate from the defensive team's ten yard line. Field goals were prohibited.
2. When a team crossed midfield, it immediately was set back twenty yards.
3. Because a solid fence surrounded the field only a few feet from the sidelines, the ball was moved in from the side ten yards (some reports say fifteen) after each out-of-bounds play, instead of starting the play right at the sideline with a loss of down. This would be the first time "hash marks" would be used in an NFL game.
4. In the case of a touchback, the ball would be brought out to the ten yard line.

The game was set for Sunday, December 18 with kickoff at 8:15 p.m. (Central Standard Time). Carr took his seat in section R (mezzanine), row F, seat 16 to watch the historic contest. As he sat down he saw an incredible sight—a soldout crowd. The capacity crowd of 11,198 had battled the elements to attend the NFL's first playoff game. The very warm fans came but they didn't see much. The confined conditions as well as the sloppy dirt really limited the play on the field. "It was very treacherous footing," remembers Glenn Presnell. "My favorite play was an off-tackle dive. One time we were close to the goal line, I ran off-tackle, as I planted my foot, it skidded out from under me and I went down. There was a hole there. I would've scored a touchdown."[35]

Despite missing Dutch Clark the Spartans held tough and fought the Bears on even terms for three quarters. Neither team scored heading into the final quarter. Then Bears halfback Dick Nesbitt intercepted an Ace Gutowsky pass and retuned it to the Spartans' seven yard line before being knocked out of bounds. Because of the special rule the ball was brought into the field ten yards, costing the Bears a down. On second down Bronko Nagurski blasted six yards to the one; on third down Nagurski tried again but this time lost a yard. So on fourth down the game's pivotal play came up, and the history of the NFL would never be the same.

Fourth and goal from the two! Nagurski got the ball a third time, faked a line smash, retreated a few steps and fired a pass to a wide open Red Grange in the end zone. Referee Bobbie Cahn signaled touchdown. "There was no way I could get through, I stopped. I moved back a couple of steps. Grange had gone around and was in the end zone, all by himself. I threw him a short pass," recalled Bronco Nagurski about the touchdown.[36]

Spartans coach Potsy Clark stormed onto the field protesting that Nagurski was not five yards behind the line of scrimmage when he threw the pass as the rules required. "We were sure that he was going to make a line plunge. He wasn't anywhere near five yards back of the line of scrimmage, which was a rule in those days," says Presnell. "It was an illegal pass. He wasn't five yards back. Of course he lined up about five yards back but when he took the ball he stared to plunge into the line. Then he jumped up. They counted it anyway."[37]

"Well, I'm right in the middle. As I recall he started up and then jumped in the air and threw the pass," remembered Ookie Miller. "They complained of course. They claimed it was illegal, but Nagurski claims he backed up far enough that he was five yards back. We worked on that play for months." Cahn was unmoved by all the protesting and held up the score. The Bears added the conversion and a few moments later a bad Spartans snap through the end zone gave the Bears a safety. Carr saw the Bears finish the game strong to win the 1932 NFL title with a 9–0 victory. "After eleven years the Bears were again champions!" wrote Halas in his autobiography. "Ralph Jones had delivered. Everybody acclaimed him. The modern T-Formation with man-in-motion had delivered."[38]

Halas had title number two. The best thing about the game was the amount of press it received, as almost every major newspaper and smaller ones ran articles on the Bears big win. Kenneth Fry writing for the United Press described the "Indoor Circus":

> Chicago Bears defeated the Portsmouth, Ohio, Spartans on the indoor gridiron at the Chicago Stadium last night, 9 to 0, for the professional football championship.

> The playing field was six inches of dirt and tanbark spread over the stadium's concrete floor. The field itself was sixty yards long, forty yards short of the rule book length. Players standing on their own goal lines punted into the other team's end zone all evening. Punts from the middle of the field landed in the mezzanine balcony and adjacent territory. One kick knocked the "BL" out of the Black Hawks hockey sign. Another hit a sour note on the organ as the organist was playing, for obscure and undetermined reason, a song about "Cutting Down the Old Pine Tree."
>
> The organist played "Illinois Loyalty" when Red Grange caught a forward pass for a touchdown. By mutual agreement neither team attempted field goals. Windows cost money.
>
> Only one punt was caught and returned during the entire contest. One went out of the bounds, one was downed. The rest landed against the walls or sent spectators scurrying for cover. Officials spent more time picking large clinkers out of the soil than they did blowing whistles.[39]

The *Portsmouth Times* called it "a sham battle on a Tom Thumb gridiron," although they did say the fans "enjoyed immensely the spectacle of an outdoor sport performed indoors." Spartans president Harry Snyder offered no excuses: "It was a nerve wracking contest. I never have seen anything like it. Of course we missed Dutch Clark but I don't know whether we could have won, if he had been here. Our quarterback made a couple of mistakes, but those were mistakes of judgements. He thought he was deciding right and went through with the play."[40]

The bottom line was that the game had more significance than its immediate effect on the NFL standings. The "Indoor Circus" would be one of the NFL's most important games. Upon returning home to Columbus, Carr also felt the significance of the game he had just witnessed. He kept only a few used tickets of games he attended in his personal scrapbook, but he made sure this one had a permanent spot in his memory and he wanted everyone to know. After placing the two-dollar ticket stub in his scrapbook he wrote, "Ticket used by me at the Championship Game between the Chicago Bears and the Portsmouth Spartans on December 18 1932."[41]

There was no doubt he could see the future of the game having a championship, so much so that he would write the statement next to the historic ticket, as it was the only time in his scrapbook that he would comment on a game. After witnessing the Indoor Circus he knew that the play on the field needed to be more exciting, and the rules had to be loosened up to allow the great athletes coming into the NFL to show off their skills. Plus, the ability to play a game indoors intrigued him too. The game of football was meant to be played outdoors and Carr knew that, but to be able to play a game indoors so fans could be comfortable was something he liked. For now that idea would have to stay in the back of his mind. It would be his vision of the pro game.

A couple of days after the game several players, writers, and fans weren't satisfied with the outcome of the indoor game. Tom Swope of the *Cincinnati Post* said of the game, "Pennant Decided in Joke Contest" and called the charity exhibition game between the Bears–Spartans in Cincinnati (December 25) the true championship contest. Carr put to rest any potential controversy by saying,

> You fellows decided to play for the championship in the Stadium. You knew in advance the field was small. You should have known that the smallness of the so-called Stadium gridiron would preclude real football and prevent both sides from executing many of the plays at your command. But since you announced that the championship would hinge on the indoor game, the Bears must be declared champions of our league. We have a standing in the eyes of the country which we must try and improve, not tear down. If we are to make the championship a box office "football" and hippodrome it, we never will increase our appeal to the public in our league cities. You made your bed and now you must lie in it, so there can be no more games between the Bears and Spartans this year which will count in the league standing."[42]

Despite some of the negative tone by the press, Carr was able to learn the most important lesson from the NFL's first ever playoff game—that the unbelievable interest generated among fans and media by a game for all the marbles at the end of the season was something the NFL needed to make permanent. The owners would also see the reaction to the indoor game, and they would respond quickly.

On December 23 Carr's office, with help from the publicity department, sent out a press release recapping the 1932 season and announcing the first statistical leaders.

> The National Football League enjoyed one of its most successful seasons in 1932 with the official race ending in a tie for the title between the Chicago Bears and Portsmouth Spartans, ending the three-year reign of the Green Bay Packers as world's champions.
>
> The Chicago Bears after getting off to a slow start finished the season as one of the most powerful aggregations the league has ever boasted and capped its performance by defeating the Spartans in a post-season playoff game played indoors at the Chicago Stadium.
>
> An unusually fine crop of newcomers came up from the college ranks to make good in their first season. Cliff Battles, halfback, and Glen Edwards, tackle, of Boston; Bob Campigolo, quarterback of Stapleton; Jack Grossman, Brooklyn back; Bill Hewitt, Bears, end; and Clarke Hinkle, Green Bay fullback, were a few of the college products who upset tradition by gaining stellar honors in their first season. Earl "Dutch" Clark, Portsmouth, quarterback, was the outstanding back of the circuit."[43]

1932 NFL Statistical Leaders

Leading rusher—Cliff Battles (Boston Braves), with 576 rushing yards
Rushing touchdowns—Bronko Nagurski (Chicago Bears), with four touchdowns
Touchdown passes—Arnie Herber (Green Bay Packers), with nine touchdowns
Passing yards—Arnie Herber (Green Bay Packers), with 630 passing yards
Most receptions—Ray Flaherty (New York Giants), with five touchdowns
Leading scorer—Dutch Clark (Portsmouth Spartans), with fifty-five points

The most amazing thing about all the major statistical leaders from the first time the NFL kept statistics is that they would all eventually be inducted into the Pro Football Hall of Fame. Carr knew it was now time to let these fantastic athletes spread their wings and fly.

20

The Pro Game Separates Itself from the College Game (1933)

In 1932 Carr saw an increase in the average attendance per game as 599,561 fans went through the turnstiles of forty-eight NFL games (forty-seven regular-season games and one postseason game). That was an increase from 9,727 fans per game in 1931 to 12,490 fans per game in 1932. With the additional positive press from the season-ending playoff game, Carr and the NFL owners had big smiles on their faces—except for one.[1]

The new kid on the block didn't seem to be rejoicing. George Preston Marshall and his partners lost $46,000 in their first season in Boston. The loss of income scared Marshall's wealthy cronies, and they wanted out. But the brash laundry magnate believed in the sport. Like his mentor Joe F. Carr he could see that professional football's best days were in front of it and not just as a profitable business. He saw the game had the potential of rivaling baseball as the number one sport in America. He would be quoted as saying "baseball, that's a common game. You have one everyday. Pro football's the national pastime."[2] Although he lost a ton of money in 1932, and his partners bailed on him, Marshall still wanted in.

The Boston Braves averaged 12,916 fans per game (77,500 total fans in six home games), which wasn't nearly as well as he thought the team would do, so Marshall looked to make a few changes. First, he didn't particularly care for the team's relationship with baseball's Boston Braves (the feeling was mutual), and he wanted his squad to have its own identity. Marshall moved his team's home games from Braves Field to Fenway Park and gave his team a new nickname—the Boston Redskins. He took the Native American theme to a new level by getting rid of Lud Wray and hiring Lone Star Dietz, former coach of Washington State and Purdue, to be his head coach. Soon Marshall would make a bigger impact on the sport he had just bought into.

As one team changed its nickname, Carr was thinking about some of the potential changes his league might be going through. His league was progressing nicely (despite the country trying to survive the Depression), but a few issues were dancing in his head. Throughout the 1932 NFL season (as well as while watching the indoor playoff game), Carr and the other owners saw that the play on the field was getting stale. As a group they began some discussions about improving the game and made a conscious effort to make their game more enjoyable for their fans. Carr thought one of the main things the league had to do was to start separating itself from the more popular college game.

In late January on one of his baseball meeting trips, Carr had a conversation with well-known sportswriter Sam Levy. Instead of chatting about America's pastime, Carr quickly turned to what Levy would describe as Carr's "first love":

> Professional football has been easily the most prosperous sporting venture of the depression period. While other sports have made hard work of hanging on this sport has moved steadily forward.
>
> Our venture was hard to sell at first. There were too many college men on newspapers who believed we were a menace. It was slow work convincing them we had a legitimate venture and a great sporting show. Now most of them are with us and I am only afraid they are going too far. Some of them are saying we will drive college football out of business. That's ridiculous. We couldn't if we wanted to and certainly we don't want to. The colleges need football and the partisanship and color of a college spectacle will save it. Moreover, we need college football. Each year it turns loose 2,500 experienced players from whom we can select the dozen or two dozen best. These fellows come to us needing no more than a year or two of seasoning to fit into our game and they come with loads of publicity, with reputations already made and with big enthusiastic followings.[3]

Levy then asked Carr about the rumors of Minneapolis planning to build a new municipal fieldhouse. "If they only knew how near our football league is to moving indoors and what a smashing success we are going to make of the pro game under cover they would not hesitate for a moment to spend the additional money needed to size the building up to the requirements of that game."[4]

Was he serious? Did he really think in 1933 that the NFL would play in a domed stadium? Although the 1932 indoor game between the Spartans and Bears wasn't a thrilling display of gridiron action on the field, Carr saw how the fans enjoyed being comfortable in their seats while a driving snowstorm occurred outside. He was always thinking of the fans and how the game could be more appealing for them. Unfortunately, most cities—large or small—didn't have any money to actually build a domed stadium. Carr and the NFL would have to wait another thirty plus years to see a pro team (Houston Oilers) play in a domed stadium (Astrodome).

Carr's crazy mind was in overdrive in 1933, and the other owners followed suit. The first thing to be discussed was what to do about all these tie games. Out of the fifty-seven regular-season games in 1932, a total of ten ended in a tie (17 percent). Giants owner Tim Mara called Carr to give his opinion on the subject and then talked to the *New York Times* on what might be done.

> In every sport but football the authorities have sought to avoid a tie score. No matter whom you are rooting for you don't want to see a game end in a tie. The game has reached such a stage now that few field goals are attempted. The one desire seems to be a touchdown.
>
> I think that if the point after touchdown were eliminated it would stimulate placements or drop kicks from the field.
>
> This [past] season we had made arrangements with the Chicago Bears in a game out there that if it ended in a tie we would experiment with an overtime period. This plan might not be feasible for collegians, but I think it would work out for the professionals. I believe that our men are in better physical condition and that it would not affect them as much. [If after overtime period the game is still tied,] . . . I guess they would have to allow the tie to remain.
>
> These statistics show how ridiculous it is to decide a game on such a mechanical thing as making the extra point. A team could have kicked off and resumed play in the time devoted to preparation of the extra point play.[5]

Mara's mind, just like Carr's, was going crazy too. Eliminating the extra point was a radical idea (which eventually didn't happen), but Mara's other arguments were right on the nose. During the 1932 season, the NFL saw just *six* field goals made—Dutch Clark led the league with half of them. In comparison the NFL saw *seven* safeties, eight if you count the one in the indoor playoff game. Something had to be done when the stats showed that teams scored more safeties than field goals. More scoring had to be encouraged, which in theory would reduce the potential of low-scoring and tie games. Carr agreed.

"Spectators are opposed to drawn-out games. They want rapid action, intermingled with thrills and glamour which have made football such a great spectacle. If the new [college] rules detract from the glamour of the game, we will have to revise them to suit our needs. It is our desire to open up the game and give the public as much action as possible. Our greatest appeal to the public is the speed with which a professional game moves."[6]

Carr could see that something had to be done and that the league couldn't wait until the summer to discuss the issues facing the owners. On top of all the chatter to make the NFL more fan friendly, Carr had several new franchise applications arrive across his desk. Several cities wanted in, including Philadelphia, Cincinnati, Cleveland (maybe to replace the struggling Portsmouth Spartans), and Pittsburgh. The Steel City had several different promoters interested, so Carr decided to kill two birds with one stone and called for a special league meeting in Pittsburgh set for February 25–26.

At 1:00 p.m. in the conference room at the Fort Pitt Hotel in Pittsburgh, President Carr called the meeting to order. Vice President Carl L. Storck took the minutes. Teams and their respective owners present were

Boston—George Preston Marshall;
Brooklyn—Martin Shenker and star quarterback Benny Friedman;
Chicago Bears—George Halas;
Chicago Cardinals—Dr. David Jones;
Green Bay—Curly Lambeau;
New York—Tim Mara and Jack Mara;
Portsmouth—Harry Snyder and Homer Selby;
Staten Island—absent.[7]

These twelve men who gathered at the Fort Pitt Hotel were about to change the course of professional football. Carr started the special meeting by suggesting the league bypass Old Business and go straight to New Business. Carr wasn't messing around; the league was there to get things done. The owners participated in a general discussion on what changes the league needed to make in order to make the game more entertaining, as well as reduce tie games, encourage more scoring, and separate their sport from the college game.

One of the first owners to talk was George Preston Marshall, who after just one year as an NFL owner wasn't shy about expressing his feelings. "Gentleman it's about time we realized that we're not only in the football business. We're also in the entertainment business. If the colleges want to louse up their game with bad rules, let 'em. We don't have to follow suit. The hell with the colleges. We should do what's best for us. I say we should adopt rules that will give the pros a spectacular individuality and national significance. Face it, we're in show business. If people don't buy tickets, we'll have no business at all."[8] After a lengthy discussion the owners adopted the following resolutions:

1. Motion by George Preston Marshall, seconded by George Halas—that goal posts be placed back at the goal line, instead of back of the end zone. Motion Carried.
2. Motion by George Preston Marshall, seconded by George Halas—that the rule covering the use of the forward pass, 5 yards behind the line of scrimmage before the ball can be thrown, be changed permitting the passer to pass the ball from any point behind the line of scrimmage. Motion Carried.
3. Motion, that when the ball is within five yards of being out of bounds, the ball would be moved into the field of play 10 yards (hash marks). Motion Carried.
4. Motion by Dr. David Jones, seconded by Benny Friedman—that the clipping penalty of 25 yards is to be retained. Motion Carried.[9]

The owners, led by the two Georges—Marshall and Halas—had not only made some important changes (which were definitely needed); they were about to separate their game from the collegiate one. Ever since the National Football League was founded in 1920 (as the American Professional Football Association), they had followed the rules of college football, but in 1933 they made important decisions and rule changes that redirected the course of the NFL. The league needed to make its "product" much more exciting and marketable. This was a big start.

To end the historic first day, the owners awarded the 1932 NFL championship to the Chicago Bears. The following morning at 8:00 a.m., Carr gathered the group to talk about a salary limit (nothing was established) and the fact that player contracts should be on file with the president. The owners then concluded the meeting by making a request, that President Carr draft a schedule for every team before the summer session in July. Because of the controversy at the end of 1931, the owners felt this would be the best way of putting together a schedule for future seasons. Carr's special meeting was a success. The president and the small gathering of sportsmen had accomplished what they wanted to do. In speaking to the press afterward, Carr expressed his happiness: "We think we have overcome the balance previously held by the defense. In fact if we can give the offense a slight edge, it doubtless would improve the game for both players and spectators."[10] But they weren't completely done remaking the NFL.

While in Pittsburgh, Carr also met with potential investors for an NFL franchise to be located in the western Pennsylvania city. The team's admission into the NFL was predicated on the removal of the state's Blue Laws, which made it illegal to hold any professional sporting event on Sundays. The state's baseball teams had suffered for years under the Blue

Law restriction, but baseball could be played any day of the week before numerous crowds. Because pro football teams normally played only one game per week, it needed the large crowds possible only on weekends, and Saturdays belonged to the colleges. The new law allowing Sunday games would go into effect that November.

Among the three different investors that inquired about an NFL team, only one had all the characteristics Carr was looking for, and he met with him for a long conversation about a franchise for Pittsburgh. Art Rooney was a thirty-two-year-old former semipro baseball and football player who had been a professional boxer as well. Rooney was also a sports promoter who had fielded the best professional football team in the city of Pittsburgh over the past couple of years and was ready to join the NFL. "NFL President Joe F. Carr approached my father [to join the NFL] because the league saw Pittsburgh as a good expansion opportunity, now that Pennsylvania 'blue laws' prohibiting Sunday play were about to be repealed," wrote Dan Rooney, son of Art Rooney, in his 2007 autobiography. "Carr and the NFL owners knew Art Rooney to be the best promoter in Western Pennsylvania. They also appreciated the fact that he was a real football man—he understood the sport and would be just the guy to cultivate a fan base in the Pittsburgh market."[11]

Arthur Joseph Rooney was born on January 27, 1901, in Pittsburgh to Daniel and Margaret Rooney. Art's father was an Irish immigrant who settled in Pittsburgh and met his future wife in the Steel City. The couple had eight children, and Daniel Rooney eventually moved his family to the north side (also known as the First Ward of Allegheny City), a working-class neighborhood made up of mostly immigrants from the British Isles. Daniel Rooney owned a tavern called Dan Rooney's Café and Saloon located at 528 General Robinson in "the Ward" as Art Rooney would call it.[12]

"It wasn't high-class, but it was a well-run place, it was very strict. No women allowed," Art Rooney would tell writer Myron Cope. "It was a great section, a wonderful section. It had a reputation as a rough and tumble section, but it [had] wonderful people."[13] The Rooney's tavern was located just a block-and-a-half east of Exposition Park, the ball field for the Pittsburgh Pirates (until 1909), so Rooney's Saloon was a popular place for sports discussion and information. Young Art—just like Carr—fell in love with the athletic life from a very early age.

"I played all sports. You went to the playground when the sun came up, and you didn't leave till the sun went down," recalled Art Rooney. "My father grew up strong and tough and streetwise. A natural athlete, he loved to compete. Baseball, football, boxing, you name it, he played it. And he played to win," says Dan Rooney. Growing up in an Irish family church was a big part of Art Rooney's life. He would be guided by the "holy trinity": faith, family, and friends. Carr could see himself in Art Rooney.[14]

In high school Rooney would become a good student and a great athlete, lettering in football, basketball, and baseball. As a halfback on the football team the local paper described his play as standing "head and shoulders above his companions. Broken field running is his chief forte." Who would have known that decades later he would gain the nickname "the Chief."[15]

After high school Rooney attended several universities—Indiana Normal of Indiana, Pennsylvania; Georgetown University; and Duquesne University—but each time he would be distracted by sports and return to the Ward. Whether it was playing semipro baseball or boxing, Rooney established himself as one of the best athletes in the area. "Boxing, football, baseball—he loved them all. But he was more than an athlete. He was a skilled organizer and a great promoter," says Dan Rooney.[16]

In 1921 (at the age of nineteen) he formed his own semipro football team called the Hope-Harvey. "The team was called Hope-Harvey because Hope was the name of the fire-engine house in The Ward and [Walter] Harvey was the doctor in The Ward. For home games we dressed and got showers at the engine house, and Harvey took care of anybody who got hurt," recalled Art Rooney. Not only did Rooney run the team but he also played (as quarterback) and coached. Recruiting players from the neighborhood as well as former college players from local universities Rooney built one of the best semipro teams in the Midwest.[17]

A couple of years after forming his team, he got a sponsor for his squad, the Loeffler Electric Store, an appliance store that wanted the team named after one of its best-selling items—the Majestic Radio. At the same time Rooney became a successful boxing promoter in the city and around the country. In 1931 Rooney married Kathleen McNulty and the two would go on to have five sons—the eldest being Dan Rooney, who would eventually follow his father's footsteps right into the Pro Football Hall of Fame. Both father and son shared the same ability to be able to communicate with anybody and show compassion for their fellow man. "Dad had the Irish gift of gab, but he wasn't just a smooth talker—he genuinely loved people and they loved him," says Dan Rooney.[18]

Rooney's affiliation with Loeffler's Electric Store ended with the coming of the 1931 season, as he renamed his team the "J. P. Rooney's" to help his brother's campaign for state legislature. Jimmy Rooney easily won his race. The J. P. Rooney's continued to play winning football, and at this time Rooney was looking to get his team into the NFL. "Our teams were as good as the teams in professional football. We were as good as the teams in the National Football League," recalled Art Rooney. The confident sports promoter might have overestimated his semipro team's talent, but Carr liked what Rooney could bring to the NFL. He was a well-connected, successful sports promoter who could finance a league franchise in a city that, according to the 1930 Census, had a population of 669,817.[19]

Carr felt positive about Rooney and gave him his word that he should prepare his team to be in the NFL. "In 1933 I paid $2,500 for a National Football League franchise, which I named the Pirates, because the Pittsburgh baseball team was called the Pirates. It wasn't until 1940, when we held a contest for a new name, that we became the Steelers," remembered Art Rooney. "I bought the franchise . . . because I figured that it would be good to have a league schedule and that eventually professional football would be good."[20]

How Art came up with the $2,500 to buy the team has been debated for the past seventy years. Besides being an athlete, sports promoter, politician, and owner, Rooney was also known as probably the best horse handicapper in the country. "He studied the sport, knew the animals, the trainers, the jockeys, the owners. Dad always told me that betting on horses wasn't just a game of chance—he wouldn't have done it if it were—it required knowledge and skill. Some people say he was the best thoroughbred handicapper in the country," wrote Dan Rooney in his autobiography.[21]

Rooney made a good living playing the horses—this is where he met Tim Mara—and most historians have claimed that this is how he paid for the NFL franchise. The myth was based on a hot streak at the track where Rooney supposedly netted anywhere from $250,000 (the consensus figure) to $380,000 at the Saratoga and Empire City racetracks. "It's been rumored that a big $250,000 payday at Saratoga enabled him to purchase the team. That's nonsense," wrote Dan Rooney in his autobiography. "Dad's legendary day at the racetrack occurred in the summer of 1937, a memorable opening day at Saratoga. [It was] the biggest payday Dad ever had at the racetrack—but it had nothing to do with buying the team. He made the deal with the NFL four years earlier."[22]

"I broke the books at Saratoga and [the rumor] kept growing, growing, and growing. That's how it came out that I won the money at the racetrack to buy the football team, which wasn't so," said Art Rooney in a 1984 NFL Films interview. "My father talked about Joe Carr a lot. He said that he was a great commissioner [president] and really did well. He was very friendly. He said that he was really a good guy," says Dan Rooney. "My father felt that the NFL was so important and having a team in Pittsburgh was important."[23]

Nobody knows how Carr felt about Rooney's horse betting but you must remember the times. "Carr persistently watched for any attempt by gamblers to move in on football. He let all managers know that if he caught any owner or manager betting on the result of a League game he would ban the individual from the League forever. The warning sufficed," recalled George Halas. "Joe hated gambling. He said it could lead only to dishonesty, and dishonesty would ruin professional football. All of us early owners were deeply appreciative of his firm stand."[24]

Although Carr hated anything to do with gambling and routinely expressed his opinion on the subject to his owners, his philosophy on horse betting was different. It was natural for any man (even if you were an NFL owner) to attend the track and put down a bet. At this time horse racing was just as popular as, if not even more than, professional football. Owners like Tim Mara, Art Rooney, George Preston Marshall (who eventually quit betting on horses), and later Charlie Bidwill all had connections with racetracks. Carr lived during a period when these men (although involved in horse racing) had prestige and creditability, because of their involvement with the ponies.

Carr retuned home after the special Pittsburgh meeting with the new rules in place for the league to improve its product. He also found a new owner for his league. The reaction to the NFL's dramatic changes in separating itself from the college game was positive, with rave reviews from the public and press:

> Joe F. Carr and his associates in the National Professional Football League are to be congratulated for recent actions in endeavoring to pep up the gridiron game for next season. It seems that the Carr-bossed organization is one that looks out for the spectator, the one who pays the freight.—Robert Hooey, *Ohio State Journal*

> Joe F. Carr, president of the league, predicted these changes will make the game more spectacular and put the "foot" back in football by encouraging kicking.—*New York Times*[25]

The positive press was met with some negativity. Ed Pollock of the *Philadelphia Public Ledger* wrote a gloomier outlook for the NFL.

> Although football fans have never caught up with all the changes in one rules book, there will be two codes published this year to multiply the confusion and misunderstanding of the spectators. In addition to the rules which will govern the college games, the professional will have their own code through which the field will be laid out and decisions rendered accordingly. . . . The decision of the pros to break away from the college game is in my opinion the worst mistake the league has made since the outlawed practice of raiding college squads for material. Football is distinctly a college game. The collegians get the crowds and have the better opportunity to educate the spectators to their rules. Disagreements in the professional code will merely lead to louder outcries against the lawmakers and the officials who must enforce the rules.

> It makes no difference whether the changes made by the professionals are good or poor. For the sake of uniformity, understanding and progress they should not have been made.[26]

The bottom line for Carr and his owners was they needed to make a break from the collegiate game. In due time, it would be the professional game at the forefront in establishing how the sport was played on the field. As Carr returned to his Columbus office, he heard some good news coming out of Portsmouth. The financially strapped Spartans started their fund-raising drive earlier and sold over 600 season tickets, securing their spot in the league. But the Spartans' roster was about to take a big hit. Dutch Clark decided to quit professional football to be the athletic director at Colorado School of Mines, to go along with his coaching duties. The Spartans wouldn't contend for the NFL title as in the previous two seasons.

In early May, President Carr began to draft the league schedule, and he asked Spartans executive Harry Snyder to help him with the task. The two men sat in Carr's Columbus office putting together the season's matchups, hoping at the summer session the owners would be pleased. After pounding his brain Carr took a break from league matters to celebrate a milestone in his son's life.[27]

On the evening of June 6, the whole Carr family watched Joe Carr Jr. graduate with honors from Holy Rosary High School. Papa Carr and his wife, Josie, were extremely proud of their son, and the family now had two high school graduates. "Buddy" was president (just like his father) of his graduating class and was so popular that the *Columbus Dispatch* wrote about his recent achievement, along with a photo that showed off the handsome student's good looks.

> Graduate Honored By Holy Rosary School
>
> President of his class and honored with the title of Rosarian, Joseph F. Carr, Jr., of 1863 Bryden Road, graduated last week from Holy Rosary High School.
>
> The honor of being Rosarian is conferred yearly on students for excellence in their four years of high school work and for outstanding service to the school in extra-curricular activities.[28]

Young Carr was following in his father's footsteps. After leaving high school, "Buddy" enrolled at the Ohio State University and studied law, making his father very proud. Carr's lack of education, or rather, his lack of opportunity to extend his education, made him want to give his son—as well as his daughter—all the means to further theirs. In just a few years, Joe and Josie would have two college graduates on their hands.

As the summer meeting approached, Carr made some final decisions on the league's franchise applications for 1933. He announced to the press that Pittsburgh (May 18) would be approved, as well as the city of Cincinnati (June 28). The Queen City's franchise would be operated by Dr. M. Scott Kearns, the coroner of Hamilton County, and William McCoy, the secretary of a local investment securities company. Carr might also have had Sid Weil, the owner of the Cincinnati Reds, involved in the ownership group because the team rented out Redland Field and would be called the Cincinnati Reds Football Club.[29]

When talking to the local press, Kearns expressed excitement about being a part of the NFL. "Professional football has been growing by leaps and bounds all over the country and we want Cincinnati to be on the football map." He also said that he would "spare no expense" to field "the best team possible."[30] The only problem was that he and his partner didn't have that much money to spend. Kearns and McCoy weren't wealthy men and built a team that just couldn't compete with the other powerful NFL clubs. Also, because of the lack of funds, the Reds spent virtually no money on adverting for home games, which meant small crowds and smaller profits.

But they were in and with the prospect of the Staten Island Stapletons folding, Carr moved on to the application of Philadelphia, which was submitted by Lud Wray, former head coach of the Boston Braves, and his partner, Bert Bell. Wray and Bell had played college football together at the University of Pennsylvania, and both wanted to get into the NFL. Wray wanted to coach again, and Bell wanted to be part of the sport he loved dearly. His purchase of an NFL franchise was the beginning of a quarter-century relationship with the National Football League.

The thirty-eight-year-old Bell was born on February 25, 1895, with the birth name of de Benneville Bell given to him by his parents John and Fleurette Bell in honor of his French grandmother. Young de Benneville was born rich and reared in the lap of luxury among the aristocracy of Philadelphia's Main Line. But his given name was a different story. "If I can lick the name de Benneville, I can handle anything," Bell frequently said. He decided to go by the name Bert for the rest of his life. His father was the attorney general of Pennsylvania, and his brother later became governor. But Bert had only one passion—football.[31]

"Football was his life," says Bert Bell Jr., son of Bert Bell. "After high school one of my grandfather's friends asked him where Bert was going to college. He said Bert will go to Penn or he'll go to hell."[32] Bert Bell did go to the University of Pennsylvania and played football as a quarterback. While at Penn he played alongside Lou Little (who went on to coach at Columbia), Heinie Miller (who played for the NFL's Frankford Yellow Jackets), and Lud Wray, one of his closest friends. After graduating from college in 1920, Bell coached at his alma mater (1920–1928) and Temple University (1930–1931) while staying in the city of Philadelphia.

Besides football Bell had another passion in his life. He fell madly in love with Frances Upton, a former Ziegfeld Follies showgirl. She had brains to go with her beauty, and she told the wealthy football lifer that she could see no future happiness being married to a man who drank too much. "All right," said Bert, "I'll never take another drink." They got married, had three children (sons Upton and Bert Jr., and daughter Jane), and he never drank again. In 1933 Bell formed a small syndicate with Wray to purchase the Frankford Yellow Jackets franchise in the NFL. The price was $2,500. Bell immediately renamed the team the Philadelphia Eagles, in honor of the bald eagle, the symbol of President Franklin D. Roosevelt's National Recovery Act. Both Wray and Bell were now in the NFL.[33]

On July 8–9 seven NFL teams and three new franchises gathered at the Blackstone Hotel in Chicago to prepare for the upcoming season. Once again the league was about to change the history of professional football. With a long agenda ahead of them, President Carr called the meeting together at 1:00 p.m. The first order of New Business was the accepting of the three new franchises. Each new member was introduced to the other owners and made short speeches on "their proposed plans of operations." None of what Art Rooney or Lud Wray (who was there representing Bert Bell) said was put into the minutes, just that they made brief statements.[34]

Staten Island officially suspended operations and Carr announced that their players would become free agents after August 1. The Stapes had enjoyed a nice run of four years in the NFL, compiling an overall record of 14–22–9. But they never finished higher than sixth place in the standings, and the Depression hit the area hard as the team averaged just over 5,000 fans for the last four home games in 1932. The league now said good-bye to the Stapes.

The NFL was now a ten-team organization and the owners made it perfectly clear what it would take to get more teams into the league. Tim Mara made a motion "that as long as the League membership remains at 10 clubs in good standing the application fee for a franchise shall be Ten Thousand ($10,000) Dollars."[35] The motion carried unanimously. In the future if anybody filed an application for an NFL franchise and were admitted it would cost ten grand to join, even before you signed a player or played a game. Carr and the owners were now serious about who could get a team into the league. It also showed to Carr that his League had come a long way from 1921 when he set the franchise fee at fifty bucks. Over the next couple of hours the moguls approved the following:

1. The Spalding J-5 unlined ball without valve as the official ball of the NFL in 1933.
2. That all clubs have two new balls ready for use before each game; second ball used if for whatever reason first one is taken out.
3. Each team in League be required to register with the President, once the colors of its uniforms.
4. Each club be compelled at all times to be properly attired and neatly attired & also visiting club will send home club at least one week in advance a copy of correct names & numbers of all players under contract at that time.
5. Visiting clubs wear a jersey distinctly different from that of the home team; in any conflict the visiting team shall provide a change for its players.
6. Each club have a football timing watch & pistol with blank cartridge for emergency use by the game officials at home games.[36]

The end of the long first day concluded with the annual election of NFL officials, and Joe F. Carr and Carl L. Storck were reelected for the thirteenth straight year as president-secretary and vice president-treasurer. Carr packed up his notes, including getting each team's official team colors:

Boston—red
Brooklyn—green and white
Chicago Bears—orange and white
Chicago Cardinals—cardinal red
Cincinnati—crimson red
Green Bay—navy blue
New York—red, white, and blue
Philadelphia—light blue and yellow
Pittsburgh—black and gold
Portsmouth—purple[37]

Some of the NFL's pioneering franchises did start with some unusual color schemes—notably Green Bay with its navy blue and Philadelphia's light blue and yellow pattern that has been recycled recently with the NFL's throwback collection. But in 1933 no team was worried about jersey sales; they were worried about just being able to afford jerseys.

On the second day, the owners were now ready to make history. At 1:00 p.m. on July 9, Carr presented the schedule for the season and it was quickly approved. After a couple months' work, Carr was satisfied with the process of putting together the league's schedule, and the owners seemed to agree. For years the owners had bounced around the idea of splitting the NFL into divisions, similar to baseball's American and National leagues. Now was the time to take that leap. According to the league minutes, George Preston Marshall made a motion suggesting that

> for the purpose of creating a new system of compiling and publishing the official standings of clubs in the League that Eastern and Western divisions be created and that the official standings for the coming season be divided into an eastern and western group:
>
> The Eastern group to consist of Boston, Brooklyn, New York, Philadelphia and Pittsburgh.
>
> The Western group to consist of Chicago Bears, Chicago Cardinals, Cincinnati, Green Bay and Portsmouth.[38]

But Marshall wasn't done with his idea of how the new NFL should look, bringing up another motion:

> That under the direction of the President and the Executive Committee the champions of the respective eastern and western groups shall meet at the conclusion of the season and play one game, the winner of which shall be designated as League champion and champion of the world; such game to be played at such time and place and under such rules and conditions as may be designated by the President and the Exec. Committee, including the division of receipts, part of which are to go to the players, part to the respective club owners whose teams are participating, and part to the league treasury.[39]

It was about time. For nearly a dozen years the NFL hierarchy had talked about arranging itself into two divisions so it could have a season-ending championship game. A championship game would do away with unseemly postseason arguments over which team had actually won the title. Disputes had erupted in 1921, 1924, 1925, and 1931. In 1932 the Spartans and Bears tied at season's end, and the NFL couldn't expect two teams to tie at the end of every year. This new setup would give the league a "second" pennant race. In theory you only had to be good in your division. Plus, the championship game at the end of the season would bring in more money and publicity. The NFL now had its version of baseball's World Series.

Both of Marshall's motions were carried. The meeting adjourned with all ten franchises, a vice president, and one president very enthusiastic about the upcoming season. The entire group could see the potential of what they had just set up, and they couldn't wait for the season to start. But before they would get going, two teams changed ownership. The Brooklyn Dodgers were sold by Bill Dwyer to two players—Chris Cagle and John "Shipwreck" Kelly—for a price that was "between $25,000 and $50,000."[40]

In Chicago, Dr. David Jones sold his Cardinals to Charlie Bidwill, who had to give up his small share of the Chicago Bears to get the team. Despite losing a good friend who helped him financially, George Halas was happy for Bidwill. "Dr. David Jones was losing interest in football. He saw a dark financial future for football and his Cardinals. Undesirable characters again sniffed about [to buy the team]. I favored my old friend Charlie Bidwill," recalled Halas.[41] After meeting with Jones on his boat, Bidwill made him an offer to buy the franchise for a reported $50,000. Charlie Bidwill was a Chicago native who graduated with a law degree from Loyola (Illinois) University. After serving in World War I he become a corporate counsel and then gradually became involved in sports around the Windy City.

Bidwill was labeled a "creative genius" as a manager for many varied sporting activities. He was president of the Chicago Stadium Operating Company, promoting every event for the arena. He was also director of the American Turf Association and proprietor of a racing stable. In his spare time he was president of the Bentley, Murray Printing Company. His sports connections and businesses made the thirty-eight-year-old Bidwill a wealthy man and a perfect owner for one of Carr's big city franchises. He also could see the big picture for the NFL.

"In brief the success of professional football depends in no small measure upon its ability to draw the workaday sports fans who either have been ignored by the colleges or who can't get away to attend Saturday games. Professional football supplies that need."[42]

On the eve of the season's opening weekend, Carr spoke to the press about what they should expect to see on NFL gridirons.

> We had our best year in 1932, despite general conditions. We have a stronger organization than ever and look for an even bigger season this fall. I may sound optimistic, and I intend to. I have seen the popularity of the professional game grow slowly but steadily. It is here to stay because it is giving the fans what they want.
>
> Professional teams are well coached, practice daily, and offer superlative football at prices less than those charged for college games. These have been the factors in the growth of attendance. We confidently expect our greatest season this fall.[43]

On the opening weekend President Carr traveled to Portsmouth to watch the Cincinnati Reds play the Spartans in their inaugural League contest. Carr's special guest that day was his son Joe Carr Jr. As a reward for graduating high school, papa Carr allowed his seventeen-year-old son to travel with him for the first time to attend an NFL game. Father and son sat in the box on the forty-five yard line, and Carr was introduced to cheers from the crowd of 5,000, but didn't give a speech. The Spartans spoiled the Reds' debut with a 21–0 whipping.[44]

Three days later Carr took a train east to witness the debut of the Pittsburgh Pirates. Because the Blue Laws of Pennsylvania weren't repealed until November 7, the Pirates (as well as Philadelphia) played their first few home games on Wednesday nights. In their first game, the Pirates had a very inexperienced lineup facing the veteran New York Giants. In front of a nice crowd of 20,000 fans, the Giants showed the Steel City squad what an NFL team should look like. The Giants dominated on both sides, winning easily 23–2. Carr saw some potential in the Pirates—especially the rather large crowd that showed up—as he chatted with head coach Jap Douds after the game. "You're not going to win any championships, but you have a fine foundation to build on." Following the game Rooney wrote in his diary, "Our fans didn't get their money's worth."[45] Fielding a team with mostly players from the University of Pittsburgh, Duquesne, and Washington and Jefferson, the Pirates finished their first season with a 3–6–2 record.

One of the players on the Pirates' team would be one of the last black players to play in an NFL game for a long time. Ray Kemp joined Joe Lillard as the only two black players in the league in 1933. Kemp had played college ball at Duquesne and was then recruited by Art Rooney to play for his J. P. Rooney's. When Rooney joined the NFL, he signed Kemp to play tackle for sixty dollars a game. "I can recall it as if it were yesterday, the tremendous ovation I received when they announced I was going in at tackle," remembered Ray Kemp about his first NFL game.[46]

"When we were traveling I ran into a lot of problems. A lot of my teammates didn't really do much about it except for one or two guys. When we were away from home, a couple of guys would come around to make sure I was alright. That sort of sustained me because there were times when it helped to know that they were standing in your corner," Kemp revealed in a 1981 interview for Black Sports in Pittsburgh. Kemp would play five games for the Steelers in 1933 before Douds didn't need him anymore. He was released by Rooney.[47]

"I received a letter saying that I had been dropped from the roster. I talked with Art Rooney and I can recall his exact words. He said 'Ray, I feel you are as good a ballplayer as we have on the club but I am not going over the head of the coach. You know how I feel about you personally," remembered Kemp. Rooney gave his coaches all the power when it came time to make roster decisions. Kemp never resented Rooney for his being released but definitely thought it showed a weakness in Rooney as the team's president. "Art gave his coaches a free hand. He didn't interfere. That's where he made his mistake for years," remembered Kemp.[48]

Rooney would agree with Kemp's assessment. "I think that was my whole mistake, letting the coaches have a free hand," recalled Art Rooney.[49] In the team's first ten years (1933–1942), Rooney had seven different head coaches. The more important issue was that he released one of only two black players in the league at the time. Before the next NFL season started, Carr's league would have no black players participating.

While Carr took road trips to games in Portsmouth (September 24) and Chicago (October 1 and October 29), he received a nice birthday note from his loving daughter, Mary. On his fifty-fourth birthday, Carr was given a short hand-written letter by his eldest child wishing him a happy birthday.

Dearest of All Dads,

Here's wishing the best and dearest Dad in the world the happiest and best birthday our Lord and the Blessed Virgin could give a wonderful father like you. I think you know by this time a little bit how grand, how swell, how wonderful you are. And you also know that this is not flattering it comes from the heart.

I offered my Rosary in Church for you this morning to our Blessed Mother, your favorite patroness to always guide you as right and make you as successful as you are today.

I won't even try to thank you for all the things you have done for me—and the unlimited happiness and joy you have brought me—ever since the moment I was born.

So here wishing you again—all the luck & every blessing possible to be blessed from the Almighty.

Always,
Your Lamb
(may you always be as proud of me as you are today)[50]

Mary Carr's love and devotion to her father was very obvious to the family and anyone who came into contact with her. Although he was gone most of the time traveling, Carr was definitely a father who had his children's love. Whether it was receiving a note from his "Lamb" or watching "Buddy" graduate from high school, he (as well as his wife, Josie) was raising his children the right way. Family, faith, and friends were being instilled in the Carr home as well as within his football league.

As for the NFL's first two-division race, the drama was kept to a minimum, as the Bears (Western) and the Giants (Eastern) won their respective divisions easily. But the new format did do its proper job—the NFL's two best teams were going to meet for the title in the league's first-ever NFL Championship Game. After winning the NFL title in 1932, George Halas didn't sit quietly basking in his glory. Before the season started, he replaced the great Ralph Jones (who resigned to go back to his old job as athletic director at Lake Forest Academy) with, of all people, himself. Then he went about restocking his squad.

Coach Halas signed former college stars halfback-kicker Jack Manders (Minnesota), end Bill Karr (West Virginia), and six feet two, 257-pound guard George Musso, from tiny Milliken College (Illinois). Musso went on to play twelve years with the Bears and was inducted into the Pro Football Hall of Fame. Every member of this rookie class would contribute to the Bears finishing with a Western-best 10–2–1 record. Out of the group Manders probably had the most impact in 1933 as he took advantage of the NFL's new rules. With the goal post moved to the front of the end zone, "Automatic Jack" led the NFL in field goals (six) and extra points (fourteen). His six field goals in 1933 matched the entire NFL's total in 1932.

While the Bears controlled the West, the New York Giants revamped themselves into the beast of the East, and they started with the search for a new signal caller. "What we needed was a quarterback. The quarterback we wanted was Harry Newman. He could throw and run, he was smart and he could be coached," says Wellington Mara, son of Tim Mara.[51] The Giants signed the Michigan All-American, who would give the Giants offense a much-needed spark since the departure of Benny Friedman. Adding to the offensive firepower was the addition of Ken Strong. After his release from the Stapletons, Strong signed with the Giants and in 1933 Steve Owen's squad scored a league-high 244 points (the Packers were second with 170).

With two games remaining, both the Bears and Giants had clinched their divisions. A week later on December 5, Carr announced that the first NFL Championship Game would take place on Sunday, December 17, at the home field of the division winner with the highest winning percentage. That meant if the Bears defeated the Packers in their season finale, they would host the game at Wrigley Field; if they lost and the Giants won, the game would be at the Polo Grounds.

To get ready for the historic game, Carr invited George Halas and Jack Mara to Columbus so they could discuss the details of the first ever title game. Both team presidents arrived in the capital city on Thursday, December 7 and headed up to the eleventh floor of the building at 16 East Broad Street. After reaching Carr's office, the two football moguls were met by Carr's secretary, Kathleen Rubadue, who led the gentlemen into the small office of President Carr.[52]

All three men were in a fantastic mood as they were about to make NFL history in putting together the league's first official championship game. The trio agreed to play the game at the home of the team with the best winning percentage; they also agreed that 60 percent of the net gate receipts of the championship game would be placed in a pool for the players, the winning club to get 60 percent of the pool and the losing club 40 percent. Carr told the two owners that he would need the roster of each team by the Thursday before the game.

After the arrangements were completed, Carr took his two special guests across the street to the statehouse to meet the governor of Ohio. Governor George White—who was a big football fan—shook hands with Halas and Mara and chatted with the group about the upcoming matchup. The *Ohio State Journal*—with a tip provided by Carr—showed up with a photographer and snapped a photo of Halas shaking hands with White. The governor wished the two men good luck in the championship game and went back to work. Carr had one final conversation with his friends and wished them well in returning home.[53]

After the meeting, newspapers around the country ran headlines claiming that the three men had just "Arranged Pro Football's World Series." The title game was set and when the Bears defeated the Packers (7–6) on December 10, it was determined that the NFL's first championship game would be played at Wrigley Field. The week leading up the title contest was busy for the whole NFL family. Dr. Harry March of the NFL's executive committee wrote an article about the popularity and history of professional football that appeared in *Literary Digest*. It was just the beginning for March as he was actually in the middle of writing a book about the history of the "postgraduate" game.[54]

As Carr was making his traveling plans to get to Chicago, he announced the officials to work the all-important game. He selected Tommy Hughitt (referee), Bobbie Cahn (umpire), Bob Karch (field judge), and Dan Tehan (head linesman). "Although I was the youngest [twenty-six years old] official in the league I was assigned to help handle the [NFL's] first title game," recalled Dan Tehan. "[I] was paid $30.00" (up from his regular salary of $25.00 per game). Wanting to avoid ending the game in darkness, Carr told the teams and the press that the game would kickoff at 1:45 p.m. (Central Standard Time), instead of the original 2:00 p.m. kickoff—which was the time on the game tickets that Halas had printed up. Carr also sent out notice that there would be a special league meeting on the day before the title game to discuss a few things for next season.[55]

The Bears were a 7-to-5 favorites to retain the championship. The game was expected to have a sellout crowd and favorable weather. On the Saturday (December 16) before the game, Carr set up shop at the Hotel Sherman to prepare for the biggest game in the fourteen-year history of the NFL. At 3:00 p.m. Carr called his special meeting with seven of the ten teams present (absent were Boston, Brooklyn, and Pittsburgh), including George Halas, Tim Mara, and Jack Mara, who must have been so anxious for the game to start that this get-together could have been considered a distraction.[56]

Carr called the meeting to discuss several general topics, one being to start the NFL season earlier so that the championship game could have the best possible weather. This was something Carr couldn't control, but he took action. "It has been proposed that we open the 1934 season just as early as possible and close it the first Sunday in December to insure playable weather for the championship game," Carr said to the press. After adjourning the meeting the whole NFL was now ready to witness history.[57]

On the afternoon of December 17 the two teams arrived at Wrigley Field to feel a cool and damp Chicago day—perfect football weather. Programs were being sold for ten cents, and the few remaining tickets went up for sale for two dollars each at the ticket office. The press box was filled to capacity with sportswriters, and the game would be broadcast locally on radio by WGN. Although the field was soft and slippery, with a stiff wind coming out of the northwest, it wouldn't hinder the offensive fireworks that were about to happen.[58]

President Carr arrived with several of the other owners and took his front row seat in box 42, tier 2, seat 8. Also at the game were college coaches Bob Zuppke (Illinois), Dick Hanley (Northwestern), and Hunk Anderson (Notre Dame). The rest of Wrigley Field was jam-packed with 26,000 fans who had no idea that what they were about to witness would keep them talking for years to come.[59]

At kickoff fog hung low over the field as the Bears took an early 3–0 lead on a Jack Manders sixteen-yard field goal. As the second quarter began Manders kicked a forty-yard field goal (thanks for moving the goal posts up) to give the Bears a 6–0 lead. Then Harry Newman got the Giants' high-scoring offense on the board. Throwing passes through the mist, Newman connected on a twenty-nine-yard touchdown pass to Red Badgro to score the first touchdown in NFL Championship Game history and give the Giants a 7–6 halftime lead.

During intermission President Carr spoke to the crowd over the field mike. He promised rule changes for next season that would make professional football more replete with thrilling plays. He was then given a big ovation. Both teams seemed to be feeling each other out in the first half, but the second half would be a different story, as the fans and the rest of the country would get a chance to see the future of the NFL. Coach Halas rallied his troops. "Halas says 'We can win this ball game. We've just been making a few mistakes out there. Just play the kind of ball that we're capable of playing and there'll be no doubt you can win this ball game,'" said George Musso in a 1999 interview with NFL Films.[60]

In the second half the fans saw the lead bounce back and forth with one exciting play after another. In the third quarter Manders kicked his third field goal to give the Bears a 9–7 advantage. The Giants then came back with a sixty-one-yard drive ending with a one-yard Moose Krause touchdown plunge to regain the lead at 14–9. The scoring had just begun, but one spectator already thought his team was going to win. "I used to sit on the bench in those days," recalled Wellington Mara, who was seventeen years old at the time. "I remember they kicked a field goal, kicked two field goals. We scored a touchdown. They kicked a field goal. We scored a touchdown. I remember saying, boy this is great. We'll trade a field goal for a TD anytime."[61]

The Bears quickly retaliated by scoring on a play made famous one year earlier in the "Indoor Circus." Deep in Giants territory, Halas called for a line plunge by Bronko Nagurski, who would then stop short and pull back to toss a pass to rookie Bill Karr. It worked perfectly for an eight-yard score. Now that you could pass from anywhere behind the line of scrimmage, this play didn't cause any uproar from the Giants. The third quarter ended with the Bears leading 16–14 and the Giants driving again. Carr and the other 26,000 spectators had just witnessed three lead changes in one single quarter. Both offenses were playing the wide-open, exciting, entertaining game that Carr and the other owners envisioned when they made the rule changes just ten months earlier. Carr was on the edge of his seat, so excited to see how this great game would end.

On the first play of the fourth quarter, with the ball at the Chicago eight yard line, Ken Strong took a handoff. But then he became trapped near the sideline and lateraled the pigskin back to a surprised Harry Newman. "Ken Strong took the ball and he went across the field. [But] he couldn't find an opening," remembered Harry Newman in a 1999 NFL Films interview. "Meanwhile, I'd gone to my right. He threw the ball back to me. The Bears all followed me. I tried to go through, find a hole. I couldn't find one. I started back. I looked and there was Ken waving his arms over the goal line. I threw the ball back to him for a touchdown."[62]

The remarkable touchdown caused the hometown crowd to moan, but also ooh and ah, because the lead changed hands once again. Late in the fourth quarter and down 21–16, the Bears came back again one final time. After a Keith Molesworth pass to Carl Brumbuagh brought the ball to the Giants thirty-three yard line, the next play saw the Bears pull off one of the most amazing plays in NFL history. Nagurski took the handoff and threw a quick jump pass to a helmetless Bill Hewitt from his left end position. After Hewitt gained fourteen yards, two Giants defenders converged on his left. Hewitt then saw teammate Bill Karr coming hard on his right and in a split second he lateraled the ball to Karr. Caught by surprise, the Giants watched the rookie from West Virginia sprint the remaining nineteen yards for a stunning touchdown.

The Windy City crowd erupted, as did George Halas on the sidelines. "We called it 'Little Pea Pass.' It worked for us many a time that play," recalled George Musso. It was the sixth lead change of the game, and it gave the Bears a 23–21 lead late in the fourth quarter. Carr asked himself, could the Giants come back one more time? He was about to see one more great play.[63]

When the Giants got the ball back again there were only a few seconds remaining. Newman faded back and threw his twelfth completion of the day (on seventeen attempts) to wingback Dale Burnett, who broke open in the Bears' secondary. Racing a few steps behind him was All-Pro center Mel Hein. Standing in between the two Giants players was the great Red Grange, and he knew quickly what Burnett wanted to do. He had just seen the Bears pull off a lateral, so Grange wasn't about to see the NFL title slip away on another.

"I could see he wanted to lateral, so I didn't go low. I hit him around the ball and pinned his arms," said Grange after the game. After the two men fell to the ground, the gun sounded ending the game. The crowd let out a big gasp and then roared for joy as the Bears won their second straight NFL title and the league's first championship game. "Red Grange saved the game for Chicago . . . that quick thinking prevented a score on the last play," said Tim Mara after the game. George Halas would always say "that play Grange made was the greatest defensive play I ever saw."[64]

The two teams left Wrigley Field knowing that they played the best they possibly could. The public and press nationwide agreed the NFL's first championship game was a big hit. The headlines and game recaps across the country proclaimed the action on the field:

> National Pro Football Honors Won by Bears in Spectacular Aerial Struggle . . . the struggle was a revelation to college coaches who advocate no changes in the rules. It was strictly an offensive battle and the professional rule of allowing passes thrown from any point behind the line of scrimmage was responsible for most of the thrills.—*New York Times*

> Fans Call Bears' Win Greatest Grid Game—*Chicago American*

> Universal comment on Sunday's game was that the Giants and Bears staged the greatest offensive battle in modern football.—Wilfrid Smith, *Chicago Tribune*

> The game was a brilliant display of offensive power . . . in one of the most spectacular games ever witnessed.—Associated Press

> Chicago Bears Capture "World Series" of Pros. . . . [The] most dramatic football game ever played.—*Burlington (North Carolina) Daily-Times*

> I advocated their forward pass rule for the colleges last year. The Bears-Giants game is proof that it produces a more open contest with resulting

thrills for the spectators.—Dick Hanley, Northwestern University head coach, who attended the game.[65]

The first NFL Championship Game was a huge success, and Carr quietly rejoiced inside. All the hard work over the past twelve months; including taking the risk of establishing new rules to break away from the more popular college game, had paid off. After the game Carr broke down the gate receipts and announced the good news to everyone involved. The net receipts of the game, after paying the tax, park rental of Wrigley Field (cost—$3,170.77), and expenses of staging the game, were $14,606.92. Of this amount, 60 percent was to go to the players based on the meeting in Columbus. The Bears would take 60 percent of that pie for winning, which came out to $210.84 dollars per player. The Giants got 40 percent, or $140.22 per player. The two franchises received $2,101.04 each and the league received $1,460.[66]

The money was secondary—although the players enjoyed the extra cash—to Carr. The tremendous publicity by the press and the enthusiasm for a title game shown by the fans is what Carr wanted to see. "[We] are primarily interested in developing a spectacular scoring game. We haven't the pageantry that goes with college games, hence as a substitute we must offer wide open play, with frequent scoring. Then too, we are not compelled to throw as tight a wall of protection around our players. They are more mature, more experienced than the collegians and thus are better able to protect themselves."[67] The NFL now had is own identity and something to sell to the public for the future.

21

Sneakers in New York (1934)

On the eve of the 1933 championship game, President Joe F. Carr reflected on a very successful season. "Professional football has been conducted upon a high plane of sportsmanship and has increased each year in popularity. This year pro football drew the largest crowds in its history," he said to the press gathered in Chicago. Counting the championship game, the NFL saw an attendance figure of 657,594 (fifty-three of the fifty-eight games reported in newspaper accounts) fans.[1]

The NFL increased the number of games played in 1933 (forty-eight in 1932 to fifty-eight in 1933) , and Carr was correct in that the league saw an increase in the total number of fans attending games—599,561 in 1932 to 657,594 in 1933—but the average per game fell just a little, from 12,490 per game to 11,337 per game. So there was plenty of work to be done. There was no time to rest on his laurels. As for the rule changes helping open up the game, Carr was extremely pleased with the increased scoring, excitement of the games, and the reduction of tie games.[2]

The NFL had a tremendous jump in field goals made, from the embarrassing six in 1932 to a whopping thirty-nine (including the three kicked in the NFL Championship Game) in 1933. The league average for scoring jumped from 16.4 points per game to 19.4, and the tie games went down from ten to just five. The new rules would pay off in a big way in 1934, when the league didn't have one tie game. Also in 1933, Carr's recruitment of a new trio of financially capable owners paid off. By selecting Bert Bell (Philadelphia), Charlie Bidwill (Chicago Cardinals), and Art Rooney (Pittsburgh) to run NFL franchises, Carr was suddenly making the league more stable than ever before.

Table 21.1. Scoring/Tie Games Comparison

Season	*Total Points Scored**	*Touchdown Passes*	*Field Goals*	*Tie Games*
1932	788 (48 games)	42 TD passes	6 FG made	10 ties
1933	1,105 (58 games)	61 TD passes	39 FG made	5 ties

*Stats include postseason

While Carr rejoiced in these positives, he would quickly have to deal with the negatives. First up was what to do with the financially strapped Portsmouth Spartans. In 1933 the team lost money for the fourth straight year—nearly $14,000 in the hole. The small town and their not-so-wealthy board of directors just couldn't support an NFL team anymore. Spartans fans were admirably loyal but were just simply too small in number to provide big gates to help pay guarantees of $4,000 or $5,000 to the Bears or Giants—as well as a share of the gate. The owners failed to pay the players after some games too. Although they didn't want to sell the team, they had no choice.[3]

"We didn't get paid for the last three or four games [in 1933]," recalled Glenn Presnell, former Spartans halfback. "We thought if we continued to play then somehow we'd get paid. But most of us didn't—at least I didn't."[4] Carr was a big fan of the city of Portsmouth and how the team was operated. But he knew that he had to get the franchise out of there. His vision of the NFL being a big-city league was just about to swallow up and spit out the second-to-last attempt of a small-town team in the NFL. The city of Green Bay would be the only small-town franchise to survive from the NFL's humble beginnings.

The Spartans would finish with a four-year record of 28–16–7; they almost won NFL titles in 1931 and 1932, and they participated in the league's first-ever playoff game—not a bad lasting legacy for the city of Portsmouth. Although all the players are now gone, the original NFL stadium that they built in 1930—Spartan Stadium—is still around and is being used every Friday night by two local high schools. Carr attended more games in Portsmouth over those four years than any other stadium (proximity to his home in Columbus was a big factor) and would miss the quintessential setting of Spartan Stadium. He now had to find a new location for the franchise.

After the 1933 NFL season, Carr attended Major League Baseball's winter meetings in New York, as he was appointed the publicity director of minor league baseball earlier that year. By 1933 minor league baseball was in danger of collapsing. There were only twelve minor leagues in operation and most of them were in shaky financial condition. Carr eventually pumped life back into baseball's farm system, and by 1939 there were forty-one minor leagues in operation, twenty-eight of which were personally organized, sponsored, and launched by Carr.

This extraordinary achievement didn't go unnoticed in later years. In 1935, Branch Rickey, who at that time was the general manager of the St. Louis Cardinals, made Carr an offer. "If you give up football," Rickey was quoted as saying. "I'll make you the biggest man in baseball." Carr responded, "If that's the price I'd have to pay, I'll have no part of it." Carr knew where his heart was and nobody could take him away from it.[5]

At the winter meetings Carr sought out H. G. Salsinger, the esteemed sports editor of the *Detroit News*. Carr knew that pro football had failed four times in Detroit. The Heralds (1920); Tigers (1921); Panthers (1925–1926), led by Jimmy Conzelman; and Benny Friedman's Wolverines (1928) all tried to capture the fancy of the Motor City but couldn't. Even with that track record, Carr still considered it a prime location for an NFL team. It was the perfect spot for the struggling Spartans.

Carr met with Salsinger, who was well respected in the city when it came to his knowledge of sports. His connections would be vital in finding an investor. Salsinger was receptive to the idea of helping the league, so President Carr commissioned him an agent. Salsinger returned to Detroit and started to put together a committee of influential sportsmen, but they were still missing a key investor who would put up the money to buy the Spartans. While having lunch at the Detroit Athletic Club, Salsinger's group saw Leo Fitzpatrick, an executive at WJR radio in Detroit. The group thought Fitzpatrick's boss was the perfect man to invest—he had money and was a big football buff. Fitzpatrick listened to the proposition, liked it, and promised to relay the information to his boss—G. A. Richards.

George Arthur Richards was a forty-five-year-old millionaire who was born in Illinois before moving to Detroit. In 1911 he became a very successful salesman for a tire company, which gradually developed into him running his own automobile dealership. Richards eventually sold his auto franchise to General Motors for a reported $100,000 to go into the emerging radio industry. The flamboyant Richards invested in two 50,000-watts stations in Detroit (WJR radio) and Cleveland (WGAR). In 1937 he would add KMPC of Hollywood, California, and his empire would be called the Richards Stations.

In 1934 Richards was an established star in the radio industry, and WJR in Detroit was the city's most popular station, nicknamed "the Good Will Station." Richards was intrigued by the offer to own a franchise and felt honored that Carr would seek him out to invest. "My father was a rather small, five feet eight, but vocal man," says Rozene Supple, daughter of George Richards. "He always enjoyed sports, so it was a perfect fit for him." Richards was a fan of the NFL and had the financial means to support a franchise. It was a perfect combination. Carr then arranged for Richards to meet with Spartans executive Harry Snyder in Detroit to discuss the compensation for transfer. "It did not take much persuasion for me to enter the pro game," Richards said in October of 1934.[6]

On March 23, one day after returning from Detroit, Snyder traveled to Columbus to confer with Carr on the negotiations relative to the transfer of the Spartans to Detroit. In his office Carr heard the terms in detail and announced that the agreement would be completed in ten days, because the Spartans shareholders had to officially sign off on the deal. On April 5 the stockholders met in the Shelby auditorium and agreed to sell. Richards and his syndicate agreed to purchase the Spartans for $15,000, which included the contracts of head coach Potsy Clark and all the players. He also agreed to pay off the remaining $6,500 (Lions media guide says $7,952.08) debt of the Portsmouth owners. Richards not only had an NFL franchise, he had an experienced, well-stocked, well-coached team.[7]

Richards announced that the franchise's front office would include William Alfs, a local Detroit attorney, as vice president; Cy Huston, who operated billiard halls and bowling centers in Ann Arbor and Detroit, as general manager; and P. M. Thomas, an executive at WJR radio, as secretary-treasurer. He then revealed that the team would play its home games at University of Detroit Stadium (capacity 25,000). It was also announced that the new franchise would drop the Spartans nickname. Just like George Halas did in Chicago, Richards honored the city's baseball team, the Tigers, by choosing the ball team's more ferocious counterpart and named the squad the Detroit Lions. A team spokesperson would say, "The lion is monarch of the jungle and we hope to be the monarch of the league."[8]

On April 10 Carr and Snyder attended a luncheon at the Statler Hotel in Detroit to officially announce the transfer and introduce the newest NFL franchise to the press. In a room filled with newspaper writers, newsreel cameras, and team executives, Carr, and Cy Huston (business manager) put their signatures on the league's paperwork. While speaking to the press (which included Tod Rockwell of the *Detroit Free-Press* and Frank MacDonell of *Detroit Times*), Carr stated he was thrilled to have Detroit back in the league and made a bold prediction for the NFL.

> I am interested in the development of the Detroit team. We have had several offers to place a team in this city, but have waited until the situation was placed in able hands. The pro game will be a success here. Detroit is recognized all over the country as a great sports town, and from what I already have learned, it will be represented by one of the best teams in the loop.

> Some outstanding critics were skeptical [of pro football] back in 1920. But a few years from now a crowd of 100,000 persons won't be unusual at a league professional game. As far back as 1925, 77,000 spectators saw the Bears and Giants play in New York.[9]

Carr's vision got the best of him. He could see the future of the game growing, but Detroit was a city that had already seen several teams fail. But in his head, Carr could see it—a stadium with 100,000 screaming NFL fans. After returning from Detroit, Carr sat down with his secretary, Kathleen Rubadue, to start sending out the *NFL Bulletins* to all team owners. The purpose of these bulletins was for the president's office to release league information on player's contracts, free agents, suspended players, rules, meetings, and anything pertaining to the NFL. Carr had started sending out a version of these bulletins as far back as 1932 and very few issues have survived. On April 26, 1934, he sent out *1934 NFL Bulletin*, number 1 (four pages in length) in which he covered, among other things, the announcement that George Preston Marshall had become the publisher at the *Washington Times*; the potential of a St. Louis franchise; a congratulatory letter to the new ownership in Detroit; and the members of the NFL Rules Committee, which included George Halas (chairman), Lud Wray, Steve Owen, Curly Lambeau, and Potsy Clark.[10]

Rubadue would type up the bulletins and mail them out. In 1934 he would send out a total of twenty-three bulletins. In the second *NFL Bulletin* (June 23), he announced the dates for the summer meeting, June 30 and July 1, at the Commodore Hotel in New York. The two-day session kicked off at 2:00 p.m. with Carr, Storck, and the ten NFL franchises all present. Carr announced that Dan Topping, a Greenwich, Connecticut, sportsman and golfer had purchased an interest in the Brooklyn Dodgers, joining John "Shipwreck" Kelly, who remained as team president. The league accepted the application of the Detroit franchise, and Carr called on Richards and Huston to give a few remarks which were "well received."[11]

Carr then introduced Bert Bell to the group, because this was his first-ever owners meeting. Bell gave a few short remarks that were "also well received." The owners must have been in a giddy mood, as they awarded the 1933 championship to the Bears next. Then a motion was brought up by Lud Wray and seconded by George Preston Marshall "that beginning with the 1934 season the game for the League Championship between the Eastern and Western be played in the Eastern section, the following year in the Western, and alternate each year."[12] The motion carried easily. This was a simple rule for the owners to make by alternating sites for the annual championship game. Since the 1933 game was played in Chicago (Western team), the 1934 game would be played in the East.

The owners then agreed to "have each club install in their home parks an electric clock that was in sight to spectators and records actual playing time during the game (cost: $150); they reelected Carr and Storck for one year; and that all officials wear arm bands, designating positions: R for referee; U for umpire; H for head linesman; and F for field judge. Arm bands are to be furnished by home club and created by President's office." All motions carried.[13]

Before the first day ended Tim Mara made a motion that the "President be authorized to purchase 100 copies of book on professional football being published by Dr. Harry March, for distribution by Pres. in manner he deems best for the League." The motion carried. Published in 1934, *Pro Football—It's Ups and Downs: A Light-Hearted History of the Post-Graduate Game* would go down as the first ever single-volume book on the history of pro football. Printed by the J. B. Lyon Company of Albany, New York, the book contained 160 pages and forty-two photos on the history of the game beginning with the "Birth of Pro Football" in western Pennsylvania and going through the 1933 season with the Bears as champions of the NFL.[14]

In short detail, and over time with inaccurate information, March wrote about the sport's important men, great players, key rules, famous games, and big moments. Within the pages were photos which included images of the six Nesser brothers, a head shot of NFL vice president Carl Storck, team photos of every NFL champion since 1920, and (on page 98) a nice studio portrait of NFL president Joe F. Carr.

The book came out in limited release for seventy-five cents in leather and one dollar in binding and was sold at the ticket offices of the New York Giants and Brooklyn Dodgers. The book was also advertised in Giants programs as a favor by his good friend Tim Mara. Carr's office bought 100 copies, and he sent them out at his discretion. As the years passed March's book became a staple for sportswriters and authors who took his book as gospel when writing future books on the history of professional football. March mainly wrote his book on memory and didn't do any real research. In the end March's book should be taken for what it's really worth—"a light-hearted history of the post-graduate game." Over time the book has become a tough volume to find. In 2009 Abebooks.com listed six copies of March's book with prices ranging from $245 to $400, with a signed one listed at $1,250.[15]

The second day began a 1:30 p.m., and the owners agreed to several rule changes: "that a player entering the game can talk to teammates; game officials tell team when last time-out is used; and any off-side penalty inside 10-yard line, is half the distance, instead of 10 yards." After the rules discussion Bert Bell brought up a motion (seconded by Tim Mara) that the "League obtain a suitable permanent trophy, to be known as the

'Ed Thorp Memorial Trophy,' said trophy to be transferred from year to year to the team winning the championship; each team winning the championship to be presented with a small replica of permanent trophy which remains property of championship club."[16]

The motion carried and it was a great gesture by the owners to honor a very successful and popular football man. Ed Thorp was a respected college football official whose family ran a sporting goods store in New York. Thorp had worked the January 1 Rose Bowl matchup between Columbia and Stanford as the side judge before dying of a heart attack on June 23 at the age of forty-eight. Thorp was good friends with Carr, Bell, and Mara, and they all thought this would be a great honor to bestow on their fallen comrade. It was also a great idea to have a formal trophy awarded to NFL teams for winning the NFL title—as the Ed Thorp Memorial Trophy became the precursor of the NFL's Super Bowl Lombardi Trophy.[17]

To wrap up the summer meeting, a motion called for "the President to develop a Professional Football Rule Book, for distribution among members, such a book to be ready on or before August 1, 1934."[18] The motion carried and Carr put together an NFL rule book for every team. Upon returning to his office Carr received a letter from the family of Ed Thorp.

My Dear Mr. Carr:

Words fail me in expressing to you the deep sense of appreciation I feel towards you for your devotion to Ed [Thorp] in having the league offer a Memorial Trophy in his name. I don't know of anything finer in the field of sports. . . . Lots of thanks. Sincerely yours,

Tom Thorp[19]

The letter from Ed Thorp's brother meant a lot to Carr; he put it in his scrapbook, where very few letters made it. When Carr sent out the newest *NFL Bulletin* on July 7, a name under the recently released players list probably didn't draw any interest from the ten NFL owners. On the seventh line under player movements, the name of Joe Lillard appeared as being cut by the Chicago Cardinals. After Ray Kemp, the release of Lillard meant there were no black players in the NFL. Starting with the 1934 season and going until the summer of 1946, when a foursome of black players (Kenny Washington and Woody Strode signed with the NFL's Los Angeles Rams; Marion Motley and Bill Willis signed with the All-America Football Conference's [AAFC's] Cleveland Browns) joined professional football teams, no black players would play in the NFL.[20]

Historians and sportswriters have claimed that there was a "gentlemen's agreement" that excluded black players from the NFL. In the league minutes from those years, there is no such rule on record. Joe F. Carr had always allowed black players to play in the league for the past thirteen seasons, as thirteen black players played in the NFL over those years. He also covered black athletes as a sportswriter, and he allowed his Panhandles team to play against black players. Even as late as 1921, on November 6, he invited the Akron Pros, with Fritz Pollard and Paul Robeson, to play his squad in his hometown of Columbus.

The disappearance of the black players in the NFL has always been a mystery that nobody wanted to solve. Owners such as George Halas and Art Rooney gave the same answers when asked the question of the supposed "gentlemen's agreement." "There weren't very many black ball players at that time." "Blacks just didn't play football." "As far as I'm concerned there was no such thing [as an agreement]. I can sincerely tell you that that was never part of our club," said Art Rooney. "In no way, shape or form," recalled George Halas in 1970. While writing his book *Pro Football: It's Ups and Downs* in 1934, Harry March wrote two pages on early black players and claimed that "there is no rule against it . . . there is no such agreement in the football League . . . such a rule would likely lead to litigation, the colored man claiming his constitutional rights of equality were being violated."[21]

No documents have been found to suggest an anti-black policy existed in the NFL. The answer may lie more in the time period of the so-called agreement. As scholar Gerald Gems wrote in 1988, "The Depression took both an economic and psychological toll on white America, as blacks were perceived as threats, or at least competitors for jobs."[22] The thought of paying a black player over a white one probably didn't make sense at this time. In the subsequent years, several owners did try to sign black players. In 1934 Rooney wanted to bring Kemp back but didn't and Halas tried to sign Ozzie Simmons (Iowa) in 1936 and Kenny Washington (University of California at Los Angeles) in 1939 to no avail.

One of the supporters of a "gentlemen's agreement" could have been George Preston Marshall, who openly expressed his anti-black opinion in public and was the last NFL owner to reintegrate his team (in 1962) after the so-called ban was lifted in 1946. "I definitely don't like to hear it. But I do think you've gotta talk about the times that this all happened," says Jordan Wright, granddaughter of George Preston Marshall. "For him it was a business decision. He didn't want to lose his fan base. Now he didn't triumph the cause of the underprivileged or the lower classes or other races. He did not. So I hate to have to defend him in that. It makes me very uncomfortable and it's a legacy that I'm stuck with. I don't like it.[23]

"I just wish people would at least put it in context of the period of the day and how it was for everybody. I don't think anybody wanted to stick their neck out. I don't think anyone wanted to say 'I'm gonna be the first person to put a black person in a prominent position in my company.' He certainly bore the weight of those bad decisions. For us it was appalling," says Wright.[24] If there was an agreement nobody actually knows what roles Carr or the other owners played in establishing the color barrier. In the end the twelve years of no black players on NFL gridirons is one of the biggest injustices in NFL history.

On July 6, 1934, the pages of the *Chicago Tribune* carried an announcement of what the newspaper described as the "most unusual football game ever scheduled." This game would be played on the evening of August 31 at Soldier Field, the city's magnificent lakefront stadium, and the participants would be a professional team, the Chicago Bears of the NFL, and a squad of college All-Americans made up of players who had just completed their eligibility in the previous season (1933).[25]

The man behind this idea was Arch Ward, the esteemed sports editor of the *Chicago Tribune*, who established Major League Baseball's All-Star Game the previous summer in Chicago. When Chicago's Century of Progress World's Fair was extended into 1934, Mayor Ed Kelly of the city asked Ward to arrange yet another unique sporting event. When the announcement of the game appeared in the *Tribune* on July 6, Ward said that "the game will stand as football's contribution to the Century of Progress Exposition."[26]

The game was to be sponsored by the *Tribune* and the proceeds were to be donated to Chicago-area charities. Ward announced that major newspapers across the country would help in conducting a national vote by fans to select the College All-Stars team and coaches. Many conferences objected to the game, but most college coaches felt it was a great honor. In the end nearly thirty newspapers worked with the *Tribune* in conducting the vote. For the player poll, the two individuals at each position receiving the highest vote totals would be invited on the team, with an additional ten or so players joining as backups.

Carr gave his blessing to the game and worked with Ward to get the exhibition contest as much publicity as he could. Halas didn't mind helping his friend Ward either, by agreeing to have his team play in the game. As the contest approached, Ward waged a relentless publicity campaign in the pages of the *Chicago Tribune* by painting the matchup of professional and collegians as an event that football fans across the country were eagerly anticipating. He also billed the College All-Stars as the "People's Team."

Balloting closed on July 25 and a total of approximately 165,000 votes had been cast. Among the stars selected were halfback Beattie Feathers (Tennessee); quarterbacks Bernie Masterson (Nebraska) and Joe Laws (Iowa);

fullback George Sauer (Nebraska); and ends Bill Smith (Washington) and Sid Gillman (Ohio State). Most of the college stars selected had just signed pro contracts—which didn't make their respective NFL teams too happy. As a matter of fact, Feathers and Masterson would be playing against their future teammates as Halas had signed the duo to play for the Bears.

As for the coach, Noble Kizer of Purdue was selected by the fans, and he would be pitted against the great football mind of George Halas. A few weeks before the game, Carr attended a baseball meeting at the Hotel New Yorker in the city and was asked to compare the two sports he had helped organize.

> This avid interest in all its phases is responsible largely for the amazing success of professional clubs because of the healthy increase in attendance at pro grid games each year since the National Football League was organized in [1920], I believe that I am making no mistake in predicting that in a few years it will outdrew baseball or any other sport, game for game.
>
> And in making this predication, I am confident that baseball's best days are in the future. That there is an increase of interest in baseball—but an increase that is not comparable to that in football.[27]

Carr's unrestrained belief in the NFL and the game of professional football never seemed to hold back his imagination. He truly believed the words he spoke when talking about the future of the sport. It was not just hollow talk to him. It was his vision, and he could see it in his mind. He could see what the sport could become.

On August 31 the *Chicago Tribune* Charity Football Game took place at Soldier Field featuring thirty-five college stars and the NFL's Chicago Bears. One hundred and thirty newspapers from twenty-two states had requested press credentials, while WGN radio carried the game. After visiting with Ward on the field, Carr was one of the 79,433 fans to jam into the stadium (sitting in section 21 of the grandstand) to see a clash of styles. From the start the crowd was mesmerized by the pageantry of the game, starting with the spotlight introduction of the collegiate squad in an otherwise darkened stadium. As for the game itself the two teams didn't give the large crowd much to cheer about. The Bears were playing their first game of the season, and the college squad had been together for only a few weeks. The game ended in a scoreless tie.

Carr hated to see games with no scoring, especially when weather wasn't an issue. Writing in the September 14 edition of the *NFL Bulletin*, he said, "COACHES should be instructed to use as much open play as possible in all of our games. The more you open the game up, the larger our crowds will be." Despite the lack of scoring in the charity game the reaction by the press and fans was very encouraging. The Associated Press wrote, "The result was a moral victory for the All-Stars, who out-played the National Football League team, out-gaining and out-maneuvering their foes with dazzling speed," and Ward included in his recap that "[It] was a football game long to be remembered." After the game the *Tribune* had $21,000 left to spread out over the three local charities. The exhibition game was a complete success. The NFL's fifteenth season began on September 9, and for the entire year it looked as if two teams in the same division would make history.[28]

The newly formed Detroit Lions roared out of the gate by winning their first seven games—all by shutouts. The city of Portsmouth would have been proud of "their boys." After three more wins, the Lions under Potsy Clark stood at 10–0. Equally as dominating were the Chicago Bears, who also won their first ten games by outscoring their opponents 240–57. Behind the blocking of Bronko Nagurski, the Bears' rookie halfback Beattie Feathers made NFL history by becoming the first player to rush for 1,000 yards in a single season. Feathers finished the 1934 season with 1,004 yards (averaging an amazing 8.44 yards per carry). With back-to-back games to be played at the end the season, the two powerhouse teams were on a collision course to decide the Western Division title.

As the season was rolling along, President Carr was faced with a crisis. The Cincinnati Reds franchise was in big trouble. Kearns and McCoy, who brought the team into the NFL in 1933, handed over the franchise to a five-man group of investors before the season started. But the team was a disaster in every single way, as they scored a paltry ten points in eight league games and attendance was lagging. Only 2,000 fans showed up for the game against the Cardinals on October 7, and three weeks later the Reds moved their game against the Lions to Spartan Stadium in Portsmouth.

The end came on November 5 when the club announced it was surrendering its franchise to the league because it could not pay its players or bills. The next day the Reds took the field for the last time. The game was a classic. At Temple Stadium against the Philadelphia Eagles, and with morale low, the Reds lost 64–0. Carr worked quickly to move the Reds franchise. He contacted the St. Louis Gunners, a very successful independent team that had been trying to get into the NFL for several years, to see if they would take on the Reds players and finish the remaining three NFL games on their schedule. They agreed.

On November 11 Carr traveled to St. Louis to attend the Gunners' first NFL game against the Pittsburgh Pirates. After speaking to the crowd of 13,700, Carr sat with St. Louis mayor Bernard Dickman to witness the Gunners pull off a surprise 6–0 win over the Pirates. The Gunners would go on to lose the remaining two games. Carr was satisfied that his league didn't have to cancel the games because of the failed Reds owners. But he wasn't too happy with himself by being so wrong in choosing the ownership to begin with. He didn't want the league to experience anymore setbacks like this.

As the season wound down the New York Giants wrapped up the Eastern Division with a mediocre 8–5 record. The only good thing was that they would be hosting the 1934 NFL Championship Game at the Polo Grounds. Carr and the rest of the league were gearing up to see who would come out of the West, with the Bears and Lions about to play two games for all the marbles—with one of the games making NFL history. Early in the season Lions owner G. A. Richards saw that his team was struggling at the box office. In their first five home games, the Lions averaged 11,600 fans per game, and with the Tigers in the World Series, Richards saw his team usually on the back page of the sports section. So he came up with an idea that changed the NFL forever.

Although NFL teams had played games on Thanksgiving before, Richards was about to take it to a whole new level. He contacted George Halas to see if he wouldn't mind playing their game in Detroit on turkey day so he could have the Lions participate in a game he could help promote as a "unique sporting event" in the Motor City. Richards wanted to make the Thanksgiving Day game an annual contest for his Lions. Halas said he would if Carr would say yes. Carr thought it was a great idea and gave the teams the go ahead. Richards advertised the game heavily and made arrangements to have the game nationally broadcast on NBC radio, thus becoming the first NFL game to be aired from coast to coast. Well-known sports announcer Graham McNamee did the play-by-play, with Don Wilson doing "color."

On November 29 in Detroit, a large crowd of 25,000 (a season high) and ninety-four stations nationally settled in to watch and hear the NFL's two best teams slug it out. Early on the Lions built a 16–7 lead, and the home fans were going crazy. In the third quarter Jack Manders kicked two field goals to narrow the lead to 16–13. Then the Bears pulled off the biggest play of the game when Joe Zeller intercepted an Ace Gutowsky pass and returned it to the Lions' four yard line. The Bears then once again turned to the play that won the famous 1932 indoor game, when Nagurski faked a line plunge, stepped back, and fired a touchdown pass to Bill Hewitt.

The Bears held on and won 19–16. Three days later the Bears won the rematch and finished the season with a perfect 13–0 record. George Halas's 1934 Bears might have been the greatest team in NFL history up to that point, as no other team had completed a season unbeaten and untied in the league's first fifteen seasons. Now they just had one game remaining to finish the job. The NFL's second annual championship game would be a rematch of the first.

Although the Giants had an up-and-down regular season, they were still one of the league's best. They had faced the Bears twice, losing 21–7 at Chicago and by one point (10–9) on November 18 at the Polo Grounds, where an NFL season-high crowd of 55,000 watched the tight contest. Tim Mara was confident in his team's chances, and he was anxious to see how the NFL's showcase game would play in the city of New York: "The public finally has come to realize that professional football is strictly on the level. The public realizes that it must be on the level or a franchise wouldn't be worth a quarter. The result is a steady growth in crowds."[29]

But what kind of crowd would show up at the Polo Grounds on December 9 ? Going into the game the Bears were a heavy favorite. The game would feature two Hall of Fame coaches (Halas, Owen) and ten future Hall of Fame players (Bears with six—Red Grange, Bill Hewitt, Walt Kiesling, Link Lyman, George Musso, and Bronko Nagurski; Giants with four—Red Badgro, Ray Flaherty, Mel Hein, and Ken Srong). The game would also see one of the strangest midgame adjustments ever, and the most explosive fourth-quarter scoring spree in NFL championship game history.

The Bears traveled to New York with two players who would miss the game; All-Pro guard Joe Kopcha and all-world rookie Beattie Feathers had injuries that prevented them from suiting up. The Giants, on the other hand, had something else in their favor. The night before the game, freezing rain and cold temperatures (that would top off at nine degrees at kickoff) made the home turf at the Polo Grounds a sheet of ice. Any speed the Bears thought they had would be negated by the frozen field.

As a very large crowd of 35,059 brave fans took their seats—including President Carr in his south-side box seat—the Giants' brain trust was about to make a decision that would go down in NFL lore. Giants end Ray Flaherty started to kick at the icy turf and then approached coach Steve Owen with an unusual idea. "[Coach] it may sound crazy, but one day when I was playing for Gonzaga the ground was just like this. We switched from cleats to basketball shoes and got some traction." Owen thought it couldn't hurt so he summoned clubhouse attendant Abe Cohen and gave him the task of going over to Manhattan College to gather up all the basketball sneakers he could and bring them back to the Polo Grounds. Just before kickoff Cohen took off to get the sneakers.[30]

The game began with the Bears taking an early lead behind the power running of Bronko Nagurski. The Giants seemed to be on their heels, sliding backward all throughout the first half, as Halas's men went into halftime with a 10–3 lead. The Bears were one half away from a perfect season. But the game was about to change. The Bears had increased their lead to 13–3 when Cohen arrived with a huge box of sneakers. The Giants grabbed them and put them on as the fourth quarter was about to start. The

Giants then exploded with a barrage of big plays. First, rookie halfback Ed Danowski threw a twenty-eight-yard touchdown pass to Ike Frankian. On their next possession, after taking over on the Bears' forty-two yard line, the Giants only needed one play to score, as Ken Strong burst up the middle for a touchdown. A short while later Strong scored again (eleven-yard run) but missed the extra point. It didn't matter. To finish the scoring, Danowski stunned the Bears with a nine-yard dash around right end.

After it was all done, the Giants and their "magic sneakers" had scored a remarkable twenty-seven fourth-quarter points. No other world championship game or Super Bowl has seen that many points by one team in the final quarter. Tim Mara's Giants were world champions for the first time since 1927 and spoiled the Bears' undefeated season. "I never was so pleased with anything in my life. In all the other contests with the Bears I always hoped the whistle would blow and end the game. Today I was hoping it would last for a couple of hours," Mara said to the *New York Times*.[31] Did the sneakers really help the Giants win? After the game there was a difference of opinions.

> I think the sneakers gave them an edge in that last half, for they were able to cut back when they running with the ball and we couldn't cut with them.—Bronko Nagurski, Bears fullback

> I'm glad to hear our basketball shoes did the Giants some good. The question now is, did the Giants do our basketball shoes any good?—Neil Cohalan, Manhattan basketball coach

> I don't think the shoes made that much difference. Any back can run through a hole.—Ken Strong, Giants halfback.[32]

Whether the shoes helped or not, the bottom line was the Giants won 30–13. In NFL history the game has simply become known as the Sneakers Game. George Halas hated the outcome but was gracious in defeat. "They deserved to win because they played a great game in that second half." For the second straight year the NFL's championship game had delivered a fantastic spectacle. Carr couldn't be more pleased. "I think we all agree it is a marvelous showing and congratulations are due everyone who had anything to do with its promotion." The following morning Carr called a special NFL meeting to award the championship trophy to the New York Giants.[33]

At 10:00 a.m. the day after the Sneakers Game, President Carr and the other NFL owners gathered in one of the conference rooms at the Victoria Hotel to hand over the first ever Ed Thorp Memorial Trophy. Carr said a few "words of congratulation" to Tim Mara and handed over the two-foot silver-plated trophy to a smiling Giants president Jack Mara. The NFL's

Thorp trophy was produced by the Rosenthal Jewelry Company of Washington, D.C., one of the largest dealers in trophies in the country, and its president, Mr. Goldnamer, was a close friend of Ed Thorp. A photo of Carr handing over the trophy to the Maras, surrounded by all the NFL owners, was snapped and published in newspapers all over the country. It was a great moment for the NFL.[34]

At the presentation meeting the owners passed a few new rule changes, as well as agreeing "that each league club be compelled to play the same number of League games starting with the 1935 season." The league was looking like a big-time sport to the press and public. It was being operated by smart and successful sports promoters-owners and with the addition of Detroit in 1934, the NFL was as close to a big-city league as ever before. Richards infused new blood with his promotional ideas (radio and annual Thanksgiving Day game), and combined with the NFL's more concerted effort to promote itself (March's book, College All-Stars charity game, and trophy presentation), the league was now at an all-time high in exposure and popularity.

22

The Postgraduate Game Is Finally a Big-City Sport (1935)

The NFL celebrated a second straight successful season under the new divisional alignment along with two exciting championship games. The league announced the gate receipts (after expenses) at $44,852.34. The Giants' players each received $621.00 for winning and the Bears each received $414.02. Including the 1934 NFL Championship Game, the NFL surpassed 800,000 fans for the first time ever. A total of 808,097 spectators attended sixty-one league games—averaging 13,247 fans per game.[1] Near the end of the 1934 NFL season Carr was asked by the United Press to reflect on his tenure as president and give his opinion on some of the all-time great players he had seen.

"Ted Nesser [is] probably the best defensive player the game has known. His ability to diagnose plays was amazing. He could play any position. As a college player, [Red] Grange was an outstanding ball carrier. Now he is an excellent blocker and a strong defensive man. Jim Thorpe could do anything that any other football player could do. He was a great ball carrier, a superb kicker, a vicious tackler and a good passer."[2]

Carr picked Thorpe as the greatest of them all. He also mentioned Bronko Nagurski, Ernie Nevers, Paddy Driscoll, Cal Hubbard, Earl "Dutch" Clark, Glen Presnell, Ken Strong, and Cliff Battles as some of the greats who'd played in the NFL. Ever since the league was founded in 1920, college players were free agents and free to sign with whichever team they wanted. But the process of signing incoming players was about to be challenged by some of the new owners in the league. At this point the NFL had nine franchises (Cincinnati/St. Louis folded) and each team was free to sign any college player they wanted. Coaches and owners would write or visit with a college player after their last collegiate contest and offer them a contract. The player usually just signed the first contract offered.

In early 1935 the issue of signing college players—and raising salaries—came to a heated discussion. After two seasons of mediocre play (a combined record of 7–12–1), Bert Bell wanted to sign some better players for his Eagles squad. He set his sights on Minnesota All-American fullback Stan Kostka. After contacting Kostka by phone, Bell traveled to Minneapolis to seal the deal. Kostka said the best offer from another team was $3,500 so Bell offered him $4,000 for the season. Big Stan said he wanted an hour to think about it. After Bell increased the offer to $6,000 Kostka was still noncommittal. Bell went back to Philly without his prize recruit who eventually signed with the Brooklyn Dodgers.

Bell became discouraged. His fellow Keystone State owner was just as frustrated with the process too. "Something has to be done about new players. Our club lost just a bit less than $10,000 last year, yet when we try to sign a new man from the college ranks, we find other clubs immediately jack up the price. It becomes a wild scramble with the players in the end getting ridiculous first-year salaries from the richer teams while the tailenders, who need new talent most, get slim pickings. If no one else introduces the matter I will propose a rule whereby the first, second, and third teams will be limited to a small number of new men," said Pirates president Art Rooney to the local press.[3]

The distribution of players was now a serious issue for President Carr, and it wasn't getting any better. The crisis was about to land on his desk in Columbus—literally. On January 1, 1935, Packers head coach Curly Lambeau was in California scouting the Rose Bowl game between Alabama and Stanford. What he saw was the greatest pass receiver in college football. Alabama end Don Hutson put on a show for Lambeau and other scouts by catching two long touchdowns while showing off his trademark speed. Lambeau, who loved the passing game, and had quarterback Arnie Herber ready to fill the Green Bay skies with spirals, needed a pass catcher. Lambeau set out to do whatever it took to sign Hutson. But he wasn't the only team interested.

"Well, when I got back from the Rose Bowl, I began hearing from all the teams. One of the people who contacted me was Curly Lambeau. Anyway, there was some bidding and as it [money] went up others dropped out. Curly offered me three hundred dollars a game. . . . Finally it was just Curly and [Brooklyn Dodgers owner] Shipwreck Kelly. Each time Curly would make me an offer, I'd wire Shipwreck and he would match it," recalled Don Hutson in an interview with author Richard Whittingham. "Finally Curly sent me a contract and I just went ahead and signed it. The day I put it in the mail, Shipwreck showed up in Tuscaloosa. He said that he had been down in Florida on vacation and that he just gotten the wires forwarded down to him.[4]

"He wanted to match the three hundred dollar offer. I told him that I couldn't because I'd already signed with Curly and had put the contract in the mail that morning because I hadn't heard from him. 'Don't worry' he said. 'Sign a contract with me, too, and let me worry about it.' Well I felt I did owe it to him after our agreement. So I signed one with Shipwreck, too," remembered Hutson.[5] Just like a script from Hollywood the two signed contracts for the services of Don Hutson arrived at 16 East Broad Street in Columbus on the same morning. As Carr opened his mail he was stunned to see that Mr. Hutson signed, not one, but two NFL contracts. This was the first time ever that this had happened at the same time. What would Carr do?

Carr glanced at the postmarks on each package. The Packers postmark read 8:30 a.m. The Dodgers postmark read 8:47 a.m. Seventeen minutes difference. Carr decided that the only fair method of settling this issue was to award Hutson to the team that had mailed their contract first. Hutson was the property of the Green Bay Packers. Lambeau cheered his good fortune, and Hutson claims it was the best thing for him. "It was probably the biggest break I ever got in football. The reason is that Brooklyn was a grind-it-out type of team, in the old Ohio State tradition, a put-out-a-lot-of-dust operation. But at Green Bay, they had a real good passer in Arnie Herber, and Lambeau was a very pass-oriented coach. He emphasized passing as well as running and so it was obviously a real break for me to end up there."[6]

Hutson's arrival in Green Bay would change the fortunes of Lambeau's team, which was struggling to find younger players to replace the legends of the 1929–1931 championship teams. Carr's decision was genius, but it did shed light on an issue of how players were coming into the league and how teams were paying first-year players. In the March 2 *NFL Bulletin* that announced the signing of Don Hutson, Carr issued a statement on the signing of players. He stated, "IN all instances where more than one club files a contract for a player, the club which files the contract FIRST in the President's office is awarded the player under our rules." It was a solid rule but why was it necessary? No player should sign two contracts (by driving up the salary) and just sit back to see which one gets to the league office first. Something had to be done, and Carr announced a special owners meeting scheduled for May 18 in Pittsburgh to formally discuss the issue. At that meeting a proposal was brought up that would change the landscape of NFL teams forever.[7]

In the April 18 *NFL Bulletin*, President Carr presented to the owners his new promotional idea for the league. Carr wrote to the owners about an agreement the league had made with a leading publishing company to produce an official NFL guide. "It should be a great means of advertising for us, and I am sure will meet the approval of the entire membership." Carr then went on to say that work on the guide had already started but that he wanted the teams to have their publicity men write an article "covering the activities and history of your club" and send a "group picture of your club, together with a photograph of the President and coach of your club."[8]

Carr's promotional idea was to publish an official guide for teams, press members, and fans. He contacted the American Sports Publishing Company in New York to help with the project. American Sports Publishing (ASP) was founded by the late A. G. Spalding and was the premier sports publisher in the country at that time. Albert Goodwill Spalding and his brother operated the world's most successful sporting goods manufacturing and retail company—Spalding Sporting Goods. After his sporting goods company became popular Spalding founded the publishing house American Sports Publishing.

The ASP produced a Spalding Guide on every sport explaining instruction, rules, and history. The guides for golf, tennis, basketball, college football, and Major League Baseball contained historical and statistical information from the previous year's season. Included in the guides would also be advertising sections for the Spalding sporting goods empire. The guides would be sold at the newsstands and sporting goods stores across the country. Carr had the best in the business to produce his publication.

The first *Official Guide of the National Football League* was published and sold in 1935 at a cost of twenty-five cents. It contained roughly fifty-eight pages of photos and information. On the cover, below the title and to the left, was a list of the nine NFL franchises and an action photo from the 1934 NFL Championship Game between the Bears and Giants. Each team had their own section with the history of the franchise with accompanying photos of the team and head shots of the team's president and head coach. The remaining pages of the guide included league statistics for the 1934 season; a review of the 1934 season with scores; all-time standings (1922–1934); a list of All-Pro teams; and a rules section. On the back cover would be the 1935 NFL schedule. On page 5, President Carr wrote a one-page "Introductory": "In the face of many obstacles, professional football has now taken its place as one of the seasonal attractions for the sport loving American public, and the initial number of the National Football League Guide is offered as a chronicle of the league's activities and a medium for promulgating the official playing rules of professional football. . . . It is hoped that the new Guide will be received in the spirit in which it is published, and that it will take its place with the other annuals that represent so successfully the various athletic sports of the United States."[9]

Before the season started Carr sent bound volumes of the *Official Guide* to each owner of the league. The first guide of the NFL was one of the most innovative promotional ideas that Carr came up with during his time as NFL president and has stood the test of time. In 2009 the NFL published for the seventy-fifth time the 688-page *Official Guide of the National Football League*—currently called the *Official NFL Record & Fact Book*. The league's official record book has become a staple for anyone interested in the league and professional football. It has become the standard bearer and final word for the history of the NFL. In 1935 any football fan could buy the first-ever guide for a whopping twenty-five cents.

On May 18 Carr and the eight NFL owners (Charlie Bidwill missed because of sickness) gathered at the Fort Pitt Hotel in Pittsburgh to discuss some pressing matters. Starting at 12:15 p.m., Carr reviewed the several promotional ideas being developed by his office, including the release of another NFL publication for the fall of 1935. B. E. Callahan Publisher (Chicago) was authorized to produce a *Who's Who in Major League Football* that would be the equivalent of the very popular baseball version they published. Former *Chicago American* sportswriter Harold "Speed" Johnson along with *Chicago Tribune* scribe Wilfrid Smith would edit the magazine.[10]

Who's Who in Major League Football would also sell for twenty-five cents on newsstands and feature photos of almost every NFL player. But Carr came up with an idea that would help sell the magazine to a broader audience, by including a special coupon in each issue. When someone flipped over the cover, the customer would see attached to the magazine's title page a small coupon marked "For Ladies Only," good for a free ticket to selected NFL games. The coupon read, "This coupon may be exchanged at any box office of any club in the National Football League for a ticket entitling a lady to a grandstand seat at any one of the official games listed on the back of this coupon during the 1935 season . . . PROVIDED the holder of this coupon is accompanied by a gentleman escort who purchases a ticket to the same game."[11]

Carr was always looking for ways to get people out to the games. By digging back to his Panhandles days, he brought back Ladies Day in order to try and get more people out to NFL stadiums. In essence a buy one, get one free ticket was a good idea, and each NFL team provided Carr one home game to accompany the promotion. The owners then got down to the most important business of the meeting. Taking the floor Eagles owner Bert Bell raised a motion that changed the NFL forever.

> Gentlemen, I've always had the theory that pro football is like a chain. The league is no stronger than its weakest link and I've been a weak link for so long that I should know. Every year the rich get richer and the poor get

> poorer. Four teams control the championships, the Giants and Redskins in the East, and the Bears and Packers in the West. Because they are successful, they keep attracting the best college players in the open market—which makes them successful.
>
> Here's what I propose. At the end of every college football season, I suggest that we pool the names of eligible seniors. Then we make our selections in inverse order of the standings, with the lowest team picking first until we reach the top-ranking team, which picks last. We do this for round after round until we've exhausted the supply.[12]

Bell proposed a smarter and more balanced way of distributing college stars within the league. Then Bell and the owners laid down five key points in the selection of players that would "for the first time become operative beginning with the 1936 season."

1. At the annual meeting in February [1936], and each succeeding year thereafter, a list of first year eligible players is to be presented to each club, and their names placed upon a board in the meeting room for selection by the various clubs. The priority of selection by each club shall follow the reverse order of the championship standing of the clubs of the preceding season; for instance, the club which finished last in either division, to be determined by percentage rating, shall have first choice, the club which finished next to last, second choice, and this inverse order shall be followed until each club has had one selection or has declined to select a player, after which the selection shall continue as indicated above until all players names appearing on the board have been selected or rejected.
2. Any first year player who is not so chosen, or whose name does not appear on the list referred to above, is eligible to sign with any club in the League.
3. If for any valid reason it would be impossible for a player to play in the city by which he has been selected, if the player can show reasonable cause why he should be permitted to play in a city other than that designated for him, then through such arrangements as can be made by sale or trade with another club, he shall be permitted to play in the city he prefers, if the President of the League approves his reasons as valid.
4. In the event of controversy between a selected player and a club, the matter shall be referred to the President, and his decision shall be accepted by all parties as final.
5. In the event a player is selected by a club and fails to sign a contract or report, he shall be placed on the reserve list of the club by which he was selected.[13]

The motion was carried unanimously. President Carr and the other owners realized this was an idea that was best for the league. The NFL could maintain what has now been labeled as "competitive balance." Back then it was just a way of not killing off the weaker franchises to stockpile the strong teams. "I thought the proposal [was] sound. It made sense. Tim Mara also approved. He and I had more to lose than any other team. With our support the proposal was adopted," recalled George Halas. "People come to see competition. We could give them competition only if the teams had some sort of equality, if the teams went up and down with the fortunes of life. Of course, that meant that no team would in the future win a championship every third year and people would start saying, 'What's happened to the Giants? They aren't the team they used to be.' That was a hazard we had to accept for the benefit of the League, of professional football and of everyone in it," commented Tim Mara about the new arrangement.[14]

Carr and the NFL owners seemed to be on the same page with this issue and it would eventually be one of the biggest foundation blocks of the big-city League. Just when it looked like President Carr could relax and celebrate the growth of his league, somebody tried to oust him from his position. G. A. Richards could see that the NFL was about to take off as a big-city sport and thought the league needed a big name running it. In Pittsburgh Richards brought with him Steve Hannigan, a promoter who was responsible for the building of Miami Beach as a tourist spot, to allow him to present his ideas for the NFL. While in the Steel City, Richards tried to influence other owners that Hannigan was the right man to run the NFL. Several owners listened (George Preston Marshall was intrigued) but none were really sold on the idea. They knew Carr was the right man, and his track record as one of the founding fathers of the NFL proved that to them. But before the meeting adjourned, Marshall raised a motion (seconded by Art Rooney) that "the salary of the President be fixed at $5,000 per year—plus Secretary and office."[15]

The president's current salary was set at $3,000 per year and had been since 1929. Marshall might have thought that if they were going to get a known promoter like Hannigan to run their league, they had to offer more than the three grand. The motion carried. The election of officials wouldn't occur until the summer scheduling meeting the following month. Carr wasn't nervous; he was in this for the long run. Upon returning to Columbus Carr spent some time relaxing with his family. It was time well spent for the fifty-five-year-old sports executive. Before leaving for the one-day summer meeting that fell on Father's Day, Mary Carr handed her beloved dad a card celebrating his special day. On the front of the envelope Mary wrote "To the Father of

All Fathers. From His Grateful Daughter—God Bless You My Darling!" Inside she wrote

> *Daddy:*
> *It isn't much I know, but since you have all the love, devotion and gratitude a daughter can give a wonderful father, after all that's what really counts.*
> *My only regret, is that one lifetime is too short to repay you for all you have done for me. To have you spared to me is all I could ask for from Our Lord, His Holy Mother and the Angels.*
> *Your Lamb*[16]

The note from his daughter made the trip to Chicago on Father's Day weekend very enjoyable for Carr. He knew he was doing great things in establishing the NFL as a big-city sport, and the support of his wife and children while he was away made it easier for him to be gone. Carr arrived at the Palmer House in Chicago on June 16 to begin the summer meeting. All nine teams were present as the league approved a new constitution and bylaws with all the additions from the previous meeting included. Then the big moment arrived for Carr with the election of league officials.

G. A. Richards was present but didn't recommend anybody for the post of president. The owners reelected Carr as president, but this time they gave him a five-year contract at the new salary of $5,000 a year. Carr was overwhelmed. Ever since he was elected as president in 1921 he had worked with a yearly contract. The owners had now voted him a long-term contract with more power and a nice pay raise. His work was appreciated by all the owners. "Richards was a real flamboyant character. He was a sharpie, a hustler. With him, everything had to be a big promotion. He wanted to fire Joe and hire Steve Hannigan to be the President. Richards said, 'Look, Joe Carr's a nice guy and he's good with paperwork but what this league needs is a promoter, a man with new ideas," remembered Art Rooney in a 1977 interview.[17]

"Needless to say, Richards didn't get much support. Halas said 'Look, Richards, Joe Carr got this league started when you were still polishing windshields. If you have any ideas about dumping him, forget it,'" said Rooney. Richards' recommendation for a new leader was futile from the start. "Although my father had different ideas of who should run the league. He seemed to like Joe Carr very much," says Rozene Supple, daughter of George Richards.[18] The confidence given by the owners to Carr just reaffirmed that he was making a difference in the sport he loved. It had been twenty-nine years since he became the team manger of the Columbus Panhandles and roamed the sidelines of a professional game for the first time. Now he was at the top of his profession. With help from a group of owners who respected his leadership, he was developing a foundation that would give the NFL a solid base for the future.

Carr celebrated the good news with a nice dinner paid for by the owners. After the feast Carr presented a rough draft of the league schedule and adjourned the meeting. The reaction to Carr's new contract and salary was favorable, although Carr was somewhat taken aback by the press calling him a "czar." Most of the headlines claimed that Carr's new contract and power put him in the same capacity as Kenesaw Mountain Landis, the baseball commissioner who was given the moniker of czar after cleaning up baseball following the 1919 World Series scandal. It was not a title Carr cared for.[19]

In *NFL Bulletin*, number 7, Carr wrote to the owners that "There has been a great demand on this office from the press in all sections of the country for the schedule, which confirms my belief that interest in the League is growing by leaps and bounds." On July 20 Carr released the full NFL schedule to teams and the press. "The schedule is by far the most attractive and evenly balanced the league has ever played." In 1935 NFL teams would play a twelve-game schedule—the first time in league history each team would play the same amount of games (fifty-three regular season games).[20]

Carr's effort to promote the league as a big-time, big-city sport was finally taking shape. As the season approached Carr made agreements for football cards to be made by the National Chicle Company; he released the *Official Guide of the National Football League*; and saw to it that Potsy Clark's instructional magazine—showing how NFL players played the game—got published. The league and its players were everywhere. It was now time to start the season. "During the off-season many new players have been added to the various clubs, and it is the opinion of every club owner in the league that the 1935 race will be the closest in the history of the professional loop," Carr said to the press. Before the regular season began, Arch Ward brought back the *Chicago Tribune* Charity All-Star Game. The success of the previous contest encouraged Ward to do it again and it proved to be a bigger hit. A crowd of 77,450 jammed Soldier Field to watch the Bears defeat the College All-Stars 5–0.[21]

Carr attended the game and on the field he saw a future president of the United States suit up for the College All-Stars. Gerald Ford, an All-American center at Michigan, played his final football game. Ford, who was offered a professional football contract by the Packers, decided to go in a different direction. But he always stayed a big football fan the rest of his life. The NFL season opened on Friday, September 13, in Philadelphia with a night game between the Pirates and Eagles at Temple Stadium. Carr attended the game with NFL owners George Preston Marshall and

Dan Topping. They saw a crowd of 20,000 screaming fans cheering at the top of their lungs. For Carr it was a fantastic sight.

After the game Carr ran into one of the country's most famous columnists—Damon Runyon—and was very excited about the future of the NFL. "It looks as if this is the big year we have been waiting for. It looks as if the pro game has definitely arrived." Carr returned home basking in the start of the 1935 season. In the newest *NFL Bulletin* he wrote, "ATTENDANCE figures for opening games in the various cities far exceeded those of many previous years. The President attended three openings, and was certainly proud of the high class manner in which the games were put on in each of the respective cities."[22]

The season looked to be a success for the ever-growing league and the 1935 campaign would belong to the city of Detroit. After four years of successful play in Portsmouth and the heart-breaking end to the 1934 campaign, the franchise known as the Detroit Lions finally put it all together by winning the Western Division with a 7–3–2 record. To top it off they defeated the mighty Bears 14–2 on Thanksgiving Day to wrap up the division title. Behind the backfield play of Dutch Clark, Glenn Presnell, Ernie Caddel, and Ace Gutowsky, the Lions rushed for 1,773 yards (second in the league) and a league-high fifteen touchdowns. The NFL's best player, Dutch Clark, led the NFL in scoring with fifty-five points as the Lions made plans to host the NFL Championship Game.

After a 4–3 start the East was once again won by the New York Giants with a 9–3 record. The turning point was a 20–3 loss on November 3 to the Bears in front of a league-high 40,000 fans at the Polo Grounds. Two weeks later the Giants won the rematch in Chicago, 3–0, and then rattled off four consecutive wins. For the third straight year Tim Mara's men would play for the NFL championship. The title game was set for December 15 at University of Detroit Stadium.[23]

Despite all the success of the Lions in 1935, the championship game would be somewhat of a letdown for Richards and the NFL. With snow showers all morning, only 15,000 fans—paying three dollars a ticket—ventured out to see the NFL crown their champion. The snowy field was muddy and slippery but it didn't slow down the Lions running game. After the kickoff the Lions completed their only two passes of the game—including a twenty-six-yard completion to Frank Christensen—that led to a two-yard touchdown run by Ace Gutowsky. After an interception the Lions scored again on a weaving sideline-to-sideline forty-yard run by Dutch Clark. Even before everyone could sit down the Lions were ahead 13–0.[24]

The two teams played a scoreless second quarter before heading into the locker rooms. President Carr spoke to the crowd at halftime and got a cheer from the pretty soaked Lions faithful. Five minutes into the third quarter, the Giants finally put a touchdown on the board behind a Ken Strong touchdown catch. But in the final period the Lions would never let the Giants come close to scoring again. Late in the game a blocked punt led to a short touchdown run by the Lions. Then a short time later an interception return set up another short scoring run by the Lions. After just two years in Detroit, the Lions were world champions. The 26–7 win was rejoiced throughout the Motor City.

Total receipts from the game totaled $33,477 with the Lions players getting $313.35 per man and the Giants getting $200 each.[25] The championship game wasn't quite as exciting as the previous two, but nonetheless it was still a success. Carr was satisfied with the totals but was still concerned about the game being affected by bad weather. Writing in the *NFL Bulletin* after the game, Carr expressed his feelings toward the championship game and how the NFL could continue to grow.

> IN addition to the splendid crowd which turned out on a very disagreeable day at Detroit, you would all have been proud to see the splendid sportsmanship and fine display of skill put on by both clubs participating in this contest. Hard fought every minute, play was extremely clean, and the newspaper men were loud in their praise of the fine exhibition.
>
> IT was gratifying to note the number of out of town newspaper men who were present at the game, all of which indicates the ever increasing interest in our League by the public, press and radio. I know we will all do our best to see that this is continued.
>
> DON'T forget that even though the regular season is over we should try to keep some Professional Football matter before the public throughout the entire year. Every time the opportunity presents itself the name of your club should be in your local papers.[26]

Carr's last statement was his way of encouraging his franchises to promote their teams as much as they could all year round—365 days. The NFL was finally becoming a big-city sport and the league needed to act like it.

23

Packers, Redskins, and the NFL Draft (1936)

Carr had now finished fifteen years on the job as president of the NFL. He had a long-term contract and was considered among his peers to be one of the finest sports executives in the country. He was on top of the world. In January of 1936 Carr was asked by the Associated Press to write a recap on the just concluded NFL season. The article appeared in newspapers all across the United States:

> The National Football League enjoyed the best season of its history during 1935. Not only was attendance the largest, but many outstanding critics thought the play by all teams was superior to any preceding year. This was due largely to the fact that the rules operative in the National League were becoming more thoroughly used by the coaches, and the players who had served in the league, together with the newcomers, seemed to have a finer grasp on them. . . .
>
> The open type of play and the revival of the field goal kicking brought about through restoration of the goal posts to the goal line has proved the wisdom of the changes made by the professional league, and is evidenced by increased interest and attendance in every city in the circuit. . . . The outlook for 1936 exceeds all previous seasons. The crop of football players that will graduate next June and become eligible for National League competition has never been so large, and with the personnel our clubs now have and the additions that can be made from the boys who graduate, each team should be stronger for 1936.[1]

Carr was once again pleased with the league's attendance figures as 745,508 fans attended the fifty-four NFL games. The figures were extremely close to the previous season with an average of 13,805 per game

(13,247 per game in 1934).[2] He was also pleased with the play on the field. It had now been three full seasons of divisional play and the implantation of the wide-open rules. In 1935 Doug Russell of the Chicago Cardinals led the league in rushing with 499 yards and Ed Danowski led the league in passing yards (794 yards) and touchdown passes (ten). But the player who made the most impact was Packers rookie end Don Hutson. Hutson led the NFL in touchdowns scored with seven. He would accomplish this feat *eight* times during his eleven-year career and go down as the NFL's greatest receiver before Jerry Rice arrived in 1985. In addition to the great individual performances the league's scoring average increased each year:

1933—1,105 points scored (19.4 points per game)
1934—1,290 points scored (21.5 points per game)
1935—1,158 points scored (21.8 points per game)

Carr's vision of a big-city, big-league sport was forming right before his eyes, and he wanted his league to keep getting bigger and better. Sitting in his two-room office in Columbus, Carr was celebrating another fine season just completed, but on January 27 he was upstaged by his own personal secretary. On the front page of the *Ohio State Journal*, Kathleen Rubadue was featured in a story about the three secretaries in town who worked for sports executives. Accompanying the story were photos of the two minor league baseball secretaries as well as Carr's NFL coworker. Carr was now the second biggest celebrity in his office.[3]

After participating in a local bowling event for charity, Carr announced that the next NFL owners meeting would be on February 8–9 in Philadelphia. Based on the motion brought up by Eagles owner Bert Bell in 1935, this meeting would mark another milestone in NFL history. The league would conduct the first-ever NFL draft. But in 1936 Carr and the owners did not call it the draft. In the league minutes they called it the "selection of players," while the press usually referred to it as the "selection of college prospects." In 1937 the league would start to call it the draft in league minutes.[4]

On the first day two new faces appeared at their first owners meeting. After eight years of professional football as an All-Pro end with the New York Yankees (1927–1928) and New York Giants (1929, 1931–1935), Ray Flaherty was hired by George Preston Marshall as the new head coach of the Boston Redskins. Flaherty was always known as one of the smartest players in the league, and it came as no surprise when Marshall signed him to lead his team. The hire would pay off in a big way as Flaherty would coach the Redskins for the next seven years and end up in the Pro Football Hall of Fame.

The other fresh face, literally, was that of twenty-year-old Wellington Mara, who joined his father, Tim, and older brother, Jack, at the gathering. Young Wellington had now been around the NFL for eleven years and knew mostly everyone involved—including President Carr. "Joe Carr was such a good man. He was a great listener. I can remember him sitting at meetings with his glasses down at the end of his nose listening intently," recalled Wellington Mara. This first meeting and the NFL draft were eye-openers for Wellington. Soon he would make the league's biggest contribution on draft days.[5]

At 1:30 p.m. in the Ritz-Carlton conference room, the whole NFL gathered to discuss league matters and, of course, the first order of business was to select players from the college ranks. Carr announced that each team would make the selection of "5 players" from a list of "approximately 90 names that are to be listed on the blackboard in the room and [each] selection of players by each club proceeded with the inverse order of the standings at the close of the season of 1935." As the ninety names appeared on the blackboard, the owners amended the bylaws to allow each club to have "nine picks."[6]

The NFL's first draft would consist of nine rounds, and who knows where the roughly ninety names came from. Most early owners claim that they just read a few of the college football magazines—such as *Street & Smith's*—or cut out of the newspaper the most current All-American team to make their selections. No team had a scouting department to help them choose. Based on the standings, the draft order went like this:

1. Philadelphia Eagles (2–9–0)
2. Boston Redskins (2–8–1)
3. Pittsburgh Pirates (4–8–0)
4. Brooklyn Dodgers (5–6–1)
5. Chicago Cardinals (6–4–2)
6. Chicago Bears (6–4–2)
7. Green Bay Packers (8–4–0)
8. Detroit Lions (7–3–2)
9. New York Giants (9–3–0)

Although the Lions were NFL champions, the order went by winning percentage, thus giving the Giants last pick in each round. But that didn't hamper them at all because they had a secret weapon at the selection meeting—Wellington Mara. In the next hour or two, the nine NFL teams selected eighty-one college stars from a variety of backgrounds and schools. With the number one overall pick, Bert Bell selected the best player in the country. Heisman Trophy winner Jay Berwanger, a halfback from the University of Chicago, went down in history as the NFL's first-ever draft pick. But he didn't belong to the Eagles very long. George Halas wanted Berwanger really bad and offered veteran tackle Art Buss to obtain the rights to get him. Bell couldn't pass up the offer, as signing Berwanger would be very difficult. Rumors had circulated that Berwanger didn't really want to play professional football, and was asking for $1,000 a game: "I haven't made up my mind yet. I haven't signed with the Bears, but I believe the decision at Philadelphia means the Chicago club has an option on my services if I decide to play pro football."[7]

In the end Berwanger didn't sign, choosing to work for a private business, and never played professional football. The second overall pick, Riley Smith, a halfback from Alabama, did and spent three productive seasons with the Redskins. Probably the most famous name to be drafted was another Alabama star, end Paul "Bear" Bryant, who was drafted in the fourth round (number thirty-one overall). Bryant didn't sign either, but, of course, went on to be one of the greatest coaches in college football history at his alma mater. Out of the eighty-one players drafted, only twenty-four signed and played in the NFL in 1936 (four more would play in 1937), with several having Hall of Fame careers.

The Bears (behind the drafting of George Halas) took two future Hall of Famers in the first draft. First rounder Joe Stydahar, a tackle from West Virginia, and ninth round selection Dan Fortmann, a guard from Colgate. The Redskins drafted end Wayne Millner in the eighth round, who would have an early impact for the Skins in 1936 by finishing fourth in the league in receptions. The fourth and last Hall of Famer to be drafted in 1936 was second rounder Alphonse "Tuffy" Leemans, a halfback from George Washington University, by the New York Giants.

Leemans was selected by the Giants on the recommendation of young Wellington Mara. Although he was only a junior at Fordham, Wellington had already immersed himself in what was going to be his life's work—guiding the New York Giants. His forte was judging talent. He kept files and notes on hundreds of college players, and one who caught his eye was Tuffy Leemans. Wellington suggested to his father that Leemans was going to be a great player and wanted to go to Washington and visit with him. Tim Mara said, "Go ahead" and off he went. "I sent a telegram [to Leemans] setting up a meeting and signed my father's name to it," Wellington Mara recalled years later. "It was to be in front of the gymnasium at George Washington. When I got there, he thought I was a kid who wanted an autograph. He looked at me, strangely suspicious, and said he was meeting Tim Mara, owner of the New York Giants. But I was able to eventually convince him that I was in fact a legitimate emissary, and he did listen to me. And, of course, we got him for the Giants." Leemans would go on to play eight great years for the Giants. The Leemans pick was just the start to young Wellington's NFL career.[8]

The NFL's first draft was a complete success (just the fact that it was now in place) and eventually it would give the NFL another building block to lean on. Over time franchises would use the draft to build their teams and create dynasties. In 1936 it would establish a more balanced league, as the NFL would see two new franchises win division titles. The rest of the Philadelphia meeting seemed secondary to the draft, but the owners also "approved cooperation with the *Chicago Tribune* for the Annual All-Star game that would include the previous year's champion to play; awarded the 1935 Ed Thorp Memorial Trophy to the Detroit Lions; approved the Spalding J-5V football as the official game ball; and lastly that the President be instructed to secure a tenth franchise holder to enter the league in 1937, if possible." The last motion was approved with an 8-to-1 vote.[9]

The Philadelphia meeting ended with another important task for President Carr. Locating a tenth franchise would be a major challenge especially since the last city he admitted was the Cincinnati–St. Louis failure. Carr would take his time in naming the tenth franchise, but eventually he would go back to one of his all-time favorite sports cities. Returning to Columbus Carr announced there would be no summer meeting, that all that was needed to be done was the drawing up of the season's schedule, which he would do from his Columbus office. The owners would now have the summer to get their teams ready to play.

The 1936 season started on September 13 with three league games watched by a total of 44,522 fans (average of 14,840 fans per game). Three weeks later with home games in Brooklyn, Pittsburgh, and Philadelphia the NFL drew 65,800 fans with an average of 21,933 per game. Carr saw that the NFL was gaining in popularity and the attendance numbers were backing him up. "Attendance figures [are] higher than ever, the nine teams more evenly matched, and the fans more interested," Carr said to the *Ohio State Journal*. But one franchise—which would win a division title—was attracting no fans.[10]

On November 1, President Carr attended the Packers–Bears matchup in Chicago. An NFL season high of 31,346 spectators showed up to watch the Packers overcome a ten-point deficit to defeat the Bears 21–10. Behind touchdowns by Don Hutson and Clarke Hinkle, the Packers were now 6–1 and in first place in the Western Division. After the game, Bears coach George Halas praised the Packers. "Today the Packers were the greatest football team we have ever played. They were all great, the Packers outfoxed and out-smarted the Bears." After four years out of any serious title contention Curly Lambeau had his squad in the driver's seat for another championship. Carr was also impressed by Lambeau's boys: "It was one of the greatest exhibitions of football that I ever witnessed. The record breaking crowd certainly got a run for its money. The Packers played super-football. Any team that can spot the Bears 10 points in the first quarter and then win out must have something. Curly Lambeau has coached a number of great Packer elevens but this year's team as it played against the Bears seems to me, the best of all. I want to extend my congratulations to Green Bay."[11]

Carr was right that Lambeau had a great team. The rest of the season the Packers went unbeaten and finished atop of the Western Division with a 10–1–1 record (the Bears finished second at 9–3–0). They would have to play the championship game on the road, but where and who would they play? The Eastern Division race came down to two teams who hadn't challenged for an NFL title before—Art Rooney's Pirates and George Preston Marshall's Redskins. After nine games the Pirates were 6–3 and leading the underachieving 4–5 Redskins coached by Ray Flaherty. But the last three games would be a nightmare for Rooney's men.

Marshall had a bigger issue than whether his squad could win out and capture a division title. The crowds in Boston were getting smaller and smaller. In five years Marshall's team had made little progress in Boston, usually taking a backseat to nearly every other sports endeavor in the city when it came to media attention. After the 1936 home opener against the New York Giants attracted a crowd of 15,000, Marshall decided to raise the price of grandstand seats from fifty-five cents to $1.10. The increase didn't endear him to fans or the press in Beantown. The *Boston Globe* wrote, "The new price arrangement found instant disfavor with the grandstand enthusiasts of 1935."[12]

The price hike exacerbated the problem. Rumors started to fly that he would move his team if attendance didn't improve. Well, it didn't; it actually got worse. The next two games (Eagles and Cardinals) attracted a total of 11,000 fans, and the rest of the season didn't get any better. Marshall wanted out of Boston and on November 9 he told the press his possible destination:

> The nice thing about owning a pro football team is that all you have to do to move is pack your trunks. I can understand why no one came to see us play Philadelphia or the Cardinals but when they are not even interested in seeing a team like the Packers [just 11,220 fans], it is time to consider moving. Why, the Packers would draw more people in Paterson, NJ, than they did here today.
>
> There are five cities that would love to have us. Yes, Washington, my home town, has put a lot of pressure on me to move down there.[13]

Marshall hated the Boston press and always lambasted them for not giving his Redskins enough coverage in the sports pages. In the summer of 1936, Marshall married former silent-movie star Corinne Griffith, and she encouraged him to move the team to Washington. Writing in her autobiography *My Life with the Redskins*, Griffith described Marshall's relationship with the Boston press. "The Boston sportswriters were loud in their dislike of pro football. They didn't like the foreign ownership, and they didn't like George."[14]

In Boston not too many people liked Marshall—who was considered an outsider—and it was time to move on. Carr was concerned about Marshall's team and the problems he was having, so he decided to make a trip east to see firsthand what was going on. At the same time the Pirates lost two straight games, and the Redskins defeated the Dodgers—in front of just 5,000 fans at Fenway Park—to set up a first place showdown. The Pirates–Redskins game (November 29) was played in Boston, and it should have been the biggest professional football game ever played in the city. But nobody cared. Carr sat with Marshall as just 7,000 fans showed up to watch the Redskins crush the Pirates 30–0.

Behind the stellar play of All-Pro halfback Cliff Battles and star tackle Turk Edwards, the Redskins were now in first place. If they defeated the Giants the following week in New York, they would clinch the Eastern Division and play host to the NFL Championship Game against the Packers. Marshall then told the press that if the Redskins won the division, he would probably move the championship game to New York. Carr was worried about what he just saw. He didn't want the NFL's signature game played in front of the sporting press and the rest of the country in a stadium with no fans. Walking off the field with Marshall after the Pirates game, he turned and said, "OK, George, you're right."[15] The following week the Redskins shut out the Giants 14–0 to clinch the Eastern Division. The next day Carr announced where the NFL Championship Game would be played and why.

> The decision to play the game in New York was reached following a canvass of the club owners involved and of the players of the two teams.
>
> Since the playoff game is largely one in which the players are rewarded for winning the divisional titles and their sole remuneration is from the players pool made up from the gate receipts of the playoff it was decided that New York was the place in which the players would benefit to the greatest degree possible under existing conditions.
>
> New York is not only the most centrally located spot, but the danger of bad weather appears less than in any other spot with the Polo Grounds offering the best equipment for inclement weather with its large covered stadium and brilliant lighting system.[16]

Marshall was happy with Carr's decision. "We'll get a much bigger gate in New York than in Boston," Marshall said to the press. "We certainly don't owe Boston much after the shabby treatment we've received. Imagine losing $20,000 with a championship team." The 1936 NFL Championship Game was set for December 13. The crowd would satisfy Marshall (as well as Carr), but the outcome did not. Behind a forty-eight-yard touchdown pass from Arnie Herber to Don Hutson and two second-half scores, the Packers defeated the Redskins 21–6. The Packers had won their fourth overall NFL title and first since 1931.[17]

As for the gate receipts, the game attracted a nice crowd of 29,545 on just a week's notice. The league announced the receipts at $33,471 with the Packers getting $250 per player and the Redskins collecting $180 per man. Four days after the game Marshall made it official to the city of Boston—the Redskins were moving to Washington. The item was buried at the bottom of the sports page in the *Boston Globe*. Carr knew it was the right thing to do, and he was happy that Marshall was totally into supporting his franchise. The brief bad publicity on the move was well worth the stability the team would get in Washington. Marshall was well-known there and had some big ideas that he wanted to try out in the nation's capital. The ideas started with the drafting of one of the NFL's greatest passers.[18]

The day (December 12) before the championship game, the owners held a special meeting and decided from now on to hold the annual college draft in December. For the second time in less than eleven months, the NFL would continue to try and balance the talent coming into the league. The owners decided that there would be ten rounds and wrote on the blackboard 100 names of college seniors to help them choose. Carr then stated "that in as much as there was a possibility of adding another franchise to the League prior to 1937 season, in fairness to the incoming member ten players should be selected for such new incumbent team. President will be authorized to select in tenth place. If event new member is admitted, player will be eligible to team. Players will go back to pool, club in order to choose, if no pro team is added." Carr would eventually draft ten players for the incoming franchise.[19]

Three potential investors from three different teams made presentations. Mr. McCardle and Mr. Henderson came all the way from Los Angeles to make a case for the Los Angeles club, but they were shot down by Bert Bell and Art Rooney, who claimed it was "inadvisable to take L.A. in as a member at this time, due to great distance of travel." Charles Murray, a sports promoter from Buffalo, said he was willing to put down the money for a franchise, and Homer Marshman, an attorney, came from Cleveland to represent his clients about getting the Cleveland Rams, a team in the independent American Football League, into the NFL. Carr said he would take both of their applications under advisement.[20]

As the owners prepared to draft, the blackboard had several big names on it, but only one really stood out. In the second round the Brooklyn Dodgers selected Duke quarterback Clarence "Ace" Parker, who would eventually be inducted into the Pro Football Hall of Fame, and the New York Giants selected several men—Ed Widseth, Ward Cuff, and Jim Poole—who would help them continue to win. But it would be the Redskins who would hit the jackpot.

Although it was the eve of the NFL Championship Game and just a week after winning the NFL's Eastern Division, the Redskins first round pick (sixth player overall) would change the fortune of Marshall's franchise. Quarterback Sammy Baugh had just finished an All-American career at Texas Christian University and was the consensus best passer in the nation. Baugh signed a contract with Marshall, and he became an instant sensation in the NFL. The NFL draft was now in place and had its first draft day "steal."

24

Heart of Gold Continues to Work (1937)

Joe F. Carr was once again pleased with another successful NFL campaign. Writing for the Associated Press he expressed his feelings toward what the league had just accomplished.

> Professional football attendance during the past year increased by more than 20-percent over the mark set the previous year, which we consider highly encouraging and even better than the increase noted in other sports.
>
> The improvement in individual performances and the increased effectiveness of our rules, tending to encourage the offense, probably played a big part in this increase in popular favor of the National Football League.
>
> There was not a single individual performance which did not exceed the previous year's record, and practically every team in the circuit gained more ground than in 1935. Two new records were established, by Arnie Herber and Don Hutson, both of Green Bay. Herber set a new forward passing mark of 77 completed passes for 1,239 yards. Hutson in catching 34 passes, also set a new high mark in that specialty.
>
> It was a year in which many new players came into the league and made good, especially in the case of Tuffy Leemans of the New York Giants, who led the league in his first season by gaining 830 yards.
>
> The Green Bay Packers won the Ed Thorp Memorial Trophy and the league championship. . . . It is the first time Green Bay has won the Ed Thorp trophy in the four years it has been in competition. . . . We look forward to one of our best seasons in 1937 for most of the clubs in the circuit are laying plans for further improvements in their personnel, and the caliber of play should be improved. It is this factor on which we base our hopes for developing new patrons.[1]

Carr was very optimistic on how the NFL was progressing in the eyes of the public. The league's increase in attendance (745,508 in 1935 to 814,815 in 1936) continued to show the NFL president that the game was in good hands.[2] Also, with the draft in place to filter future college stars into the league, the NFL was about as stable as it ever could be. The game was now ready to take off to another level. Little did Carr know that in nine months he almost wouldn't be around to see his league take the next step.

Two months after the Packers won the 1936 NFL title, Carr scheduled the next owners meeting for February 12–13 at the Hotel Sherman in Chicago. On the first day the NFL's executive committee met to discuss a few items. First up was the selection of the NFL's tenth franchise. After much homework Carr recommended the Cleveland Rams as the league's newest team. Carr's infatuation with the city of Cleveland as an NFL destination revealed itself again. He knew the city would embrace the NFL as long as the new owners—led by attorney Homer Marshman—were dedicated to fielding a competitive team. The owners placed the Rams in the Western Division.

The owners then approved "that clubs play a schedule of 11 games in 1937; guarantee of visiting teams [from] $4,000 to $5,000; awarded the Ed Thorp Memorial Trophy to the Green Bay Packers; and approved Spalding J-5 ball for '37." After a dinner break the 1937 NFL schedule was approved. The second day saw the owners pass "that the President-Secretary salary increase [from $5,000] to $8,000 per year. The Vice-President/Treasurer from $1,000 to $1,500 per year." Carr and Carl Storck's hard work as NFL executives was once again rewarded with pay raises. To end the meeting the owners officially approved the move of the Boston franchise to Washington, as George Preston Marshall's team would now be called the Washington Redskins.[3]

After two years of just nine teams the NFL was now back to a ten-team circuit. Although the Cleveland Rams would get off to a horrible start on the field—going just 1–10 in 1937—the NFL would remain a ten-team loop (expect for 1943 when World War II reduced the NFL to eight teams) for the next thirteen years, until 1950 when the league expanded to thirteen teams. The league was stable, and Carr returned home to Columbus knowing that he had made the right decision in placing a franchise in Cleveland. It was a perfect sports city and the area was known for its passion for football. This time it was going to work. As he walked through the door at 1863 Bryden Road, Carr didn't know that he would be spending more time at home than on the road in 1937.

In Washington the newly minted Redskins were getting a complete makeover from the husband-and-wife team of George Preston Marshall and Corinne Griffith. As Marshall set up shop in the nation's capital, he wanted to make the Redskins the biggest event in the city on fall Sundays. "He took his tip from show business and at that time Corinne was around and she was helpful in that. She was very savvy, very smart." says Jordan Wright, granddaughter of George Preston Marshall. "First, he instituted these halftime shows, which were big spectaculars. It was like all a of sudden the place would turn into a circus with all kinds of entertainers and of course the marching band. Corinne then wrote the fight song, 'Hail to the Redskins.'"[4]

In order to get fans out to Griffith Stadium in Washington, Marshall hired a full 110-piece marching band to play music and to play the team's new fight song. The band and the fight song became an instant hit with fans and made Redskins games the place to be on Sundays in D.C. "Football is a game of pageantry. It derives as a spectacle from the gladiator shows of the Romans in the pages of history," said George Preston Marshall. "He encouraged men and women to attend games. It was the thing to do. Celebrities would be in his box and they'd be all over. Women would be in their furs and men in their hats. It was pretty exciting," says Wright. "It would be a big show as well as the game."[5]

"If you get women and the kids steamed up over a football game, you have papa hooked," Marshall would say about attracting the whole family.[6] Washington was about to take the NFL by storm and by the end of the 1937 season Marshall would be basking in the glory of his move south. As for Carr, 1937 wouldn't be so cheerful. On June 4 his estranged sister Mary Carr died at her home in Toledo of a heart attack. She was sixty-two years old. She left behind three grown children—sons Robert and Joseph and a daughter, Dorothy—who over the past couple of years had begun to write to Carr in Columbus.

From 1935 to 1938, Robert and Dorothy Pratt wrote to their uncle at least four times discussing their situation in Toledo. On September 16, 1935, Dorothy wrote to Carr asking him for a favor:

My dear Uncle Joe,

I won't take up much of your time with a long letter but as usual I have a favor to ask. As the football season approaches, we are looking forward to seeing some of the games in Detroit and are wondering if you would be kind enough to send us a pass as you did for Joe [her brother] last year. You don't know how I dislike to have it appear that the Pratt family is always asking favors from you when we can do nothing to repay you, and I suppose if I had as much pride as my Mother, I wouldn't do this. If it is impossible for you to do this, please don't hesitate to say so. Although we would appreciate it very much, I don't want you to be put to any inconvenience.

We are all feeling just fine. Mother looks very well and I just wish that once in a while she could meet her family. I know she misses them a lot and would give a great deal to talk to them once in a while. Bob has started back to school, and I guess we will all be glad when he has finished his last year. I am glad tho', that he can finish, because it will mean that at least one member of our family has made the grade.

Jerry [her husband, Gerald Walsh] and I are both well and just as happy as ever. We both send our regards and hope that you will not think us too "nervy" to ask the above favor.

Affectionately,
Dorothy[7]

Carr responded on September 18:

My dear Dorothy:

I have your letter under date of September 16, and at the outset let me tell you how glad I was to hear from you, and especially to learn that your Mother and all at Toledo are well.

I, too, regret that we do not see one another more often, but you may be sure you are constantly in our thoughts, and the happiness of all of you is first in our desires.

In reference to the pass would advise, I overlooked the fact that Joe had returned to Florida, and today mailed him a pass for himself and one. When it comes please return it, and I will have another made out as you requested in your letter. If you do this at once, I will take care of it immediately.

Trusting you are well and happy, and asking you to extend the love of all the Carrs in Columbus to all in Toledo, I am as ever,

Your loving uncle,
Joe F. Carr[8]

The exchange of letters showed that Carr still cared for his relatives despite the detached relationship he had with his sister. Sending the courtesy pass to attend NFL games was just a small gesture worth doing. On December 23, 1935, Carr wrote, maybe for the last time ever, a letter to his sister in Toledo.

My dear Sister:

Am in receipt of your splendid letter under date of December 19, and as usual was mighty glad to hear from you, and found much pleasure in reading one of your composed and well written epistles.

Have not been in Toledo since I saw you last, nor have I been through there at a time when I could see you. Several times I traveled from Detroit, but always on the sleeper, so I trust this will account for me not stopping off. It is needless for me to tell you you are uppermost in my mind at all times. Was in Chicago last week and had a very nice visit with John [brother], although I could see him for just a short time. Everybody there seems to be well and happy, and things are coming along as good as can be expected. Everybody in Columbus is busy and well, and after all that is the most important thing. . . . Well, Mayme, I suppose you are busy getting ready for Christmas like everybody else. I am inclosing herewith a little remittance which I trust will be acceptable. I hope you and yours will have all the good things I want you to have, and whenever you get a chance come down and see us.

With love from all in Columbus to all in Toledo, I am as ever,

Your loving brother,
Joe F. Carr[9]

Carr's relationship with his siblings was always one of distance and eventually put a mental strain on him. Although Carr didn't spend a lot of time with his sister, he truly cared for her and wanted her to be happy. When she died Carr was visibly shaken, and this may have led to his own health issues three months later. At this time the Carr siblings numbered four—John Karr of Chicago and Michael, Joe, and Edward of Columbus.

On July 9 President Carr released the NFL schedule to the teams and press. The season was to begin on September 5 with the Eagles playing at Pittsburgh. The starting date would be the earliest in NFL history. As the season approached, Carr made his annual trip to the Windy City to attend the *Chicago Tribune* Charity All-Star Game (August 31). On the field during the pregame warm-ups, Carr talked over WGN radio about the upcoming season. A crowd of 84,560 fans showed up to watch the College All-Stars upset the Green Bay Packers, 6–0, behind a forty-seven-yard touchdown pass from Sammy Baugh (Texas Christian University) to end Gaynell Tinsley (Louisiana State University). This was just the start of a remarkable year for "Slinging Sammy."[10]

On September 10 Carr traveled to Cleveland to watch the Rams play their first NFL game against the Detroit Lions. On a warm Friday night, the city pulled out all the stops for the franchise's debut. Before the contest the city held a parade that went down Euclid Avenue and ended at Municipal Stadium. Inside, the flag was raised by Company C of the 11th United States Infantry, which was stationed at Great Lakes. To kick off the game, Mayor Harold Burton threw out the first pass—a la baseball's ceremonial first pitch. The *Cleveland Plain Dealer* wrote, "Mayor Burton drew back his arm, and let the football fly. He isn't much with a baseball—but he tosses a mean spiral."[11]

Carr was impressed to see 24,800 spectators in the stands as the Rams took the field to a loud ovation. It would be the only real cheer of the night for the hometown fans. The Lions scored three touchdowns in the first half to take a 21–0 lead. At halftime President Carr was asked to speak to the crowd from the field. The press box at spacious Cleveland Stadium was several levels up, and it took Carr a good ten to fifteen minutes to get down to the field. During his walk Carr felt tired and light-headed and had a sharp pain in his chest. Being the strong-willed Irishman he was, Carr made it to the field and delivered his speech. After watching the Lions finish off the Rams, 28–0, Carr felt a little better on the train ride home. A little over a week later his life would change.

After returning from Cleveland, Carr went back to work and had a phone conversation with his friend Bill McKinnon—a sports columnist with the *Columbus Dispatch*. While chatting to McKinnon about the Rams NFL debut a few days earlier, he was asked about his health. Carr said he was "fine, thanks to the good Lord." But Carr wasn't fine. He was tired, worn, and had trouble with severe chest pains. Soon his health took a turn for the worse and sent the fifty-seven-year-old sports executive to the hospital. Carr had suffered a mild heart attack, and on September 20, 1937, he checked himself in at Grant Hospital. The news of Carr's condition made the front page of the *Dispatch*.

Joe Carr Ill at Grant Hospital

> Joseph F. Carr, of 1863 Bryden Road, one of the most outstanding figures in professional athletics in the United States is in Grant Hospital suffering from a heart ailment, attendants said Tuesday. Mr. Carr entered the hospital Monday.[12]

Carr's family physican, Dr. Edward E. Campbell (who replaced his good friend Dr. Bob Drury, who passed away in 1933), discovered the heart condition that affected the president. "Well, he was diagnosed having a smaller size heart and the doctor predicated a prognosis that he would not live too long," says Michael Carr, grandson of Joe F. Carr. Carr's condition stabilized, and on September 22 the hospital reported him in "fair condition" and that he was resting in his own room.[13]

Carr's heart condition was very serious, and the whole Carr family was nervous that he wouldn't make it. "There is a history of heart problems in that side of the family," says James Carr, grandson of Joe F. Carr. "Coupled with that he was a smoker; we know that's bad now. Back then there just wasn't an awareness of the health risks. Plus he was a hard worker and it was probably dealing with all these heavy hitters in the NFL, it was pretty stressful. All those things contributed to that."[14]

"[The family] were terrified. When he had the heart attack my grandmother said 'Oh Joe, you won't live long.' That's all she could do. She prayed," says Michael Carr. "They were at the hospital night and day and they knew there was nothing they could do. It's just bide their time. They certainly rallied around him and hoped for the best." Carr survived the heat attack, but he was in no shape to work or do any everyday chores. He was tired and very weak, and was told to get some much-needed rest. The family would set up shop at Grant Hospital.[15]

A week later (September 29) the hospital reported his condition "as much improved last night," but he was still pretty much useless, spending all his time resting in bed. As Carr was spending his days regaining his strength, the NFL season continued on with some large attendance numbers. Out of the fifty-five regular season games in 1937, twenty attracted a crowd of at least 20,000 fans. On October 31 at the Polo Grounds in New York, the Bears–Giants contest had 50,449 fans show up. In its eighteen-year history, the NFL saw its greatest year at the gate in 1937. The numbers were very impressive.[16]

1. New York Giants (seven home games) = 250,025 (35,717 fans per game)
2. Chicago Bears (five home games) = 113,760 (22,752)
3. Washington Redskins (six home games) = 113,022 (18,837)
4. Detroit Lions (six home games) = 112,984 (18,830)
5. Brooklyn Dodgers (five home games) = 87,873 (17,574)
6. Pittsburgh Pirates (seven home games) = 91,629 (13,089)
7. Green Bay Packers (six home games**) = 77,332 (12,888)
8. Cleveland Rams (five home games) = 55,800 (11,160)
9. Chicago Cardinals (three home games) = 25,812 (8,604)
10. Philadelphia Eagles (five home games) = 23,698 (4,739)

** Packers played two home games in Milwaukee

After the first two months of the season, the Western Division was led by the undefeated Chicago Bears (5–0), while the Eastern was led by the Giants (4–1) and Redskins (4–2). The race to get to the NFL Championship Game was now heating up. On October 30 Dr. Campbell announced that Carr "will leave Grant Hospital next week after a month's treatment for a heart ailment and that Carr is in fine shape." A week and a half later on November 11, Josie, with the help of Mary and Joe Jr., took her husband home to continue his recovery. The family would rally around him with all their hearts.[17]

"When my grandfather had the serious heart condition, my father [Joe Carr Jr.] would accompany him wherever and whenever. To ensure that he was taken care of," says Gregory Carr, grandson of Joe F. Carr. "Things like, making sure he was taking his pills, his diet. That he was getting enough sleep. When my grandfather started traveling again my father went with him. He was like a sophomore in college and it was difficult.

A stressful thing for him. But he made the accommodations necessary to go to law school and travel with my grandfather at the same time." While Buddy helped his father get around, Josie and Mary took care of his needs at home. For most of the next eight months Carr would spend his time at home.[18]

As Thanksgiving arrived, the NFL's title matchup came into focus. The Bears cruised to the Western Division title behind the play of super fullback Bronko Nagurski, as Halas's squad finished with the NFL's best record, at 9–1–1. In the Eastern Division it came down to the Giants and Redskins—who were led by rookie quarterback Sammy Baugh. On November 28 the Redskins (7–3 record) defeated the Packers 14–6 in front of 30,000 screaming D.C. fans to set up a winner-take-all matchup with the Giants (6–2–2 record) in New York on the NFL's final weekend.

Marshall's first year in Washington was a big success. The six home games averaged nearly 20,000 fans per game, and his team was once again in the hunt for a championship. Even the local press was captivated by the city's newest attraction. *Washington Evening Star* sportswriter Bill Dismer wrote, "Definitely, the Redskins have 'caught on.' Whether it is the novelty of a major league professional eleven, the magic of All-America names, or the craving for football again after a long, hot summer, coach Ray Flaherty and his men have completely captured the fancy of all who have seen them."[19]

Despite being bedridden Carr must have felt extremely proud when he heard that the largest NFL crowd since 1925 (the Red Grange game in New York) showed up to watch the December 5 game in the Big Apple. A crowd of 58,285 jammed into the Polo Grounds to watch a rookie guide his team to a divisional title. Baugh completed eleven of fifteen passes and one touchdown while All-Pro halfback Cliff Battles rushed for 170 yards and two touchdowns as the Skins pounded the Giants 49–14. The forty-nine points were just eleven points shy of what the Giants had given up all year (sixty points in the previous ten games). For the second straight year the Redskins would be in the NFL Championship Game.

The 1937 title game would pit the Redskins against the Chicago Bears on December 12 at Wrigley Field. As championship week arrived, Carr actually did a few presidential tasks. He announced the officials for the game, with Bill Halloran as referee, and notified the other owners that Vice President Carl L. Storck would preside over the owner's meeting and draft to be held the day before the championship game. But as the NFL family gathered in Chicago, rumors began to fly about the future of the ill president.[20]

Three days before the title game, an Associated Press report was released that Carr would resign as league president. The report claimed that two teams favored Carr to retire to an advisory role because of his ill health. One of the owners was Detroit's George A. Richards, who always wanted a "bigger" name to be president. The other owner seemed to be George Preston Marshall. Although Marshall had a good relationship with Carr, the health issues facing the president worried him. Carr was still resting at home and unable to travel, so Marshall was keeping his options open just in case the league had to replace the current president. Upon hearing the reports, Carr spoke up: "There is absolutely nothing to the reports. I'm feeling fine, but I've got to take it easy for a while."[21]

The rumors quickly faded, but Carr's presidency had hit a crossroad. His health was important to him, as well as his family, but he didn't want to give up the thing he loved the most—the NFL. There was still too much work to be done. He would listen to his doctor, get the rest he needed, and get back to work as quickly as he possibly could. It was the Irish way.

The day before the championship game at the Hotel Sherman in Chicago, Vice President Storck presided over his first league meeting with all ten teams in attendance. It would be a sad moment for Joe F. Carr. Ever since taking over as president he had presided at *thirty-eight* consecutive league meetings, never missing one in seventeen seasons, until now. A heart attack was the only thing that could keep him away. But he knew the league was strong enough to move on and get things done. That's what they did.

After roll call the owners prepared themselves for the draft. Before they started Wellington Mara unveiled a board with 166 college players eligible to be drafted. Done by himself, Mara created maybe the first-ever scouting service and didn't keep it to himself. The whole league benefited from his knowledge and hard work, something the early owners had gotten the grasp of. Led by President Carr's philosophy, the entire organization was thinking "league first"—what was best for the league. "You had a collection of very strong-minded, strong-willed people," says Virginia McCaskey, daughter of George Halas. "Yet, they realized that in order to succeed as an entity, they had to give up some of their personal considerations and that's the way it should be."[22]

The owners went on to draft 110 players over twelve rounds, with the Cleveland Rams selecting Indiana halfback Corbett Davis number one overall. Future Hall of Famers, tackle Frank "Bruiser" Kinard (third round by Brooklyn), and center Alex Wojciehowicz (first round by Detroit), were chosen. But it was a brainy halfback from the University of Colorado that everybody wanted to see where he would be drafted. Byron "Whizzer" White was the best running back in the nation in 1937 and seemed to be a lock to go number one overall. But White had just won a Rhodes scholarship from the University of Oxford and told the NFL he would be attending the school in the fall of 1938. So as the draft's first round began, it came as a surprise when Art Rooney selected White with the number four overall pick. Most of the owners thought he had just wasted a pick. Rooney thought differently.

The meeting ended with the owners giving Wellington Mara a round of applause for all his work with the draft. Storck completed his first meeting with no headaches.[23] It was now time to decide a champion. Game day began with a brutally cold morning, as the temperature reached a high of just fifteen degrees, which limited the paying crowd to just 15,870—very disappointing considering the large crowds that showed up during the regular season. The cold weather didn't affect the play on the field. The first quarter fireworks included three touchdowns as the hometown Bears took a 14–7 lead. After a scoreless second, the fans were about to witness more wide-open action.

Early in the third quarter Sammy Baugh hooked up with All-Pro end Wayne Millner for a fifty-five-yard touchdown to tie the game. But Chicago took back the lead with a thirteen-play, seventy-three-yard march that ended with a four-yard touchdown pass from Bernie Masterson to Eggs Manske. Baugh then struck back quickly by throwing a seventy-eight-yard scoring strike to Millner on the first play after the kickoff. After forcing a Bears punt Baugh drove the Redskins eighty yards on eleven plays, ending the drive with a thirty-five-yard touchdown pass to Ed Justice to give the Skins a 28–21 lead.

Baugh had just thrown three touchdowns in the third quarter alone. The rookie from Texas Christian University wasn't fazed by the magnitude of the title game. After all the offensive explosions, the fourth quarter came down to the Redskins defense keeping the Bears out of the end zone. After a couple of goal line stops Ray Flaherty's boys captured the NFL Championship. In his first year in Washington George Preston Marshall had brought the city a world title. Rookie sensation Sammy Baugh finished the game completing eighteen of thirty-three passes for a championship game record of 354 yards and three touchdowns. Baugh was now the NFL's brightest star.

Carr was thrilled with the play on the field in Chicago as the exciting, high-scoring game received rave reviews from the press. The attendance figure was another story. The cold weather definitely played a major factor in keeping the fans away, but Mother Nature was one thing Carr couldn't control. As Carr prepared to spend the holidays at home, his league was approached with a very tantalizing offer. Several wealthy businessmen from Miami contacted Damon Runyon, the well-known columnist-writer, to see if the NFL would be interested in hosting its annual championship game in the Florida city. Ruynon contacted Carr to relay the offer of roughly $40,000 to host the NFL's marquee game. Carr released a statement:

> The offer is a flattering one, but the big question is whether the winners of the eastern and western divisions would care to take the game from their home towns, where the fans had supported the teams all season.
>
> Those behind the venture in Miami stated that they would like to make it the outstanding sports spectacle of the country. If the National league could see fit to have the game for the world's professional football championship shuttled there, they are very anxious to get the playoff as an annual sports feature at the winter center.[24]

The generous offer showed Carr that the NFL was growing in stature, but he was reluctant to take the game away from the fans that really supported the league. The league's fans were more important than the money. He announced that the decision on the offer wouldn't be made until the owners met in February at the league's winter meeting. In other NFL news, Lions quarterback Dutch Clark was given the first annual Gruen Award for the player who demonstrated the highest standard of play "with outstanding sportsmanship and significant service for the advancement of professional football." A group of five nationally known sports editors voted. Included in that group were Alan Gould (Associated Press), George Daley (*New York Herald-Tribune*), H. G. Salsinger (*Detroit News*), Warren Brown (*Chicago Herald-Examiner*), and Ed Bang (*Cleveland News*). Carr liked the idea of having a league Most Valuable Player award and decided in 1938 to make it an official award with sportswriters in NFL cities voting.[25]

The year 1937 was Carr's most difficult as NFL president. The mild heart attack he suffered in September incapacitated him for nearly all of the season, and he couldn't travel or work from his office. Despite the ill health, by the end of the year Carr was capable of making some key decisions as he eased back into his role as league president. Although he was diagnosed with a heart ailment, the tough-minded son of an Irish immigrant had only one thing on his mind: get back to his role as NFL president.

25

"Greatest Show in Football" (1938)

While resting at home Carr began thinking about his future. He desperately wanted to get back to work, but he would have to be patient in returning to his normal routine. One of the things he did in January of 1938 was write his annual recap of the NFL season for the Associated Press.

> Fresh from its finest season in both attendance and spectacular play, the National Professional Football League looks forward to even greater things in 1938. Our selective draft system, under which the weaker teams are given first opportunity to negotiate with graduating college stars, showed its effect for the first time during 1937, and was a heavy factor in providing the tight, colorful race.
>
> The Eastern Division surprised everyone by jumping up on even terms with the western half in strength this year while Washington's victory in the playoff game gave the East the national title for the first time in years [since 1934].
>
> The league will continue to play an open game, and increase scoring possibilities. The goal posts will remain on the goal line to permit more field goals, and forward passes from anywhere behind the line of scrimmage will be permitted as in the past. . . . The league's attendance showed a 15 per cent increase and reached a new high.
>
> We think we are providing the greatest show in football——a game which must be played by experts, but one from which the ordinary fan can get a 'kick.'"[1]

Carr's assessment of the NFL was always positive and continued to show how far the NFL had come since it was founded in 1920. The league's attendance had once again increased to nearly one million fans (967,812) in the fifty-five regular season games and one championship game. That was up from the 814,815 fans in 1937.[2] As for scoring the NFL saw 1,424 points scored in the fifty-five regular season games and an all-time high of 25.9 points per game. Stars like quarterbacks Sammy Baugh (Redskins), Ace Parker (Dodgers), Arnie Herber (Packers), and Dutch Clark (Lions); running backs Cliff Battles (Redskins), Clarke Hinkle (Packers), and Tuffy Leemans (Giants); center Mel Hein (Giants); and ends Don Hutson (Packers), Bill Hewitt (Eagles), and Wayne Millner (Redskins) provided the NFL with star power that created a product worth seeing for sports fans in the ten NFL cities. Carr just needed to get better physically to see his league take its next big leap.

Although he still couldn't travel, Carr kept busy with his presidential tasks. Besides releasing his article to the Associated Press, he announced that the next owners meeting would be held on February 19 in Philadelphia and that Vice President Storck would once again preside. It would be the second straight league gathering that he would miss. The ten teams met at the Ritz-Carlton and seemed to get little done. The owners prohibited teams from postseason exhibition games except for the team that wins the championship, and they formally turned down the city of Miami's offer to host the annual championship game. The owners felt that taking away the title game from their hometown fans was too much to give up just to make a little more money.

It seems money wasn't much of a problem for one owner. While at the meeting Art Rooney offered Whizzer White, his first round pick, a record contract of $15,000 for the 1938 season. "No player ever put out as much effort as White. I've seen many players with greater ability but none tried harder and gave 100 per cent effort at all times," said Art Rooney. Several of the other moguls lost their hats. But White was serious about his studies at Oxford and turned down Rooney, although he did leave the door open a little. "I wrote him, though, asking would he still be interested if I should change my mind [this] next summer," said Whizzer White.[3]

As winter ended President Carr was allowed to leave his house to work in his office at 16 East Broad. It felt good to be back to his old routine, and like the hard worker he was, he got straight to work. One of the first things he did upon returning to his office was make plans for the NFL's next promotional project. Besides using radio, the *Official Guide of the National Football League,* trading cards, Ladies Day coupons, and other ways of trying to promote the league, Carr came up with another idea to get the NFL product out to more fans. He wanted to have a promotional film produced to show what the NFL was about and how the game was played. The film would be shown in movie theaters all across the country and would give the NFL more publicity than ever before.

Carr contacted G. A. Richards, who had been living the past year out in Hollywood for health reasons, to see if he knew of a film company that could shoot and produce the documentary on the NFL. Richards suggested Industrial Pictures, Inc., located in his adopted hometown of Detroit. Industrial Pictures was a fairly new production company that had just completed an eight-minute film on the Bryce Canyon National Park sponsored by the Ford Motor Company. Ford showed off its newest vehicles that could get you around the vast Bryce Canyon Park for reasonable prices. Carr was intrigued with the novice company, plus they could give his "football film" all the attention it needed.

After Carr contacted Industrial Pictures, the film company agreed to join the project. Industrial hired Juett Box as director and Oscar Ahbe as cameraman for the entire shoot. Carr then went looking for a sponsor for the film and found the perfect partner. Wheaties breakfast cereal was founded in 1924 in Golden Valley, Minnesota, and used sports as a tool to promote its healthy product. In 1927 the company put up billboards advertising their cereal at Nicollet Park, the minor league baseball stadium located in Minneapolis. Soon the cereal was advertising itself as "the Breakfast of Champions." In 1934 Lou Gehrig became the first athlete to appear on a box of Wheaties. In subsequent years, Babe Zaharias became the box's first female athlete (1935), and Jesse Owens became the box's first black athlete (1936).

Carr knew that Wheaties was the ideal sponsor for his film. The combination of the NFL's good, clean sportsmanship reputation and the cereal's clean, good-for-your-body product was perfect. Carr contacted the executives at General Mills, Inc., to see if they would want to sponsor the NFL film. It was an easy decision for General Mills as they gave Carr a yes and drew up a fifteen-page contract for Carr and the owners to sign. The contract claimed the film was being made as "it is the desire of the Clubs and the League to promote, advertise and popularize the game of professional football, particularly as played by the Clubs of the League, so as to increase the public following of the Clubs and the public interest in and attendance at League games . . . and the Clubs and the League are desirous of accomplishing said end by the media of [this] motion picture."[4]

The NFL and General Mills agreed to the following:

> I. Company [General Mills] will arrange and pay for the production of an educational sound motion picture film featuring the preparation, training, fundamentals and execution of professional football, as played by the Clubs of the League during the 1938 playing season. Said film shall be produced by such technique as Company in its discretion deems best, shall be from four to five thousand feet in length, shall be non-commercial but may contain implied or inferred references to Company's product WHEATIES by such means as the appearance of WHEATIES advertising signs on practice fields

> and such means as Company, with the cooperation and relying upon the ingenuity of the Clubs, shall devise.
>
> II. Company's responsibility shall be limited to the expenditure of Thirty-five Thousand Dollars ($35,000.00) in the production, editing and processing of the said film. Company agrees to furnish each member Club of the League with one print of such film as the Club's own property and Company will maintain for its own use a print or the number of prints adequate for distribution to places where Company can produce exhibition without cost to itself.
>
> III. The Clubs and the League will cooperate with Company, its agents and employees in making playing fields, practices, action and players available for the filming and will likewise cooperate in procuring appropriate endorsements from such of their players as use and are willing to endorse Company's product WHEATIES. . . .
>
> THE UNDERSIGNED, As President of the NATIONAL FOOTBALL LEAGUE, hereby approves of the foregoing agreement on behalf of the League and hereby accepts for himself and his successors in office during the existence of this agreement all delegations and responsibilities therein outlined which apply to the President of the League in such capacity.[5]

The contract was then signed by President Carr and all ten owners. The deal was now complete; the NFL would have its own promotional film—some twenty-six years before the league formed NFL Films. Carr could see the NFL's continued growth, and he wanted to use everything in his power to promote the game. By using film and the increasing popularity of movie theaters, he took another bold gamble in trying to get the NFL to a broader audience. None of the other owners objected to this new idea, and they let Carr's media background take charge.

Now that the film was in motion, Carr got back to putting the schedule together for the 1938 season. While assembling the games Carr gave permission to a few teams to play games in non-NFL cities such as Buffalo, New York, Erie, Pennsylvania, and Charleston, West Virginia, to help further the NFL's potential fan base. Carr set up the Charleston game between the Philadelphia Eagles and Pittsburgh Pirates mainly for the new NFL film. He wanted to show off the league to a new audience in front of the rolling cameras. On July 7 Carr released the NFL schedule and its fifty-five regular-season games. The season was to start on September 9, and the 1938 NFL Championship Game would be played on the home field of the Eastern Division winner.

As the summer began, Carr arranged for the film director hired by Industrial Pictures to shoot the training camp of the Detroit Lions. It would be the opening segment of the NFL promotional film. Lions head coach Dutch Clark agreed to be the technical advisor for the film. He allowed the film company to shoot his team going through camp—starting with the players' physicals and weigh-in and continuing onto the field where they filmed the players standing in their positions and running the plays of a typical NFL team. Clark was even asked to demonstrate the drop-kick (he was the best in the league at drop-kicking), which was shot in super slow motion for added effect. Lions' owner G. A. Richards made a surprise visit to camp and would be mentioned in the movie. Filming was also done at every other team's training camps and would continue throughout the regular season with at least one league game shot for each team. The film would conclude with the season-ending 1938 NFL Championship Game.

On August 1 the NFL heard some fantastic news. After months of going back and forth, Byron "Whizzer" White announced that he would sign a one-year contract with the Pittsburgh Pirates, for $15,000. The money was too good to pass up. White was also able to convince the powers that be at Oxford to delay his entrance into the school until January of 1939. "If it was still a choice between the scholarship and pro football my decision would be the same as it was in June when I picked Oxford, but now it is definite I can still play football and go to England." Carr's league gained another star player and all eyes would be on the $15,000 star.[6]

A week after the White signing was announced, Carr received some more good news and this time it was not about football. On August 9 Joe Carr Jr. received notification that he was 1 of 259 people to pass the Ohio state bar exam taken in June. He was now ready to be a full-time lawyer.[7] Before the season began, NFL publicity director Ned Irish of New York talked to the press about the upcoming season and the league's newest star.

"The league has grown up. This is the first time I remember it starting a season with the same teams and the same coaches it had the previous year. . . . I don't see how he can miss. He is a great back. The only thing that can get him down is the schedule. The Pirates play four games in 11 days in September. This will tire a fellow used to playing only once a week."[8]

A week before the season started Carr was given the okay to travel. His first excursion was to Chicago to see the *Tribune* Charity All-Star Game (August 31) hosted by his good friend Arch Ward. The College All-Stars, led by Purdue quarterback Cecil Isbell (signed by the Packers), defeated the NFL's Washington Redskins 28–16, in front of another fantastic crowd for the charity game—74,250. Carr was excited about attending his first football game since his mild attack suffered in Cleveland in 1937. He was back doing the thing he loved the most—being president of the NFL.

While in Chicago, President Carr called a league meeting at the Palmer House with members of the NFL's finance committee. At the meeting were Carr, Homer Marshman (Cleveland), Tim Mara (New York), Art Rooney (Pittsburgh), Dan Topping (Brooklyn), and Charles Bidwill (Chicago), who was substituting for George Halas. The owners just went over a few fine points within the league and then went their separate ways. Carr returned to Columbus feeling a little tired, but was happy that he was able to travel for a few days without any health problems, showing the owners he was still capable of performing all his tasks as NFL president.[9]

After pretty much missing all the action of the 1937 season, the fifty-nine-year-old Carr was excited about the beginning of the 1938 campaign (he celebrated his fifty-ninth birthday on October 23). He was back in the groove working at his job and depending less on his immediate family. The season got off to a great start, and Carr was back in the spotlight. After rumors of gambling in sports, Paul Mickelson of the Associated Press wrote a nice story about how Carr was operating the NFL on the "straight-and-narrow" and even called for the sport to honor their pioneers.

> Fortunately for the professional pigskin chasers, they are directed by Mr. Joe Carr, an honest gentleman from Columbus, O., who is as uncompromising in his demand for integrity as Kenesaw Mountain Landis, whose iron hand brought respect and faith to organized baseball. Joe, in many respects, is even better equipped for necessary detective work than stern Judge Landis. He's a man who gets around, talks to the high and the low, and never forgets a name, face or action. He has the confidence and affection of every club owner and player he represents. . . . When the pro footballers get around to installing their heroes in the hall of fame, Sammy [Baugh] will be there along with such pioneers as Carr, Chicago's George Halas and those ceaseless workers from Green Bay, who helped keep the game alive.[10]

At this time pro football did not have a hall of fame. Major League Baseball had established their museum in 1936 and eventually inducted their first class of players in 1939 when it opened its doors for the first time. Mickelson was one of the first sportswriters to suggest a football hall of fame, but nobody was really listening. It would be another twenty-five years until the doors of the Pro Football Hall of Fame opened. At least Mickelson believed Carr was deserving of induction.

Midway through the season, Carr was once again seeing big crowds attending NFL games. Since 1934 the NFL had seen the average attendance at games increase every year:

1934: 13,247 fans per game
1935: 13,805 fans per game
1936: 14,814 fans per game
1937: 17,282 fans per game

The 1938 season seemed to be no different, and it looked like the league would see 1 million total fans for the first time. On Sunday, October 16, the

NFL's four league games in Chicago, Detroit, New York, and Green Bay attracted 109,548 fans (average of 27,387 per game), which put a big smile on the face of President Carr. "We are trying to make professional football bigger every year. We are trying to give it more spectaculrism [*sic*] and put on a real show. We have formed our rules with that end in view. We want, and are getting, an abundance of spectator interest," said Carr to the International News Service.[11] Throughout the 1938 season the NFL saw seven games attract crowds of more than 35,000 fans, including a season high of 57,461 fans at the Polo Grounds for the December 4 matchup between the Redskins and Giants. The NFL was now putting on the "greatest show in football." It made the league's old guard very happy about the future of the sport. Even George Halas cheered the increase in popularity: "Fans see one game and are sold on professional football. New stars each season, continued brilliant jobs by old favorites, keep the old fans coming back and new ones taking an initial interest. Poor games are the exception and there certainly aren't any pushovers in the circuit. At one time, the Bears were the only team to practice daily, but not anymore. Nowadays, every team works hard in practice and plays harder to win."[12]

Deep inside, Carr rejoiced at the NFL's current success. Looking back at the eighteen years as NFL president, including his heart attack the previous year, Carr must have felt extremely proud of how popular the league had become. From the early days of franchise instability and players jumping from team to team, the NFL in 1938 was showing signs of being that established sports organization that would eventually capture America's heart. Carr had to be proud of the work he and the other owners had done. The potential of seeing close to 1 million fans in a single season made Carr rest easier at night.

In the middle of November, the city of Charleston, West Virginia, prepared itself for the arrival of the NFL. During the summer Carr announced that several non-NFL cities would host a few league games to help showcase the sport. Local sports promoter Henderson Peebles thought his city of roughly 67,914 citizens (1940 federal census) would enjoy seeing the NFL up close and personal. Carr contacted Peebles and scheduled the game in Charleston between the Pittsburgh Pirates, with the league's newest star, Whizzer White, and the Philadelphia Eagles for Saturday, November 19. Peebles secured Laidley Field (capacity of roughly 10,000) and set ticket prices at $2.00 for general admission and $1.50 for reserved seats. He also blocked off a section of bleacher seats priced at fifty cents for students. As the game approached, Carr informed Peebles that it would be part of the NFL's promotional film. He wanted the game captured on film to show the increasing popularity of the pro game. "The pictures that are to be taken in Charleston will be part of a five reel educational and entertaining picture on football which later will be shown in the theaters throughout the country and will be available for display in elementary and high schools, colleges, noon-day luncheons, clubs and other groups," Carr said.[13]

In a letter to Peebles, he reiterated his attention of sending the film crew to Charleston.

Dear Mr. Peebles:

I sincerely hope you and your associates appreciate the unusual opportunity afforded Charleston—for national advertising purposes—by the visit of the newsreel and motion picture men this coming weekend. The mere scheduling of the Pittsburgh-Philadelphia National League professional game for Charleston has already brought your city considerable publicity, but that is a small item compared to the advantages offered by the picture men.

These films will be shown throughout the United States—wherever football is played and in addition to the action shots of Whizzer White, Dave Smukler [Eagles fullback] and other luminaries of the gridiron many views of the crowd and celebrities in attendance will be photographed.

Charleston is the capital city of West Virginia and with such a marvelous chance to bring it to the attention of millions of people. . . . The importance of this motion picture invasion of your city cannot by over-emphasized.

Get busy now and have your leading citizens dressed up and on parade Saturday. Motion picture fans and gridiron enthusiasts from coast to coast will be seeing them on screen a few months from now.

With best wishes and greetings to my many Charleston friends, I remain as ever, Sincerely your friend,

Joe F. Carr,
President[14]

The film crew from Industrial Pictures with director Juett Box and cameraman Oscar Ahbe traveled to Charleston to begin shooting. Arriving on Wednesday before the game, Box and Ahbe scouted the stadium to find the best angles to film the game. Box was impressed by the layout, and speaking to the *Charleston Gazette*, he talked about the experience of shooting the NFL's first promotional film.

This is certainly a great break for Charleston. When you consider we have only operated in Brooklyn, Cleveland, Washington, Detroit, Philadelphia and Pittsburgh and it puts Charleston right up with the big boys. President Joe Carr, of the National League, told me nothing was too good for Charleston so we are going to "shoot the works!"

Hundreds of fans hear and read of "spinner players," "double wing backs," "off tackle slants," and "lateral passes" and not 10 percent of them know what they mean. We take pictures of these plays, in slow motion, as

> they are executed by the pros in practice. Later we take shots of the same plays as they are run off in a regular game.
>
> Tomorrow [Thursday] we expect to photograph the Eagles in action at Laidley Field. We'll catch them in various offensive and defensive maneuvers and then Saturday we'll film the same plays as they "try" to execute them against the Pirates. Present plans call for a reversal of this procedure on Pittsburgh, as we expect to make our shots of them Sunday afternoon here, the day after the game.
>
> I hope you have a banner crowd and we want every celebrity in the state to be on hand when we start grinding.[15]

As the game approached the weather didn't cooperate, as a rain storm hit Charleston starting Friday afternoon, and it rained all day Saturday. Peebles conferred with owners Art Rooney and Bert Bell about postponing the game. They thought it was a good idea and told him to call Carr to ask permission to move the game. Carr told Peebles that a lot had gone into putting on the game, and that postponing the game until Sunday was fine with him. The forecast for Sunday was much better. As the two teams took the field on Sunday, what the two owners saw didn't make them happy. Only 6,500 fans came out to watch the NFL in Charleston. What a letdown. The small crowd did see an entertaining game—a 14–7 Eagles win—highlighted by Whizzer White's seventy-nine-yard touchdown run.

Carr was disappointed with the attendance in Charleston but was happy the two teams played well. He was also pleased the film crew got a lot done in their time in West Virginia. The film was nearly complete with only the 1938 championship game and President Carr's introductory stand-up to shoot.

As for the championship races, once again they were tight. In the Western Division, it was a two-team race between the Green Bay Packers (who won it all in 1936) and Detroit Lions (who won it all in 1935). On November 13 the Packers defeated the Lions 28–7 in front of 45,139 fans in Detroit to give them an 8–2 record. After the Packers lost to the Giants the following week, the Lions won back-to-back games to trail the Pack by just one game going into the final regular season game. If the Lions defeated the Eagles, they would tie the Packers at 8–3.

On December 4 the Eagles, who had a record of 4–6, upset the Lions in the Motor City, winning 21–7. The Packers claimed the Western Division title for the second time in three years. In the Eastern Division, it was a two-horse race too—between the defending champs, the Washington Redskins, and the New York Giants. Both teams dominated their remaining opponents, setting up a season finale matchup on the same day the Lions lost to the Eagles. The game was hyped in New York as the NFL's game of the year, and the city of New York didn't disappoint. An NFL season high of 57,461 fans jammed the Polo Grounds to see who would capture the Eastern Division.

The Giants (7–2–1) held a one-game lead in the division over the Redskins (6–2–2). After all the hype, the game was a blowout. Behind the play of the Giants' defense, which scored two touchdowns (one on a ninety-six-yard interception return by Ward Cuff), the Gotham squad crushed the champs 36–0. Tim Mara's team had won its fourth division title in six years of divisional play. They would host the Packers in the title game at the Polo Grounds on December 11. Carr was excited about the matchup, and he packed his bags for New York. After missing the previous championship game, the league's president wasn't going to miss this one.

Carr arrived in the Big Apple early and checked into the Hotel New Yorker. The day before the game, the league held its annual draft and owners meeting. Once again Wellington Mara provided the list of college seniors to be drafted. Texas Christian University (TCU) center Ki Aldrich went number one overall to the Chicago Cardinals, but quarterbacks Sid Luckman of Columbia—who led the Chicago Bears to four NFL titles in his twelve years—and little Davey O'Brien of TCU were the big stars chosen. Luckman went number two overall, with O'Brien number four to the Philadelphia Eagles. Carr enjoyed running the owners meeting again and felt right back at home. After the meeting he announced the winner of the NFL's first annual Most Valuable Player (MVP) award voted on by six sportswriters from six NFL cities. The jury consisted of Harry Ferguson (United Press sports editor); H. G. Salsinger (*Detroit News*), Shirley Povich (*Washington Post*), Warren Brown (*Chicago Herald & Examiner*), Ed Bang (*Cleveland News*), and Lawton Carver (International News Service). Mel Hein, New York Giants center, was voted the first ever NFL MVP.[16]

The six-feet-two, 225-pound center-linebacker was the best lineman in the NFL and an easy choice. Rookie Whizzer White led the NFL in rushing but gained only 567 yards with four rushing touchdowns. Packers end Don Hutson had a solid year (thirty-two catches for 548 yards and nine touchdowns), but Hein was the best player on the best team. Hein led a defense that gave up a league-low 79 points (just 7.2 points per game) in eleven games and surrendered just eight touchdowns all season (three rushing, five passing).

On the day of the championship game, Carr headed over to the Polo Grounds with the other owners as the whole NFL was prepared to see the Packers and the Giants face off for the 1938 NFL championship. As they entered the stadium what they saw had never ever been seen at the previous five title matchups. The Polo Grounds was jammed packed with a record NFL Championship Game crowd of 48,120 fans. The anticipation of excitement was brewing in the stands. Carr walked out onto the football field with the game officials—led by referee Bobbie Cahn—smiling from ear to ear. He couldn't believe his eyes as he looked up to see nearly 50,000 fans settling in their seats to watch the NFL's marquee game.[17]

While speaking with the officiating crew, the director and cameraman of Industrial Pictures came by to film the president with his whistle blowers. As pregame drills continued for both teams, President Carr was introduced to Giants center Mel Hein. As photographer's flashbulbs popped, Carr presented Hein with a gold watch as a symbol for winning the NFL's MVP award. Both men smiled for the cameras. As the 2:00 p.m. kickoff approached, Carr took his seat full of pride and relief. After going through the most difficult year of his life in 1937, he was now back on top, watching his league take another giant step forward. The NFL was no longer taking the baby steps it took back in the twenties to gain respect. The league had now become a respectable sport across the country, and the NFL Championship Game had become one of the premier sporting events. It had come full circle. Now it was time to give the fans a show.

On the Packer's second possession, Giants end Jim Lee Howell blocked Clarke Hinkle's punt to set up the game's first score, a Ward Cuff fourteen-yard field goal. The hometown Giants extended their lead following another blocked punt with Tuffy Leemans scoring on a six-yard touchdown run. The extra point attempt failed, to give the Giants a 9–0 first quarter lead. The fireworks were now about to start. In the second quarter, the teams exchanged scores, as the Packers cut into the lead with a forty-yard scoring strike from Arnie Herber to Cecil Mulleneaux. The Giants responded with a twenty-one-yard touchdown pass from Ed Danowski to rookie Hap Barnard. The first half ended with Hinkle making up for his punting mistake by plowing over for a one-yard score. The two teams went into the Polo Grounds locker room with the Giants holding a slim 16–14 lead.

During the intermission the crowd was buzzing as the 1938 title game was becoming a classic. Carr still continued to smile from ear to ear as he sat nervously in his seat. He had dreamed about this moment his whole life. Sitting in a NFL stadium with a capacity crowd watching two teams play their hearts out, giving the paying fans their money's worth. If this was the future of the NFL, Carr knew it had a bright path ahead. He knew this game was going to be bigger than baseball. He could see it. His vision of 100,000 crazy football fans filling a state-of-the-art stadium, witnessing the league's ultimate game wasn't far behind. The NFL as he could see it was complete. Little did he know this would be the last NFL game he would ever see.

In the third quarter, the Packers finally took the lead on a short field goal. Leading by one point (17–16), the Packers then couldn't stop Giants halfback Hank Soar. The versatile Soar carried the ball five times and caught one pass to carry the Giants to the Pack's twenty-three yard line.

Then Danowski fired a bullet into double coverage to Soar, who made a leaping grab at the goal line and dragged Clarke Hinkle into the end zone for the go-ahead score. After the successful extra point, the Giants held a 23–17 lead going into the fourth quarter. The crowd was on the edge of their seats to see if the league's best defense could hold on. Four times in the final period the Packers invaded Giants territory and threatened to pull it out. Each time the Giants defense, led by NFL MVP Mel Hein, turned them away. The gun sounded with the Giants winning their third NFL championship.

The game was a resounding success. The players shared in the gate receipts of $58,331.80 with the Giants getting $504.45 per player while the Packers each received $368.81. Umpire Tom Thorp said, "It was the best played and most exciting game I have ever worked in or seen." After the game, Giants head coach Steve Owen commented on his team's fantastic defensive effort in the fourth quarter: "Those kids of mine just made up their minds that [the] famous Packer attack was going to be stopped. And how they stopped them."[18] Carr's return to the NFL in 1938 was personally fulfilling for him as he was able to overcome his health issues to watch his league reach a new level. Unfortunately it might have taken too much out of him.

26

Death of a President (1939)

Joe F. Carr had just finished his eighteenth season as NFL president. The year before while relaxing at home Carr decided to write some of his memories down from the nearly two decades of running the NFL:

> Post-graduate football has developed from a sandlot experiment to a million-dollar enterprise. The average value of the ten clubs in the league is well over $100,000. I know of at least three club-owners who would not part with their franchise for three times that amount.
>
> We who have given a good deal of time to developing post-graduate football have steadfastly maintained that the American public would respond enthusiastically to this great sport so long as it was cleanly handled, and kept above reproach.
>
> It's too bad someone said the motion picture industry is just in its infancy. I should like to say that about post-graduate football. I believe we are facing a new era, one that will bring football happiness to millions of people in the United States. Every year thousands of fans join our family and learn to like the game as we play it.
>
> But I love the game, and I'll be right back there this fall, for my eighteenth season of National League Football, hoping you're getting as much fun out of watching the game as I get out of running it.[1]

Heading into 1939 the NFL was more stable and popular than ever before. Carr had the league poised for even more growth. In 1938 the attendance reached an all-time high of 1,178,536, topping the 1 million mark for the first time in league history (in 1939 the NFL would see over 1 million paid admissions for the first time ever). Counting the championship game (fifty-six games total), the NFL averaged 21,045 fans per game, topping 20,000 per game for the first time ever too. That was up from the 17,282 in 1937.[2]

On January 1 Carr announced that the NFL's promotional movie titled *Champions of the Gridiron* would be released sometime in March. Produced by Industrial Pictures of Detroit, the nearly one-hour film was almost ready to be shown in theaters across the country. In the opening scene of the film, Carr is sitting at his desk in his Columbus office and introduces what the following movie is all about.

> In presenting *Champions of the Gridiron*, the National Football League, in conjunction with General Mills Incorporated, has produced an entertaining and instructive picture that should appeal to every member of the family. In this picture you will see most of the outstanding college stars of the past few years. Many of whom are the greatest football players of all time, now playing postgraduate football. For those whose only interest in the game is that of a spectator, these experts will analyze and demonstrate intricate plays in order to make the enjoyment of watching football more complete.
>
> To perspective football players in elementary schools, high schools, and colleges, these champions will demonstrate how the game should be played to obtain the maximum of efficiency, with the greatest amount of safety. For this great fall sport has a minimum of hazards for personal injury if properly played.
>
> Above all, the object of this picture is to demonstrate to the people of America that clean, competitive athletics, combined with the proper nourishing food and good habits will develop healthy, rugged bodies and clean active minds. Such as have made the youth of America the finest in all the world.[3]

Carr was excited about the potential of the promotional movie. It would give the NFL more exposure as the film would play in movie houses from coast to coast. Carr started lining up premieres in NFL cities, as well as other parts of the country, including his hometown of Columbus. As the movie was nearing completion Carr sent out word to the league that the next owners meeting would take place in Chicago over a four-day period, from February 9–12. This would be the longest meeting in NFL annals and a historic one for President Carr. But a week before the gathering, rumors once again started to swirl about the position of president of the NFL.

A news report surfaced, stating that the NFL was in negotiations to hire James A. Farley, current postmaster general, as the new NFL "czar" to replace Joe F. Carr. The report claimed that Farley would leave his current post to run the NFL for $75,000 a year.[4] The rumors were started by George Preston Marshall, who was a close friend of Farley and wanted him to be the head man of the NFL. Marshall tried to recruit Lions owner G. A. Richards to support his cause, but Richards (who always wanted a big name to run the league) wasn't biting. Speaking to the United Press, Richards expressed his honest opinion about the rumor:

> Marshall just thought the Farley thing up for a little publicity. He'll think up anything to get his name in the paper. Just as soon as this thing falls through he'll think up something else just as ridiculous.
>
> Did you read the salary figure? Just seventy-five thousand dollars that's all. Where is that coming from? Who is going to put up that sort of money? Not three years ago my fellow owners pooh-poohed a suggestion of mine that we hire a nationally known man to head the league because I thought we would have to pay twenty-five thousand dollars to get him. And they voted down my suggestion that we pay a big publicity firm five thousand dollars to publicize the sport. Said they couldn't afford it.
>
> Farley is a magnificent organizer and knows sport from top to bottom. He would be perfect for the spot but I would hate to have to hang from my thumbs, or by my wrists even until the money for his first year's salary is raised.[5]

The money was too outrageous for any of the other owners to really think about hiring Farley. Marshall's idea was just too far-fetched, and none of the moguls took him seriously. During the first day of the meeting, they would prove to Marshall that they already had the right man for the job. So excited about attending the meeting, Carr arrived in Chicago before any of the other owners. The four-day conference at the Congress Hotel began at 3:00 p.m. on Thursday, February 9. On the first day the owners went over a few issues, including meeting with Arch Ward to discuss the ever popular *Chicago Tribune* Charity All-Star Game, and announcing the resignation of publicity director Ned Irish. But the biggest issue brought forth was about to blindside the current president.[6]

In a motion brought up by Cardinals owner Charlie Bidwill, seconded by Eagles owner Bert Bell, the owners presented an idea "that President-Secretary Joe F. Carr be re-elected for a period of 10-years, effective Feb. 1, 1939, and that his salary be placed at $10,000 per year plus $1,200 for his secretary, plus necessary expenses for his office." The proposal carried unanimously. The owners then voted unanimously to "re-elect Vice-President-Treasurer Carl L. Storck for ten years effective Feb. 1, 1939 at a salary of $3,000 per year." Just a week earlier there were rumors of replacing Carr. Now the owners were rewarding him with a long-term contract that proved to the whole sporting world that Carr was the man to see the NFL into the next decade.[7]

Although Carr's original five-year contract he signed in 1935 was almost up, the new extended deal took him by surprise. He knew he wanted to continue in his role as NFL president, but his health was an issue and probably made some of the owners a little nervous. In the end the owners knew they only wanted Carr to run their organization, and as long as he was physically capable, then the job was his until he wanted to retire. The salary increase was just a bonus. The first day ended with President Carr very excited about his future.

Over the following days the owners prepared a rough outline of the 1939 NFL schedule and approved a few new guidelines on and off the field. On the third day Stuart Rothman of General Mills "discussed the distribution of the football picture; reiterating his promise to the President that he would furnish each club a 35mm print as well as a 16mm print." Also that day George Halas presented a resolution on behalf of the Professional Football Writers Association of America, "resolving, that the National [Football] League, to assist in the establishment and promotion of a legitimate off-season publicity feature, set up a cash purse, trophy or prize, to be presented to the player voted by the Writers to be the most valuable to his team in the championship race, and be it further resolved that said award be made annually in the name of the NFL." In 1938 the NFL had established a Most Valuable Player (MVP) award—won by Giants center Mel Hein—and that player received a watch. For this fall the player would get something more substantial, like a permanent trophy or a cash prize; the owners agreed to let President Carr come up with a proper award.[8]

The reelection of Carr as NFL president was well received across the country as sports headlines everywhere announced the exciting news. Most of the headlines proclaimed that "the football-for-profit magnates wasted little time in deciding to keep the fiery, whitehaired Carr in the chair he has occupied since 1921 . . . for a 10-year term."[9] Upon returning to Columbus Carr got back to work. A month after the Chicago meeting, the NFL's promotional film *Champions of the Gridiron* made its premiere in theaters across the country. It was also made available for free to colleges, schools, and athletic and fraternal clubs. After five months of shooting, the nearly one-hour film—which was produced from 300,000 feet of film, narrated by Harry Wismer of WJR radio in Detroit (owned by Lions owner G. A. Richards), and supervised by Dutch Clark—was released to glowing reviews. After a private showing Carr was extremely pleased with what he saw.

"This film displays the greatest numbers of star players ever gathered in football films. It not only provides exceptional entertainment but also makes simple, the games technique as played by the leading elevens in this country . . . contains more action, thrilling entertainment and instructional matter than any football film ever shown. This film is certain to be very popular with football fans, young and old and others who may be strangers to the gridiron spectacle."[10]

The film featured footage of all ten NFL teams in actual games and practices, as well as close-ups—shot in both slow-motion action and regular speed. NFL stars such as Sammy Baugh, Don Hutson, Mel Hein, Whizzer White, Ed Danowski, Ace Parker, Dutch Clark, and Jack Manders are predominantly featured throughout the movie. The film concludes with the thrilling finish of the 1938 NFL Championship Game won by the New York Giants over the Green Bay Packers. Several NFL cities had free viewings, including a showing in New York for 100 Big Apple sportswriters and radio personalities. In attendance was newly hired Navy football coach Swede Larson, who was very impressed by the film: "The National Football League would be doing great public service to show this film in every high school in the country. It is the finest football movie I have ever seen."[11]

The promotional film was a hit. While sitting at his desk in Columbus, Carr wrote a letter to Bert Bell and talked to Art Rooney on the phone about having the summer meeting in Pittsburgh next month. He also made arrangements to premiere the film in his hometown. Cosponsored by the *Ohio State Journal* and the Agonis Club of Columbus, *Champions of the Gridiron* was set up to be shown at the RKO Palace Theater on Saturday, May 13, just a block west from Carr's office at 16 East Broad. At 9:30 a.m. "several thousand people" crammed into the Palace Theater to watch the NFL's newest promotional idea. Attending the premiere were the *Ohio State Journal* Quarterback Club, Agonis Club, Central Ohio Football Officials Association, and many coaches and players of Central Ohio colleges, universities, and high schools. One of the coaches watching was Ohio State head coach Francis Schmidt, who was also impressed by the film. "It was the most complete showing of its kind that I have ever seen."[12]

All the hard work of putting together the promotional film was paying off for President Carr, as the movie was reaching a big audience. It had done what he thought it would do. Little did he know it would be the last presidential duty he would accomplish in office. A few days after the Saturday premiere of *Champions of the Gridiron*, Carr completed a long week of work at the NFL headquarters and looked forward to a quiet weekend at home. It had been a very productive off-season up to this point, and Carr had reached the pinnacle of his career. The vision he had for the NFL as a big-time, big-city sport was taking shape right in front of his eyes. As Carr reflected on his nearly two decades as NFL president, he must have felt very proud of how the NFL had grown up from its small-town disorganized roots to having a prominent place in the sporting world. But suddenly the NFL family was about to have its world shattered.

On Friday, May 19, Carr arrived at his home at 1863 Bryden Road, tired but cheerful, to spend dinner with his wife and two children. The busy schedule had finally caught up to him, and he needed some rest. After an uneventful evening, Joe and Josie went to bed. Mary, age twenty-five, and Joe Jr., age twenty-three, went to bed shortly afterward. But just after midnight, Joe F. Carr awoke with severe chest pains. Feeling ill and struggling to breathe, he was driven by the family several blocks downtown to Mt. Carmel Hospital to be admitted for tests. Josie contacted their family physician, Dr. Edward Campbell, who arrived to evaluate the famous sports executive.

In a scene similar to the one in the fall of 1937, the Carr family surrounded their loved one and prayed for his health. Fully conscious and aware, Carr spent a restless Friday night in the hospital, but he rebounded in the morning with what the hospital reported as "a fairly comfortable day."[13] While at the hospital, Joe Carr Jr. called Bill McKinnon, sportswriter for the *Columbus Dispatch*, and one of his father's close friends, and told him of the situation. While talking to McKinnon he made one request: "Dad just went over to Mt. Carmel for a rest of 10 days or so. Nothing serious but his physician believes he should take it easy for a while. Dad would like it if you wouldn't mention his present confinement."[14]

But the situation was serious. Just when it looked like Carr dodged another bullet, he went into full cardiac arrest. With Josie, Mary, and Joe Jr. by his side, Carr was pronounced dead. At 4:50 p.m. on Saturday, May 20, 1939, the president of the NFL passed away.[15] He was fifty-nine years old. It almost seems unfair that Carr—who had just been given a ten-year contract—at the height of his career was suddenly struck down and gone. The combination of his smaller sized heart and his very busy schedule was too much. The family—including his two brothers in Columbus—were stunned. Josie and the two children started to grieve.

"He had a stressful job and it took a toll on him," says James Carr, grandson of Joe F. Carr. "Plus he was a very heavy smoker of cigars, which can take a toll on your heart. Back then all they told you to do was rest, so he tried to rest as best he could. It finally caught up to him. At the time of his death he had become a very significant, important man, not only in the city of Columbus but throughout the country. So he was a pretty big deal at the time of his death. It's pretty amazing the kind of man that he was. It cast a very broad shadow."[16]

As the family dealt with the personal loss, the NFL family was also stunned by the sudden passing of their president. As the news started to spread across the country, NFL owners expressed their feelings toward the man that guided their sport for the past two decades. In Chicago Charlie Bidwill praised Carr, and George Halas felt the loss of his close friend.

> The loss of Mr. Carr is irreparable. Professional football's remarkable growth and popularity today is not the result of the efforts of any one owner or

> group of owners. It is due entirely to Mr. Carr's fair and impartial administration of its affairs and his steadfast belief in the game.—George Halas, owner of the Chicago Bears[17]

> Mr. Carr had the happy faculty of seeing the other fellow's side of every disagreement. He fought diligently against every reform that might make an enemy for professional athletics and athletes. He was professional football's balance wheel. Mr. Carr's integrity and sportsmanship alone were responsible for professional football overcoming the antagonistic attitude that existed among many sports leaders at the time the National League was founded. It will be impossible to replace him.—Charlie Bidwill, owner of the Chicago Cardinals[18]

> Gee, I can hardly believe that Joe Carr is dead. I was talking to him last week. He appeared to be in the best of health and said he felt great. He was planning to come to Pittsburgh for a league meeting next month. Carr's passing means a personal loss and a loss to professional football which cannot be replaced. He will be missed by those connected with the sport.—Art Rooney, owner of the Steelers[19]

Ever since the league was founded in 1920 the NFL hadn't experienced a gloomier day than May 20. The following morning on the Lord's Day the whole country awoke to the headlines of "Joe Carr: Noted Football Executive Dies." In his hometown of Columbus the newspaper's front pages revealed the sad news.

> "Joe Carr, Nationally Known in Sports, Dies"—*Ohio State Journal*
> "Joe Carr, Vet Sports Organizer, Dies at 59, Headed Pro Loop"—*Columbus Citizen*
> "Joe Carr, Noted Figure in Sports World, Is Taken by Death after Heart Attack"—*Columbus Dispatch*[20]

As the sports world digested the shocking news the Carr family prepared to say good-bye to their fallen hero. As hundreds of condolences arrived, Josie, with help from her son Joe Jr., planned for the funeral to take place on Wednesday (May 24) at Holy Rosary Church—located a few blocks from their Bryden Road home. Before he passed away, Carr drew up a will that left an estate, valued at $43,174.49, to his wife and two children. He also made plans for his body to be buried at the new Catholic cemetery in the south end of Columbus—St. Joseph's Cemetery. On the day before the funeral, the Carr family announced the eight active pallbearers:

1. William McGrath, former director of athletics of Columbus parochial schools

2. Nick Barack, secretary of Agonis International
3. Harry Murray, executive at Pennsylvania Railroad
4. George M. Trautman, president of the American Baseball Association
5. Bob Hooey, sportswriter *Ohio State Journal*
6. Roy Swabby, employee at Ohio National Bank
7. George Halas, president and coach of the Chicago Bears
8. Carl L. Storck, vice president of the NFL[21]

The evening before the funeral, all the NFL owners traveled to Columbus to pay their last respects to President Joe F. Carr. On May 24 the capital city of Ohio saw one of the greatest collections of sports executives ever. "The visitors at the funeral were not just football people. They were journalists; they were baseball people; they were basketball people. They were promotional people. They were politicians," says Gregory Carr, grandson of Joe F. Carr. "His influence was pretty significant and at that time one of the top sports influences in the country." Carr's secretary Kathleen Rubadue, who always felt close to the Carr family, was also in shock. "She was definitely sad about the whole thing," says Robert Knapp, son of Kathleen Rubadue. "Later on she never really said a whole lot about that."[22]

The NFL owners who attended (joining Halas and league executive Storck) were designated as honorary pallbearers—Dan Topping (Brooklyn Dodgers); Charlie Bidwill (Chicago Cardinals); Tom Lipscomb (Cleveland Rams); William Alfs (Detroit Lions); Curly Lambeau (Green Bay Packers); Tim and Jack Mara (New York Giants); Art Rooney (Pittsburgh Pirates); George Preston Marshall (Washington Redskins); Jim McCurdo (Philadelphia Eagles). Other sports executives and newspaper writers who attended were Arch Ward, Branch Rickey, childhood friend Bob Quinn, Bill McKinnon, Lew Byrer, and Lee MacPhail. In all there were more than 300 people jammed into Holy Rosary Church that morning.

After a private viewing at Egan-Ryan Chapel, Carr's body was brought to Holy Rosary for the service that started promptly at 10:00 a.m. Josie, with Mary and Joe Carr Jr.—as well as Carr's brothers Michael and Edward—sat bravely in the front row as fifteen visiting priests sat in the sanctuary. The casket was surrounded by "one of the most impressive and largest floral displays ever afforded to a national figure."[23] A choir that featured thirty boys sang poignantly as the large crowd finally took their seats. Father John J. Murphy of Holy Rosary gave the eulogy:

> Mr. Carr's life work was in the field of national recreation. . . . Recreation is a useful, important and necessary part of life. It is not man made; it is from Nature which means that it is from God who, though he needed it not, set the example by resting on the seventh day of Creation. . . . Again, his work

> had to do largely with athletic competition. We cannot lose sight of the fact that this type of recreation carries with it a delicate condition. While in other occupations success may be distributed; that is, in business, in industry, in professional life, there is honor, there is success, there is victory for many. In the world of competitive athletics one group can win only because the other group loses. To encourage, to sustain in the face of loss and defeat, was the peculiarly trying task of Joe Carr. It is human nature that in losing we seek a change of administration. Yet with him through years of administration, admiration, appreciation and prestige increased.
>
> The reasons Mr. Carr was successful were based in the principles on which his life was founded. He believed that there always must be rules to guide the game and life, that there must be truth, nobility and kindness. His was a personality to be admired, nourished, cherished, envied and loved.
>
> Joe Carr chose to put his talents to use in the field of recreation and in that chosen field there is none who could surpass him.[24]

The moving words by Father Murphy brought tears to everyone's eyes, including Josie and her two children. They knew that their husband and father was now in the hands of God and that he was in good hands. After the ceremony, the thirty-six honorary pallbearers formed two lines to form an aisle through which the eight active pallbearers would carry Carr's casket out of the church and into the hearse that would take him to St. Joseph's Cemetery. "It was an awesome ceremony. I mean it was probably the biggest funeral the city's ever seen," says Michael Carr, grandson of Joe F. Carr. "I saw the pictures. I mean there was flowers all over. Unbelievable. He was everything they said he was."[25]

Most of the crowd piled in their cars to follow Carr's body, driving the ten miles south down High Street to St. Joseph's Cemetery. The large crowd then gathered in the St. Agnes section (plot 229) to hear the final rites given by Father Murphy. Carr was then buried next to his newly planted headstone that simply read—Joseph F. Carr. No dates or poem. "The headstone itself is pinkish granite and it's got inlays of various flowers and foliates on the corners of it," says Gregory Carr. "The center has a Gaelic cross with the I.S. insignia with my grandfather's name emblazoned upon the front of it. It's set on a granite footer to maintain the integrity of the gravestone."[26]

"[The gravesite] for us this is a holy place. We're talking about my grandfather here. Not only was he the founder of the NFL, but we kind of looked to him as the founder of our family," says James Carr. "The very individual in our family who's like at the head of the table. That's how I look at him and I admire him. So it's a pretty intense place for our family." The very simple but stoic headstone was now the final resting place for one of the NFL's founding fathers. For the Carr family, it was a sad but perfect way to say good-bye. Before the NFL owners left Columbus, they made one announcement: that vice president and treasurer Carl L. Storck would be acting president until a formal meeting was scheduled sometime in July for Pittsburgh, where a permanent replacement would be named.[27]

Just when it seemed that the Carr family could take a break from all the sadness more bad news came to them from Chicago. Two weeks after saying good-bye to Joe F. Carr, the family learned that John Karr, Joe's big brother, had passed away from a heart attack at the age of sixty-nine. John's health kept him from attending his brother's funeral and eventually became worse soon after his brother was buried. The original Carr family was now down to two—Michael and Edward.

Although it had only been a month since President Carr passed away, the owners still had a league to run, and Carr would have wanted them to move forward as quickly as possible. It was the Irish way. On July 22 the NFL owners and coaches met at the Fort Pitt Hotel in Pittsburgh to discuss league matters; to set up the NFL schedule for 1939; and choose a new president. All of the owners showed up except for G. A. Richards, who remained in California due to health issues, and George Preston Marshall. Carl Storck presided over the meeting, which began with a permanent proposal to honor Carr's work for the NFL. Storck presented a motion about the future of the league's MVP award. Carr presented Hein with a watch but in the last owners meeting Carr was given the responsibility of coming up with a more dignified award. At this moment George Halas stood up and brought forth a motion saying:

> I would like to submit a resolution here in regard to the same award. . . . It is a resolution stating that the most valuable award should be called the Joe F. Carr Memorial Award.
>
> Where as the untimely death of Joe F. Carr, founder and president of the NFL, prevented action by Mr. Carr on the resolution adopted this Feb. 1939 meeting of National League, where in Mr. Carr was asked to designate a suitable award for National League MVP, it is proposed that the MVP resolution be amended as following:
>
> That the NFL's Most Valuable Player award be designated the Joe F. Carr Memorial Award. That the Joe F. Carr Memorial Award be given annually to the player named the Most Valuable in the National League championship race. That the selection of the MVP be made by the Professional Football Writers of America.[28]

The motion carried unanimously. "You are giving the Award in the name of the man who has done more for professional football than any living man, and any man for a long, long time," spoke Curly Lambeau at the meeting. It was a thoughtful and honorable gesture by the whole NFL to honor their late president. The MVP award was Carr's idea, who thought it could rival major league baseball's annual award, which was getting a lot of publicity at this time, so naming the award after him made perfect sense. The owners then turned to electing a new president. Because of the sudden death of Carr, the owners didn't have much time to interview potential candidates and with the absence of outspoken owners G. A. Richards and George Preston Marshall, they nominated Carl L. Storck as president. The owners approved Storck's election and gave him a one-year contract.

After a lifetime of service the forty-five-year-old NFL employee was now replacing a legend and a close friend. "When Joe Carr passed away my parents were very upset and didn't know what was going to happen," says Dolores Seitz, daughter of Carl Storck. "They felt a loss because they were very close and they were so in sync with their thinking. My father was not happy that he got it [to be president] the way he did." After being elected, Storck's first assignment from the owners was to "provide and present Mrs. Joe F. Carr a leather-bound memorial [book] detailing her husband's life work with services to the League."[29] It was another small gesture to help honor Carr's life work. The owners also agreed to pay Carr's remaining 1939 salary to his widow. As the meeting adjourned the league took a huge breath of relief. Although the league had lost its heartbeat, the organization was in good hands. Carr had handpicked most of the owners to guide the NFL into the future. He would have also been pleased that the owners selected Storck to help continue his legacy.[30]

Since Storck had put in nearly twenty years of service, it made sense for the owners to select him as the next president. Storck moved the NFL office temporarily to his hometown of Dayton, leaving Kathleen Rubadue by herself in the old office at 16 East Broad Street. In less than a year, Rubadue would leave the NFL and get married. Just as with Carr, the NFL was Storck's life, and he could continue to promote Carr's ideals without any setbacks. As the 1939 season approached, it seemed strange to not see Carr at an opening weekend game. For the first time since 1921, the NFL would play a league game without Joe F. Carr in office. In the *Official Guide of the National Football League: 1939*, former superstar Red Grange wrote an article on the progress of professional football. He pointed out one individual responsible for its growth.

> In singling out the individual, who was most responsible for the growth of pro football, I think I can safely place the name of the late Joe F. Carr in nomination. Mr. Carr served as president of the league from the time it was founded in 1920 [1921] until his untimely death last May. Joe was a kindly, sympathetic, stubborn and, more important than anything else, an honest gentleman. He insisted from the start that pro football would one day be one of America's outstanding sports, despite the fact that colleges decried the game and prospective customers refused to be stamped. Joe remained un-

daunted, however, and fought doggedly for the recognition of an ideal. Mr. Carr, it seems to me, had more than an ideal when the league was founded. He had vision and common sense, too.

Down through the years, it is a matter of record that Joe Carr gave everyone, no matter what their capacity, a square deal. Players coming into the league knew they would be treated fairly. The fact that former league players like myself, who are now engaged in business and professional life, are the league's greatest boosters, I think is a fine tribute to Carr's ability. A lot of folks talk about the Golden Rule. Carr put it into practice. He treated others as he wanted to be treated by them.

The league is going to miss Joe Carr, but, I am firmly convinced he left it the heritage of a sound foundation, built on principles of honesty and common sense, that will be his invisible monument in years to come.[31]

Yes, a foundation had been built by Carr that would endure, and yes the league was in good hands. On Sunday, September 10, the NFL played its first game without Carr as president. Some 15,075 fans showed up at Titan Stadium in Detroit to watch the Lions defeat the Chicago Cardinals 21–13. There was no report of a moment of silence or any tribute to the fallen president. Four weeks after the NFL's opening weekend, President Storck sent Josephine Carr a letter presenting her with the memorial book authorized by the NFL owners.

Dear Mrs. Carr and Family:

I have been authorized by the club owners of the National Football League to present you with a Memoriam of your late husband and father, for the loving services he rendered to all of us. I am forwarding it to you under separate cover.

I sincerely hope you will accept our kind condolences and good wishes.

Very sincerely yours
Carl L. Storck
President[32]

The five-page memorial book was about an inch thick and was bound in a thick black leather binding. The five pages praised Carr's career and included facsimile signatures of all ten NFL owners and the original signature of President Storck. The book—which cost about $100 to publish—was so special to Josie and the Carr family that the original book and letter are still with the Carr family after seventy years.[33]

As the 1939 season rolled on the NFL saw another milestone. On October 22 the Philadelphia Eagles played the Brooklyn Dodgers at Ebbets Field in front of 13,057 fans. Little did the crowd know that this would be the first NFL game broadcast on television. Carr would have been thrilled to see his league take another big step forward, even if it would take another twenty plus years for TV to make the NFL a money-making extravaganza. At the end of the season, the league saw a rematch of the 1938 championship game, with the Packers and Giants winning their divisions. This time the game was played in Green Bay.

The outcome was different too. The Packers destroyed the Giants 27–0 to win their fifth NFL title. After the season the Football Writers of America voted for the NFL's Joe F. Carr Memorial Award. Although his team finished with just a 5–5–1 record, the Cleveland Rams rookie tailback-quarterback Parker Hall won the award. As the end of the decade arrived, the NFL was now at a crossroad. Carl L. Storck had replaced Carr, but he was signed for only one year. How would the NFL handle the aftermath of Carr's death?

27

Aftermath

Like life the NFL would move on without its former president. But for the Carr family, it was a different story. At the age of fifty-nine, Josephine Carr was now a widow and she handled her husband's death with tons of courage and grace. She continued to live at the family home on Bryden Road the rest of her life while taking care of her family. Her son, Joseph Carr Jr., continued his work as a prominent lawyer and also started a family. He married a local woman, Marjorie Naddy, and the couple had seven children—all boys—although two died very early. Joseph F. Carr III and Francis Carr passed away before they reached their tenth birthdays. Buddy eventually moved his family out of the Bryden Road home to a more spacious residence at 252 Preston Road, which was less than a mile and a half away from his mother.

Despite his success as a lawyer in Columbus, Joe Jr. always maintained his love for the NFL, and in his heart he wanted to continue his father's lifework. "He idolized his father and what he wanted to do was follow in his footsteps. He wanted to become more active and work in the NFL," says James Carr, grandson of Joe F. Carr. "My grandfather discouraged him from doing that. He told my dad to 'stick with the law, son, stick with the law.' I think he was sorely disappointed that he couldn't follow in his father's footsteps. I think his first love and his first choice would have been working with the NFL. But that was not to be."[1]

As Buddy built a family and a career, his sister was having a hard time with the death of their father. Although she had her mother and brother there for support, she seemed to be struggling the most with the loss. "She was devastated. After she received her college degree she pretty much stayed at home. She stayed at home and dedicated her life to family matters. She was very dedicated to her family," says James Carr. "She was a very loving person, a very loyal person. A very bright lady who spoiled us later on. But she was devastated by the loss of her father." The loss of her beloved father had a lasting impact on her. She never married, and for the rest of her life she dedicated herself to whatever the Carr family needed.[2]

As the Carr family moved forward, so did the NFL. But this time the owners weren't on the same page. In 1939 the NFL passed over 1 million paid fans in attendance (1,071,200) for the fifty-five regular-season games, as the sport continued to show more growth. With the league at an all-time high in popularity, the owners became divided in their opinion on who should be at the forefront leading them. Once again several owners started a discussion about hiring a "big-name" executive to run their organization. They wanted a "commissioner" to run the league similar to what Major League Baseball had with Kenesaw Mountain Landis. Heading into the 1940 off-season, the owners interviewed a few big names about the position.[3]

George Preston Marshall and G. A. Richards combined their efforts into recruiting a big-name person to succeed Carr. In December of 1939, they had a conversation with FBI director J. Edgar Hoover about taking the job. "Sorry but I cannot consider the proposition at this time," Hoover said in a telegram. The owners then quickly moved to their most popular choice. About the same time they approached Hoover, the owners chatted with Arch Ward, the promotional genius who also was the sports editor at the *Chicago Tribune*, about the job. George Halas approached Ward and offered him the position with an unbelievable offer of $25,000 a year for ten years. But Ward was not interested, saying, "[I] could not overlook the splendid opportunities in my position with the *Chicago Tribune*." The owners were now 0-for-2, and time was slipping away before the spring meeting to select a president.[4]

Storck was confident he would be reelected despite the rumors of the owners wanting a bigger name. "I warmed up to the work for the start. If the league re-elects me and requests that I make the office a full-time job I feel sure I would be more inclined to comply with their wishes than I was last spring." Storck was still working for General Motors, but spending all his time as NFL president was something he wanted to do. "I will continue to carry on and give the league my best efforts; it is likely that I will retain the president's office in my home at Dayton."[5]

On April 13 in New York the owners met to prepare for the 1940 NFL season and to vote on who would be the next NFL president. Instead of a multiyear contract, the league was back to the one-year deals that dominated the early years. Marshall, who most owners expected to oppose Storck's reelection, remained silent when Carr's protégé was selected for one more year. After the meeting Marshall talked to the press: "I think

Storck is a fine executive but I can name a better one. However, I know of no available candidate now . . . all is harmony, and we've done more on the first day at this meeting than any one I ever attended before."[6]

Storck's hard work was rewarded again, but he would be on a short leash. Some of the NFL owners—led by outspoken George Preston Marshall—didn't think he was the right person to lead the league. The year 1940 would be Storck's last as NFL president. Marshall's frustration from the off-season continued into the NFL season. His Redskins dominated the regular season, winning the Eastern Division with a 9–2 record. In the NFL Championship Game the Redskins hosted the Chicago Bears (who won the Western Division with an 8–3 record), who they defeated 7–3 late in the season. After that game Marshall had called the Bears a "bunch of crybabies." Little did Marshall know he would regret saying those words. In the championship game on December 8, the Bears pummeled the Redskins 73–0, unleashing the modern T-formation on the NFL and giving Halas his fourth NFL title.

Shortly after the season several owners continued their onslaught of hiring a "big-name sports executive" to be their next leader. Poor Carl L. Storck—who had been involved with the NFL since it was founded in Canton, Ohio, in 1920—was the sacrificial lamb. "My father was so honest and always jovial and friendly with everyone in the NFL. He got along with everyone," says Dolores Seitz, daughter of Carl L. Storck. Except for one. "[Marshall] is the only one I ever knew that he did not. He was the new guy on the block and he was going to come in and change everything to his way of thinking," says Seitz.[7]

In the end Marshall won out. Before the spring meeting Marshall and the owners made another offer to Arch Ward. He declined again, but this time he offered an alternate. He recommended Notre Dame athletic director Elmer Layden—who became famous on the field as one of the Four Horsemen of Notre Dame during the Roaring Twenties. He was the big name the NFL was looking for, although he had never been an executive in the professional ranks. As the meeting approached, Storck defended his reputation and his lifetime of work with the NFL.

> This morning two club owners came to me as a committee to see how I stood. That was the first time they had ever consulted me on the matter of a commissionership. I told them how would you feel in my place? I told them I haven't a letter in my files criticizing my work as president for two years. They made the rules and I simply enforced them. I've been in this league for 20 years—not for the money but because I loved it.
>
> I told the league I would serve as president under Layden only on the provision that I get a contract which defines my duties. I have nothing against Layden, but I don't think he knows what a contract or a waiver means. And while they say they have, I tell you they haven't got enough votes for him yet.

> For 15 years I worked for nothing. Two years ago when I became president I didn't quit my job with General Motors because I was afraid something like this would happen.[8]

But it was too late. Marshall had the votes. Knowing he didn't want to work under Layden, Storck resigned as president. The owners hired Elmer Layden to be the NFL's first commissioner. He signed a five-year contract for $20,000 a year. Storck left the NFL with a broken heart. "I am convinced that Layden is not qualified to handle the job, due mostly to his lack of administrative experience in professional sports. Layden was steamrolled into his job when George Halas and Arch Ward saw an opportunity to put it across."[9] Even if the owners wanted a more well-known name to run their organization, the ousting of Storck—after his lifetime of work—was not the proper thing to do. Over time Storck would never get over leaving the NFL the way he did.

"He was heartbroken. That's what I always thought my father died of was heartbreak," says Dolores Seitz, daughter of Carl L. Storck. "He was just stunned I guess. It was shortly after that he had the stroke. I thought leaving the NFL is what caused the stroke. I do think what he did helped the NFL. I think it helped the NFL become bigger and more important." In the end Storck died from a broken heart. On March 13, 1950, just nine years after resigning from the NFL, Storck died from numerous health issues in a Dayton nursing home. He was just fifty-six years old.[10]

Storck was right about Layden. Despite his success on the gridiron, Layden lacked the leadership skills to help further the NFL. Although the NFL was greatly effected by World War II, with players serving overseas, Layden failed to recognize the growing field of television to help promote the NFL. When Layden's five-year contract expired, the owners looked at one of their own to lead them. In 1946 they hired Bert Bell as NFL commissioner. The man Carr gave an NFL franchise to in Philadelphia back in 1933 moved the league's office from Chicago to the city of Brotherly Love. His leadership guided the NFL to greater heights through the "fabulous fifties" and made the NFL a staple on television. The league was now in good hands.

On August 30, 1950, Josie Carr, the beloved widow of Joe F. Carr, died at her home of natural causes at the age of seventy. She was buried next to her husband. Seven years later, the Carr family was once again struck by a death in the family. On July 2, 1957, Joseph F. Carr Jr. died of a sudden heart attack at the age of forty-one. Just like his father, Buddy was stricken with a weak heart that took his life much too soon. He left behind his sister, Mary; his wife, Marjorie; and five young boys. On July 5 after a small ceremony at St. Catharine Church in Columbus, Joe Carr Jr. was buried next to his father at St. Joseph's Cemetery.

28

Pro Football Hall of Fame (1963)

In 1961 paid attendance in the NFL exceeded 4 million for the first time ever. The year before saw the country's second professional league formed, with the American Football League (AFL) playing in eight cities—giving pro football twenty-one different franchises from coast to coast. Professional football was now a big-time business. The founders and pioneers of the sport could rejoice. Ever since Major League Baseball opened its Hall of Fame in Cooperstown, New York, in 1939, there had been talk of football having its own shrine. Cities such as Latrobe, Pennsylvania, and Buffalo, New York, wrote proposals to build a museum but nothing happened. Then the city where the NFL was founded suddenly got to work.

On December 6, 1959, Clayton Horn, the editor of the *Canton Repository*, instructed one of his sportswriters—Chuck Such—to issue a Hall of Fame challenge to the city of Canton. The headline read, "Pro Football Needs a Hall of Fame and Logical Site Is Here." This headline raised a lot of eyebrows around the city, but none rose higher than those of H. H. Timken Jr., the chairman of the board at Canton's largest industry, the Timken Rollar Bearing Company. He called Such to offer his support and assigned the company's recreation director, Earl Schreiber, to the project. Other cities which also applied for the potential site at this time were Detroit and Pittsburgh. But it was too late; Canton was well in front of everybody, and on January 25, 1961, at the NFL's owners meeting in New York, the city of Canton made a formal bid for the Pro Football Hall of Fame.[1]

William Umstattd, chairman of the executive committee at Timken, accompanied Schreiber to New York for the meeting to be held at the

Warwick Hotel. They showed the NFL owners a scale model of the proposed hall (not one owner looked at it) and gave a short three-minute presentation in which Umstattd estimated the cost of the Hall of Fame to be $350,000. He also said the city of Canton would donate $250,000 while Mr. Timken himself would donate $100,000. At this point the owners began to listen. Three months later at an NFL meeting in San Francisco, Canton was selected as the Hall of Fame city.

A fund-raising campaign started on December 7, 1961, and in less than three months, the city raised $378,026 through community pledges. Pro football had found a home for its Hall of Fame, where the greats of the sport would live on forever. Dick McCann, an executive with the Washington Redskins, was selected as the Hall of Fame's first director. Canton's hard work became a reality with a ground breaking ceremony on August 11, 1962, when NFL commissioner Pete Rozelle (who had replaced the recently deceased Bert Bell in 1960) shoveled the first dirt. The ceremony also launched the annual Hall of Fame game series at Fawcett Stadium—the high school field that was located across the street from the site of the Hall of Fame.

At the end of the 1962 season, the Hall of Fame selected fourteen men to help vote for the charter class of enshrinees. The selection committee would select seventeen charter members from a list of the game's great players and contributors. The committee consisted of twelve sportswriters (one from each NFL city) and two former NFL stars:

1. Lewis Atchison (*Washington Star)*
2. Jimmy Conzelman (former NFL player-coach)
3. Arthur Daley (*New York Times*)
4. Art Daley (*Green Bay Press-Gazette)*
5. Herb Good (*Philadelphia Inquirer*)
6. Sam Greene (*Detroit News*)
7. Chuck Heaton (*Cleveland Plain Dealer*)
8. Charles Johnson (*Minneapolis Star*)
9. Jack McDonald (*San Francisco News-Call Bulletin)*
10. Paul Menton (*Baltimore Evening Sun*)
11. Bob Oates (*Los Angeles Herald-Examiner*)
12. Davey O'Brien (former NFL quarterback)
13. Jack Sell (*Pittsburgh Post-Gazette)*
14. George Strickler (*Chicago Tribune*)

The committee poured over eighty potential candidates for election, and after reviewing all of the names, they finally made their choices. On January 29, 1963, the Hall of Fame held a press conference to reveal the seventeen names. Hall of Fame director McCann spoke of these great men.

> The selectors can be proud of their dedicated efforts. When you look back over the great long line of pro football players (and contributors) it wasn't an easy task to settle upon just a few. Many have been great. But this is a long, firm stride toward catching up with the past.
>
> These are the milestone men of pro football. Their deeds and dogged faith wrote the history of this great game.[2]

McCann then rattled off the seventeen names—eleven players and six contributors. The names of the first Hall of Fame class read like the names on the Declaration of Independence. These were the founding fathers of professional football. The eleven players were

1. Sammy Baugh
2. Dutch Clark
3. Red Grange
4. Mel Hein
5. Pete Henry (deceased)
6. Cal Hubbard
7. Don Hutson
8. Johnny "Blood" McNally
9. Bronko Nagurski
10. Ernie Nevers
11. Jim Thorpe (deceased)

Hearing the names of the six contributors would have been personally gratifying to the late Joe F. Carr, as they all worked closely to make professional football and the NFL a successful and stable sports organization. They were also his close friends.

1. Bert Bell (deceased in 1959)
2. George Halas
3. Curly Lambeau
4. Tim Mara (deceased in 1959)
5. George Preston Marshall

The sixth and final contributor was Joe F. Carr. Twenty-four years after his death Carr was going to join sixteen other pioneers to be immortalized in the sport's ultimate shrine. For the panel of selectors, Carr's election was a simple choice. Voter Paul Menton of the *Baltimore Evening Sun* said it best about the man who cleaned up professional football. "One man was largely responsible for stopping these shenanigans, bringing money men into the sport, blending the group into a solid league which slowly gained respect. That's why I think Joe F. Carr, the National League's first president for some eighteen years before his death, deserves the honor of being the first person picked for the new Hall of Fame."[3]

The seventeen charter members were scheduled to be inducted at the Hall of Fame dedication on September 7, 1963, although the Carr family would not be invited. "There was supposed to be an invitation extended to her [daughter Mary Carr] and us boys so that we could be part of the induction ceremony," says James Carr, grandson of Joe F. Carr. "But there was no invitation extended."[4] But several families—especially those of deceased members—weren't involved in the first ceremony. The families of Jim Thorpe, Pete Henry, and Bert Bell didn't attend to accept the honor for their loved ones either. The Hall of Fame wanted star power for the first ceremony, so David Lawrence, special assistant to the U.S. president; Philip Hart, senator from Michigan; Byron "Whizzer" White, who went from the gridiron to become a U.S. Supreme Court justice; Harry Abendroth, major general; and other celebrities served as presenters for the Hall of Famers.

To represent the Carr family, the Hall of Fame selected Earl Schreiber, president of the Hall of Fame, to act as presenter for Carr, and Dan Tehan, former NFL official who was hired by the late Joe F. Carr, accepted the honor on behalf of the Carr family. "Let me say it was a great thrill to receive on behalf of the Carr family, the Joe Carr replica at Canton as his memory was honored by induction into the professional Football Hall of Fame," recalled Dan Tehan in a 1964 interview.[5] On the day of the dedication, the city of Canton rolled out the red carpet. On a beautiful September day the Hall of Fame's first induction weekend—nicknamed "Pro Football's Greatest Weekend"—started at 9:30 a.m. with a parade through the city that ended at the steps of the Hall of Fame. Then immediately after the parade the induction ceremony was held in Fawcett Stadium in front of a crowd of over 6,000 football fans. After a welcome by Canton mayor James Lawhun, the ceremony got started with the induction of George Halas, who remembered his first trip to Canton back in 1920.

> On my trip down here, my memory was stirred back quite a few years when I think of the wonderful men who did so much to develop football in this area and throughout the country. Such fellas like the Nesser brothers, Ralph Hay, Frank McNeil, Leo Lyons, Joe Carr of the Columbus Panhandles, who was president of the National Football League from 1921 to 1939, some 18 years and you may be sure that some of those years were pretty tough. They were pioneers and this is the land where football set its roots and here is the Hall of Fame where its history and traditions will be preserved and remembered.[6]

The roll call continued with names such as Grange, Mara, Nevers, Hubbard, Henry, Clark, and Lambeau, and then it was time for Joe F. Carr to take his turn to enter the hallowed place of the Pro Football Hall of Fame. Hall of Fame president Schreiber praised the son of an Irish immigrant.

> Joe Carr was the engineer of organized pro football. The little railroader put it on the right track for its ride from rags to riches. He started as manager of the Columbus Panhandles, a railroad yard team whose lineup had almost nobody but Nessers. Turning to newspaper work he became a force in organized baseball, and he was sure pro football could be developed along the same lines. His urging led to formation of the league, in its second year he took over as president. His faith had blinkers but not once did his eyes leave the rails which gleamed ahead towards his major league goal. Not once, till death shattered them. Too bad you say he's not here to proudly survey results of his devotion. Yes, but actually he's already seen it. Like he kept trying to tell so many of these people and so many others. Joe Carr saw it all down the tracks through the mist a long time ago. Receiving for Joe Carr, Sheriff of Cincinnati, Dan Tehan, football official in this league for thirty-four years . . . Dan Tehan.[7]

Dan Tehan walked to the podium to accept for Carr and he kept it short and sweet: "Honored guests, ladies and gentlemen, it's a distinct honor for the committee to select me to receive the replica of Joe Carr for the National Football Hall of Fame. It was Joe Carr who gave me the opportunity to be a small part of the greatest football league in the world. Thank you."[8]

After accepting for Carr, he left the podium and posed for photos next to the bronze bust of his mentor. The sculpted bust of Carr shined in the Canton sun and would eventually be moved into the Hall of Fame to preserve his immortality as one of the league's pioneers. "It's so incredible when people are honored by being inducted. To me it's just amazing because very few people have that privilege of having their likeness and their deeds that they did live on through a museum," says James Carr. "I'm amazed and I feel a lot of pride in my grandfather for doing what he did. The things that he did and his tenacity and his hard work, and his absolute love of football and the NFL. I'm very proud to have my grandfather honored in that way."[9]

For the Carr family it was bittersweet. Although they weren't there in person, they did appreciate with all their hearts that their loved one, Joe F. Carr, was being given the highest honor anyone involved in professional football could receive. Joe F. Carr was a charter member of the Pro Football Hall of Fame, and he would be forever honored with a bronze bust in Canton. Future generations of football fans, as well as the Carr family, could travel to the Hall of Fame and see the bronzed likeness of the man who gave the NFL a solid foundation that would be built upon to make football the most popular sport in the country.

29

The Legacy of Joe F. Carr

After her father passed away in 1939, Mary Carr spent the rest of her life taking care of her family. She did not marry, but she lived a rather healthy life at the home at 1863 Bryden Road and spent most of her time spoiling her nephews. "She would visit us every weekend. We would always walk over there to pick her up on a Friday evening and she would stay Friday evening, Saturday, and Sunday. Then Sunday evening we'd take her back home. Once we got our driver's license we continued that routine," says Gregory Carr, grandson of Joe F. Carr. "This time with her was a wonderful opportunity to learn about our grandfather. To have such close communication with my aunt who knew just about everything there was to know about my grandfather was a wonderful experience."[1]

"Inside the house it was like going back in a time capsule because the interior of the house was kept exactly the same as it had been when my grandfather and grandmother were living there," says James Carr, grandson of Joe F. Carr. "All the furniture, all the carpet, all of that sort were exactly the way that it was back then. It was a very happy time coming over to see her."[2]

Throughout her adult life when the opportunity arose, Mary Carr tried to preserve her father's legacy as one of the pioneers of the NFL. In November of 1959 *Time* magazine ran a story on the NFL with Giants linebacker Sam Huff featured on the cover. Within the article on Huff, the magazine briefly discussed the origins of the NFL. Mary was so touched by the magazine's interest in the NFL, she wrote a letter to the magazine talking about her father's involvement with the league. In the December 21, 1959 edition the letter was printed in the Letters to the Editor section.

Sir:

It was my father, the late Joe F. Carr, who organized the National Professional Football League, was elected its president in 1921, and remained president until his death in May 1939.

My father was responsible for the success and integrity of pro football, and it was he who sold "postgraduate" football to the late Timothy J. Mara, George Halas, Arthur J. Rooney, George Preston Marshall, "Curly" Lambeau, and the late Charles Bidwill, the late George A. Richards and the late Bert Bell.

MARY CARR, Columbus[3]

For her entire life she continued to love her father. On March 24, 1983, Mary Carr passed away quietly at her home on Bryden Road at the age of sixty-nine.

As the years have passed on, the name of Joe F. Carr has seemed to vanish from the scene—despite the tremendous growth of the NFL. Back in 1939 the NFL named its Most Valuable Player (MVP) award after the late Joe F. Carr, and the players who won the initial awards were some of the greatest players in the early years of the NFL.

1938—Mel Hein (New York Giants)**
1939—Parker Hall (Cleveland Rams)
1940—Ace Parker (Brooklyn Dodgers)**
1941—Don Hutson (Green Bay Packers)**
1942—Don Hutson (Green Bay Packers)**
1943—Sid Luckman (Chicago Bears)**
1944—Frank Sinkwich (Detroit Lions)
1945—Bob Waterfield (Cleveland Rams)**
1946—Bill Dudley (Pittsburgh Steelers)**
** Hall of Famer

Six different future Hall of Famers won the award in the first nine years the award was given. Then mysteriously in 1947 the writers stopped voting for the award, and the name of Joe F. Carr all but disappeared off the league's MVP award. When the United Press in 1951 and the Associated Press in 1957 started selecting the NFL MVP again, the award was not named after the former league president. It seems to be a crime that one of the league's founding fathers doesn't have his name attached to such an award or some honor associated with the NFL. Looking back at the career and legacy of Joe F. Carr, the list of accomplishments is very impressive:

1. He created the first "Constitution and Bylaws of the National Football League."

2. He developed the NFL's standard player's contract.
3. He set up territorial rights to preserve gate receipts for home teams.
4. He helped rename the league the National Football League in 1922.
5. He established peace with colleges and universities by setting up the rule that no college player could play in the NFL until after his class had graduated.
6. Along with the owners and coaches, he helped establish rules on the field that helped the NFL separate itself from the college game.
7. He established statistics for NFL players starting in 1932.
8. He split the NFL into two divisions and created the NFL Championship Game in 1933.
9. He wrote the first ever *Official NFL Record & Fact Book* (originally titled *Official Guide of the National Football League*) in 1935.
10. Along with the owners, he created the NFL draft in 1936.
11. He sold and developed the NFL's first ever promotional film—*Champions of the Gridiron*—in 1938 (released in 1939).

In his nearly nineteen years as NFL president, Joe F. Carr helped build a foundation that is still being used today. "It's the number one sport in the world. It's almost a trillion dollar business with the media. The Super Bowl is the number one sporting event in the world. That pretty much speaks for itself," says Gregory Carr, grandson of Joe F. Carr. "It was just overwhelming to me. As I got older I could see exactly what happened and how it developed and why it developed because of my grandfather," says Michael Carr, grandson of Joe F. Carr. "I really believe to this day it would not be the NFL if it wasn't for my grandfather. It had been disorganized and had structural problems. They would have trouble getting teams in large cities. They wouldn't have the direction. Just the strong-willed direction that my grandfather provided, I just don't think it would've been the same."[4]

Carr's dogged determination combined with his unwavering belief in the game of professional football made him the perfect man to lead the NFL in its early years. His vision of what the NFL could be during its formative years never wavered and he kept to his plan of building a foundation of a big-city organization. His recruitment of franchise owners in these big cities also paid off in a big way. "[They let] the man with the expertise run the league. The owners were comfortable in taking the second chair and saying to my grandfather 'OK you do it.' But another factor was that they were all very good friends," says James Carr. "He was good friends with George Halas, he was good friends with Art Rooney and he was very good friends with Tim Mara. That deep friendship that developed between my grandfather and the owners led to a type of trust in which they felt, 'OK Joe, you're the man. You have the experience. You can do the job, go ahead and do it and you're not going to get interference from us.' There was a trust buildup due to these friendships."[5]

"Well they all loved football. They weren't in it for the money. My father, Bert Bell, his life was football," says Bert Bell Jr., son of Bert Bell. "My grandfather really liked the people he worked with. He definitely liked the people that were involved in the NFL. They all got along with each other back then," says Jordan Wright, granddaughter of George Preston Marshall. "I don't think anybody could've dreamed of what it had grown into. [My father] had that commitment and the love of the game. He used to say he didn't really work at it because it was so important to him and he was so pleased that what he believed in had come to fruition in the present success of the NFL and we were all the benefactors," says Virginia McCaskey, daughter of George Halas.[6]

"I have a theory that the NFL has been blessed with the right commissioners who had the right talents at the right time," says Dan Rooney. "Joe Carr is the most underrated guy in the Hall of Fame. He came up with the rules and uniform player contracts. Bert Bell had been everything including a coach. Pete Rozelle turned it into what it is today and Paul Tagliabue took it to the next level. Now Roger Goodell, and he worked for both Pete and Paul."[7]

Over the NFL's first nine decades, Carr is one of only eight men who have held the position of president-commissioner. The eight men include Jim Thorpe, Joe F. Carr, Carl L. Storck, Elmer Layden, Bert Bell, Pete Rozelle, Paul Tagliabue, and Roger Goodell. Only Rozelle's twenty-nine year run (1960-1989) as commissioner was longer than Carr's tenure. Each man has contributed greatly to building professional football to its current status as the world's most popular sport. For Joe F. Carr, his lasting legacy is that he helped move the NFL from its small-town roots to the big city—giving the sport the proper place to become a successful business. Along the way he helped recruit a fantastic group of sportsmen and businessmen to run these big-city franchises. In a 1969 interview with author Myron Cope, Chicago Bears owner George Halas spoke of the early owners "league first" philosophy that Carr instilled: "One of my principles was always to do anything that was to the benefit of the league, and that was the case with all of the other teams, too. They were not selfish. They did not think just in terms of 'What's good for me?' They thought in terms of the league, and that's one of the reasons why the league has been so successful—why the game has grown into the greatest sport in the country."[8]

Carr's leadership and unbelievable vision of what the sport could become has endured for nearly a century. When looking back at Carr's legacy, some people might say, "Isn't it a shame that he didn't live to see professional football become the country's number one sport." But just like former Hall of Fame president Earl Schreiber said in his presenter's speech in 1963, "actually he's already seen it. Like he kept trying to tell so many of these people and so many others. Joe Carr saw it all down the tracks . . . through the mist . . . a long time ago."[9]

Appendix: Dates and Locations of NFL Meetings Presided by NFL President Joe F. Carr (1921–1939)

Date	Location
April 30, 1921	Portage Hotel (Akron, Ohio)
June 18, 1921	Hollenden Hotel (Cleveland, Ohio)
August 27, 1921	LaSalle Hotel (Chicago, Illinois)
January 28, 1922	Courtland Hotel (Canton, Ohio)
June 24–25, 1922	Hollenden Hotel (Cleveland, Ohio)
August 20, 1922	Triangle Park (Dayton, Ohio)
January 20, 1923	Sherman House (Chicago, Illinois)
July 28–29, 1923	Hotel Sherman (Chicago, Illinois)
January 26–27, 1924	Hotel Sherman (Chicago, Illinois)
July 25–26, 1924	Hotel Sherman (Chicago, Illinois)
January 24–25, 1925	Hotel Statler (Cleveland, Ohio)
February 25, 1925 (Exec. Mtg.)	Columbus, Ohio
August 1–2, 1925	Hotel Sherman (Chicago, Illinois)
February 6–7, 1926	Hotel Statler (Detroit, Michigan)
July 10–11, 1926	Benjamin Franklin Hotel (Philadelphia, Pennsylvania)
February 5–6, 1927	Astor Hotel (New York, New York)
April 23, 1927	Hotel Statler (Cleveland, Ohio)
July 16–17, 1927	Hotel Northland (Green Bay, Wisconsin)
September 4, 1927	Hotel Statler (Cleveland, Ohio)
February 11, 1928	Hotel Statler (Cleveland, Ohio)
July 7, 1928	Biltmore Hotel (Providence, Rhode Island)
August 12, 1928	Statler Hotel (Detroit, Michigan)
February 2, 1929	Hotel Sherman (Chicago, Illinois)
July 27–28, 1929	Seaside Hotel (Atlantic City, New Jersey)
January 25, 1930	Van Cleve Hotel (Dayton, Ohio)
July 12–13, 1930	Seaside Hotel (Atlantic City, New Jersey)
July 11–12, 1931	Edgewater Beach Hotel (Chicago, Illinois)
July 9–10, 1932	Ritz-Carlton Hotel (Atlantic City, New Jersey)

February 25–26, 1933	Fort Pitt Hotel (Pittsburgh, Pennsylvania)
July 8–9, 1933	Blackstone Hotel (Chicago, Illinois)
December 16, 1933	Hotel Sherman (Chicago, Illinois)
June 30–July 1, 1934	Commodore Hotel (New York, New York)
December 10, 1934	Victoria Hotel (New York, New York)
May 18, 1935	Fort Pitt Hotel (Pittsburgh, Pennsylvania)
June 16, 1935	Palmer House (Chicago, Illinois)
February 8–9, 1936	Ritz-Carlton Hotel (Philadelphia, Pennsylvania)
December 12, 1936	Hotel Lincoln (New York, New York)
February 12–13, 1937	Hotel Sherman (Chicago, Illinois)
August 31, 1938	Palmer House (Chicago, Illinois)
December 9–10, 1938	Hotel New Yorker (New York, New York)
February 9–12, 1939	Congress Hotel (Chicago, Illinois)

Notes

Many sources and interviews were used for this book, including the Joe F. Carr Scrapbook that the Carr family has kept for over eighty years. I made a copy of each page of the scrapbook and those pages produced two binders. The two binders have a total of 564 pages. I gave each page a number so within the notes, each reference to the scrapbooks is titled JFC Scrapbook, Binder 1 or 2, with the page number. After the release of this book I will donate a copy of the two binders to the Pro Football Hall of Fame. I also used many of the publications from the Professional Football Researchers Association (PFRA), which I have been a member of since 1993. I want to thank the late Bob Carroll, former executive director of the PFRA and editor of the PFRA publication *Coffin Corner*, for giving me permission to use the PFRA's publications and articles—especially the series *Bulldogs on Sunday* (1892–1939)—in this book.

Another vital source was my access to all the "NFL Meeting Minutes" (1920–1939) during Carr's time as NFL president. These minutes are permanently located in the archives at the Pro Football Hall of Fame in Canton, Ohio.

Also, I was able to obtain two years of the *NFL Bulletins* (1934–1935), which were originally released by Carr's NFL office in Columbus, Ohio. The *NFL Bulletins* came from the Bert Bell family collection that went up for public auction several years ago. The original copies of these *Bulletins* have been donated to the Pro Football Hall of Fame.

All attendance figures were taken from Bob Carroll, Michael Gershman, David Neft, and John Thorn, eds., *Total Football II: The Official Encyclopedia of the National Football League* (1999), as well as Bob Gill and Tod Maher, *The Pro Football Encyclopedia* (1997). Both of these great encyclopedias use actual newspaper accounts of the games to report attendance figures. The figures are not actual paid admissions, just reported figures from game recaps.

INTRODUCTION

1. Carr's cheery greeting to *Journal* writer Emerson Davis from the *Ohio State Journal*, December 6, 1931.
2. *Chicago Tribune*, July 9, 1933. *Columbus Citizen*, November 24, 1932.
3. Joe F. Carr file, Pro Football Hall of Fame, newspaper article, January 27, 1933.
4. Population numbers came from U.S. Bureau of the Census, *Population of States and Counties of the United States: 1790–1990* (Washington, D.C.: Author, 1996). The population numbers are for the counties the NFL franchises resided in—since most teams did have fans commute from different areas to attend games from 1920 to 1940.
5. U.S. Bureau of the Census, *Population of States and Counties*.

CHAPTER 1: THE IRISH WAY (1841–1878)

1. The family name of Karr (sometimes the spelling was K-e-r-r) was used by the family from the birth of Michael Karr in 1841 to 1900 when they went by the current spelling of Carr. *Columbus City Directories 1866–1939*.
2. 1840 Irish Census. James Carr, author interview, July 31, 2004.
3. 1850–1860 Irish Census.
4. 1860 Ohio Census.
5. Ed Lentz, "As it Were," *This Week in Westland*, August 30, 1993, 12.
6. Gregory Carr, author interview, July 31, 2004.
7. 1870 Columbus City Directory.
8. Michael Carr, author interview, July 31, 2004.
9. The information on Margaret Hurley came from the Ohio Census, obituary, *Ohio State Journal*, July 20, 1898, and Margaret Mooney, author interview, July 31, 2004.
10. James Carr, author interview, July 31, 2004.
11. *Diocese of Columbus: The History of Fifty Years, 1868–1918*, 176–186. **[AU1:]**
12. *History of St. Patrick's Church* (Columbus: Saint Patrick Press, 1994), 1–17. **[AU2]**
13. The information on the Karr children came from Ohio Censuses, baptismal records at St. Patrick Church (Columbus, Ohio), and family tree research done by Margaret Mooney, great-niece of Joe Carr.

CHAPTER 2: GROWING UP IN COLUMBUS, OHIO (1879–1893)

1. 1880 Columbus City Directory.
2. Margaret Mooney, author interview, July 31, 2004.
3. Joseph Francis Carr was born on October 23, 1879, in Columbus, Ohio, according to his baptismal record. On the baptismal record his last name is spelled K-e-r-r. The original baptismal record was found and is kept at St. Joseph's Cathe-

dral in Columbus, Ohio. Rev. Michael M. Meara performed the baptism for the Carr family. A copy also exists at the Pro Football Hall of Fame.

4. 1880 Ohio Census. The information on Bridget Karr was given by Margaret Mooney, author interview, July 31, 2004, and James Carr, author interview, July 31, 2004.

5. Robert Quinn (1870–1954) was the general manager for the Columbus Senators for fifteen years (1902–1917) before spending twenty-nine years in Major League Baseball with four different teams. After his retirement, Quinn spent four years as the president of the Baseball Hall of Fame (1948–1951). *Ohio State Journal*, March 13, 1954.

6. Robert Drury, obituary, *Ohio State Journal*, August 19, 1933.

7. 1900 United States Census. Jim Heavey, author interview, March 28, 2009.

8. *Chicago Daily Tribune*, October 21, 1911. In October 1917 John Karr had another police raid of his cigar shop in Chicago for gambling; see *Chicago Daily Tribune*, January 18, 1917; September 18, 1917.

9. Heavey, interview.

10. *Ohio State Journal*, undated article titled "The Good Ole Days." JFC Scrapbook, Binder 1, p. 57.

CHAPTER 3: THE LOVE OF A FAMILY IS REPLACED BY A LOVE OF SPORTS (1894–1906)

1. The gold school medal that Joseph F. Karr won was excellence in Bible history (written on the front). The actual medal is 2 and 5/16th inches in length and 1 and 1/2 inches wide and belongs to the Carr family in Columbus.

2. Machinist information came from newspaper article written by Russ Needham, *Columbus Citizen*, January 9, 1931. Gregory Carr, author interview, July 31, 2004. Michael Carr, author interview, July 31, 2004.

3. James Carr, author interview, July 31, 2004.

4. *Ohio State Journal*, July 23, 1898. *Columbus Dispatch*, July 21, 1898.

5. The information about the Carr family name came from the Carr family and research done by Margaret Mooney. Also, Columbus City Directories, 1864–1940.

6. Margaret Mooney, author interview, July 31, 2004.

7. *Ohio State Journal*, May 24, 1939.

8. *Canton Repository*, May 21, 1939.

9. Chris Willis, *The Columbus Panhandles: A Complete History of Pro Football's Toughest Team, 1900–1922* (Lanham, MD: Scarecrow Press, 2007), 6–9.

10. *Columbus Dispatch*, February 6, 1905. *Columbus Press-Post*, February 6, 1905.

11. Gregory Carr, interview.

12. Columbus City Directories, 1899–1914.

13. Information on the Massillon–Canton game is from Bob Carroll, *The Tigers Roar: Professional Football in Ohio, 1903–09* (North Huntingdon, PA: Pro Football Researchers Association, 1990), 45–80.

14. Michael Carr, interview.

CHAPTER 4: THE COLUMBUS PANHANDLES AND THE GREAT NESSER BROTHERS (1907–1909)

1. Robert W. Peterson, *Pigskin: The Early Years of Pro Football* (New York: Oxford University Press, 1997), 45–46.
2. Joe F. Carr, as told to Michael Fanning, "Post-Graduate Football," unpublished, 1938, 18.
3. Carr, "Post-Graduate Football," 18.
4. All the information on the Nesser family background comes from Chris Willis, *The Columbus Panhandles: A Complete History of Pro Football's Toughest Team, 1900–1922* (Lanham, MD: Scarecrow Press, 2007), xx–xxiii.
5. James Carr, author interview, July 31, 2004. Irene Cassady, author interview, May 7, 2005.
6. Cassady, interview.
7. Kate Benson, author interview, September 14, 2002.
8. *Ohio State Journal*, December 7, 1917. Babe Sherman, author interview, July 6, 2000.
9. Sherman, interview.
10. Football salary info came from newspaper article titled "A Voice from Past: One-Time Grid 'Iron Man' Supports Two-Platoon System." Article came from Nesser family scrapbook.
11. Cassady, interview.
12. Joann Franke, author interview, April 22, 2007.
13. *Buffalo Evening-News*, November 20, 1922.
14. Cassady, interview.
15. Cassady, interview. James Carr, author interview, August 1, 2004.
16. *Columbus Dispatch*, October 14, 1907. This is the first-ever mention in a Columbus newspaper of Joe Carr as Panhandles team manager in 1907.
17. *Ohio State Journal*, October 21, 1907.
18. *Columbus Dispatch*, November 10, 1907. This is the first-ever team photo of the Panhandles and Joe Carr to appear in a Columbus newspaper.
19. *Columbus Press-Post*, November 11, 1907.
20. *Ohio State Journal*, November 13, 1907.
21. Ted Schneider, author interview, May 7, 2005.
22. *Ohio State Journal*, November 18, 1907.
23. Carr, "Post-Graduate Football," 16.
24. *Columbus Press-Post*, October 5, 1908.
25. *Ohio State Journal*, October 8, 1908.
26. *Columbus Dispatch*, November 29, 1908.
27. *Columbus Dispatch*, November 30, 1908.
28. *Ohio State Journal*, November 30, 1908.
29. Carr quote came from article called "Nesser Stuff" from the Columbus Panhandles file at the Pro Football Hall of Fame.
30. Cassady, interview.
31. Cassady, interview.
32. Football ad appeared in the *Canton Daily News*, October 25, 1909.

33. *Canton Repository*, November 1, 1909.
34. *Ohio State Journal*, November 4, 1909.
35. *Ohio State Journal*, November 8, 1909.
36. *Columbus Citizen*, November 13, 1909. This was the first ever newspaper article written by a Columbus newspaper on the five Nesser brothers.
37. *Dayton Journal*, November 15, 1909. *Ohio State Journal*, November 15, 1909.
38. *Ohio State Journal*, November 17, 1909.

CHAPTER 5: STARTING A FAMILY (1910–1913)

1. Sally Nesser, author interview, June 2, 2003. Connie Shomo, author interview, June 2, 2003.
2. *Ohio State Journal*, October 20, 1910.
3. *Ohio State Journal*, October 24, 1910. *Columbus Citizen*, January 9, 1931.
4. *Ohio State Journal*, October 27, 1910.
5. *Ohio State Journal*, October 28, 1910.
6. *Ohio State Journal*, October 30, 1910.
7. *Columbus Dispatch*, November 25, 1910.
8. *Richmond Palladium*, June 13, 1907. *Richmond Evening Item*, March 2, 1908. *Richmond Palladium*, March 2, 1908.
9. Martha Sullivan, author interview, March 4, 2007. Additional Sullivan family information on homes and occupations was found in Richmond City Directories, 1857–1913.
10. Michael Carr, author interview, July 31, 2004.
11. June 27, 1911, wedding invitation, courtesy of Carr family.
12. Sullivan, interview.
13. Joe Colburn, author interview, June 4, 2006.
14. *Ohio State Journal*, October 15, 16, 17, 1911.
15. *Akron Beacon-Journal*, October 16, 1911.
16. *Ohio State Journal*, November 13, 1911.
17. *Ohio State Journal*, November 21, 1911.
18. *Columbus Citizen*, November 27, 1911.
19. *Ohio State Journal*, November 29, 1911.
20. *Wellston Telegram*, November 31, 1911.
21. *Dayton Journal*, December 4, 1911.
22. Gregory Carr, author interview, July 31, 2004.
23. Jack Cusack, *Pioneer in Pro Football* (Forth Worth, TX: Author, 1963), 3–5.
24. *Hamilton Evening Journal*, November 15, 1912.
25. *Columbus Citizen*, October 12, 1912.
26. *Canton Repository*, October 16, 1912.
27. *Canton Daily News*, October 21, 1912.
28. *Newark (Ohio) Advocate*, November 22, 1912.
29. *Ohio State Journal*, September 2, 1913. *Columbus Dispatch*, September 2, 1913.
30. Martha Sullivan, author interview, November 21, 2004.

31. *Canton Daily News*, October 27, 1913.
32. *Ohio State Journal*, December 2, 1913.
33. *Columbus Dispatch*, December 7, 1913.
34. *Ohio State Journal*, December 15, 1913.
35. *Ohio State Journal*, December 15, 1913.

CHAPTER 6: PRO FOOTBALL'S MOST FAMOUS TRAVELING TEAM (1914–1916)

1. Joy Dolan, author interview, March 15, 2008.
2. Margaret Mooney, author interview, July 31, 2004. Dolan, interview.
3. James Carr, author interview, July 31, 2004. Michael Carr, author interview, July 31, 2004.
4. *Ohio State Journal*, September 24, 1914.
5. *Akron Beacon-Journal*, October 5, 1914. *Canton Repository*, October 5, 1914.
6. *Ohio State Journal*, October 7, 1914.
7. *Ohio State Journal*, October 19, 1914.
8. *Canton Repository*, October 21, 1914.
9. *Canton Repository*, October 26, 1914.
10. *Ohio State Journal*, November 16, 1914.
11. *Columbus Citizen*, November 21, 1914.
12. Irene Cassady, author interview, May 7, 2005.
13. *Newark (Ohio) Advocate*, August 11, 1915.
14. *Ohio State Journal*, October 2, 1915.
15. *Marion Daily Star*, October 6, 1915.
16. *Canton Daily News*, October 12, 1915.
17. *Canton Repository*, October 13, 1915.
18. *Canton Daily News*, October 18, 1915.
19. *Toledo Daily Blade*, October 21, 1915.
20. *Toledo News-Bee*, October 25, 1915.
21. *Massillon Independent*, October 30, 1915.
22. *Columbus Dispatch*, November 1, 1915.
23. James Brigham, author interview, March 11, 2006.
24. *Columbus Citizen*, August 8, 1948.
25. *Ohio State Journal*, November 8, 1915.
26. *Ohio State Journal*, November 15, 1915.
27. *Youngstown Vindicator*, November 21, 1915.
28. *Fort Wayne Journal-Gazette*, November 26, 1915.
29. *Fort Wayne Journal-Gazette*, November 26, 1915.
30. *Columbus Dispatch*, November 30, 1915.
31. *Ohio State Journal*, December 1, 1915.
32. *Columbus Dispatch*, December 2, 1915.
33. Jack Cusack, *Pioneer in Pro Football* (Forth Worth, TX: Author, 1963), 9.
34. Bob Carroll, *The Ohio League, 1910–1919* (North Huntingdon, PA: Professional Football Researchers Association, 1997), 44–45.

35. *Portsmouth Daily Times*, September 21, 1916.
36. *Ohio State Journal*, October 14, 1916.
37. *Detroit Free Press*, October 20, 1916.
38. *Cleveland Plain Dealer*, October 23, 1916.
39. *Columbus Dispatch*, October 26, 1916.
40. *Canton Repository*, October 28, 1916.
41. *Canton Repository*, October 28, 1916.
42. *Canton Repository*, October 29, 1916.
43. *Canton Daily News*, October 30, 1916.
44. *Canton Daily News*, October 30, 1916.
45. *Canton Daily News*, Oct. 30, 1916.
46. *Toledo Daily Blade*, November 2, 1916.
47. *Toledo Daily Blade*, November 4, 1916.
48. *Toledo News-Bee*, November 6, 1916.
49. *Toledo News-Bee*, November 6, 1916.
50. *Massillon Independent*, November 8, 1916.
51. *Columbus Citizen*, November 14, 1916.
52. *Cleveland Plain Dealer*, November 25, 1916.
53. *Ohio State Journal*, December 6, 1916.
54. *Columbus Dispatch*, December 11, 1916.

CHAPTER 7: MAKING A NAME FOR HIMSELF (1917–1919)

1. *Fort Wayne Journal-Gazette*, December 5, 1916. *Brownsville (Texas) Herald*, January 4, 1917.
2. *Portsmouth Daily Times*, March 29, 1917.
3. *Massillon Independent*, September 25, 1917.
4. *New Castle (Pennsylvania) News*, October 17, 1917.
5. *Akron Beacon-Journal*, October 11, 1917.
6. *Canton Daily News*, October 21, 1917.
7. *Canton Repository*, October 22, 1917.
8. *Youngstown Vindicator*, October 24, 1917.
9. *Youngstown Vindicator*, October 27, 1917.
10. *Canton Daily News*, October 31, 1917.
11. *Toledo News-Bee*, November 8, 1917.
12. *Toledo News-Bee*, November 7, 1916.
13. *Ohio State Journal*, November 30, 1917.
14. *Canton Daily News*, December 3, 1917.
15. *Canton Daily News*, December 8, 1917.
16. *Ohio State Journal*, September 24, 1918.
17. Dolores Seitz, author interview, June 9, 2007.
18. Seitz, interview.
19. Seitz, interview.
20. Seitz, interview.
21. *Ohio State Journal*, July 5, 1919.

22. James King, author interview, June 1, 2003.
23. King, interview.
24. Jack Cusack, *Pioneer in Pro Football* (Forth Worth, TX: Author, 1963), 30. Bob Carroll, *The Ohio League, 1910–1919* (North Huntingdon, PA: Professional Football Researchers Association, 1997), 78.
25. Carroll, *The Ohio League*, 78–79.
26. Carroll, *The Ohio League*, 79.
27. *Akron Beacon-Journal*, September 5, 1919.
28. *Ohio State Journal*, October 2, 1919. *Ohio State Journal*, October 3, 1919. *Ohio State Journal*, October 4, 1919. *Ohio State Journal*, October 7, 1919. *Ohio State Journal*, October 8, 1919.
29. Carroll, *The Ohio League*, 88.
30. *Columbus Citizen*, November 15, 1919.
31. Carroll, *The Ohio League*, 94–95.
32. Carroll, *The Ohio League*, 95–96.

CHAPTER 8: THE AMERICAN PROFESSIONAL FOOTBALL ASSOCIATION (1920)

1. Joe F. Carr's proposed new professional football league appeared in newspapers in Ohio and it was eight months before the NFL's first-ever meeting in Canton, Ohio, at the automobile dealership of Ralph Hay. *Massillon Evening Independent*, January 8, 1920. *Portsmouth Times*, January 9, 1920.
2. *Sandusky (Ohio) Star-Journal*, January 15, 1920.
3. Dan Forrestal, *The Kernel and the Barn: The 75-Year Story of the Staley Company* (New York: Simon and Schuster, 1982), 42.
4. George S. Halas, with Gwen Morgan and Arthur Veysey, *Halas: An Autobiography* (Chicago: Bonus Books, 1986), 31–32.
5. Virginia McCaskey, author interview, 1999.
6. Halas, *Halas*, 53–55.
7. Bob Carroll and PFRA Research, *Bulldogs on Sunday, 1920* (North Huntingdon, PA: Pro Football Researchers Association, n.d.), 3–4.
8. Carroll and PFRA, *Bulldogs on Sunday*, 3–4.
9. Carroll and PFRA, *Bulldogs on Sunday*, 3–4.
10. Halas, *Halas*, 60.
11. "APFA League Meeting Minutes," September 17, 1920. The original minutes that were typed by Art Ranney (Akron) are now currently on display at the Pro Football Hall of Fame.
12. Mike Rathet and Don Smith, *Their Deeds and Dogged Faith* (New York: Rutledge Books and Balsam Press, 1984), 25.
13. George Vass, *George Halas and the Chicago Bears* (Chicago: Henry Regnery, 1971), 6–7.
14. APFA League Minutes, September 17, 1920.
15. *Canton Repository*, September 18, 1920. *Ohio State Journal*, September 18, 1920.
16. *Akron Beacon-Journal*, October 7, 1920.

17. Fritz Pollard, archival interview, NFL Films, 1976.
18. *Des Moines (Iowa) News*, December 9, 1920.
19. *Cedar Rapids (Iowa) Evening Gazette*, December 24, 1920.
20. Forrestal, *The Kernel and the Barn*, 48.
21. *Buffalo Courier*, December 26, 1920.
22. *Ogden Standard-Examiner*, December 19, 1920.
23. Halas, *Halas*, 66.

CHAPTER 9: PRESIDENT ELECT (1921)

1. "APFA Meeting Minutes," April 30, 1921.
2. Bob Carroll and PFRA Research, *Bulldogs on Sunday, 1921* (North Huntingdon, PA: Pro Football Researchers Association, n.d.), 3. Joe Carr's first salary was mentioned in Howard Roberts, *The Story of Pro Football* (New York: Rand McNally, 1953), 42. The $1,000 salary was never mentioned in the "NFL Meeting Minutes."
3. James Carr, author interview, September 14, 2002, and July 31, 2004.
4. JFC Scrapbook, Binder 1, p. 162.
5. "APFA Meeting Minutes," April 30, 1921.
6. Ray Didinger, "The Man Who Had a Dream," *Pro! The Official Program of the National Football League* 7, no. 5 (September 18, 1977), 12C.
7. *Ohio State Journal*, May 2, 1921.
8. *Canton Daily News*, May 2, 1921. "APFA Meeting Minutes," June 18, 1921.
9. *Canton Daily News*, June 19, 1921.
10. "APFA Meeting Minutes," June 18, 1921.
11. "APFA Meeting Minutes," August 27, 1921.
12. David Zimmerman, *Curly Lambeau: The Man behind the Mystique* (Hales Corner, WI: Eagle Books, 2003), 28–29.
13. Zimmerman, *Curly Lambeau*, 28–29.
14. Zimmerman, *Curly Lambeau*, 28–29.
15. Chuck Johnson, *The Green Bay Packers: Pro Football's Pioneer Team* (New York: Thomas Nelson, 1961), 43, 48.
16. Zimmerman, *Curly Lambeau*, 30.
17. "APFA Meeting Minutes," August 27, 1921.
18. *Columbus Citizen-Journal*, May 24, 1939.
19. *Oakland Tribune*, August 28, 1921.
20. George S. Halas, with Gwen Morgan and Arthur Veysey, *Halas: An Autobiography* (Chicago: Bonus Books, 1986), 69–70.
21. Copy of the October 6, 1921, letter between Staley and Halas appears in Dan Forrestal, *The Kernel and the Barn: The 75-Year Story of the Staley Company* (New York: Simon and Schuster, 1982), photo spread.
22. Halas, *Halas*, 71–73.
23. Halas, *Halas*, 71–73.
24. *Columbus Citizen*, December 9, 1921.
25. Carroll and PFRA, *Bulldogs on Sunday, 1921*, 13.

CHAPTER 10: THE NATIONAL FOOTBALL LEAGUE (1922)

1. Lester Higgins, archival interview, NFL Films, 1976. *Massillon Evening Independent*, December 20, 1921.
2. *Massillon Evening Independent*, January 21, 1922.
3. Bob Carroll and PFRA Research. *Bulldogs on Sunday, 1922* (North Huntingdon, PA: Pro Football Researchers Association, n.d.), 5–15.
4. Richard Whittingham, *Bears: In Their Own Words* (Chicago: Contemporary Books, 1991), 157–158.
5. Whittingham, *Bears*, 157–158. *Fort Wayne Sentinel*, February 4, 1922.
6. Carroll and PFRA, *Bulldogs on Sunday, 1922*, 1–3.
7. George S. Halas, with Gwen Morgan and Arthur Veysey, *Halas: An Autobiography* (Chicago: Bonus Books, 1986), 76.
8. Halas, *Halas*, 76.
9. "APFA Meeting Minutes," January 28, 1922.
10. James Carr, author interview, July 31–August 1, 2004.
11. "APFA Meeting Minutes," January 28, 1922.
12. *Columbus Citizen*, February 1, 1922.
13. Halas, *Halas*, 91.
14. Carroll and PFRA, *Bulldogs on Sunday, 1922*, 14.
15. Bryan Cummings, *Airedales: The Oorang Story* (Calgary, Alberta, Canada: Detselig Enterprises, 2001), 57.
16. Bob Lingo, author interview, June 25, 2000.
17. *Oorang Comments and Oorang Catalog 26*. (LaRue, OH: Oorang Kennels, n.d.), 123.
18. Lingo, interview.
19. Cummings, *Airedales*, 90–91.
20. Lingo, interview.
21. *Akron Beacon-Journal*, January 24, 1995.
22. Lingo, interview.
23. "NFL Meeting Minutes," June 24–25, 1922. *Rock Island Independents vs Chicago Bears Official Program*, Sunday December 9, 1923. Code of Ethics statement appeared in 1922 NFL programs.
24. "NFL Meeting Minutes," June 24–25, 1922.
25. "NFL Meeting Minutes," August 20, 1922.
26. Guy Chamberlin, archival interview, Pro Football Hall of Fame, 1965 (audio interview).
27. Halas, *Halas*, 82.
28. *Green Bay Press-Gazette*, November 6, 1922.
29. *Columbus Citizen*, November 27, 1922.
30. *Ohio State Journal*, December 24, 1922.

CHAPTER 11: DEFENDING PROFESSIONAL FOOTBALL (1923)

1. Larry Names, *The History of the Green Bay Packers: The Lambeau Years, Part One* (Wautoma, WI: Angel Press, 1987), 85–86.

2. Names, *The History of the Green Bay Packers*, 85–86.
3. Names, *The History of the Green Bay Packers*, 85–86. The attendance figures are from the newspaper accounts of the game and Bob Carroll, Michael Gershman, David Neft, and John Thorn, eds., *Total Football II: The Official Encyclopedia of the National Football League* (New York: HarperCollins, 1999), 1746–1753.
4. Chuck Johnson, *The Green Bay Packers: Pro Football's Pioneer Team* (New York: Thomas Nelson, 1961), 50–51.
5. George S. Halas, with Gwen Morgan and Arthur Veysey, *Halas: An Autobiography* (Chicago: Bonus Books, 1986), 86.
6. Martha Sullivan, author interview, March 4, 2007.
7. Sullivan, interview.
8. "NFL Meeting Minutes," January 20, 1923.
9. "NFL Meeting Minutes," January 20, 1923.
10. Bob Carroll and PFRA Research, *Bulldogs on Sunday, 1923* (North Huntingdon, PA: Pro Football Researchers Association, n.d.), 2.
11. JFC Scrapbook, Binder 1, p. 21.
12. "NFL Meeting Minutes," July 28–29, 1923. This is the first time that the "NFL Meeting Minutes" mention Joe F. Carr taking a salary—which is for $1,000 a year.
13. "NFL Meeting Minutes," July 28–29, 1923.
14. JFC Scrapbook, Binder 1, p. 36. *Chicago Tribune*, July 30, 1923.
15. Carroll and PFRA, *Bulldogs on Sunday, 1923*, 3.
16. Ralph Hay's letter to the fans of the Canton Bulldogs appeared in *Hammond Pros vs Canton Bulldogs Official Program*, Sunday, September 30, 1923.
17. *Ohio State Journal*, September 30, 1923.
18. William Guthery, author interview, June 26, 2000.
19. *Ohio State Journal*, October 15, 1923.
20. Joe F. Carr's Gridiron Gossip columns appeared every Friday in the *Ohio State Journal*. Those quoted are from October 19, October 26, and November 2, 1923.
21. Amos Alonzo Stagg's comments appeared in the *Ohio State Journal*, November 2, 1923; *Waterloo (Iowa) Evening Courier & Reporter; Galveston (Texas) Daily News* and *San Antonio Express*, November 2, 1923.
22. Joe F. Carr's statement responding to the comments made by Amos Alonzo Stagg appeared in the *Ohio State Journal*, November 2, 1923, and the *Lincoln (Nebraska) Star Journal*, November 3, 1923. Some text illegible.
23. *Columbus Citizen*, November 8, 1923.
24. *Ohio State Journal*, December 7, 1923.
25. Attendances figures from Carroll et al., *Total Football II*.
26. Carroll and PFRA, *Bulldogs on Sunday, 1923*, 7–8.
27. *Ohio State Journal*, December 21, 1923.

CHAPTER 12: BABY STEPS FOR PRESIDENT CARR (1924)

1. "NFL Meeting Minutes," January 26–27.
2. "NFL Meeting Minutes," January 26–27.

3. "NFL Meeting Minutes," January 26–27.
4. "NFL Meeting Minutes," July 25–26.
5. "NFL Meeting Minutes," July 25–26.
6. Howard Barnes, *A Documentary Scrapbook of Football in Frankford* (Philadelphia: Historical Society of Frankford, 1985), 1, 27, 51.
7. *Canton Repository*, August 24, 1924.
8. *Ohio State Journal*, September 28, 1924. *Ohio State Journal*, October 4, 1924.
9. *Ohio State Journal*, October 17, 1924.
10. Attendance figures from Bob Carroll, Michael Gershman, David Neft, and John Thorn, eds., *Total Football II: The Official Encyclopedia of the National Football League* (New York: HarperCollins, 1999).
11. *Columbus Citizen*, November 10, 1924. *Columbus Dispatch*, November 10, 1924.
12. Attendance figures for Frankford Yellow Jackets games from newspaper accounts and Carroll et al., *Total Football II.*
13. Attendance figure for Chicago Bears–Cleveland Bulldogs game, *Davenport (Iowa) Democrat & Leader*, December 8, 1924.
14. *Ohio State Journal*, December 14, 1924.
15. Carr's 1924 NFL recap article, *Ohio State Journal*, December 21, 1924.
16. JFC Scrapbook, Binder 1, p. 54.

CHAPTER 13: THE NFL COMES TO NEW YORK CITY (1925)

1. John S. Sullivan information from interview with Martha Sullivan, March 24, 2007.
2. "NFL Meeting Minutes," January 24–25, 1925.
3. "NFL Meeting Minutes," January 24–25, 1925.
4. "NFL Meeting Minutes," January 24–25, 1925.
5. George S. Halas, with Gwen Morgan and Arthur Veysey, *Halas: An Autobiography* (Chicago: Bonus Books, 1986), 94.
6. *New York Times*, June 11, 1940. *Massillon Independent*, October 28, 1908. *Massillon Independent*, June 2, 1916.
7. Background information on Tim Mara from Arthur Daley, *Pro Football's Hall of Fame* (New York: Tempo Books, 1963), 146–147, and Carlo DeVito, *Wellington: The Maras, the Giants, and the City of New York* (Chicago: Triumph Books, 2006), 5–10.
8. Daley, *Pro Football's Hall of Fame*, 146.
9. Dave Klein, *The New York Giants: Yesterday, Today, Tomorrow* (Chicago: Henry Regnery Company, 1973), 16–17.
10. The conversation in Gibson's office between Carr and Mara regarding the establishment of an NFL franchise in New York is found in Daley, *Pro Football's Hall of Fame*, 143.
11. Klein, *The New York Giants*, 18–19.
12. Klein, *The New York Giants*, 18–19. Daley, *Pro Football's Hall of Fame*, 142.
13. *New York Times*, May 15, 1925. More information about the meeting was published in the *Massillon Independent*, June 2, 1925; *Ohio State Journal*, May 15, 1925; *Oneonta (New York) Star*, May 15, 1925.

14. *New York Times*, September 10, 1925.
15. Jim Terzian, *New York Giants* (New York: Macmillan, 1973), 159.
16. "NFL Meeting Minutes," August 1–2, 1925.
17. "NFL Meeting Minutes," August 1–2, 1925.
18. In 1925 Joe F. Carr's salary was raised to $2,500 a year. "NFL Meeting Minutes," August 2, 1925. Halas, *Halas*, 94–95.
19. *New York Times*, September 10, 1925. Ticket prices from *New York Times*, October 18, 1925.
20. Klein, *The New York Giants*, 19.
21. Richard Whittingham, *Illustrated History of the New York Giants* (Chicago: Triumph Books), 2005, 1.
22. Whittingham, *Illustrated History of the New York Giants*, 1. *New York Times*, October 19, 1925.
23. Attendance figures from Bob Carroll, Michael Gershman, David Neft, and John Thorn, eds., *Total Football II: The Official Encyclopedia of the National Football League* (New York: HarperCollins, 1999).
24. Carroll et al., *Total Football II*.
25. *New York Times*, November 16, 1925. *Columbus Dispatch*, November 16, 1925.

CHAPTER 14: THE GALLOPING GHOST AND POTTSVILLE CONTROVERSY (1925)

1. John M. Carroll, *Red Grange and the Rise of Modern Football* (Urbana: University of Illinois Press, 1999), 69.
2. *Decatur (Illinois) Review*, November 12, 1925.
3. Huff, Zuppke, Yost, and Pegler quoted in Carroll, *Red Grange and the Rise of Modern Football*, 69–79.
4. *Ohio State Journal*, November 17, 1925.
5. *Ohio State Journal*, November 18, 1925.
6. *Columbus Citizen*, November 20, 1925.
7. *Ohio State Journal*, November 22, 1925.
8. *St. Patrick Church Bulletin*, November–December 1925.
9. *Ohio State Journal*, November 23, 1925. *Portsmouth Times*, November 24, 1925. *Ohio State Journal*, November 25, 1925.
10. JFC Scrapbook, Binder 1, p. 58.
11. *Ohio State Journal*, November 28, 1925.
12. JFC Scrapbook, Binder 1, p. 63.
13. Carroll, *Red Grange and the Rise of Modern Football*, 93.
14. Richard Whittingham, *The Chicago Bears: An Illustrated History* (New York: Rand McNally, 1982), 42.
15. Whittingham, *The Chicago Bears*, 42.
16. Red Grange, as told to Ira Morton, *The Red Grange Story: An Autobiography* (Urbana: University of Illinois Press, 1993), 94.
17. Carroll, *Red Grange and the Rise of Modern Football*, 98–99.
18. Richard Whittingham, *What a Game They Played* (Lincoln: University of Nebraska Press, 2001), 133.

19. Carroll, *Red Grange and the Rise of Modern Football*, 108.
20. Carroll, *Red Grange and the Rise of Modern Football*, 108.
21. Carroll, *Red Grange and the Rise of Modern Football*, 108.
22. Carroll, *Red Grange and the Rise of Modern Football*, 108.
23. *Columbus Dispatch*, December 10, 1925.
24. Guy Chamberlin, archival interview, Pro Football Hall of Fame, 1965 (audio interview).
25. *Pottsville Republican*, November 19, 1987.
26. *Pottsville Journal*, December 2, 1925.
27. *Philadelphia Ledger*, December 10, 1925.
28. *Decatur (Illinois) Review*, December 17, 1925.
29. *Chicago Tribune*, December 30, 1925.
30. *Chicago Tribune*, December 16, 1925.
31. *Columbus Citizen*, December 30, 1925. *Decatur (Illinois) Review*, December 30, 1925.

CHAPTER 15: THE GRANGE LEAGUE (1926)

1. Figures for the 1925–1926 Grange tour and the George Halas quote are from John M. Carroll, *Red Grange and the Rise of Modern Football* (Urbana: University of Illinois Press, 1999), 125–126.
2. George S. Halas, with Gwen Morgan and Arthur Veysey, *Halas: An Autobiography* (Chicago: Bonus Books, 1986), 121.
3. "President's Report," "NFL Meeting Minutes," February 6–7, 1926.
4. "President's Report."
5. *Frankford Yellow Jacket News* 3, no. 17 (July 1926), 2. The *Frankford Yellow Jacket News* is a monthly newsletter published by the Frankford Athletic Association.
6. Dave Klein, *The New York Giants: Yesterday, Today, Tomorrow* (Chicago: Henry Regnery Company, 1973), 34.
7. Halas, *Halas*, 121.
8. "NFL Meeting Minutes," February 6–7, 1926.
9. "NFL Meeting Minutes," February 6–7, 1926.
10. *Lincoln (Nebraska) Star*, February 9, 1926. *Waterloo (Iowa) Evening Courier*, February 9, 1926.
11. Dr. Harry March quote is from JFC Scrapbook, Binder 1, p. 112.
12. Joe F. Carr interview with *Chicago Tribune* sportswriter Don Maxwell (Speaking of Sports) is from JFC Scrapbook, Binder 1, pp. 66–68.
13. Newspaper article titled "Pro Football War Looms" with quote from Chris O'Brien is found in NFL files at the Pro Football Hall of Fame.
14. *Ohio State Journal*, February 16, 1926.
15. *Liberty Magazine*, February 20, 1926. JFC Scrapbook, Binder 1, p. 130.
16. *New York Times*, March 8, 1926.
17. JFC Scrapbook, Binder 1, pp. 119–120.
18. Joe F. Carr letter to NFL owners appeared in *Frankford Yellow Jacket News* 3, no. 14 (April 1926), 3.

19. Joe F. Carr's visit to speak at the Frankford Athletic Association was advertised and covered in *Frankford Yellow Jacket News* 3, no. 16 (June 1926), 1–3.
20. "NFL Meeting Minutes," July 10–11, 1926.
21. Dinner menu is from *Frankford Yellow Jacket News* 3, no. 17 (July 1926), 1. "NFL Meeting Minutes," July 10–11, 1926.
22. Joe Ziemba, *When Football Was Football: The Chicago Cardinals and the Birth of the NFL* (Chicago: Triumph Books, 1999), 148.
23. Myron Cope, *The Game That Was* (New York: World, 1970), 73.
24. Cope, *The Game That Was*, 73.
25. Cope, *The Game That Was*, 73.
26. "NFL Meeting Minutes," July 10–11, 1926.
27. *New York Times*, July 13, 1926.
28. *New York Times*, July 17, 1926.
29. Joe F. Carr quote on the NFL in 1926 is from newspaper article titled "Joe May Be Otto's Rival" dated July 28, 1926, from Carr file at Pro Football Hall of Fame.
30. *Canton Repository*, October 18, 1926.
31. Photo of Joe F. Carr at Chicago Cardinals–Frankford Yellow Jackets game appeared in 1926 Frankford Yellow Jackets home program dated November 13, 1926.
32. Jim Reisler, *Cash and Carry: The Spectacular Rise and Hard Fall of C. C. Pyle, America's First Sports Agent* (Jefferson, NC: McFarland, 2009), 98.
33. Richard Whittingham, *Bears: In Their Own Words* (Chicago: Contemporary Books, 1991), 164.
34. Reisler, *Cash and Carry*, 100.
35. Halas, *Halas*, 127.
36. Richard Whittingham, *Illustrated History of New York Giants* (Chicago: Triumph Books, 2005), 10.
37. *San Antonio Light*, December 13, 1926.
38. Halas, *Halas*, 132.

CHAPTER 16: TRAVELING FOR A CAUSE (1927–1928)

1. "NFL Meeting Minutes," February 5–6, 1927.
2. "NFL Meeting Minutes," February 5–6, 1927.
3. "NFL Meeting Minutes," February 5–6, 1927.
4. "NFL Meeting Minutes," February 5–6, 1927.
5. "NFL Meeting Minutes," February 5–6, 1927.
6. Gregory Carr, author interview, July 31, 2004.
7. Description of the Carr home at 1863 Bryden Road came from family interviews and tours of the residence by the author on several occasions.
8. James Carr, author interview, August 1, 2004.
9. Martha Sullivan, author interview, November 21, 2004.
10. St. Patrick's Church *Monthly Calendar* newsletters, dated October 1927, August 1929, November 1929, April 1931. Newsletters were found in the archives at St. Patrick Church, Columbus, Ohio.

11. James Carr, interview.
12. Sullivan, interview.
13. James Carr, author interviews, September 14, 2002, and August 1, 2004.
14. Sullivan, interview.
15. History of the New Hayden Building from National Register of Historic Places application file prepared by Judy Williams.
16. *Ohio State Journal*, October 7, 1900.
17. James and Gregory Carr, author interviews, April 20, 2007. 1927 Columbus City Directory.
18. A picture of Joe F. Carr's name on the door of the NFL office at 16 East Broad Street in Columbus, Ohio, was shot for the 1938 NFL film *Champions of the Gridiron*.
19. Description of the NFL office is taken from photos, as well as a tour of the eleventh floor by the author on April 20, 2007.
20. All notes and Joe F. Carr's detailed outline of the reorganized NFL are from "NFL Meeting Minutes," April 23, 1927.
21. "NFL Meeting Minutes," April 23, 1927.
22. "NFL Meeting Minutes," July 16–17, 1927.
23. "NFL Meeting Minutes," July 16–17, 1927.
24. *Chester (Pennsylvania) Times*, August 18, 1927.
25. C. C. Pyle quote from "NFL Meeting Minutes," September 4, 1927.
26. Richard Whittingham, *What a Game They Played* (Lincoln: University of Nebraska Press, 2001), 25.
27. Attendance figures from Bob Carroll, Michael Gershman, David Neft, and John Thorn, eds., *Total Football II: The Official Encyclopedia of the National Football League* (New York: HarperCollins, 1999).
28. *Bridgeport (Connecticut) Telegram*, October 18, 1927.
29. All attendance figures from Carroll et al., *Total Football II*.
30. *Ohio State Journal*, December 25, 1927.
31. "NFL Meeting Minutes," February 11, 1928.
32. "NFL Meeting Minutes," July 7, 1928.
33. "NFL Meeting Minutes," August 12, 1928.
34. Dick Reynolds, "The Steam Roller Story," *Providence Journal-Bulletin*, n.d., 5.
35. Reynolds, "The Steam Roller Story," 5.
36. Reynolds, "The Steam Roller Story," 5.
37. *Ohio State Journal*, November 20, 1928.
38. Sullivan, interview.
39. Reynolds, "The Steam Roller Story," 22.
40. *Dallas Morning News*, November 4, 1928. JFC Scrapbook, Binder 1, pp. 226–229.
41. *Ohio State Journal*, December 25, 1928.

CHAPTER 17: HOW DO WE GET TO THE BIG CITIES AND STAY? (1929–1930)

1. "NFL Meeting Minutes," February 2, 1929.
2. "NFL Meeting Minutes," February 2, 1929.

3. Carl L. Storck letter to Joe F. Carr, dated February 7, 1929, is from "NFL Meeting Minutes," February 2, 1939. Letter found in the files at the Pro Football Hall of Fame.

4. *Ohio State Journal*, February 10, 1929. A photo of C. C. Pyle and Joe F. Carr accompanied the article on Pyle's visit to Columbus, Ohio.

5. Information on Kathleen Rubadue-Knapp is from her son Robert Knapp and the Columbus City Directories.

6. Robert Knapp, author interview, April 19, 2009.

7. Knapp, interview.

8. Knapp, interview.

9. *Columbus Dispatch*, January 14, 1982. This is the only known interview done by Kathleen Rubadue-Knapp on being the first NFL secretary.

10. James Carr, author interview, August 1, 2004. Knapp, interview.

11. Martha Sullivan, author interview, March 4, 2007.

12. Knapp, interview.

13. Richard Whittingham, *Illustrated History of the New York Giants* (Chicago: Triumph Books, 2005), 15–16.

14. Joe Ziemba, *When Football Was Football: The Chicago Cardinals and the Birth of the NFL* (Chicago: Triumph Books, 1999), 160.

15. Ziemba, *When Football Was Football*, 160.

16. Ziemba, *When Football Was Football*, 160.

17. *Chester (Pennsylvania) Times*, July 29, 1929.

18. "NFL Meeting Minutes," July 27–28, 1929.

19. John Hogrogian, "The Staten Island Stapletons," *Coffin Corner* 7, no. 6 (1985), 2–5.

20. "NFL Meeting Minutes," July 27–28, 1929.

21. "The National Football League Financial Report" (January 1 to July 15, 1929). The report was found in the files at the Pro Football Hall of Fame.

22. Hogrogian, "Staten Island Stapletons," 4–5.

23. Denis J. Gullickson, *Vagabond Halfback: The Life and Times of Johnny Blood McNally* (Madison, WI: Trails Books, 2006), 65–66.

24. David Zimmerman, *Curly Lambeau: The Man behind the Mystique* (Hales Corner, WI: Eagle Books, 2003), 74.

25. Gullickson, *Vagabond Halfback*, 68.

26. Zimmerman, *Curly Lambeau*, 82.

27. Zimmerman, *Curly Lambeau*, 82.

28. Zimmerman, *Curly Lambeau*, 82.

29. Larry Names, *History of the Green Bay Packers, Part One* (Wautoma, WI: Angel Press, 1987), 179.

30. "NFL Meeting Minutes," January 25, 1930.

31. "NFL Meeting Minutes," January 25, 1930.

32. *Dayton Journal*, January 26, 1930.

33. *Portsmouth Times*, February 21, 1930.

34. Carl Becker, *Home & Away: The Rise and Fall of Professional Football on the Banks of the Ohio, 1919–1934* (Athens: Ohio University Press, 1998), 214–216.

35. Ticket prices from *Portsmouth Times*, September 24, 1930. Program price is from several 1930–1933 Portsmouth Spartans programs.

36. "NFL Meeting Minutes," July 12–13, 1930.
37. "NFL Meeting Minutes," July 12–13, 1930.
38. "NFL Meeting Minutes," July 12–13, 1930.
39. Patrick Tehan, author interview, April 18, 2009.
40. Joe Quinn, "A Man for All Season," *Referee 1*, no. 6 (November–December 1976), 35.
41. *Mansfield (Ohio) News-Journal*, November 22, 1954.
42. Joe F. Carr's visit to see the NFL debut of the Portsmouth Spartans is from *Portsmouth Times*, September 12, 1930; *Portsmouth Times*, September 15, 1930.
43. Becker, *Home & Away*, 220.
44. All attendance figures for 1930 night games are from Bob Carroll, Michael Gershman, David Neft, and John Thorn, eds., *Total Football II: The Official Encyclopedia of the National Football League* (New York: HarperCollins, 1999).
45. *Portsmouth Times*, October 24, 1930.
46. All attendance figures for 1930 Brooklyn Dodgers games are from Carroll et al., *Total Football II.*
47. Richard Whittingham, *The Chicago Bears: An Illustrated History* (New York: Rand McNally, 1982), 75.
48. *Ohio State Journal*, November 28, 1930.
49. *Charleston (West Virginia) Daily Mail*, November 30, 1930.
50. Joe F. Carr letter to Dutch Sternaman, dated November 28, 1930, is from Whittingham, *The Chicago Bears*, 75. The original letter is owned by the Sternaman family.
51. *Portsmouth Times*, December 15, 1930. Gullickson, *Vagabond Halfback*, 80.
52. *Portsmouth Times*, December 16, 1930.
53. *Fresno (California) Bee*, December 16, 1930.
54. *Chester (Pennsylvania) Times*, October 23, 1930. *Lima (Ohio) News*, November 19, 1930.
55. *Portsmouth Times*, December 15, 1930. *Zanesville (Ohio) Times-Recorder*, December 15, 1930.

CHAPTER 18: SMALL-TOWN GREEN BAY IS TITLETOWN (1931)

1. All attendance figures come from actual newspaper articles; also from Bob Carroll, Michael Gershman, David Neft, and John Thorn, eds., *Total Football II: The Official Encyclopedia of the National Football League* (New York: HarperCollins, 1999). Additional figures are from Bob Gill and Tod Maher, *The Pro Football Encyclopedia* (New York: Macmillan, 1997), 99–110.
2. JFC Scrapbook, Binder 1, p. 319. *Milwaukee Tribune*, May 15, 1931.
3. JFC Scrapbook, Binder 2, pp. 424–425.
4. JFC Scrapbook, Binder 1, p. 315. *Cleveland Plain Dealer*, June 6, 1931.
5. JFC Scrapbook, Binder 1, p. 315.
6. "NFL Meeting Minutes," July 11–12, 1931.
7. "NFL Meeting Minutes," July 11–12, 1931.
8. "NFL Meeting Minutes," July 11–12, 1931.

9. *Columbus Citizen*, July 30, 1931.
10. 1931 NFL Schedules is from *Portsmouth Times*, September 11, 1931. *Stevens Point (Wisconsin) Daily Journal*, July 14, 1931.
11. George S. Halas, with Gwen Morgan and Arthur Veysey, *Halas: An Autobiography* (Chicago: Bonus Books, 1986), 147–148.
12. Facts about Carr threatening to fine the Packers are from *Appleton (Wisconsin) Post-Crescent*, October 15, 1931.
13. *Portsmouth Times*, October 20, 1931.
14. Game recap, attendance figure, and appearance of Mayor James Walker, *New York Times*, November 2, 1931.
15. *Portsmouth Times*, December 7, 1931.
16. *Portsmouth Times*, December 7, 1931.
17. *Ohio State Journal*, December 8, 1931.
18. *Portsmouth Times*, December 8, 1931.
19. *Portsmouth Times*, December 13, 1931.
20. Lambeau and Hubbard quotes are from Chuck Johnson, *The Green Bay Packers: Pro Football's Pioneer Team* (New York: Thomas Nelson & Sons, 1961), 140, 142.
21. *Ohio State Journal*, December 14, 1931.
22. Martha Sullivan, author interviews, November 21, 2004, and March 4, 2007.
23. Sullivan, interviews.

CHAPTER 19: INDOOR CIRCUS (1932)

1. *Portsmouth Times*, December 23, 1931.
2. *Portsmouth Times*, January 8, 1932.
3. *Ohio State Journal*, January 12, 1932.
4. *Portsmouth Times*, January 12, 1932.
5. *Syracuse Herald*, February 16, 1932.
6. *Portsmouth Times*, March 2, 1932.
7. Jordan Wright, author interview, July 11, 2009.
8. Wright, interview.
9. Wright, interview.
10. Wright, interview.
11. George S. Halas, with Gwen Morgan and Arthur Veysey, *Halas: An Autobiography* (Chicago: Bonus Books, 1986), 151.
12. Lou Little letter to Bert Bell, dated April 4, 1932, is from author's collection.
13. "NFL Meeting Minutes," July 9–10, 1932.
14. "NFL Meeting Minutes," July 9–10, 1932.
15. "NFL Meeting Minutes," July 9–10, 1932.
16. Halas, *Halas*, 148–149.
17. Portsmouth Spartans ticket prices from *Portsmouth Times*, October 1, 1932, and November 27, 1932.

18. John Torinus, *The Packer Legend* (Neshkoro, WI: Laranmark Press, 1983), 45.
19. *Portsmouth Times*, September 18, 1932.
20. *Portsmouth Times*, September 26, 1932.
21. Thom Loverro, *Washington Redskins: The Authorized History* (Dallas, TX: Taylor, 1996), 7.
22. Population from Federal Census. *Portsmouth Times*, October 7, 1932.
23. *Portsmouth Times*, October 7, 1932.
24. Charles K. Ross, *Outside the Lines: African Americans and the Integration of the National Football League* (New York: New York University Press, 1999), 37.
25. *Mason City (Iowa) Globe-Gazette*, November 24, 1933.
26. *Green Bay Press-Gazette*, October 17, 1932.
27. *Wisconsin State Journal*, November 28, 1932.
28. Halas, *Halas*, 167.
29. Virginia McCaskey, author interview, August 8, 2005.
30. McCaskey, interview.
31. Western Union Telegram dated December 14, 1932, is from author's collection.
32. *Portsmouth Times*, December 15, 1932.
33. Charles "Ookie" Miller, author interview, NFL Films, 1999.
34. McCaskey, interview. Glenn Presnell, author interview, NFL Films, 1999.
35. 1932 NFL playoff game kickoff time is from *Portsmouth Times*, December 16, 1932. Joe F. Carr seat in Chicago Stadium for game is from his personal ticket stub from JFC Scrapbook, Binder 2 (page 361). Presnell, interview.
36. John M. Carroll, *Red Grange and the Rise of Modern Football* (Urbana: University of Illinois Press, 1999), 170–171.
37. Presnell, interview.
38. Miller, interview. Halas, *Halas*, 169.
39. *Stevens Point Daily Journal*, December 19, 1932.
40. *Portsmouth Times*, December 19, 1932.
41. JFC Scrapbook, Binder 2, pp. 361, 366.
42. JFC Scrapbook, Binder 2, pp. 361, 366.
43. *Portsmouth Times*, December 23, 1932.

CHAPTER 20: THE PRO GAME SEPARATES ITSELF FROM THE COLLEGE GAME (1933)

1. Attendance figures are from Bob Carroll, Michael Gershman, David Neft, and John Thorn, eds., *Total Football II: The Official Encyclopedia of the National Football League* (New York: HarperCollins, 1999).
2. Thom Loverro, *Washington Redskins: The Authorized History* (Dallas, TX: Taylor, 1996), 8.
3. Joe F. Carr quote is from newspaper article in the Sport Chatter column by Sam Levy, from Carr file at Pro Football Hall of Fame, dated January 27, 1933.

4. Sport Chatter column by Sam Levy.
5. *New York Times*, January 10, 1933. *Portsmouth Times*, January 11, 1933.
6. JFC Scrapbook, Binder 2, p. 331.
7. "NFL Meeting Minutes," February 25–26, 1933.
8. Arthur Daley, *Pro Football's Hall of Fame* (New York: Tempo Books, 1963), 154.
9. "NFL Meeting Minutes," February 25–26, 1933.
10. "NFL Meeting Minutes," February 25–26, 1933. *Charleston (West Virginia) Daily Mail*, February 27, 1933.
11. *Pittsburgh Sun-Telegraph*, February 27, 1933. Dan Rooney, as told to Andrew E. Masich and David F. Halaas, *Dan Rooney: My 75 Years with the Pittsburgh Steelers and the NFL* (New York: Da Capo Press, 2007), 14.
12. Art Rooney background information from Andrew O'Toole, *Smiling Irish Eyes: Art Rooney and the Pittsburgh Steelers* (Haworth, NJ: St. Johann Press), 1–40.
13. Myron Cope, *The Game That Was* (New York: World, 1970), 124–25.
14. Cope, *The Game That Was*, 125. Rooney, *Dan Rooney*, 10.
15. O'Toole, *Smiling Irish Eyes*, 14.
16. Rooney, *Dan Rooney*, 11
17. Cope, *The Game That Was*, 127.
18. Rooney, *Dan Rooney*, 10.
19. Cope, *The Game That Was*, 126. 1930 United States Census.
20. Cope, *The Game That Was*, 126.
21. Rooney, *Dan Rooney*, 12.
22. Rooney, *Dan Rooney*, 12.
23. Art Rooney, archival interview, PBS-TV, 1984. Dan Rooney, interview, NFL Films, 1999.
24. George S. Halas, with Gwen Morgan and Arthur Veysey, *Halas: An Autobiography* (Chicago: Bonus Books, 1986), 151.
25. *Ohio State Journal*, February 28, 1933. *New York Times*, February 27, 1933.
26. *Philadelphia Public Ledger*, March 1, 1933.
27. *Portsmouth Times*, May 7, 1933.
28. *Columbus Dispatch*, June 11, 1933. Graduation invitation from JFC Scrapbook, Binder 2, pp. 412–413.
29. *Portsmouth Times*, May 19, 1933. *Portsmouth Times*, June 28, 1933.
30. *Cincinnati Times-Star*, June 21, 1933. *Cincinnati Post*, June 21, 1933.
31. Ray Didinger and Robert Lyons, *The Eagles Encyclopedia* (Philadelphia, PA: Temple University Press, 2005), 6.
32. Bert Bell Jr., author interview, May 2, 2009.
33. *New York Times*, February 1, 1973.
34. "NFL Meeting Minutes," July 8–9, 1933.
35. "NFL Meeting Minutes," July 8–9, 1933.
36. "NFL Meeting Minutes," July 8–9, 1933.
37. "NFL Meeting Minutes," July 8–9, 1933.
38. "NFL Meeting Minutes," July 8–9, 1933.
39. "NFL Meeting Minutes," July 8–9, 1933.

40. *Ohio State Journal*, August 23, 1933.
41. Halas, *Halas*, 150.
42. JFC Scrapbook, Binder 2, pp. 461–462.
43. JFC Scrapbook, Binder 2, p. 441.
44. *Portsmouth Times*, September 18, 1933.
45. *Pittsburgh Press*, September 21, 1933.
46. Ray Kemp quotes are from 1981 interview with Black Sports in Pittsburgh.
47. Kemp, Black Sports in Pittsburgh interview.
48. Kemp, Black Sports in Pittsburgh interview.
49. Cope, *The Game That Was*, 138.
50. Mary Carr's hand-written letter is from JFC Scrapbook, Binder 2, pp. 427–429.
51. Wellington Mara, archival interview, NFL Films, 1999.
52. *Columbus Citizen*, December 7, 1933.
53. *Ohio State Journal*, December 8, 1933.
54. *Chicago Tribune*, December 8, 1933. *Literary Digest*, December 9, 1933.
55. *Columbus Citizen*, December 15, 1933.
56. "NFL Meeting Minutes," December 16, 1933. *Columbus Citizen*, December 16, 1933.
57. "NFL Meeting Minutes," December 16, 1933. *Chicago Tribune*, December 15, 1933.
58. Joe F. Carr's actual game ticket from the 1933 NFL Championship Game is from JFC Scrapbook, Binder 2, p. 445.
59. JFC Scrapbook, Binder 2, p. 445. *New York Times*, December 18, 1933.
60. George Musso, author interview, NFL Films, 1999.
61. Mara, archival interview.
62. Harry Newman, author interview, NFL Films, 1999.
63. Musso, interview.
64. *Chicago Tribune*, December 18, 1933. John M. Carroll, *Red Grange and the Rise of Modern Football* (Urbana: University of Illinois Press, 1999), 175.
65. Newspaper headlines and quotes from *New York Times*, December 18, 1933; *Chicago American*, December 18, 1933; *Chicago Tribune*, December 18, 1933; *Burlington (North Carolina) Daily-Times*, December 18, 1933.
66. *Portsmouth Times*, December 19, 1933.
67. *Pittsburgh Press*, February 27, 1933.

CHAPTER 21: SNEAKERS IN NEW YORK (1934)

1. *Columbus Citizen*, December 16, 1933.
2. Attendance figures are from Bob Carroll, Michael Gershman, David Neft, and John Thorn, eds., *Total Football II: The Official Encyclopedia of the National Football League* (New York: HarperCollins, 1999).
3. Carl Becker, *Home & Away: The Rise and Fall of Professional Football on the Banks of the Ohio, 1919–1934* (Athens: Ohio University Press, 1998), 302.

4. Glenn Presnell, author interview, NFL Films, 1999.

5. Ray Didinger, "The Man Who Had a Dream," *Pro! The Official Program of the National Football League* 7, no. 5 (September 18, 1977), 12C.

6. Rozene Supple, author interview, October 30, 2009. Richards quoted in *Ohio State Journal*, October 27, 1934.

7. *Portsmouth Times*, March 23, 1934. *Hamilton Daily Journal*, April 7, 1934. *2009 Detroit Lions Media Guide.*

8. Charlie Sanders, with Larry Paladino. *Tales from the Detroit Lions* (Sports Publishing: Champaign, IL, 2005), 96. *Detroit Free Press*, April 10–11, 1934. *Detroit Times*, April 11, 1934.

9. *1934 NFL Bulletin*, no. 1 (April 26, 1934).

10. *1934 NFL Bulletin*, no. 2 (June 23, 1934).

11. *1934 NFL Bulletin*, no. 2.

12. *1934 NFL Bulletin*, no. 2.

13. *1934 NFL Bulletin*, no. 2. Harry A. March, *Pro Football: Its Ups and Downs* (Albany, NY: J. B. Lyon, 1934).

14. March, *Pro Football*. Abebooks.com (checked in August 2009).

15. "NFL Meeting Minutes," June 30–July 1, 1934.

16. *Lowell (Massachusetts) Sun*, June 23, 1934.

17. "NFL Meeting Minutes," June 30–July 1, 1934.

18. JFC Scrapbook, Binder 2, pp. 510–512.

19. *1934 NFL Bulletin*, no. 3 (July 7, 1934).

20. Art Rooney, archival interview, PBS-TV, 1984. Charles K Ross. *Outside the Lines: African Americans and the Integration of the National Football League* (New York: New York University Press, 1999), 44. March, *Pro Football*, 151.

21. Gerald Gems, "Shooting Stars: The Rise and Fall of Blacks in Professional Football," *Professional Football Researchers Association*, 1988 Annual, 11.

22. Jordan Wright, author interview, July 11, 2009.

23. Wright, interview.

24. *Chicago Tribune*, July 6, 1934.

25. *Chicago Tribune*, July 6, 1934.

26. *Pittsburgh Press*, August 9, 1934.

27. *1934 NFL Bulletin*, no. 19 (September 14, 1934). Thomas Littlewood, *Arch: A Promoter, Not a Poet: The Story of Arch Ward* (Ames: Iowa State University Press, 1990), 93–94.

28. *Columbus Citizen*, December 4, 1933.

29. Richard Whittingham, *Illustrated History of the New York Giants* (Chicago: Triumph Books, 2005), 36.

30. *New York Times*, December 10, 1934.

31. *New York Times*, December 10, 1934.

32. *New York Times*, December 10, 1934. *1934 NFL Bulletin*, no. 23 (December 20, 1934).

33. "NFL Meeting Minutes," December 10, 1934. *New York Times*, December 11, 1934. *1934 NFL Bulletin*, no. 23 (December 20, 1934).

34. *1934 NFL Bulletin*, no. 23 (December 20, 1934).

CHAPTER 22: THE POSTGRADUATE GAME IS FINALLY A BIG-CITY SPORT (1935)

1. Attendance figures are from Bob Carroll, Michael Gershman, David Neft, and John Thorn, eds., *Total Football II: The Official Encyclopedia of the National Football League* (New York: HarperCollins, 1999). *1934 NFL Bulletin*, no. 23 (December 20, 1934).
2. *Elyria (Ohio) Telegram*, September 19, 1934.
3. Art Rooney quote found in 1935 NFL newspaper file at the Pro Football Hall of Fame.
4. Richard Whittingham, *What a Game They Played* (Lincoln: University of Nebraska Press, 2001), 121–122.
5. Whittingham, *What a Game They Played*, 121–122.
6. Whittingham, *What a Game They Played*, 121–122. Mike Rathet and Don Smith. *Their Deeds and Dogged Faith* (New York: Rutledge Books and Balsam Press, 1984), 89–90.
7. *1935 NFL Bulletin*, no. 3 (March 2, 1935).
8. *1935 BFL Bulletin*, no. 5 (April 18, 1935).
9. *Official Guide of the National Football League: 1935* (New York: American Sports Publishing, 1935).
10. "NFL Meeting Minutes," May 18, 1935. *Who's Who in Major League Football* (Chicago: B.E. Callahan Publisher, 1935).
11. *Who's Who in Major League Football*. NFL coupon attached inside cover next to cover page.
12. *New York Times*, February 1, 1973.
13. "NFL Meeting Minutes," May 18, 1935.
14. George S. Halas, with Gwen Morgan and Arthur Veysey. *Halas: An Autobiography* (Chicago: Bonus Books, 1986), 158.
15. "NFL Meeting Minutes," May 18, 1935.
16. Mary Carr Father's Day card and envelope from Carr family collection.
17. Ray Didinger, "The Man Who Had a Dream," *Pro! The Official Program of the National Football League* 7, no. 5 (September 18, 1977), 14C.
18. Didinger, "The Man Who Had a Dream," 14C. Rozene Supple, author interview, October 30, 2009.
19. *Columbus Dispatch*, June 17, 1935. *Chicago Tribune*, June 17, 1935.
20. *1935 NFL Bulletin*, no. 7 (July 17, 1935).
21. *Ironwood (Michigan) Daily Globe*, July 19, 1935.
22. *New York American*, September 17, 1935. *1935 NFL Bulletin*, no. 12 (September 27, 1935).
23. Attendance figure from Carroll et al., *Total Football II*.
24. Carroll et al., *Total Football II*. Ticket price from actual game ticket for 1935 NFL Championship Game.
25. *1935 NFL Bulletin*, no. 14 (December 19, 1935).
26. *1935 NFL Bulletin*, no. 14 (December 19, 1935).

CHAPTER 23: PACKERS, REDSKINS, AND THE NFL DRAFT (1936)

1. *Oshkosh (Wisconsin) Northwestern*, January 13, 1936.
2. Attendance figures are from Bob Carroll, Michael Gershman, David Neft, and John Thorn, eds., *Total Football II: The Official Encyclopedia of the National Football League* (New York: HarperCollins, 1999).
3. *Ohio State Journal*, January 27, 1936.
4. "NFL Meeting Minutes," February 8–9, 1936.
5. Wellington Mara quote from conversation with Giants PR director Pat Hanlon.
6. "NFL Meeting Minutes," February 8–9, 1936.
7. *Chicago Tribune*, February 11, 1936.
8. Richard Whittingham, *Illustrated History of the New York Giants* (Chicago: Triumph Books, 2005), 43.
9. "NFL Meeting Minutes," February 8–9, 1936.
10. Attendance figures are from Carroll et al., *Total Football II*. *Ohio State Journal*, October 13, 1936.
11. Both George Halas and Joe F. Carr quotes are from newspaper clipping found in 1935 NFL file at the Pro Football Hall of Fame.
12. Michael Richman, *The Redskins Encyclopedia* (Philadelphia, PA: Temple University Press, 2008), 4.
13. Richman, *The Redskins Encyclopedia*, 4.
14. Corinne Griffith, *My Life with the Redskins* (New York: A. S. Barnes, 1947), 20.
15. Dan Daly and Bob O'Donnell, *The Pro Football Chronicle* (New York: Macmillan, 1990), 70.
16. *Ironwood (Michigan) Daily Globe*, December 7, 1936.
17. Thom Loverro, *Washington Redskins: The Authorized History* (Dallas, TX: Taylor, 1996), 12–14.
18. Richman, *The Redskins Encyclopedia*, 5.
19. "NFL Meeting Minutes," December 12, 1936.
20. "NFL Meeting Minutes," December 12, 1936.

CHAPTER 24: HEART OF GOLD CONTINUES TO WORK (1937)

1. *Appleton (Wisconsin) Post-Crescent*, January 18, 1937.
2. Attendance figures are from Bob Carroll, Michael Gershman, David Neft, and John Thorn, eds., *Total Football II: The Official Encyclopedia of the National Football League* (New York: HarperCollins, 1999).
3. "NFL Meeting Minutes," February 12–13, 1937.
4. Jordan Wright, author interview, July 11, 2009.
5. Howard Roberts, *The Story of Pro Football* (New York: Rand McNally, 1953), 200. Wright, interview.

6. Roberts, *The Story of Pro Football*, 200.

7. Dorothy Walsh letter to Joe F. Carr, dated September 16, 1935. Letter is from the Carr family collection.

8. Joe F. Carr letter to Dorothy Walsh, dated September 18, 1935. Letter is from the Carr family collection.

9. Joe F. Carr letter to Mary (Carr) Pratt, dated December 23, 1935. Letter is from the Carr family collection.

10. *Monessen Daily Independent*, July 10, 1937. *Chicago Tribune*, September 1, 1937.

11. *Cleveland Plain Dealer*, September 8 and 11, 1937.

12. *Columbus Dispatch*, September 21, 1937.

13. Michael Carr, author interview, July 31, 2004. *Columbus Citizen*, September 22, 1937.

14. James Carr, author interview, July 31, 2004.

15. Michael Carr, interview.

16. *Ohio State Journal*, September 28, 1937. Attendance figures are from Carroll et al., *Total Football II*.

17. *Ohio State Journal*, October 30, 1937.

18. Gregory Carr, author interview, July 31, 2004.

19. *Washington Evening Star*, August 29, 1937.

20. *Ohio State Journal*, December 8, 1937.

21. *Columbus Dispatch*, December 9, 1937. *Ohio State Journal*, December 10, 1937.

22. "NFL Meeting Minutes," December 11, 1937. Virginia McCaskey, author interview, August 8, 2005.

23. "NFL Meeting Minutes," December 11, 1937.

24. *Columbus Dispatch*, December 23, 1937. *Ohio State Journal*, December 24, 1937. *Columbus Dispatch*, February 20, 1938.

25. *Ohio State Journal*, December 27, 1937.

CHAPTER 25: "GREATEST SHOW IN FOOTBALL" (1938)

1. *Oshkosh (Wisconsin) Northwestern*, January 4, 1938.

2. Attendance figures are from Bob Carroll, Michael Gershman, David Neft, and John Thorn, eds., *Total Football II: The Official Encyclopedia of the National Football League* (New York: HarperCollins, 1999).

3. *Danville (Virginia) Bee*, February 16, 1938.

4. Original contract between the NFL and General Mills is from Carr family archives.

5. NFL–General Mills contract.

6. *Greeley (Colorado) Daily Tribune*, August 1, 1938.

7. *Massillon Evening Independent*, August 9, 1938.

8. *Ohio State Journal*, August 29, 1938.

9. "NFL Meeting Minutes," August 31, 1938.

10. *Ohio State Journal*, October 19, 1938.

11. Joe F. Carr quote is from 1938 newspaper clipping from Carr family archives.

12. *Columbus Dispatch*, October 21, 1938.
13. *Charleston Gazette*, November 13, 1938.
14. Joe F. Carr letter is from *Charleston Gazette*, November 17, 1938.
15. *Charleston Gazette*, November 17, 1938.
16. *Columbus Citizen*, December 10, 1938.
17. *New York Times*, December 12, 1938.
18. *New York Times*, December 12, 1938.

CHAPTER 26: DEATH OF A PRESIDENT (1939)

1. Joe F. Carr, with Michael Fanning, "Post-Graduate Football," unpublished, 1938, 33.
2. Attendance figures are from Bob Carroll, Michael Gershman, David Neft, and John Thorn, eds., *Total Football II: The Official Encyclopedia of the National Football League* (New York: HarperCollins, 1999).
3. Joe F. Carr speech is from the 1938 NFL film titled *Champions of the Gridiron* (released in 1939).
4. *Lowell (Massachusetts) Sun*, February 1, 1939.
5. *Wisconsin State Journal*, February 2, 1939.
6. "NFL Meeting Minutes," February 9, 1939.
7. "NFL Meeting Minutes," February 9, 1939.
8. "NFL Meeting Minutes," February 9, 1939.
9. *Ohio State Journal*, February 10, 1939. *Ohio State Journal*, May 9, 1939.
10. *Uniontown (Pennsylvania) Morning Herald*, March 14, 1939.
11. *Connellsville (Pennsylvania) Daily Courier*, May 26, 1939.
12. *Ohio State Journal*, May 14, 1939.
13. *Ohio State Journal*, May 21, 1939.
14. *Columbus Dispatch*, May 21, 1939.
15. Certificate of Death, State of Ohio, 1939, file 30845.
16. James Carr, author interview, July 31, 2004.
17. *Chicago Tribune*, May 21, 1939.
18. *Chicago Tribune*, May 21, 1939.
19. *Pittsburgh Sun-Telegraph*, May 21, 1939.
20. Headlines are from *Ohio State Journal*, May 21, 1939; *Columbus Citizen*, May 21, 1939; *Columbus Dispatch*, May 21, 1939.
21. Estate value from newspaper clipping from Carr family archives. List of pallbearers is from *Columbus Citizen*, May 24, 1939.
22. Gregory Carr, author interview, July 31, 2004. Robert Knapp, author interview, April 19, 2009.
23. *Ohio State Journal*, May 25, 1939.
24. *Ohio State Journal*, May 25, 1939. *Official Guide of the National Football League: 1939* (New York: American Sports Publishing, 1939), 7.
25. Michael Carr, author interview, July 31, 2004.
26. Gregory Carr, interview.

27. James Carr, interview.
28. "NFL Meeting Minutes," July 22, 1939.
29. "NFL Meeting Minutes," July 22, 1939.
30. Dolores Seitz, author interview, June 9, 2007. "NFL Meeting Minutes," July 22, 1939.
31. *Official Guide of the National Football League: 1939*, 82.
32. Carl L. Storck letter to Josephine Carr, dated October 7, 1939, is from Carr family archives. Five-page leather-bound Memorial book is also from Carr family archives.
33. "NFL Meeting Minutes," July 22, 1939.

CHAPTER 27: AFTERMATH

1. James Carr, author interview, July 31, 2004.
2. James Carr, interview.
3. *2009 NFL Record & Fact Book* (New York: Time, Inc. Home Entertainment, 2009), 540.
4. Dan Daly and Bob O'Donnell, *The Pro Football Chronicle* (New York: Macmillan, 1990), 83–84.
5. *Galveston (Texas) Daily News*, December 25, 1939. *Lima (Ohio) News*, April 15, 1940.
6. *Coshocton Tribune*, April 13, 1940.
7. Dolores Seitz, author interview, June 9, 2007.
8. *Helena (Montana) Independent*, April 5, 1941.
9. *Helena (Montana) Independent*, April 5, 1941.
10. Seitz, interview.

CHAPTER 28: PRO FOOTBALL HALL OF FAME (1963)

1. *Canton Repository*, December 6, 1959.
2. *Columbus Dispatch*, January 29, 1963.
3. *1962 Official Pro Football Hall of Fame Program.*
4. James Carr, author interview, July 31, 2004.
5. *Mansfield (Ohio) News-Journal*, November 22, 1964.
6. George Halas, Hall of Fame acceptance speech, 1963.
7. Earl Schreiber, Hall of Fame presenter speech, 1963.
8. Dan Tehan, Hall of Fame acceptance speech (on behalf of Joe Carr), 1963.
9. James Carr, interview.

CHAPTER 29: THE LEGACY OF JOE F. CARR

1. Gregory Carr, author interview, July 31, 2004.
2. James Carr, author interview, August 1, 2004.

3. *Time*, December 21. 1959.
4. Gregory Carr, interview. Michael Carr, author interview, July 31, 2004.
5. James Carr, interview.
6. Bert Bell Jr., author interview, May 2, 2009. Jordan Wright, author interview, July 11, 2009. Virginia McCaskey, author interview, August 8, 2005.
7. Dan Rooney quote from article by Geoff Hobson, "Godell Hitting Stride," www.bengals.com, April 4, 2007.
8. Myron Cope, *The Game That Was* (New York: World, 1970), 282–283.
9. Earl Schreiber, Hall of Fame presenter speech, 1963.

Bibliography

PRIMARY SOURCES

Newspapers

Akron Beacon-Journal
Appleton (Wisconsin) Post-Crescent
Boston Globe
Boston Post
Bowling Green Daily Sentinel-Tribune
Bridgeport (Connecticut) Telegram
Buffalo Evening News
Burlington (North Carolina) Daily-Times
Canton Daily News
Canton Repository
Cedar Rapids (Iowa) Evening Gazette
Charleston (West Virginia) Daily Mail
Chicago American
Chicago Daily Tribune
Cincinnati Enquirer
Cincinnati Post
Cleveland News
Cleveland Plain Dealer
Columbus Citizen-Journal
Columbus Dispatch
Columbus Press-Post
Coshocton (Ohio) Tribune
Dayton Journal
Decatur (Illinois) Review

Des Moines News
Detroit Free Press
Fort Wayne Journal
Fort Wayne News-Sentinel
Fresno (California) Bee
Galveston (Texas) Daily News
Green Bay Press-Gazette
Hamilton (Ohio) Evening Journal
Helena (Montana) Independent
Ironwood (Michigan) Daily Globe
Lincoln (Nebraska) Star
Marion (Ohio) Daily News
Mason City (Iowa) Globe-Gazette
Massillon Evening Independent
Milwaukee Journal
Modesto (California) Evening News
Newark (Ohio) Advocate
New Castle (Pennsylvania) News
New York Times
Oakland Tribune
Ogden (Utah) Standard Examiner
Ohio State Journal
Oshkosh (Wisconsin) Northwestern
Philadelphia Public Ledger
Pittsburgh Press
Pittsburgh Sun-Telegraph
Portsmouth (Ohio) Daily Times
Richmond (Indiana) Evening-Item
Richmond (Indiana) Palladium
Rochester Times-Union
San Antonio Express
Sandusky (Ohio) Star-Journal
Shelby (Ohio) Globe
Stevens Point (Wisconsin) Daily Journal
Toledo Daily Blade
Toledo News-Bee
Uniontown (Pennsylvania) Morning Herald
Washington Post
Waterloo (Iowa) Evening Courier-Reporter
Wellston (Ohio) Telegram
Youngstown Telegram
Youngstown Vindicator
Zanesville (Ohio) Times-Recorder

Author Interviews

Bell, Bert Jr. May 2, 2009.
Blackburn, Leo. July 1, 2000.

Brigham, James. March 11, 2006.
Carr Family Location Shoots. August 1, 2004.
Carr, James. September 14, 2002, and numerous e-mails.
Carr, Joe F., Grandsons Family Roundtable, with Gregory Carr, James Carr, and Michael Carr. July 31, 2004.
Cassady, Irene. May 7, 2005.
Chaboudy, Louis. July 1, 2000.
Colburn, Joe and Katherine. June 4, 2006.
Deters, Nancy. April 18, 2009.
Dolan, Joy. March 15, 2008.
Franke, Joann. April 22, 2007.
Guthery, William. June 26, 2000.
Heavey, Jim. March 28, 2009.
Horrigan, Joe. May 6, 2005.
Johnson, Jeanne. April 18, 2009.
King, James. June 1, 2003.
Knapp, Robert. April 19, 2009.
Lingo, Bob. June 26, 2000.
McCaskey, Virginia. 1999 and August 8, 2005.
Mooney, Margaret. July 31, 2004, and August 22, 2007.
Mulbarger, Bill. June 4, 2006.
Nesser Family Reunion. September 14, 2002.
Nesser, Sally. June 2, 2003.
Presnell, Glenn. February 21, 1999.
Ruh-Manhart, Sharon. July 22, 2006.
Schneider, Ted. May 7, 2005.
Seitz, Dolores. June 9, 2007.
Sherman, Babe. July 6, 2000.
Shomo, Connie. June 2, 2003.
Steverson, Norris. July 5, 2002.
Sullivan, Martha. November 21, 2004, and March 4, 2007.
Supple, Rozene. October 30, 2009.
Tehan, Patrick. April 18, 2009.
Wright, Jordan. July 11, 2009.

Archival Interviews

Bowser, Arda. NFL Films, 1994.
Broda, Hal. NFL Films, 1976.
Chamberlin, Guy. Pro Football Hall of Fame, 1965 (audio interview).
Clark, Dutch. Detroit TV Station, 1962.
Halas, George. NFL Films, 1976.
Halas, George. NFL Films, 1981.
Higgins, Lester. NFL Films, 1976.
Johnson, Pearce. NFL Films, 1991.
Lyman, Link. Pro Football Hall of Fame, 1964 and 1965 (audio interviews).
Mara, Wellington. NFL Films, 1999.
Martin, Ike Roy. NFL Films, 1976.

Miller, Charles. NFL Films, 1999.
Musso, George. NFL Films, 1999.
Newman, Harry. NFL Films, 1999.
Pollard, Fritz. NFL Films, 1976.
Rooney, Art. PBS-TV, 1984.
Rooney, Dan. NFL Films, 1999.
Thorpe, Grace. *Akron Beacon-Journal*, 1995.

SECONDARY SOURCES

Books

Anderson, Heartley W., with Emil Klosinski. *Notre Dame, Chicago Bears and "Hunk."* Orlando, FL: Daniels Publishing, 1976.

Barnes, Howard. *A Documentary Scrapbook of Football in Frankford*. Philadelphia: Historical Society of Frankford, 1985.

Becker, Carl. *Home & Away: The Rise and Fall of Professional Football on the Banks of the Ohio, 1919–1934*. Athens: Ohio University Press, 1998.

Braunwart, Bob and Bob Carroll. *The Alphabet Wars: The Birth of Professional Football, 1890–1892*. North Huntingdon, PA: Pro Football Researchers Association, 1981.

Carroll, Bob. *The Ohio League, 1910–1919*. North Huntingdon, PA: Pro Football Researchers Association, 1997.

Carroll. Bob. *The Tigers Roar: Professional Football in Ohio, 1903–09*. North Huntingdon, PA: Pro Football Researchers Association, 1990.

Carroll, Bob, Michael Gershman, David Neft, and John Thorn, eds. *Total Football II: The Official Encyclopedia of the National Football League*. New York: HarperCollins, 1999.

Carroll, Bob and Bob Gill. *Bulldogs on Sunday, 1919*. North Huntingdon, PA: Pro Football Researchers Association, n.d.

Carroll, Bob and PFRA Research. *Bulldogs on Sunday, 1920*. North Huntingdon, PA: Pro Football Researchers Association, n.d.

Carroll, Bob and PFRA Research. *Bulldogs on Sunday, 1921*. North Huntingdon, PA: Pro Football Researchers Association, n.d.

Carroll, Bob and PFRA Research. *Bulldogs on Sunday, 1922*. North Huntingdon, PA: Pro Football Researchers Association, n.d.

Carroll, Bob and PFRA Research. *Bulldogs on Sunday, 1923*. North Huntingdon, PA: Pro Football Researchers Association, n.d.

Carroll, John. *Fritz Pollard: Pioneer in Racial Advancement*. Urbana: University of Illinois Press, 1992.

Carroll, John M. *Red Grange and the Rise of Modern Football*. Urbana: University of Illinois Press, 1999.

Coenen, Craig R. *From Sandlot to the Super Bowl: The National Football League 1920–1967*. Knoxville: University of Tennessee Press, 2005.

Cohen, Richard M., Jordan Deutsch, Roland Johnson, and David Neft. *The Scrapbook History of Pro Football*. Indianapolis, IN: Bobbs-Merrill, 1976.

Cohen, Richard M. and David Neft. *Pro Football: The Early Years (An Encyclopedic History, 1895–1959)*. Ridgefield, CT: Sports Products, 1978.
Columbus (Ohio) City Directories, 1864–1940.
Cope, Myron. *The Game That Was*. New York: World, 1970.
Cummins, Bryan. *Airedales: The Oorang Story*. Calgary, Alberta, Canada: Detselig Enterprises, 2001.
Curran, Bob. *Pro Football's Rag Days*. New York: Bonanza Books, 1969.
Cusack, Jack. *Pioneer in Pro Football*. Fort Worth, TX: Author, 1963.
Daley, Arthur. *Pro Football's Hall of Fame*. New York: Tempo Books, 1963.
Daly, Dan and Bob O'Donnell. *The Pro Football Chronicle*. New York: Macmillan, 1990.
Davis, Jeff. *Papa Bear: The Life and Legacy of George Halas*. New York: McGraw-Hill, 2005.
Dent, Jim. *Monster of the Midway: Bronko Nagurski, the 1943 Chicago Bears, and the Greatest Comeback Ever*. New York: Thomas Dunne Books/St. Martin's Press, 2003.
DeVito, Carlo. *Wellington: The Maras, the Giants, and the City of New York*. Chicago: Triumph Books, 2006.
Didinger, Ray and Robert Lyons. *The Eagles Encyclopedia*. Philadelphia: Temple University Press, 2005.
Dietrich, Phil. *Down Payments: Professional Football as Viewed from the Summit, 1896–1930*. North Huntingdon, PA: Pro Football Researchers Association, 1995.
Eichinger, Fred. *The History of Shelby Football, 1894–1985*. N.p: Author, n.d.
Forrestal, Dan, J. *The Kernel and the Bean: The 75-Year Story of the Staley Company*. New York: Simon and Schuster, 1982.
Frederick, Chuck. *Leatherheads of the North: The True Story of Ernie Nevers & the Duluth Eskimos*. Duluth, MN: X-Communication, 2007.
Gill, Bob and Tod Maher. *The Pro Football Encyclopedia*. New York: Macmillan, 1997.
Godin, Roger. *The Brooklyn Football Dodgers*. Haworth, NJ: St. Johann Press, 2003.
Grange, Red, as told to Ira Morton. *The Red Grange Story: An Autobiography*. Urbana: University of Illinois Press, 1993.
Green, Jerry. *Detroit Lions: NFL Great Teams' Great Years*. New York: Macmillan, 1973.
Griffith, Corinne. *My Life with the Redskins*. New York: A. S. Barnes, 1947.
Gullickson, Denis J. *Vagabond Halfback: The Life and Times of Johnny Blood McNally*. Madison, WI: Trails Books, 2006.
Halas, George S., with Gwen Morgan and Arthur Veysey. *Halas: An Autobiography*. Chicago: Bonus Books, 1986.
Hanson, Carl and Denis J. Gullickson. *Before They Were The Packers: Green Bay's Town Team Days*. Black Earth, WI: Trails Books, 2004.
Johnson, Chuck. *The Green Bay Packers: Pro Football's Pioneer Team*. New York: Thomas Nelson & Sons, 1961.
Klein, Dave. *The New York Giants: Yesterday, Today, Tomorrow*. Chicago: Henry Regnery, 1973.
Klosinski, Emil. *Pro Football in the Days of Rockne*. New York: Carlton Press, 1970.
Lentz, Ed. *Columbus: The Story of a City*. Charleston, SC: Arcadia Publishing, 2003.

Little People's A B C. New York: Graham & Matlock, Co., n.d.

Littlewood, Thomas. *Arch: A Promoter, Not a Poet: The Story of Arch Ward.* Ames: Iowa State University Press, 1990.

Loverro, Thom. *Washington Redskins: The Authorized History.* Dallas, TX: Taylor, 1996.

Maltby, Marc S. *The Origins and Early Development of Professional Football.* New York: Garland Publishing, 1997.

March, Harry A. *Pro Football: Its Ups and Downs.* Albany: J. B. Lyon, 1934.

McCaskey, Patrick and Mike Sandrolini. *Bear with Me: A Family History of George Halas and the Chicago Bears.* Chicago: Triumph Books, 2009.

McClellan, Keith. *The Sunday Game: At the Dawn of Professional Football.* Akron, OH: University of Akron Press, 1998.

Miller, Jeffrey. *Buffalo's Forgotten Champions: The Story of Buffalo's First Professional Football Team and the Lost 1921 Title.* Philadelphia: Xlibris Corporation, 2004.

Murray, Mike. *Lions Pride: Sixty Years of Detroit Lions Football.* Dallas, TX: Taylor, 1993.

Names, Larry. *The History of the Green Bay Packers: The Lambeau Years, Part One.* Wautoma, WI: Angel Press, 1987.

Names, Larry. *The History of the Green Bay Packers: The Lambeau Years, Part Two.* Wautome, WI: Angel Press, 1987.

Official Guide of the National Football League: 1935. New York: American Sports Publishing, 1935.

Official Guide of the National Football League: 1939. New York: American Sports Publishing, 1939.

Oorang Comments and Oorang Catalog 26. LaRue, OH: Oorang Kennels, n.d.

O'Toole, Andrew. *Smiling Irish Eyes: Art Rooney and the Pittsburgh Steelers.* Haworth, NJ: St. Johann Press, 2004.

Pervin, Lawrence A., *Football's New York Giants: A History.* Jefferson, NC: McFarland, 2009.

Peterson, Robert W. *Pigskin: The Early Years of Pro Football.* New York: Oxford University Press, 1997.

Rathet, Mike and Don Smith. *Their Deeds and Dogged Faith.* New York: Rutledge Books and Balsam Press, 1984.

Reisler, Jim. *Cash and Carry: The Spectacular Rise and Hard Fall of C. C. Pyle, America's First Sports Agent.* Jefferson, NC: McFarland, 2009.

Richman, Michael. *The Redskins Encyclopedia.* Philadelphia: Temple University Press, 2008.

Roberts, Howard. *The Chicago Bears.* New York: G. P. Putnam's Sons, 1947.

Roberts, Howard. *The Story of Pro Football.* New York: Rand McNally, 1953.

Rooney, Dan, as told to Andrew E. Masich and David F. Halaas. *Dan Rooney: My 75 Years with the Pittsburgh Steelers and the NFL.* New York: Da Capo Press, 2007.

Ross, Charles K. *Outside the Lines: African Americans and the Integration of the National Football League.* New York: New York University Press, 1999.

Schmidt, Raymond. *Football's Stars of Summer: A History of the College All-Star Football Game Series of 1934–1976.* Lanham, MD: Scarecrow Press, 2001.

Scott, Jim. *Ernie Nevers: Football Hero.* Minneapolis, MN: T. S. Denison, 1969.

Sullivan, George. *Pro Football's All-Time Greats: The Immortals in Pro Football's Hall of Fame*. New York: G. P. Putnam's Sons, 1968.
Terzian, Jim. *New York Giants*. New York: Macmillan, 1973.
Tootle, James R. *Baseball in Columbus*. Chicago. Arcadia Publishing, 2003.
Torinus, John. *The Packer Legend*. Neshkoro, WI: Laranmark Press, 1983.
U.S. Bureau of the Census. *Population of States and Counties of the United States: 1790–1990*. Washington, D.C.: Author, 1996.
Vass, George. *George Halas and the Chicago Bears*. Chicago: Henry Regnery, 1971.
Ward, Arch. *The Green Bay Packers*. New York: G.P. Putnam's Sons, 1946.
Warner, Glenn S. *Football for Players and Coaches*. Carlisle, PA: Carlisle Indian School, 1912.
Wheeler, Robert. *Pathway to Glory: Jim Thorpe*. New York: Carlton Press, 1975.
Whitman, Robert. *Jim Thorpe and the Oorang Indians: NFL's Most Colorful Franchise*. Defiance, OH: Hubbard, 1984.
Whittingham, Richard. *Bears: In Their Own Words*. Chicago: Contemporary Books, 1991.
Whittingham, Richard. *The Chicago Bears: An Illustrated History*. New York: Rand McNally, 1982.
Whittingham, Richard. *Illustrated History of the New York Giants*. Chicago: Triumph Books, 2005.
Whittingham, Richard. *Sunday Mayhem: A Celebration of Pro Football in America*. Dallas, TX: Taylor, 1987.
Whittingham, Richard. *What a Game They Played*. Lincoln: University of Nebraska Press, 2001.
Who's Who in Major League Football. Chicago: B.E. Callahan Publisher, 1935.
Willis, Chris. *The Columbus Panhandles: A Complete History of Pro Football's Toughest Team, 1900–1922*. Lanham, MD: Scarecrow Press, 2007.
Willis, Chris. *Old Leather: An Oral History of Early Pro Football in Ohio, 1920–1935*. Lanham, MD: Scarecrow Press, 2005.
Ziemba, Joe. *When Football Was Football: The Chicago Cardinals and the Birth of the NFL*. Chicago: Triumph Books, 1999.
Zimmerman, David. *Curly Lambeau: The Man behind the Mystique*. Hales Corner, WI: Eagle Books, 2003.

Articles

Barnett, Bob. "1936: The First Draft." *Coffin Corner* 5, no. 6 (1983).
Carroll, Bob and Bob Braunwart. "The Panhandles: Last of the Sandlotters." *Coffin Corner* 1, no. 8 (1979).
Carroll, Bob and Bob Braunwart. "The Taylorville Scandal." *Coffin Corner* 2, no. 6 (1980).
Carroll, Bob, Bob Braunwart, and Joe Horrigan. "The Oorang Indians." *Coffin Corner* 3, no.1 (1981).
Didinger, Ray. "The Man Who Had a Dream." *Pro! The Official Program of the National Football League* 7, no. 5 (September 18, 1977).
Gems, Gerald. "Shooting Stars: The Rise and Fall of Blacks in Professional Football." *Professional Football Researchers Association*, 1988 Annual.

Gladen, Todd. "William Joseph Butler." Columbus Panhandle File. Pro Football Hall of Fame. Unpublished article.
Hogrogian, John. "Staten Island Stapletons." *Coffin Corner* 7, no. 6 (1985).
Horrigan, Joe. "Joe Carr." *Coffin Corner* 6, no. 5 (May–June 1984).
Olsen, Linda. "The Panhandle Division: An Early History." *Keystone* 23, no. 4 (Winter 1990), 9–10.
Quinn, Joe. "A Man for All Season." *Referee* 1, no. 6 (November–December 1976).
Reynolds, Dick. "The Steam Roller Story." *Providence Journal-Bulletin* (n.d.). Article published by the donation of Gilbane Building Company, Providence, Rhode Island.
Rhoades, Howard P. "Necessary Nessers: A Remarkable Family of Football Stars." *Baseball Magazine* XVIII, no. 3 (January 1917).
Whitney, Alan. "A Long Way from the Starchworks." *Chicago*, November 1955.

Scrapbooks and Unpublished Documents

Carr, Joe F., with Michael Fanning. "Post-Graduate Football." Unpublished, 1938.
JFC Scrapbook. Binders 1 and 2.

Index

About the Author

Chris Willis has worked at NFL Films as head of the research library since 1996. His first book, *Old Leather: An Oral History of Early Pro Football in Ohio, 1920–1935*, was published in 2005 by Scarecrow Press. *Old Leather* was given the 2005 Nelson Ross Award by the Professional Football Researchers Association for recent Achievement in Football Research and Historiography. His second book, *The Columbus Panhandles: A Complete History of Pro Football's Toughest Team, 1900-1922*, was published in 2007 by Scarecrow Press.

As the resident historian at NFL Films, Chris oversees all aspects of research for the company and their producers. In 2002 he was nominated for an Emmy for his work on the HBO Documentary *The Game of Their Lives: Pro Football in the 1950s*. He is also a member of the College Football Historical Society and the Professional Football Researchers Association (PFRA). Several of his articles, including "The Pro Football Hall of Fame—The Beginning," "The Bodyguard and Johnny U," "Ralph Hay: Forgotten Pioneer," and "Joe Carr's Vision," have been published in the PFRA publication *Coffin Corner*. In 1997 and 1998 Chris gave oral presentations at the Pro Football and American Life symposiums held at the Pro Football Hall of Fame.

Before starting at NFL Films, Chris graduated with a B.S. in physical education from Urbana (Ohio) University—while playing four years on the Urbana football team—and attended one year of graduate school at The Ohio State University in sports history. Chris Willis is a native of Columbus, Ohio, and currently resides in Moorestown, New Jersey.